How create anger
to [illegible], Hamlet in
just a few words

Horror
Menvale? Moreover
Newcastle
Finally
As we have seen / Also see

The Third Reich's Elite Schools

The Third Reich's Elite Schools

A History of the Napolas

by

HELEN ROCHE

OXFORD
UNIVERSITY PRESS

OXFORD
UNIVERSITY PRESS

Great Clarendon Street, Oxford, OX2 6DP,
United Kingdom

Oxford University Press is a department of the University of Oxford.
It furthers the University's objective of excellence in research, scholarship,
and education by publishing worldwide. Oxford is a registered trade mark of
Oxford University Press in the UK and in certain other countries

First Edition published in 2021

Impression: 1

Published in the United States of America by Oxford University Press
198 Madison Avenue, New York, NY 10016, United States of America

British Library Cataloguing in Publication Data
Data available

Library of Congress Control Number: 2021940026

ISBN 978-0-19-872612-8

DOI: 10.1093/oso/9780198726128.001.0001

Printed and bound by
CPI Group (UK) Ltd, Croydon, CR0 4YY

This book is dedicated to my mother,

Elizabeth Roche,

without whom (in so many ways) this book would never have been possible.

Preface

Combining the intricacies and peculiarities of thousands of sources and millions of words of notes, amassed over the course of a decade, was never going to be an easy task—but it was never anything less than fascinating. Even when the project seemed like a mountain whose summit would forever be unattainable, with the onward path shrouded by mists and uncertainty, my belief that this book both could and should be written never dwindled.

At the same time, in my more ironic moments, I did wonder at the quirk of fate that had led me to dedicate a significant proportion of my life to researching a very specific type of boys' boarding school. Could it be that my own educational 'socialization' in an English girls' boarding school had lent the topic its initial fascination? After all, homesickness, (psychologically) sadistic staff in charge of boarding, and scarcely pleasant forms of bullying were equally present at a Catholic all-girls ex-convent school in the late 1990s and early 2000s. Was I, like the two most prominent historians of the Napolas, Harald Scholtz and Horst Ueberhorst, doomed to revisit my own cloistered adolescent past (even if, unlike their own *almae matres*, my school had no connection whatsoever with National Socialism)?

I was also very much aware that my own personal subjectivities (British, female, more or less millennial) would not only shape the way in which I perceived my subject—for instance, did my musicological family background, and my training and sometime experience as a professional musician, mean that I had over-privileged accounts of music-making at the NPEA in my notes, whereas another scholar might have taken more interest in theatre or art?—but also the way in which the former Napola-pupils with whom I corresponded perceived me. As mentioned in my first book, *Sparta's German Children* (2013), which was based on the Classics PhD-project from which my interest in the more general history of the NPEA first arose, rather than perceiving a Briton as the erstwhile 'enemy', many of my eyewitnesses felt more willing to trust me precisely because they saw my intentions as untrammelled by native German shibboleths (such as the 'Frankfurt School', the 'Bielefeld School', or the all-encompassing shadow of 'political correctness'—for more on this kind of rhetoric, see Chapter 12). Something about my 'outsider' status made it possible for me to engage with many former pupils on a different level—leading ultimately to the strange happenstance that I might be the only person to whom they could unconstrainedly reminisce, knowing that I would not only understand exactly who or what they were talking about, but could even refresh their own memory of arcane facts now known only to a few survivors—for instance, that the great plough-horse at the Napolas' seaside retreat near Kolberg had been named Blücher, or that the caretaker there was called *Vater* Heck . . . .

And then, there were the strange coincidences which revealed to me how very many people in Germany had been in some way touched or affected by the NPEA, even if they had never actually attended one—the museum curator whose mother turned out to have been an NPEA secretary; the audience-member at a public history lecture who told me afterwards that his father had been the mechanic at the local Napola, servicing all of the school's many cars, trucks, and motorbikes; the archaeologist colleague whose father had been selected to take the NPEA entrance exam, but whose conservative Catholic grandfather had been adamantly opposed to the idea, and had sent him to the *Gymnasium* a year early instead . . . .

In the end, I had amassed so much material on the schools that I could probably have written this book at least three times over, using completely different sources in each iteration. At the same time, one book can only ever be so long, and there were countless spheres—de-Christianization, wartime alumni networks, musical activities, English-teaching, mining 'missions', the American exchanges, and the old boys' networks, to name but a few—where I despairingly had to acknowledge that only the merest fraction of the material could find its way into the final manuscript, and that to do the theme justice, each topic would really need a subsequent article all of its own. From this perspective, when it came to themes on which I had already published in detail, such as sport, the NPEA in conquered Eastern Europe, the English public-school exchanges, post-war eyewitness testimonies, or the Spartan ideal, I deliberately chose not to duplicate most of this material, instead recommending readers to consult the volumes and articles in question for a more in-depth analysis.

Finally, throughout the process, I was given the opportunity to realize just how crucial the personal archives of former pupils are to preserving the full historical record of these fascinating and contested institutions. If anyone who reads this happens to be an eyewitness, relative, or descendant, who is wondering what they should do with Napola-related effects, then my heartfelt plea would be: do your utmost to find an archive that will take the material in (even contact me if you have to . . .). Only then will the schools' true variety, and the multifarious nature of their life and afterlife, be properly preserved for posterity.

*

Unsurprisingly, my first and most crucial debt of gratitude lies with the many former NPEA-pupils who were prepared to share their memories of their schooldays with me as eyewitnesses (*Zeitzeugen*). Many of them went out of their way to correspond with me over a period of several years, to welcome me into their homes, and even to share relevant personal documents with me for the first time. In particular, I would like to thank the late Dr. Uwe Lamprecht for allowing me unprecedented access to his personal archive, without which this book would necessarily have been far less comprehensive and less colourful; I will always be grateful to him and his wife Ursula for their generosity. In this regard, Arne and Dorothea Heinich, Dietrich Schulz, Klaus and Hannelore Schikore, and Hans and Luise Rettkowski also deserve special mention. I am also very grateful to the members of the NPEA Berlin-Spandau, NPEA Köslin, and Schulpforta old boys' networks for their invaluable assistance, and the fascinating opportunities which they granted me to experience some of their meetings at first hand.

The decade or so which I have spent working on this project has ended up spanning many different phases of my professional and personal life. During my time at Cambridge, first as a graduate student, and then as a Research Fellow, I had the good fortune to be a member of Sir Richard Evans' German History Research Seminar, and I will always be grateful for the sage advice and guidance which he gave me in the project's early stages, and for the opportunity to present my work-in-progress at the seminar regularly as it developed. At Cambridge, Jo Whaley and Brendan Simms have also always been willing to provide valuable mentorship as my career as a modern historian has progressed, along with Moritz Föllmer, Suzanne Marchand, and Christina Morina beyond the fens.

Meanwhile, during darker times, Henrike Lähnemann saved my life (both literally and metaphorically), for which I will forever be in her debt; nor will I ever forget the assistance provided by the Margaret Beaufort Institute, Cambridge Women's Aid, Natassa Varka, Victoria Griggs, Jane Gaffney, Antony Warren, Ian de Massini, and John McKean, Cora Xu, and the Cambridge University Writing Group, as well as Ric Whaite, whose support during my first year at Durham was invaluable. I was also incredibly fortunate to have the opportunity to spend several months at UCL working with Mary Fulbrook, Stephanie Bird, and Stefanie Rauch as part of their AHRC-funded research project on 'Compromised Identities: Reflections on Perpetration and Complicity under Nazism', before moving on to the History Department at Durham, where I am similarly blessed with the nicest, most supportive, and most intellectually stimulating colleagues imaginable.

In terms of practical assistance, I would like to acknowledge here the generous support of the *Deutscher Akademischer Austauschdienst* and the DAAD Cambridge Research Hub, the John Stewart of Rannoch Research Fund, and the *Volkswagenstiftung*, which enabled my external participation in Detlef Schmiechen-Ackermann's relevant research project at the Institut für Didaktik der Demokratie, Leibniz-Universität Hannover. My research trips to Berlin and to Vienna were facilitated respectively by Christian Wendt, who arranged for my stint as a visiting scholar with the FU-Berlin's 'TOPOI' Excellence Cluster, and by Sybille Steinbacher and Johanna Gehmacher, who made me wonderfully welcome at the Universität Wien. Professor Steinbacher was also instrumental in facilitating my contribution to an issue of *Beiträge zur Geschichte des Nationalsozialismus* on 'Sport in National Socialism', which was crucial to the development of some of the key ideas in this book—as was Michael Rowe's invitation to give a paper on the project at the Institute of Historical Research's German History Seminar in London, and Norbert Frei's invitation to present a paper at the Jena Center for Twentieth-Century History's symposium, '*Wie bürgerlich war der Nationalsozialismus?*'. Meanwhile, my many archival trips to Germany would not have been possible without the generosity of all those who welcomed me into their homes for days or weeks at a time, especially Bernhard and Josephine Cook-Müller, Christine and Gebhard Enßle, Dorothee and Lisa Kattner, and Derrick and Gudrun Mitchell.

At various stages, Max Haberich, Nathaniël Kunkeler, and Tim Schmalz have provided stalwart and much-appreciated research assistance, while the aid of various archivists at the many archives throughout Germany and further afield was also a *sine qua non* for the project's success. For reasons of space, I can only single out the following: Sven Schneidereit at the Bundesarchiv in Lichterfelde, whose ever-cheerful and enduringly helpful demeanour when on duty in the reading-room is always a saving grace; Günter Biele at the Sächsisches Hauptstaatsarchiv in Dresden, who made it possible for me to catalogue the holdings of the NPEA Klotzsche old boys' network; Wolfram Theilemann at the Stadtarchiv in Nordhausen, who has since involved me in other fascinating local history projects; and Ulrich Burkhart and Hanum Louloudis at the Zentralarchiv des Bezirksverbands Pfalz in Kaiserslautern, who run the most relaxed and friendly archive that I have ever encountered in Germany or elsewhere—even providing their readers with tea and coffee!

I am also very much indebted to those other historians of the NPEA who provided me with excellent advice and even, in some cases, hospitality: Steffi Flintrop, Andreas Förschler, Thomas Fritz, Marie Hagenbourger, Tim Müller, Juliane Tiffert (née Kühne), Adolf Morlang, Michal Šimůnek, and Steffen Wagner—many of whom also very generously gave me access to their own private archives, as well as giving me much food for thought. Steffen Wagner at Weierhof, Reinhard Käsinger at Neubeuern, and Detlev Kraack, Arne Rogg-Pietz, and Heide Beese at Plön also gave me tours of their respective schools and archives (culminating, in the case of the Plön Gymnasium, with an impromptu discussion of the Scottish referendum with an upper-school English class!). Paige Roberts and Mary Mulligan at Andover, Matt Edmonds at St. Andrews, and Sophie Arnfield at Tabor Academy all provided me with invaluable material and insights on the US exchange programme, as did emeritus professor John Stephan. Meanwhile, Christine McCrudden and Julian Girdham kindly responded to my questions about exchanges in the British Isles (as did numerous archivists at English public schools, most of whom are acknowledged in my 2013 article on the topic, which addresses the material which they provided more directly).

Finally, I am very grateful to all those who advised me on the project and the manuscript as it took shape—I benefited greatly from fruitful exchanges with

Richard J. Evans, Johanna Gehmacher, Ben Goossens, Detlef Schmiechen-Ackermann, Nicholas Stargardt, Sybille Steinbacher, Dietmar Süß, and Michael Wildt, as well as receiving extremely helpful comments on the manuscript from Moritz Föllmer, Lisa Pine, Daniel Siemens, and Brendan Simms, and the anonymous OUP readers. Many thanks are also due to everyone at OUP who has been involved with the project over the years, especially Robert Faber, Stephanie Ireland, and Cathryn Steele, as well as to Tess McCann, for her excellent work in putting the maps together, and Tom Zille, for checking my translations (and for generally making the world a better place). As ever, any remaining infelicities and errors are my responsibility alone.

In conclusion, most importantly of all, I must thank a few of those who have had to live with the book and its genesis on a daily basis—firstly, my mother Elizabeth Roche, to whom this book is dedicated, and without whose extensive and inexhaustible practical assistance its completion might never have been possible; Rob Hanson, whose decision to join the Durham University Writing Group was ultimately so fortuitous, and who has since had to bear with my reading many bits of the manuscript to (or at) him during the writing process—and, last but not least, my darling Alex, whose genuine interest in my work is a constant delight, and whose unceasing affection and support brings me strength and happiness every day.

Contents

List of Illustrations

N.B. Although the majority of the images used here portray pupils at NPEA Rügen, former pupils from other Napolas generally agree that they convey the flavour of analogous activities at other schools throughout the Napola system, and very similar images can be found in the photographic collections of pupils from many other NPEA.

A Note on Terminology

NPEA vs. Napola

The official abbreviation for the designation *Nationalpolitische Erziehungsanstalt* (singular) and *Nationalpolitische Erziehungsanstalten* (plural) was NPEA (i.e. the initials of *National-Politische Erziehungs-Anstalt*). However, although the school authorities disliked the widespread use of the more colloquial (uncapitalized) abbreviation 'Napola' (i.e. *Na[tional]-Pol[itische] A[nstalt]*—plural: 'Napolas'), and attempted to legislate against its use (see the Introduction), at times, they would still use this abbreviation themselves—perhaps because it was simply so much easier to pronounce. Thus, the term 'Napola' can regularly be found in official media coverage on the schools, including an article published in April 1938 by the Inspectorate's very own press officer, Helmut Trepte.[1] Moreover, it can also be found in official correspondence by and with various government agencies, and was also constantly used as a contemporary term of art by present and former pupils.[2]

From this perspective, Gisela Miller-Kipp's frequently asserted (yet flawed) contention—that the use of the abbreviation 'Napola' is historically incorrect—simply cannot stand.[3] While it may even be true, as Miller-Kipp suggests, that the term at one time also officially applied to the extremely short-lived '*Nationalpolitische Lehrgänge*' (National Political Courses), this was by no means the way in which the term was usually understood even during the Third Reich, let alone in the post-war period.[4] The evidence therefore overwhelmingly suggests that contemporary pupils, staff, bureaucrats, journalists, and members of the general public alike would all have assumed that the abbreviation referred to a *Nationalpolitische Erziehungsanstalt*.[5] Hence, I have used the two abbreviations more or less interchangeably in the pages which follow.

Ausleseschule vs. *Eliteschule*

In German-language scholarship, since the publication of Harald Scholtz's monograph *Nationalsozialistische Ausleseschulen* in 1973, the Napolas have often been described not as 'elite schools' (*Eliteschulen*), but as '*Ausleseschulen*'.[6] The subtleties of this term cannot be rendered both completely and concisely in English, due to the racially loaded, Social Darwinist connotations of the noun '*Auslese*' during the Third Reich—the closest two-word approximation would be something like 'selective schools'. Although the prevalence of the term '*Ausleseschulen*' in the scholarly literature can in some measure be attributed to political and/or polemical motivations, which sought to sever the schools' connection with the culpability of Nazi 'elites' in the wake of denazification (as discussed in the Introduction), or which sought to repudiate the idea that National Socialist pedagogy could ever have been capable of cultivating a 'true' elite, it is also indisputable that the NPEA were commonly referred to as '*Ausleseschulen*' during the Third Reich. In this regard, even the Napola authorities did not necessarily wish either to seem too 'elitist', or to risk giving the impression that a high-flying career was automatically guaranteed for all NPEA graduates.[7]

Nevertheless, as Lisa Pine has cogently remarked in her relatively recent survey of education in Nazi Germany, any kind of highly selective education is, by its very nature, 'elitist' in some measure.[8] Moreover, it is also undeniable that the Napolas did explicitly aim to train the future elite of the Third Reich in all walks of life. Therefore, to cut this terminological Gordian knot, and to ensure that the book's title will be comprehensible (rather than confusing) to an Anglophone audience, I have followed Pine's lead in using the term 'elite schools'.[9]

Place-Names in Eastern Europe and the Balkans

When discussing locations in present-day Czechia, Poland, and other countries in Eastern Europe and the Balkans where place-names were once German or were forcibly 'Germanized' during occupation, I will give the current name in brackets when the location is first mentioned, thereafter using the designation which was officially in use at the time in question, as indicated by the sources. However, the names of specific schools in these regions, such as NPEA Köslin or NPEA Loben, will always be rendered using the German form of the name, since the official name of the school was never (for example) NPEA Koszalin or NPEA Lubliniec.

Terms of Art

The following terms and abbreviations will not routinely be translated or glossed—see the glossary for further information:

Anstaltsleiter: headmaster/principal.
Erzieher: member of teaching staff—ranks included ***Zugführer***, ***Hauptzugführer***, or ***Hundertschaftsführer***.
Geländespiele: cross-country wargames.
Jungmann: Napola-pupil—see also ***Napolaner***.

Zug: class or year-group.
NPEA für Mädchen/Mädchen-NPEA: NPEA for girls.
HJ: Hitler Youth.
BDM: the female branch of the Hitler Youth.

N.B. To calculate the worth of Reichsmarks in any given year in present-day Euros, the following tool is invaluable: https://www.dm-euro-rechner.de/die-reichsmark/.

As an example, a machinist employed at an NPEA during the 1930s would have received a monthly salary of around 225 RM (2,700 RM per year).

Notes

1. Helmut Trepte, 'Die Napolas', *Berliner Tageblatt*, 14 April 1938 [Bundesarchiv Lichterfelde (BArch), R 4902/1490]; cf. 'Was will die Napola?', *Bremer Nachrichten*, 5 January 1944 [Niedersächsisches Landesarchiv—Hauptstaatsarchiv Hannover (NLA-HStAH), ZGS 2/1 Nr. 155].
2. Cf. e.g. BArch, NS 38/3913, letter dated 16 June 1937; BArch, R 187/270b, Bl. 121; NLA-HStAH, Hann. 180 Hannover B Nr. 95.
3. E.g. Gisela Miller-Kipp, '"Klasse Schule—immer genug zu essen, wenig Mathematik". Elitebildung im "Dritten Reich" oder über die Herstellung von Elite-Bewusstsein', in Jutta Ecarius and Lothar Wigger, eds, *Elitebildung—Bildungselite. Erziehungswissenschaftliche Diskussionen und Befunde über Bildung und soziale Ungleichheit* (Opladen, 2006), 44–66, 48, n. 12; Gisela Miller-Kipp, 'Elitebildung in den Elite-Schulen des "Dritten Reiches". Praxis und Systemfunktion', in *'Es war ein Welt von Befehl und Gehorsam.' Nationalsozialistische Elitebildung und die Adolf-Hitler-Schule Sachsen in Pirna-Sonnenstein (1941 bis 1945)* (Pirna, 2008), 17–36, 21, n. 15; more recently: Gisela Miller-Kipp, 'Review of Rainer Hülsheger, *Die Adolf-Hitler-Schulen 1937–1945: Suggestion eines Elitebewusstseins*', *H-Soz-u-Kult, H-Net Reviews* (February 2016). Unfortunately, this error has subsequently been perpetuated in other recent publications, such as Tim Müller, 'A Legal Odyssey: Denazification Law, Nazi Elite Schools, and the Construction of Postwar Memory', *History of Education* 46, no. 4 (2017), 498–513, 499, n. 11.
4. On the *Nationalpolitische Lehrgänge* themselves, see Barbara Schneider, *Die höhere Schule im Nationalsozialismus. Zur Ideologisierung von Bildung und Erziehung* (Cologne, 2000), ch. III.3.4.
5. *Nationalpolitische Erziehungsanstalt Plön. Rundbrief*, Nr. 25 (October 1943), 23.
6. Harald Scholtz, *Nationalsozialistische Ausleseschulen. Internatsschulen als Herrschaftsmittel des Führerstaates* (Göttingen, 1973).
7. Cf. Staatsarchiv Hamburg, 361-2 VI Nr. 604, Deutscher Gemeindetag, letter dated 25 June 1935. For accounts of the NPEA during the Third Reich which did use the term 'elite', see e.g. Willy Beer, 'Elite und Norm', *Deutsche Allgemeine Zeitung*, 20 July 1939 [BArch, NS 5/VI/18842]; Willi Jung, *Deutsche Arbeiterjugend. Auslese, Förderung,*

Aufstieg (Berlin, 1940), 31; 'Elitebildung', *Das Reich*, 27 April 1941 [BArch, NS 5/VI/18842].

8. Lisa Pine, *Education in Nazi Germany* (Oxford, 2010), 71.
9. Quite apart from the untranslatable elements of the term *Auslese*, defining the NPEA as 'selective schools' in English would utterly fail to convey a true sense of the schools' programme; rather, it would make them sound relatively innocuous—something along the lines of an English grammar school.

Introduction

The Napolas in Historical Context

Berlin, October 1940: SS-Lieutenant-General August Heißmeyer, the Inspector of the National Political Education Institutes (NPEA), expounded his megalomaniac expectations for the development of the system of elite boarding schools under his control to the Head of the Reich Chancellery.[1] Within the next five years, in order to safeguard the survival of the Reich in accordance with the Führer's will, the number of NPEA in existence must rise from a mere twenty-one to a grand total of one hundred. The schools would then be able to produce around three thousand graduates each year, most of whom would go on to take up leading positions in the Wehrmacht, Party, and state. To get this expansion programme off the ground, fifteen new schools would have to be founded in the next financial year alone, and 14.25 million Reichsmarks would need to be allocated for this purpose in the Reich budget for 1941. Moreover, as soon as Germany had triumphed in the Second World War, all of the NPEA which had already been founded would necessarily have to be supplied with brand new campuses, in keeping with their vital imperial mission to provide leaders for all of the peoples which Germany had now conquered. Only then, Heißmeyer averred, could Hitler's anxieties concerning the overall stability of the Third Reich be assuaged.

Less than a year later, Heißmeyer had begun to enlist the assistance of numerous architects and state construction officials in order to realize these far-reaching proposals, including plans for a monumental 'model campus' on the outskirts of Berlin which could be shown off to foreign dignitaries visiting the Nazi capital.[2] At a conference of relevant architects and officials in July 1941, Heißmeyer declared that the buildings which they were to design and construct must be magnificent, worthy of the Reich's greatness, and able to withstand the elements for hundreds of years; they were to be the 'pillars' upholding the educational system in every Gau.[3] The following year, the Inspector also outlined plans for further schools to be founded not only in occupied Flanders, Holland, and Luxembourg, but also in Norway and (supposedly neutral) Switzerland.[4]

By April 1944, it seemed as if some of the Inspector's grandiose plans might come at least partly to fruition; twelve out of the desired fifteen NPEA had indeed been founded in 1941, and Heißmeyer was now proudly able to boast that, since the outbreak of war, the number of schools in existence had risen to forty-three.[5] By now, many of the Eastern and Western occupied territories—present-day

The Third Reich's Elite Schools: A History of the Napolas. Helen Roche, Oxford University Press. © Helen Roche 2021.
DOI: 10.1093/oso/9780198726128.003.0001

Czechia, Poland, the Netherlands, Belgium, and Luxembourg—had had schools established to train 'racially suitable' future leaders from their native populations alongside children from the German heartland of the 'old Reich'.[6] Even as the war situation worsened, and Germany began to suffer defeat after defeat, the Reich and Prussian Finance Ministries were still willing to pump millions of Reichsmarks into the Napola system; the final school to be founded, NPEA Bohemia in Kuttenberg (Kutná Hora), officially opened its doors as late as 21 April 1944.[7]

And yet, less than eighteen months later, with the National Socialist regime utterly vanquished and Germany enduring fourfold foreign occupation, those schools whose buildings still survived at all had often been ransacked and damaged beyond all recognition. Thus, during a local government inspection of the former site of the school at Potsdam, one of the few remaining NPEA administrators lamented that he had been wholly unable to prevent either the local populace or resident Soviet troops from continually looting the building—making off with everything from roof-tiles to kitchen utensils and books from the abandoned library.[8] A few months on, rain and snowmelt from the damaged roof had made most of the rooms uninhabitable, and the women who had been billeted there routinely used the school's ruined furniture to fuel their cooking-fires.[9] Like all of the Third Reich's other Ozymandian imperial dreams, Heißmeyer's hubris and his putative educational empire had finally come to naught.[10]

Perhaps it is unsurprising, then, that even in Germany, few today are fully aware of the role which the NPEA played in the Third Reich's machinery of political and racial domination—or even that they existed at all. For, unlike the National Socialist training academies or 'Order Castles' (*Ordensburgen*) for adult Party cadres which were newly built at Crössinsee, Sonthofen, and Vogelsang, or the Adolf-Hitler-Schools which later inhabited their vast building complexes—still well known as some of the most notorious surviving instances of Nazi monumental architecture—the Napolas rarely formed such a 'visible' part of the Third Reich's educational landscape, either literally or metaphorically.[11] On occasion, this could lead to embarrassing (if somewhat amusing) misunderstandings—for instance, the time when the *Westdeutscher Beobachter*, a leading West-German regional daily, printed an article celebrating the schools' achievements in the state's annual winter charity campaign entitled 'Italian Youth Raise Money for the Winter Help'—having evidently assumed that the so-called 'Napola'-pupils must have originated from Naples.[12] In similar vein, since the term 'Educational Institute' (*Erziehungsanstalt*) was often used to denote some kind of reformatory or institution for young offenders, many members of the general public might consider the 'inmates' at the schools to be potentially dangerous—as did one group of visitors to NPEA Oranienstein, who were keen to espy the artistic delights of the baroque palace in which the school was situated (including frescoes by van Dyck), yet did not dare to pass beyond the gates: 'Not without reserve, they asked one of the group of pupils (*Jungmannen*) who were romping around outside the magnificent wrought-iron courtyard railings how they came to be allowed to move around so freely here. The little chap answered them mischievously, "These are only the mild cases; the more serious ones are locked up!"'[13]

From this perspective, NPEA staff and bureaucrats at the Inspectorate alike were continually irritated by the fact that, in publicity terms, the schools appeared to be perpetually living up to their own motto: 'Be more than you seem' (*Mehr sein als scheinen*).[14] To add insult to injury, after only a few months of existence, the Adolf-Hitler-Schools (AHS), rival Party elite boarding schools founded by Reich Youth Leader Baldur von Schirach and Reich Organization Leader Robert Ley in 1937, had become far better known, due to their extremely slick and wide-ranging propaganda campaign.[15] Yet the fact that most Germans, even those who lived in the vicinity of an NPEA, had little notion of what exactly went on there, and that even members of the SS who wished to send their sons to a Napola might have no idea of the schools' real name, or how to go about making an application—not to mention the grisly rumours that the sporting education at the schools was so excessive that 'most of the poor lads suffer from a heart condition'—were primarily the Inspectorate's own fault.[16] Instead of placing the schools in the public eye and informing the public about their aims and ethos on a regular basis, the Inspectorate stringently restricted and censored all publications about the NPEA, and, until 1937, staff at the schools were forbidden from even giving public talks about the Napolas, or showing the films which had been made of their activities.[17] It seems that these rules were (slightly) loosened only after the AHS' competing advent on the elite-school scene; even so, the themes of presentations by staff were still strictly limited to discussion of their own personal work at their particular school, rather than the Napola system as a whole.[18]

So, what exactly were the NPEA, and why did they matter—why, indeed, should they matter to us now? In the following section, I give a brief outline of the Napolas' aims and ethos (as a basis for subsequent observations), before making a case for the originality of my approach, and defining the schools' significance for the history of the Third Reich as a whole. I also give a concise overview of the various debates to which this first comprehensive study of the schools will contribute, and the ways in which it builds upon existing scholarship.

In the following section, I then go on to sketch the programmatic intentions of the key figures involved in the Napolas' founding and subsequent development—Reich Education Minister Bernhard Rust; the first Inspector of the NPEA, Joachim Haupt, and the second (and last) Inspector, August Heißmeyer—touching upon the extent to which the schools' programme drew upon pre-National Socialist educational traditions, including the turn-of-the-century youth movements, reform pedagogy, and the militaristic methods of the Prussian cadet schools. In this connection, we will also examine the schools' educational aims—in particular, their commitment to the 'socialist' elements of National Socialism, in the form of free or heavily subsidized places for poorer members of the racially defined German national community under Nazism, the so-called *Volksgemeinschaft*. Finally, I conclude by briefly outlining the book's structure (chapter-wise), and the nature of the sources used in its construction.

*

Put simply, the National Political Education Institutes (*Nationalpolitische Erziehungsanstalten*), most commonly known as NPEA or Napolas, were Nazi Germany's principal training institutions for the future elite of the Third Reich.[19] Self-confessedly modelled on an amalgam of the English public schools, the Prussian cadet schools, and the harsh educational practices of ancient Sparta, the NPEA aimed to take boys from the age of 10, and turn them into leaders in all walks of life—whether military, political, or intellectual.[20] The schools were open to pupils of any background—in fact, they offered a generous scheme of free or heavily subsidized places, which were also a key element in their propaganda, since the schools deliberately aimed to foster talented children from poorer backgrounds, particularly the sons of workers and farmers. Nevertheless, it seems that middle-class children still predominated.[21]

Prospective pupils were subjected to a rigorous and gruelling selection process, which not only tested their supposed level of 'racial purity' and their academic abilities, but also placed extreme emphasis on physical prowess and sheer courage. Those who successfully passed all aspects of the selection examination would then join their Napola's first 'platoon' (*Zug*—class), learning to live in a highly militarized and enclosed boarding-school community.[22] The schools provided an extensive variety of activities—academic lessons, though taken seriously, took a back seat compared with physical education, which included the opportunity to ride, glide, sail, drive, and ski, as well as engagement in pre-military training, such as small-bore shooting and cross-country war-games.[23] Pupils also had the chance to visit many European countries (as the Reich's 'cultural ambassadors'), and to take part in exchanges with British public schools and American academies. Older boys also spent extended periods working in factories, mines, or on German farms in the conquered Eastern territories—in order to understand the lives of 'the people', whom they would one day rule in peace and lead in war.[24]

Needless to say, the Napolas were also hothouses for the propagation of Nazi ideology, and countless former pupils died on the battlefields of World War II. As the Third Reich began to disintegrate, lessons were subject to ever greater disruption, and conditions at the schools generally worsened, although the situation was still often far less dire at the NPEA than it would have been at 'normal' secondary schools.[25] In general, boys were called up ever younger to serve as anti-aircraft auxiliaries or teenage soldiers. Some, convinced of the rightness of the German cause, continued to fight on even after Germany had capitulated to the Allies in May 1945.

This monograph presents an entirely original synthesis of primary source-material collated over the past decade from eighty archives in half a dozen countries worldwide, as well as drawing upon eyewitness testimonies from over one hundred former Napola-pupils, with whom I have been corresponding since 2009. Hence, it illuminates school life at the NPEA, and the multifarious political projects within which the schools were enmeshed, in greater detail, and with far greater subtlety, than any previously existing studies. In particular, it highlights the significant 'variety within unity' exhibited by individual schools within the NPEA system—including the very first Napolas which were founded in former Prussian cadet schools; those with a long-standing humanistic tradition; those established in the German federal states beyond Prussia and in annexed Austria, and those founded to aid 'Germanization' in the occupied Eastern and Western territories—as well as the (often overlooked) NPEA for girls.

The book follows a tripartite structure, beginning with an account of the Napolas' place in the Third Reich's educational landscape, their institutional development, and their everyday life or *Alltagsgeschichte* (Part I). Part II then moves on to explore the varying regional circumstances and long-standing traditions which influenced the ethos of the different schools within the Napola system in detail. This differentiation is especially important, given that most previous scholarship has tended to lump all of the Napolas together indiscriminately—and, indeed, to obliterate the differences between the Napolas and other, better-known Nazi elite educational institutions, such as the Adolf-Hitler-Schools and the Reich School of the NSDAP at Feldafing (for a full discussion of the relationship between the NPEA and the AHS, see the Conclusion).[26] Finally, Part III depicts the effects of total war on the schools, and the whole system's dramatic disintegration during the final months of World War II; in conclusion, the epilogue documents the fate of the Napolas and their adherents in post-war German society.

Throughout the following chapters, we shall see that, when approached appropriately, the Napolas form a fascinating microcosm; a petri-dish in which many of the Third Reich's most fundamental tendencies can be found in magnified form. These include—but are certainly not limited to:

- The constant conflicts caused by polycratic infighting over which political faction (including the Education Ministry, the SA, the Party, or the military) should gain control over the schools—and the infinite rapacity of Himmler and the SS, which fuelled it most (Chapter 1).
- The complex relationship between the centre of the Nazi state and its periphery—both in terms of the tensions between the central government in Berlin and the federal states within Germany itself, and between Austria and Germany within the context of the ever-expanding 'Greater German Reich' (Chapters 5 and 7).

- The contradiction between National Socialist claims to honour past traditions, particularly in the form of religion and humanism, and their wholesale erosion, rejection, and destruction (Chapter 6).
- The institutionalization of radically unequal, yet complementary, forms of gender politics and socialization (Chapter 9).
- The related ideology and rhetoric of the racial *Volksgemeinschaft*, which was made corporeal in hyper-concentrated and distilled form in the student body itself, and the regime's racially underpinned dreams of a new Nazi European order, created through a radical programme of Germanization policy in both Eastern and Western Europe (Chapter 8).
- And, last but not least, the Nazi regime's grandiose claim to control the future by controlling and shaping the lives of Germany's youth, so that, in Hitler's own words, 'They will never again be free throughout their entire lives', instead becoming 'fleet as greyhounds, tough as leather, and hard as Krupp-steel' in his service.[27]

As we shall see, the Napolas lay at the forefront of many political and sociocultural developments under National Socialism—whilst simultaneously reflecting many others. Thus, the schools' history can provide a fresh perspective on Nazi subjects' everyday behaviour and political expectations, whilst also illuminating many themes which are considered to be of key importance by scholars of the Third Reich today. For instance, the dictatorship's concern with providing its 'Aryan' citizens with opportunities for personal advancement, individual enjoyment, and self-expression was reflected in the schools' expansive programme of sporting and artistic extracurricular activities—as was the seductiveness of the regime and the lure of the *Volksgemeinschaft*, of being able to define oneself positively and dominatingly against the negative pole of the racial 'Other'.[28] In this instance, the Napolas' '*schöner Schein*', their seductive glamour,[29] was arguably even more attractive because the comradeship on offer at the NPEA was far more 'racially exclusive' than that which most school-children in the Third Reich might experience. Thus, an even more marked sense of superiority could be fostered amongst the student body, not just in opposition to societal outcasts, but in opposition to members of the Hitler Youth, or even pupils from other types of elite school as well.[30]

I would therefore suggest that the student body at the Napolas should be seen as a form of distilled or hyper-selective '*auserlesene*' *Volksgemeinschaft*; that is, pupils allegedly represented very many of the ideals prioritized in the idea of the Nazi national community—racial, physical, and political—but in microcosm. Traits such as purported 'racial purity', sporting capacity, strength and (relative) physical perfection, political uniformity, and above all, the will to achievement, to ever greater *Leistung*, which were demanded of National Socialist citizens in general, can be found at the Napolas in particularly refined and exaggerated form.

Meanwhile, what Norbert Frei has termed the '*gefühlte Gleichheit*' (experienced egalitarianism) of the *Volksgemeinschaft* can be found within the schools' micro-community in abundance:[31] that is, a feeling of equality, comradeship, and belonging, despite material and social inequalities in pupils' family background. Indeed, we might argue that, of all the National Socialist institutions which offered German citizens educational opportunities or the prospect of greater social mobility, the Napolas came closest to realizing many of the 'aspirations of dictatorship', not merely in terms of their enhanced capacity to indoctrinate German youth, but also because they realized certain facets of the promise of the Nazi 'social revolution' in a way that was more than merely illusory.[32]

All in all, then, we can see the Napolas as a prism through which many key aspects of Nazism are refracted—some with particular intensity; others at a level which mirrored that of the Third Reich at large. For this reason, I would argue—as Jürgen Finger has suggested in his recent monograph on Nazi educational politics in Württemberg—that we can indeed gain extremely valuable insights into the nature of the Third Reich through treating '*Bildungsgeschichte als Zeitgeschichte*'—that is, treating the history of education as contemporary history.[33] All too often—and not only in German history or German studies—we find research on educational history or the history of childhood and youth being pushed to the margins, corralled away into a subfield all its own, and to some extent spurned or ignored by 'mainstream' political or social historians.[34] Yet, in fact, what could be more telling than the ways in which a state seeks to indoctrinate its youth, or the particular virtues which it seeks to instil in its citizens of the future?[35] The utility of such an approach is also suggested by the fact that there now exist a number of monographs on individual aspects of the Third Reich, including Detlef Brandes' and Johannes Koll's analyses of Nazi occupation policies in the conquered Czech lands and the Netherlands respectively, or Annette Mertens' study of religious expropriations in Germany and Austria after the Anschluss, which have already pointed towards the Napolas' key role in many spheres of National Socialist policy.[36]

Seen from this perspective, the history of education can grant us crucial insights into the nature, goals, and priorities of many a regime—and how much more so in the case of the training of the putative political elite? Had National Socialism endured for longer, the graduates of the Napola system would indeed have ruled Europe. And, even in both post-war Germanies and in Austria, a significant number of them still went on to gain extremely prominent military, economic, and political positions—for instance, the ex-pupils with whom I have corresponded during the course of my research have included a former Austrian Justice Minister, a NATO-Commander-in-Chief for Central Europe, and Erich Honecker's former righthand man in the East German Youth Organization, the FDJ.

I would therefore suggest that this study can provide a model, not only for treating *Bildungsgeschichte* as *Zeitgeschichte*, but also for treating *Bildungsgeschichte* as *Alltagsgeschichte*—demonstrating that, in a meaningful sense, the history of an era, a regime, or a dictatorship can indeed be written through the medium of the history of education or the history of childhood and youth—fusing institutional history with experiential history of the kind which has already been successfully pioneered in works such as Nicholas Stargardt's ground-breaking studies of childhood and war under Nazism, or the new C. H. Beck history series entitled 'The Germans and National Socialism' (*Die Deutschen und der Nationalsozialismus*).[37]

*

So, how far does this approach chime with previous discussions of the NPEA, and with further debates on society and pedagogy in the Third Reich more generally?

Despite the more or less recent appearance of a number of path-breaking MA and PhD theses, including Andreas Förschler's study of the NPEA in Backnang, Stefanie Flintrop's self-published doctoral dissertation on the Napolas for girls, Tim Müller's analysis of the NPEA and denazification, and Juliane Tiffert's examination of Napola school trips in South-Western Europe, the state of published scholarship on the Napolas for the most part remains preserved in aspic,[38] still held in thrall to the views put forward by Horst Ueberhorst and Harald Scholtz half a century ago, in the late 1960s and early 1970s.[39] Ueberhorst's sourcebook on the Napolas, *Elite für die Diktatur* (Elite for the Dictatorship), first appeared in 1969, and Harald Scholtz's monograph treating all of the Nazi elite schools, entitled *Nationalsozialistische Ausleseschulen* (National Socialist Selective Schools), was published four years later, in 1973—yet these two publications have still remained the unquestioned 'standard works' on the schools right up to the present day.[40]

This is not problematic merely because both works are considerably outdated, and rely upon a tiny fraction of the currently accessible sources (for instance, neither historian had access to documents held in what was then the German Democratic Republic), nor even because Scholtz's analysis is rooted in that contemporary vein of criticism which resolutely refused to take National Socialist ideological and pedagogical aspirations seriously (*Ideologiekritik*).[41] Rather, as Tim Müller has cogently argued, the fact that both scholars had themselves been educated at Nazi elite schools—in Ueberhorst's case, at NPEA Oranienstein; in Scholtz's case, at an Adolf-Hitler-School—led them deliberately to obfuscate the Napolas' history, in accordance with the positive 'post-war myths' which had been purposefully cultivated by former adherents of the NPEA as part of their denazification strategy (see Chapter 12).[42] Thus, Scholtz's desire both to play down the 'elite' status of what he preferred to term 'selective' schools at all costs, and to portray the Napolas' educational programme as 'pathetic', inefficient, and lacking in any pedagogical coherence—a judgement which has largely been unquestioningly accepted in subsequent scholarship—was ultimately driven by his own exculpatory political agenda:[43] namely, '[to distance] the Napolas and Adolf-Hitler-Schools from Nazi sites of indoctrination, such as the *SS-Junkerschulen* and *NS-Ordensburgen* [and] to correct the negative post-war image of the Adolf-Hitler-Schools by aligning it more closely with that of the Napolas'.[44]

Meanwhile, Ueberhorst's sourcebook, which is still used uncritically by many scholars and students as a substitute for undertaking archival research of their own on the NPEA, is even more deeply steeped in many of the most virulent tropes of defensive myth-building which former staff and pupils deployed during the immediate post-war period.[45] Thus, not only is the collection wholly biased towards material from Ueberhorst's old school, Oranienstein, but the (at times misleading) selection of documents and their framing or excerpting can easily lead to skewed interpretations.[46] As a case in point, both Scholtz and Ueberhorst provide an analysis of the Napolas which were founded in the 'Greater German Reich' which is historically untenable, ascribing beneficent motives to the NPEA Inspectorate, and distancing the institution from Himmler's Germanization policies in a fashion which does not bear the slightest resemblance to the facts which can now be reconstructed (nor even to those available at the time).[47] Thus, while both of these works may provide a starting-point for the uninitiated, they should no longer be treated as a central foundation for future analyses.

Therefore, in opposition to such politically motivated misconceptions, I would argue that the time is now ripe to take the Napolas' pedagogical aspirations and antecedents seriously—in line with more recent scholarly developments in German educational history, which has now dismissed the school of thought which argued that all National Socialist pedagogy must be deemed worthless 'un-pedagogy' (*Un-Pädagogik*) or 'non-education' (*Non-Bildung*), sedulously denying the existence of any continuities with previous types of pedagogy.[48] As the following chapters will show, despite having begun their life in somewhat experimental fashion, and having undergone various changes in direction and curricular adjustments over the years, the NPEA certainly did possess a coherent programme—the system was scarcely chaotic or shambolic in the way that Scholtz and his acolytes have consistently implied. Moreover, while all of the Nazi elite schools were undeniably sites of political indoctrination, the education on offer at the Napolas generally appears to have been less academically ineffective than that offered by the other elite schools, and acceptance was certainly defined more by one's ability than one's parents' political affiliation (which would have been unthinkable at the AHS).[49] Indeed, it appears that, at least until the advent of World War II (and even beyond), above-average intellectual capability was considered an essential criterion for attendance at most NPEA, even if this was still only one of a number of considerations which were taken into account holistically when assessing prospective pupils' suitability.[50]

Overall, in less than a decade, the Napolas had genuinely managed to create a system of schools which could in some sense be considered analogous to the British public schools—complete with the requisite more-or-less majestic campuses, catalogues of sporting victories, and long-standing institutional loyalties—their establishment had taken mere years, rather than decades or centuries. Thus, while one may ardently *wish* that the Napolas had achieved nothing, to deny that they did so *because* of that desire is to indulge in a form of historical obfuscation.[51] The education which the schools provided was arguably effective to a substantial degree, when considered on its own terms. Those terms may appear deplorable to a twenty-first-century observer, but to leave the question unexplored is to lose a key opportunity both to analyse the intentions of the Nazi dictatorship, and to explore how readily National Socialist educational ideologies could be put into practice, given favourable circumstances and a ready-made arena.

From this perspective, recent work on the *Ordensburgen* and the Adolf-Hitler-Schools has begun to take important steps in this direction—siting National Socialist elite education squarely within the context of key debates concerning the social and political history of the Third Reich as a whole.[52] As we shall see, the NPEA were arguably more effective and influential than either of these institutions—indeed, much of the AHS' educational programme was simply copied from that of the Napolas (see the Conclusion). Nevertheless, taking these volumes' lead, this book also treats the NPEA as one of those institutions which existed at the inclusive end of the regime's spectrum of mechanisms of inclusion or 'selection' (*Auslese*), forming the 'racial elite' at the apex of the *Volksgemeinschaft*—the other side of the coin of all those mechanisms of exclusion and eradication (*Ausmerze*) which were created in order to realize the regime's genocidal logic.[53]

In addition, this work also finds itself in dialogue with new transnational approaches to the Third Reich, demonstrating that, given the Napolas' imperial reach and expansionist drive, their history should also be considered from a transnational perspective.[54] Through trips, exchanges, and, ultimately, through the Nazi regime's war of conquest, their influence did indeed literally extend 'from the Arctic Ocean to Rio de Janeiro; from the Russian border to New York'.[55] Furthermore, the study engages with recent historiographical advances in regional history, women's history, and the history of religious persecution and colonial domination during the Third Reich, as well as engaging with key debates concerning the nature of the *Volksgemeinschaft*.[56] Finally, following the lead of other ground-breaking studies in German history which have appeared since the turn of the millennium, the book's range also encompasses continuities beyond the twentieth century's traditional temporal caesuras.[57] Thus, it not only considers pre-National Socialist influences on the NPEA (thereby demonstrating Nazism's fundamental accommodability with existing traditions), but also traces the impact of the schools' education and the fates of staff and pupils beyond the so-called 'zero hour' of Germany's defeat in 1945.[58]

*

In an essay published for an Anglophone readership in 1935, entitled 'The Educational Ideals of the German National Socialist Movement', Joachim Haupt, the first Inspector of the NPEA, described the Napolas as 'boarding establishments... designed to combine formal learning with political social training, and to act as a sort of advance guard on the road to the national socialistic reform of education'.[59] In similar vein, a few years later, Reich Education Minister Bernhard Rust hailed the NPEA as 'the granite foundations of future national political education...they have become the pioneer and paradigm of National Socialist schooling'.[60]

In the view of the Education Minister and both Inspectors of the NPEA, only a boarding-school environment could sufficiently realize the National Socialist pedagogical mission of unifying the competing educational influences of the parental home, school, and Hitler Youth.[61] From this perspective, the Napola programme did indeed offer something new, since elite boarding schools were a relative rarity in the German educational landscape. Unlike Britain, with its many public schools, Germany could boast only a few venerable boarding institutions such as Schulpforta and the Saxon ducal schools at Grimma and Meißen, the aristocratic '*Ritterakademien*', the former cadet schools, and the newly conceived *Landerziehungsheime* or country boarding schools, as well as (often religious-run) boarding schools in areas where the rural population was so scattered as to make it difficult for children to commute to school every day from outlying farms and villages.

In general, the architects of the NPEA system were keen to stress the utter originality or '*Neuartigkeit*' of their brainchild at all costs, whilst disavowing the importance of previous educational traditions. This distancing from all previous paradigms also operated at the level of the vocabulary used at the schools; adherents of the Napolas were explicitly ordered to avoid using terminology from the 'civilian' system as far as possible—a 'deliberate setting-aside of terms and designations used in schools at large'.[62] Although, from a curricular standpoint, the NPEA generally followed academic syllabuses analogous to those of other German secondary schools (see Chapter 2),[63] the Napolas' novelty was held to lie more specifically both in their stringent selection process, and in their claim to provide a form of 'total education' (*Gesamterziehung*) which could mould pupils' characters whilst indoctrinating them politically and steeling them physically, encompassing them at all times within the school 'community' or *Gemeinschaft*.[64] Thus, the purely military methods of the cadet schools were considered to be no more fitting a model for the Napolas' educational praxis as a whole than the methods of any normal day-school would have been.[65]

As we shall see in Chapter 4, the NPEA did in fact inherit many traditions and practices from the Royal Prussian Cadet Corps—but the validity of these was always contested and open to interpretation.[66] At the same time, new models of child-centred boarding education, such as those put forward by Hermann Lietz and other adherents of reform pedagogy at the *Landerziehungsheime* and other private boarding schools during the Weimar era, were explicitly dismissed by Heißmeyer et al. as being far too liberalistic and averse to militarization.[67] Meanwhile, although the NPEA programme might have possessed some affinities with pedagogical theories put forward by Nazi educationalists such as Ernst Krieck, there is very little evidence to suggest that these theories ever exerted a meaningful influence on the schools' praxis and their day-to-day functioning.[68] Thus, despite the ostensible connections which some commentators have perceived between Krieck's tract entitled *Nationalpolitische Erziehung* (*National Political Education*), first published in 1932, and the 'National Political Education Institutes'—in part simply due to their shared use of the adjective '*nationalpolitisch*', and their general adherence to certain key tenets of the Nazi educational *Weltanschauung*—these similarities appear to have possessed little significance in practice; not least because Krieck himself explicitly condemned boarding-school education within the pages of the tome in question.[69]

Rather, as in many other spheres of education in the Third Reich, most NPEA praxis bypassed such academic theory-building entirely and, when in search of inspiration, went straight to the Nazi 'Gospel'—*Mein Kampf*.[70] In accordance with the Führer's pseudo-philosophical outpourings, the NPEA aimed to create the National Socialist 'new man', whilst simultaneously drawing not only upon those utopian ideals encapsulated within the turn-of-the-century youth movements, but also upon that sphere of educational theory which Nazi educators most affected to despise—reform pedagogy.[71] Thus, while many aspects of the Napolas' programme, especially the extracurricular activities such as camps, wargames, harvest 'missions', and borderland activism, had their basis in the practice of the interwar youth movements (as Rüdiger Ahrens' seminal study has shown, many of these groups were very much attuned to the more right-wing currents in Weimar politics), many reform-pedagogical teaching methods were equally susceptible to authoritarian adaptation at the NPEA.[72] These might include self-directed projects, a general emphasis on pupils' gaining greater independence and responsibility, and the cultivation of a varied range of artistic and practical skills and talents (see Chapter 3).[73] From this perspective, we can ultimately see the NPEA programme as a highly effective fusion combining all of the most seductive elements of reform pedagogy, youth-movement praxis, and the militarized education offered at the Prussian cadet schools.[74]

Whatever their antecedents, however, the ultimate aim of the NPEA in the eyes of their creators was to train their pupils into regime-loyal subjects who would be capable of serving the Nazi state in any type of leadership role—even though programmatic texts on the schools were always at pains to stress that attendance at a Napola by no means entitled graduates to a stellar career or a favoured position in the Reich's political hierarchy.[75] Although there existed variations in selection criteria between individual schools, as well as in their curricula, the basic demands made of prospective pupils were always relatively consistent: they had to be 'healthy, irreproachable racially and in terms of their character, and gifted with above-average intelligence'.[76] Exceptions to these requirements on grounds of political expediency appear to have been rare in the extreme, and the schools were constantly concerned to emphasize that they were far from mere institutions for 'charity cases'; children from disadvantaged backgrounds would only be admitted if they fulfilled all of the schools' other essential admission criteria (see Chapter 2).[77]

Nevertheless, in accordance with Point 20 of the NSDAP Party programme, numerous press articles and programmatic documents written by or on behalf of the school authorities also stressed that the social status of applicants, in particular their parents' wealth or standing, made no difference whatsoever to their ability to gain a place at the schools.[78] A particularly favoured conceit was the idea that the 'spirit of socialism' ruled supreme at the Napolas, so that (for example), the son of a Major might live and work alongside the son of a foreman in a tram garage.[79] As Heißmeyer put it in an interview with the Reich Youth Press Service in September 1936, 'It would be a betrayal of National Socialism if we were to make the education of our future leaders a question of wealth or pedigree'.[80]

To this end, a generous means-tested system of free and subsidized places was devised, which ensured that approximately 10 per cent of pupils were charged no fees at all, with a series of incremental steps rising from Class B (*c.*240 RM per year, or 20 RM per calendar month) to Class M (*c.*1,440 RM per year, or 120 RM per calendar month), according to parents' net income.[81] Free places were also offered to certain categories of Prussian and Reich civil servants.[82] Individual schools were additionally encouraged to seek support from local government, town councils, firms, and Party organizations to sponsor subsidized places for boys from their local area, in order to provide even more opportunities for the children of financially disadvantaged citizens—and some of these initiatives do seem to have achieved some degree of success.[83] In addition, those NPEA with so-called '*Aufbauzüge*' attached—classes starting at around 13, for those boys who had missed out on being selected at the age of 10 in the *Volksschule* (primary school)—offered a far higher ratio of free places, in a deliberate attempt to bring a larger proportion of working-class youth into the schools.[84]

In this connection, it is worth noting that the Inspectorate made it a point of honour that no *Jungmann* should be expelled simply because his parents or guardians were unable to pay the school-fees, and, in 1936, Heißmeyer concluded an agreement with Reich Organization Leader Robert Ley that, in cases where the local Mayor, Party offices (*Kreisleitung*), or Gauleitung were unable to stump up the funds for a scholarship or a sponsored place, Ley's German Labour Front (DAF) would foot the bill.[85]

Such social assistance not only covered the payment of school fees, however, but also extended to all areas of school life. The Napolas provided their pupils with all of the requisite uniforms and equipment, so that—as in the Hitler Youth—variations in social status among the *Jungmannen* could never be revealed by differences in dress.[86] All pupils received exactly the same amount of pocket money (around 10 RM per month), and their families were strictly forbidden from sending further tips or top-ups to supplement this.[87] Moreover, each *Anstaltsleiter* (headmaster) was charged with the duty of forcing all social distinctions to vanish from his NPEA, and 'particularly worthy, but socially badly-off *Jungmannen*' were to be provided with funding at his discretion to smooth their path, without their having to ask for it, and without their schoolmates knowing anything about it. This institutional generosity might include paying for journeys home in the holidays, or subsidizing particularly expensive school trips. In 1934, the NPEA authorities requested 3,000 RM to be set aside in the 1935 Prussian state budget for this specific purpose.[88]

The Inspectorate even made arrangements with bodies such as the Reich Student Affairs Office (*Reichsstudentenwerk*) that less well-off *Jungmannen* would be put forward for their funding-streams without having to participate in a special course or *Lehrgang* (which all 'normal' applicants would have been expected to undergo as a matter of course). *Jungmannen* were also given especially detailed careers advice, both by the *Reichsstudentenwerk* and by the SS-Central Office, while those exhibiting particular potential for and interest in the diplomatic service would be automatically put forward as candidates for the Foreign Office's fast-track course, as well as being presented to Foreign Minister Joachim von Ribbentrop in person at their graduation.[89] Thus, at least during the pre-war years, the idea that attending an NPEA could open doors which would previously have been completely inaccessible to boys from a lower-class background seems to have had some foundation in fact. This contention is also supported by the fact that, in cases where relevant statistics exist, it appears that the majority of Napola graduates pursued careers in the professions and in leadership positions which were at least equal to, and at times of higher social standing, than those pursued by their parents.[90] Moreover, as H. W. Koch has argued, the representation of children from working-class backgrounds at the NPEA during the late 1930s was significantly greater than that offered by any other form of higher education in Germany, either prior to the Third Reich, or for many decades thereafter.[91]

*

In the chapters which follow, many of these themes will be explored in greater depth. However, while it would be possible to gain a basic overview of the Napolas' functioning purely by reading Part I, especially the two longer core chapters on daily life and extracurricular activities at the NPEA, and the chapters in Part II have deliberately been written in such a way that they can each be read separately as individual case studies if so desired (as could the chapters on the schools' wartime and post-war fate in Part III), the reader will undoubtedly gain the most value from the volume if they read it from start to finish.

Within the following section (Part I—'Genesis'), Chapter 1 explores the foundation and subsequent development of the NPEA and their administration, including staff recruitment. Although both the Wehrmacht and the SS became ever more concerned to gain control of the Napolas for their own ends, neither achieved their aim, and the Education Ministry continued to retain some control of the schools, even in the face of Himmler's wrath. As with so many political institutions during the Third Reich, the constant wrangling of hostile factions formed an inevitable backdrop to the system's expansion.

The next two core chapters then move on to focus in detail on everyday life at the Napolas. Chapter 2 describes the various processes by which pupils were selected for the entrance exam, the nature of the exam itself, and pupils' first impressions of their new environment when they arrived, as well as giving an account of general routine at the schools, and the various types of activities in which pupils consistently took part—whether academic, sporting, pre-military, or purely recreational. Chapter 3 then treats the creative and artistic education which the Napolas offered, as well as less routine occurrences, such as festivities, trips abroad, exchanges with schools in other countries (British public schools and US academies), and the so-called *Einsätze* (missions), during which pupils were sent to live and work with farmers, miners, or factory-workers, in order to experience their way of life at first hand.

The following six chapters (Part II—'Variety within Unity') then go on to analyse the different types of school within the Napola system in more detail. Chapter 4 looks at the process of 'Napolisation' which took place at the Weimar Republic's *Staatliche Bildungsanstalten*, the successor institutions of the former Prussian cadet schools. The chapter considers how far the NPEA represented a resurrection of the cadet-school tradition, and the schools' connection with more broadly existing affinities between Prussianism and National Socialism. Chapter 5 then examines the tensions between the central government in Berlin and the German federal states when it came to the foundation of non-Prussian NPEA in Saxony, Anhalt, and Württemberg, and the Napolas' relationship with broader impulses towards centralization within the National Socialist state.

Meanwhile, Chapter 6 considers the Napolas' marginalization of religious and oppositional educational foundations, looking in detail at the Napolisation of Ilfeld and Schulpforta, the first 'humanistic' NPEA to be founded, as well as the fates of those schools at Haselünne, St. Wendel, and Neubeuern, which were far more ruthlessly expropriated. Chapter 7 then goes on to explore the transformation of the Viennese *Bundeserziehungsanstalten* into Napolas in the wake of the Anschluss, whilst also depicting Heißmeyer's 'Klostersturm' or expropriation of the Austrian monasteries, due to his rapacious desire to find suitable campuses for new schools—both processes conform to patterns of Nazification policy in Austria more generally during this period. Chapter 8 then considers the schools'

Germanizing mission in the Eastern and Western occupied territories within the context of broader mechanisms of Nazi colonial domination during World War II, while Chapter 9 looks at the curricula and contested nature of the NPEA for girls, which fundamentally reflected competing National Socialist attitudes to the 'woman question' more generally.

Moving on to Part III ('Nemesis'), Chapter 10 depicts the deterioration in the quality of school life in wartime, including the 'missions' which pupils had to perform as anti-aircraft auxiliaries or leaders in the children's evacuation programme (KLV). Chronic shortages of everything from steel to salt, from teaching staff to stable-hands, increasingly thrust the schools into a whirlwind of administrative chaos, as Germany's fortunes in World War II gradually worsened. Chapter 11, the only chapter based primarily on eyewitness testimony, then charts the long series of evacuations, treks, and (in some cases) desperate last stands in which pupils took part, as the Allies advanced further and further into the heart of Germany in Spring 1945. Meanwhile, Chapter 12 looks beyond 1945 to examine the ways in which staff and pupils managed to 'master their pasts', both in the immediate aftermath of the war, in the context of Allied denazification processes, and beyond, analysing the strategies which former pupils have employed in creating their own form of 'collective memory', and the formation of their old boys' networks. Finally, the Conclusion considers the effectiveness or otherwise of the schools' pedagogical approach on its own terms, comparing the Napolas' performance with that of other mechanisms of education and indoctrination within the Nazi state, including normal 'civilian' secondary schools, the Hitler Youth, and the Adolf-Hitler-Schools.

Given the patchy survival of sources on the NPEA—not least due to mass burnings of documents at many schools by staff and pupils as the Allied forces advanced in spring 1945—I have endeavoured throughout my research for this book to seek out as broad a source-base as possible, synthesizing material from as many archives and libraries as was practically feasible, in order to ensure that any generalizations I might make would be well-founded. Every institution which I visited added at least one or two more pieces to the overall mosaic. While the official archival correspondence from the NPEA administration and government organizations and ministries can illuminate the schools' hierarchy and institutional framework, surviving documents pertaining to individual schools, in particular their newsletters, can more readily provide insights into daily life at the Napolas. Of course, I have routinely subjected all of my sources to the most stringent criticism, especially given that media and newsletter reports necessarily portray the ideal face of the system or the Napola in question, rather than presenting some form of unvarnished reality. Nevertheless, in conjunction with surviving private documents, these school newsletters can still give us an unparalleled window onto the schools' endeavours, as well as revealing crucial variations in their individual ethos.[92] Chapter 11 aside, I have tended only to use retrospective eyewitness testimonies and memoirs corroboratively; however, in Chapter 12, I also treat the themes of Napola collective memory which repeatedly arise in these sources in some detail.[93]

From this perspective, it is quite possible that some of the eyewitnesses with whom I have corresponded may consider the conclusions of this account disappointing. Some had clearly hoped that my work might vindicate their own post-war perceptions of the Napolas' status, and prove that the NPEA were—due to their lack of explicit Party affiliation—'not a Nazi school' (see Chapter 12). All of the surviving evidence, however, points resolutely in the opposite direction. The NPEA were indeed instruments of the Nazi state, and their aims and ideology were steeped in the tenets of Nazism, although they did not succumb to anti-intellectualism and pure indoctrination in so grave a measure as the Adolf-Hitler-Schools.

Yet, as Heidi Rosenbaum has shown, it is unsurprising that my correspondents and interviewees follow the pattern prevalent in their generation of remembering their schooldays as 'normal' and 'unpolitical', even when their everyday life was shaped by the Napola (and hence by Nazism) on every level.[94] Because much of the schools' ideological indoctrination was covert rather than overt, and in any case largely corresponded to views with which they would have been instilled throughout their childhood, pupils would often genuinely have perceived nothing especially political about their schooling at the time. It is only hindsight, which reformats these recollections from direct representation of the child's contemporary perceptions and emotions to an adult reconception of those same events and experiences, that allows such memories to be accepted by ex-pupils as indicating that their education was in fact thoroughly politicized. Hence, many eyewitnesses are unable (or unwilling) to transform their 'happy', 'normal' memories of their schooldays into a more unpalatable, if more objective, perspective on the past. This should not necessarily be considered the mere product of conscious dissimulation, but rather as a means of reconciling unbearable cognitive dissonance; a protection mechanism aimed above all at preserving the self.[95]

Ultimately, however, the Napolas were undoubtedly intended to provide an ideal National Socialist education. And—unlike the only comparable system of Nazi elite schools, the AHS—the NPEA can also fairly be said to have realized much of their potential during the six years of peace following the Nazi seizure of power. Even during the war years, the schools continued to proliferate and expand at an astonishing rate, despite endemic war-related shortages of personnel, building materials and supplies. The desperation with which the regime sought to uphold the Napola system during a time of total war, at enormous cost, also proves how extraordinarily vital the Nazi regime perceived these schools to be—both for the German war effort, and for the regime's confidently envisaged post-war future.

Notes

1. Bundesarchiv Lichterfelde (BArch), R 43-II/956b, Bl. 47–50, letter from Heißmeyer to Lammers dated 22 October 1940 confirming his position, following a personal meeting with Lammers which had taken place on 18 October.
2. BArch, R 4606/2022, letters dated 19 March 1941, 5 December 1941; on the further development of these plans, see related correspondence in this file; also BArch, R 2/27762, letter dated 31 July 1942. Heißmeyer also planned to turn the schools' retreat at Burg Strechau in Styria into a fully functioning centre for special courses and conferences (BArch, R 2/27788, report dated 12 July 1943).
3. Staatsarchiv Ludwigsburg (StAL), FL410–4 Bü 109, 'Arbeitstagung im Reichsfinanzministerium Berlin und in der Nat.polit. Erziehungsanstalt in Ballenstedt vom 15.-18.7.1941', 3.
4. BArch, NS 19/2741, Bl. 28, letter from Heißmeyer to Berger dated 24 July 1942.
5. BArch, R 1501/131026, letter dated 25 May 1944. If we also include the one NPEA which had to be closed before the war, Wahlstatt, this means that the total number of Napolas founded, by the Inspectorate's own reckoning, was forty-four. However, many of these schools were only '*im Aufbau*'—that is, they were still at an early stage in the process of being built up from a couple of initial year-groups into a full-size secondary school.
6. See Chapter 8.
7. Cf. Šimůnek, Michal, 'Poslední "vůdcovska škola" nacistické diktatury: tzv. Nacionálně politický výchovný ústav Čechy (Nationalpolitische Erziehungsanstalt Böhmen) v Kutné Hoře, 1943–1945 [Die "NPEA Böhmen" in Kuttenberg 1943–1945: Letzte "Führerschule" der national-sozialistischen Diktatur]', *Acta Universitatis Carolinae* 51, no. 1 (2011), 59–81.
8. Brandenburgisches Landeshauptarchiv (BLHA), 204A MdF Nr. 2128, letter dated 4 September 1945; on the fate of other school buildings and campuses during the immediate post-war period, see Chapter 12.
9. BLHA, 204A MdF Nr. 2128, letter dated 5 April 1946.
10. In this context, Heißmeyer's ambitions had much in common with other wartime SS projects anticipating the 'final victory', including the 'Generalplan Ost'. As Bastian Hein has shown, these plans were frequently characterized, firstly, by a radicalism which went well beyond that of other Nazi state agencies; secondly, they were never mere 'chimeras' which possessed no foundation in reality, but were often able to proceed well beyond the planning stage; finally, the drive for their implementation remained largely unaffected by the severe military setbacks which Germany suffered both in winter 1941–2, and after Stalingrad; rather, their evolution often continued almost until the bitter end—cf. Bastian Hein, *Elite für Volk und Führer? Die Allgemeine SS und ihre Mitglieder 1925–1945* (Munich, 2012), 297–300.
11. Cf. 'Schule der Auslese. Die nationalpolitischen Erziehungsanstalten', *Neues Wiener Tageblatt*, 13 June 1939 [BArch, R 3903/2248]. Indeed, we might ascribe the relative dearth of recent studies on the NPEA, in comparison with the *Ordensburgen* and Adolf-Hitler-Schools, to this literal lack of visibility. For a more wide-ranging comparison of the Napolas with both of these institutions, see the Conclusion.

12. BArch, NS 2/64, Bl. 123; cf. *Der Deutsche Volkserzieher* 3 (1938), 429; BArch, R 4901/8, Bl. 61, correspondence dated 4 March 1938. The Inspectorate was similarly incensed when the NPEA were termed 'Napoli-schools' in an official report by a British educational commission.
13. Gustav Skroblin, 'Vom Sinn der Gemeinschaftserziehung in den Nationalpolitischen Erziehungsanstalten', *Frauen-Warte* 6 (1941) [BArch, NS 5/VI/18842]. N.B. All translations are the author's own.
14. Cf. 'Vier Jahre NPEA. Nationalsozialistische Erziehungsanstalten—Musterstätten der Gemeinschaftserziehung: Eine Unterredung mit SS-Obergruppenführer Heißmeyer', *Rote Erde*, 20 April 1937 [BArch, R 4902/1490]; F. Kopp, 'Glauben, Gehorchen, Kämpfen! Vom Weg und Ziel der "Nationalpolitischen Erziehungsanstalten"', *Völkischer Beobachter*, 14 March 1939 [BArch, NS 5/VI/18842]; 'Oldenburger Jungen auf der Nationalpolitischen Erziehungsanstalt', *Oldenburgische Staatszeitung*, 4 February 1941 [Bundesarchiv Koblenz, ZSg. 117 Nr. 290].
15. BArch, NS 2/64, Bl. 121ff.; Helmut Trepte, 'Die Napolas', *Berliner Tageblatt*, 14 April 1938 [BArch, R 4902/1490]. For a full discussion of the Napolas' relationship with the AHS, see the Conclusion.
16. Cf. e.g. 'Jungen der Napola spielen mit im Film. "Kopf hoch, Johannes!" wird gegenwärtig von Victor de Kowa gedreht', *Thüringer Gauzeitung*, 29 July 1940 [Kreisarchiv Nordhausen]; Bundesarchiv-Militärarchiv Freiburg, RS 14/4 (Teil 2), letter dated 19 February 1940; Hellmann, 'Nationalpolitische Erziehungsanstalten', *Mitteldeutsche Nationalzeitung*, 18 February 1936 [BArch, NS 5/VI/18840].
17. Österreichisches Staatsarchiv (ÖStA), BEA 7, letter dated 12 September 1938; StAL, E 202 Bü 1746, letter dated 19 January 1937; cf. BArch, R 43/II-956b, Hempel, 'Bergwerkseinsatz des Zuges "Walter Clausen" (6. Zug) der Nationalpolitischen Erziehungsanstalt Plön' (24 June 1942), §14; BArch, R 2/27788, letter dated 19 June 1942.
18. StAL, E 202 Bü 1746, letter dated 19 January 1937; cf. StAL, E 202 Bü 1747, letter dated 6 September 1939.
19. For a discussion of these abbreviations and their contemporary usage, see the Note on Terminology above. I shall use both abbreviations interchangeably in the pages which follow, for reasons of stylistic variation.
20. For a detailed analysis of Spartan influences at the schools, see Helen Roche, *Sparta's German Children: The Ideal of Ancient Sparta in the Royal Prussian Cadet Corps, 1818–1920, and in National Socialist Elite Schools (the Napolas), 1933–1945* (Swansea, 2013); on British public-school influences, see Helen Roche, '*Zwischen Freundschaft und Feindschaft*: Exploring Relationships between Pupils at the Napolas (*Nationalpolitische Erziehungsanstalten*) and British Public Schoolboys', *Angermion: Yearbook for Anglo-German Literary Criticism, Intellectual History and Cultural Transfers/Jahrbuch für britisch-deutsche Kulturbeziehungen* 6 (2013), 101–26, 104–8; on the cadet-school tradition at the NPEA, see Chapter 4.
21. Four girls' schools were also founded (Hubertendorf-Türnitz in Austria, Achern, Colmar-Berg in Luxembourg, and Heythuysen in the Netherlands respectively); their aims and programme are discussed in detail in Chapter 9. However, given their marginal position within the Napola system as a whole, I have based the following overview on the state of affairs at the boys' schools alone.

22. For a detailed account of the selection process and daily life at the schools, see Chapter 2.
23. For a concise depiction of sporting and pre-military activities at the schools, see also Chapter 2; for a more in-depth analysis, see Helen Roche, 'Sport, Leibeserziehung und vormilitärische Ausbildung in den Nationalpolitischen Erziehungsanstalten: Eine "radikale" Revolution der körperlichen Bildung im Rahmen der NS-"Gesamterziehung"?', *Beiträge zur Geschichte des Nationalsozialismus* 32 (2016), 173–96.
24. For more on all of these activities, see Chapter 3.
25. On the deterioration of the situation at the schools in wartime, see Chapter 10.
26. For an exception to this rule, see Elke Fröhlich, 'Die drei Typen der nationalsozialistischen Ausleseschulen', in Johannes Leeb, ed., *'Wir waren Hitlers Eliteschüler'. Ehemalige Zöglinge der NS-Ausleseschulen brechen ihr Schweigen* (Munich, 2005), 241–63.
27. The quotation '*und sie werden nicht mehr frei ihr ganzes Leben*' is taken from a speech which Hitler gave to the Hitler Youth in Hagen in December 1938, and has subsequently become a commonplace when discussing National Socialist pedagogy and the regime's totalitarian claims on youth; '*flink wie Windhunde, zäh wie Leder und hart wie Kruppstahl*' is a citation from *Mein Kampf* (Munich, 1943 edn, 392).
28. Cf. Moritz Föllmer, 'The Subjective Dimension of Nazism', *The Historical Journal* 56, no. 4 (2013), 1107–32; Moritz Föllmer, *Individuality and Modernity in Berlin: Self and Society from Weimar to the Wall* (Cambridge, 2013); Pamela E. Swett, Corey Ross, and Fabrice d'Almeida, eds, *Pleasure and Power in Nazi Germany* (Basingstoke, 2011); Frank Bajohr and Michael Wildt, eds, *Volksgemeinschaft. Neue Forschungen zur Gesellschaft des Nationalsozialismus* (Frankfurt am Main, 2009); Martina Steber and Bernhard Gotto, '*Volksgemeinschaft*: Writing the Social History of the Nazi Regime', in Martina Steber and Bernhard Gotto, eds, *Visions of Community in Nazi Germany: Social Engineering and Private Lives* (Oxford, 2014), 1–25.
29. Cf. Peter Reichel, *Der schöne Schein des Dritten Reiches. Gewalt und Faszination des deutschen Faschismus* (Hamburg, 2006).
30. Cf. e.g. Walter Flemming, 'Ehemalige Schüler der Nationalpolitischen Erziehungsanstalt Ilfeld/Südharz äußern sich über ihre Erlebnisse in der Anstalt. Walter Flemming—Interview durch eine Studentin' (1984), 35; Manfred F., private correspondence, 4 September 2011; Eckhard R., private correspondence, 25 February 2012. We might compare such feelings of superiority with Katrin Kollmeier's observations on 'the ordering of inequality' within the Hitler Youth organization—cf. Katrin Kollmeier, *Ordnung und Ausgrenzung. Die Disziplinarpolitik der Hitler-Jugend* (Göttingen, 2007), 13–14.
31. Norbert Frei, '"Volksgemeinschaft". Erfahrungsgeschichte und Lebenswirklichkeit der Hitler-Zeit', in *1945 und wir. Das Dritte Reich im Bewußtsein der Deutschen* (Munich, 2009), 121–42.
32. Cf. David Schoenbaum, *Hitler's Social Revolution: Class and Status in Nazi Germany* (New York, 1966); further literature on this theme will be discussed in the relevant sections below.
33. Jürgen Finger, *Eigensinn im Einheitsstaat. NS-Schulpolitik in Württemberg, Baden und im Elsass 1933–1945* (Baden-Baden, 2016), 21–45.

34. Cf. e.g. Kristine Alexander and Simon Sleight, 'Introduction', in Kristine Alexander and Simon Sleight, eds, *A Cultural History of Youth in the Modern Age* (London, forthcoming); also Martha Saxton, 'Introduction to the First Volume of *The Journal of the History of Childhood and Youth*', in Heidi Morrison, ed., *The Global History of Childhood Reader* (New York, 2012), 103–4; Paula S. Fass, 'Introduction: Is There a Story in the History of Childhood?', in Paula S. Fass, ed., *The Routledge History of Childhood in the Western World* (New York, 2013), 1–14.
35. For similar sentiments, see Nicholas Stargardt, 'German Childhoods: The Making of a Historiography', *German History* 16, no. 1 (1998), 1–15, esp. 12–14; Charles Lansing, *From Nazism to Communism: German Schoolteachers under Two Dictatorships* (Cambridge, MA, 2010), 7–8; Machteld Venken and Maren Röger, 'Growing up in the Shadow of the Second World War: European Perspectives', *European Review of History/revue européenne d'histoire* 22, no. 2 (2015), 199–220, esp. 203.
36. Detlef Brandes, *'Umvolkung, Umsiedlung, rassische Bestandsaufnahme'. NS-'Volkstumspolitik' in den böhmischen Ländern* (Munich, 2012); Johannes Koll, *Arthur Seyß-Inquart und die deutsche Besatzungspolitik in den Niederlanden (1940–1945)* (Vienna, 2015); Annette Mertens, *Himmlers Klostersturm. Der Angriff auf katholische Einrichtungen im Zweiten Weltkrieg und die Wiedergutmachung nach 1945* (Paderborn, 2006).
37. Nicholas Stargardt, *Witnesses of War: Children's Lives under the Nazis* (London, 2006); Nicholas Stargardt, *The German War: A Nation under Arms, 1939–45* (London, 2015); titles in the C. H. Beck series thus far include Tim Schanetzky, *'Kanonen statt Butter': Wirtschaft und Konsum im Dritten Reich* (Munich, 2015), Moritz Föllmer, *'Ein Leben wie im Traum': Kultur im Dritten Reich* (Munich, 2016), and Dietmar Süß, *'Ein Volk, ein Reich, ein Führer': Die deutsche Gesellschaft im Dritten Reich* (Munich, 2017). On the significance of educational *Alltagsgeschichte* for the study of Fascism, see Luca la Rovere, 'Totalitarian Pedagogy and the Italian Youth', in Jorge Dagnino, Matthew Feldman, and Paul Stocker, eds, *The 'New Man' in Radical Right Ideology and Practice, 1919–45* (London, 2018), 19–38; on the importance of exploring the history of children's everyday life in Nazi Germany, see also Heidi Rosenbaum, *'Und trotzdem war's 'ne schöne Zeit'. Kinderalltag im Nationalsozialismus* (Frankfurt am Main, 2014), esp. 11–14.
38. Andreas Förschler, 'Die Nationalpolitische Erziehungsanstalt Backnang. Eine Eliteschule im Dritten Reich' (MA thesis, Stuttgart, 2002); Stefanie Jodda-Flintrop, *'Wir sollten intelligente Mütter werden'. Nationalpolitische Erziehungsanstalten für Mädchen* (Norderstedt, 2010); Tim Müller, 'From Racial Selection to Postwar Deception: The Napolas and Denazification' (PhD thesis, McMaster University, 2016). Although the latter contains some factual errors in the chapters on the Third Reich itself, due to the limited nature of the archival research which the author was able to undertake, Müller's analysis of the post-war period is extremely useful, and some of the most valuable sections of the thesis have now been published in his article 'A Legal Odyssey: Denazification Law, Nazi Elite Schools, and the Construction of Postwar Memory', *History of Education* 46, no. 4 (2017), 498–513. Other works by local historians and school and university students are of variable quality; most only treat a single school, and many of the authors in question tend to make erroneous generalizations

about the entire Napola system based on their limited research; most make no attempt whatsoever to engage with broader historiographical debates concerning culture and society in the Third Reich in general. However, the most useful examples of this type of publication include Arnulf Moser's *Die Napola Reichenau. Von der Heil- und Pflegeanstalt zur nationalsozialistischen Eliteerziehung (1941–1945)* (Konstanz, 1997), Adolf Morlang's *'Neuer Stil im alten Schloss'. Die Napola/NPEA Oranienstein 1934–1945* (Diez, 2002), and Matthias Paustian's *Die Nationalpolitische Erziehungsanstalt Plön 1933–1945* (Rostock, 1995). In cases where I consider works of this type to possess scholarly value, I have cited them in the relevant sections discussing individual schools; those which have been published are also listed in the bibliography. For a more detailed critique of the extant literature, see also Roche, *Sparta's German Children*, 4–5.

39. Gisela Miller-Kipp's highly tendentious contributions to the debate on Nazi 'elite' education are particularly noteworthy in this regard (as discussed in this volume's Note on Terminology); cf. n. 50. For discussion of an analogous 'timewarp' problem concerning scholarship on the Waffen-SS, see Martin Gutmann, *Building a Nazi Europe: The SS's Germanic Volunteers* (Cambridge, 2017), 7: 'Perhaps as a result of the monopolization of Waffen-SS literature by former Waffen-SS members and their apologetic supporters, serious historians long wrote the topic off. With the exception of [a few studies], the history of the military arm of the SS was neglected for almost fifty years. As the historiography of the Nazi regime and its war crimes has become a lot more complicated over the past few decades, dealing with everything from race, class, gender, and sexuality to transnationalism, historians' assumptions about the origins and role of the Waffen-SS were frozen in time'. Although Klaus Schmitz's monograph *Militärische Jugenderziehung. Preußische Kadettenhäuser und Nationalpolitische Erziehungsanstalten zwischen 1807 und 1936* (Frankfurt am Main, 1997) avoids these pitfalls to some extent, Schmitz's fairly brief treatment of the NPEA (pp. 245–304) only considers the first three years of the schools' existence, and is far more concerned with the minutiae of ministerial power-politics than with elucidating the nature of everyday life at the schools.
40. Horst Ueberhorst, *Elite für die Diktatur. Die Nationalpolitischen Erziehungsanstalten 1933–1945: Ein Dokumentarbericht* (Düsseldorf, 1969); Harald Scholtz, *Nationalsozialistische Ausleseschulen. Internatsschulen als Herrschaftsmittel des Führerstaates* (Göttingen, 1973).
41. On the prevalence of *Ideologiekritik* during this period, see Lutz Raphael, 'Pluralities of National Socialist Ideology: New Perspectives on the Production and Diffusion of National Socialist *Weltanschauung*', in Martina Steber and Bernhard Gotto, eds, *Visions of Community in Nazi Germany: Social Engineering and Private Lives* (Oxford, 2014), 73–86, 73–4; on prevailing scholarly views concerning the necessity of discarding such forms of criticism and taking National Socialist ideology seriously, see e.g. Richard J. Evans, *The Coming of the Third Reich* (London, 2003), Preface; Richard J. Evans, 'The Emergence of Nazi Ideology', in Jane Caplan, ed., *Nazi Germany* (Oxford, 2008), 26–47; Peter Fritzsche, *Life and Death in the Third Reich* (Cambridge, MA, 2008), 15; Thomas Rohkrämer, *Die fatale Attraktion des Nationalsozialismus. Zur Popularität eines Unrechtsregimes* (Paderborn, 2013), 10–12; Gudrun Brockhaus, 'Einführung: Attraktion der NS-Bewegung—Eine interdisziplinäre Perspektive', in Gudrun Brockhaus, ed., *Attraktion der NS-Bewegung* (Essen, 2014), 7–28, 8–9.

42. Müller, 'Legal Odyssey', 512; Müller, 'Postwar Deception', 23.
43. Scholtz, *Ausleseschulen*, esp. 8–10, 57, 61–2, 76–7, 97ff., 107–8; for similar criticisms of Scholtz's portrayal of the Adolf-Hitler-Schulen, see Wolfgang and Barbara Feller, *Die Adolf-Hitler-Schulen. Pädagogische Provinz versus ideologische Zuchtanstalt* (Weinheim, 2001). For more recent overviews of education in the Third Reich which have tended to take Scholtz's negative interpretation of the NPEA at face value, see e.g. Richard J. Evans, *The Third Reich in Power* (London, 2006), esp. 282–5; Lisa Pine, *Education in Nazi Germany* (Oxford, 2010), ch. 4.
44. Müller, 'Postwar Deception', 23.
45. e.g. Ueberhorst, *Elite*, 9–13, 28–30, 36–7, 41–4, 93–4, 137, 399; cf. Müller, 'Legal Odyssey', 512; also Chapter 12.
46. For criticism of Scholtz's similarly limited sourcebase, see Feller and Feller, *Adolf-Hitler-Schulen*, 230–1. While Erhard Naake's two extant discussions of the NPEA—his unpublished doctoral dissertation, entitled 'Zur Theorie und Praxis der Erziehung in den Nationalpolitischen Erziehungsanstalten und ähnlichen faschistischen "Eliteschulen"' (Jena, 1971), and his article 'Die Heranbildung des Führernachwuchses im faschistischen Deutschland', *Zeitschrift für Geschichtswissenschaft* 21, no. 2 (1973), 181–95—are completely imbued with politicized antifascist jargon and Communist assumptions (including a concerted attempt to prove that fascist tendencies in elite pedagogy were being cultivated in present-day West Germany), Naake's critique of Ueberhorst's work on this score does possess some basis in reality—including the fact that the sourcebook presents exculpatory denazification documents as 'evidence' for the schools' programme (cf. Naake, 'Heranbildung', 187).
47. For a more detailed discussion of these failings, see Helen Roche, '*Herrschaft durch Schulung*: The *Nationalpolitische Erziehungsanstalten im Osten* and the Third Reich's Germanising Mission', in Burkhard Olschowsky and Ingo Loose, eds, *Nationalsozialismus und Regionalbewusstsein im östlichen Europa: Ideologie, Machtausbau, Beharrung* (Berlin, 2016), 127–51, 148–50.
48. For an excellent survey of these historiographical debates, which were known (in analogy with the so-called *Historikerstreit*) as the *Bildungshistorikerstreit* (Educational Historians' Dispute), see Jeanette Bair, 'Nationalsozialismus als Gegenstand bildungshistorischer Forschung—Ein Überblick über Neuanfänge, Kontinuitäten, Brüche und ihre disziplinäre Rezeption', in Klaus-Peter Horn and Jörg-W. Link, eds, *Erziehungsverhältnisse im Nationalsozialismus. Totaler Anspruch und Erziehungswirklichkeit* (Bad Heilbrunn, 2011), 13–26. For a similar approach to the history of the Adolf-Hitler-Schools, see Feller and Feller, *Adolf-Hitler-Schulen*.
49. See Chapter 2. Thus, in contrast with the Adolf-Hitler-Schools, prospective pupils' parents were not investigated politically as a matter of course, and Hitler Youth reports were not generally considered a necessary part of the application process either (Geheimes Staatsarchiv Preußischer Kulturbesitz, I. HA Rep 151 IC, Nr. 7422/1 and I. HA Rep 151, Nr. 1094, Bd. 2; Landesarchiv Berlin, A Rep. 343 Nr. 1252, Bl. 184–5). The decision over whether parents had to provide certificates of political reliability appears to have lain with individual *Anstaltsleiter* (cf. BArch, R 3016/65, *Deutsche Justiz*, 26 November 1937, Nr. 47, Ausg. A S. 1830). In general, such demands seem to have been a rarity (although Bensberg and Ballenstedt provide exceptions to the rule).

50. *Pace* the numerous effusions to the contrary by Gisela Miller-Kipp, who has even claimed (with no evident historical justification, and in plain contradiction of much of the surviving archival evidence discussed in Chapter 2) that 'one only needed to possess a certain level of age-appropriate general knowledge; to put it plainly: anyone could get in who hadn't been dropped on the head'—cf. Gisela Miller-Kipp, '"Klasse Schule—immer genug zu essen, wenig Mathematik". Elitebildung im "Dritten Reich" oder über die Herstellung von Elite-Bewusstsein', in Jutta Ecarius and Lothar Wigger, eds, *Elitebildung—Bildungselite. Erziehungswissenschaftliche Diskussionen und Befunde über Bildung und soziale Ungleichheit* (Opladen, 2006), 44–66, 54. This fallacious assumption may also be due to Miller-Kipp's persistent (and erroneous) tendency to lump all of the elite schools together, thus treating the academically far less rigorous Adolf-Hitler-Schools as more or less identical with the NPEA.
51. Cf. Wolfang Keim, 'Kontinuitäten und Traditionsbrüche. Die Inkorporation des Weimarer Erziehungswesens in den NS-Staat', in Albert Moritz, ed., *'Fackelträger der Nation'. Elitebildung in den NS-Ordensburgen* (Cologne, 2010), 47–80, 68–9; also Ulrich Herrmann and Jürgen Oelkers, 'Zur Einführung in die Thematik "Pädagogik und Nationalsozialismus"', in Ulrich Herrmann and Jürgen Oelkers, eds, *Pädagogik und Nationalsozialismus* (Weinheim, 1989), 9–17, 10.
52. Particularly notable in this regard are the contributions to the following pair of edited volumes: Albert Moritz, ed., *'Fackelträger der Nation'. Elitebildung in den NS-Ordensburgen* (Cologne, 2010), and Klaus Ring and Stefan Wunsch, eds, *Bestimmung: Herrenmensch. NS-Ordensburgen zwischen Faszination und Verbrechen* (Dresden, 2016).
53. Cf. Kiran Klaus Patel, '"Auslese" und "Ausmerze". Das Janusgesicht der nationalsozialistischen Lager', *Zeitschrift für Geschichtswissenschaft* 54 (2006), 339–65; Stefan Schnurr and Sven Steinacker, 'Soziale Arbeit im Nationalsozialismus—*Auslese* und *Ausmerze* im Dienste der *Volkspflege*', in Klaus-Peter Horn and Jörg-W. Link, eds, *Erziehungsverhältnisse im Nationalsozialismus. Totaler Anspruch und Erziehungswirklichkeit* (Bad Heilbrunn, 2011), 253–73; also my forthcoming article with Lisa Pine, entitled '*Zwischen Auslese und Ausmerze*: The Biopolitics of Education in the Third Reich's "Special Schools" and "Elite Schools"'. On the importance of considering such mechanisms of inclusion as well as exclusion, see Roche, '*Herrschaft durch Schulung*'.
54. Cf. Gutmann, *Nazi Europe*, 9; Jochen Böhler and Robert Gerwarth, 'Non-Germans in the Waffen-SS: An Introduction', in Jochen Böhler and Robert Gerwarth, eds, *The Waffen-SS: A European History* (Oxford, 2017), 1–15, 4; Daniel Siemens, *Stormtroopers: A New History of Hitler's Brownshirts* (New Haven, 2017), intro. In this context, my study also aims to facilitate future transnational (or trans-chronological) comparisons between the NPEA and other types of elite school, without exploring these explicitly (which would be impossible within this book's remit).
55. See Chapter 3. Indeed, as Luca la Rovere has noted, the Italian Fascist ideologue Julius Evola even saw the NPEA as a model for the boarding schools founded by Mussolini's Fascist youth movement, the GIL (la Rovere, 'Totalitarian Pedagogy', 33, n. 52).
56. N.B. I have deliberately chosen not to take an explicitly masculinity studies-defined approach to the boys' schools; however, future analyses from this perspective could certainly be fruitful, taking recent studies of the Wehrmacht and the SS by Thomas

Kühne and Christopher Dillon as a model; cf. Christopher Dillon, *Dachau and the SS: A Schooling in Violence* (Oxford, 2015); Thomas Kühne, *The Rise and Fall of Comradeship: Hitler's Soldiers, Male Bonding and Mass Violence in the Twentieth Century* (Cambridge, 2017).

57. Works which demonstrate the importance of bridging such caesuras include Föllmer, *Identity and Modernity*; Mary Fulbrook, *Dissonant Lives: Generations and Violence through the German Dictatorships* (Oxford, 2011); Frank Biess, *Homecomings: Returning POWs and the Legacies of Defeat in Postwar Germany* (Princeton, 2006); on Nazism's essential adaptability to pre-existing traditions, see Raphael, 'Pluralities'.
58. See in particular the following section, and Chapters 4, 6, 7, and 12.
59. Joachim Haupt, 'The Educational Ideals of the German National Socialist Movement', *The Yearbook of Education* (1935), 923–30, 928. On Haupt's biography, see Chapter 1; also Christoph Sperling, *Joachim Haupt (1900–1989). Vom Aufstieg eines NS-Studentenfunktionärs und Sturz des Inspekteurs der Nationalpolitischen Erziehungsanstalten* (Berlin, 2018).
60. '"Erziehen heißt Charakter bilden". Reichsminister Rust im Zeltlager der nationalpolitischen Erziehungsanstalten', *Berliner Zeitung*, 5 July 1938 [BArch, R 8034-II/9296]. Elsewhere, Rust also described the NPEA as 'experimental institutes for our ideas'—cf. 'The Development of German Education, 1934/35', *Internationale Zeitschrift für Erziehung* (1935), 297–300, 300.
61. Joachim Haupt, *Nationalerziehung* (Langensalza, 1936), 15; BArch, R 2/12710, Heißmeyer, 'Denkschrift'. As we shall see in the Conclusion, the Napolas' experiment in this regard provided the model for a new system of non-elite state boarding schools which were subsequently created during wartime—the *Deutsche Heimschulen*.
62. StAL, E 202 Bü 1747, letter from Calliebe dated 3 September 1939; 'Arbeitstagung im Reichsfinanzministerium', 5.
63. Most of the NPEA followed the curriculum of a *Realgymnasium*, while four of them (Ilfeld, Schulpforta, Haselünne, and Neubeuern) followed the curriculum of a humanistic *Gymnasium*—for more on the schools' academic curricula, see Chapter 2; cf. Bernhard Rust, 'Die Grundlagen der nationalsozialistischen Erziehung', *Hochschule und Ausland*, 13, no. 1 (1935), 1–18, 8–12, and relevant correspondence in BArch, R 5/3362.
64. Cf. Heißmeyer, 'Denkschrift'; August Heißmeyer, 'Erziehung zur soldatischen Moral. Das Ziel der Nationalpolitischen Erziehungsanstalten', *Die Innere Front NSK. Pressedienst der NSDAP—Sonderdruck* (1942).
65. BArch, R 4901/8, Bl. 23–5.
66. e.g. Reichsjugendpressedienst, 'Neuer Erziehungsbegriff', *Deutsche Allgemeine Zeitung*, 6 October 1936 [BArch, NS 5/VI/18840]; cf. Schmitz, *Militärische Jugenderziehung*, 245.
67. Heißmeyer, 'Denkschrift', 10; cf. Hans H. Bielstein, 'Die Berthold-Otto-Schule und die Nationalpolitischen Erziehungsanstalten—ein Vergleich der Erziehungsformen' (Prüfungsarbeit, 1935), Bibliothek für Bildungsgeschichtliche Forschung (DIPF), GUT ASS 86.
68. Cf. Edith Niehuis, *Das Landjahr. Eine Jugenderziehungseinrichtung in der Zeit des Nationalsozialismus* (Nörten-Hardenberg, 1984), ch. 10.1.
69. Ernst Krieck, *Nationalpolitische Erziehung* (1932), 87; cf. Scholtz, *Nationalsozialistische Ausleseschulen*, 64.

70. Herrmann and Oelkers, 'Einführung', 13; cf. Hermann Giesecke, *Hitlers Pädagogen. Theorie und Praxis nationalsozialistischer Erziehung* (Weinheim, 1993), esp. 72–3; Barbara Schneider, *Die höhere Schule im Nationalsozialismus. Zur Ideologisierung von Bildung und Erziehung* (Cologne, 2000), 318–19. For examples of Rust and Heißmeyer using Hitler's adumbrations in *Mein Kampf* to frame their pedagogical programme, see Rust, 'Grundlagen'; August Heißmeyer, *Die Nationalpolitischen Erziehungsanstalten* (Berlin, 1939).
71. Cf. e.g. Jorge Dagnino, Matthew Feldman, and Paul Stocker, eds, *The 'New Man' in Radical Right Ideology and Practice, 1919–45* (London, 2018).
72. Rüdiger Ahrens, *Bündische Jugend. Eine neue Geschichte 1918–1933* (Göttingen, 2015).
73. Keim, 'Kontinuitäten und Traditionsbrüche', 67; cf. Wolfgang Keim, 'Bildung versus Ertüchtigung. Gab es einen Paradigmenwechsel im Erziehungsdenken unter der Nazi-Diktatur?', in Hartmut Lehmann and Otto Gerhard Oexle, eds, *Nationalsozialismus in den Kulturwissenschaften: Band 2—Leitbegriffe—Deutungsmuster—Paradigmenkämpfe—Erfahrungen und Transformationen im Exil* (Göttingen, 2004), 223–58; Wolfgang Keim, '100 Jahre Reformpädagogik-Rezeption in Deutschland im Spannungsfeld von Konstruktion, De-Konstruktion und Re-Konstruktion—Versuch einer Bilanzierung', in Wolfgang Keim, Ulrich Schwerdt, and Sabine Reh, eds, *Reformpädagogik und Reformpädagogik-Rezeption in neuer Sicht. Perspektiven und Impulse* (Bad Heilbrunn, 2016), 19–69. It was not for nothing that, in April 1932, the National Socialist Teachers' League (NSLB) had organized a rally at the Berlin Sportpalast under the banner 'Pestalozzi—Fichte—Hitler'—cf. Konrad Jarausch, *The Unfree Professions: German Lawyers, Teachers, and Engineers, 1900–1950* (Oxford, 1990), 99.
74. On the prevalent National Socialist tendency to incorporate all of these ideological 'languages' into a holistic *Weltanschauung*, see Raphael, 'Pluralities', 75–80.
75. e.g. BArch, R 3903/2249, 'Erziehungsziel/Aufnahmebedingungen der Nationalpolitischen Erziehungsanstalt Wahlstatt', letter dated 18 December 1934.
76. This particular wording is taken from the 1942–3 'Merkblatt für die Aufnahme in Nationalpolitische Erziehungsanstalten' (BArch, R 187/270b, Bl. 107–10), but the same type of formulation is used in the majority of the documents detailing entrance requirements, including those pertaining to individual schools, and those relating to the NPEA for girls (see Chapter 9).
77. One might contrast the state of affairs at the Adolf-Hitler-Schools, which were far readier to admit pupils who were the sons of high-ranking Nazis, even if their personal achievements left something to be desired—for more on this, see Feller and Feller, *Adolf-Hitler-Schulen*. N.B. The following five paragraphs draw on my paper entitled 'Schulische Erziehung und Entbürgerlichung', in Norbert Frei, ed., *Wie bürgerlich war der Nationalsozialismus?* (Göttingen, 2018), 154–72.
78. Cf. e.g. 'Auslese der Jugend', *Der Angriff*, 28 October 1936 [BArch, NS 5/VI/18840]; 'Insgesamt 21 nationalpolitische Erziehungs-Anstalten im Reich. Heißmeyer über den Erziehungsplan', *Niedersächsische Tageszeitung*, 7 February 1939 [Niedersächsisches Landesarchiv—Hauptstaatsarchiv Hannover, Hann. 180 Hannover B Nr. 95]; 'Jetzt wieder Neuaufnahmen. Die Nationalpolitischen Erziehungsanstalten. Für Kinder unbemittelter Eltern Ausbildung auf Staatskosten—Erziehung zum Gemeinschaftsgedanken', *Völkischer Beobachter*, 7 February 1939 [BArch, R 4902/1490].

79. 'Deutsche Menschen aus deutschem Geist. Vom Wirken der Nationalpolitischen Erziehungsanstalten', *Kattowitzer Zeitung*, 5 August 1940 [BAK, ZSg. 117 Nr. 290]; A. Nees, 'Schloss Oranienstein. Erst Kloster, Prachtschloß, Kadettenanstalt, zweimal von Franzosen verwüstet. Seit zwei Jahren: Nationalpolitische Erziehungsanstalt. Deutsche Jugend von Sumatra bis Südslawien, von Amerika bis zum deutschen Osten im alten Oranierschloß—Ein neuer Schultyp hat sich bewährt', *'Neueste Zeitung' Illustrierte Tageszeitung, Frankfurt a. M.*, 27 March 1936 [Landeshauptarchiv Koblenz, Bestand 662,008 Nr. 15].
80. K. G. Walberg, 'Die Nationalpolitische Erziehungsanstalt', *Reichsjugendpressedienst*, 8 September 1936 [BArch, NS 5/VI/18840].
81. Cf. BArch, R 2/19991, 'Erläuterungen zu dem Muster eines Kassenanschlages für eine Nationalpolitische Erziehungsanstalt'. The amounts set for each class might shift from year to year, but the principle of gradated contributions remained the same.
82. Cf. in particular BArch, R 3003/24494.
83. On local initiatives organized by individual Napolas, see for example NPEA Ballenstedt: Landeshauptarchiv Sachsen-Anhalt, Abteilung Dessau, Z 140, Nr. 1495; NPEA Klotzsche: Sächsisches Hauptstaatsarchiv Dresden (SHStAD), 11125 Nr. 21366; NPEA Oranienstein: Landeshauptarchiv Koblenz, Bestand 503 Landratsamt Nr. 113. On centrally organized initiatives directed by the Reich Education Ministry, see Staatsarchiv Hamburg, 361-2 VI Nr. 604; also *Nachrichtendienst des Deutschen Gemeindetages*, Jg. 1937, Nr. 20 (November 1937), 819: Übernahme von Patenschaften für Landjahrkameradschaftsführer zum Besuch Nationalpolitischer Erziehungsanstalten (Hessisches Staatsarchiv Marburg, Bestand 180 Marburg—Landratsamt Marburg—Nr. 5544).
84. BArch, NS 45/35, 'Vom Wesen der Nationalpolitischen Erziehungsanstalten'; cf. BArch, R 5/5280, letter dated 11 April 1942.
85. SHStAD, 11125 Nr. 21351, Bl. 148–9, letter from Heißmeyer dated 30 April 1936.
86. Cf. Fritzsche, *Life and Death*, 98–108, on the importance of such social levelling on a material as well as a psychological level (with particular reference to the Hitler Youth and the Reich Labour Service).
87. BArch, R 187/270b, Bl. 104; Kurt Wehrhan, 'Nationalpolitische Erziehung, insbesondere die nationalpolitischen Erziehungsanstalten', *Die neue deutsche Schule* 9 (1935), 99–105.
88. Geheimes Staatsarchiv Preußischer Kulturbesitz (GStAPK), I. HA Rep. 151 Nr. 1093, Bl. 193, 'Anmeldung für den Staatshaushalt 1935', 30 October 1934.
89. ÖStA, BEA 49, letter dated 4 February 1939; StAL, E 202 Bü 1747, agreements dated 26 January 1939 and 31 January 1939; *Der Jungmann. Feldpostbericht der NPEA Oranienstein*, 9. Kriegsnummer, 86.
90. See Roche, 'Erziehung und Entbürgerlichung' for a more detailed analysis of this phenomenon. For information on pupils' career choices during wartime, see BArch, NS 19/1531, Berger, 'Denkschrift an Reichsführer-SS. Erziehernachwuchs 1942' (March 1942); BArch, NS 19/490, Heißmeyer, 'Bericht über die Studien- und Berufsberatung an den NPEA der Donau und Alpenländer und Bayern' (10 January 1944); also Chapter 10.
91. H. W. Koch, *The Hitler Youth: Origins and Development 1922–1945* (New York, 1975), 186.

92. Although, to paraphrase William Weaver's discussion of school magazine articles written by public school-boys at Rugby during the nineteenth century, pupils 'clearly did not have unlimited latitude in expressing their own viewpoints or publicly deviating from the official...line; their writings were bounded by what they thought that parents, classmates, masters, and the headmaster wanted to hear', that does not mean that reports by *Jungmannen* were completely 'scripted' by staff. Indeed, the evidence suggests that essays and journal entries which pupils had initially crafted during independent school projects often found their way into school newsletters without substantial editing (apart from merely orthographic corrections). Rather, just as the 'Children of the American Revolution' analysed by Susan A. Miller enthusiastically conformed to adult agendas because the two groups' 'racial' and social interests fundamentally converged, the *Jungmannen* who authored these accounts also arguably possessed agency and pursued self-expression in their writing, even if they did so precisely through adhering to Nazi norms and values—cf. William N. Weaver, '"A School-Boy's Story": Writing the Victorian Public Schoolboy Subject', *Victorian Studies* 46, no. 3 (2004), 455–87, 461; Susan A. Miller, 'Assent as Agency in the Early Years of the Children of the American Revolution', *The Journal of the History of Childhood and Youth* 9, no. 1 (2016), 48–65, 49; see also Kristine Alexander, 'Agency and Emotion Work', *Jeunesse: Young People, Texts, Cultures* 7, no. 2 (2015), 120–8 (on obedience as an expression of youthful agency), and Lyndsey Dodd, 'Children's Citizenly Participation in the National Revolution: The Instrumentalization of Children in Vichy France', *European Review of History/revue européenne d'histoire* 24, no. 5 (2017), 759–80 (on the potential authenticity of propagandistic texts written by children).
93. I have already discussed the potential advantages of analysing such eyewitness testimonies in detail elsewhere—cf. Helen Roche, 'Surviving "*Stunde Null*": Narrating the Fate of Nazi Elite-School Pupils during the Collapse of the Third Reich', *German History* 33, no. 4 (2015), 570–87; also Roche, *Sparta's German Children*, 9–13.
94. Rosenbaum, *Kinderalltag*, 14, 31, 154.
95. We might usefully compare the Nietzschean aphorism on cognitive dissonance: 'Memory says, "I did that." Pride replies, "I could not have done that." Eventually, memory yields'—Friedrich Nietzsche, *Jenseits von Gut und Böse* (1886), Aphorism 68. On the idea that children who had been indoctrinated under Nazism generally tended to remember the factual (rather than the ideological) content of their National Socialist schooling in later life, see Heinz-Elmar Tenorth, 'Grenzen der Indoktrination', in Peter Drewek et al., eds, *Ambivalenzen der Pädagogik. Zur Bildungsgeschichte der Aufklärung und des 20. Jahrhunderts—Harald Scholtz zum 65. Geburtstag* (Weinheim, 1995), 335–50.

PART I

GENESIS

1

Foundation and Administration

The Napolas' Position within the Polycratic Nazi State

The Napolas were essentially the brainchild of their first Inspector, SA-man Joachim Haupt, one of North Germany's most radical National Socialist student activists during the Weimar Republic, and former schoolmaster Bernhard Rust, one of the Party's stalwart 'old fighters', who had held the position of Gauleiter in Südhannover-Braunschweig for many years before being appointed first as Prussian Culture Minister (1933) and then Reich Education Minister (1934) in the wake of the Nazi seizure of power.[1] The two men had first joined forces after Haupt was sacked from his teaching position at the *Schleswig-Holsteinische Bildungsanstalt* (Stabila) in Plön in 1931, due to his continuing penchant for pro-Nazi activism and speech-making. Keen to alleviate the young educator's plight, Rust undertook to provide Haupt with a job as the editor of the *Niedersächsische Tageszeitung*, a Party daily newspaper run by the local Gauleitung.[2] Following Rust's elevation to ministerial heights, Haupt and his close friend Reinhard Sunkel, who had attended the Prussian cadet school at Lichterfelde together, became the Minister's right-hand men, forming part of the team of young and enthusiastic Nazi aides with which Rust habitually surrounded himself; Sunkel was appointed as Rust's personal adjutant, while Haupt was granted the position of permanent secretary (*Ministerialdirektor*) in the Education Ministry.[3]

Haupt, who would become moderately well-known for his numerous tracts treating National Socialist pedagogical themes, saw the creation of the NPEA as a perfect opportunity to unify his educational conceptions regarding the importance of all-male warrior-bands (probably inspired by his time in the Freikorps), his affection for the quasi-pederastic pedagogy of the 'Aryan' ancient Greeks, and the importance which he accorded to 'selection' (*Auslese*) within the school system as a whole.[4] However, Haupt's career was destined to come to a sticky end, along with the influence of the SA over the Napolas which his tenure as Inspector had facilitated—a state of affairs which had initially led to the NPEA at Plön being named the 'Ernst-Röhm-School' in honour of the SA chief (needless to say, this designation was swiftly obliterated after the Night of the Long Knives).[5] In Autumn 1935, Haupt was accused of cultivating allegedly homosexual relationships with pupils at a number of schools, including Schulpforta and NPEA Plön.[6]

The Third Reich's Elite Schools: A History of the Napolas. Helen Roche, Oxford University Press.
DOI: 10.1093/oso/9780198726128.003.0002

While the charges appear to have been trumped up, inasmuch as there seems to have been scant proof that Haupt had done anything more than engage in more or less homoerotic friendships with the boys in question—indeed, the accusations were very probably a stratagem of Himmler's to remove Haupt from the scene, and enable the installation of an Inspector who would be loyal to the SS first and foremost (see further below)—it was certainly true that Haupt had scarcely acted in a fashion in keeping with his appointed position of trust and responsibility. Taking schoolboys on a skinny-dipping trip to the Wandlitzsee using a car and chauffeur belonging to the Napola administration, or writing gushing letters praising the blue-eyed gaze of his 'ephebes', were scarcely actions calculated to endear Haupt to the highly homophobic Nazi authorities—especially when he had at first refused to take his arrest by the Gestapo seriously, even going so far as to deliberately insult his interrogator.[7] After a protracted procedural process, Haupt not only lost his position as Inspector of the NPEA, but was also kicked out of the NSDAP *tout court*.[8] Though he may not exactly have been the final casualty of the Röhm Putsch, Haupt had nevertheless fallen foul of the National Socialist tendency to instrumentalize sexuality-related denunciations against members of the SA—a fact which, both in the context of the power struggles for control of the NPEA as well as those within the Nazi state more generally, ultimately led to the SS gaining ever more power within the system.[9]

Within this context, the aims of the following chapter are threefold. Firstly, it provides a concise exposition of the schools' foundation, and relevant administrative developments (which will be discussed in more detail in the relevant chapters in Parts II and III), as well as a brief delineation of the bureaucratic tasks handled by the inspectorial staff. Secondly, it investigates the schools' relationship with other organizations within the Nazi state, focusing in particular on the inevitable problems caused by the polycratic wrangling of competing institutions within the state apparatus.[10] Indeed, the prevalence of such internecine power struggles in itself speaks volumes for the significance accorded to the NPEA within the Nazi regime, despite the fact that recent comprehensive studies of the SS, the SA, and the Reich Education Ministry make no concerted mention of the Napolas at all.[11] Especial attention will be paid in this regard to Himmler's determined (though ultimately not wholly successful) efforts to place the entire Napola system under the sway of the SS, with the aim of turning the NPEA into dedicated SS-training schools, just as the Adolf-Hitler-Schools were intended to provide dedicated cadres for the Party organization.[12] Finally, we shall explore the Inspectorate's methods of recruitment and control of NPEA *Erzieher* and *Anstaltsleiter*, and the ensuing attempts to create a cadre of ideologically sound and fanatically loyal staff who would conform completely to the National Socialist inspirational ideal of the 'leader-' or 'educator-personality'. A brief conclusion then contextualizes these observations more broadly within relevant literature on the Third Reich and its administration.

*

As Rust himself at least partially admitted, Haupt had been the driving force behind the initial founding of the NPEA, despite the fact that the Education Minister was able to take much of the public credit for the schools' existence, and their subsequent successes.[13] It appears that the idea of creating 'National Political Education Institutes' out of the three former Prussian cadet schools at Plön, Potsdam, and Köslin, which had been turned into civilian *Staatliche Bildungsanstalten* (state boarding schools or Stabilas) under the Weimar Republic, was a spontaneous move, rather than the outcome of an assiduously prepared programme—at least, the notion of creating schools of this type does not appear in any prominent National Socialist pedagogical or programmatic literature, or even in Haupt's own oeuvre, prior to 1933.[14] From this perspective, Klaus Schmitz has argued that the sudden triumph of the Nazis and their rapid accession to government led Rust and Haupt to take immediate and more or less unpremeditated action in this regard, since the first official announcement that the Stabilas in question would be transformed into Napolas took place only a few days before all of the Stabila-pupils were due to return to school for the 1933–4 academic year.[15] The announcement concerning the Napolas' creation was deliberately made on Hitler's birthday, 20 April 1933, since the schools' foundation represented a form of institutional 'birthday gift' from Rust to the Führer.[16]

Right from the start, Rust was concerned above all that the NPEA should be under his direct control, following a military-style chain of command, rather than being subject to any of the bureaucratic branches of his Ministry.[17] The resulting office which he created to deal with Napola-related bureaucracy, known as the *Landesverwaltung der Nationalpolitischen Erziehungsanstalten in Preußen* (State Administration of the National Political Education Institutes in Prussia—henceforth abbreviated as *Landesverwaltung*) was therefore headed by Rust in his capacity as 'Chief of the National Political Educational Institutes' (*Chef der Nationalpolitischen Erziehungsanstalten*), with Haupt acting as his deputy.[18] Although the *Landesverwaltung* was only formally established on 27 December 1933, with Haupt receiving his official appointment as Inspector of the NPEA on 7 April 1934, the process of turning the Stabilas into Napolas had already been in train since the beginning of the summer term in May 1933 (see Chapter 4).[19] Thus, in a series of reminiscences published to celebrate NPEA Plön's tenth anniversary, the school's *Anstaltsleiter*, SA-*Standartenführer* Hermann Brunk, recalled having been approached by Haupt in March 1933 to see if he would theoretically be willing to 'take on' an NPEA, before receiving official instructions from Rust on 24 May 1933 to take over the *Schleswig-Holsteinische Bildungsanstalt* and 'train the German lads there into National Socialists'.[20] A former SA-activist and police officer who had fallen foul of the Weimar authorities, Brunk boasted proudly of his utter dearth of pedagogical qualifications and professional experience for such a task—a lack which (as we shall see), he shared with the other early *Anstaltsleiter*, SS-gynaecologist Adolf Schieffer and former Wehrmacht-officer and war-novelist Ulrich Sander.[21] It was only on 1 July 1933, however, that Rust officially dismissed the previous Stabila directors, so that Brunk, Schieffer, and Sander could consider their positions fully secure.[22]

According to Brunk's highly self-congratulatory and self-aggrandizing account of NPEA Plön's first days, despite his highly unorthodox background, the 'police-major' was nevertheless able to win over the staff and pupils at the Stabila with relative ease.[23] Soon after his arrival at Plön on 27 May 1933, Brunk ordered that all of the pupils' fashionably long, unmilitary-style haircuts (which he dubbed 'revolution quiffs') should be summarily shorn; he also banned all non-HJ youth groups, including the Scouts (*Pfadfinder*), and made sure that all of his charges, whether pupils or staff, were garbed in some semblance of the Hitler Youth uniform.[24] Brunk also claimed to have coined the designation '*Jungmann*' for pupils at Plön, which then became common usage for pupils at all of the NPEA.[25] Finally, on 28 October 1933, in the SA-chief's own presence, Brunk was able proudly to preside over the renaming of the school after Ernst Röhm, at Rust's behest—an 'honour' which swiftly suffered the most extreme form of *damnatio memoriae* after Röhm's assassination and the SA's fall from favour the following summer.[26]

*

Once the initial foundation stage at Plön, Potsdam, and Köslin was over, the Prussian Finance Ministry was faced with a veritable spate of financial demands from Rust and the *Landesverwaltung*, including requests for new administrative appointments to deal with the ever-rising tide of Napola-related bureaucracy, and preparations for new foundations. Thus, the relevant documents preserved at the Geheimes Staatsarchiv Preußischer Kulturbesitz in Berlin-Dahlem paint a programmatic portrait of the Napola system's initial expansion, as well as revealing those areas of education which were considered most crucial when making requests for extra funding.[27] These included (but were not limited to) paramilitary sports (*Wehrsport*) and boxing, music, and 'borderland activities' to strengthen 'ethnic German' sentiment in the areas abutting Germany's post-Versailles borders.[28]

From this point onwards, we can discern a series of phases of new foundations, each of which was fundamentally interlinked with the administrative expansion of the NPEA bureaucracy (see Figure 1.1). Even in the initial decree announcing the foundation of the *Landesverwaltung* in December 1933, the three remaining Stabilas in Berlin-Spandau, Naumburg, and Wahlstatt had been nominated for

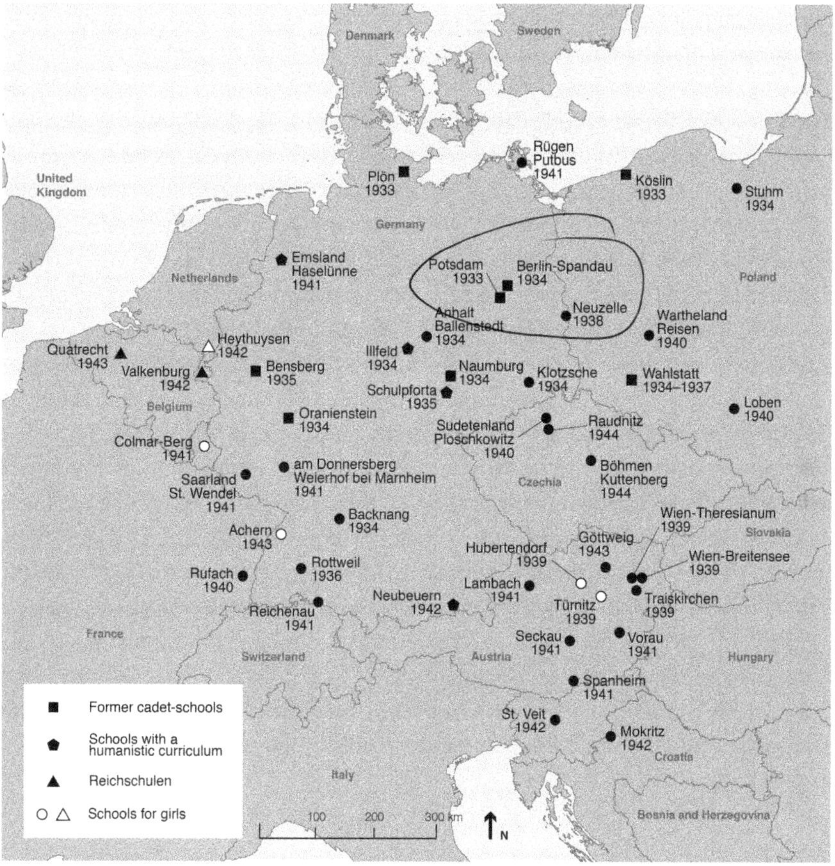

Figure 1.1 Locations of the Napolas and *Reichsschulen* and their dates of foundation (superimposed upon modern European state boundaries).

Napolisation at Easter 1934; in the same year, Schloss Oranienstein (the site of another former Prussian cadet school) followed suit, with Stuhm and Ilfeld close behind, as the first East-Prussian Napola and the first Napola with a 'humanistic' curriculum respectively.[29] Furthermore, by this time, three of the federal states beyond Prussia had begun to take matters into their own hands, founding Napola-style schools on their own initiative in Saxony, Anhalt, and Württemberg (see Chapter 5).[30] For reasons which will be discussed below, 1935–7 were relatively quiet years, with the final former Prussian cadet school at Schloss Bensberg in the Rhineland opening its doors in 1935, along with the forced Napolisation of Germany's premier humanistic boarding school, Schulpforta, in the same year (see Chapter 6).[31]

It was in 1938, following the Anschluss, that the first great administrative upheaval took place, with the takeover of the Viennese *Bundeserziehungsanstalten*, the Austrian First Republic's equivalent of the Weimar Republic's Stabilas (see Chapter 7). These were the first NPEA to be fully financed by the Reich, rather than by the Prussian Finance Ministry, as well as providing the catalyst for the foundation of the first NPEA for girls (see Chapter 9). Along with the planned foundation of NPEA Sudetenland in the wake of the Munich agreement, which would also be funded from the Reich budget (see Chapter 8), these developments meant that Rust could no longer countenance the Napola administration's bearing a title which implied that it was still a purely Prussian institution. On 26 October 1938, Rust therefore decreed that the name of the *Landesverwaltung* would henceforth be changed to the 'Inspectorate of the National Political Education Institutes' (*Inspektion der Nationalpolitischen Erziehungsanstalten*).[32] On 4 November 1938, the Inspectorate was also fully integrated into the Reich Education Ministry (as opposed to the Prussian Culture Ministry).[33]

Even during wartime, the pace of the Napola system's expansion only increased, with a dozen new Napolas being founded in 1941 alone, many of which were contained within the newly annexed territories of the rapidly expanding 'Greater German Reich' (see Chapters 7 and 8).[34] On 1 April 1941, the NPEA in Saxony, Anhalt, and Württemberg were also finally incorporated into the Reich administration, as part of the regime's centralization drive or '*Verreichlichung*' (see Chapter 5). Finally, even as the tide of the war turned, new Napolas were still being founded in occupied territories both East and West, with the very last foundations in Kuttenberg (Kutná Hora) and Raudnitz (Roudnice na Labem) taking place as late as 1944 (see Chapter 8).

*

Needless to say, the constant growth of the responsibilities accruing to the *Landesverwaltung* and, subsequently, the Inspectorate, led to a concomitant intensification of administrative labour, and the relevant archival files contain numerous demands that the NPEA offices be supplied with extra staff, in order to cope with the ever-increasing workload.[35] Thus, from a staff of fewer than a dozen at the *Landesverwaltung*'s humble beginnings in 1934, by 1936, the number of employees had swelled to twenty (including secretaries, a chauffeur, and a cleaning lady).[36] This ballooning bureaucracy was only brought to a halt by the exigencies of wartime; even so, the Inspectorate did all in its power (with variable success) to keep the Napola system running as smoothly as possible until the bitter end, even as Allied bombing raids devastated Berlin (see Chapter 10).[37]

The tasks which the NPEA administration had to carry out were multifarious, including responsibilities pertaining to public relations, financial affairs, and managing individual schools' requirements and requests for equipment or renovation; much of the surviving bureaucratic documentation concerns questions of personnel, recruitment, and budgetary issues. At first, the NPEA authorities had to deal with numerous teething troubles, such as the refurbishment and replacement of antiquated facilities and equipment at the former Stabilas, whilst constantly having to negotiate with the parsimonious Prussian Finance Minister, Johannes Popitz.[38] From a less than uniform beginning, however, trial, error, and greater centralization increasingly began to unify standards and expectations at the NPEA within Prussia, while those in the federal states were placed under increasing pressure to conform to the Prussian paradigm (see Chapter 5). Pro forma templates for budgets and building-works would frequently be circulated, alongside unified catalogues of the necessary uniform, equipment, and vehicles required at each type of school, right down to the number of horses prescribed for each NPEA.[39] Indeed, two surviving files at the Staatsarchiv Ludwigsburg demonstrate that, by the late 1930s, the Inspectorate was both keen and able to dictate many of the minutiae of school life and administration right down to the very last detail.[40] Not only did headmasters and teaching staff from all of the schools have to meet frequently; bursars and other support staff at the NPEA would also be requested to attend regular administrative conferences, in the interests of unifying best practice at all of the Napolas throughout the Reich.[41] Numerous documents in the relevant federal and regional archives also attest to the constant building-works and renovations which were continuously being carried out at the NPEA, since the Inspectorate had reluctantly acquiesced to the idea that, for the time being at least, it would be impracticable to build new schools from scratch, rather than using existing buildings.[42] In future, however, it was envisaged that all of the existing NPEA would move into purpose-built campuses (situated in sufficiently impressive landscapes), with the buildings on each site reflecting each school's individual character.[43] Perhaps it was hardly surprising, then, that (according to Popitz) the twelve existing Napolas in 1934–6 cost 325 per cent more to maintain than all of the remaining 350 state secondary schools (*höhere Schulen*) in Prussia.[44] However, as we shall see below, the problems and bad blood caused by this apparently insatiable greed on the part of Rust and the NPEA authorities would have serious implications for the Napolas' future.

Finally, one of the most important tasks of all for the NPEA administration was the scouting out of prospective buildings for future foundations. As we shall see in Part II, much of this activity from the Anschluss onwards was directed towards the deliberate expropriation of convents, monasteries, and religious schools, as well as mental hospitals and asylums (on the latter, see Chapter 10). However, such initiatives could also lead to fruitful cooperation with local Gauleiter, or serve more localized political ends, such as the Mayor of Freiburg's (ultimately unsuccessful) bid to establish Baden's first Napola in his city, in order to counteract the power of 'political Catholicism' in the surrounding area, or Gauleiter Simon's sponsorship of a new-build NPEA in Trier to strengthen his region's position as 'the western cornerstone of the Reich'.[45] In line with Rust's own native Lower-Saxon local patriotism, plans were also afoot to build Napolas on the Bückeberg and on the shores of the Steinhuder Meer, but in the end, the only NPEA ever to be built from scratch was the school at Ballenstedt, which was constructed at the initiative of Anhalt's Minister-President Freyberg, rather than that of the Reich Education Ministry (see Chapter 5).[46]

*

Nevertheless, whether such collaborations were taking place in the newly occupied territories, or within the borders of the '*Altreich*', Germany's heartland, these initiatives were often seen as a prime opportunity for Gauleiter and other functionaries to curry favour with the regime—one of the many crucial forms of power-relationship which the Napolas were constantly cultivating with other institutions within the Nazi state. As we shall see in the following chapters, the NPEA were sedulously encouraged to build relationships with Party organizations within their local and regional communities, as well as with universities and training colleges in the vicinity. Thus, at a headmasters' conference in December 1936, it was suggested that the Napolas in Backnang and Rottweil should make contact not only with as many tertiary education institutions as possible in the surrounding area, but also with the Gauleitung in Swabia, Württemberg, and Baden; with the regional south-western branches of the SA and SS; the Stuttgart NSKK Motor-Brigade; the Württemberg and Baden branches of the Hitler Youth, the Reich Agrarian Organization (*Reichsnährstand*) and the Reich Labour Service (RAD), as well as neighbouring battalions of the German Labour Front (DAF), the Wehrmacht, and regional government offices.[47] *Erzieher* and pupils at many of the schools would routinely undertake work experience in local Party offices such as the *Kreisleitung*, learning how the administrative side of the regime functioned;[48] they would also participate in political rallies and events, assist with charitable drives and the distribution of propaganda, or simply undertake joint endeavours such as cross-country war-games with regional branches of the SA or the National Socialist Motor-Corps (NSKK).[49]

While Rust and Haupt's initial plans for the NPEA had foreseen the armed forces (*Reichswehr*) and the SA as the principal parties who would patronize, support, and advise the schools,[50] after the Night of the Long Knives in summer 1934, SA involvement with the Napolas at the highest level was swiftly and predictably sidelined. Indeed, it appears that, at least from 1934 onwards, *Jungmannen* were prohibited from joining the SA whilst they were still attending the schools, along with the SS and other similarly 'adult' Party organizations.[51] Nevertheless, many of the Napolas continued to possess *Anstaltsleiter* and *Erzieher* who were loyal to the SA—as NPEA Neuzelle proudly noted in a report from 1937 on the school's relationship with the local Stormtroopers, 'the connection between the NPEA and the SA is simple and heartfelt, since there is a personal union between the two in the person of the *Hundertschaftsführer* and the Troop-leader (*Truppführer*). Most of the *Zugführer* are also SA-men'.[52] Under the aegis of SA-*Standartenführer* Brunk, Plön, the NPEA formerly named after Ernst Röhm, still maintained particularly close connections with the SA in Nordmark and their leader, Joachim Meyer-Quade, as well as the prominent royal SA-enthusiast Prince August-Wilhelm of Prussia, who had attended the school in its former incarnation as a cadet school during his time at the Prussian cadet corps.[53] Meanwhile, SA-*Brigadeführer* Paul Holthoff, the *Anstaltsleiter* at NPEA Bensberg, even came under suspicion from the SS for attempting to effect an SA re-takeover of the NPEA during the war years—a supposition which may not have been wholly groundless.[54]

Despite occasional tensions with local Party authorities or the Gau leadership, by and large, the Gauleiter tend to have been staunch supporters of the NPEA—especially those which were founded in Austria and the occupied territories (see Chapters 7 and 8).[55] Indeed, at Weierhof in the Palatinate, Gauleiter Bürckel was so taken with the Napola paradigm that he attempted to found an elite school of his own in the image of the NPEA (see Chapter 6). Gauleiter and other dignitaries from various branches of the NSDAP were frequent visitors to the schools, and the Party might also undertake to help the NPEA with their extensive pre-selection process (see Chapter 2).[56]

Even the Hitler Youth, which entertained a more or less rivalrous relationship with the NPEA, benefited from ongoing collaboration with the elite schools. Thus, despite various teething troubles, from March 1936 onwards, the *Landesverwaltung* mandated that all *Jungmannen* should become members of autonomous Hitler Youth troops at their NPEA.[57] Finally, on 7 November 1936, prior to the enforcement of the Hitler Youth Law (*Gesetz über die Hitlerjugend*) the following month, which compulsorily conscripted all German youths into the HJ, an official contract came into effect between the Reich Youth Leadership (*Reichsjugendführung*) and the *Landesverwaltung*, legally mandating Hitler Youth duties as part of school life at the Napolas.[58] Thenceforward, older *Jungmannen* would routinely spend some of their 'free' time leading local Hitler Youth groups in neighbouring towns or villages.[59] Sometimes, this could lead to problems when the Napola-pupils were unable to understand their youthful charges' thick local dialects, or simply deemed them incorrigibly stupid or lazy, due to their lack of desire to undertake their duties with the requisite élan or fanaticism.[60]

However, these small niggles on a personal level paled in comparison to the constant institutional wrangling for advantage or dominance (*Kompetenzstreiten*) with which the Inspectorate had to deal. These quarrels could range from minor squabbles with the Directorate of the *Reichsbahn* (the German national railway) over whether the sons of railwaymen should get free train-fares to travel to school if they attended a Napola, or disputes with the Reich Finance Ministry over whether a dentist's couch should be an obligatory piece of equipment for every single NPEA sickbay, to the ongoing struggles with the Prussian Finance Ministry over the number and remuneration of officials in the *Landesverwaltung*—all of which could become extremely heated.[61] However, such financial troubles ultimately led to a very dangerous development indeed from Rust's perspective—and yet one which, at least initially, the Education Minister had welcomed with open arms—the increasingly extensive involvement of the SS in the schools' administration.[62]

*

After Rust and Haupt's decision to go ahead on their own initiative and turn Schulpforta into a Napola in 1935 without having obtained Prussian Finance Minister Johannes Popitz's prior permission, Popitz had put his foot down and insisted that no further Napolas should be founded on Prussian soil unless and until he saw fit (hence the relative dearth of new foundations between 1935–7).[63] At the same time, the hitherto seemingly bottomless well of Popitz's readiness to fund even the most costly NPEA building-projects revealed itself to be illusory, so that a real financial crisis appeared to be threatening the Napolas' survival.[64] Rust therefore turned to Himmler for support, and, following Haupt's dismissal, which (oddly enough) had also been facilitated by a number of SS officials bringing evidence against him, accepted the appointment of SS-*Obergruppenführer* August Heißmeyer as Haupt's successor on 10 February 1936.[65] Heißmeyer (b. 1897) had joined the NSDAP in 1925, and, after a swift rise through the ranks of first the SA and then the SS, had already gained the coveted position of Head of the SS Central Office (*SS-Hauptamt*) in 1935. His appointment was therefore deliberately intended to ensure that Himmler would be able to exert ever more control over the NPEA as time progressed.[66]

Himmler appears to have first gained the impression that the Napolas might make a fitting educational addition to his ever-growing empire on a visit to NPEA Köslin in June 1934.[67] Thenceforward, with Heißmeyer as his (mostly) willing righthand man, the Reichsführer-SS began to undertake every possible stratagem to bring the schools more fully under his sway. Himmler's henchmen would even routinely undertake to spy on the Education Minister to assess the level of his paranoia and the exact state of his deteriorating health (Rust suffered from chronic trigeminal neuralgia, caused by a war-wound which he had sustained during his service at the front in World War I).[68] At its most extreme, this state of affairs led to a hefty power-struggle between Heißmeyer and his most prominent rival in the SS hierarchy, Gottlob Berger, over Heißmeyer's allegedly divided loyalties and ongoing commitment to the Reich Education Ministry's aims.[69] Berger had taken over from Heißmeyer as the head of the *SS-Hauptamt* in 1941, while Heißmeyer had been given an eponymous educational department of his own (the *SS-Dienststelle Obergruppenführer Heißmeyer*) as a form of consolation prize. Berger insistently claimed behind the Inspector's back that Heißmeyer was secretly seeking to strengthen the Reich Education Ministry's position, whilst watering down plans to install suitably loyal SS teachers at the schools, and hindering SS control of Himmler's 'key trump card'—the schools which were being founded in the occupied Netherlands (see Chapter 8).[70] Spurred on by these accusations, Himmler insisted virulently that Heißmeyer must ensure that the ultimate goal of ousting Rust and replacing the Education Minister with the Reichsführer-SS as 'Inspector General of the NPEA' be fulfilled with all possible haste; indeed, he even went so far as to have a pro forma letter drafted for Rust to sign, handing over the Inspectorate of the NPEA wholesale to the Reichsführer-SS.[71] Nevertheless, even after the SS had begun to gain ever more power over the NPEA in the occupied territories, in early 1943, Berger was still complaining to SS colleagues that 'everyone who knows the National Political Education Institutes knows that our influence is desperately small'.[72]

Such a comment might seem surprising, when one surveys the sheer amount of change in an SS-favourable direction which had been effected in the intervening years since Heißmeyer's advent as Inspector in 1936. It was not just that Himmler and other SS dignitaries made frequent visits to the NPEA, with the Reichsführer-SS even attempting to engage in personal recruitment for the SS when he spoke to the massed ranks of *Jungmannen* at the schools' annual manoeuvres.[73] Rather, the Inspectorate had started up a conveyor-belt style relationship between the NPEA and the newly founded *SS-Mannschaftshäuser*—fraternities which housed SS-loyal university students in an ideologically controlled environment during their time in higher education—and Heißmeyer was also in the process of creating an SS-run old boys' network which would corral all NPEA graduates into an overarching 'Order', constructed along SS lines (see Chapter 10, n. 25).[74] Furthermore, from 1936 onwards, 'Racial Experts' (*Rassereferenten*) from the SS Race and Resettlement Office (*Rasse und Siedlungs Hauptamt*/RuSHA) began to play a crucial role in the Napola selection process.[75] An arcane system of racial categories was introduced to assess candidates' 'racial suitability', and, while at first the racial advisors might defer to the judgement of individual *Anstaltsleiter*, by 1941, their decision had become absolutely binding.[76] Essentially, this development meant that any pupil who was accepted at an NPEA would already have passed all of the racial requirements necessary to attain SS-membership—a crucial step towards realizing Himmler's ultimate desire to turn the Napolas first and foremost into preparatory schools for his SS training academies (*Junkerschulen*).[77]

Moreover, similar measures were increasingly being taken to screen the *Erzieher* as well, as the Inspectorate began to move towards recruiting new staff solely from the ranks of the SS; at many of the schools, existing staff were also strongly encouraged to join the SS if they had not done so already.[78] By March 1944, Heißmeyer had also drawn up a proposal that all *Erzieher* at the schools should be given ranks and uniform insignia equating to those used in the General SS (*Allgemeine SS*).[79] Meanwhile, from 1936 onwards, teaching staff at the NPEA were encouraged to attend SS ideological training courses laid on either by the RuSHA or, from 1941 onwards, by Heißmeyer's own *SS-Dienststelle*.[80] Extant reports suggest that the *Erzieher* who attended these courses generally participated enthusiastically, welcoming the opportunity to improve the Napolas' 'comradely' relations with the SS, and even expressing the desire that this relationship should be taken much further.[81]

Finally, just as in the SS more generally, the teaching staff at the Napolas gradually became subject to the most extreme control of all—over when, and to whom, they might get married.[82] Thus, the 'nanny Inspectorate' might require all of the schools to provide annual birth and marriage statistics for their staff, demand certificates of racial purity for teachers' future wives, or even order any *Erzieher* who were still bachelors to wed within the year.[83] Thus, Gerd Siegel, an *Erzieher* who was working at NPEA Oranienstein, noted in a letter to his wife on 3 March 1939 that Heißmeyer had publicly ordered three unwed teachers at the school to 'marry before my next visit, or you'll be sacked!'[84] In a programmatic speech written the previous year, Heißmeyer noted that when he had taken over the NPEA, it had been assumed that the staff duties were so onerous that *Erzieher* were better off unmarried, since they would have no time to devote to their wives and families.[85] In order to combat this untenable state of affairs, and ensure that the especially fine 'breeding stock' of the Napola staff would be in a position to do their bit to safeguard the 'biological properties and demographic position of our race', the Inspector decreed that cheap apartments should be made available for all married staff.[86] Ultimately, it was envisaged that every school would have its own 'staff village' (*Erzieherdorf* or *Erziehersiedlung*) with twenty dwellings for teaching staff and twenty for support staff, so that no *Erzieher* (apart from trainee teachers) would be compelled to leave their wives behind and sleep within the school walls, unless they were on duty that night.[87] Indeed, Gerd Siegel's own correspondence with his wife vividly illustrates the toll taken on staff who were forced to spend long periods away from their wives and families in order to fulfil their school duties—as did the admission of an *Erzieher* at NPEA Oranienstein that his wife's complete nervous breakdown, which left him in charge of their three small boys during her convalescence at a sanatorium in 1943, was ultimately down to his having constantly put his 'Oranienstein-fanaticism' ahead of the needs of his family.[88]

In sum, then, the ideal Napola *Erzieher* was no longer merely a young, fit, idealistic teacher-cum-*Führer*—as at home 'on the water...as on the saddle of a horse [or] a motorcycle...; as conversant with skis as with...sails, rifles, foils, and boxing-gloves'.[89] Rather, he also had to be prepared to submit to Heißmeyer's demand (and, by extension, that of the Reichsführer-SS) that he father a large brood of 'racially pure' German children for the good of his nation.

*

However, these were not the only demands which the Inspectorate began to make of teaching staff after Heißmeyer's advent as Inspector. While Rust and Haupt had not been particularly concerned about whether staff were members of the NSDAP, so long as they possessed the requisite character traits and enthusiasm (indeed, one of the first *Anstaltsleiter*, Ulrich Sander of NPEA Potsdam, had never been a Party member),[90] Heißmeyer explicitly stated that every *Erzieher* should be a member of the Party and a convinced National Socialist; staff were also supposed to possess membership of one of the Party's subsidiary organizations, and be a Reserve Officer in the Wehrmacht or the Waffen-SS.[91] Nevertheless, a statistical analysis of fifty-nine relevant NPEA personnel documents held at the Geheimes Staatsarchiv Preußischer Kulturbesitz shows that only 12 per cent of *Erzieher* serving at the Prussian Napolas in 1937 had joined the Nazi Party prior to its seizure of power, while almost half (46 per cent) had not even gained the politically dubious status of 'March windfalls' (*Märzgefallene*); that is, they had not joined the Party between the Nazi seizure of power and the temporary ban on new membership (*Aufnahmestopp*) which came into force in May 1933. Meanwhile, a small but significant proportion of the staff in question (8 per cent) had no NSDAP affiliation at all.[92]

From this perspective, it does not seem that all of the *Erzieher* who joined the teaching staff at the NPEA were motivated to take up positions there solely due to their unbridled Nazi convictions. Rather, in many cases, trainee teachers (*Referendare*) appear to have been headhunted; the *Landesverwaltung* made an agreement with teacher-training colleges that suitable trainees would be recommended to the NPEA authorities, and the schools' final Vice-Inspector, Otto Calliebe, also founded a Napola-specific regional teacher-training seminar (*Bezirksseminar*) at the NPEA in Potsdam.[93] Trainees who opted to do some of their work-experience at a Napola might spend up to two years at an NPEA—but they would have to be prepared both for an incredibly gruelling schedule, and potential hazing (or even terrorization) from their pupils if they were unable to exert the requisite authority, as well as being constantly subjected to the school and the Inspectorate's control over their lives, including the minutiae of their personal appearance.[94] This meant that it could be a problem to retain trainee teachers for whom the daily grind of constantly being on duty from morning till night, as well as having to take part in all of the boys' physical and sporting activities (including cross-country war-games), could seem a bridge too far—especially when the pay at the NPEA was not always significantly better than that at a civilian day-school.[95]

The all-encompassing nature of a teaching job at the NPEA was partly dictated by the schools' military-style hierarchy, with the *Anstaltsleiter* occupying the position of ultimate command, the *Unterrichtsleiter* or Director of Studies as his second-in-command in charge of academic affairs, and a series of ranks beneath, ranging from two to four *Hundertschaftsführer* (lit. centurions), who might be placed in charge of crucial spheres such as boarding affairs, premilitary training, and school trips, to the many rank-and-file *Zugführer* who had to take responsibility for each individual class.[96] Taking on the role of 'duty *Zugführer*' (*Zugführer vom Dienst*) was often a particularly thankless task, since it could involve a 5.30am start, overseeing the wake-up call and supervising the boys as they washed, dressed, and did their early-morning sport; making sure that everything was in order throughout the whole school during the day, and that all pupils were doing what they should be in the right place at the right time; conducting the frequent massed 'inspections' before mealtimes; and dealing with any crises which might arise or visitors who might arrive.[97] Even when staff were not specifically undertaking this 'duty' role, they were effectively working non-stop (except when they were asleep): teaching lessons; attending to their pupils' multifarious needs and problems; marking homework; keeping their physical fitness up to scratch; and attending all of the many meetings, lectures, and 'political evenings' which the school put on (see further Chapter 2).[98]

Yet, at the same time, for those trainee teachers who managed to stay the course, the sense of constant challenge, as well as the elevated academic ability and enthusiasm of pupils at the NPEA, and the excellence of the Napola facilities when compared with those at most civilian schools, often proved a decisive spur to commit to a career in the Napola system.[99] It was not for nothing that Gerd Siegel admitted to his wife in October 1938 that, 'if I'm honest, then I have to say that the life at this school seems more agreeable than any other living conditions that I've ever found myself in'.[100] The potentially all-consuming vocation of a Napola-*Erzieher* could therefore appear to have significant advantages as well as drawbacks, even for those trainee teachers who were more interested in pursuing the teaching profession at all costs, rather than being specifically devoted to the cause of National Socialist elite education.

*

Finally, how did the *Anstaltsleiter* fit into this picture? As mentioned above, the first NPEA-headmasters were uniformly characterized by their lack of pedagogical experience, and were self-confessedly chosen by Rust purely due to their personal character, their leadership qualities, and their 'militant pasts' as political activists, which made them far better suited than most professional pedagogues to direct the schools' manifold paramilitary activities.[101] At first, Rust deliberately gave the *Anstaltsleiter* a great deal of leeway to shape their respective schools as they saw fit, so that a coherent system could be created organically through a mixture of individual pedagogical experimentation and frequent communal consultation.[102] However, as time went on and the Napola 'experiment' began to take on a concrete form, it was more common for the newer *Anstaltsleiter* (such as Lothar Dankleff, Hans Eckardt, and Arnold Janssen) to have proven themselves by working their way up through the ranks of various Napolas as *Erzieher*, before being given the task of leading a school of their own.[103] It was also noticeable that, following Heißmeyer's arrival on the scene as Inspector, the previous preponderance of SA-*Anstaltsleiter* was replaced by a swing towards favouring SS candidates instead.[104]

The role of the *Anstaltsleiter* was multifarious, but primarily administrative and 'inspirational'—by and large, he was not expected to teach; academic affairs were the province of his subordinate, the *Unterrichtsleiter*.[105] The *Anstaltsleiter*'s most important tasks involved ensuring that the school was properly maintained and taking responsibility for its financial solvency; representing the school's interests to the wider world, including dealing with parents, local government, and the Party and HJ leadership; and securing a sufficient number of new pupils each year. He also had to coordinate his Napola with the Inspectorate and the other NPEA, and direct and inspire his subordinates politically and personally, whilst additionally engaging in what would now be termed 'blue sky thinking'.[106] All in all, he was supposed to act as a 'fatherly friend' to the *Jungmannen*, and a highly civil and sympathetic comrade to his *Erzieher*.[107]

In order to unify the disparate 'experiments' of the schools' initial years, the *Anstaltsleiter* also had to attend regular conferences or meetings every couple of months or so, at which every conceivable aspect of NPEA life and administration would be discussed—from detailed debates concerning the requisite health insurance for the *Jungmannen* or the minutiae of different types of uniform, to decisions regarding the ideal curriculum for various academic subjects, or the best way to carry out cross-country war-games.[108] These meetings were held at a different school every time, so that the varied circumstances at each Napola could be experienced at first hand; depending on the amount of accommodation available, the conferences might also involve a camping-trip for all concerned, since every school was supposed to send three *Erzieher* and a couple of *Jungmannen* to each conference, as well as the *Unterrichtsleiter* and the *Anstaltsleiter* himself.[109] At times, the conferences would be designed to address specific guiding themes, such as the gathering held in November 1938 at NPEA Stuhm, which focused on 'Questions of Religious Education'.[110] Over the years, the decisions made at these conferences led to the creation of more or less unified guidelines and curricula, which then formed a basis upon which new ideas (and new school foundations) would build.[111] Although such meetings became much harder to hold in wartime, the headmasters' conferences still carried on sporadically until at least 1943.[112]

In practice, this system, which still granted a good deal of power and leeway to individual headmasters, meant that the influence of an *Anstaltsleiter* on his NPEA could be just as important in moulding its ethos as its previous tradition had ever been; hence, the character and interests (or obsessions) of an individual headmaster could easily make their mark upon an entire school.[113] Thus, the aforementioned *Anstaltsleiter* Brunk of NPEA Plön infected the Napola with his own unsavoury taste for Germanic mysticism and quasi-occult political ceremonies, as well as catering to his alarming fixation with toughening the *Jungmannen* up at all costs. Prospective pupils were chosen more with respect to their potential sporting ability than any other consideration, and any pupil who did not earn 180 points or more in the Reich Youth Sporting Competition (*Reichsjugendwettkampf*) each year was in serious danger of expulsion.[114] Two *Jungmannen* from Plön who were selected to go on the school's US exchange programme in 1935–6 discovered that Brunk's militarization had entered their marrow to such a degree that, even once they were aboard the liner which would take them to the New World, wearing elegant suits rather than their habitual uniform, every whistle and shout of 'Achtung!' made their legs jump together until eventually they realized that Brunk was no longer around to 'harshly disturb our peace'.[115] Even when on leave from active service in 1942, Brunk insisted on spending almost the entire eight days of his brief furlough putting the *Jungmannen* through their paces with a series of drills and wargames.[116] Meanwhile, *Anstaltsleiter* Bernhard Pein of NPEA Spandau appears to have been one of the most openly antisemitic of all the *Anstaltsleiter*—which may explain why some pupils from Spandau became particularly involved in antisemitic activism during his tenure (see Chapter 2).[117] However, the headmasters' exalted position did not always leave them beyond reproach in other ways—*Anstaltsleiter* Adolf Schieffer ultimately lost both his SS-membership and his position at NPEA Schulpforta after engaging in an unfortunate affair with the school cook.[118]

*

From this perspective, then, the NPEA and their administration arguably tended to manifest in microcosm many aspects of the Nazi state more generally—not least the obsession with the creation of military-style hierarchies, in accordance with the so-called 'Führer-principle'.[119] Thus, Reich Minister Rust personified the classic *Führer–Gefolgschaft* (leader-follower) model for his bureaucratic and pedagogic subordinates on the macro-level, just as the *Anstaltsleiter* performed this role on the micro-level at each individual NPEA.[120]

At the same time, the Napola administration also provides a particularly multifaceted case study of the constant polycratic wrangling which so often lay at the heart of the Nazi state—that seemingly chaotic tangle of competing competencies which made the regime a veritable 'institutional jungle'.[121] Nevertheless, we might concur with more recent analyses of the Third Reich's bureaucracy which suggest that such *Kompetenzstreiten* did not necessarily lead to utter inefficiency and anarchy—rather, they could also (or simultaneously) contribute to administrative stabilization, whilst furthering the regime's overall interests and prestige.[122] In this particular instance, we might argue that, despite the Napolas' ostensible 'crises', Himmler's obsession with gaining control of the NPEA actually ensured that they retained a significant position within the Nazi state, as well as enabling the schools' transnational reach to continue to expand until the final months of World War II. If the SS and the Reich Education Ministry had not both been fighting *for* the interests of the NPEA against all other potentially hostile parties, including the Prussian and Reich Finance Ministries, then their financial and material difficulties might ultimately have triumphed, relegating the schools to a mere insignificant footnote in the Third Reich's educational history.

In addition, even the relative power and respective positions of the SA and SS within the National Socialist regime's organizational hierarchy over time is mirrored in microcosm by the SA's initial power and influence over the Napolas, as reflected by Haupt's appointment as the schools' first Inspector, and the dedication of NPEA Plön to Ernst Röhm, followed by Röhm's *damnatio memoriae* and Haupt's dismissal on trumped-up homosexuality charges. The consequent rise of SS influence over the schools following Heißmeyer's inspectorial appointment, reflecting Himmler's increasingly virulent attempts to gain control of the Napola system in its entirety, can also be seen as symptomatic of the Reichsführer's growing will to power within the state. The very fact that Gottlob Berger deemed the Napolas to be important enough to attempt to wrest away from Heißmeyer as a way to gain Himmler's favour, using the dirtiest tricks at his disposal, also indicates the schools' increasing significance within the SS, as well as without. Moreover, as we shall see in Chapter 8, the almost absolute power which Himmler and the SS were ultimately able to exert over the *Reichsschulen* in occupied Holland and Flanders corresponds more broadly to the emergent ascendency of the Reichsführer-SS in the occupied territories. Furthermore, one might even suggest that, by the early 1940s, the stringent racial selection undertaken at the NPEA meant that their pupils were far more 'elite' according to the SS' own criteria than were many members of the *Allgemeine SS*.[123]

Finally, although it might not be possible to place most Napola-*Erzieher* in the same bracket as those 'uncompromising', highly educated and ideologically motivated killers analysed by Michael Wildt in his seminal study of the leaders of the SS Security Service (SD), since many staff may simply have been enticed by the prospect of a steady teaching job after the frequent and demoralizing unemployment crises of the Weimar years (which tended to affect younger trainee teachers disproportionately), the decision to stay in the NPEA system could easily lead to a radicalization of teachers' existing political views, due to the schools' constant programme of ongoing National Socialist and SS indoctrination.[124]

Overall, therefore, we can arguably identify both the Inspectorate, and the NPEA system as a whole, as what the sociologist Lewis A. Coser has termed 'greedy institutions'—a designation which has been used to great effect by Daniel Siemens and Stefan Kühl in analysing the role of the SA and the *Einsatzgruppen* (killing squads) respectively.[125] Such institutions are characterized above all by the control which they exert over their members, and the excessive nature of their 'omnivorous' demands on members' loyalty and compliance, attempting to 'encompass within their circle the whole personality' of each individual member, whilst still ostensibly appealing to his voluntary commitment.[126] As the control of the SS over the schools and their *Erzieher* began to wax ever more powerful under

Heißmeyer's dominion, NPEA staff and personnel became similarly entangled with Himmler's concept of the total, all-encompassing 'Order', which ultimately exposed all of the schools' employees to what Peter Longerich has dubbed Himmler's 'voyeuristic' manipulation of their most intimate personal choices, especially those regarding sexual relations, marriage, and childbirth.[127]

However, as we shall see in the following chapter, the control which the NPEA were able to exert over their youthful charges during their time at the schools was even more extensive, encompassing almost every single aspect of pupils' daily lives. From this perspective, the NPEA were more than a merely 'greedy institution'—they were also a form of 'total institution'.[128]

Notes

1. For further biographical information on Haupt, see Geheimes Staatsarchiv Preußischer Kulturbesitz (GStAPK), I. HA Rep. 151, Nr. 1093, Bl. 98; also Klaus Schmitz, *Militärische Jugenderziehung. Preußische Kadettenhäuser und Nationalpolitische Erziehungsanstalten zwischen 1807 und 1936* (Frankfurt am Main, 1997), 253–9; Alfred Heggen, 'Joachim Haupt (1900–1989): Ein früher NSDAP-Aktivist in Schleswig-Holstein', *Zeitschrift der Gesellschaft für Schleswig-Holsteinische Geschichte*, 134 (2009), 193–203; Christoph Sperling, *Joachim Haupt (1900–1989). Vom Aufstieg eines NS-Studentenfunktionärs und Sturz des Inspekteurs der Nationalpolitischen Erziehungsanstalten* (Berlin, 2018); on Rust, see Anne C. Nagel, *Hitlers Bildungsreformer. Das Reichsministerium für Wissenschaft, Erziehung und Volksbildung, 1934–1945* (Frankfurt am Main, 2012). Ulf Pedersen's biography of Rust, entitled *Bernhard Rust: Ein nationalsozialistischer Bildungspolitiker vor dem Hintergrund seiner Zeit* (Braunschweig, 1994), is disappointingly more of a rehabilitatory apologion than a creditable work of scholarship, perhaps due to the author's having collaborated with Rust's family in order to gain access to hitherto unexplored documents. See also Helen Roche, *Sparta's German Children: The Ideal of Ancient Sparta in the Royal Prussian Cadet Corps, 1818–1920, and in National Socialist Elite Schools (the Napolas), 1933–1945* (Swansea, 2013), 189, 193.
2. Sperling, *Joachim Haupt*, 69–71; relevant documents relating to Haupt's dismissal can be found in the Archiv Gymnasium Schloss Plön (AGSP). On the history of the Stabilas in general, see Chapter 4.
3. Schmitz, *Militärische Jugenderziehung*, 253–8; Roche, *Sparta's German Children*, 193–4; Nagel, *Hitlers Bildungsreformer*, 122.
4. Schmitz, *Militärische Jugenderziehung*, 247, 287; Roche, *Sparta's German Children*, 193–5; cf. Helen Roche, '"Anti-Enlightenment": National Socialist Educators' Troubled Relationship with Humanism and the Philhellenist Tradition', *Publications of the English Goethe Society* 82, no. 3 (2013), 193–207, 203–5. Haupt's tract entitled *Sinnwandel der formalen Bildung* (1935), published under the pseudonym 'Winfrid', was particularly popular in this regard.

5. Cf. Alfred Heggen, 'Die offizielle Einweihung der Nationalpolitischen Erziehungsanstalt "Ernst Röhm" in Plön am 28. Oktober 1933', *Jahrbuch für Heimatkunde im Kreis Plön* 37 (2007), 46–62.
6. For a detailed description of the accusations and Haupt's reaction to them, see Sperling, *Joachim Haupt*, 113–29.
7. Sperling, *Joachim Haupt*, 117–18, 127–8, 145.
8. Sperling, *Joachim Haupt*, 134–49.
9. On the trope of the homosexual SA-activist, see Daniel Siemens, *Stormtroopers: A New History of Hitler's Brownshirts* (New Haven, 2017), 172–5; cf. Sperling, *Joachim Haupt*, 156.
10. On the polycratic nature of the Nazi state and its bureaucracy more generally, see e.g. Christiane Kuller, '"Kämpfende Verwaltung". Bürokratie im NS-Staat', in Dietmar Süß and Winfried Süß, eds, *Das 'Dritte Reich'* (Munich, 2008), 227–45; also Jane Caplan, *Government without Administration: State and Civil Service in Weimar and Nazi Germany* (Oxford, 1988); Rüdiger Hachtmann and Winfried Süß, eds, *Hitlers Kommissare. Sondergewalten in der nationalsozialistischen Diktatur* (Göttingen, 2006); Sven Reichardt and Wolfgang Seibel, *Der prekäre Staat. Herrschen und Verwalten im Nationalsozialismus* (Frankfurt am Main, 2011).
11. Cf. Peter Longerich, *Heinrich Himmler* (Oxford, 2012); Siemens, *Stormtroopers*; Nagel, *Hitlers Bildungsreformer*. Longerich's study only mentions the NPEA once in the context of Himmler's foster-son Gebhard being sent to a Napola, though he had to leave a few months later (p. 375—N.B. the schools are erroneously named here as 'National Socialist educational establishments'); Nagel's monograph, meanwhile, only contains one brief paragraph on the NPEA (pp. 158–9).
12. On the Napolas' relationship with the Adolf-Hitler-Schools, and the political wrangling involved in their inception, see the Conclusion.
13. GStAPK, I. HA Rep. 151, Nr. 1093, Bl. 98; Schmitz, *Militärische Jugenderziehung*, 259, 261.
14. Schmitz, *Militärische Jugenderziehung*, 259.
15. Schmitz, *Militärische Jugenderziehung*, 261–2. During this period, the academic year in Germany habitually began at Easter, rather than in Michaelmas.
16. Cf. Schmitz, *Militärische Jugenderziehung*, 261. Ironically, however, Hitler never visited any of the Napolas, ultimately bestowing his name and patronage on the Adolf-Hitler-Schools instead.
17. Schmitz, *Militärische Jugenderziehung*, 265.
18. Landesarchiv Berlin (LAB), A Pr. Br. Rep. 042 Nr. 1612, Bl. 28.
19. Bundesarchiv Lichterfelde (BArch), R 4901/8, Bl. 21; GStAPK, I. HA Rep. 151, Nr. 1093, Bl. 98; Institut für Zeitgeschichte, München (IfZ), MA 1438, draft memo dated 10 November 1933. For more on the details of the transformation process, see Chapter 4.
20. Staf., *10 Jahre NPEA Plön. Sonderheft der Kameradschaft* (Kiel, 1943), 3–4. On Brunk's background and his arrival at Plön, see also Matthias Paustian, *Die Nationalpolitische Erziehungsanstalt Plön 1933–1945* (Rostock, 1995), 20–2.
21. 10. *Jahre Plön*, 3–4.

22. GStAPK, I. HA Rep. 151, Nr. 1093, Bl. 7.
23. 10. *Jahre Plön*, 4–5.
24. 10. *Jahre Plön*, 4–6, 11.
25. 10. *Jahre Plön*, 7.
26. 10. *Jahre Plön*, 30–3; Heggen, 'Einweihung'. In his tenth-anniversary account, Brunk had to be extremely careful not to mention the name-change, or to stress the presence of SA dignitaries at the festivities, which can cause his narration of the celebrations to seem somewhat stilted. On the Night of the Long Knives and the SA's fall from grace more generally, see Siemens, *Stormtroopers*; Peter Longerich, *Die braunen Bataillone. Geschichte der SA* (Munich, 1989).
27. See in particular GStAPK, I. HA Rep. 151, Nr. 1093.
28. For more on pre-military training at the NPEA, see Chapter 2; on artistic education and the schools' 'borderland missions', see Chapter 3.
29. BArch, R 4901/8, Bl. 21; on the foundation of Stuhm and Wahlstatt, see further Helen Roche, '*Herrschaft durch Schulung*: The *Nationalpolitische Erziehungsanstalten im Osten* and the Third Reich's Germanising Mission', in Burkhard Olschowsky and Ingo Loose, eds, *Nationalsozialismus und Regionalbewusstsein im östlichen Europa: Ideologie, Machtausbau, Beharrung* (Berlin, 2016), 127–51, esp. 131–3. On Ilfeld, see Chapter 6; also Helen Roche, 'Die Klosterschule Ilfeld als Nationalpolitische Erziehungsanstalt', in Detlef Schmiechen-Ackermann et al., eds, *Die Klosterkammer Hannover 1931–1955. Eine Mittelbehörde zwischen wirtschaftlicher Rationalität und Politisierung* (Göttingen, 2018), 605–26.
30. It was only on 1 April 1937 that the affairs of the federal NPEA began to be officially centralized, although efforts in this direction were already being made from 1935 onwards; cf. Niedersächsisches Landesarchiv—Staatsarchiv Oldenburg, Best. 134 Nr. 2353, Bl. 3; BArch, R 4901/5272, Bl. 3.
31. In Württemberg and Anhalt, 'branch-schools' (*Zweiganstalten*) were founded in Rottweil (for Backnang) and in Köthen (for Ballenstedt) in 1936, while, in 1938, NPEA Neuzelle finally gained full independence from NPEA Potsdam. For a more detailed discussion of Schulpforta's Napolisation, see also Helen Roche, '"Wanderer, kommst du nach Pforta…": The Tension between Classical Tradition and the Demands of a Nazi Elite-School Education at Schulpforta and Ilfeld, 1934–45', *European Review of History/revue européenne d'histoire* 20, no. 4 (2013), 581–609.
32. BArch, R 4901/8, Bl. 67, 71; cf. relevant correspondence in GStAPK, I. HA Rep. 151 IC, Nr. 7308.
33. Cf. BArch, R 2/19991, letter from Sowade dated 14 January 1939.
34. Cf. 'Zehn Jahre Nationalpolitische Erziehungsanstalten—Feierliche Appell in Potsdam—Reichsminister Rust und SS-Obergruppenführer Heißmeyer sprachen', *Deutsches Nachrichtenbüro*, 26 May 1943 [BArch, R 4902/1490]. The NPEA founded during this year included Rügen (Putbus), Loben, Seckau, Vorau, Spanheim (St. Paul), Saarland (St. Wendel), Reichenau, Rufach, Achern, Colmar-Berg (Luxembourg), Weierhof (am Donnersberg), and Emsland (Haselünne).
35. Cf. BArch, R 4901/8; GStAPK, I. HA Rep. 151 IC, Nr. 7308; also GStAPK, I. HA Rep. 151, Nr. 1094—Bd. 2, Bl. 225–7.
36. e.g. GStAPK, I. HA Rep. 151 Nr. 1093, Bl. 156–8; BArch, R 4901/8, Bl. 45.

37. For an account and relevant diary entries by an *Anstaltsleiter* who had been seconded to the NPEA administration towards the end of the war, which vividly depicts the chaotic and highly dangerous conditions under which the Inspectorate was working by this point, see Hans Eckardt, *Rückschau auf mein Leben* (n.d.).
38. Cf. e.g. GStAPK, I. HA Rep. 151 IV, Nr. 2736, Bl. 28–35; also Chapter 4. For an example of Popitz's parsimony in practice, see GStAPK, I. HA Rep. 151, Nr. 1079, letter from Popitz to Rust dated 13 March 1935. Nevertheless, it is still salutary that Rust managed to push through so much expenditure for the NPEA despite Popitz's general inclination towards austerity measures in the education sector—on financial tensions between Popitz and Rust more generally, see Nagel, *Hitlers Bildungsreformer*, 90–100. On Popitz's life in general, and his subsequent (rather muted) opposition to the regime, see Anne C. Nagel, *Johannes Popitz (1884–1945). Görings Finanzminister und Verschwörer gegen Hitler. Eine Biographie* (Cologne, 2015).
39. e.g. BArch, R 2/12711, 'Raumprogramm für die Neubauten der Nationalpolitischen Erziehungsanstalten mit grundständigem Zug'; GStAPK, I. HA Rep. 151, Nr. 3929, Bl. 57ff.; Sächsisches Hauptstaatsarchiv Dresden (SHStAD), 11177 Nr. 496, 'Vermerke über die Arbeitstagung der Sachbearbeiter in Bauangelegenheiten der Nationalpolitischen Erziehungsanstalten am 15. Juli 1941 im Reichsfinanzministerium in Berlin'; BArch, R 2/19991, 'Erläuterungen zu dem Muster eines Kassenanschlages für eine Nationalpolitische Erziehungsanstalt'; GStAPK, Rep. 151, Nr. 1093, Bl. 152; BArch, R 2/12712, 'Aufstellung der in den Nationalpolitischen Erziehungsanstalten benötigten Pferde'. For the problems which these requirements could cause for schools in the less wealthy federal states, see Chapter 5.
40. Staatsarchiv Ludwigsburg (StAL), E 202 Bü 1746 and 1747.
41. Cf. e.g. Österreichisches Staatsarchiv (ÖStA), BEA 7, 'Arbeitsplan für die Rentmeisterbesprechung vom 8.-10. Juni 1939', programme dated 11 March 1939.
42. August Heißmeyer, *Die Nationalpolitischen Erziehungsanstalten*, 10 (BArch, NS 31/121). For examples of such building- and renovation-related documents, see e.g. LAB, A Pr. Br. Rep. 042, Nr. 1614, letter from Sowade dated 21 June 1937, and the numerous files pertaining to NPEA Potsdam-Neuzelle held at the Brandenburgisches Landeshauptarchiv.
43. 'Vermerke über die Arbeitstagung'; Otto Schäfer, 'Ziel und Gestalt der nationalpolitischen Erziehungsanstalten', *Nationalsozialistisches Bildungswesen* 7, no. 1 (1942), 19–31, 24–5; see also Calliebe and Neuhaus, 'Die Bauten der Nationalpolitischen Erziehungsanstalten in Preußen', *Zentralblatt der Bauverwaltung/Zeitschrift für Bauwesen* 59, no. 50 (1939) [Sonderdruck, BArch, R 2/27762].
44. BArch, R 2/28072, letter from Popitz to Rust dated 30 June 1936. One of the worst offenders in creating this financial sinkhole was NPEA Stuhm—renovations on site cost literally millions of Reichsmarks during this period (cf. BArch, R 2/28071–28077).
45. On Freiburg, see Generallandesarchiv Karlsruhe (GLAK), Bestand 235, Nr. 35344; on Trier, see Landeshauptarchiv Koblenz (LHAKO), Bestand 860—Staatskanzlei Rheinland-Pfalz—Nr. 2116; LHAKO, Bestand 442—Bezirksregierung Trier—Nr. 18800; LHAKO, Bestand 662,003—NSDAP Kreisleitung Trier-Westland—Nr. 68; GStAPK, I. HA Rep. 151, Nr. 13483; 'Stärkung des westlichen Eckpfeilers des Reiches. Nationalpolitische Erziehungsanstalt in Trier. Die ersten Bauraten bewilligt /

Feststellung in drei bis vier Baujahren / Unterredung mit Gauleiter Pg. Simon', *Nationalblatt*, 25 January 1938 [BArch, R 8034-II/9296]. The building works foundered due to financial problems, and the prospect of their completion faded ever further into the distance after the outbreak of World War II.

46. On the plans for the two Lower-Saxon NPEA, see Niedersächsisches Landesarchiv—Hauptstaatsarchiv Hannover (NLA-HStAH), Hann. 180 Hannover B Nr. 95; GStAPK, I. HA Rep. 151, Nr. 13476–13477; Niedersächsisches Landesarchiv, Staatsarchiv Wolfenbüttel (NLA-StAW), 12 Neu 13 Nr. 19574; on the plans for the Bückeberg in particular, see the relevant documents held at the Stadtarchiv in Hameln (my thanks to Annette Blaschke for this reference); on the plans for the Steinhuder Meer development, which would also have replaced the Napola in Ilfeld, see Roche, 'Klosterschule Ilfeld', 623–4.
47. StAL, E 202 Bü 1746, Gräter, 'Bericht des Anstaltsleiters der Nationalpolitischen Erziehungsanstalt Backnang über die Teilnahme bei der Anstaltsleiterbesprechung am 2.12.1936 in der Nationalpolitischen Erziehungsanstalt in Berlin-Spandau', 4.
48. e.g. Schliack, 'Bericht über einen dreiwöchigen Aufenthalt auf der Kreisleitung in Nauen (Osthavelland)', *Spandauer Blätter* 3 (20 August 1935), 10; StAL, E 202 Bü 1747, 'Voraussichtlicher Jahresplan für die Zeit Ostern 1939—Ostern 1940'; BArch, R 43-II/956b, Wolf, 'Bericht über den politischen Einsatz der Nationalpolitischen Erziehungsanstalt Stuhm im Kreis Leipe (Lipno), Sommer 1941' (August 1941), Bl. 106–7; Hauptzugführer Eckardt, 'Erzieher und Ortsgruppenleiter', *Mitteilungen der Nationalpolitischen Erziehungsanstalt Naumburg/Saale*, 18. Kriegsnummer (October 1943), 17–18.
49. See Chapters 2 and 3. However, in an account entitled 'Geländeübung der Anstalt mit den Verbänden der Partei' published in an issue of NPEA Plön's school newsletter from June 1938, the author pointedly remarked that the NSKK had taken inordinate pleasure in using up the dummy hand-grenades far too quickly—cf. *Die Kameradschaft. Blätter der Nationalpolitischen Erziehungsanstalt Plön* 4, no. 1 (June 1938), 16.
50. IfZ, MA 1438, draft memo by Haupt dated 10 November 1933; cf. BArch, R 4901/8, letter from Rust to Popitz, 5 January 1934, Bl. 27.
51. StAL, E 202 Bü 1746, 'Niederschrift über die Anstaltsleiterbesprechung am 2.-3. Dezember 1936 in Berlin-Spandau', 4; Wilhelm Rautenberg, 'Von der Klosterschule zur Nationalpolitischen Erziehungsanstalt. Ilfeld April 1932–April 1935', in Rudolf Marggraf, ed., *Die Nationalpolitische Erziehungsanstalt Ilfeld. Sammlung der von 1934 bis 1944 herausgegebenen Ilfeld-Blätter—Ein Beitrag zur Zeitgeschichte. Band II: Januar 1943 bis April 1944/45* (1998), 487–517, 503. Rautenberg claims that this measure was taken by Rust (partly at his son Hans-Bernhard's instigation, after he had been accused of dereliction of his SS duties) in order to prevent SA and SS 'service' from impinging on pupils' school schedules and their free time.
52. 'NPEA. und SA.', *Mehr sein als Scheinen. Nationalpolitische Erziehungsanstalt Potsdam-Neuzelle: Arbeitsbericht* (March 1937), 10.
53. See the relevant entries in *Die Kameradschaft*, e.g. A. Hintze, 'SA-Nordmarktreffen', *Die Kameradschaft* 1, no. 2/3 (November 1935), 11–12. From this perspective, the NPEA fit the paradigm which Daniel Siemens has recently posited; namely, that the

SA did not wholly lose significance or influence in the Nazi state even after the Night of the Long Knives (cf. Siemens, *Stormtroopers*).

54. Cf. BArch, R 187/270b, Bl. 130–4; on SS suspicions of Holthoff's intentions, see e.g. BArch, NS 19/2741, esp. Bl. 22–30.
55. On NSDAP authorities' non-cooperation with the NPEA, see e.g. BArch, R 2/31684; BArch, R 2/12736; BArch, R 2/27779, letter dated 20 September 1943; BArch, R 2/12723; Gerd Cremer, 'Die Entlassung von Dr. von Drygalski, wie ich sie erlebte', in Marggraf, *Ilfeld*, Bd. II, 516–17.
56. Cf. e.g. BArch, R 187/557, Bl. 349–55; Hauptstaatsarchiv Stuttgart, E 200b Bü 178, letter dated 8 January 1945; Niedersächsisches Landesarchiv—Staatsarchiv Osnabrück, Rep 430 Dez 400 Nr. 397, letter from Gaupersonalamtsleiter, Gauleitung Weser-Ems, to Kreispersonalamtsleiter dated 17 December 1943; NLA-HStAH, Hann. 180 Lüneburg Acc. 3/88 Nr. 26, letter dated 6 November 1935; Landeshauptarchiv Sachsen-Anhalt, Abteilung Magdeburg, Rep. C 28 II, Nr. 2361, Bl. 134; StAL, PL 502/13 Bü 142, Gaupersonalamt der NSDAP, Hauptstelle Führernachwuchs, Rundschreiben Nr. 15 (3 December 1943).
57. 'Eingliederung der Schüler der Nationalpolitischen Erziehungsanstalten in die HJ. Ein Interview mit dem Inspekteur, SS-Gruppenführer Heißmeyer', *Reichsjugendpressedienst*, 19 March 1936 [BArch, NS 5/VI/18840].
58. 'Die HJ. in den Nationalpolitischen Erziehungsanstalten', *Reichsjugendpressedienst*, 7 November 1936 [BArch, NS 5/VI/18840]; Meister, 'H.J.-Arbeit im Rahmen der Anstalt', *Der Jungmann* 1, no. 3–4 (December 1936), 72–3. N.B. The schools in Saxony, Anhalt, and Württemberg were more Hitler-Youth oriented from the beginning, and hence initially had more in common with the Adolf-Hitler-Schools—see further Chapter 5.
59. e.g. 'Zusammenarbeit mit der HJ.', *Potsdam-Neuzelle: Arbeitsbericht* (March 1937), 10–11; Schülke, 'DJ.-Dienst der 1. Hundertschaft', *Die Brücke. Nachrichten der Nationalpolitischen Erziehungsanstalt Köslin* 11, no. 4/5 (February 1939), 75; 'Aus der HJ-Arbeit', *Pflug und Schwert* 1 (1943), 15; H.B., private correspondence, October 2013.
60. e.g. Kurt Meyer, *Gelobt sei, was hart macht! Fröhliche, unbeschwerte, aber harte Jahre auf der NPEA* (2003), 40; 'Unsere Arbeit in der Hitler-Jugend', *Nationalpolitische Erziehungsanstalt/Reichsschule für Volksdeutsche Rufach-Achern* (December 1941), 16–17.
61. Cf. BArch, R 5/3362; BArch, R 2/12711, letters dated 13 February 1942, 3 March 1942, 13 March 1942; GStAPK, I. HA Rep. 151 IC, Nr. 7308, Bl. 8–11.
62. On *Kompetenzstreiten* between the SS and the Wehrmacht, see also Chapter 10.
63. Schmitz, *Militärische Jugenderziehung*, 267–68. Popitz also gave the *Landesverwaltung* an ultimatum in December 1936, warning that at least one NPEA would have to be closed by the beginning of the next financial year in order to safeguard the existence of the remaining schools; this demand ultimately led to the closure of NPEA Wahlstatt—cf. BArch, R 43-II/956b, Bl. 10–12.
64. Schmitz, *Militärische Jugenderziehung*, 271.
65. Sperling, *Joachim Haupt*, 153, 155; cf. BArch, NS 19/2741, Bl. 22. Sperling notes that Heißmeyer was officially able to retain his SS rank by treating his bureaucratic inspectorial rank in the Education Ministry as an honorary one.

66. Roche, *Sparta's German Children*, 194–5.
67. Fr. Eichler, 'Der Reichsführer der SS, Pg. Himmler, weiht die 3 Sturmfahnen der N.P.E.A.', *Die Brücke* 7, no. 3 (August 1934), 41–4. Himmler promised the staff and pupils that he would not forget the NPEA, and expressed his fulsome praise for the school's good work. The author of the report ironically closed with the wish that the school would soon 'come under Himmler's protection'. On Himmler's additional attempts to add the Hitler Youth to his empire, see Gerhard Rempel, *Hitler's Children: The Hitler Youth and the SS* (Chapel Hill, 1989).
68. BArch, NS 19/2498, Bl. 1. On Rust's health problems, see Roche, *Sparta's German Children*, 196.
69. Cf. BArch, NS 19/2010, letter from Berger to Wolff dated 22 April 1942; BArch, NS 19/2741, Bl. 22–4, 42–3. On the feud between Berger and Heißmeyer more generally, see also Longerich, *Himmler*, 499; also the relevant essays in Roland Smelser and Enrico Syring, *Die SS. Elite unter dem Totenkopf: 30 Lebensläufe* (Paderborn, 2000). On Berger's life and career, see also Joachim Scholtyseck, 'Der "Schwabenherzog". Gottlob Berger, SS-Obergruppenführer', in Michael Kißener and Joachim Scholtyseck, eds, *Die Führer der Provinz. NS-Biographien aus Baden und Württemberg* (Konstanz, 1997), 77–110.
70. BArch, R 2/12711, letters dated 26 January 1941, 24 March 1941; BArch, NS 19/2741, Bl. 47.
71. BArch, NS 19/2741, Bl. 43.
72. BArch, NS 19/239, letter from Berger to With dated 25 February 1943; cf. BArch, R 43-II/956c, Bl. 3. Even in 1944, the most obvious outward manifestation of SS control was merely cosmetic—the addition of the SS eagle to pupils' uniforms; cf. Dietrich Schulz, *Meine Napolazeit in Putbus 1941–1945* (2013), 20.
73. BArch, NS 19/4005, Heinrich Himmler, 'Rede des Reichsführer-SS vor den Leitern, Erziehern und den Jungen der 8., 7. und 6. Klassen der Nationalpolitischen Erziehungsanstalten am 3.7.38 im Zeltlager Ahrenshoop' (1938); Anon., *Sommerübung 1938* (unpublished manuscript, 1938); on the manoeuvres more generally, see Chapter 2.
74. Heißmeyer, *Die Nationalpolitischen Erziehungsanstalten* (BArch, NS 31/121); StAL, E 202 Bü 1747, letter dated 15 February 1939; on the *Mannschaftshäuser*, see Bastian Hein, *Elite für Volk und Führer? Die Allgemeine SS und ihre Mitglieder 1925–1945* (Munich, 2012), 161–3. During wartime, this scheme transmuted into a genuine desperation to get pupils to join the military branches of the SS—see Chapter 10.
75. For a detailed description of all of the stages in the selection process as a whole, see Chapter 2.
76. BArch, NS 47/40, agreement dated 17 March 1939; BArch, NS 2/134; BArch, NS 2/68, Bl. 94; BArch, R 187/270b, Bl. 122.
77. On the immense significance attached to such racial selection processes for members of the SS, see Longerich, *Himmler*, 302; Hein, *Elite*, 92–150.
78. Cf. e.g. BArch, R 187/270b, Bl. 121. For an example of a senior *Erzieher* at NPEA Backnang resisting the pressure to join the SS, see StAL, F 455, Nr. 4.
79. BArch, NS 19/3096, Bl. 2–3. Thus, trainee teachers (*Referendare*) would be given the rank of NPEA-*Untersturmführer* (Second Lieutenant), *Assessoren* (junior masters) would be given the rank of NPEA-*Übersturmführer* (Lieutenant), graduating after two years' service to *Hauptsturmführer* (Captain); the rank of *Studienrat* (master) would

then be equated to that of *Sturmbannführer* (Major), and the rank of *Oberstudienrat* (senior master) would be equated to that of *Obersturmbannführer* (Lieutenant Colonel). Meanwhile, *Unterrichtsleiter* and *Anstaltsleiter* would be given the rank of *Standartenführer* (Colonel), *Oberführer* (Senior Colonel), or *Brigadeführer* (Brigadier), depending on the exact extent of their responsibilities; these ranks would by extension be applied to senior bureaucrats working for the Inspectorate.

80. Cf. BArch, NS 2/64, Bl. 121ff.; SHStAD, 11125 Nr. 21351, Bl. 56–9; also Hans-Christian Harten, *Himmlers Lehrer. Die Weltanschauliche Schulung in der SS 1933–1945* (Paderborn, 2014), 173–5.
81. e.g. BArch, NS 2/64, 'Äußerungen über den Schulungskurs in Neubabelsberg, der vom SS-Rasse- und Siedlungshauptamt für Erzieher der Nationalpolitischen Erziehungsanstalten vom 10.-15. Januar 1938 abgehalten wurde' (1938), Bl. 122–43.
82. On marital control in the SS, see Longerich, *Himmler*, ch. 13.
83. e.g. StAL, E 202 Bü 1747, letter from the Inspectorate to all NPEA dated 2 May 1939; ÖStA, BEA 7, letter dated 28 February 1938; ÖStA, BEA 164, letter from the Inspectorate demanding a certificate of racial heritage (*Abstammungsnachweis*) for Liselotte Oberwandling, the future wife of *Erzieher* Helmut Gradnitzer; IfZ, ED 735–8–2, letter from Heißmeyer to an *Erzieher* at Oranienstein dated 5 April 1939; Wasmann Nachlass, letter from Heißmeyer to Wasmann dated 4 March 1940. Some Napolas went so far as to have reports on these marriage and birth statistics published in their school newsletters as well, e.g. 'Eheschließung und Kinderzahl der Bensberger Erzieher', *Rundbrief der NPEA Bensberg*, 13. Kriegsfolge (15 March 1942), 8; Zugführer Baumann, 'Eheschließung und Kinderzahl der Rottweiler Erzieher', *Im Gleichschritt* 3, no. 10 (November 1942), 236–7.
84. Gerd Siegel, 'Ein ehemaliger Erzieher der NPEA Bensberg schrieb an seine Frau (Auszüge aus einem intensiven Briefwechsel)', letter dated 3 March 1939; in his post-war memoirs, Siegel trivializes this incident and presents it in a comic light—cf. Gerd Siegel, *Wechselvolle Vergangenheit* (Göttingen, 1980), 117.
85. Heißmeyer, *Die Nationalpolitischen Erziehungsanstalten*, 15–16.
86. Heißmeyer, *Die Nationalpolitischen Erziehungsanstalten*, 15; cf. GStAPK, I. HA Rep. 151 IC, Nr. 12393; GStAPK, I. HA Rep. 151, Nr. 3929, Bl. 66; BArch, R 2/28072, report dated 9 May 1936. At times, this could lead to staff 'playing the system' and deliberately getting married as quickly as possible simply in order to be granted a free apartment—cf. BArch (ehem. BDC), Personalakten Arnold Janssen (DOB 8.4.1907), letter dated 9 February 1937 from 27. SS-Standarte to SS-Abschnitt XII, Frankfurt/Oder.
87. StAL, FL410–4 Bü 109, 'Arbeitstagung im Reichsfinanzministerium Berlin und in der Nat.polit. Erziehungsanstalt in Ballenstedt vom 15.-18. Juli 1941', 12.
88. Siegel correspondence; LHAKO, 700,238 Nr. 9, *Sammelbericht* Nr. 5 (10 July 1943).
89. Friedrich Lübbert, 'Die körperliche Erziehung in den Nationalpolitischen Erziehungsanstalten', *Leibesübungen und körperliche Erziehung* 11 (1938), 273–9, 274. On the extreme demands made on teachers' physical fitness at the NPEA, see Helen Roche, 'Sport, Leibeserziehung und vormilitärische Ausbildung in den Nationalpolitischen Erziehungsanstalten: Eine "radikale" Revolution der körperlichen Bildung im Rahmen der NS-"Gesamterziehung"?', *Beiträge zur Geschichte des Nationalsozialismus* 32 (2016), 173–96. Personnel documents held at the Geheimes

Staatsarchiv Preußischer Kulturbesitz demonstrate clearly that, even for many academic *Erzieher*, sport was a favoured subsidiary subject, with many staff having passed the PE-teaching examination (*Turnlehrerprüfung*) during their teacher-training (cf. GStAPK, I. HA Rep. 90A, Nr. 1765); particularly talented trainees at the Reich Academy for Physical Training (*Reichsakademie für Leibesübungen*) would also be nominated as potential candidates for PE-teaching positions at the NPEA (SHStAD, 11125 Nr. 21351, 'Bericht über die Reifeprüfung in Potsdam-Neuzelle, Spandau, Naumburg, Schulpforta, 28. Februar 1938', Bl. 197–8). On official conceptions of the ideal NPEA-*Erzieher* more generally, see BArch, NS 2/134, Bl. 21; Heißmeyer, *Die Nationalpolitischen Erziehungsanstalten*, 14–15; GLAK, Bestand 235, Nr. 35344, decree dated 8 March 1938; 'Vermerke über die Arbeitstagung', 1–2.

90. Politisches Archiv des Auswärtigen Amts, report dated 21 January 1934 (describing a visit to Sander at NPEA Potsdam on 19 January 1934); Schmitz, *Militärische Jugenderziehung*, 290.
91. BArch, NS 19/2741, Heißmeyer, 'Bericht' (11 July 1942), Bl. 17. In this report, Heißmeyer states that *Erzieher* were not supposed to have any confessional affiliation either.
92. GStAPK, I. HA Rep. 90A, Nr. 1765. For more on the *Aufnahmestopp* and its implications, see the introduction by Wolfgang Benz and the essays by Juliane Wetzel and Björn Weigel in Wolfgang Benz, ed., *Wie wurde man Parteigenosse? Die NSDAP und ihre Mitglieder* (Frankfurt am Main, 2009).
93. GLAK, Bestand 235, Nr. 35344, Rust, 'Zusammenarbeit zwischen Hochschulen für Lehrerbildung und Nationalpolitischen Erziehungsanstalten', decree dated 8 March 1938; on the *Bezirksseminar*, see SHStAD, 11125 Nr. 21351, Bl. 163; Otto Calliebe, 'Gedanken zur Entwicklung der Nationalpolitischen Erziehungsanstalten (NPEA)' (1969), 3, 9. Sometimes, trainee teachers appear to have specifically requested to do work experience at an NPEA—cf. Hessisches Hauptstaatsarchiv Wiesbaden, Bestand 425 Nr. 479, letter dated 9 July 1935; NLA-StAW, 12 Neu 13 Nr. 19574, 'Ausbildung von Studienreferendaren an Nationalpolitischen Erziehungsanstalten'. Participants in the Education Ministry's 'Land Service' (*Landjahr*) programme could also undertake to do voluntary work experience at an NPEA; cf. BArch, NS 38/5254.
94. Cf. SHStAD, 11125 Nr. 21351, 'Bericht über die Dienstbesprechung der Nationalpolitischen Erziehungsanstalt in Backnang (Württemberg) vom 10.-12. Nov. 1937', Bl. 189; on the gruelling nature of the schedule for *Erzieher*, see e.g. GStAPK, I. HA Rep. 151, Nr. 1095, Bl. 152–4. On the terrorizing of trainee teachers by pupils, see e.g. Hugo Selke, *Auch eine Jugend in Deutschland. Meine Schulzeit in Ilfeld und Schulpforte 1935–1939* (1990), 18–19; Hans Lindenberg, *Montagskind. Erinnerungen*, Vol. 1 (1990), 98; for a former member of staff's account of his own experiences as a *Referendar*, see Friedrich Dubslaff, *Erinnerungen* (n.d.), 1–8. For an example of the extent of inspectorial control over teachers' appearance, see Vice-Inspector Adolf Schieffer's expatiation on the correct way for *Erzieher* to wear their belt-buckles: StAL, E 202 Bü 1746, letter from Schieffer dated 8 November 1937. Many similar prescriptions are also contained in this file and StAL, E 202 Bü 1747.
95. Cf. BArch, R 43-II/956b, Bl. 10–12; BArch, R 2/12711, letter dated 4 September 1943; BArch, R 2/12583, letter from Heißmeyer to Reinhardt dated 11 May 1941; Hans Günther Zempelin, *Des Teufels Kadett: Napola-Schüler von 1936 bis 1943. Gespräch*

mit einem Freund (Frankfurt am Main, 2000), 58. For detailed information on teachers' paygrades, see BArch, NS 6/499; BArch, R 2/12711; BArch, R 2/12583; BArch, R 2/10857a.

96. Cf. Otto Schäfer, 'Ziel und Gestalt der nationalpolitischen Erziehungsanstalten', *Nationalsozialistisches Bildungswesen* 7, no. 1 (1942), 19–31, 22–3. Other ranks included *Hauptzugführer* (and, on occasion, *Haupthundertschaftsführer*, the title assumed by Gerhard Lüders, the headmaster at NPEA Rügen, since he was still subject to control by the *Anstaltsleiter* of the Napola's 'mother-school' at NPEA Spandau).
97. For examples of a 'life in the day' of a *Zugführer vom Dienst*, see Heinrich Tangermann's account, reprinted in Helmut-Albrecht Kraas, ed., *Napola Neuzelle (ehem. Kreis Guben/Mark Brandenburg)—eine Dokumentation*, Vol. 2 (1993–4), 55–7; Siegel correspondence, letter dated 5 November 1938.
98. e.g. Siegel correspondence, *passim*.
99. Siegel correspondence, letters dated 2 September 1938, 4 September 1938; Arne Heinich, interview with Paul Nitsche (a former music-teacher at NPEA Bensberg), n.d. (*c.* June 1981).
100. Siegel correspondence, letter dated 18 October 1938.
101. Cf. GStAPK, I. HA Rep. 151, Nr. 1093, Bl. 7; Helmut Trepte, 'Die Nationalpolitische Erziehungsanstalt', *Internationale Zeitschrift für Erziehung* 3, no. 4 (1934), 489–92, 490; Staatsarchiv Hamburg, 113–15 B V 115, letter from Rust dated 25 October 1937; 'Rechtsanwalt Glauning, Pressereferent im REM—Wissenschaft, Erziehung und Volksbildung', *Völkischer Beobachter*, 30 January 1938 [Bundesarchiv Koblenz, ZSg. 117 Nr. 285].
102. BArch, R 5/3362, Bernhard Rust, 'Rede des Reichsministers Rust' (21 April 1941), 4–5; 'Die Nationalpolitischen Erziehungsanstalten: Vier Jahre Arbeit für eine nationalsozialistische Erziehung!', *Volksaufklärung und Schule*, 47/8 (1938), 2–4, 3.
103. Cf. e.g. BArch (ehem. BDC), Personalakten Hans Eckardt (DOB 16.12.1908), R 9361/III 36120; BArch, (ehem. BDC), Personalakten Lothar Dankleff (DOB 26.1.1905), SSO 135; GStAPK, I. HA Rep. 151, Nr. 1078, Bl. 71.
104. See the relevant personnel files held in the former Berlin Document Center archive at the Bundesarchiv in Lichterfelde.
105. Cf. StAL, E 202 Bü 95, letter dated 25 November 1937; SHStAD, 11125 Nr. 21351, Barth, 'Bericht über meinen Besuch der Nationalpolitischen Erziehungsanstalten Ballenstedt, Ilfeld, Naumburg und Schulpforta vom 19.-22. Oktober 1936', Bl. 43–9; Heißmeyer, 'Die Nationalpolitischen Erziehungsanstalten', 12.
106. Schäfer, 'Ziel und Gestalt', 22.
107. Schäfer, 'Ziel und Gestalt', 22. As we shall see in Chapter 2, some *Anstaltsleiter* managed to maintain such positive relationships with their pupils and staff rather better than others.
108. Cf. 'Anstaltsleitertagung der Nationalpolitischen Erziehungsanstalten in Ostpreußen vom 23. bis 27. Juni 1937', *Weltanschauung und Schule*, 1/7 (1937), 553–6.
109. e.g. StAL, E 202 Bü 1747, letter from Brunk dated 31 May 1937.
110. Cf. SHStAD, 11125 Nr. 21351, Bl. 251–2.
111. For examples of minutes and reports from the conference in December 1936, see StAL, E 202 Bü 1746, 'Niederschrift'; 'Bericht des Studienrats Dr. Max Hoffmann

über die Tagung der Anstaltsleiter der Nationalpolitischen Erziehungsanstalten in Berlin-Spandau am 1. und 2. Dezember 1936'; Gräter, 'Bericht'; SHStAD, 11125 Nr. 21351, Bl. 14–20.

112. See the programme for the conference which took place from 21–4 July 1943 in *Nationalpolitische Erziehungsanstalt Plön: Rundbrief*, Nr. 25 (October 1943), 33–4.
113. Cf. e.g. Eckardt, *Rückschau*, 114.
114. Schmidt, 'Bericht über die Reichsjugendsportwettkämpfe am 24.5.41', *Plön: Rundbrief*, Nr. 17, 11, 19; *Plön: Rundbrief*, Nr. 21 (November 1941), 28.
115. 'Plöner Jungmannen in den Vereinigten Staaten von Nordamerika', *Die Kameradschaft* 1, no. 4 (March 1936), 19–25, 20.
116. Olaf Burmähl, 'Staf in Plön', *Plön: Rundbrief* 22 (August 1942), 41–2.
117. For examples of Pein's antisemitic outpourings, see e.g. Pein, 'Sommerferien 1935', *Spandauer Blätter* 3 (20 August 1935), 5–6; Pein, 'Der Anstaltsleiter: Liebe Gäste, Ehemalige, Kameraden und Jungmannen', *Spandauer Blätter* 7 (20 October 1936), 4–7.
118. BArch (ehem. BDC), Personalakten Adolf Schieffer (DOB 16.8.1886).
119. Cf. Gerhard Hirschfeld and Lothar Kettenacker, *The 'Führer State': Myth and Reality. Studies on the Structure and Politics of the Third Reich* (Stuttgart, 1981); Christopher Dillon, *Dachau and the SS: A Schooling in Violence* (Oxford, 2015), esp. ch. 5.
120. Cf. Nagel, *Hitlers Bildungsreformer*, 79–80.
121. Moritz Föllmer, *'Ein Leben wie im Traum': Kultur im Dritten Reich* (Munich, 2016), 73; cf. Nagel, *Hitlers Bildungsreformer*; Schmitz, *Militärische Jugenderziehung*, 246.
122. Kuller, 'Bürokratie', 233–4.
123. Cf. Hein, *Elite*, ch. 4, 312–13.
124. Cf. Michael Wildt, *An Uncompromising Generation: The Nazi Leadership of the Reich Security Main Office* (Madison, 2009); Axel Nath, *Die Studienratskarriere im Dritten Reich* (Frankfurt am Main, 1988); Konrad Jarausch, *The Unfree Professions: German Lawyers, Teachers, and Engineers, 1900–1950* (Oxford, 1990); Charles Lansing, *From Nazism to Communism: German Schoolteachers under Two Dictatorships* (Cambridge, MA, 2010); Schmitz, *Militärische Jugenderziehung*, 292.
125. Siemens, *Stormtroopers*, xxvii; Stefan Kühl, *Ganz normale Organisationen. Zur Soziologie des Holocaust* (Berlin, 2014), 315–16.
126. Lewis A. Coser, *Greedy Institutions: Patterns of Undivided Commitment* (New York, 1974), 4–6 (cited in Siemens, *Stormtroopers*, xxvii). These organizations tend to brook no division between work and free time, allowing their members no other frame of reference with which to engage with the wider world (cf. Kühl, *Organisationen*, 316–17).
127. Kühl, *Organisationen*, 314; Longerich, *Himmler*, 742. On the control and selection processes exerted over personnel at the schools, see e.g. GStAPK, I. HA Rep. 151 Nr. 1094 Bd. 2, Bl. 154; BArch, R 2/12583, letter from Calliebe dated 15 May 1941; also ÖStA, BEA 58 and BEA 101, which include documentation indicating that support staff also had to supply the school authorities at the Austrian NPEA with certification of their 'racial purity' in order to be permitted to retain their positions after the Anschluss (see also Chapter 7).
128. See further Chapter 2 (n. 285); also Erving Goffman, 'On the Characteristics of Total Institutions', in *Asylums: Essays on the Social Situation of Mental Patients and Other Inmates* (London, 1961); Roche, *Sparta's German Children*, ch. 5.

2
'Selection', Teaching, and Everyday Life

Once a pupil had successfully endured the Napolas' arduous selection or '*Auslese*' process, he would find himself completely in thrall to the schools' programme of 'total education' (*Gesamterziehung*). Every day, from his rude awakening and the obligatory early-morning run or swim, through the usual timetable of lessons, sport, or pre-military training, and even during his free time, each *Jungmann* lived according to the schools' strict schedule of 'duties' (*Dienst*), and was fully subject to Napola discipline. The NPEA authorities proudly boasted on numerous occasions that, as boarding schools, the Napolas could effect a far more all-encompassing socialization than could the traditional trio of Nazi pedagogical influences—namely, the parental home, school, and the Hitler Youth. Rather, the NPEA effectively replaced and combined all of these elements in order to create the Napola '*Gemeinschaft*'—an elitist microcosm of the *Volksgemeinschaft* as a whole. In this sense, the NPEA arguably lay in the vanguard of National Socialist educational experimentation, since they were successfully able to suffuse all aspects of pupils' lives with ideological indoctrination—often so subtly that, even today, former pupils are unable to perceive exactly how politicized their education at the schools truly was.[1]

From this perspective, the aims of this chapter are threefold. Firstly, it provides an experiential account of the selection process and everyday life at the NPEA, presenting what we might term a 'thick description' of the schools' *Alltagsgeschichte*. Secondly, it investigates the content and indoctrinatory effects of teaching at the Napolas, especially those lessons which were explicitly dubbed 'national-political', as well as the role of sport and physical training, which formed a core aspect of the schools' curriculum. Finally, it considers the educational experience which the schools offered within the context of broader literature on pedagogy and society in the Third Reich.

We shall begin with an account of the lengthy process of pre-selection and the NPEA entrance exam, before moving on to treat pupils' experiences of the settling-in process, everyday life, and their relationship with the schools' support staff and teaching staff. We then explore the Napolas' academic and physical education curriculum in detail, before closing with a depiction of the culmination of pupils' school career, the school-leaving exam or *Reifeprüfung*, and the ensuing graduation ceremony (*Abiturientenentlassung*). The conclusion then provides a brief contextualization of the schools' overall programme within the framework of existing scholarship on the Third Reich, seeking to comprehend the Napolas'

The Third Reich's Elite Schools: A History of the Napolas. Helen Roche, Oxford University Press. © Helen Roche 2021.
DOI: 10.1093/oso/9780198726128.003.0003

programme in terms of its pedagogical and political effectiveness vis-à-vis other Nazi institutions; the extent to which the NPEA betrayed continuities with pre-National Socialist thinking in terms of reform pedagogy, and the ways in which the schools constituted a microcosm of broader trends which are more generally observable within the Nazi state and its educational policy.

Zwischen Auslese und Ausmerze: The NPEA Selection Process

As previously discussed, it is indisputable that the Napolas were highly elitist '*Ausleseschulen*', in the sense that the schools' intake of pupils was intensely selective. However, the selection criteria at the NPEA were very different from those imposed by their forerunners. At the Weimar Republic's *Staatliche Bildungsanstalten*, for instance, although the terms '*Schülerauslese*' (selection of pupils) and '*Ausleseprinzip*' (selective principle) were commonly used throughout the 1920s, candidates' intellectual abilities were still the primary criterion underpinning the selection process.[2] However, at the Napolas, although above-average academic ability was still a clear desideratum, 'character' and physical fitness were prioritized above 'mere book-learning', in accordance with Hitler's hierarchy of pedagogical virtues (as delineated in *Mein Kampf*).[3]

Moreover, in order to be accepted at a Napola, pupils and their families had to connive in the process of what Peter Fritzsche has termed 'racial grooming', supplying the school authorities with evidence that their antecedents had been sufficiently 'Aryan' for the requisite number of generations.[4] Thus, Peter K., a former pupil of NPEA Spandau, remembered that 'before I was considered, my father had to prove that I was of "Aryan" descent. He had to provide a family tree going back three generations. It took him quite a few weeks to obtain the required certified documents. I remember that it involved some travelling to obtain church records. Phoning and letter writing to remote country locations, even if you had an address, did not necessarily find you the office where the records were kept. I remember him having frustrations.'[5] Hans Lindenberg, who attended NPEA Potsdam, recalled that, even after he had been accepted at the Napola, further research still had to be undertaken, this time clarifying the 'racial integrity' of his family tree as far back as his great-great-great grandparents—as it turned out, an almost impossible task.[6]

Most existing accounts of the Napola selection process take a somewhat piecemeal approach, focusing above all on the criteria specified in school prospectuses and official press releases (*Aufnahmebedingungen*), and on the experiences of boys being observed first in their own civilian school classrooms as part of the pre-selection process, and then at the week-long NPEA entrance examination, the *Aufnahmeprüfung*.[7] This lacuna exists in part because the '*Auslese*' procedure was far more complex than pupils themselves could ever know—for most prospective *Jungmannen*, the first that they would experience of the selection process would be the appearance of a couple of unanticipated observers at the back of their primary-school classrooms. However, the effort which had been expended in the various stages of the pre-selection process prior to this point would already have been immense, involving the collaboration of thousands of individual teachers and educational officials, numerous provincial school boards, and even, on occasion, the creation of bespoke teacher-training programmes. This section will therefore map the entire procedure of 'registration' (*Meldung*) and pre-selection (*Vormusterung*) in greater detail, before treating the Napola entrance examination from a variety of different perspectives.

Although we can certainly discern occasional frictions between the NPEA and individual officials in regional government, as well as those internal and external tensions created by the increasing involvement of the SS in the 'racial' aspects of the selection process (as discussed in Chapter 1), the collaboration between the Napolas and local government appears for the most part to have run fairly smoothly.[8] Ultimately, it would have been impossible to keep the NPEA running at all without an enduringly effective system of cooperation between individual Napolas, primary schools, District School Boards (*Kreisschulräte*), and regional governments all over Germany. Moreover, the '*Auslese*' procedures appear to have been largely uniform throughout the different regions of the Reich, with only small variations existing between individual schools.[9] At least in the pre-war years, the process seems to have produced a genuine *Auslese*, with an extremely high attrition rate recorded at every stage. During World War II, however, tensions appear to have increased over which Napolas could claim which 'recruitment districts' (*Musterungsbezirke*) as their territory, since the system was expanding at such a rapid rate that it was becoming increasingly difficult to find a large enough number of sufficiently qualified candidates within the ever-shrinking region allotted to each individual school—not to mention the constant need to compete with the growing number of Adolf-Hitler-Schools and other types of elite school, which were now all seeking candidates for their own intake.[10]

A great deal of rich documentary material concerning this process, including statistical evidence, is to be found in federal state archives such as the Niedersächsisches Hauptstaatsarchiv in Hannover, the Hessisches Hauptstaatsarchiv in Wiesbaden, the Landeshauptarchiv Sachsen-Anhalt in Magdeburg, or the Landesarchiv Nordrhein-Westfalen in Münster. These documents shed a significant light upon the constant efforts of NPEA *Anstaltsleiter* (or their representatives) to manipulate local government officials within their sphere of influence into executing their directives to the letter: trying to get 'their' recruitment districts to compete against each other, or shaming them by revealing how badly their recruitment campaigns had gone compared to those of other districts in the area—a phenomenon which can arguably be seen as a hallmark of the Nazi political style more generally.[11]

These reports also indicate that the total number of boys who were 'pre-registered' by their primary schools did not always match the number who actually turned up to the pre-selection tests—a telling indication that, however much the NPEA and government authorities might desire that all concerned should comply with their demands, the situation on the ground might in fact be rather different.[12] As we shall see, this even meant that in some cases the *Anstaltsleiter* would instruct schools not to inform parents that their sons had been pre-selected until after the event. At the same time, it does not appear that the NPEA ever directly forced parents into sending their children to a Napola, despite some eye-witnesses' claims to the contrary.[13] If such coercion did occur, then, it seems probable that this would have taken place on the initiative of individual local government officials, who might have been desperate to gain this kind of accolade for their district—or simply to get the NPEA authorities off their back by providing the Napola in question with at least one suitable candidate. However, none of my archival research to date has yielded concrete documentary evidence that coercion of this kind existed at all.

In the interests of concision, the following narrative depicting the usual course of the selection process is based on a composite reading of all of the available data taken from individual case-studies, rather than treating a plethora of individual Napolas' experiences in great detail.[14] It is important to note in this connection that, although it was not unknown for parents to register their children as prospective candidates for an NPEA themselves, this was neither the norm, nor the schools' preferred *modus operandi*. Indeed, in a memo prepared by *Hundertschaftsführer* Otto Brenner of NPEA Ballenstedt in April 1944, the author deemed applications by parents and guardians, as well as recommendations by Party functionaries or by current or former *Jungmannen*, to be far less valuable than those recommendations which had been guided by the long-standing experience of primary-school teachers.[15] In a report dated 25 May 1940, Wilhelm Kemper, the *Unterrichtsleiter* at NPEA Bensberg, also expressed reservations about those 'private registrations' (*Privatmeldungen*) which were sent to the NPEA by parents acting on their own initiative. Kemper claimed that, in that year's round of admissions, only 17 per cent of those boys who had been privately recommended had been admitted—a sorry comparison with the number of pupils who had been pre-selected by their primary schools and deemed eligible to enter the Napola, which usually amounted to around 50 per cent.[16] At times, reports and recommendations by Hitler Youth leaders were also deemed to be relatively unhelpful for the Napolas' purposes in this regard.[17]

*

For any *Anstaltsleiter*, one of the most pressing administrative problems to contend with would be primary-school teachers' numerous misapprehensions concerning which types of boys should be pre-selected for the NPEA, and at what age. Correspondence in the archival collections cited above abounds in ever-more detailed memos attempting to counteract teachers' ignorance on this score—including the erroneous idea that the Napolas' aim was to provide an education for 'charity cases', regardless of their ability and potential; that only boys with blond hair and blue eyes had a chance of admission, or that boys who were physically under-developed or suffered from medical problems or congenital defects could be deemed worthy of consideration.[18] Problems might also be caused by primary-school teachers taking offence if prospective candidates whom they had recommended for the NPEA were too frequently rejected, or by their coming to believe that the selection process was simply too competitive for them to bother making recommendations in future.[19] However, if teachers attempted to suggest too many candidates, the majority of whom were completely unsuited for selection according to the Napolas' stringent criteria, this could also cause the NPEA administrative headaches later on.

For an *Anstaltsleiter* who wished to garner the cream of the crop of potential applicants from the 'recruitment districts' assigned to him, then, the first task was an essentially PR-related one. He would need to ensure that relevant articles and notifications, soliciting and encouraging applications and pre-selection registrations from all primary schools in the relevant areas, would be published in regional state-government dispatches, and in the local press.[20] Most importantly, he would need to supply every District School Board (*Kreisschulrat*) in the region with relevant literature, especially memos on the aims of the NPEA and their selection criteria, which could then be passed on to all primary-schools in that district (*Kreis*) in order to guide teachers in their decision-making.[21] Such media initiatives at the local level might be complemented by articles in the national press, or the widespread screening of propaganda movies about the NPEA, such as the supporting film *Unsere Jungen* (1940), or the feature film *Kopf hoch, Johannes!* (1941), which was directed by the renowned regisseur Victor de Kowa.[22] These cinematic offerings were intended to raise public awareness of the Napolas' mission, and to drum up support and applications by boys who had been fascinated and intrigued by the positive portrait of boarding-school life at the Napolas depicted therein. That this drive was successful, at least in part, can be demonstrated by the fact that many former pupils recall having been inspired to apply after having seen a showing of one or other of these films at the cinema.[23] On one occasion, a group of fifty school-girls who had seen one of the Napola-films in 1942 were even moved to address a gratuitous fan letter 'To an Unknown *Jungmann* at NPEA Spandau', where the missive was received with much hilarity, and reprinted in the school newsletter to amuse former pupils at the front.[24] Individual NPEA might also record amateur 'school films' (*Anstaltsfilme*) depicting their everyday life and 'missions', which could then be screened for the benefit of prospective parents or teachers at local schools.[25]

Finally, it was considered crucial to develop strong personal relationships with local primary-schools—and teacher-training colleges—to ensure that teachers would know exactly what the NPEA were looking for in prospective candidates.

Napola-*Erzieher* might offer to come and give talks at local teachers' meetings, hold screenings of the *Anstaltsfilme* mentioned above, or they might invite '*Erzieher*-comrades' from schools in the region to visit the Napola for a day or two, or even to attend the pre-selection examinations.[26] The NPEA in Württemberg also set up partnerships with teacher-training colleges (*Hochschulen für Lehrerbildung*) in Esslingen and Karlsruhe, making arrangements for trainee teachers to come and visit the NPEA at Backnang and Rottweil so that they could get a sense of the Napolas' aims and ethos.[27] Teacher-training colleges throughout Germany were also requested to submit the names of trainee teachers who appeared to be particularly attuned to the Napolas' pedagogical needs to the Inspectorate on a regular basis.[28]

Once an *Anstaltsleiter* had prepared the ground as carefully as possible, hopefully ensuring that teachers at the schools in his 'recruitment districts' would recommend the 'right' type of candidate, the next step was to send out requests for pre-selection registrations (*Meldungen*) to the District School Boards—these requests would then be distributed to all of the relevant schools in each Board's catchment area. This stage of the process necessarily involved a great deal of correspondence, largely in order to hector or cajole local officials into ensuring that the requisite quotas of prospective applicants from each district would be met. Those districts which had not yet responded, or which had claimed that there were no suitable candidates for pre-selection to report, would often be browbeaten into supplying the desired information.[29] Teachers would frequently be warned not to inform parents of pupils' pre-selection at this stage; instead, they were told to describe the pre-selection test simply as a 'medical examination', either to avoid arousing 'false hope', or in the fear that parents might then withdraw their children from the process, whether because they were opposed to the idea of their son being sent to boarding school or to a Napola *tout court*, or because they had other plans for him.[30] Although the *Anstaltsleiter* might stress that 'there will never be any compulsion [for families] to apply', teachers were nevertheless instructed not to allow parents' views on whether they wished their sons to be selected or not to sway them, but simply to base their judgement upon their own perception of pupils' suitability and capability.[31]

Assuming that they believed some of their pupils to be suitable candidates, the teachers, via their schools, would then send their recruitment recommendations back to the District School Board. Thus, in 1938, the District Schools Officer for Marburg forwarded a number of teachers' observations to NPEA Bensberg for consideration, containing judgements such as: 'Siegfried Cohrs...is a healthy German youth who inspires good hope for his future. He is also musical; he plays the mouth organ. His admission is to be recommended', or 'Heinz Gröte is the fourth of five children. His father was a secretary with the local magistrate, but due to a nervous disorder is now in a mental hospital in Lüneburg. The children are healthy. His mother wants to send the lad to the local town commercial college for further training. He also makes an inspiring impression, is alert and eager to learn. His character appears to be impeccable. The sponsorship of Heinz Gröte via a National Political Education Institute would probably bear fine fruit.'[32]

Once a list of suitable candidates from all of the Napola's 'recruitment districts' had been compiled, the *Anstaltsleiter* would need to arrange for a '*Vormusterung*' (pre-selection) or '*Ausleselager*' (selection camp) to take place. This process often involved liaising with the local health authorities (*Gesundheitsämter*), in order to supply doctors who could undertake a preliminary medical examination of all of the candidates who had been recruited for the pre-selection test, so that those with obvious medical defects could be excluded from consideration prior to the actual *Aufnahmeprüfung*.[33] Either the prospective candidates from each *Kreis* would be gathered together at a school which was located centrally within the district, and subjected to physical, medical, and academic tests,[34] or a team of two experienced Napola-*Erzieher*, usually including at least one *Hundertschaftsführer* and a medic (or, later, a 'racial inspector' from the SS) would visit each school in the district individually.[35] In the latter case, the *Anstaltsleiter* would arrange a timetable for the visit with the schools in question, so that the *Hundertschaftsführer* could visit the relevant classes, and gain a personal impression of the boys who had been pre-selected on paper, attempting as far as possible to give the impression that this was merely a run-of-the-mill school inspection.[36] Thereafter, the pre-selection committee would take charge, observing pupils' demeanour in physical education and academic lessons, whilst the school-teachers would attempt to showcase the abilities of those candidates whom they (or the committee) believed were most worthy of note. The medic would then examine the boys' general state of health and their constitution; the *Hundertschaftsführer* would have them play games which tested their strength, speed, and dexterity, and, to close, the prospective candidates would be invited to converse with the committee.[37] Finally, successful candidates' parents might receive an invitation to visit the NPEA, in order to see the place where their son might end up being educated for themselves, and the parents of current Napola-pupils might additionally be enlisted to help calm prospective parents' anxieties.[38]

The visit by the Napola pre-selection committee tends to be the point at which most former pupils first realized that they might have been selected as potential candidates for an NPEA. Most seem to have been under the impression that the pre-selection team were only being informed by their form-teachers about the most likely candidates in each class during the course of their brief visit, without ever apprehending that they had initially been judged by their teachers long before, and that the appearance of the Napola-*Erzieher* in person was merely the culmination of an extremely long and convoluted series of bureaucratic recruitment mechanisms.[39] The deal would only be finally sealed, however, with the receipt of an official missive from the NPEA in question, requesting boys' attendance at the week-long entrance examination (parents were supposed to accompany their sons, if at all possible), and containing detailed instructions about how to reach the Napola, what to bring, as well as all the minutiae of timings, financial questions, and insurance fees.[40] Parents would be given the opportunity to tour the NPEA while their sons settled in, and they were also asked to meet the *Anstaltsleiter* and the *Hundertschaftsführer* in person, before departing that afternoon and leaving their children to their fate.[41]

*

The reasons for boys and their families to accept the invitation to the *Aufnahmeprüfung* (or for applying to an NPEA in the first place, in the case of those who had sent in 'private' applications) were multifarious.[42] A few boys were inspired by the fact that their families had some connection with the schools already—Günter L.'s uncle had been a caretaker at the cadet school in Wahlstatt, for instance, while Hinrich Kattentidt's father worked as the head of the building department (*Baudezernent*) for the Klosterkammer in Hannover, which bore some responsibility for the upkeep of the Napola in Ilfeld.[43] Many parents also realized that the chance to send their children to an NPEA could provide their offspring with prospects far beyond anything they could offer themselves—whether in terms of social mobility, and the fact that their child would have a much better chance of continuing into higher education, or in terms of the opportunity to provide their child with an all-expenses-paid schooling which would simultaneously obviate many of their own financial anxieties.[44]

Considerations of political expediency, or even health concerns, could also play a role: Hans-Joachim Männig remembered that his parents were especially happy to send him to NPEA Schulpforta not only because it was a *Gymnasium*, but also because their current abode in an industrial region plagued by brown coal dust was exacerbating his severe asthma, which Schulpforta's pleasant situation in the Saale valley promised to alleviate.[45] Meanwhile, Dietrich Schulz of NPEA Rügen recalled that his mother, who was a 'passionate devotee of Hitler', wanted both of her children to receive 'the best possible education and training from a National Socialist perspective'. His sister Christiane was therefore sent to the NPEA for girls at Hubertendorf-Türnitz in Austria, while Dietrich himself was supposed to end up at an Adolf-Hitler-School. However, when Dietrich surreptitiously 'lost' the AHS-application form on the way to the post, his mother applied to NPEA Berlin-Spandau on his behalf instead—a choice which accorded with Dietrich's newfound appreciation of films such as *Kadetten* and *Kopf hoch, Johannes!*, as well as his respect and admiration for both his grandfather, a former member of the Kaiser's royal guard, and his father, who had fought as a soldier in the Great War.[46]

Strangely enough, since parents might be requested to provide the aforementioned certificate of Aryan ancestry (*Ariernachweis*) prior to registration, but in most cases did not have to provide any form of certification regarding their own political reliability, it was not unknown for the sons of parents who held oppositional views towards the Nazi regime to be invited to take the entrance examination, and then subsequently admitted to an NPEA.[47] For instance, Hans Habermann and his brother were both pupils at NPEA Schulpforta, even though their father, Max Habermann, the leader of the German White-Collar Workers' Union, ended up being tangentially involved in the July plot in 1944, and would have been the official union representative in the post-war German government if Stauffenberg's coup had succeeded.[48] Moreover, attendance at a Napola could even afford some form of protection to families who might otherwise have fallen foul of the regime—in this vein, Hans-Hoyer von P. of NPEA Rügen recalled that his aristocratic mother had apparently been able to evade retribution by the Gestapo, following a denunciation by the family's cook for allegedly listening to the BBC and making uncomplimentary remarks about Hitler, by playing her trump card during the ensuing interrogation: 'What do you think you're playing at; my sons are at a Napola!'[49] Manfred F., a former pupil of NPEA Spandau, also recalled that, after his primary-school teacher had seen one of the films about the Napolas and suggested to his parents that this could be a good opportunity for him, they were highly doubtful, and discussions subsequently raged within the family regarding the best course of action. Finally, his parents decided to agree that Manfred could undertake the entrance exam, since they believed that there was no real chance of his being accepted, given that his father was not a member of the NSDAP. They were extremely surprised by the final outcome.[50]

Conversely, among 'ethnic German' communities and settler families in the East, a zealous enthusiasm for National Socialism and the idea of the 'Greater German Reich' might make the idea of a Napola-education seem particularly appealing. Kurt Schwechheimer, the son of a settler family from Riga who ended up attending NPEA Wartheland, noted that his mother was the driving force behind his acceptance at the Napola: 'Although she was Estonian, she was much more of a German than our father'.[51] Eugen K., also a former pupil of NPEA Wartheland, remembered that when a delegation of *Erzieher* from the Napola turned up at his school in January 1940 and described the benefits which he could gain if he were admitted there, 'I was immediately fired up. As an expatriate German (*Auslandsdeutscher*), I thought of everything that came from the Reich as unquestionably fine anyway.'[52]

Some boys were even enthused enough by the propaganda campaign laid on by the Napola-*Erzieher* that they would dare to apply on their own initiative; thus, Karl Dürrschmidt (formerly of NPEA Neubeuern) remembered that he had been so captivated with the idea of attending the Napola that he had signed up for the selection test without consulting his parents, and then had to spend hours subsequently convincing them to accept this *fait accompli* against their better judgement.[53] Meanwhile, Hugo Selke, a former pupil of NPEA Ilfeld, recalled having been absolutely fascinated by Ernst von Salomon's novel

Die Kadetten (*The Cadets*), and, when he saw a marching column of boys in a cadet-like uniform in his home town, enquired where they came from. It turned out that they were *Jungmannen* from the Napola at Stuhm, which lay close by. Selke immediately set off on his bike, rode to Stuhm, and asked the *Anstaltsleiter* whether he could join the school. Probably due to the rule that no *Jungmann* was supposed to live too close to the Napola which he attended, NPEA Stuhm, Plön, and Köslin were ruled to be out of the question, but Ilfeld, as the first humanistic Napola, was suggested instead.[54]

Whatever the reasoning behind families' acceptance of the invitation to the entrance exam, however, now was the time for the 'racial grooming' and the gathering of relevant paperwork to begin in earnest, in readiness for the ultimate test of prospective pupils' mettle: the *Aufnahmeprüfung*.[55]

*

While pupils' memories of their experiences during the entrance examination are necessarily fragmentary and impressionistic, a surviving 'Order of the Day' (*Tagesbefehl*) from NPEA Oranienstein portrays in minute detail how the *Aufnahmeprüfung* there in March 1939 was organized administratively. The official timetable for the first day runs as follows:

> Arrival of the candidates on Monday, 6 March between 10am–1pm and potentially 2–4pm. The candidates report at this time to *Hundertschaftsführer* Goos in the *Hundertschaftsführer*'s office in the Schloss. *Jungmannen* from *Zug* (Class) 1/3 and the *Stubenältesten* (room-captains) will be on hand to assist him. *Hundertschaftsführer* Goos is responsible for a sufficient number of *Jungmannen* being available to meet trains at the station.
>
> *Anstaltsleiter*'s office hours for the parents: Dietrich-Eckart-Zimmer between 10am–1pm and 2–4pm. The waiting-room for the parents is in the Oraniensaal. *Zugführer* Brenner and *Jungmann* Kraft will be on duty in the Oraniensaal.
>
> Guided tours of the school for the parents between 11am and 1pm and between 3pm and 4pm. [List of tour guides.]
>
> The house masters of *Zug* I/1c and *Zug* I/2 will be available in their respective *Zug* common rooms.
>
> Lunch on Monday 6 March at 1.15pm. Assignment of tables to each *Zug* by the Duty *Zugführer*.
>
> Lessons for the candidates' classes (*Prüfungszüge*): 4.10pm–5.45pm (German and Arithmetic)
>
> Medical examination: 6pm (duration 2 hours). Beginning with I/1c. (Duration for each *Zug* c.20 minutes.)
>
> The candidates for I/3 go to *Zug* I/2 (Examination Director *Zugführer* Klitschmüller) and do their entire duties in this *Zug*...[56]

> Upon arrival it must immediately be ascertained which candidates will not be collected on 11 March 1939. The Examination Director (*Prüfungsleiter*) will establish which trains these candidates will need to catch. The candidates who are travelling alone will be escorted to the station by *Jungmannen*. Responsible: *Hundertschaftsführer* Goos. The money for the return journey must immediately be cashed in by the candidates upon their arrival on Monday and taken out again on Saturday after the third lesson....[57]

The subsequent appendices to this 'Order of the Day' provide an exhaustively detailed list of the arrangements for the rest of the *Aufnahmeprüfung*. This included notifications concerning which *Zugführer*, *Erzieher*, and *Stubenältester* would be in charge of which cohorts of candidates, allocating each of these to a *Zug* in groups of twenty, arranged alphabetically according to their surnames. Accommodation would be overseen by the *Stubenältester*, and lessons would take place under the watchful eye of the *Zugführer* and the *Prüfungsleiter* (Examination Director), with academic lessons (focusing on German, Arithmetic, and Biology) taking place each morning between 8am and 12 noon.[58] In the afternoons, the candidates would undergo a packed programme of physical activities, including gymnastics, swimming, boxing, and cross-country war-games, as well as tests of character (see below).[59] By the fourth day of the examination, *Erzieher* were instructed to have amassed sufficient written material to facilitate an initial judgment on pupils' academic capabilities, using a unified framework which would be distributed beforehand.[60] They would then have to attend a staff meeting to discuss their initial assumptions as to which candidates were 'indubitably suitable', which were 'impeccably unsuitable', and which were 'questionable'.[61] At the end of the examination, all of the *Erzieher* would attend a second staff meeting, at which final decisions would be made, and all of the report forms would then be submitted to the *Unterrichtsleiter* by 7pm on the following Monday.[62] In her journal, the house-matron at Oranienstein, Emmy Spornhauer, chronicled the toll which such a gruelling schedule could take on the Napola support staff: overseeing more than two hundred high-spirited youngsters until nearly 10pm, including observing their football games and gymnastic exercises, watching over them at meals and in the dormitories, dealing with their washing, supervising their homework and private reading periods, and organizing creative activities for them, had left her 'completely shattered'.[63] Small wonder, then, that Hans Lindenberg should remark, looking back in the 1990s, that the *Aufnahmeprüfung* was the longest examination he had ever undergone in his entire life to date—even the examination which he had subsequently had to pass in order to become a naval officer cadet had only lasted three days.[64]

Contemporary accounts by *Erzieher* nevertheless suggest that staff at the Napolas tried to make the entire examination process as enjoyable as possible, attempting to vanquish the candidates' anxieties and draw them out, rather than making them feel like 'guinea pigs'.[65] Friedrich Dubslaff, an *Erzieher* at NPEA

Naumburg, described the process from the teachers' perspective: tasks were deliberately chosen in order to test the candidates' intellectual and physical qualities, such as number games, close analysis of pictures or song lyrics, or written compositions with titles such as 'My penknife tells a story', as well as exercises on the climbing bars to test boys' strength, or getting candidates to balance on a thick pole which would be placed across the body of the school swimming pool and making them attempt to walk across it, even if they could not swim (see further below). Care would be taken to make allowances for deficiencies in candidates' education up to that point, and their familial circumstances, when considering both their academic ability and their character.[66]

Sometimes, it was also considered helpful to throw the group of candidates in at the deep end metaphorically as well as literally, observing their capacity to employ lateral or abstract thinking when faced with challenges which were completely alien to them. Thus, candidates at NPEA Ballenstedt who had never learnt any Latin before might be given a few elementary lessons in the dead language to see how they fared, and whether they had a flair for language-learning.[67] In similar vein, Hans Lindenberg still remembered one of the 'trick questions' which he had been given during his own *Aufnahmeprüfung* at NPEA Potsdam: 'Eleven sparrows are perching on a bench. If I shoot one dead, how many sparrows are left perching on the bench?'[68] Other aspects of the examination would involve spoken and written dictation, arithmetic problems, and *viva voce* examinations on subjects such as Biology, History, and Geography.[69] In addition, candidates would often have to undergo a one-to-one *viva* with the *Anstaltsleiter* himself at some point during the week.[70]

The crowning test of all, however, was the so-called '*Mutprobe*' or 'test of courage'. This would take different forms at different schools, but the overall aim was to see whether candidates would be prepared instantly to undertake without hesitation an action which could seem frightening, potentially to the point of impossibility, thus showing their true mettle. This might involve jumping from one of NPEA Oranienstein's third-floor balconies into a safety blanket held by a group of *Jungmannen* below, without being able to tell if there would be a safe landing before one jumped; leaping from a high diving-board into water if one could not swim, or swinging across a local river on a rope.[71] Boys might also be forced to box or wrestle each other, or urged to climb an icy 10-metre-high wall and push their comrades who had already reached the top back down into the snow.[72] This could potentially lead to a crop of minor injuries each year, as Dieter Eschenhagen noted in connection with a *Mutprobe* which was favoured at NPEA Loben—jumping down from the climbing bars in the school gymnasium.[73] Overall, the teachers and the older *Jungmannen* who were supervising the examination were constantly seeking to discern which boys were distinguishing themselves as future *Jungmann*-material in terms of their physical prowess, quick thinking, and their strength of character, and which were conversely revealing themselves to be egotists, 'nature lovers', or 'Mummy's boys', without the requisite will or capacity to subordinate themselves entirely to the school community.[74]

Even when they were not under the watchful eye of the *Erzieher*, however, the candidates might have to endure various forms of hazing from the older *Jungmannen* who were helping out with the examination—whether through the resurrection of cadet-school traditions which involved attacking the candidates' dorms by night, as at NPEA Naumburg, or through rituals such as the '*Tristtaucherprüfung*' ('ducking in the lavatory test'), as at NPEA Stuhm.[75] Needless to say, the sanitized accounts by 'prospective *Jungmannen*' (*Jungmann-Anwärter*) which were eventually published in some school newsletters made no mention of these 'extracurricular' trials—such as W. Galler's encomium to the 'paradise' at NPEA Oranienstein, which picturesquely described his visit there as 'a dream finding its fulfilment'.[76]

Once the candidates had returned home, there then came the anxious time of waiting for the letter of rejection or acceptance from the NPEA, and, in successful cases, the preparations for the new school year.[77] However, in a sense, for these newly minted *Jungmannen*, the truly testing period had only just begun. For instance, at NPEA Potsdam, new pupils were not even allowed to leave the school for the first few weeks of the year, until they had proved that they could represent the Napola fittingly in public.[78] Moreover, not only would the new boys often be subjected to far more brutal forms of hazing by their seniors (see below), but for the first six months at the school (known as the *Probehalbjahr*), they were still very much on probation, and attrition rates were expected to rise as high as 5 per cent—although the Napola authorities were concerned to make switching to a civilian school as painless as possible for those pupils who were ultimately asked to leave.[79]

However, for those *Jungmannen* who had successfully gained admission and for whom remaining at the Napola seemed fairly assured, what did school life hold in store?

Settling In and Everyday Life

From being one of the best at lessons and sport in their local primary school or Hitler Youth group, the new *Jungmannen* were swiftly catapulted into a wholly new way of life; one which entailed almost complete regimentation and subordination, both to staff and to older pupils.[80] They would swiftly need to accustom themselves to the Napolas' strict timetable of *Dienst* (duties and exercises)—for instance, a normal weekday at one of the schools would look something like this:

6.45 Reveille, followed by early-morning sport

7.20 Breakfast

7.35	Saluting the flag / Morning rollcall
7.45	First lesson
8.40	Second lesson
9.35	Third lesson
10.20	Second breakfast / Mid-morning break
10.40	Fourth lesson
11.35	Fifth lesson
12.45	Lunch / Break
14.30	Various forms of outside *Dienst* / sport,
	including free time on two afternoons a week
16.25	Mid-afternoon break
16.45	Study period
	including free time / activities on two afternoons a week
18.50	Evening rollcall
19.00	Dinner
19.20	Free time / Orderly duties
22.00	Lights out[81]

A typical day would begin with the *Jungmannen* being awoken by a bugle fanfare; pupils would have to leap out of their beds immediately and rush to wash and dress for early-morning sport, before undergoing the first inspection and rollcall of the day (see Figures 2.1 and 2.2). The whole school would then march to the dining hall, wait for the command to be seated, and eat their 'first breakfast' as quickly as possible, in order to be ready in time for the first lesson.[82] Although the *Jungmannen* might be provided with better food than some boys would have been used to at home (at least during the peacetime years), the fare was usually rather plain, and often did not wholly satisfy the hunger of growing adolescents.[83] Thenceforward, each minute of the day was regimented and allotted to a certain lesson or activity, and the times when one could relax one's guard and entertain private thoughts, let alone undertake individualistic endeavours, were designedly few and far between.

While some pupils might find it fairly easy to settle in, others were left to conceal any homesickness or weakness as best they could.[84] For instance, Peter B. of NPEA Plön recalled that he used to long each day for the evening so that he could go and cry secretly in the lavatories: 'It often comforted me, then, that in the neighbouring cubicles I could also hear others weeping.'[85] Meanwhile, Joachim Doedter remembered that when he started at NPEA Neubeuern, he had been so desperate to get sent home that he had planned to climb a tree in order to break

Figure 2.1 Pupils at NPEA Rügen hurry to wash and brush their teeth before breakfast.

Figure 2.2 Rollcall and saluting the flag at NPEA Rügen, *c.*1942.

his arm deliberately; this plan was only foiled when his best friend Siegfried, whose mother was a friend of Joachim's own mother, mentioned the plot in one of his letters home. In the end, Joachim simply stopped taking optional exeats in order to avoid the 'cramp in his soul' which always afflicted him upon his return to the Napola after a few days at home.[86] Conversely, Martin Meissner was so unhappy at NPEA Ilfeld that he ran away from the Napola twice; after his second abscondment, the school authorities decided that he should continue his education elsewhere.[87]

While most boarding schools at the time would arguably have had a similar effect on some of their pupils—acute homesickness when a child leaves home and has to adjust to institutional life for the first time is very common in most Western cultures—there were other taxing aspects of the new Napola lifestyle which are more uniquely attributable to the schools' militaristic ethos, many of which can be traced directly back to the traditions of the Royal Prussian Cadet Corps.[88] Some of the most alienating aspects of the new order undoubtedly pertained to the extremely strict rules regarding tasks such as organizing the clothes and other belongings in one's *Spind* (cupboard), or making one's bed: Günter Graffenberger of NPEA Stuhm remembered that all of the clothes and towels had to be so accurately folded in the *Spind* that one could lay a ruler alongside them, and any deviation at all from perfection could lead to the entire contents of the cupboard being dashed to the floor by one's superiors until all was deemed sufficiently shipshape.[89] Similarly, Henning Lenthe recalled that the intricacies of exact bed-making were so demanding that, even though pupils at his Napola, Köslin, were allowed to have naps in their free time, none of them would actually dare to do so, since it would mean having to make one's bed all over again when one awoke.[90] Another former pupil from NPEA Weierhof even recollected that, when a young substitute teacher decided to check up every night on whether pupils' toothbrushes and combs were completely clean, most of the boys simply decided to buy an extra toothbrush and comb purely 'for show', whilst continuing to use the original ones in their usual capacity.[91]

All in all, whether in lessons, during prep time, or preparing for lights-out in their (often extremely large and far from homely) dormitories, the *Jungmannen* would be constantly under the watchful eye of their *Erzieher*.[92] Every morning, lunchtime, and evening, pupils would undergo a rollcall, during which the duty *Zugführer* would scrutinize their punctuality, cleanliness, and tidiness, as well as making important announcements and giving commands relating to the day ahead. The orderliness and cleanliness of the boys' quarters would also be constantly subject to inspection, including their day-rooms, dormitories, and washrooms, as well as their cupboards, uniforms, and shoes.[93] As we shall see, failure to pass these inspections with any but the most flying colours could lead to extremely harsh punishments, whether from teachers or more senior boys. Pupils would also be constantly exposed to the Nazification of everyday life at the schools, whether through being compelled to listen communally to propaganda broadcasts, attending regular National Socialist 'morning celebrations' (see Chapter 3), or, at some Napolas, being made to practise the 'Hitler Greeting' ad nauseam.[94]

The militarization of school life was also palpable, not just in terms of the preponderance of militaristic vocabulary and titles—such as the use of the term *Zug* ('platoon') instead of 'class', or the hierarchy based on cadet-school military ranks—but also when it came to pupils having to take it in turns to 'stand guard' at the school gates, or the ways in which classes were organized.[95] Whenever a *Jungmann* addressed a member of staff, he had to do so using the title appropriate to his rank, and, at the beginning of each lesson, the *Jungmannen* would always have to stand to attention as the teacher entered, as depicted in an English textbook devised specifically for the Napolas' use:

> I salute: a soldier salutes, a civilian greets. What do you do?[96]
>
> When the master enters the class-room, the monitor says: 'This is the first form. Thirty-two boys are present. One boy is in the hospital. One boy is on leave. Smith is absent. I do not know where he is.'...
>
> [Ensuing commands by the *Erzieher*, which would also have included the 'Hitler Greeting':][97]
>
> 'Class—alert! Attention! ('Shun!') Eyes—right! Eyes—front! Stand at ease! Sit down!'[98]

The textbook in question also waxed lyrical regarding the details of the school uniform:

> [Fred] has a fine uniform. He has a brown shirt and black shorts. In winter he has a black blouse. The big boys have no blouse. They have a brown tunic and brown breeches. On their shoulders they have shoulder-straps.
>
> Round his waist Fred has a belt. Soldiers have belts. On the belt-lock there is the emblem of the '*Jungvolk*'. On the belt-lock of the big boys there is the German emblem. It shows an eagle carrying the swastika.
>
> Like all German boys Fred has a shoulder-belt. When he leaves, he has a black cap. He likes his uniform very much.[99]

Hans Schoenecker remembered that the initial distribution and handling of the uniforms, all of which were provided by the school, was treated as a kind of 'cultic ritual', and contemporary accounts of pupils trying on their uniforms for the first time indicated that many boys were somewhat obsessed by this crucial rite of passage.[100] The respect regularly accorded to the uniformed *Jungmannen* by strangers in the street also provided a fillip for their feelings of elitism: Gerd Stehle, a graduate of NPEA Köslin's fast-track airforce-cadet class (*Fliegerzug*) commented that it felt like an 'internal Reich Party Rally' to have soldiers, or even NCOs, salute one in the street, since they had clearly made the calculation that it was better to salute in haste and enjoy one's leisure than to end up being punished for not saluting an unknown uniform which might subsequently turn out to belong to a superior form of official.[101]

Many former pupils' worst memories of the schools' more militarized aspects, however, concern the brutal hazing which could take place, both at the hands of teachers and older *Jungmannen*. For instance, leaving even a single piece of clothing misaligned in one's cupboard could lead to the culprit and all of his comrades being subjected to the dreaded 'masked ball' (*Maskenball* or *Kostümfest*), a form of hazing which dated back to cadet-school days. This practice involved getting changed into and out of many different types of uniform within an incredibly short space of time, before having to present a completely ship-shape cupboard to the superior in charge (usually an impossible task, given the fact that items of uniform would by this time have been hastily strewn all over the room during the multiple changes).[102] Some former pupils even judged that the 'masked balls' which they had suffered at the NPEA were worse than any that they had subsequently experienced in their military training after they had left school.[103] The *Jungmannen* might also be subjected to so-called 'punishment drills' (*Strafexerzieren*) if some offence had been committed (whether bed-wetting, lack of orderliness, or some other prank or misdemeanour, especially one which they had failed to confess)—these could take the form of gruelling night marches, endless press-ups or assault-course-type activities on muddy fields, or other forms of unpleasant physical drill.[104]

Meanwhile, older pupils higher up the school hierarchy were also often capable of abusing their powers—for instance, Hartmut Vahl of NPEA Schulpforta remembered the petrified thrall in which his room-captain (*Stubenältester*) held his youthful subordinates, and the night-beatings ('terror in the dormitory') which they suffered at the hands of their seniors.[105] Jürgen Schach von Wittenau remembered that, upon his arrival, his *Stubenältester* at NPEA Rügen had betrayed similarly sadistic tendencies:

> Kartz was our dictator. Taller than us, very pale, with black hair falling over his forehead, with piercing unfriendly eyes. Physically much stronger than we were and sexually premature, he turned us into slaves by sheer force and cunning and tried to impress us by telling dirty stories of a topic yet foreign to our aspirations, and by proudly displaying his relevant organs. This, of course, did not shatter us, because at the age of ten any glimpse into what we considered the world of the grown-ups was welcome even if we failed to understand why respected people were so keen on having sex which to us was nothing but the inexplicable law of procreation. What *did* torture us was the cruelty with which Kartz treated us, especially those who were not courageous enough to resist....

> Kartz used to walk up to me asking with a silky voice: 'Have you had your daily thrashing yet? No? OK, I'll see to it...' And he got down to business, sometimes helped by his friend Wolf with whom he used to roam about singling out victims for their mutual pleasure. Unlike Kartz, Wolf had a round face and was muscular in a rubber-like way. Unlike Kartz, he always smiled benevolently when hitting someone or twisting his arm. When Kartz saw me writing or reading a letter, he would grab it and read it out aloud and make fun of the intimate details, much applauded by the dutiful mirth of my companions. When a parcel from [home] arrived with some goodies to complement our fare, eggs, sugar, sausage, it was quite usual to share the contents. Always hungry, we used to mix an egg with sugar, stir and beat the mix and drink it with avid pleasure. But in our study it was Kartz who claimed supremacy. He opened the parcels first and decided how the contents were to be distributed.[106]

In some cases, these 'sadistic undertones' could cause pupils to suffer severe psychological trauma, and might even lead to their leaving the school.[107]

Committing an offence which would involve one's whole dormitory, room, or class being punished by the school authorities could also lead to subsequent mass-beatings by one's comrades, in order to teach the offender a lesson—the so-called *Klassen-*, *Stuben-*, or *Hordenkeile*. However, such 'punishments' could also be meted out as a fitting penance for those who were generally considered to be too 'weak' (*Flaschen*), or those who were deemed to be letting the side down in matters of sport or 'comradeship'.[108] In order to survive, then, boys had somehow to establish themselves within the unofficial school hierarchy or *Hackordnung*, standing up to their bullies, and proving themselves to have become truly assimilated into the Napola '*Gemeinschaft*'. Thus, Jürgen Schach von Wittenau was able to triumph over his bullies as follows:

> I finally realized that I wasn't the one to fight my adversaries on the battlefield. But what could I do to lose the image of a natural victim? I had to develop some initiative to catch the attention of the other boys. I had to gain a new reputation. An idea struck me. In those days, all of us had inkpots for our pens. Ballpoint pens hadn't been invented, fountain pens few of us had. I did, though, and sported the luxury of owning an extra-large bottle of green ink rather than the black or blue one we boys usually had. One day, I picked up the bottle from my desk, raised it and looked at it thoughtfully.
>
> Kartz watched me: 'What are you doing?'
>
> I muttered: 'I am wondering if someone has the guts to drink it.'
>
> 'Why should anyone drink it?'
>
> 'Well, because it needs more courage than having a fight. I don't think you'd do such a thing.'

'You think I haven't the guts, do you? You are asking for some reminder of who is the boss here? Don't you remember?'

He frowned menacingly. The other boys looked up in suspense.

'Well, you're the boss. But you wouldn't drink it!'

'You think I wouldn't? You think I'm afraid of your bloody ink?' He grabbed the bottle. He unscrewed it. He drank it. All the green ink gone down in a matter of seconds. 'See?'

'Hey', cried Bartelt, one of the other boys, 'good show, man, but, what's gonna happen now, Kartz? We want to see. Won't you go to the latrine?'

Kartz decided: 'OK, let's have a pee.'

All of us followed him and stood around him as he unbuttoned his pants and let go. Alas, nothing unusual. We returned to our room and discussed the matter, and I remarked that ink was made from a poisonous plant, not mortal but.... Kartz was silent. He looked a bit paler than usual. Had he poisoned himself? He wasn't sure, and since he wasn't sure, he felt a bit seedy. He didn't talk to me.

There was a definite change of attitude to me among my companions. I hadn't done much. But I wasn't the faceless newcomer any longer, ready to be pushed around. I was one of them.[109]

Meanwhile, opportunities to gain power through official channels also existed through the NPEA leadership hierarchy for *Jungmannen*, which began by giving pupils fairly lowly assignments, such as administrative service in the library, 'Shoeshine-room Duty' (*Schuhputzraumdienst*), or mealtime 'Table Duty' (*Tischdienst*), before allowing them to take on positions with more responsibility, such as *Stubenältester* or *Jungmann vom Dienst* (Duty *Jungmann*). Finally, pupils could aspire to the coveted positions of *Jungmannzugführer*, *Jungmanngruppenführer*, or even *Jungmann-Hundertschaftsführer*—roles which could be seen as equivalent to those of form prefect, senior prefect, and head boy in English parlance.[110] The *Jungmann-Hundertschaftsführer* from each Napola would also be invited to week-long conferences at which they would listen to presentations on relevant challenges and problems, and discuss how to manage their responsibilities through best practice.[111] As Dietrich Schulz of NPEA Rügen put it:

Jungmannen had to be brought up to be leader-personalities, who were in a position to command and make independent decisions, and were meant to be 'an example worthy of imitation' to the troop or collective entrusted to them. Everyone in the *Zug* (class) would be *Jungmann vom Dienst* once, and had to prove his leadership abilities. He also had to decree punishments. The education to absolute obedience was all bound up with that. Special achievements in lessons, sport and institutional duties (*Anstaltsdienst*) were honoured with promotion to the rank of *Jungmann- Gruppen-/Zug-* and *Hundertschaftsführer*.[112]

At least in theory, these boys in the highest year-groups would take charge of the younger boys in their care, acting as counsellors, and seeking to make their daily round run as smoothly as possible.[113] However, it is undeniable that some pupils were inspired to aspire to these roles less because of the heightened pastoral responsibility which they afforded, and more because of the special insignia which they added to one's uniform epaulettes.[114]

Even during their relatively circumscribed periods of 'free time', pupils were still subject to a certain amount of control. Thus, an 'order of the day' from NPEA Oranienstein dated 3 December 1938 decreed that '*Jungmannen* often receive books as gifts from their parents at Christmas whose acquisition the school cannot condone, or the acquisition of which is not absolutely necessary. The *Zugführer* should therefore immediately undertake to give the *Jungmannen* positive advice on compiling their wishlist of books for Christmas. Herewith a reminder that possession of Hitler, *Mein Kampf*, Rosenberg, *Myth* [*of the Twentieth Century*], and Chamberlain, *Foundations* [*of the Nineteenth Century*] is essential for *Jungmannen* in the upper school'.[115] Armin Eise also recalled that, when he and a group of other friends in his class at NPEA Bensberg had decided to build a 'fortress' in the woods, their activity had been frowned upon because it smacked of 'cliquishness'. Two of the *Erzieher* therefore led the rest of the class to find the group and overpower them, subsequently rebuking them for not having observed one of the first rules of the art of war—setting a guard: 'Our plan had backfired, but the unit was complete again. The *Zug* marched in closed ranks back to the school'.[116] Less controversial pastimes might include reading school-approved literature (see Figure 2.3), going for walks, writing letters home, playing cards and boardgames, amateur journalism, or photography, model-making, and amateur radio.[117] For the younger boys, handicraft activities, make-shift sports such as 'sock-ball' or 'coat-hanger hockey', and playing with model cars or model railways, were *de rigueur*.[118]

Sometimes, however, these pastimes could spill over into rather more questionable, or even dangerous, pranks: Kurt Schwechheimer remembered deliberately smuggling a hen into a physics lesson to annoy his teacher at NPEA Wartheland, as well as seeking to distil alcohol in secret, while Arnulf Putzar of NPEA Spandau recalled a friend of his being inspired by the V2 rocket to steal some saltpetre, black powder, and sulphur from the chemistry lab. Instead of rolling down the gentle incline of the desk and flying out of the open window, the 'rocket' which he had created with these ingredients simply made an almighty stink and burned a hole right through the desk before water could be fetched to extinguish the blaze.[119] It has even been suggested that one game of 'Sioux versus Apaches' which was unexpectedly disturbed by an *Erzieher* at NPEA Bensberg led to embers of the 'camp fire' being left aglow, leading to a conflagration which destroyed an entire wing of Schloss Bensberg in March 1942.[120] Meanwhile, among older boys, the habit of taking the school motorcycles for an unauthorized turn around the

Figure 2.3 The reading room at NPEA Rügen, 1943.

grounds in order to experience the thrill of a short ride on a fast machine might be too much to resist, as at NPEA Ballenstedt—a practice which might also be combined with the clandestine consumption of cigarettes and alcohol.[121]

At times, *Jungmannen* would even engage in activities which we might be tempted to term a form of low-level resistance to their political circumstances, or *Resistenz*. This tendency is revealed most readily in the spoof 'newspapers' which were circulated by graduating classes (*Abiturzeitungen*), such as NPEA Spandau's 1938 send-up of the Nazi official newspaper, the *Völkischer Beobachter*, entitled *Der Napola Beobachter*. The '*NB*' not only mocked staff mercilessly, satirizing the absurdities of one senior master's formless rhetorical style with an article entitled 'Thus spake Notker the Stammerer'. Rather, the paper also included a perfect parody of the programme for one of the Nazi pseudo-religious political ceremonies to which pupils were so frequently subjected (see Chapter 3), imitating the call and response of massed speech-choirs and the pathos of their manipulative rhetoric; the fictional ceremony culminated with a celebratory bonfire of all of the pupils' old exercise-books.[122] Many of these 'newspapers' also included highly satirical small-ads which lampooned the Nazi regime's racial obsessions—thus, the Spandau '*NB*' edition mocked contemporary 'racial science' by advertising a fake Latin-course which did not require candidates to possess any knowledge of Latin at all, entitled '*Kleines Latinum? Keine Sorge*':

> *Little Latin? No worries!* No vocabulary-cramming! No grammar! No mindless learning by heart! My new historico-racial teaching method makes Latin a

pleasure. A daily-repeated summary of Roman history imparts to the pupil not only an exact knowledge of 'Etruscan alien domination' and the 'ancient Roman farming nobility', but also a deep insight into the essence of the Latin language. Silvias Mehlmahler. Director of the 'Alopan' Linguistic Institute, Berlin.[123]

Another satirical pamphlet, prepared by a group of Spandau *Jungmannen* as a gift for their beloved *Erzieher* 'Karlchen' Euler, included a pitch-perfect send-up of the convoluted language of the NPEA Inspectorate's frequent decrees—this time, in the form of a health-and-safety advisory edict on how to shave appropriately.[124]

Other forms of adolescent rebellion at the NPEA might include growing one's hair longer than the prescribed military-style length, secretly playing or listening to jazz (or even, during wartime, to the BBC), or faking IDs in order to get into underage films.[125] Music and song could also be used as a way to mock the Napola authorities, or even the regime itself—Kurt Meyer remembered the shock that he and a group of classmates received when they realized that the pub where they were singing a spoof version of the Nazi anthem, the Horst-Wessel-Lied, beginning 'Raise high the pan! The roast potatoes await...' ('*Die Pfanne hoch! Die Bratkartoffeln warten...*'—as opposed to '*Die Fahne hoch! Die Reihen fest geschlossen*' / 'Raise high the flag! The ranks are tightly closed...') was the haunt of the local SA.[126] Thus, while I have only encountered one contemporary instance of a *Jungmann* 'going rogue', turning completely against his NPEA upon graduation, and being excluded from the school community thenceforth, these contemporary sources strongly suggest that life within the Napolas' walls did not necessarily transform pupils into completely Nazified automata, nor did it rob them entirely of the capacity for independent thought.[127] Nevertheless, such rebellion or mockery could usually only be expressed in very circumscribed terms.

What, then, of pupils' engagement with the wider world beyond the Napolas' gates?

Contact with the Outside World

As we might expect, the Napolas' allocation of school holidays, or *Ferienordnung*, was highly circumscribed. Pupils were given eighteen days of holiday at Easter and Christmas, a few days in the autumn, and six weeks in the summer, a substantial proportion of which might be consumed by the schools' extensive programme of trips and 'missions' (see Chapter 3).[128] From this perspective, then, how far were the *Jungmannen* genuinely isolated from the outside world—and how far did the NPEA succeed in cutting pupils off from their families?

An account in NPEA Plön's school newsletter describing the 'vivid hustle and bustle' at the Napola at the beginning of June 1938 depicts a melting pot full of 'former pupils in the most varied uniforms, NSLB officials, Swedish exchange-students, and miners, together with the *Erzieher* and *Jungmannen*'—a reflection of the schools' considerable reach beyond their immediate environs.[129] In this context, it is also worth noting that the NPEA could never exist in total isolation from the communities within which they were situated; in fact, each school arguably provided plentiful trade and employment opportunities in its local area.[130] Indeed, when a substantial amount of building work was in train, the NPEA might even be able to contribute usefully to regional unemployment-reduction schemes.[131] Meanwhile, the many positions which the schools needed to fill on the technical and support side, which required each Napola to employ a veritable army of locally based automobile and motorcycle mechanics, grooms, cobblers, handymen, gardeners, caretakers, secretaries, cooks, cleaners, maids, nurses, and washerwomen, also provided valuable regular employment for many individuals within the locality.[132] Moreover, as we shall see in the following chapter, the schools often contributed to their local economy and culture through charitable drives and the provision of musical or theatrical entertainment, or, in some cases, through targeted assistance in local Party politics. At some Napolas, Party organizations or sports groups from the surrounding area might also be granted access to NPEA facilities.[133]

However, the schools were also quite capable of making a rather more negative impression—for example, an issue of NPEA Stuhm's school newsletter published in 1939 mentioned that the local inhabitants (unflatteringly dubbed '*Stumaken*') had bent the wrought-iron letters of the sign at the school's entrance so that it read '*Nationalpolnische Erziehungsanstalt*', replacing the term 'National Political' with 'National Polish'—an extremely tendentious epithet in the context of the heightened nationalist tensions in the area. Meanwhile, rumours abounded in Plön that the headmaster of the NPEA was a horrific martinet who beat pupils within an inch of their lives, and kept them shackled in damp caves and cellars in the basement of Plön castle.[134] In addition, given that the *Jungmannen* tended to think of themselves as a cut above the native inhabitants, tensions and fights with local Hitler Youths were not unknown, not least when it came to rivalries over the 'fairer sex'.[135]

*

Indeed, for the *Jungmannen* themselves, one of the most crucial forms of interaction with the outside world were those dancing lessons (*Tanzstunden*) which boys from the upper school were permitted to host, using girls from local schools as dancing partners—Manfred Klotz recalled that, at least at the beginning of the first lesson, these could easily degenerate into a kind of sprint, as pupils desperately sought to pick the most attractive of the girls as their partner.[136] However, as one might expect, boys' pubertal urges, and their encounters with the opposite sex, were also subject to strict control by the school authorities. Inspectorial regulations decreed that every dormitory should have enough space between each bed to prevent 'sexual transgressions', and that every corner of the dormitories and showers should be easily surveillable from the door.[137] Any clandestine sexual activity, especially of a homosexual nature, would in all likelihood lead not only to a severe reprimand, but to immediate expulsion.[138] The *Jungmannen* therefore constantly had to tread the flimsy tightrope between the schools' official moral stance on sexuality—'stay pure and be mature' (*rein bleiben und reif werden*), and their natural curiosity about their own adolescent development, and sexual attraction.[139] Thus, visits by girls from the *Mädchen-Napolas* were highly popular (see Chapter 9), and the friendships which were forged with local BDM-girls or land-girls (*Landjahrmädchen*) were often remembered with great fondness (see Figure 2.4).[140] At NPEA Neuzelle, two of the *Erzieher* apparently married BDM-leaders from the neighbouring BDM Domestic Science School (*BDM-Haushaltungsschule*), where two *Jungmannen* also met their future wives—an outcome which the school authorities may in some measure have intended.[141]

In the absence of regular opportunities to meet members of the opposite sex, however, the *Jungmannen* might also end up having massive crushes on those females who did regularly venture within the walls of the NPEA—especially the nurses who were employed in the school sickbay.[142] Helmuth J. of NPEA Klotzsche remembered that he and one of his 18-year-old classmates were both utterly in love with the 20-year-old nurse at their school; his friend eventually succeeded in 'winning' her, and the resulting relationship endured beyond his

Figure 2.4 Pupils from NPEA Rügen folk-dancing with girls from the BDM, 1943.

graduation.[143] While Reinhard Wagner coyly noted that the bevy of maids at the Napola were 'not without an effect, especially on the older *Jungmannen*' at NPEA Rottweil, one pupil at NPEA Mokritz appears to have genuinely fallen in love with a female intern who was working on the kitchen staff at the school in 1944; as their love letters and her post-war memoirs reveal, their tendresse lasted until he was eventually killed in battle at the end of World War II.[144] Bodo Helms of NPEA Potsdam-Neuzelle even claimed that he and his classmates were so desperate to see their house-matron's legs and peek under her skirt that they sawed the bottom off the legs of her chair when she was due to sit at their table at dinner. The unfortunate lady allegedly tipped backwards upon sitting down, hit her head, and injured herself, and the would-be voyeurs were almost expelled.[145] Sometimes, however, the boot could be on the other foot; in a letter to his mother dated 6 February 1945, Dieter Pfeiffer noted that, upon his return to NPEA Spanheim, 'unfortunately an office girl at our school has fallen for me. She wasn't my cup of tea though.'[146]

*

But what of the most important outside connection of all—that with one's familial home, and with one's parents? From one perspective, like many boarding-school pupils of this era, during term-time, the *Jungmannen* perceived their parents above all as a vital source of much-needed extra food and pocket money.[147] As previously mentioned, *Jungmannen* were nominally supposed to live at least thirty kilometres away from their school, and parental visits to the Napola were always supposed to be approved beforehand by the school authorities.[148] While it was generally compulsory for boys to write a letter or postcard home every week, and most surviving letters home from the NPEA seem perfectly normal and childish, almost entirely concerned with the needs and minutiae of day-to-day life, rather than revealing any overt politicization, there nevertheless exists some evidence that the Napolas' ideological ethos could begin to erode parent-child relationships. Thus, one pupil from NPEA Neuzelle recalled getting into an argument with his mother over the fact that she had started 'hamstering'—in this instance, buying a large amount of soap from a Jewish department store before rationing began in earnest.[149] More disturbingly, Günter Graffenberger remembered that his time at the Napola had more or less destroyed his relationship with his own parents, who were completely opposed to the Nazi regime. At the beginning of the war, Günter's father had been imprisoned in Stutthof concentration camp, and later chose to fight in a punishment battalion rather than remain incarcerated there. During the school holidays, when Günter's father was home on leave, his mother would vainly beg her husband and son not to talk politics, detesting the strife which she knew would inevitably ensue. Subsequently, on the evening of 20 July 1944, when the report of the failed attempt to assassinate Hitler came through on the family radio, his mother's unthinking response, 'what a shame', led Günter to shriek at her in rage as she trembled before him: how dare she say such a thing in front of her son, who was being educated at a Napola! Both

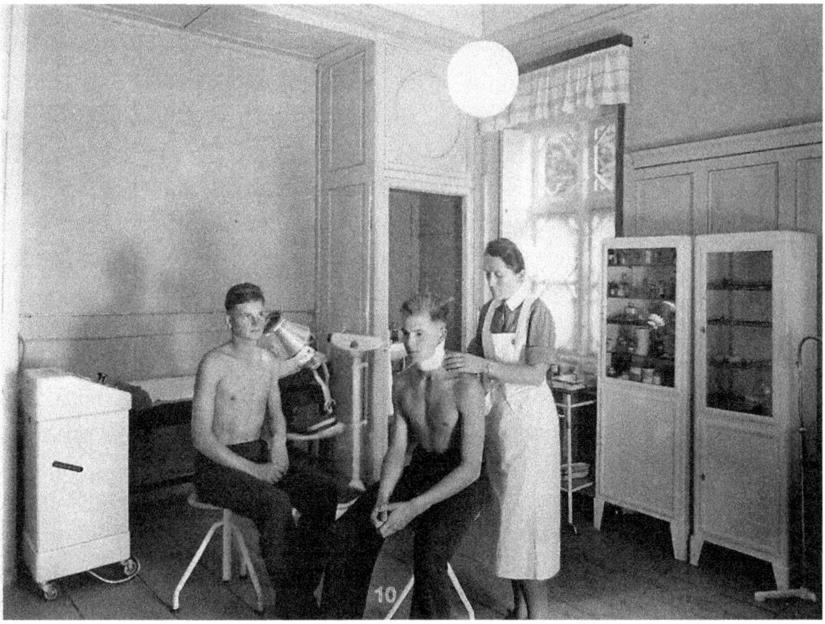

Figure 2.5 The sickbay at NPEA Rügen, with a nursing sister in attendance, *c.*1942.

mother and son were faced with the unpleasant realization that their political views were now utterly irreconcilable, and the end of the holiday could not come quickly enough for either of them.[150]

Of course, the NPEA would endeavour to calm parents' fears and doubts—not only attempting to convince them of the extent of the schools' care for their sons, and the high standard of medical support which the Napolas could provide (see Figure 2.5), but also assuring them that the school would do nothing to harm the parent-child relationship.[151] *Erzieher* might also correspond regularly with parents to allay their anxieties, and persuade them that their sons were as safe and well as could be once they had been entrusted to the schools' capable care.[152] In addition, parents could subscribe to the Napola school newsletters, and parents' days were a frequent feature of the school calendar.[153] However, it was perhaps inevitable that the *Jungmannen* would ultimately turn for solace during term-time to more easily accessible adults within the school itself—in particular, their house-matrons and their *Erzieher*.

Pupils' Personal Relationships with House-Staff and Teaching Staff

The most commonly acknowledged 'parental ersatz', perhaps unsurprisingly, were the so-called 'house-mothers' or 'house-matrons' (*Heimmütter*/*Hausdamen*), whose purpose was to impart a more 'familial' tone to the education of the youngest two year-groups, before they came completely under the grip of the Napolas' military-style 'formation training' (*Formationserziehung*).[154] The role of these undersung and overworked 'substitute mothers' was remarkably multifarious; for instance, at NPEA Oranienstein, the much-beloved *Hausdame* Emmy Spornhauer had to supervise the *Jungmannen* in their dormitories and in the washrooms, and even attend their cross-country war-games at dead of night; she would help out in the sickbay, deal with laundry, rehearse plays and musical performances with her charges, read aloud to them, organize arts and crafts activities for them and teach them to sew, attend their 'political evenings', and help them decorate the school for celebrations and events.[155] At some schools, the *Hausdame* was more directly responsible for teaching the *Jungmannen* 'good etiquette', sitting with the younger boys at mealtimes and criticizing their table manners.[156] Former pupil Walter Flemming remembered that at NPEA Ilfeld, the 'house-mother' would usually walk through the dormitories before lights-out, bidding her charges goodnight, and giving them a friendly stroke on the hand or a pat on the back. Flemming saw this comforting ritual as a welcome compensation for the far harsher tone of the male *Erzieher*.[157] During the winter months, the house-mother might also bring salves for the small boys' chilblained hands, or even some welcome 'bird feed' (*Spatzenfutter*)—i.e., a clandestine bedtime snack.[158]

On the paternal side, it was usually the *Erzieher* or *Anstaltsleiter* who provided the requisite ersatz—after all, these men could have a hugely influential positive or negative impact on boys' day-to-day lives. Some *Anstaltsleiter* inspired an almost worshipful adoration in their pupils—for instance, the headmaster of NPEA Plön, Hermann Brunk, was hailed by Harald R. in his private journal as 'the greatest educator of youth of whom I know'.[159] *Anstaltsleiter* Paul Holthoff of NPEA Bensberg, meanwhile, went out of his way to write personally to a *Jungmann* who had been taken ill with scarlet fever whilst sojourning at the Dutch *Reichsschule* in Valkenburg, sending special Christmas wishes to the boy's hospital bed in Heerlen.[160] Conversely, however, *Jungmannen* could be extremely harsh judges of those *Anstaltsleiter* whom they felt did not live up to their expectations; for instance, *Anstaltsleiter* Adolf Schieffer at NPEA Schulpforta was notorious for being an 'unapproachable functionary', in contrast to his predecessor, Kurt Person, and pupils at NPEA Naumburg had similar reservations regarding *Anstaltsleiter* Alfred Männich, the little-loved successor of the school's first headmaster, the charismatic August Hellmann.[161] Meanwhile, pupils at NPEA Rügen simply nicknamed their headmaster, *Hauptundertschaftsführer* Gerhard Lüders, 'the jackass' (*der Trottel*), deriding his unauthoritative lisp and his frequent foul temper.[162]

The same dichotomy in terms of affection or contempt also held true when it came to pupils' relationship with their *Erzieher*—as mentioned above, one class of pupils at NPEA Spandau were so devoted to their *Zugführer*, 'Karlchen' Euler, that they presented him with a published version of their 'class diary' from 1938 onwards, and celebrated his birthday with flowers, songs, and poems, having 'barely forgiven him' for getting married.[163] Hans Lindenberg also recalled that one of his *Erzieher* at NPEA Potsdam was famed for his night-time candlelit story-telling sessions in the biology lab, while Harry Bolte of NPEA Ilfeld recollected how impressed he and his classmates had been with the comradeship of one *Erzieher*, Winkelmann, who did not hesitate for a moment to subject himself to all of the same trials and tribulations as his *Jungmannen* during their weeks of land service in Slovakia.[164]

However, although the discipline and punishments exerted by the *Erzieher* were supposed neither to go any further than those which a firm but fair father might exert, nor to bear any hint of cane-happiness or '*Prügelpädagogik*', many former *Jungmannen* recall being subject to incompetent, or even cruel, *Erzieher* who would do their best to make their pupils' lives a living hell.[165] At NPEA Spanheim, for instance, a contemporary class diary reveals that the *Jungmannen* in Dieter Pfeiffer's class were constantly plagued, both in and out of lessons, by their intensely short-tempered and potentially sadistic *Zugführer* Matzke, who sometimes even treated them as unpaid servants (getting them to heat his bathwater or collect his medicaments, for instance).[166] Meanwhile, Walter Becker recalled that the maths-teacher at NPEA Naumburg, nicknamed 'Lucki' or 'Luzifer' Luckinger, ultimately had to be taken to task by a commission of inspectors from Berlin, who were unimpressed by his striking about him with his board-ruler and taunting his charges with expostulations such as 'I'll smack you into the wall so hard that the homicide squad'll have to scrape you off with a spade!'[167] Peter Gerlach remembered that at Naumburg, there was also a music-teacher with paedophiliac tendencies who attempted to get pupils to sit on his lap during his private lessons—however, he was subsequently forced to leave.[168]

From this perspective, then, the 'substitute parenting' which the Napolas offered could be highly problematic, and yet the *Erzieher* at the schools were ultimately in control of almost every aspect of pupils' lives during term-time. This total control was even more dangerous, however, when we consider the influence which these thoroughly Nazified teachers could have on the content of the academic lessons which the *Jungmannen* had to attend every day—which formed an equally important part of their everyday life. Hence, in the following section, we will explore the curriculum and the content of academic lessons at the NPEA in more detail.

Teaching and Academic Lessons

As we might expect, the respect accorded to the various academic subjects at the NPEA followed the usual National Socialist hierarchy of values—hence,

Biology, History, Geography, and German were particularly privileged, due to their respective contributions to Nazi ideology, while religious instruction was gradually excised from the curriculum (see Chapter 6).[169] While different schools might follow slightly different curricula, especially with regard to the programme of language-teaching which they offered—*Anstaltsleiter* Hellmann of NPEA Naumburg even brought in Czech and Serbian as optional modern languages, in order to facilitate the school's Germanizing mission in Eastern Europe—broadly speaking, the Napolas followed the curriculum of a normal *Deutsche Oberschule* (secondary school).[170] Meanwhile, four of the NPEA—Ilfeld, Schulpforta, Haselünne, and Neubeuern—followed the curriculum of a 'humanistic *Gymnasium*' throughout, treating ancient Greek as a core subject as well as Latin. In part, the Napola authorities had decided not to attempt to create an entire syllabus from scratch (as at the Adolf-Hitler-Schools) because they wanted to make it as easy as possible for unsuccessful pupils to transfer back into the civilian school system unproblematically.[171] Thus, barring a couple of exceptions—such as Schlunke's *First English Textbook*, and a modern history textbook which had been put together by a working group at NPEA Naumburg—the Napolas generally used the same selection of textbooks as other secondary schools throughout the Reich.[172]

At the same time, the Napola authorities made sure that every school was liberally supplied with the latest literature and state-of-the-art teaching materials (see Figures 2.6 and 2.7). For instance, at NPEA Rottweil, in one year alone, over 16,000 RM was allocated for spending on relevant volumes for the staff library, and a total of 3,400 RM was allotted to books for the pupils' library, while around 12,000 RM was allocated for apparatus in each scientific subject, and just over 4,000 RM for other materials, including maps and atlases.[173] Many of the key principles of modern pedagogy were also instrumentalized to make lessons as interesting for the *Jungmannen* as possible—indeed, some schools even experimented with novel forms of test, such as NPEA Naumburg's *Zugwettkampf* (Class Contest), which featured not only sporting and artistic challenges, but also contests in debating, dictation, and mental arithmetic, or NPEA Plön's Crystal-Maze-style competition, in which eight teams of seven *Jungmannen* from the upper year-groups had to rush from one 'station' to another throughout the school buildings and grounds, carrying out different types of intellectual and physical tasks, and winning or losing minutes overall according to how well they had done on each test.[174] Teachers were also supposed to be constantly available to their pupils for questions concerning their specialism, especially as the *Jungmannen* reached the upper school and began to think about their future in higher education; moreover, *Erzieher* and *Jungmannen* were encouraged to form voluntary working groups to explore topics of particular interest in more detail in their spare time.[175] The Napolas were also among the very first schools in Germany not only to build up a substantial collection of films for use in lessons, but also to produce their own sound-films.[176] Meanwhile, in order to unify curricular

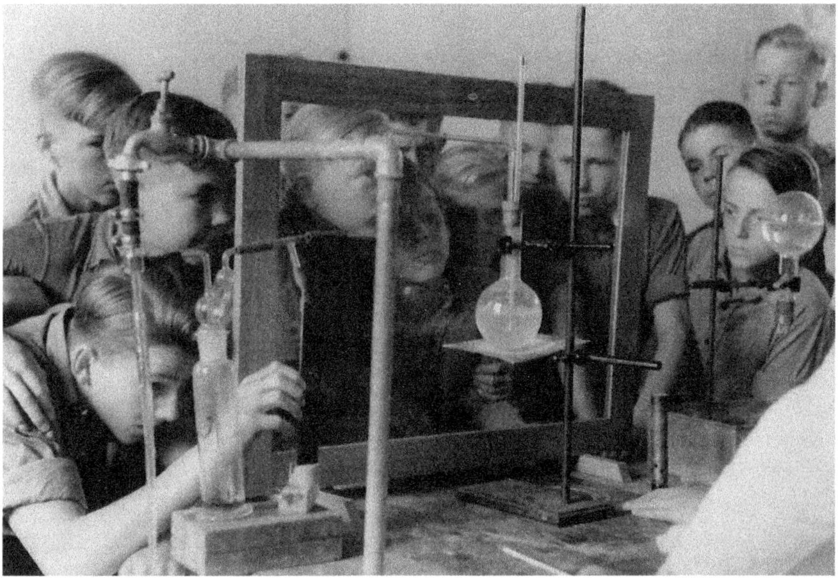

Figure 2.6 and Figure 2.7 Biology and Chemistry lessons at NPEA Rügen during the early 1940s.

expectations and coordinate teaching practices throughout the Napola system, in addition to the regular headmasters' conferences, discipline-specific conferences were frequently held for *Erzieher* in every subject—generally involving short presentations on relevant issues by teachers from various schools, as well as discussion of best practice. The Reich Education Ministry's general guidelines for the subject in question were usually taken as a starting point, before homing in on ideas or adjustments which were more specific to the needs of the NPEA.[177]

Interestingly, even during the Third Reich, there seems to have been a desire at the schools to counteract the idea that education at the Napolas was simply about who had the biggest biceps.[178] As *Hundertschaftsführer* Dr. Jung of NPEA Haselünne declared, 'it goes without saying that the quick-witted weakling finds no place among us, but neither does a lad who only has peak physical performances to offer'.[179] However, while no *Jungmann* would ever be allowed to repeat a year (*sitzenbleiben*), but would be expelled instead if he failed the school year—a fact which often caused less academically gifted pupils no small anxiety—the truth was, as one former *Erzieher* at NPEA Bensberg stressed, that the selection process intentionally did not pick out a highly intellectual '*Auslese*', especially since boys who wore spectacles were not allowed to apply.[180] Moreover, the schools' many 'missions', 'manoeuvres', camps, and school trips, which were not only considered just as important as the curriculum of academic lessons, but were also treated as a crucial supplement to these (see Chapter 3), meant that the number of lessons for each subject in any given year might be cut short when compared with the number of lessons on offer at a civilian school.[181]

Nevertheless, while any group of *Jungmannen*, taken on average, were unlikely to be the most academically gifted of their age-group, in the pre-war years, they would still for the most part have been above average academically, as well as being good all-rounders when it came to their contribution to sporting and extracurricular activities. However, it was inevitable that the advent of war should have brought about a marked decline in academic standards, both in terms of the level of intellectual achievement required for acceptance at a Napola, and in terms of the standard of teaching on offer at the schools (see Chapter 10). Even so, many former pupils would later claim that the academic education which they had received at the NPEA had stood them in much better stead than that of many pupils from normal secondary schools, when both groups returned to complete their secondary education after the end of World War II.[182]

*

We will now briefly consider the Nazification of the various academic subjects at the Napolas, beginning with the sciences, and moving on to the social sciences and humanities, before treating the schools' main curricular innovation—the introduction of 'National Political Instruction' (*nationalpolitische Unterricht*). Although all school subjects were necessarily saturated with National Socialist ideology during the Third Reich, even at civilian schools, these 'national political' lessons appear to have been exceptional, inasmuch as political indoctrination was their primary focus.[183] The section will conclude with a brief glance at the effects which such indoctrination appears to have had on pupils' actions and attitudes, whether during school trips to visit ghettos in Eastern Europe, or on ostensibly 'innocent' trips to the Napolas' seaside hostel on the Frisian Island of Föhr.

As we might expect, Biology, of all the sciences, was the most subject to ideologization, due to its connections with Social Darwinism and Nazi racial theory. Thus, at a conference for Napola Biology-*Erzieher* held at Rankenheim in March 1938, plans for the individual year-groups included instructions to treat the animal and plant world primarily from the perspective of their nourishment of the German *Volk*, and the ensuing implications for Germany's concept of empire and the NSDAP's Four Year Plan. Meanwhile, 'Struggle' (*Kampf*) was to be treated as a 'principle of life', and human biology was supposed not only to focus on the current and historical cultural spheres of the various 'races', especially the 'Nordic-Germanic' race, but also to highlight theories of ethnicity, population politics, and racial genetics.[184] Even the younger boys' excursions into parks or meadows in search of flora, fauna, and other natural phenomena were ultimately intended to bring home to them the unshakeable truths of Darwinism and Mendelian genetics.[185] When preparing for their school-leaving examination (*Reifeprüfung*), pupils would often have to study books by racial theorists and eugenicists such as Hans F. K. Günther (the so-called 'Race Pope'), Lothar Gottlieb Tirala, and Egon Freiherr von Eickstedt.[186] To supplement such reading, the schools were lavishly supplied with state-of-the-art scientific equipment, including microscopes, compilations of slides, vivaria housing animals for live experiments, and collections of biological curiosities (see Figure 2.6).[187] One former pupil at NPEA Rottweil recalled a huge display case which stood outside the biology classroom, containing not only a human embryo suspended in embalming fluid, but also a range of model skulls depicting the characteristics of the different races, including (most fascinatingly of all for the *Jungmannen*) a real human skull which represented the 'Indogermanic' race.[188]

Since classes in 'Racial Theory' (*Rassenlehre*) also formed an integral part of Biology teaching, former pupils also recall being taught at great length about the physical characteristics of the different 'races'—Nordic, Falic, Dinaric, Alpine, Mediterranean, and East-Baltic—as well as the so-called 'Jewish race', which was always portrayed in the most uncomplimentary terms (see further below).[189] The *Jungmannen* might be regularly subjected to racial testing during these lessons to determine which 'race' they belonged to—including having their heads measured with callipers to find the longest and widest skulls in the class; relevant observations would then be noted according to Güntherian craniometric principles, in an attempt to determine the racial 'index' of each year-group.[190] Pupils were often very relieved to find that they belonged to an approved type of mixed race, such as 'Nordic-Falic', and subsequent teasing might also take on a racial tone; thus, Reinhard Wagner of NPEA Rottweil remembered that his friend Wetzel was 'good-naturedly' mocked for being a 'Mediterranean husk with a Nordic heart', due to his swarthy appearance.[191]

Meanwhile, Chemistry lessons served to instil not only the usual information about relevant formulas and chemical reactions, but also to hammer home the alleged racial superiority indicated by the primacy of German organic chemistry, and the idea that Germany's precarious situation when it came to autarchy in raw materials (especially fuels, fats, and fibres) could only be solved by the invention and production of sufficient ersatz-materials; Jewish boycotts could then be blamed for the worsening foreign exchange rate which was causing this vicious cycle.[192] In similar vein, Physics was often instrumentalized to serve militaristic ends, focusing on topics such as ballistics, telegraphy, and the physics of flight.[193] Even Mathematics could at times be put to analogous uses—*Jungmannen* might be deliberately given calculations related to ballistics and windspeeds in order to complement their first-hand experience of small-bore shooting, or set assignments for homework from a series of pamphlets entitled 'Luftwaffe and School' (*Luftwaffe und Schule*), which contained arithmetic problems solely based on air force-related topics.[194]

Meanwhile, new methods of teaching 'racialized' Geography focused in particular on 'the fateful connection between race and place', characterizing the *mores* of different peoples within and outside Germany as inevitably linked to their racial make-up.[195] Much of the syllabus might be taken up with preparations for revanchist school trips (see Chapter 3), or tied to 'contemporary questions' in geo-politics, such as the possible weaknesses of the British Empire, the problematic nature of various international treaty agreements, and German colonialism, including the 'struggles' of 'ethnic Germans' in the 'lost' territories of Eastern Europe.[196] In History, a racialized perspective was also par for the course—extolling the cultural achievements of the 'Nordic' races, and attributing the downfall of civilizations to the cardinal sin of 'racial mixing'.[197] At NPEA Emsland, History was also hymned as being 'better suited than any other lesson to awaken political awareness and train the political will'.[198] Historical phenomena such as medieval fortresses could not be treated in purely aesthetic or cultural terms, therefore, but rather had to be analysed solely in terms of their expression of political power. From the medieval period onwards, the Germans had to be portrayed as the 'political man' par excellence—since they had created not only the First Reich, the Hanse, and the Order of Teutonic Knights, but also the glorious new contemporary Reich; the true victor over all the preposterous anarchy and particularism of more recent eras.[199]

German lessons were also strongly oriented towards the idea of Germany's 'racial fate', ranging from ancient Germanic sagas, Greek tragedies, and German folktales to Luther, Nietzsche, and the romantic classics—all interpreted in sufficiently ideological fashion.[200] Often, the teaching in German, History, Geography, and Art would all be to some extent interwoven, in order to provide a sufficiently wide-ranging 'political training of the will', informed by modern racial theory.[201] Finally, modern languages and Latin were also taught with such perspectives in mind—as was ancient Greek, at the few 'humanistic' Napolas which offered the subject.[202] Although Latin remained an important part of the curriculum at all of the NPEA for the whole of their existence, English gained the lion's share of attention, not least due to considerations of political expediency, since a sound knowledge of the language would enable the *Jungmannen* to make connections more easily with pupils and staff at elite schools in Britain and the United States (see Chapter 3).[203]

*

However, the most ideological subject of all was the 'national political teaching' (*nationalpolitische Unterricht*) or 'ideological instruction' (*Weltanschauliche Schulung*) for the upper year-groups, which went by a number of names at various schools at different times, perhaps due to the fact that this form of teaching was primarily the responsibility of each individual *Anstaltsleiter*.[204] Thus, the lessons were known as the 'political seminar' at NPEA Naumburg; 'political teaching' at NPEA Spanheim; 'national political education' or 'political working groups' at NPEA Plön, and 'national politics' at NPEA Potsdam.[205] Over the years, as one might expect, the SS also gradually gained greater influence over the syllabus of these classes; in 1938, NPEA Inspector August Heißmeyer appointed SS-*Standartenführer* Dr. Caesar, the Director of the Education Department (*Schulungsamt*) at the SS Central Office (*SS-Hauptamt*), to be his advisor in questions of ideological instruction at the NPEA.[206]

A document prepared by the then Vice-Inspector Hermann Brunk in November 1936, detailing best practice with regard to political training and schools' collaboration with the Party, stated that the *Erzieher* who were placed in charge of political classes should, if at all possible, be 'long-standing Party comrades', who would not only be intellectually *au fait* with all of the key tenets of the National Socialist *Weltanschauung*, but would also be able to enthuse the *Jungmannen* with their tales of experiences from the Party's 'time of struggle' prior to the Nazi seizure of power.[207] The document also instructed all of the Napolas which had not already done so to establish a lecture series featuring representatives of the various Nazi organizations, including the Party itself, the SA, SS, and HJ, as well as the NSKK (National Socialist Motor Corps), DAF (German Labour Front), and NSV (National Socialist People's Welfare Organization).[208] This would not only ensure that staff and pupils were fully apprised of the historical development, tasks, and aims of the NSDAP and all of its subsidiary organizations, but would simultaneously provide each school with a circle of political 'patrons' who would take a keen interest in the Napola's work and participate in its everyday life. This circle could also include 'men, and possibly women; from border regions and expatriate communities; from the arts and academia; from the economy, and from the state government and regional administration. Nevertheless, the lecture evenings should still primarily serve the purpose of political education.'[209] Finally, schools were requested to send in a report detailing all of the political training which had previously taken place, both for staff and pupils; a list of relevant lectures which had already been held, including the name of the speaker and the topic; experiences gained, and plans for the following year, as well as the nature of the contacts which had been cultivated with local Party offices.[210]

The content of the 'ideological' classes themselves could take many different forms: intensive study of key ideological texts such as Hitler's *Mein Kampf* and Alfred Rosenberg's *Myth of the Twentieth Century* was extremely common, as were discussions of recent political speeches, or the tenets of the NSDAP Party Programme.[211] NPEA Stuhm's syllabus stated that, in the first year of instruction, the 'political working groups' at the school would learn the basics of political knowledge, in particular the history of the National Socialist movement, the Party manifesto, and the problematic position of Germans living in nations beyond the Reich's borders; in the second year, they would learn about all of the different organizations of the Nazi state, the regime's reconstruction of Germany, and the measures which were being taken to realize the National Socialist new order, including the racial and biological 'recovery' and 'restructuring' of German society. In the final year, combined with trips abroad (see Chapter 3), the *Jungmannen* would be acquainted with the nature of their political adversaries (*Gegner*), and their aims and methods of combat; pupils would give presentations considering how best to rebut hostile worldviews, whether represented by Jewry, Bolshevism, Freemasonry, Liberalism, Catholicism, or 'reaction'.[212] In order to learn how propaganda worked, it was considered most valuable for pupils to read works of 'hostile literature', forcing the *Jungmannen* to engage with them from an antagonistic point of view.[213] From this perspective, one former pupil of NPEA Neuzelle remembered having to do an intensive course on Marxism, Leninism, and Stalinism, which included the *Communist Manifesto*, *Das Kapital*, and the idea of 'Socialism in One Country', which he claimed had even served him well in later life.[214]

Less formal political education would often take place on one evening a week, under the aegis of the *Zugführer*; *Jungmannen* from the younger year-groups might receive this kind of instruction too.[215] Pupils would be encouraged to discuss relevant events which had come up in the news, or during everyday school life (such as questions of how to lead a fully National Socialist existence, or be truly 'comradely'). They would especially be encouraged to bring up opinions which they might have heard on school trips, or during the holidays, which they '[felt] instinctively to be false, or even dangerous', but did not know how to rebut—such as doubts regarding the veracity of state media reports, or the effectiveness of Nazi economic policies.[216] At NPEA Neuzelle, for instance, the teacher would often play the part of a political 'moaner', whose opinion the *Jungmannen* would either have to learn to counter convincingly or make appear ridiculous, in order to ensure that pupils would have the relevant ideological arsenal at hand to attack such opinions in real life, rather than remaining 'passive National Socialists' who would sit idly by while their ideology was threatened.[217] In addition, *Jungmannen* might each be asked to give a five-minute presentation on the politics and current affairs of a different part of the globe, using material from newspapers and periodicals to inform their political analyses of relevant foreign policy; discussions of domestic politics and the rectitude of Nazi policies would generally be led by the *Zugführer*.[218] Pupils would also be encouraged to study privately in their 'communal libraries', which would be liberally supplied with works on all of the relevant subjects, including 'racial science' (*Rassenkunde*), 'military science' (*Wehrwissenschaft*), and politics.[219] Other activities might include close analysis of recent political speeches, parsing the meaning of key terms such as 'freedom', 'duty', and 'leadership' in accordance with National Socialist conceptions of morality.[220] In preparation for the '*Waffenleite*' or secular confirmation ceremony which all *Jungmannen* would undergo in their mid-teens (see Chapter 3), pupils might also take part in a form of ideological small-group 'confirmation class' (*Besinnungsstunde*).[221]

Finally, pupils would also have to engage every day with those political slogans or '*Tischsprüche*' which were read out before meals were served as a kind of secular (or even anti-religious) substitute for grace. A calligraphic collection of these 'table slogans' from NPEA Plön reveals a curious mixture of revanchist adages, ideological catch-phrases, and pseudo-religious or proverbial home truths, including watchwords such as 'Our power lies in our discipline'; 'Power is Duty. Freedom is Responsibility'; 'Eternal peace is a dream, and not even a very attractive one', 'Religion is the crutch of a corrupt political system', or 'The worst man of all is the one who is always right'.[222] Sometimes, each table would be asked to come up with their own slogans, and the *Tischspruch* might be read out by one *Jungmann*, or by the table *en masse*. Kurt Meyer even claimed in his memoirs that, contrary to the spirit if not the letter of this practice, tables would compete to come up with the shortest possible adage, so that all of the ravenous *Jungmannnen* could be served more speedily. Whereas in the preceding months, slogans such as 'You are nothing! Your people is everything', or 'Loyalty is the core of honour', had been the norm, now, far more laconic phrases such as '*Arbeit adelt*' ('Work ennobles'), or even '*Kämpfe*!' ('Fight!') became *de rigueur*. Finally, when all of the *Jungmannen* on one table simply shouted 'Hmm!' in unison, they were deemed to have won the contest once and for all.[223]

*

That such forms of ideological indoctrination should have had a substantial effect on pupils' political views is unsurprising—for instance, former *Jungmannen* who went on to study for a higher degree might even complain to their *alma mater* that the university courses they were attending were ridiculously 'unpolitical', or that the lectures were 'as un-influenced by our worldview as they were before the seizure of power, and often even down-right inimical to our feeling and thinking.'[224] One former pupil from NPEA Naumburg also rejoiced in the fact that, although he had been worried that his education might not have been so academically rigorous as that of some of his comrades who were 'cunning old foxes' in French or Latin, during a training course, he had gained the best mark of all for his essay on 'War as a Test of our People': 'My success was all the sweeter because everyone else knew that I was from an NPEA.'[225]

However, even during their time at the schools, this gradual saturation with Nazi ideology, and not least with virulent antisemitism, could have a concrete effect on pupils' ideas and actions. Thus, in an edition of the NPEA Spandau school newsletter which was published in August 1935, we find an article which provides abundant evidence of antisemitic actions being deliberately planned and carried out by Napola-pupils, with the connivance and encouragement of their *Erzieher*.[226] That summer, a group of forty-five *Jungmannen* had been taken on a trip to the Napolas' new seaside retreat at Wyk auf Föhr, a village on the second largest of the North Frisian Islands off the German coast of the North Sea. Here, they were horrified to discover that the local population was so politically 'slack', particularly with regard to the 'Jewish question', that 'representatives of the "chosen" people' were to be found everywhere on the island—two Jewish children's homes were even in evidence:

> If only the Jews had at least taken a back seat!
>
> We saw them on the spa promenade, they sat in the reading room, wallowed here and there on the beach, and gave us admirable opportunity to study [racial] types. But they didn't keep themselves to themselves, instead, they were having fun.... They sat with Aryans...and went for walks and attended public events with *Volksgenossen* [racial comrades—i.e. 'Aryan' citizens]. When we thought that these '*Volksgenossen*' would be ashamed, we were mistaken. On the contrary, they seemed to feel quite at ease in [Jewish] company.

The author of the report, *Jungmann* Trübenbach (Unterprima) goes on to describe how this state of affairs led the Napola-pupils to take matters into their own hands: 'Was nothing to be done against this plague of Jews, which ought to sicken every upstanding *Volksgenosse*? Everywhere else in the Reich, yes, but in Wyk, not a sign. The task which we set ourselves was to jolt the local population awake and recall them to their duty.'

After some of the local population took exception to a group of Jewish children leading the procession at a children's festival, the *Jungmannen* decided to make the first move in their planned antisemitic propaganda campaign (see Figure 2.8). Paper and paints were sought, and the leading artist among the boys got to work drawing Jewish caricatures, whilst one of the *Erzieher* provided suitably 'effective' slogans, such as 'Jews! Germany's patience is at an end!' or 'In 1864, you didn't wish to be enslaved by the Danes; do you wish to be enslaved by the Jews today?'

Figure 2.8 Antisemitic propaganda posters created by pupils at NPEA Spandau during their stay on the Frisian island of Föhr, August 1935.

Glue was cooked up out of potato flour, and, that night, a band of pupils sallied out to place the posters at strategic points around the town. Enraged enquiries by the local police officer at the hostel where the *Jungmannen* were staying the next morning were met with innocent and astonished faces: 'Putting up posters? Us? Impossible! *We* sleep at night-time!'[227] Meanwhile, on the following nights, the *Jungmannen* not only pasted placards on all of the town's most important buildings, but also painted slogans such as 'Jews not wanted!' on the pavements—and, outside the house of a man they believed to have taken down one of their posters, they scrawled 'Red Jewish lackey!' (*Roter Judenknecht*).

However, the *pièce de résistance* of the Napola-pupils' propaganda effort came one Sunday when an air-show was planned, at which many important figures were expected to appear. The boys painted for three days straight, until they had fifty placards ready; meanwhile, the *Hundertschaftsführer* gave speeches to the Party and the SA on such topics as 'political Catholicism', Jewry, and Freemasonry, which began to attract large audiences of interested locals:

> Interest in the Jewish question was awakened. We found not only volunteers to help with our poster-pasting sessions and thankful audiences at the meetings, but the people also engaged with these questions personally. The sales of *Der Stürmer* and *Das Schwarze Korps* rose so much that the shopkeepers couldn't supply enough of them. Furthermore, the bathing administration took note, and since this time no 'non-Aryans' have been permitted to attend public events in the town. The Party comrades there regretted very much that we had to leave, and promised to continue the work which we had set in train. The result of our

> five-week agitation proved to us that a small circle of people, when working at the right time and with the right means, can achieve great success and gain many supporters. Interest in the sphere of the Jewish question was present, and the inhabitants of Wyk wanted to continue to work in our spirit. Thus was our task completed, for we had intended nothing more.

Last but not least, two of the most highly prized posters from the propaganda campaign had the dubious honour of being reprinted in the *Spandauer Blätter*.

That the transformation effected by the Spandauer was indeed as dramatic as Trübenbach claims can be at least partially inferred from archival documents treating Wyk's Jewish population, which have been systematically examined by Dirk Warkus-Thomsen in his article on the fate of the two Jewish children's homes in the town.[228] Wyk had previously had a long history, dating back to the Kaiserreich, of being one of the most Jewish-friendly bathing resorts in Germany. The town had even continued to provide a safe haven for Jews during the Third Reich well after other resorts which had long welcomed Jews, such as Nordeney, had been declared '*Judenfrei*' (Jew-free), due to a programme of radical antisemitic activism among local SA and Party cadres, coupled with the Bathing Administration's fear of being branded a 'Jewish Bathing Resort' (*Judenbad*), and thus losing custom to other more radically anti-Jewish resorts.[229] However, the gradual, yet inexorable, process of driving all Jews, including the inhabitants of the children's homes, out of Wyk—and off the island of Föhr in its entirety—seems first to have been initiated by the Mayor only *after* the Spandauers' 'action', and may also have been spurred on by subsequent complaints from the authorities at NPEA Plön.[230]

The second example of an overtly antisemitic report by a Napola-pupil is taken from the November 1938 issue of the NPEA Köslin school newsletter. Entitled 'Jews in Poland: in the anteroom of Asia (fleeting impressions from the Jewish Quarter in Sosnowice)', the piece was written by a pupil in the 7th class, who would probably have been around 17. The author, *Jungmann* Boneß, begins by drawing a very unfavourable comparison between the well-maintained modern high street in the centre of Sosnowice, and the tangle of crooked alleys which made up the Jewish quarter, only five minutes' walk away. He writes:

> Arduously, we…push through a swarm of filthy individuals, nagging and haggling. I can't refrain from describing a typical example of this type: A black, greasy top hat conceals a little stiff peaked cap, which is worn simultaneously. A swarm of rampant black greasy frizzly hair streams from underneath and mutates imperceptibly into copious sideburns. The *pièce de résistance* is constituted by a 'foot-muff', i.e. a beard…. The mouth with its bulging lips and never-brushed teeth is in constant motion. A brown-skinned, short, thick neck leads into a broad body, completely enshrouded in a sack-like, greasy, much-tattered

> kaftan, from which the knock-kneed short flat feet still poke out. Short, drooping arms with gesticulating hands, often holding gnarled sticks, complete this unlovely picture.[231]

As we can see from this depiction, Boneß has completely internalized the negative Nazified image of the 'common-or-garden' Jew, and approaches his subject with a seemingly anthropological or ethnographic interest, fuelled by contempt. There is no trace of sympathy or fellow-feeling with the people whom he is observing, and indeed, he goes on to extend his disparagement to every type of Jew that he sees, whether they be young or old, male or female:

> Mostly some of them stand around, mumbling loudly and casting frowning, poisonous glances our way. Others cling to us with sinister importunacy, in order to 'do a little deal' with us (*um 'ä Geschäftsche' zu tätigen*). In between pale Jewboys buzz about..., rouged floozies ('*Schicksen*') with ever-painted nails, and abysmally ugly old women with snarled grey hair, crooked gait and usually a strongly pronounced Jewish nose. Here and there a few abject-looking peasants, the objects of exploitation by this sinister community. On the street, deals are being done; an elderly disciple of the Talmud has set himself up with a giant basket full of foul rubber balls. But then, a Jew can make a business out of anything....

No opportunity is lost here to use the most negative language, connoting disgust, filth, fear, or even suggestions of sexual depravity—as well, of course, as references to the supposed Jewish global economic conspiracy. This tendency becomes even more marked in the following description of the Jewish market hall, which is portrayed as incredibly unhygienic, full of vagrants, stink, and unbearable noise. Metaphorical filth becomes ever more interchangeable with physical filth, as Boneß describes seeing thousands of flies swarming over a long table full of unprotected cuts of meat, some of which are apparently beginning to decay; or a single room in the cellar which serves as home to an entire family, from which an evil odour arises, and the stink of mouldering flesh. Thus, although we encounter no actual violence or specific antisemitic action in Boneß's narrative, this trip nevertheless seems to denote an active attempt by the school authorities to instil loathing and repugnance for Jews by taking pupils to see them in their supposedly 'natural habitat' (as if they were mere animals in a zoo or nature reserve).

Such excursions appear to have been common at many of the NPEA; other surviving accounts document the experiences of *Jungmannen* at Bensberg, Klotzsche, Loben, Naumburg, Neuzelle, Rottweil, and Schulpforta, who made similar trips; many of these testimonies also concern visits to those 'ghettos' which had been deliberately created as part of Nazi occupation (and ultimately extermination) policy in Eastern Europe after the outbreak of World War

II. Similarly virulent attitudes towards Jews (as well as other 'out-groups', including Poles, Russians, and people of colour) can also be found scattered throughout the selections of correspondence sent in by alumni and *Erzieher* fighting on all fronts during the war, which were subsequently reprinted in the Napolas' school newsletters (see Chapter 10). It therefore seems likely that the ideological indoctrination instilled at the NPEA would have had the effect of heightening Napola graduates' tendency to act violently towards those deemed to be 'enemies' of the regime during wartime, even if direct proof of such tendencies would be less easy to find.[232]

However, the other form of concentrated preparation for warfare which the *Jungmannen* were constantly forced to undergo—in this instance physical, rather than ideological—was equally deeply encoded within the Napolas' curriculum, in the form of their all-encompassing sporting and pre-military training.[233]

Sport, Physical Education, and Premilitary Training at the NPEA

As we have seen, in order to pass the Napola selection tests successfully, physical fitness was an absolute *sine qua non*; moreover, both the abundant variety of sporting activities on offer at the NPEA, and the state-of-the-art facilities and equipment with which they were supplied at vast state expense, contributed significantly to the attraction which the schools exerted on potential pupils.[234] Sporting contests were a constant feature of the calendar at any Napola, whether as an obligatory part of the annual speech day—which also provided the perfect opportunity to display the pupils' sporting achievements to parents, alumni, and distinguished guests alike—or in the form of matches and competitions with local schools or branches of the Hitler Youth.[235] Indeed, sport seems to have been crucial both to the Napolas' interactions with their local communities and the outside world more generally, and to their relationship with other NPEA, given that the schools' annual *Wettkämpfe* (contests) and *Manöver* (manoeuvres), at which all of the Napolas competed with each other keenly, were seen as an important part of forging individual schools' identity.

Team-games such as football and handball aside, the programme of physical education at the Napolas was fundamentally divided into two branches—'basic training' (*grundständige Leibesübungen*), which focused in particular on gymnastics, athletics, and swimming, and 'supplementary training' (*zusätzliche Leibesübungen*), which included boxing, fencing, riding, rowing, sailing, skiing, gliding, learning to drive cars and motorcycles, and martial arts such as wrestling or ju-jitsu. In general, the basic training focused on 'natural forms of exercise' (such as running, jumping, and throwing), although apparatus-gymnastics was also highly prized, due to its supposedly 'German nature', and its cultivation of physical control, agility, and courage.[236] However, even in this instance, particularly when working with the youngest pupils, teachers were concerned to develop boys' interest by treating the apparatus in the first instance as the kind of natural obstacle which they might encounter in a cross-country war-game—or by using tests of speed and endurance to foster competition among the *Jungmannen*.[237] Swimming was also deemed to be of especial importance; every Napola was supposed to have a swimming bath, and many NPEA even possessed an indoor pool of their own. It was stipulated from the outset that every new pupil who could not swim upon arriving at the school at Easter must be able to earn his *Freischwimmerzeugnis* (a certificate proving that he could swim freely for twenty minutes) by the end of the summer term, only eight weeks or so later. Broadly speaking, this drive seems to have been successful, with reports from NPEA Potsdam confirming that, in 1935, only two of the twenty non-swimmers in a cohort of forty-three new boys in the first year had failed to achieve this goal;[238] in 1940, by their second year, 95 per cent of pupils at NPEA Spandau had succeeded in gaining the status of 'free-swimmers', and by their fourth year, 99 per cent of pupils there could swim for an hour without stopping, while 80 per cent had also earned the badge of the German Life-Saving Association (*DLRG-Abzeichen*).[239]

Meanwhile, the 'supplementary' activities represented one of the Napolas' chief claims to fame; after all, what civilian school could offer every single pupil the opportunity to glide, ride, drive, sail, or ski? Even the Airforce, Motor, Naval, and Cavalry branches of the Hitler Youth could never provide individuals with a fundamental training in every single one of their disciplines.[240] Of course, the schools' varied locations had a significant impact on the sporting activities that they could offer; thus, Napolas situated near lakes or rivers, such as Plön or Oranienstein, necessarily provided more opportunities for water sports; meanwhile, Napolas in mountainous regions, such as Ilfeld in the Harz, would partake more regularly in skiing competitions.[241] Nevertheless, every effort was made to offer a full range of activities to pupils at all of the schools (at least until the war years began to take their toll, due to the compulsory requisitioning of horses and motor vehicles).[242] In the 5th and 6th *Zug*, *Jungmannen* were able to gain an elementary training in all of the 'supplementary' activities (apart from driving); boxing was often compulsory. Then, in conjunction with their *Erzieher*, they would choose two disciplines on which to focus during the final three years of their time at the Napola.[243]

The enthusiasm with which many of the *Jungmannen* greeted these multifarious opportunities is revealed very clearly in the accounts published in the schools' newsletters—for instance, the breathless excitement with which boys described their first ever flight in a glider, or their first experience in a sailing boat: 'It was heavenly, whizzing through the waves... during the storm'.[244] Although some of the new activities might seem more exciting in theory than in practice—for instance, the driving lessons were much more concerned with theory, and with driving safely once one had passed one's test, than with long rides in fast machines, and rowing training might consist as much of exercises using rowing machines on dry land as those using boats on the water—pupils' overall impression seems to have been a favourable one.[245]

*

Like almost all physical education during the Third Reich, the Napolas' curriculum aimed at the inculcation of hardiness in preparation for war—a fact which is incessantly highlighted in all of the relevant sources' insistence on the importance of toughness, courage, tenacity, and readiness to fight.[246] Indeed, the Napolas were arguably especially privileged in their ability to provide their pupils with an all-encompassing pre-military training (see Figure 2.9), and graduates of the

Figure 2.9 Shooting practice at NPEA Rügen, *c.*1944.

schools were particularly prized as recruits by the various branches of the armed forces (see Chapter 10).[247]

From this perspective, the schools' frequent cross-country war-games (variously known as *Geländespiele*, *Geländesport*, or *Geländedienst*)—including night-time exercises—which usually took place on a weekly basis at individual Napolas, served as an especially effective form of paramilitary training.[248] In the lower school, the war-games focused on harnessing boys' youthful enthusiasm for adventure, teaching them how to spy without being observed, using the lie of the land and the undergrowth to creep around the enemy unseen, and providing them with simple objectives such as capturing the opposing side's camp or 'munitions dump'. Each boy had a red or blue 'life-thread' (*Lebensfaden*) tied to his wrist, and if it were torn off, he was pronounced officially 'dead', thus providing an easy way of reckoning up the winners and losers in any hostile encounter. The ensuing (usually wild) 'battles' were often framed with tales from local history, such as the peasants' revolt, or, in borderland areas, skirmishes with groups such as Polish nationalists or Dutch separatists in the more recent past; they also involved orienteering, reconnaissance patrols, marching with heavy backpacks, and the internalization of instant obedience to commands from one's superiors.[249] The military-style orders for each mission stipulated in detail its aims and the requisite role-play scenario, as well as the uniforms to be worn by each party, timings, and other minutiae, such as where the 'dead' were to gather once they had been 'killed'.[250] After the end of each mission, the group would be given a critique of their performance, and told how they could improve in future.[251]

Perhaps the most obvious example of the Napolas' 'education for war', however, was the annual military-style *Manöver* (manoeuvres), which included massed *Geländespiele* involving between two thousand and three thousand *Jungmannen* in the older year-groups, and which were often observed by some of the highest dignitaries in the land, including Heinrich Himmler, Bernhard Rust, and members of the Wehrmacht High Command (OKW).[252] Following an initial experimental 'Autumn Exercise' (*Herbstübung*) in 1934, involving all of the Prussian Napolas and NPEA Ilfeld, the first *Manöver* including all of the Napolas took place on the Lüneburg Heath (*Lüneburger Heide*) in 1936.[253] Although the manoeuvres planned for East Prussia in 1937 had to be cancelled due to the logistical difficulties of transporting three thousand *Jungmannen* such a long way, the 1938 and 1939 manoeuvres were able to take place unproblematically in Mecklenburg and Carinthia respectively.[254] These *Manöver* were also reported in great detail in the National Socialist media, including newsreels, not least because they would often involve concluding speeches by regime grandees such as the *Reichsführer-SS*.[255]

The logistics involved in organizing the manoeuvres were, quite simply, immense. Surviving correspondence from the Inspectorate of the NPEA regarding the 1939 summer manoeuvres in Carinthia appears to have involved micro-managing every possible aspect with military precision and exactitude—including crucial questions such as whether the schools' mobile field-kitchens (*Gulaschkanonen*) should be towed on trailers or placed in lorries; what colour epaulettes each school must wear, and exactly which bakeries, butchers, and dairies each Napola should patronize, as well as precise arrangements for the requisite journeys on special trains, and even designations regarding which administrator would be responsible for 'pumps, latrines, [and the] supply of straw'. Each aspect of the manoeuvres—the military exercises, the sporting activities, and the camp—would be the responsibility of a different headmaster, and those schools with full-time medical staff would be required to send their doctors too.[256] In May of that year, it was estimated that it would cost 20,000 RM simply for all of the Prussian Napolas to take part in the Carinthian manoeuvres, while the participation of the newly founded Austrian NPEA would probably cost a further 12,000 RM.[257] During the Second World War, however, the schools had to content themselves with holding 'Summer Solstice Competitive Games' (*Sonnenwendwettkämpfe*) each year at NPEA Naumburg, since massed military exercises in far-flung regions of the Reich were no longer sustainable or practicable in wartime.[258]

An account of the 'Autumn Manoeuvres' in 1936, published in the periodical *Weltanschauung und Schule*, gives a good overall impression of the programme.[259] To settle in, the *Jungmannen* would spend three days getting to know the local area, staying in villages, farms, and barns, and putting on entertainments for the resident population. There then followed a three-day military exercise, which, far from being an indiscriminate rough-and-tumble, was supposed to involve militaristic precision and use of terrain—with numerous umpires observing both sides to ensure that they followed the rules of the game.[260] All kinds of espionage and trickery would be attempted during the exercise; pupils might disguise themselves as stupid country bumpkins to see whether the enemy guardpost might reveal fatal information about their team's strength and disposition when questioned, and they would also use all of the modern technology at their disposal (including morse telegraphy, field telephones, and motorcycles).[261] In one instance, at dead of night, an enemy patrol from the opposing team (led by NPEA Naumburg) even gained access to NPEA Potsdam-Neuzelle's only truck, which was filled with all of the school's provisions (including a huge preserving jar containing two hundred portions of Mirabelle plums), and drove it off as booty, to the chagrin of all concerned, including the *Erzieher* and *Anstaltsleiter*.[262] Forever after, one of NPEA Potsdam-Neuzelle's battle cries would be 'Revenge for the Mirabelles!', and Potsdam, Neuzelle, and Naumburg became sworn foes at the manoeuvres from thenceforward.[263]

The final day of the military exercise would generally end in a set-piece battle—thus, in 1936, the massed ranks of the 'Blues' formed up in Frederician ranks, school by school, to storm the heights south of Tellmer, which were being held by the 'Reds', with the *Anstaltsleiter* leading the way.[264] Indeed, the headmasters' 'life-threads' were particularly coveted trophies—Dieter Pfeiffer recalled that, in his memory of one final battle, he could still see the Oranienstein *Anstaltsleiter*, Friedrich Lübbert, holding high his broken thumb and yelling 'Lads, avenge my thumb!'; the offending digit had been broken during a tussle with NPEA Rottweil's acting *Anstaltsleiter*, Paul Steck.[265] Throughout the exercise, teachers were just as likely to be attacked as *Jungmannen*; one *Erzieher* at NPEA Potsdam remembered losing not just his life-thread, but also his glasses, to a hefty attack by a massive sixth-former from NPEA Naumburg.[266]

After the fighting was over, the next task for each Napola was to prepare the site where all of the schools would be camping for the next three days of sporting contests—including the creation of sufficient vehicle tracks, washing places, and latrines. Each school competed to make its 'camp gate' as artistic as possible, using natural materials such as heather, moss, and wood, attempting to evoke the symbolism of their respective *Heimat*.[267] Thus, NPEA Ballenstedt's gate might depict the Napola's local coat of arms back in Anhalt, while NPEA Köslin might create a sailing-ship, in allusion to the school's location by the sea.[268] There then followed a packed programme of competitions, including contests in 'military sports', such as orienteering and assault courses, as well as athletics contests and football and handball tournaments. More 'fun' competitions included a relay race which involved not only the *Jungmannen* of a given age-group and their *Erzieher*, but also the school cook, chauffeur, and bursar, with the *Anstaltsleiter* bringing up the rear. All of these competitions, however, focused on team-building rather than highlighting individual achievement, and the evening 'ceremonies' (*Feierstunden*), each put on by an individual Napola in order to celebrate local culture, were also designed to foster the schools' overall cohesion and fellow-feeling. The grand finale, however, was heralded by the arrival of Education Minister Rust and other dignitaries and high-ranking military personnel, who would be treated to an impressive show, including demonstrations of motorsports, riding, gymnastics, boxing, wrestling, and tug-of-war, as well as the finals of the handball and football tournaments, and team contests in competitive semaphore, morse telegraphy, and the speed-laying of field telephone-lines.[269]

The military flavour of all of these activities can perhaps best be demonstrated by the following extract from a journal kept by a pupil at NPEA Backnang during the 1938 manoeuvres in Mecklenburg:

> Day 3: The wargame begins. At 8am sharp, the red armbands and life-threads are given out. Five minutes later we already find ourselves on the march in the direction of Rostock. At the 'Lüsewitzer Krug' inn, we enter the woods and take up reserve positions. Cyclists, trucks, and motorcycles chase along the road overhead and we have to lie here 'idly'. 100m to the right of us, the Reds' leader, *Anstaltsleiter* Brunk, has set up camp. Finally our *Jungmann-Zugführer* arrives and gives me and a comrade an exploratory mission. We leave all unnecessary

> baggage and break out in the direction of Impfendorf. In the woods, we bump into a platoon of Rottweil boys and 'deal with' an enemy cyclist. Then we press on and reach the railway line between Pastow and Groß-Lüsewitz. Our task is complete and we report what we have seen and heard to *Anstaltsleiter* Brunk. Then again waiting and again more waiting. Suddenly we are retrieved from our position and hurled to the 'Front' with an omnibus. There we're involved in a few short skirmishes, but they're pointless. Then suddenly we're commanded to retreat. I'm fighting a losing battle along with a couple of comrades. From 2–6pm there's a pause in the fighting. We rest up in Groß-Lüsewitz. After four hours, the battle continues. We march to the Billenhagen Forestry. There we're back in the reserves. It starts to rain and we get out our tent canvasses and coats. For about six hours, we stay in the woods and wait for our assignment to the Front.[270]

Testimonies such as this one, along with reports in school newsletters with titles such as 'The First Battle!', or 'Military Bulletin No. 5 from the Blue Team at the Napolas' Autumn Manoeuvres!', clearly capture the seductive martial excitement of these occasions, and are littered with proof of pupils' enthusiasm and lust for battle, as well as the militarization of their very thoughts and vocabulary. Above all, however, such personal accounts demonstrate the effectiveness of these forms of pre-military training in accustoming the *Jungmannen* to the theory and practice of warfare.[271]

The Napolas' School-Leaving Examination and Graduation Ceremony

Once pupils had managed to fulfil all of the gruelling physical and mental tasks demanded of them during the entirety of their school career at the NPEA, then, what lay in store for them at its end?

Before he could graduate, each *Jungmann* would have to pass the Napolas' school-leaving examination or *Reifeprüfung*—just as he would have done at a civilian school. However, the form of examination at the NPEA was rather different, and was perceived in some quarters as testing the worth of the education offered by the *Anstaltsleiter* and *Erzieher* as much as that of the *Jungmannen* themselves.[272] The written exam, which followed the model of normal school-leaving examinations, might include topics such as:

- Hindenburg and Ludendorff's plans for a large-scale offensive in the East, and the practical implementation of the campaigns against Russia.
- Goethe's engagement with the technical and political world of the nineteenth century.

- With reference to Alfred Bäumler's article 'The Reformation, the world-historical turning-point of the Middle Ages', discuss the ways in which the author perceives the reform movement and Luther's action as possessing validity in the present.[273]
- How does modern physics conceptualize the construction of atoms and the origin of light? Take into account the meaning of the physical worldview from our perspective.
- Pure and applied research, presented using the example of German light alloys.[274]

However, once the written exams had been completed, all of the *Anstaltsleiter* and *Unterrichtsleiter* would travel round to the various schools, acting as an examination commission for the *viva voce* exams. This would allow the headmasters and Directors of Studies to gain an overview of the standard of achievement at each school, whilst learning from personal experience which methods might work well, and which badly.[275] The aim of this *viva* was not so much to examine pupils' academic knowledge as to test their political acumen; at NPEA Naumburg, for instance, three candidates at a time would have to sit around a table and discuss key themes such as 'Race and Religion', 'The Difference between Racial and Imperialist Foreign Policy', and 'Our Current Colonial Situation', dealing pointfully with objections raised by the examiners. At most of the Napolas, pupils would also be asked to prepare a twenty-minute presentation on a special subject of their choice, and then be examined separately on biological or 'national political' questions.[276] Claus Cordsen of NPEA Bensberg recalled that his *viva* in March 1939 on his special subject, Chemistry, consisted entirely of his giving a ten-minute talk on the chemical process used to produce synthetic rubber, including demonstrations at the blackboard; the examination committee appeared to be bored and uninterested, leaving the *Anstaltsleiter* and the Chemistry teacher to conduct the exam single-handed.[277] Meanwhile, a surviving cache of English exam questions prepared by Rudolf Wasmann at NPEA Bensberg gives an idea of the standard—and the political nature—of such *viva voce* tests:[278]

> (1) Nature and meaning of intonation. The characteristic traits of English intonation.
>
> (2) Give a summary of the following letter to the Editor of THE TIMES. What strikes you when reading this letter?
>
> To the Editor of the *Times*.
>
> Sir,
>
> - Many thousands of Britischers [*sic*] were more than glad to read Mrs. Blagden's letter of protest. It is true that the tone, manner, and quality of the news are both bellicose and provocative very much too often.

We all went through the long period of B.B.C. announcements as regards the 'sanctions' with what patience we could muster, and then, as the B.B.C. had not learnt its lesson, there came the provocative language about great Continental nations and the constant use of the word 'insurgents' to describe the forces of General Franco in Spain. Most serious newspapers have long used the word 'Nationalists'. Even on the evening of February 18, with Barcelona taken days ago, the B.B.C.-announcer could find no-better word than 'insurgents'. Many people in England, and 90 per cent. outside it, could have assured the B.B.C. from the beginning of the certain triumph of General Franco in Spain, but once again, to use a sporting phrase, the B.B.C. has put its money on the wrong horse. It really grieves Englishmen who do know the Continent and are realists that the B.B.C. should appear still so far from learning its patent lessons. Will it not make a real effort to appreciate and try to understand the thought of Spain, of Italy, and even of Germany? Can it not realize that Signor Mussolini wants peace and not war? Surely he proved that at Munich last September.

Yours very faithfully,
A. T. Parsons.

*

Finally, for those *Jungmannen* who had passed both parts of the examination successfully (which appears to have been the vast majority), there then ensued the celebratory school-leaving ceremony in Berlin—the so-called *Abiturientenentlassung*, which was generally combined with a winter sport festival at NPEA Spandau.[279] During their spare time, the graduands might be allowed to see the sights of the city (perhaps even attempting to snatch a glimpse of the Führer himself), or be given the opportunity to attend performances at Berlin's many theatres and concert halls.[280]

The graduation ceremony would usually take place either at the Napola in Berlin-Spandau, or at Schloss Charlottenburg; as we might expect, the exact type of dress uniform which the *Jungmannen* would have to wear, and the timing and manner of their advent, were all planned right down to the last detail.[281] Following a festive celebration at which the hundreds of graduands were ceremonially received by Reich Education Minister Rust, accompanied by all of the usual pomp and circumstance of Nazi political ritual—fanfares, Führer-slogans, and National Socialist hymns—the *Jungmannen* would then have to listen to exhortatory speeches by Rust, and receive greetings from other Nazi hierarchs, such as Hermann Göring, even if such notable grandees could not always be present in person.[282] Afterwards, they would all march in massed ranks into the Tiergarten, through the Brandenburg Gate, and down Unter den Linden, placing wreaths first on the war memorial, and then on the graves of Horst Wessel and Herbert Norkus, the two most famous 'martyrs' of the National Socialist movement.[283]

Now, they were *Jungmannen* no longer, but graduates of the NPEA, ready to take their first unconstrained steps into the wider world beyond their school walls.

Conclusions

Some scholars have dubbed the Third Reich an '*Erziehungsstaat*'; a state which consistently privileged the idea of 'training' over more traditional forms of academic 'education' (*Bildung*), fulfilling the regime's fundamental mission to turn all 'politically acceptable' German citizens into *Volksgenossen*.[284] Indeed, the Napolas' programme of 'total education' and 'formation training' shared a great many commonalities with those programmes which were put into practice at other forms of educational 'total institution' during the Third Reich's early years, such as the Reich Labour Service (RAD), the 'Year on the Land' (*Landjahr*), the 'National Political Training Courses' (*Nationalpolitische Lehrgänge*), and the Party and SS training academies (the *Ordensburgen* and *Junkerschulen*). All of these organizations adopted a similarly military-style structure and ideologically guided curricular focus, underpinned by a rigorous rationale of increasingly racialized '*Auslese*' and '*Ausmerze*' (selection and eradication).[285] Such institutions invariably possessed hierarchies, timetables, and structural elements borrowed from the military, including roll calls, flag parades, and sentry duties, as well as insisting that participants should wear uniforms, and constantly steel their bodies through physical and martial exercise.[286] The socialization processes at these institutions also featured inescapable forms of mutual control, with members of the 'troop' accepting self-imposed discipline, as well as that inflicted by higher authorities—all the while placing continual emphasis on the necessity of complete submission to the demands of 'comradeship'.[287]

Moreover, just like these other National Socialist institutions, the Napolas drew not only upon pre-existing military, nationalist, and authoritarian patterns of thought, but also upon more recent developments in the pedagogical sphere.[288] While, as we have seen, the NPEA were always supplied with the most up-to-date literature, teaching materials, and equipment, the schools also experimented with modern pedagogical methods, including those adapted from the Reform Pedagogy movement and the pre-National Socialist youth movements (as discussed in the Introduction).[289] In similar fashion to the SS training-courses at the *Junkerschulen*, the intimate connection of 'learning' with 'comradeship' at the Napolas combined 'progressive' teaching methods with the inculcation of National Socialist ideology.[290] Just as the SS-courses at the *Junkerschule* Bad Tölz aimed to cultivate 'fanatical political soldiers' who would nevertheless be able to engage in independent study, 'think for themselves', and ground their opinions in relevant literature, the better to 'muzzle doubters and rumour-spreaders', rather than mindlessly regurgitating the material presented by the teacher or falling back on 'superficial buzzwords',[291] the political instruction at the NPEA was especially dangerous because it, too, ostensibly taught intellectual skills which any teacher would wish their students to display—yet in a context so saturated with ideology that the *Jungmannen* who had been taught in this fashion could only interpret their material using Nazified modes of thought.[292]

Hence, the Napolas' overall ability to indoctrinate their pupils ideologically was far more effective than that of most other Nazi educational institutions, including the civilian school system.[293] While organizations such as the *Landjahr* and the Reich Labour Service attempted to inculcate their adherents with National Socialist ideology in similar fashion, they nevertheless appear to have fallen far short of their goals, not only because their entire programme was far shorter—in the case of the *Landjahr*, eight months, rather than the Napolas' eight years—but also because the *Erzieher* had no unified framework of instruction to follow, especially given that they had to cater to all intellectual levels, and could provide their students with little more than a superficial 'scaffolding of facts and simple argumentative structures'.[294] More than either of these institutions, much less the regular Hitler Youth or the civilian school classroom, where teachers' and pupils' spheres of action were far more circumscribed and open to outside influences, the NPEA were able to construct a closed conception of the world for their pupils, within which National Socialist values and forms of judgement were applied universally, and which was explicitly designed to repel any contrary information from the outside world.[295] While civilian schools were constantly 'caught in the field of tension between ideology, pragmatism, and politics', and were often reduced to '*Sofortmaßnahmen*' (emergency measures) when it came to turning the regime's ideological tenets into educational praxis,[296] the NPEA could generally take immediate and unrestricted action to put these into practice—thus placing the Napolas at the vanguard of the planned National Socialist pedagogical reform. Put quite simply, the Napola education was all-encompassing, yet, since the NPEA did not entirely seek to abolish traditional academic standards and forms of assessment, they were nevertheless able to avoid the wholesale anti-intellectualism and academic nihilism of the Adolf-Hitler-Schools.[297]

From this perspective, the Napolas were ultimately able to indoctrinate their youthful charges more successfully, and for far longer, than most other Nazi educational institutions (including both the *Ordensburgen*, which only offered shorter training courses for 25–30-year-olds, and the Adolf-Hitler-Schools, which functioned for no longer than a couple of years in normal peacetime conditions). Moreover, the Napolas were far better able to achieve the distinctively National Socialist goal of 'erasing the individual identity and implanting a purely collective one' than most of the 'camp'-type National Socialist total educational institutions, due to the schools' all-embracing nature, and their selectivity.[298] Long before they had reached the age of military majority, the *Jungmannen* had 'merged their individual selves into a real or imagined group of comrades' just as eagerly as the

Wehrmacht soldiers investigated by Thomas Kühne, completely buying into the ideal of National Socialist comradeship—'a powerful discourse that pressured individuals to sacrifice themselves on the altar of a racially purified and ideologically united genocidal *Volksgemeinschaft*'.[299] From this standpoint, not only would former *Jungmannen* who became members of the armed forces—which meant almost every Napola-graduate, following the outbreak of World War II—have been likely to feel fewer qualms about the atrocities inflicted during the regime's 'total war'; they would also have fallen precisely into what Kühne has termed the 'born soldier' category of Wehrmacht recruits (see further Chapter 10).[300] Yet these Napola-graduates had not been born, but rather made, by the militaristic toughening and ideological indoctrination inflicted upon them throughout their school career.

Finally, we can see that the NPEA embody in microcosm many of the more general characteristics of the Nazi state—not just in terms of their comprehensive mechanisms of socialization and ideologization, but also in terms of the schools' constant privileging of racial 'selection' and martial prowess. However, as we shall see in the following chapter, the schools' programme of education ranged far more widely than mere classroom teaching and physical training—pupils would also be given the opportunity to travel the globe, experience the life of the working man, and cultivate their manifold artistic talents. Nevertheless, just like the academic instruction and the physical education programme, all of these ostensibly attractive 'extracurricular' activities only existed in order to serve the Napolas' ideological ends.

Notes

1. See the Introduction. The NPEA for girls (*NPEA für Mädchen*) followed a similar curriculum, but with slightly different emphases—for a detailed account of these, see further Chapter 9; also Stefanie Jodda-Flintrop, *'Wir sollten intelligente Mütter werden'. Nationalpolitische Erziehungsanstalten für Mädchen* (Norderstedt, 2010).
2. For a detailed discussion of the *Staatliche Bildungsanstalten*, see Chapter 4; cf. the relevant correspondence in Landesarchiv Nordrhein-Westfalen, Abteilung Rheinland, Duisburg (LNRW-D), BR 5 Nr. 20251; also 'Aufnahmeprüfung an den Nationalpolitischen Erziehungsanstalten', *Weltanschauung und Schule*, 1/5 (1937), 300–3. For an example of the change in selection criteria at the former *Landesschule* at Schulpforta after its transformation into an NPEA, see Helen Roche, '"Wanderer, kommst du nach Pforta…": The Tension between Classical Tradition and the Demands of a Nazi Elite-school Education at Schulpforta and Ilfeld, 1934–45', *European Review of History/revue européenne d'histoire* 20, no. 4 (2013), 581–609, 593. On the changing connotations of '*Auslese*', one might compare the increasing racialization of the term '*Volksgemeinschaft*', which came to bear a very different meaning under the Third Reich from that which it had possessed in many quarters prior to the Nazi seizure of power—cf. e.g. Michael

Wildt, 'Die Ungleichheit des Volkes. "Volksgemeinschaft" in der politischen Kommunikation der Weimarer Republik', in Frank Bajohr and Michael Wildt, eds, *Volksgemeinschaft. Neue Forschungen zur Gesellschaft des Nationalsozialismus* (Frankfurt am Main, 2009), 24–40.

3. Adolf Hitler, *Mein Kampf* (Munich, 1943), 452.
4. Peter Fritzsche, *Life and Death in the Third Reich* (Cambridge, MA, 2008), Chapter 2.
5. Peter K., *A Prussian Goldminer's Tale: From Childhood, through Boyhood to Manhood and Marriage* (2013), 5.
6. Hans Lindenberg, *Montagskind. Erinnerungen*, Vol. 1 (1990), 39. For similar problems encountered by members of the SS in this regard, see Bastian Hein, *Elite für Volk und Führer? Die Allgemeine SS und ihre Mitglieder 1925–1945* (Munich, 2012), 133–4.
7. This holds true when considering extant academic accounts, as well as published memoirs by former pupils. On the *Aufnahmebedingungen* per se, see the Introduction.
8. For examples of such frictions, see Brandenburgisches Landeshauptarchiv (BLHA), Rep. 2A II Gen Nr. 1294, Bl. 44–5; Landeshauptarchiv Sachsen-Anhalt, Abteilung Magdeburg (LHASA-MD), Rep. C 28 II, Nr. 2361, Bl. 19–20, 28–30.
9. For instance, at NPEA Ballenstedt, *Jungmannen* currently attending the Napola might be asked to assist their *Erzieher* with the pre-selection examinations. N.B. Matters were slightly different for those NPEA in the conquered Eastern and Western territories during World War II, and at the Napolas for girls (see further Chapter 8 and Chapter 9). On the differences between the NPEA in Saxony, Anhalt, and Württemberg and those in Prussia prior to the unification of the Napola system in 1941, see Chapter 5.
10. From this perspective, we might compare the expansionist dreams of the NPEA with the regime's equally grandiose dreams of Eastern colonization—there simply did not exist enough people within the Reich who were both willing and able to become settlers in the occupied Eastern territories, just as there did not exist enough willing and qualified youths to fill the projected number of places at all of the Napolas, especially during a time of total war.
11. One could just imagine the local government Twitter-feed in the age of social media: 'Just got our recruitment report in from @NPEA_Oranienstein—so pleased with our results: 25% of our boys got in! ☺'
12. In order to get around this problem, some Napolas began to cast the invitation to the pre-selection tests as a 'compulsory call-up notice' (*Einberufungsbefehl*), in the hope that candidates and their families would assume that they had no choice but to attend—cf. Brenner, 'Erfahrungsbericht, zusammengestellt von Hundertschaftsführer Brenner [NPEA Ballenstedt]. Betr: Jungmannen-Auslese', April 1944 (LHASA-MD, Rep. C 28 II, Nr. 2361, Bl. 130–7).
13. Of course, it might well appear to be in eyewitnesses' interest to suggest that their sojourn at a Nazi elite-school had been a matter of coercion rather than individual or parental choice—hence, such adumbrations should be treated with a certain degree of scepticism.
14. For an analysis of some more detailed case studies, see my forthcoming collaborative article with Lisa Pine, provisionally entitled '*Zwischen Auslese und Ausmerze*: The Biopolitics of Education in the Third Reich's "Special Schools" and "Elite Schools"', based on our contributions to a panel at the German History Society Conference in September 2019. N.B. For simplicity's sake, I have referred here to 'primary schools'

and 'primary-school teachers' throughout, since the majority of the Napolas' efforts at recruitment were aimed in this direction. However, those NPEA with *Aufbauzüge*, which received an extra intake of pupils at around the age of 14, also had to engage with teachers at middle-schools (*Hauptschulen* or *Mittelschulen*).

15. Brenner, 'Erfahrungsbericht', Bl. 130.
16. Niedersächsisches Landesarchiv—Hauptstaatsarchiv Hannover (NLA-HStAH), Hann. 180 Lüneburg Acc. 3/88 Nr. 26, report by Kemper dated 25 April 1940.
17. Cf. e.g. Staatsarchiv Ludwigsburg (StAL), E 202 Bü 1746, letter from Gräter dated 3 November 1936.
18. Cf. e.g. BLHA, Rep. 2A II Gen Nr. 1294, Bl. 25–6, 'Merkblatt für die Lehrer der Volksschulen', also Bl. 36; NLA-HStAH, Hann. 180 Lüneburg Acc. 3/88 Nr. 26, letters from Holthoff and Kemper, NPEA Bensberg, dated 14 June 1938, 20 June 1939, 22 May 1940.
19. E.g. NLA-HStAH, Hann. 180 Lüneburg Acc. 3/88 Nr. 26, letter dated 6 May 1940.
20. E.g. 'Nationalpolitische Erziehung. Neuaufnahmen zu Ostern 1936 in Bensberg', *National-Zeitung*, 29 December 1935 [BArch, NS 5/VI/18840]; 'Erziehung zu ganzen Männern. Aufnahme in die Nationalpolitischen Erziehungsanstalten', *Stuttgarter NS-Kurier*, 23 November 1936 [StAL, E 202 Bü 1746]; cf. Brenner, 'Erfahrungsbericht', Bl. 130.
21. E.g. Hessisches Staatsarchiv Darmstadt (HStAD), G15 Alsfeld M 437; LHASA-MD, Rep. C 28 II Nr. 2361, Bl. 57–8; Landesarchiv Nordrhein-Westfalen, Abteilung Westfalen, Münster (LNRW-M), Regierung Arnsberg, Nr. 31779 and Nr. 31780, letter dated 14 August 1940; Niedersächsisches Landesarchiv—Staatsarchiv Oldenburg (NLA-StAOL), Best. 134 Nr. 2353, Bl. 79–81.
22. Cf. 'Jungen der Napola spielen mit im Film. "Kopf hoch, Johannes!" wird gegenwärtig von Victor de Kowa gedreht', *Thüringer Gauzeitung*, 29 July 1940 [Kreisarchiv Nordhausen]; also Harald Scholtz, '*Unsere Jungen*. Ein Film der Nationalpolitischen Erziehungsanstalten', *Filmdokumente zur Zeitgeschichte*, G 128 (1969), 285–302; Klaus-Peter Horn, '"Unsere Jungen". Zur Darstellung der Praxis der Nationalpolitischen Erziehungsanstalten im Film', in Klaus-Peter Horn et al., eds, *Pädagogik im Militarismus und Nationalsozialismus. Japan und Deutschland im Vergleich* (Bad Heilbrunn, 2006), 141–9. On youth propaganda films in the Third Reich more generally, see e.g. Barbara Stelzner-Large, *Der Jugend zur Freude? Untersuchungen zum propagandistischen Jugendspielfilm im Dritten Reich* (Weimar, 1996).
23. E.g. Arne Heinich, *'Niemand entgeht seiner Zeit': Erziehung, Lernen und Leben in der Nationalpolitischen Erziehungsanstalt (Napola) Bensberg bei Köln. September 1942 bis April 1945* (Norderstedt, 2007), 19; Eckhard R., private correspondence, 25 February 2012; Karl-Heinz Lübke, private correspondence, 29 September 2011.
24. 'Nachtrag', *Spandauer Blätter* 28, Kriegsausgabe 13 (April 1942), 45–6.
25. E.g. Staatsarchiv Freiburg (StAF), G 225/1 Nr. 127, letter dated 19 February 1943.
26. E.g. LHASA-MD, Rep. C 28 II Nr. 2361, Bl. 100; Brenner, 'Erfahrungsbericht', Bl. 130–1; Niedersächsisches Landesarchiv—Staatsarchiv Osnabrück (NLA-StAOS), Rep 430 Dez 400 Nr. 3131, esp. Kreisschulrat Lührmann, 'Bericht über die Besichtigung der Nationalpolitischen Erziehungsanstalt Bensberg vom 30. Oktober bis 2. November 1938'.
27. Cf. Generallandesarchiv Karlsruhe (GLAK), Bestand 235, Nr. 35344, esp. 'Besuch der Nationalpolitischen Erziehungsanstalten Backnang und Rottweil', report dated 27

June 1938 (interestingly, the comments on the NPEA by the representatives of the teacher-training college were not uniformly favourable); StAL, F 400 Bü 223, 'Zusammenarbeit mit Hochschulen für Lehrerbildung'.

28. StAL, F 400 Bü 223, decree dated 5 November 1938.
29. Cf. e.g. the correspondence contained in Landesarchiv Berlin, A. Rep. 044–08–535; LNRW-M, Regierung Arnsberg, Nr. 31779 and Nr. 31780; NLA-HStAH, Hann. 180 Lüneburg Acc. 3/88 Nr. 26.
30. E.g. NLA-HStAH, Hann. 180 Lüneburg Acc. 3/88 Nr. 26, letter dated 6 May 1940; Holthoff, 'Anhang: Warum soll die Meldung der Jungen durch die Erzieher ohne jede Rücksicht auf die Eltern und deren Pläne erfolgen? Warum sollen die Eltern von der Meldung nicht in Kenntnis gesetzt werden?'; cf. NLA-StAOL, Best. 134 Nr. 2352, Bl. 37. NPEA Emsland, however, appears to have practised an opposing strategy, asking teachers explicitly to tell parents that their sons had been pre-selected, in order to prevent the waste of effort occasioned by the recruitment of pupils whose parents would ultimately oppose their changing schools: cf. NLA-HStAH, Hann. 180 Lüneburg Acc. 3/88 Nr. 26, letter from NPEA Emsland dated 10 March 1942.
31. E.g. Holthoff, 'Anhang'; Staatsarchiv Hamburg (StAH), 3361–2 VI Nr. 604, letter dated 16 November 1944.
32. NLA-HStAH, Hann. 180 Lüneburg Acc. 3/88 Nr. 26, letter from Kreisschulrat Marburg dated 18 January 1938.
33. On collaboration with local *Gesundheitsämter*, see e.g. StAH, 3361–2 VI Nr. 604, letter dated 6 September 1944; for reports on the results of the *Vormusterung*, see e.g. LNRW-M, Regierung Arnsberg, Nr. 31780, NPEA Oranienstein, 'Bericht über die Aufnahmeprüfung', report dated 27 March 1940.
34. Cf. NLA-HStAH, Hann. 180 Lüneburg Acc. 3/88 Nr. 26, letter from NPEA Naumburg dated 1 August 1937.
35. Cf. Otto Calliebe, 'Gedanken zur Entwicklung der Nationalpolitischen Erziehungsanstalten (NPEA)', (1969), 7–9.
36. Calliebe, 'Gedanken', 7–9.
37. Calliebe, 'Gedanken', 8–9.
38. Calliebe, 'Gedanken', 9; cf. HStAD, G 15 Lauterbach 577, letter dated 11 November 1939.
39. For an example, see Hans Schoenecker, *Lebenserinnerungen 1928–1960* (2007), 10.
40. E.g. Landeshauptarchiv Koblenz (LHAKO), Bestand 662,008 Nr. 14, letter dated 11 February 1937.
41. LHAKO, Bestand 662,008 Nr. 14, letter dated 11 February 1937; cf. Schoenecker, *Lebenserinnerungen*, 12.
42. N.B. It should be noted that all of the accounts cited below stem from personal recollections or memoirs from the post-war period, and may therefore to some extent serve an exculpatory function.
43. Günter L., private correspondence (publicity flyer), 15 December 2012; Hinrich Kattentidt, private correspondence, 29 January 2013; cf. Helen Roche, 'Die Klosterschule Ilfeld als Nationalpolitische Erziehungsanstalt', in Detlef Schmiechen-Ackermann et al., eds, *Die Klosterkammer Hannover 1931–1955. Eine Mittelbehörde zwischen wirtschaftlicher Rationalität und Politisierung* (Göttingen, 2018), 605–26, 625.

44. For examples, see Armin Eise, 'Betrachtungen', 1–2; Manfred Klotz, *Trotzdem groß geworden! Jugenderfahrungen eines kleinen Mannes* (Norderstedt, 2000), 93–6; Dietrich Geyer, *Reußenkrone, Hakenkreuz und roter Stern. Ein autobiographischer Bericht* (Göttingen, 1999), 46; Manfred B., 'Antworten zu den Nationalpolitischen Erziehungsanstalten im Nazi-Deutschland: Nationalpolitische Erziehungsanstalt Rottweil' (private correspondence, 5 March 2015). The concerns of long-suffering mothers with many children to look after often loom large in these accounts; Rüdiger B. of NPEA Spandau also recalled that it was decided that it would be better for him to go to boarding school because his mother had just filed for a divorce (private correspondence, 8 February 2011).
45. Hans-Joachim Männig, 'Schulpforta: NPEA im Krieg', *Die Pforte. Schulpforta-Nachrichten. Zeitschrift des Pförtner Bundes e.V.* 51 (1998), 15–19.
46. Dietrich Schulz, *Meine Napolazeit in Putbus 1941–1945* (2013), 1. On the Napolas' involvement with filming *Kadetten*, see Chapter 4 below.
47. NPEA Bensberg was one of the few Napolas which, like the Adolf-Hitler-Schools, did demand that applicants' political reliability be certified—this was evidently a decision which was left to individual *Anstaltsleiter* to determine. On the sons of oppositional parents attending an NPEA, see Arnulf Moser, *Die Napola Reichenau. Von der Heil- und Pflegeanstalt zur nationalsozialistischen Eliteerziehung (1941–1945)* (Konstanz, 1997), 60; also Hans Günther Zempelin, *Des Teufels Kadett: Napola-Schüler von 1936 bis 1943. Gespräch mit einem Freund* (Frankfurt am Main, 2000), 43–4; Harald Schäfer, *NAPOLA: Die letzten vier Jahre der Nationalpolitischen Erziehungsanstalt Oranienstein bei Diez an der Lahn 1941–1945. Eine Erlebnis-Dokumentation* (Frankfurt am Main, 1997), 67, n. 55.
48. Interview with Hans Habermann, 13 November 2017; cf. Peter Hoffmann, *The History of the German Resistance, 1933–1945*, 3rd edn (Montreal, 1996), 33–4.
49. Hans-Hoyer von P., private correspondence, 2 April 2013.
50. Manfred F., private correspondence, 4 September 2011.
51. Kurt Schwechheimer, *Mein Leben* (unpublished typescript, n.d.), 12–13.
52. Eugen K., private correspondence, 28 April 2017.
53. Karl Dürrschmidt, *Mit 15 in den Krieg. Ein Napola-Schüler berichtet* (Graz, 2004), 10–11. We might connect such initiatives with broader drives in Nazi youth policy to alienate and separate children from their parents (see further below).
54. Hugo Selke, *Auch eine Jugend in Deutschland. Meine Schulzeit in Ilfeld und Schulpforte 1935–1939* (1990), 5.
55. A letter from Vice-Inspector Calliebe written in May 1939 suggests that, over time, the Inspectorate became more concerned not to 'embitter' parents by forcing them to expend time, effort, and money in order to provide a whole swathe of genealogical documents before their son's admission to a Napola was fully assured (the Inspectorate had decided that candidates' fathers' personal assurance concerning their 'Aryan ancestry' should be deemed sufficient at the pre-examination stage). From this perspective, Calliebe suggested that all of the NPEA should refrain from requesting any document which might force parents to spend money in its acquisition (including passport photographs) until after a firm acceptance had been agreed (StAL, E 202 Bü 1747, letter from the Inspectorate dated 19 May 1939). Until the 1940s, however, parents were still required to pay the relevant expenses for travel and board and lodging,

although some Napolas might offer refunds or provide financial assistance for less well-off families. Later on, the NSV would cover all of these costs, if required, except the 0.20 RM cost of insuring each candidate, which meant that parents could no longer use lack of funds as an excuse for not allowing their children to attend the examination (cf. Brenner, 'Erfahrungsbericht', Bl. 131–2).

56. Privatarchiv Adolf Morlang (PAAM), 'Extraanlage zu "Tagesbefehlen" 1939, Nachlass Zgf. Kurt B. (1906–79), ab 1936 NPEA Oranienstein', 1.
57. 'Extraanlage', 7.
58. 'Extraanlage', 2–5.
59. 'Extraanlage', 6. Interestingly, although these tests were not officially designated in the Order of the Day as '*Mutproben*', the activities described match these 'tests of courage' exactly.
60. 'Extraanlage', 4.
61. 'Extraanlage', 5.
62. 'Extraanlage', 7.
63. [Emilie] Spornhauer, *Tagebuch* (LHAKO, Bestand 662,008 Nr. 13), entries dated 31 March 1935 to 5 April 1935. On 6 April 1935, she noted that eighty of the 230 pupils had passed the entrance examination. For an official account of the *Aufnahmeprüfung* in 1935, see *Unterrichtsleiter* Köster's article in *Der Jungmann. Nationalpolitische Erziehungsanstalt Oranienstein/Lahn* 1, no. 1 (December 1935), 47, which states that around 150 pupils out of a total of five hundred had passed the examination that year, from a field of two thousand applications and registrations. The numerical discrepancy may be explained by the fact that the examination took place in two 'shifts'. Köster also encouraged current *Jungmannen* to recommend primary-school pupils whom they knew and who might be suitable candidates for the following year's examination, and to encourage them to apply to the NPEA by telling them positive tales of school life there.
64. Lindenberg, *Montagskind*, 40.
65. Hundertschaftsführer Dubslaff, 'Probewochen 1943', *Mitteilungen der Nationalpolitischen Erziehungsanstalt Naumburg/Saale*, 16. u. 17. Kriegsnummer (July/September 1943), 14–17; see also 'Erlebnisse und Erfahrungen während der Probewochen (Aus Aufsätzen des Zuges 4a)' in the same issue, 21–2, and Brenner, 'Erfahrungsbericht'.
66. Dubslaff, 'Probewochen'.
67. Brenner, 'Erfahrungsbericht', Bl. 136. These accounts provide an effective rebuttal of previous castigations by scholars such as Gisela Miller-Kipp (as mentioned in the Introduction) to the effect that the NPEA cared nothing whatsoever for the academic abilities of their pupils, and that their entrance tests were wholly intellectually exiguous (cf. e.g. Gisela Miller-Kipp, '"Klasse Schule—immer genug zu essen, wenig Mathematik". Elitebildung im "Dritten Reich" oder über die Herstellung von Elite-Bewusstsein', in Jutta Ecarius and Lothar Wigger, eds, *Elitebildung—Bildungselite. Erziehungswissenschaftliche Diskussionen und Befunde über Bildung und soziale Ungleichheit* (Opladen, 2006), 44–66.
68. Lindenberg, *Montagskind*, 40 (the solution being that all of the other sparrows would have flown away as soon as the gun had fired).
69. Cf. Dubslaff, 'Probewochen'; Lindenberg, *Montagskind*, 40.
70. E.g. Heinich, *Bensberg*, 34; Lindenberg, *Montagskind*, 40.

71. E.g. Lindenberg, *Montagskind*, 40; Selke, *Schulzeit*, 6.
72. E.g. Schoenecker, *Lebenserinnerungen*, 13–14; Eckhard R., private correspondence, 25 February 2012.
73. Dieter Eschenhagen, 'Auch ich war ein Eliteschüler Hitlers' (Oldenburg, 2000), 4–5.
74. E.g. Köster, 'Aufnahmeprüfung 1935', 47; 'Erlebnisse und Erfahrungen', 21–2.
75. E.g. '10 Jahre NPEA. Naumburg—ein Überblick. Von der "Stabila" zur "Napola"', *10 Jahre Nationalpolitische Erziehungsanstalt Naumburg an der Saale* (1944), 7–9; Eckhard R., private correspondence, 25 February 2012.
76. 'Der Nachwuchs erzählt', *Der Jungmann* 4, no. 6–7 (December 1938), 65–6.
77. E.g. Schoenecker, *Lebenserinnerungen*, 14.
78. Lindenberg, *Montagskind*, 51.
79. Cf. StAL, E 202 Bü 1746, letter dated 27 April 1937; StAL, E 202 Bü 1747, letter dated 29 April 1939; Heinz Winkler and Hans Worpitz, *Die Nationalpolitischen Erziehungsanstalten (NPEA) und ihre Jungmannen. Berichte, Entwicklungen und Erlebnisse von Jungmannen der NPEA Loben/Annaberg* (2003), 41; Bundesarchiv Lichterfelde (BArch), R 4901/5272, Bl. 1. On expected attrition rates, see BArch, R 2/19991, 'Erläuterungen zu dem Muster eines Kassenanschlages für eine Nationalpolitische Erziehungsanstalt'; in the 'room programme' for new-build NPEA, the administrative authorities actually calculated the amount of space needed for each year-group by reckoning that one or two *Jungmannen* would drop out of each class (*Erziehungsgemeinschaft*) every year for the first five years at the school (BArch, R 2/12711, 'Raumprogramm für die Neubauten der Nationalpolitischen Erziehungsanstalten mit grundständigem Zug').
80. Lindenberg, *Montagskind*, 55.
81. Adapted from Otto Schäfer, 'Ziel und Gestalt der nationalpolitischen Erziehungsanstalten', *Nationalsozialistisches Bildungswesen* 7, no. 1 (1942), 19–31, 25–6.
82. E.g. Georg Hempel, 'Der Wert der Fahrt für die Nationalpolitischen Erziehungsanstalten' (1935), 2–3; Reinhard Wagner, *Mehr sein als scheinen. Vier Jahre Jungmann in der NPEA Rottweil* (Ditzingen, 1998), 34–5. Wagner noted that some pupils might attempt to get out of early-morning sport by spending too long on the lavatory.
83. That the NPEA authorities were keen to ensure that their charges benefited from a sufficiently balanced diet is suggested by experiments carried out by the Reich Department of Health (*Reichsgesundheitsamt*) at NPEA Potsdam—cf. BArch, R 86/3563 and R 86/3564; also R 86/3529. For both 'breakfasts', boys would usually be provided with bread and butter with jam or honey and coffee. A fairly substantial three-course meal would be served at lunchtime, followed by more rolls and coffee at the afternoon break, and, in the evening, a light supper—see also Schlunke, *First English Textbook* (Potsdam, n.d.), 21–2.
84. For instance, Friedrich-Wilhelm J.s' mother wrote in her diary on 4 May 1941: 'Friedrich-Wilhelm's first letters and postcards have arrived from the NPEA in Naumburg. Now he has to accustom himself to the strict atmosphere and life away from home. Despite everything, he seems to be having a lot of fun, especially when marching out with fife and drum'—cf. Friedrich-Wilhelm J., *In jenen Jahren*, 11.
85. Peter B., private correspondence, September 2011.

86. Joachim Doedter, 'Erinnerungen—Heimweh'.
87. Martin Meissner, *Times Past. Memoirs Ending When I Was Thirty-One Years Old* (2008), ch. 3. The fairly compassionate and conciliatory letter which Martin's form-teacher sent to his mother after his departure also exemplifies the sheer amount of bureaucracy involved even when a boy left the school after a relatively brief period of time. This included sending on the pupil's police de-registration, his school report, and the settling of any relevant bills and accounts, as well as making arrangements for remaining belongings to be returned, and the potential buying-back of any textbooks which would not be needed at his new school (Zugführer Seidel to Frau K. Meissner, correspondence dated 22 September 1939).
88. See Chapter 4; also Roche, *Sparta's German Children*.
89. Günter Graffenberger, *Vom Memel bis Stockholm: Erinnerungen eines auslandsdeutschen Journalisten* (Osnabrück, 2002), 25. Dirk van de Walle of NPEA Ilfeld recalled that, on this score, his Napola-training stood him in good stead when he came to join the SS later on: 'We all had our own cupboard with whatever one owned and one of the first shows of military authority came with a *Stuben- und Spindappell* (an inspection of our room and cupboard). As expected by such a first inspection, the responsible inspector just pulled the cupboard over emptying everything onto the floor. Arriving at my cupboard he opened the door and stood perplexed at what he saw. He called his superior, the sergeant on duty, in order to have a witness of this impossibility; he shouted: "whose is this and where did you learn this?" "In the Napola, sergeant!" Convincing enough, both gave me the job to fix their own cupboard immediately. I must say that after two years of Napola discipline nothing in one's cupboard was 1 mm. out of place'—cf. Dirk van de Walle, *Memories of My Youth in National Socialist Germany* (2018), 24–5.
90. Henning Lenthe, *Lenthe Familiengeschichte Teil 2—Henning mit Eltern und Geschwistern von 1934–1955* (1997), 50. At a headmasters' conference (*Anstaltsleitertagung*) in 1937, it was suggested that the youngest boys should not be required to make their beds if sufficient non-teaching staff were available to undertake this task: cf. StAL, E 202 Bü 1746, 'Niederschrift über die Anstaltsleitertagung in der Nationalpolitischen Erziehungsanstalt in Stuhm bezw. in dem Zeltlager am Geserichsee vom 23.-27. Juni 1937'.
91. Steffen Wagner (private archive), Interview with Karl S.
92. Cf. e.g. Walter Flemming, 'Ehemalige Schüler der Nationalpolitischen Erziehungsanstalt Ilfeld/Südharz äußern sich über ihre Erlebnisse in der Anstalt. Walter Flemming—Interview durch eine Studentin' (1984), 9–10.
93. Schäfer, 'Ziel und Gestalt', 26–7.
94. E.g. Steche, *Jahresbericht der Nationalpolitischen Erziehungsanstalt Ilfeld über das Schuljahr 1934/35* (1935), 18–19; Karl-Josef Franke, *Erinnerungen aus den Jahren 1941–1945* (n.d.), 38.
95. On the use of the cadet-school ranking system, see Chapter 4; on the militarization of school life more generally, see Österreichisches Staatsarchiv (ÖStA), BEA 164, letter dated 9 December 1938. On one recently promoted *Hauptzugführer* getting shirty with a *Jungmann* who had still addressed him merely as '*Zugführer*', see Joachim Doedter, *Erinnerungen NPEA Neubeuern 1942–1945*, 6–7. On guard duty or '*Wache*', see e.g. Peter Gerlach, *Lebenserinnerungen* (2007), 55.

96. Schlunke, *First English Textbook*, 33.
97. Cf. Gottfried Wirths, *Vom Jagdschloss zur National-Politischen Erziehungs-Anstalt. Geschichte des Bensberger Schlosses / Tagebuch* (n.d.).
98. Schlunke, *First English Textbook*, 4–5, 14.
99. Schlunke, *First English Textbook*, 16. It is worth noting that the different schools often sported slightly different uniforms—some favoured the form of Hitler-Youth style kit described here, while others' were more cadet-like in their style or colours. Thus, one former pupil of NPEA Spandau recalled his pride in the fact that his school's olive-green uniforms did not resemble those of the Hitler Youth—cf. Wilfried von Kalckstein, *Jahrgang 1920: Gestempelt und geprägt* (Rodowo, 2012), 52.
100. Schoenecker, *Lebenserinnerungen*, 14; cf. Th. Kleinschmidt, 'Unsere neue Uniform!' *Die Brücke: Nachrichten von der Nationalpolitischen Erziehungsanstalt Köslin* 7, no. 3 (August 1934), 52–3; *Mitteilungen der Nationalpolitischen Erziehunganstalt Naumburg/Saale*, 18. Kriegsnummer (October 1943), 16. On the importance of uniforms for constructing elite identities under Nazism, see e.g. Daniel Mühlenfeld, 'The Pleasures of Being a "Political Soldier": Nazi Functionaries and Their Service to the "Movement"', in Pamela E. Swett, Corey Ross, and Fabrice d'Almeida, eds, *Pleasure and Power in Nazi Germany* (Basingstoke, 2011), 204–33, 212; Christopher Dillon, *Dachau and the SS: A Schooling in Violence* (Oxford, 2015), 202.
101. Gerd Stehle, *Fliegen—nichts als fliegen. Pilot in Krieg und Frieden* (Berg am Starnberger See, 2001), 51.
102. For a description, see Arnold Janssen, 'Die Kunst der Strafe im Erziehungswesen auf der Mittelstufe einer Nationalpolitischen Erziehungsanstalt: Ein Ausschnitt aus der Erziehertätigkeit' (1934), 53, Bibliothek für Bildungsgeschichtliche Forschung (DIPF), GUT ASS 628.
103. E.g. Walter Becker, *Erinnerungen an die NAPOLA Naumburg. Ein über die 'Kadette Naumburg' hinausgehender Beitrag zur Geschichte der NPEA* (Neustrelitz, 2000), 185.
104. E.g. Erhard W. Schmidt, *Großvater packt aus* (2006), 17–19.
105. Hartmut Vahl, *Napola Schulpforta 1943–1945. Erinnerungen eines Schülers* (Hamburg, 2000), 6–7, 12–13.
106. Jürgen Schach von Wittenau, *Blown Away (or: Just Keep Walking…)* (n.d.), 55–6.
107. Cf. Hartmut Schlottke, *Osten—Westen: Danzig Finale. Erinnerung an eine verlorene Zeit 1930 bis 1945* (n.d.), 37–40.
108. E.g. Eschenhagen, 'Eliteschüler Hitlers', 8a. Eschenhagen comments that this sort of bullying was often passed down from one generation of *Jungmannen* to another—those who had suffered it desired to inflict that same suffering in their turn. For similar types of bullying at the Prussian cadet schools, see Roche, *Sparta's German Children*—although the forms of hazing employed there were arguably far more brutal and torturous, even leading in some cases to pupils' death.
109. Schach von Wittenau, *Blown Away*, 56–7.
110. On the cadet-school equivalents of these ranks, see Chapter 4.
111. See the relevant documents in Helmut-Albrecht Kraas, ed., *Napola Neuzelle (ehem. Kreis Guben/Mark Brandenburg)—eine Dokumentation*, Bd. 1 (1993–4).
112. Dietrich Schulz, private correspondence, 30 December 2009.
113. Klotz, *Trotzdem groß geworden*, 104.
114. Cf. Flemming, 'Interview', 36.

115. PAAM, Nachlass Kurt B., Tagesbefehl 34/38 (3 December 1938), §4.
116. Armin Eise, 'Betrachtungen', 5.
117. E.g. Schäfer, *NAPOLA*, 87; Eugen K., private correspondence, 28 April 2017; von Kalckstein, *Jahrgang 1920*, 53.
118. E.g. Spornhauer, *Tagebuch*; Lindenberg, *Montagskind*, 91; Bach and Bergfeldt, 'Spiel mit der Eisenbahn', *Die Brücke* 11, no. 4/5 (February 1939), 86; 'Die große Schlacht zwischen Autounion und Mercedes', *Spandauer Blätter* 7 (20 October 1936), 32. The NPEA Inspectorate deliberately intended every school to have enough space for a dedicated play-room for the younger boys, with sufficient cupboards for modelling equipment, stamp and photograph albums, cameras, tennis rackets, construction kits, and model railway sets; cf. BArch, R 2/27776, letter dated 26 September 1941; BArch, R 2/27779, letter dated 1 September 1943.
119. Schwechheimer, *Mein Leben*, 46, 80–6; Arnulf H. K. Putzar, *Im Schatten einer Zeit* (Schwerin, 1998), 75.
120. Georges Vermandel, '"Lausbuben" vernichteten europäisches Kulturgut. Der Brand im Nordflügel des Bensberger Schlosses im März 1942—Damaliger Ablauf nach 50 Jahren erstmals genau rekonstruiert—Ein "Jungenstreich"', *Rheinisch-Bergischer Kalender* 65 (1995), 30–5. The fall-out of this incident led to concentration-camp prisoners being used to repair the extensive damage to the building—see further Chapter 10.
121. StAH, 213–11 Nr. 0162/40.
122. *Der Napola Beobachter*—1. Ausgabe, 6. Jg., Spandauer Ausgabe (17 February 1938).
123. *Der Napola Beobachter*.
124. *Die Meute. Das Buch einer Gemeinschaft* (Lötzen, n.d.), 101–8.
125. Gerd-Bruno Ludwig and Ernst-Christian Gädtke, eds, *Jahrgang '45. 1937 bis 1944 und 60 Jahre danach. Erlebt, berichtet und reflektiert von Überlebenden eines Jahrgangs der NPEA Spandau* (2004), 12–13, 59–61; Friedrich-Wilhelm J., *In jenen Jahren*, 17; Lindenberg, *Montagskind*, 133; Schulz, *Napolazeit*, 21; Winkler and Worpitz, *Loben*.
126. Kurt Meyer, *Gelobt sei, was hart macht! Fröhliche, unbeschwerte, aber harte Jahre auf der NPEA* (2003), 22. For an example of pupils using the medium of song to mock the school authorities at NPEA Schulpforta, and being harshly punished for their temerity, see Chapter 10.
127. Cf. LHAKO, 700,238 Nr. 9, letter dated 6 January 1943. For an example of a highly intellectual *Jungmann* from a deeply Christian background struggling to reconcile National Socialist ideology with his finer feelings, see Harald R., *Tagebuch*.
128. StAL, E 202 Bü 1747, 'Voraussichtlicher Jahresplan für die Zeit Ostern 1939—Ostern 1940'; Sächsisches Hauptstaatsarchiv Dresden (SHStAD), 11125 Nr. 21351, Bl. 164.
129. *Die Kameradschaft. Blätter der Nationalpolitischen Erziehungsanstalt Plön* 4, no. 2/3 (April 1939), 4. On the international exchanges and 'mining missions' which would have led to some of these more exotic-sounding encounters, see Chapter 3.
130. For similar reflections on the embedded social status of the *Ordensburgen*, see Thomas Roth and Stefan Wunsch, 'Vogelsang in der Region. Die NS-Ordensburg im Fokus der regionalgeschichtlichen Forschung', in Albert Moritz, ed., *'Fackelträger der Nation'. Elitebildung in den NS-Ordensburgen* (Cologne, 2010), 136–98.
131. E.g. Landeshauptarchiv Sachsen-Anhalt, Abteilung Dessau, K 13 Ballenstedt, Nr. 401, Bl. 283.

132. For lists of roles required within each school, see 'Erläuterungen zu dem Muster eines Kassenanschlags'; for a list of the actual staff employed at NPEA Spandau in 1938, see 'Aus der Gefolgschaft', *Spandauer Blätter* 12 (3 February 1938), 16–19. Many schools made a significant effort both to make their support staff feel included, and to assure them that they were a valuable asset to the school community. This might include presenting them with awards for loyal service (indeed, some staff at the longer-established NPEA had worked there since the cadet-school days), taking them on expenses-paid trips out, and organizing in-house parties and entertainments for them. In addition, some Napolas occasionally gave their personnel the opportunity to describe their activities and experiences in their school newsletters—e.g. 'Von der Betriebsgemeinschaft', *NPEA Neuzelle*, 18. Kriegsbrief (June 1944), 47–53. Although there is too little space to go into detail here, it would be fascinating fully to explore the experiences of the predominantly female personnel in what has normally been considered to be the wholly masculine world of the NPEA. An initial step in this direction, following my discovery of a journal belonging to NPEA Oranienstein's house-matron at the Landeshauptarchiv Koblenz, has recently been made by Adolf Morlang: 'Als Frau in einer Männerwelt: Das Tagebuch der sog. "Hausdame" der NPEA Oranienstein', *Heimatjahrbuch Rhein-Lahn-Kreis* (2016), 64–7.
133. E.g. *Nationalpolitische Erziehungsanstalt Stuhm im Aufbau* (Königsberg, 1938), 64–5.
134. *Stuhmer Altkameradschaft*, 4. Rundbrief (1939), 17–18; Staf., *10 Jahre NPEA Plön. Sonderheft der Kameradschaft* (Kiel, 1943), 39. In this connection, *Anstaltsleiter* Brunk of Plön, the headmaster in question, noted that the rumours had reached such a pitch that the Gestapo had 'had to get involved'.
135. E.g. Stehle, *Fliegen*, 48. On the prevalence of such elitism at the NPEA more generally, see e.g. Eckhard R., private correspondence, 25 February 2012.
136. Klotz, *Trotzdem groß geworden*, 118; cf. Wagner, *Mehr sein als scheinen*, 160–6; Selke, *Schulzeit*, 36.
137. Geheimes Staatsarchiv Preußischer Kulturbesitz (GStAPK), I. HA Rep. 151, Nr. 3929, Bl. 23–5; GStAPK, I. HA Rep. 151 IV, Nr. 2735, Bl. 166–8; BArch, R 2/28072, report dated 9 May 1936; BArch, R 2/12730, 'Bericht über die durchgeführte eingehende Geschäftsprüfung bei der Nationalpolitischen Erziehungsanstalt Stuhm' (21 April 1942); Zentralarchiv des Bezirksverbands Pfalz, T 21 Nr. 27, 'Bericht über die Besichtigung der nationalpolitischen Erziehungsanstalt Oranienstein bei Diez an der Lahn am 15. und 16. Oktober 1936'.
138. E.g. Klaus Kleinau, *Im Gleichschritt, marsch! Der Versuch einer Antwort, warum ich von Auschwitz nichts wusste. Lebenserinnerungen eines NS-Eliteschülers der Napola Ballenstedt* (Hamburg, 2000), 39; Manfred B., 'Antworten zu den Nationalpolitischen Erziehungsanstalten im Nazi-Deutschland. Nationalpolitische Erziehungsanstalt Rottweil', private correspondence, 5 March 2015; Karl-Josef Franke, *Erinnerungen*, 52; Wagner, *Mehr sein als scheinen*, 84.
139. Gerlach, *Lebenserinnerungen*, 50; Schoenecker, *Lebenserinnerungen*, 15; Helmuth J., 'Stellungnahme zum Weihnachtsrundbrief 1976', 5–7 (SHStAD, 13771 Nr. 7). On adolescents' experience of such tensions in Nazi culture more generally, see Heidi Rosenbaum, *'Und trotzdem war's 'ne schöne Zeit': Kinderalltag im Nationalsozialismus* (Frankfurt am Main, 2014), 232, 241.

140. E.g. Gerd-Bruno Ludwig, 'Landliebe', in Ludwig and Gädtke, *Jahrgang '45*; Manfred B., 'Antworten'; Friedrich G., private correspondence, 16 December 2012.
141. Kraas, *Napola Neuzelle*, Bd. 2, 42; cf. Zugführer Blanke, 'Feiern in Räumen unserer Gemeinschaft', *NPEA Neuzelle*, 6. Kriegsbrief (April 1941), 18–19.
142. E.g. Dürrschmidt, *Mit 15 in den Krieg*, 19; Hans-Hoyer von P., private correspondence, 4 December 2009.
143. Helmuth J., 'Stellungnahme', 8.
144. Wagner, *Mehr sein als scheinen*, 25; Helga Rasch, *Mokritz—Mein Jugendtraum und was aus ihm wurde: Erinnerungen* (Deutsches Tagebucharchiv Emmendingen, 75.2).
145. Bodo Helms, *Von Anfang an dabei. Mein abenteuerliches Fliegerleben 1939–1980* (Berg am Starnberger See, [2000]), 28–9.
146. Dieter Pfeiffer, *War Phoebes Opa wirklich zehn Jahre im Knast? Der ganz persönliche Blick zurück: Eliteschüler—Soldat—Kriegsgefangener. Eine Hilfe zum Verstehen oder Respektieren. Dankbarkeit für das, was danach kam* (2004), 11.
147. The correspondence between State Secretary Hans Pfundtner and his son Reinhardt exemplifies this type of parental relationship perfectly (BArch, R 1501/5656).
148. Cf. Schäfer, *NAPOLA*, 16, 197; Geyer, *Reußenkrone*, 51. Parents who flouted this rule would be given short shrift by the school authorities.
149. G. Drescher, *Erinnerungen—NPEA Neuzelle* (Institut für Zeitgeschichte, Munich [IfZ], ED 735-5), 16.
150. Graffenberger, *Vom Memel bis Stockholm*, 35–7.
151. E.g. 'Elternstunde', *Nationalpolitische Erziehungsanstalt Sudetenland: Blätter*, 2. Folge (New Year [*Jahreswende*] 1941–2), 34–7. While it is true that the medical provision at the schools appears to have been above average in general, the gruelling physical demands of the curriculum could lead to pupils developing congenital weaknesses or suffering unfortunate accidents (e.g. Kalckstein, *Jahrgang 1920*, 59; Schmidt, *Großvater packt aus*, 19; *Im Gleichschritt* 2, no. 4 (May 1941), 105; Gerd Siegel, 'Ein ehemaliger Erzieher der NPEA Bensberg schrieb an seine Frau (Auszüge aus einem intensiven Briefwechsel)', letter to Herr Koch dated 3 May 1942; *Oraniensteiner Rundbrief*, Nr. 14 (15 July 1943). In at least one instance of this kind, the boy's father attempted to sue one of the schools for medical malpractice—cf. GStAPK, I. HA Rep. 151, Nr. 1095, Bl. 197–205. For an example of a school doctor's annual report on one of the NPEA in Württemberg, see Staatsarchiv Sigmaringen, Wü 66/12 T 3 Nr. 13—in general, outbreaks of illnesses such as diphtheria and scarlet fever were not uncommon.
152. E.g. Rudolf Wasmann, Nachlass (copies courtesy of Arne Heinich). Wasmann was an *Erzieher* at NPEA Bensberg.
153. E.g. IfZ, ED 735-8-3, invitation to a parents' afternoon at NPEA Potsdam dated 21 September 1941; see also Chapter 3.
154. 'Niederschrift über die Anstaltsleitertagung'.
155. Spornhauer, *Tagebuch*; for a former pupil's view, see Zempelin, *Des Teufels Kadett*, 109–10.
156. E.g. Schoenecker, *Lebenserinnerungen*, 23–4; Kraas, *Napola Neuzelle*, Bd. 2, 58.
157. Flemming, 'Interview', 30.
158. 'Die Stunde der Hausmutter', *Ilfelder Blätter*, 22. Kriegsheft (March 1942), [423].
159. Harald R., *Tagebuch*, 17, entry dated 24 August 1943; see also below.

160. LNRW-D, RW 0023 Nr. 282, letter dated 19 December 1942. On the *Reichsschulen* in Holland and Bensberg's special relationship with them, see Chapter 8.
161. Selke, *Schulzeit*, 13–14.
162. Klaus Schikore, private correspondence, May 2011.
163. *Die Meute*, esp. p. 40.
164. Lindenberg, *Montagskind*, 68; Harry Bolte, *Ilfelder Erinnerungen 1936–1943* (n.d.), 10.
165. On disciplinary ideals at the NPEA, see in particular Janssen, 'Die Kunst der Strafe'.
166. Hans Dieter Pfeiffer, ed., *Nationalpolitische Erziehungsanstalt Spanheim in Lavanttal, Kärnten, Österreich, 1941–1945. Persönliche Niederschriften als eine Brücke des Verstehens* (n.d.), diary entries for February, March, April, June, and July 1943. For other examples of sadistic *Erzieher*, see Helmut Wigelbeyer, *Schicksal am Fluss. Autobiographischer Roman* (Berlin, 2012); Eschenhagen, 'Eliteschüler Hitlers', 6; Wagner, *Mehr sein als Scheinen*; cf. Peter Meuer, *Linien des Lebens: Eine Kindheit und Jugend im Schwäbischen und anderswo* (Stuttgart, 1991), 93.
167. Becker, *Naumburg*, 172.
168. Gerlach, *Lebenserinnerungen*, 53–4.
169. On the excision of religious studies, see also Roche, '"Wanderer, kommst du nach Pforta"', 595–6; Roche, 'Klosterschule Ilfeld'. On the ideologization of school-teaching in general, see Lisa Pine, *Education in Nazi Germany* (Oxford, 2010), ch. 3; also Kurt-Ingo Flessau, 'Schulen der Partei(lichkeit)? Notizen zum allgemeinbildenden Schulwesen des Dritten Reichs', in Kurt-Ingo Flessau, Elke Nyssen, and Günter Patzold, eds, *Erziehung im Nationalsozialismus. '...und sie werden nicht mehr frei ihr ganzes Leben!'* (Cologne, 1987), 65–82; Benjamin Ortmeyer, *Schulzeit unterm Hitlerbild. Analysen, Berichte, Dokumente* (Frankfurt am Main, 1996), 49–54; Wolfgang Keim, *Erziehung unter der Nazi-Diktatur Band II: Kriegsvorbereitung, Krieg und Holocaust* (Darmstadt, 1997); Richard J. Evans, *The Third Reich in Power* (London, 2006), 261–5.
170. For examples of the variety of slightly different curricula offered by (or even within) individual schools, see e.g. Hauptstaatsarchiv Stuttgart, M 600/37 Bü 415; StAL, E 202 Bü 1746, decree dated 20 March 1937; StAL, E 202 Bü 1749, 'Nationalpolitische Erziehungsanstalt Rottweil—Merkblatt für die Aufnahme Frühjahr 1940'. On Hellman's initiative, see '10 Jahre Arbeit an der deutschen Jugend—ein Querschnitt. Erziehung durch Unterricht und Leibesübungen', *10 Jahre NPEA Naumburg*, 32–9, 34; Becker, *Naumburg*, 126. On the Napolas' Germanizing programme in Eastern Europe, see further Chapter 3 and Chapter 8.
171. Cf. BArch, R 43-II/956b, Heißmeyer to Lammers, 'Bericht über die Arbeit der Nationalpolitischen Erziehungsanstalten', Bl. 51–78, Bl. 54–5.
172. Schlunke, *First English Textbook*; Fachgemeinschaft für Geschichte an der Nationalpolitischen Erziehungsanstalt Naumburg an der Saale, *Aufriß der deutschen Geschichte im 19. und 20. Jahrhundert. Von der französischen bis zur nationalsozialistischen Revolution und zur Gegenwart* (Leipzig: Teubner, 1941). At the headmasters' conference at NPEA Spandau in December 1936, the idea that the schools should put together their own series of textbooks had been mooted by *Anstaltsleiter* Prinz of NPEA Stuhm, but was ultimately postponed until after further consideration by *Erzieher* at the conferences held for individual subjects over the course of the next

year (StAL, E 202 Bü 1746, 'Niederschrift über die Anstaltsleiterbesprechung am 2.-3. Dezember 1936 in Berlin-Spandau', 5). For examples of the lists of textbooks which were used at various schools, see IfZ, ED 735–9; StAL, E 202 Bü 1746, catalogue of expenditure for NPEA Rottweil.

173. See the relevant catalogue of expenditure in StAL, E 202 Bü 1746.
174. 'Leistungsprüfung im Zugwettkampf', *10 Jahre NPEA Naumburg*, 64–9; SHStAD, 11125 Nr. 21351, *Mitteilungsblätter der Nationalpolitischen Erziehungsanstalten* 2 (December 1936), Bl. 33. Apparently the idea of broadening this type of competition to all of the schools, and having an annual academic contest to match the schools' annual sporting contests (see below) never bore fruit—cf. Rudolf Marggraf, ed., *Die Nationalpolitische Erziehungsanstalt Ilfeld. Sammlung der von 1934 bis 1944 herausgegebenen Ilfeld-Blätter—Ein Beitrag zur Zeitgeschichte* (1998), Bd. I, VIII. See also 'Die Bildungsaufgabe', *Nationalpolitische Erziehungsanstalt Potsdam-Neuzelle: Arbeitsbericht* (March 1937), 3–5.
175. E.g. Hundertschaftsführer Dr. Jung, 'Unsere unterrichtliche Erziehung', *Emsland: NPEA Haselünne* 2 (April 1944), in Marggraf, *Ilfeld*, Bd. II, 317–19, 319.
176. Cf. StAL, E 202 Bü 1746, 'Verzeichnis der im Filmarchiv der Nationalpolitischen Erziehungsanstalten vorhandenen Filme'; StAL, E 202 Bü 1747, letter dated 13 December 1939; Weber, 'Unser Tonfilm—Unser Schatz', *Spandauer Blätter*, Heft 8 (16 December 1936), 26–8. The film-catalogue included collections of ideological teaching-films from the SS-*Schulungsamt* (Education Department), such as 'Jewry I' (*Judentum I*), 'Freemasonry II' (*Freimaurerei II*), and 'Blood and Soil I and II' (*Blut und Boden I und II*).
177. See, for example, the relevant documents in StAL, E 202 Bü 1746 and 1747, especially the notes and programme from the biology teachers' conference held at Rankenheim, March 1938 (see further below).
178. Eichberger, 'Vom äußeren Leben unserer Anstalt', *Der deutsche Erzieher* (1937), 235–7, 236.
179. Jung, 'Unsere unterrichtliche Erziehung', 317; cf. Heinrich Olms, 'Jugend im Krieg—Bewährungsprobe der nationalsozialistischen Erziehung. "VB."-Gespräch mit dem Inspekteur der "Napola", SS-Obergruppenführer Heißmeyer', *Völkische Beobachter*, 5 November 1939 [BArch, NS 5/VI/18842].
180. Arne Heinich, interview with Rudolf Wasmann, 21 February 1987. For an example of a pupil's anxieties regarding expulsion, see Dieter Pfeiffer, ed., *So war es. NPEA Bensberg: Nationalpolitische Erziehungsanstalt Bensberg 1935–1945*, Vol. 1 (1998), 207, Hans Freiherr von Zedlitz diary, entry for 5 March 1937: 'Today, my first maths test missed the mark. Once again, not focused enough. In the last few weeks I simply haven't been able to pull myself together any more. So I've already made a mess of three tests. My fear is about what will happen at Easter. If I fail at Easter, I don't want to have to remain at home. Sometimes I feel so alone, as if there isn't a single person whom I can trust. I just don't know where it will end.'
181. Cf. Johannes Eggers, 'Ein Halbjahr 2 Wochenstunden organische Chemie auf der Nationalpolitischen Erziehungsanstalt' (DIPF, GUT ASS 259, 1936), 1.
182. See Chapter 12; also Helen Roche, 'Surviving "*Stunde Null*": Narrating the Fate of Nazi Elite-School Pupils during the Collapse of the Third Reich', *German History* 33, no. 4 (2015), 570–87.

183. From this perspective, the ideological instruction appears to have been much closer to that employed on SS training-courses at the *Junkerschulen*—cf. Hans-Christian Harten, *Himmlers Lehrer. Die Weltanschauliche Schulung in der SS 1933–1945* (Paderborn, 2014).
184. StAL, E 202 Bü 1746, notes from 'Biologentagung Rankenheim' (March 1938).
185. E.g. Zugführer Dr. Reichelt, 'Vom Biologieunterricht', *Rundbrief der NPEA Bensberg*, 16. Kriegsfolge (18 April 1943), 24–5; Werner Hauer, 'Über die Gestaltung eines vorbereitenden Lehrganges im Biologie-Unterricht der Sexta an der Nationalpolitischen Erziehungsanstalt Naumburg' (DIPF, GUT ASS 479, 1936).
186. Gerhard Hoop, 'Biologie', *Plön Rundbrief* 21 (November 1941), 22.
187. On the outfitting of the biology laboratory at NPEA Oranienstein, see GStAPK, I. HA Rep. 151, Nr. 1095, Bl. 149. Hans Günther Zempelin also remembered that Oranienstein was the only school in the district which owned life-size wax models of the human muscles and bowels, as well as a microscope-projector which allowed slides from a microscope to be projected onto a screen. There were enough microscopes to be shared one between every two pupils, and, in the chemistry and biology laboratories, every work-bench boasted its own gas and electricity connection point, which was unusual at that time (*Des Teufels Kadett*, 76).
188. Martin Itschert, cited in Marieluise Conradt, *Vom Königlichen Württembergischen Lehrerseminar zum Staatlichen Aufbaugymnasium des Landes Baden-Württemberg. 1912 bis 1994 in Rottweil: eine Schulchronik* (Rottweil, 1994), 41.
189. Wagner, *Mehr sein als scheinen*, 109–11; Eschenhagen, 'Eliteschüler Hitlers', 6–7; Hans Rettkowski, 'Das/mein Erbe der Napola. Vortrag im RC Oldenburg-Ammerland am 2.11.2000' (2000), 5. *Jungmannen* might then go on to use this kind of terminology to describe their peers or their teachers—just as they themselves might have been judged by such racial criteria during the selection process (see Chapters 1 and 2).
190. 'Schädelmessungen', *Die Brücke* 7, no. 1 (April/May 1934), 3–4.
191. Wagner, *Mehr sein als scheinen*, 111, 46. That many pupils at the NPEA did not necessarily fit the 'Aryan' stereotype (blond and blue-eyed), can be seen particularly clearly in a collection of passport photos from NPEA Potsdam-Neuzelle held at the Brandenburgisches Landeshauptarchiv: BLHA, Rep. 41 Amtsbezirk Neuzelle Nr. 15, Wehrmeldeamt Guben.
192. E.g. Eggers, 'Chemie', 2–3.
193. E.g. Helmut Blon, 'Die Lehre vom Schuss. Äußere Ballistik. Abschlußarbeit von Jungmann Helmut Blon, Nationalpolitische Erziehungsanstalt Rottweil, 1942' (StAS, Wü 161/5 T 1 Nr. 20); 'Der vierte Zug morst!', *NPEA Neuzelle*, 10. Kriegsbrief (February 1942), 20–1; E. Seidel, 'Vom Physikunterricht', *Der Deutsche Erzieher* (1937), 241; 'Die naturwissenschaftliche und mathematische Erziehung an der Nationalpolitischen Erziehungsanstalt', *Die Brücke* 16, no. 1 (February 1944), 25–9.
194. E.g. Kurt Meißner, 'Fragen der Schießlehre im mathematischen Unterricht der Oberstufe', *Ballenstedt: Schriftenfolge der Nationalpolitischen Bildungsanstalt in Ballenstedt am Harz* 2 (Christmas 1936), 18–22; 'Im neuen Schulpforta. Das alte Gymnasium als Nationalpolitische Erziehungsanstalt', *Frankfurter Zeitung*, 20 May 1943 [BArch, NS 5/VI/18843].
195. E.g. Dr. Walter Gollhardt, 'Nationalpolitische Erziehung im Geschichts-, Deutsch- und Erdkundeunterricht', *Ballenstedt* 2 (Christmas 1936), 11–18, 16.

196. E.g. Hans Joachim Schütze, 'Geopolitische Betrachtung SO-Europas im Erdkundeunterricht der Klasse 8', *Ballenstedt* 4 (Easter 1938), 7–13; Heinz Wiedemann, 'Noch etwas zur Stuhmer Antike', *Stuhmer Altkameradschaft*, 7. Rundbrief (1940), 17–18; Karl Heinrich Henschke, 'Heimatkundlicher Unterricht auf der Unter- und Mittelstufe der Höheren Schule: Nationalpolitische Erziehungsanstalt Köslin und Berlinisches Gymnasium zum Grauen Kloster' (DIPF, GUT ASS 546, 1937), 15.
197. E.g. Gollhardt, 'Nationalpolitische Erziehung', 12; 'Geschichtliche und erdkundliche Erziehungsarbeit an der Nationalpolitischen Erziehungsanstalt', *Die Brücke* 16, no. 1 (February 1944), 30–3. For more on this tendency in National Socialist history-teaching in general, see Helen Roche, '*Blüte und Zerfall*: "Schematic Narrative Templates" of Decline and Fall in *völkisch* and National Socialist Racial Ideology', in Lara Day and Oliver Haag, eds, *The Persistence of Race: Change and Continuity in Germany from the Wilhelmine Empire to National Socialism* (Oxford, 2017), 65–86; also Gilmer W. Blackburn, *Education in the Third Reich: A Study of Race and History in Nazi Textbooks* (Albany, 1985). For a case study of the instrumentalization and racialization of ancient history at the NPEA, see Roche, *Sparta's German Children*, 203–13.
198. Jung, 'Unsere unterrichtliche Erziehung', 318.
199. Jung, 'Unsere unterrichtliche Erziehung', 318.
200. E.g. 'Deutschkundliche Erziehung in der NPEA', *Die Brücke* 16, no. 1 (February 1944), 23–4; StAL, E 202 Bü 1747, 'Arbeitsplan für den Deutschunterricht an den Nationalpolitischen Erziehungsanstalten' (an edited version is also available online at https://homepages.uni-tuebingen.de/gerd.simon/SchulungNAPOLA.pdf).
201. 'Geschichtliche und erdkundliche Erziehungsarbeit', 30. On the ideological nature of artistic education at the NPEA, see Chapter 3.
202. E.g. Schlunke, 'Arbeitsplan für den Englischunterricht an den Nationalpolitischen Erziehungsanstalten' (n.d.); 'Latein in den Nationalpolitischen Erziehungsanstalten', *Deutsche Allgemeine Zeitung*, 5 December 1941 [BArch, NS 5/VI/18842]; on specific aspects of Latin- and Greek-teaching, see Roche, *Sparta's German Children*, 203–13; also more generally Helen Roche, 'Classics and Education in the Third Reich: *Die Alten Sprachen* and the Nazification of Latin- and Greek-Teaching in Secondary Schools', in Helen Roche and Kyriakos Demetriou, eds, *Brill's Companion to the Classics, Fascist Italy and Nazi Germany* (Leiden, 2018), 238–63.
203. Cf. Röttger, 'Warum Latein auch an Nationalpolitische Erziehungsanstalten?', *Der Deutsche Erzieher* 11 (1941), 326–7; on the exchanges with British public schools, see also Helen Roche, '*Zwischen Freundschaft und Feindschaft*: Exploring Relationships between Pupils at the Napolas (*Nationalpolitische Erziehungsanstalten*) and British Public Schoolboys', *Angermion: Yearbook for Anglo-German Literary Criticism, Intellectual History and Cultural Transfers/Jahrbuch für britisch-deutsche Kulturbeziehungen* 6 (2013), 101–26.
204. Cf. SHStAD, 11125 Nr. 21351, Brunk, 'Arbeit im Winter, politische Ausbildung und Zusammenarbeit mit der Partei' (report dated 4 November 1936), Bl. 173–5. The winter term was specifically ear-marked for bringing staff and pupils up to speed politically, since it was far less disrupted by 'missions', camps, and other extracurricular trips away from the local area.
205. Cf. Becker, *Naumburg*, 60; Pfeiffer, *Spanheim*, 18, diary entry dated 27 October 1942; W. Ruge, 'Nationalpolitische Erziehung in Plön', *Die Kameradschaft* 2, no. 1 (May

1936), 12–14; Politisches Archiv des Auswärtigen Amts, R 62972, report dated 23 January 1934 (which suggests that *Anstaltsleiter* Sander of NPEA Potsdam was the first headmaster to introduce the subject). Some eyewitnesses go out of their way to deny that such 'political' lessons ever existed at all; however, this may well be because the classes were only ever intended for the older year-groups, and in some cases ceased during wartime due to lack of staff, so that pupils who only attended the lower year-groups of an NPEA would never have experienced them.

206. StAL, E 202 Bü 1747, letter dated 17 October 1938. On ideological instruction in the SS in general, see Harten, *Himmlers Lehrer*.
207. Brunk, 'Arbeit im Winter', Bl. 173–4.
208. Examples of these programmes abound in the relevant sections of school newsletters—for instance, at NPEA Ilfeld in December 1938, *Hundertschaftsführer* Meyer reported that the school had welcomed SS-*Gruppenführer* Koppe (speaking on the SD); *Oberregierungsrat* Blume (on 'Freemasonry'), University-Professor Franz (on 'Jewry'), and the fathers of two current pupils, who spoke on South-Eastern Europe—Meyer, 'Bericht aus dem Anstaltsleben', *Ilfelder Blätter*, Jg. 1938–9, Heft 1 (December 1938), [139–41]. In 1934, NPEA Plön even invited Richard Crossman, who was then based at New College, Oxford, to give one of the lectures there—cf. Zugführer Prinz, 'Der politische Abend', *Die Kameradschaft* 1, no. 1 (May 1935), 22–4; *10 Jahre Plön*, 39–40.
209. Brunk, 'Arbeit im Winter', Bl. 174. The schools were also supposed to cultivate contacts with local branches of the NSDAP, mutually sending representatives to each other's high-profile events and festivities (Bl. 174–5).
210. Brunk, 'Arbeit im Winter', Bl. 175.
211. E.g. Brunk, 'Arbeit im Winter', Bl. 173; 'Aus der Winterarbeit der 2. Hundertschaft', *Die Brücke* 13, no. 3 (March 1941), 81–6.
212. For a syllabus of very similar instruction at the SS-training courses analysed by Hans-Christian Harten, see *Himmlers Lehrer*, 439–78, esp. 459. These courses were divided up into separate subjects, however, including '*Gegnerkunde*' (Adversary Lore) and '*Nationalsozialistische Institutionskunde*' (National Socialist Institutional Lore).
213. Zugführer Ulrich Tittel, 'Die Politische Schulung', *Nationalpolitische Erziehungsanstalt Stuhm im Aufbau* (Königsberg, 1938), 33–5. On *Gegnerforschung* in the Third Reich and in the SS more generally, see e.g. Harten, *Himmlers Lehrer*; Lutz Hachmeister, *Der Gegnerforscher. Die Karriere des SS-Führers Franz Alfred Six* (Munich, 1998); Bastian Hein, *Elite für Volk und Führer? Die Allgemeine SS und ihre Mitglieder 1925–1945* (Munich, 2012), 225–40; Stefanie Steinbach, *Erkennen, erfassen, bekämpfen—Gegnerforschung im Sicherheitsdienst der SS* (Berlin, 2018).
214. Drescher, *Erinnerungen*, 32–3; see also the relevant notes from the course in Kraas, *Napola Neuzelle*, Bd. 1.
215. This type of '*Zugabend*' or '*Heimabend*' could also take a less explicitly political form, such as a musical or social evening, or it might involve a multi-media presentation by the whole class on a specific ideological theme—cf. Hauptzugführer Liebich, 'Der Zugabend als charakterformende Kraft', *Die Brücke* 16, no. 2 (May 1944), 54–5; 'Unsere Heimabende', *Spandauer Blätter* 25, Kriegsausgabe 10 (September 1941), 15–17.

216. Zugführer Herrfurth, 'Nationalpolitische Schulung im 4. Zug', *NPEA Neuzelle*, 11. Kriegsbrief (June 1942), 17–18; Minx, Mürbe, and v. Schmeling, 'Unsere Zugabende', *Die Brücke* 13, no. 3 (March 1941), 81–2.
217. Herrfurth, 'Nationalpolitische Schulung', 17.
218. Herrfurth, 'Nationalpolitische Schulung', 17.
219. Michel, Gildemeister, and Fischer, 'Unsere Gemeinschaftsbücherei', *Die Brücke* 13, no. 3 (March 1941), 83.
220. Zugführer Boldt et al., 'Aus der Arbeit des 6. Zuges', *Die Brücke* 13, no. 3 (March 1941), 84–6.
221. W. Grützmacher, 'Vorbereitung auf die Seitengewehrverleihung', *Die Brücke* 13, no. 3 (March 1941), 86.
222. *Tagessprüche an der NPEA Plön* (n.d.).
223. Meyer, *Gelobt sei, was hart macht*, 5.
224. Hellmuth Frank, letter reprinted in 4. *Rundbrief der Nationalpolitischen Erziehungsanstalt Bensberg* (*c.* March/April 1940).
225. *Mitteilungen der Nationalpolitischen Erziehungsanstalt Naumburg/Saale*, 14. Kriegsnummer (December 1942), 22, letter from Bergermann dated 11 November 1942.
226. Trübenbach, 'Unsere politische Tätigkeit in Wyk a. Föhr', *Spandauer Blätter* 3 (20 August 1935), 11–12 (all of the quotations in the following paragraphs refer to this account). The *Anstaltsleiter*'s preface to this volume of the newsletter, taken from a speech given at the start of the summer holidays (Pein, 'Sommerferien 1935', 5–6) also draws attention to the fact that pupils had previously been exposed to Jewish 'effrontery' (*Frechheit*), and encourages them to take action against the host of enemies in their midst. Harald Scholtz goes so far as to interpret the ensuing 'action' at Wyk as a spontaneous reaction directly caused by Pein's speech, though this would be impossible to substantiate beyond all reasonable doubt; cf. Harald Scholtz, *Nationalsozialistische Ausleseschulen. Internatsschulen als Herrschaftsmittel des Führerstaates* (Göttingen, 1973), 105.
227. According to official correspondence, the illegal bill-posters were never brought to justice, so the Napola-pupils' denial of any involvement appears to have been taken seriously—cf. Dirk Warkus-Thomsen, '"Jüdische Kinder gehören in jüdische Heime." Von einem jüdischen Kinderheim und einer "Judenaustreibung" in Wyk auf Föhr', in Gerhard Paul and Miriam Gillis-Carlebach, eds, *Menora und Hakenkreuz. Zur Geschichte der Juden in und aus Schleswig-Holstein, Lübeck und Altona 1918–1998* (Neumünster, 1998), 387–96. On the prevalence of illegal antisemitic actions by Party activists elsewhere, including an incident at the bathing resort of Nordeney, which might be compared to those taken by the Spandauer (though on a significantly graver scale), see Frank Bajohr and Dieter Pohl, *Der Holocaust als offenes Geheimnis. Die Deutschen, die NS-Führung und die Alliierten* (Munich, 2006), 25–6. Often, such actions—including anti-Jewish poster campaigns—were unpopular with the inhabitants of the resorts in question, although generally for financial rather than philosemitic reasons—cf. Frank Bajohr, *'Unser Hotel ist judenfrei'. Bäder-Antisemitismus im 19. und 20. Jahrhundert* (Frankfurt am Main, 2003), 122–3.
228. Warkus-Thomsen, '"Jüdische Kinder gehören in jüdische Heime"'.
229. Bajohr, *'Unser Hotel ist judenfrei'*, 19, 117–19.

230. Warkus-Thomsen, '"Jüdische Kinder gehören in jüdische Heime"', 391–2; cf. Archiv Gymnasium Schloss Plön, letter from the school's 'Lagerleiter' dated 8 September 1938.
231. Boneß, 'Juden in Polen: im Vorzimmer Asiens (Augenblicksbilder aus dem Sosnowicer Judenviertel)', *Die Brücke* 11, no. 3 (November 1938), 47–8.
232. N.B. To undertake a full correlation of those Napola graduates whose full names we possess with potential perpetrators of atrocities on the Eastern front (and elsewhere) would be technically possible, but would be so time-consuming as to form the basis of an entire long-term research project in its own right. This is therefore an enquiry which has necessarily had to remain beyond the scope of this particular monograph.
233. N.B. The following five paragraphs draw upon the third section of an article already published in Vol. 32 of the journal *Beiträge zur Geschichte des Nationalsozialismus* (2016)—readers are advised to consult the original article for a more detailed account of the schools' physical education programme, and its broader significance within the context of school life at the NPEA, as well as a full sports-historical bibliography: cf. Helen Roche, 'Sport, Leibeserziehung und vormilitärische Ausbildung in den Nationalpolitischen Erziehungsanstalten: Eine "radikale" Revolution der körperlichen Bildung im Rahmen der NS-"Gesamterziehung"?', in Frank Becker and Ralf Schäfer, eds, *Sport und Nationalsozialismus* (Göttingen, 2016), 173–96.
234. For an example of a pupil deciding that he wished to attend a Napola because of the sporting opportunities thus afforded, see Hinrich Kattentidt, private correspondence, 27 December 2012.
235. E.g. *Spandauer Blätter* 7 (October 1936), 10–11; *Spandauer Blätter* 10 (July 1937), 9; *Ilfelder Blätter* 5 (Christmas 1937), [111]; *Ilfelder Blätter*, 1938/39, no. 1 (December 1938), [141].
236. Friedrich Lübbert, 'Die körperliche Erziehung in den Nationalpolitischen Erziehungsanstalten', *Leibesübungen und körperliche Erziehung* 11 (1938), 273–9, 276.
237. Kurt Bockhacker, 'Die Erziehung durch Leibesübungen im Rahmen der Gesamterziehung an der Nationalpolitischen Erziehungsanstalt Oranienstein bei Diez a. d. Lahn' (DIPF, GUT ASS 122), 19–20; Arno Erkenbrecher, 'Die körperliche Erziehung in der Unterstufe der Nationalpolitischen Erziehungsanstalt Potsdam-Neuzelle' (DIPF, GUT ASS 277, 1935), 18–19. In general, Bockhacker's thesis provides a very useful overview of the theory and practice of physical education at an NPEA.
238. Erkenbrecher, 'Erziehung', 25.
239. *Spandauer Blätter* 21 (September 1940), 9.
240. Cf. Michael Buddrus, *Totale Erziehung für den totalen Krieg: Hitlerjugend und nationalsozialistische Jugendpolitik Teil 1* (Munich, 2003), 186–94. Interestingly, in some cases, the Napola special courses merely provided better access to a programme of activities (such as boxing, wrestling, or gliding) which would always have formed part of boys' HJ-training; however, in other cases, they seemed to foster sports with a more distinctively pseudo-aristocratic ethos, which one might more readily associate with an elite boarding school (my thanks to Nick Stargardt for raising this point).
241. Cf. Heinrich Heine, 'Versuch einer Einordnung des Ruderns als "angegliederte" Leibesübung in den Rahmen der Gesamterziehung an der Nationalpolitischen Erziehungsanstalt Oranienstein' (DIPF, GUT ASS 511, 1936), 25.

242. On the NPEA Inspectorate's concerted (and sometimes almost desperate) attempts to provide the schools with ski huts converted from customs-houses on the former German-Austrian border, in order to ensure that all of the schools would have sufficient access to winter sports courses, see ÖStA, BEA 25. The accommodation could also be used for mountain hiking training in the summer months (ÖStA, BEA 7, letter from Sowade dated 30 March 1939).
243. Lübbert, 'Erziehung', 276. Some of these involved outside instructors—particularly gliding, which often involved courses run in collaboration with the *Deutscher Luftsportverband* or the *NS-Fliegerkorps*. However, most were taught by the NPEA *Erzieher* themselves.
244. *Spandauer Blätter* 3 (August 1935), 12–18; *Spandauer Blätter* 40 (June 1944), 21.
245. Cf. Heine, 'Versuch'; Mittelstaedt, 'Ausbildung im Kraftfahren' (StAL, E 202 Nr. 1746). See also Dorothee Hochstetter, *Motorisierung und 'Volksgemeinschaft': Das Nationalsozialistische Kraftfahrkorps (NSKK) 1931–1945* (Munich, 2005), 274.
246. Lübbert, 'Erziehung', provides a particularly telling example of this tendency; see more generally Berno Bahro, *Der SS-Sport. Organisation—Funktion—Bedeutung* (Paderborn, 2013).
247. For more on this, see Hajo Bernett, *Sportunterricht an der nationalsozialistischen Schule. Der Schulsport an den höheren Schulen Preußens 1933–1940* (Sankt Augustin, 1985), 94–6. According to the Inspectorate's 'Ausbildungspläne im Geländedienst und im Kleinkaliberschießen' from December 1940, cross-country war-games at the schools were ultimately supposed to adhere to the training guidelines for infantry in the Wehrmacht (Bernett, *Sportunterricht*, 94).
248. Cf. e.g. 'Der Geländesport an der NPEA Backnang', *Der Deutsche Erzieher* 5 (1937), 244; BArch, NS 45/35, 'Vom Wesen der Nationalpolitischen Erziehungsanstalten', 4–5. While such war-games were also undertaken by the Hitler Youth, their frequency and scale were rarely so intense—cf. Buddrus, *Totale Erziehung*, ch. 3; Roche, 'Sport, Leibeserziehung und vormilitärische Ausbildung'.
249. E.g. 'Kampf um Hohenfels', *Der Jungmann* 1, no. 3–4 (December 1936), 7: 'Just as the medieval inhabitants of the fortress catapulted the enemy with burning oil and beehives, so we did the same with cold water'; BArch, R 43-II/956b, 'Bericht über den politischen Einsatz der Nationalpolitischen Erziehungsanstalt Stuhm im Kreis Leipe (Lipno), Sommer 1941', 5; Spornhauer, *Tagebuch*, entry dated 27 November 1934. See also Erkenbrecher, 'Erziehung', 37–43, which gives an excellent account of the aims and teaching of *Geländedienst*. Once World War II broke out, the *Geländespiele* would often take on a more contemporary flavour, featuring missions such as capturing downed pilots, renegade traitors, or spies patrolling through the woods—cf. e.g. Dietrich Jeschke, *Erinnerungen* (2005), 9.
250. For an example of these orders, see 'Geländespiel am 6.10.43—Lage Rot', in Kraas, *Napola Neuzelle*, Bd. 1. However, the language of 'killing' ('*töten*' or '*killen*') could lead to problems if civilians ever became unwittingly involved in the action; for instance, an account from NPEA Stuhm's school newsletter in autumn 1943 reported that the farmer's wife at a farm where one of the 'enemy spies' had taken refuge assumed that the boys on the other team really meant to kill their comrade, and the *Jungmannen* ended up surrounded by a group of women as she shrieked: 'Don't kill him, don't kill him; I'll go to the police!'—*Stuhmer Altkameradschaft*, 16. Rundbrief

(October 1943), 11. On another occasion, a group of farmers near NPEA Rottweil chased off a 'reconnaissance patrol' with pitchforks, having mistaken them for escaped French PoWs—cf. *Zugschronik Jahrgang 1943, NPEA Rottweil* (1943); Wagner, *Mehr sein als scheinen*, 142.

251. E.g. Putzar, *Im Schatten einer Zeit*, 36.
252. For an account of one such, see 'Treffen aller Napolas', *Das Schwarze Korps*, 3 August 1939.
253. On the initial manoeuvres, see 'Herbstübung 1934', *Die Kameradschaft* 1, no. 1 (May 1935), 16–22; *10 Jahre Plön*, 19–28.
254. Flemming, 'Interview', 16. On the initial plans for the cancelled 1937 manoeuvres, see StAL, E 202 Bü 1746, relevant correspondence from July and August 1937.
255. For examples of media reports from each year, see 'Herbstübung und Zeltlager der nationalpolitischen Erziehungsanstalten. DAF-Kundgebung als Auftakt der Reichstagung des Amtes für Berufserziehung und Betriebsführung', *Völkischer Beobachter*, 29 September 1936 [BArch, NS 5/VI/18840]; 'Die große Sommerübung der Nationalpolitischen Erziehungsanstalten. "NPEA Stuhm" kehrt als Sieger von der großen Sommerübung heim', *Danziger Vorposten*, 21 July 1938 [BArch, NS 5/VI/18841]; Werner Kindt, 'Sommerübung von 3000 Schülern. Das Lager der "Napola" am Fuße der Karawanken', *Deutsche Allgemeine Zeitung*, 13 July 1939 [BArch, R 8034-II/9296]. For an eyewitness account of Himmler's visit by a former pupil, see Selke, *Schulzeit*, 55–6; for a typescript of one of Himmler's speeches, see BArch, NS 19/4005, 'Rede des Reichsführer-SS vor den Leitern, Erziehern und den Jungen der 8., 7. und 6. Klassen der Nationalpolitischen Erziehungsanstalten am 3.7.38 im Zeltlager Ahrenshoop' (1938).
256. StAL, E 202 Bü 1747, letters from the Inspectorate dated 31 May 1939, 7 June 1939, 14 June 1939.
257. BArch, R 2/12732, letter from Sowade dated 17 May 1939.
258. For an account of the Solstice Games in 1941, see 'Bericht über die erste Teilnahme der Anstalt an Anstaltswettkämpfe Naumburg 1941', *Putbusser Kameradschaft. Blätter der Nationalpolitischen Erziehungsanstalt Rügen*, Rundbrief 1 (July 1943), 3–5.
259. 'Herbstübung der Nationalpolitischen Erziehungsanstalten', *Weltanschauung und Schule* 1, no. 1 (1936), 27–34.
260. An account in the NPEA Köslin school newsletter describes the umpires' role in more detail: each Napola was supposed to bring two or three umpires so that any break-away group, including significant reconnaissance patrols, could be suitably observed. The umpire would have to make sure that no participants had double-knotted their 'life-threads', that they were not straying too close to railway lines, and that they were playing by the printed 'rules of the game'; not behaving in too brutal a fashion, or failing to observe the 'breaks in play'. They would also run the 'Casualty Collection Point' or *Totensammelstelle* for those who had lost their 'life-thread', as well as helping to count up the winners and losers to see who had won the final victory at the end of the game—cf. Zugführer Dr. Pirwitz, 'Als Schiedrichter im Geländespiel!', *Die Brücke* 12, no. 3 (October 1939), 49–51. During the longer exercises, the 'dead' would also be 'resurrected' by being given a new thread, so that the fight could go on; cf. Anon., *Erlebnisse als [Erzieher] der NPEA Potsdam* (IfZ, ED 735-3), 121.

261. E.g. Kubaschek, 'Spionage', *Pförtner Blätter* 1, no. 3 (December 1936), 62–3; Wendt, 'Der Hauptkampftag im Manöver 1938', *Die Brücke* 11, no. 3 (November 1938), 58; H.B., private correspondence, October 2013.
262. Heinrich Tangermann, *Das war es* (1965, reprinted in Kraas, *Napola Neuzelle*, Bd. 2, 48–9); cf. Anon., *Erlebnisse*, 119. Potsdam and Neuzelle only officially separated into two discrete institutions on 1 April 1938.
263. It was very common for the different Napolas to come up with battle cries of this kind, such as NPEA Köslin's 'Kussalin Ahoi!', NPEA Stuhm's 'Sankt Uuuuhm!', or NPEA Potsdam's 'Horridoh!' On the notorious 'Mirabelle heist', see Flemming, 'Interview', 17; *Mitteilungen der Nationalpolitischen Erziehungsanstalt Naumburg/Saale*, 22. Kriegsnummer (July 1944), 32 (letter from Horst Barth): 'So after the second or third bottle, the Captain and I suddenly recognized each other. We realized that we were both "Napolaner". He asked: "Which school"—I: "Naumburg," he: "Revenge for Mirabelles!" And then we both had to laugh uproariously. The Potsdamer must really have taken our nocturnal raid very hard back then.' On the two schools' enduring enmity, also known as the 'Mirabelle war' (*Mirabellenkrieg*), see e.g. 'Anstaltsübungen', *10 Jahre Naumburg*, 40–5, 41; *Potsdamer Kameradschaft* 61 (June 1997), 5 (letter from Hartwig Hosang).
264. 'Herbstübung der Nationalpolitischen Erziehungsanstalten', 29.
265. Cf. Dieter Pfeiffer, 'Jungmann in vier Nationalpolitischen Erziehungsanstalten—Wahlstatt, Bensberg, Traiskirchen, Spanheim—1936–1943', *Der Freiwillige* 39, no. 9 (1993), 22–4, 24.
266. Anon., *Erlebnisse*, 121.
267. 'Herbstübung der Nationalpolitischen Erziehungsanstalten', 29–30.
268. *Die Meute*, 78.
269. 'Herbstübung der Nationalpolitischen Erziehungsanstalten', 31–3.
270. Anon., *Sommerübung 1938* (unpublished manuscript, 1938).
271. Cf. e.g. *Spandauer Blätter* 1 (December 1934), 13–25. Once again, many former pupils are prone to dismiss the idea that the *Geländespiele* were really intended as paramilitary training, and equate these war-games instead with activities which any common-or-garden scout troop or youth group might participate in. However, even if this perception accurately represents pupils' own experience at the time, it certainly does not reflect the aims and intentions of the school authorities in making these activities a core part of the curriculum.
272. August Heißmeyer, *Die Nationalpolitischen Erziehungsanstalten*, 21–2 (BArch, NS 31/121). A proposal was put forward in early 1939 which suggested replacing the traditional *Reifeprüfung* with a form of ten-month-long 'attainment competition' (*Leistungskampf*) in the final year, covering all subjects holistically based on themes decided by the Inspectorate in advance (this appears to have been part of a much broader plan to reconfigure the schools' organization completely and replace 'classes' with 'teams' so that the Napolas no longer followed the model of a normal secondary school). However, the idea subsequently seems to have been taken no further, much to the relief of the more academically minded *Anstaltsleiter* (cf. StAL, E 202 Bü 1747, Männich, 'Änderungsvorschlag für die Reifeprüfung an den Nationalpolitischen

Erziehungsanstalten', memo dated 24 February 1939, and subsequent correspondence). On a similar form of examination being put into practice at the Adolf-Hitler-Schools, see the Conclusion.

273. Fast, 'Einige Prüfungsthemen unserer Abschlußbildung des Zuges Helmut von Moltke (7a)', *Stuhmer Altkameradschaft*, 14. Rundbrief (November 1942), 6.
274. Zugführer Mosch, 'Nochmals: Abschlußbildung 1942', *Stuhmer Altkameradschaft*, 15. Rundbrief (January 1943), 5.
275. Cf. SHStAD, 11125 Nr. 21351, Bl. 189–91; Calliebe, 'Gedanken', 5. The structure of the examination was left up to the individual *Anstaltsleiter*. For an eyewitness account of a written examination, see Selke, *Schulzeit*, 63.
276. SHStAD, 11125 Nr. 21351, Bl. 197–8: 'Bericht über die Reifeprüfung in Potsdam-Neuzelle, Spandau, Naumburg, Schulpforta, 28. Februar 1938'. This form of examination was deemed to have been conceptually sound, but poorly carried out. The *Anstaltsleiter* of NPEA Klotzsche also noted in his report that the written work at the schools which he visited in 1938 was generally only of 'average' standard, in part due to the recent reduction of the number of school years at all secondary schools, which necessarily meant that all of the candidates had effectively missed out on an entire year of instruction.
277. Claus Cordsen, *Meine Erinnerungen an Bensberg. Nationalpolitische Erziehungsanstalt in den Jahren 1935–1939* (1998), 58.
278. Wasmann Nachlass, questions for *Jungmann* Büscher (copy courtesy of Arne Heinich). Scribbled notes on the page below read as follows: 'Göbbels in one of his last essays refers to the biassed news [*sic*], sensational, that sends the English to bed with a feeling of fear. The English are conscious of the left tendencies of the BBC / The writer blames the BBC for not making a study of the totalitarian states.' Perusal of the *Times* digital archive shows that this was indeed a genuine letter to the editor, dated 23 February 1939.
279. E.g. 'Abiturientenentlassung', *Spandauer Blätter* 9 (1 May 1937), 12–16.
280. 'Abiturientenentlassung', 12; Werner Andrä, 'Abiturienten-Entlassung in Berlin (14.-16. März 1938)', *Die junge Front. Kameradschaftsblätter der Staatlichen Nationalpolitischen Erziehungsanstalt Klotzsche, Rudolf-Schröter-Schule* 1, no. 1 (1938), 12–13.
281. On these arrangements, see StAL, E 202 Bü 1746, letter from Schieffer dated 5 March 1938; StAL, E 202 Bü 1747, letter dated 2 March 1939. The expense involved in travelling to Berlin could be a sore point with the school authorities at the non-Prussian Napolas, however—see further Chapter 5.
282. On the prevalence of such political rituals at the NPEA in general, see Chapter 3. For media reports of the graduation ceremonies and Rust's speeches, see e.g. 'Reichsminister Rust verabschiedet Abiturienten. Entlassungsfeier in der Nationalpolitischen Erziehungsanstalt Spandau', *Völkischer Beobachter*, 23 March 1937 [BArch, NS 5/VI/18841]; 'Feierstunde im Charlottenburger Schloß. Reichsminister Rust entließ 300 Reifeprüflinge der Nationalpolitischen Erziehungsanstalten', *Völkischer Beobachter*, 17 March 1938 [BArch, R 8034-II/9296]; 'Rust sprach in Spandau. Entlassungsfeier der Nationalpolitischen Erziehungsanstalten', *Völkischer Beobachter*, 18 March 1939 [BArch, R 8034-II/9296].

283. Andrä, 'Abiturienten-Entlassung', 13; 'Entlassung des Jahrganges 1939 der Nationalpolitischen Erziehungsanstalten in Berlin-Spandau', *Spandauer Blätter* 15 (May 1939), 14–15. This issue also includes speeches by some of the graduands from Spandau, which grant an interesting insight into their political attitudes. For an example of a graduation speech by the headmaster of NPEA Spandau to the whole school, see 'Es spricht der Anstaltsleiter', *Spandauer Blätter* 5 (20 March 1936), 4–5.
284. Cf. Pine, *Education*, 23, citing Stefan Schnurr, 'Vom Wohlfahrtsstaat zum Erziehungsstaat. Sozialpolitik und soziale Arbeit in der Weimarer Republik und im Nationalsozialismus', *Widersprüche* 8 (1988), 47–64; also Heinz-Elmar Tenorth, '"Erziehungsstaaten". Pädagogik des Staates und Etatismus der Erziehung', in Dietrich Benner, Jürgen Schriewer, and Heinz-Elmar Tenorth, eds, *Erziehungsstaaten. Historisch-vergleichende Analysen ihrer Denktraditionen und nationaler Gestalten* (Weinheim, 1998), 13–54; Kiran Klaus Patel, *Soldiers of Labor: Labor Service in Nazi Germany and New Deal America, 1933–1945* (Cambridge, 2005), 260.
285. On the concept of the 'total institution', see Erving Goffman, 'On the Characteristics of Total Institutions', in *Asylums: Essays on the Social Situation of Mental Patients and Other Inmates* (London, 1961). On the application of this model to German military boarding schools, see e.g. Roche, *Sparta's German Children*, 111–21; Kiran Klaus Patel has also used the concept in his analysis of the RAD (*Soldiers of Labor*, ch. 3.1.2). On the institutions listed above, see e.g. Patel, *Soldiers of Labor*; Edith Niehuis, *Das Landjahr. Eine Jugenderziehungseinrichtung in der Zeit des Nationalsozialismus* (Nörten-Hardenberg, 1984); Barbara Schneider, *Die höhere Schule im Nationalsozialismus: Zur Ideologisierung von Bildung und Erziehung* (Cologne, 2000), 372–5; Klaus Ring and Stefan Wunsch, eds, *Bestimmung: Herrenmensch. NS-Ordensburgen zwischen Faszination und Verbrechen* (Dresden, 2016); Harten, *Himmlers Lehrer*, ch. II.3.
286. Cf. Patel, *Soldiers of Labor*, 207–21; Niehuis, *Landjahr*, esp. ch. 9.1; also Jürgen Schiedeck and Martin Stahlmann, 'Totalizing of Experience: Educational Camps', in Heinz Sünker and Hans-Uwe Otto, eds, *Education and Fascism: Political Identity and Social Education in Nazi Germany* (London, 1997), 54–80.
287. Cf. Patel, *Soldiers of Labor*, 206–7; Thomas Kühne, *The Rise and Fall of Comradeship: Hitler's Soldiers, Male Bonding and Mass Violence in the Twentieth Century* (Cambridge, 2017), esp. 81–3, 116; also Thomas Kühne, *Belonging and Genocide: Hitler's Community, 1918–1945* (New Haven, 2010), ch. 2; Fritzsche, *Life and Death*, 98–103; also the locus classicus: Sebastian Haffner, *Defying Hitler: A Memoir* (London, 2002), chs 36–9.
288. Cf. Patel, *Soldiers of Labor*, 260; Niehuis, *Landjahr*, 10, 247; Pine, *Education*, 137.
289. For a similar analysis of the *Ordensburgen*, see Dieter Barteszko, 'Bollwerke im Höhenrausch—Die Ordensburgen des "Dritten Reiches"', in Ring and Wunsch, *Bestimmung: Herrenmensch*, 66–79; on similarities with the Adolf-Hitler-Schools in this respect, see also the Conclusion.
290. Cf. Harten, *Himmlers Lehrer*, 571, 584–5.
291. Cf. Harten, *Himmlers Lehrer*, 311–12.
292. Needless to say, the many Napola graduates who attended the *Junkerschulen* were likely to perform extremely well on these types of courses—in a sense, their prior

training at the NPEA meant that they were already the perfect participants from an ideological as well as a physical perspective.

293. On the 'boundaries of indoctrination' at civilian schools, see Heinz-Elmar Tenorth, 'Grenzen der Indoktrination', in Peter Drewek et al., eds, *Ambivalenzen der Pädagogik. Zur Bildungsgeschichte der Aufklärung und des 20. Jahrhunderts—Harald Scholtz zum 65. Geburtstag* (Weinheim, 1995), 335–50; cf. Evans, *Third Reich in Power*, 266–72. See also Lutz Raphael, 'Die nationalsozialistische Ideologie', in Paul Ciupke and Franz-Josef Jelich, eds, *Weltanschauliche Erziehung in Ordensburgen des Nationalsozialismus. Zur Geschichte und Zukunft der Ordensburg Vogelsang* (Essen, 2006), 15–32.
294. Patel, *Soldiers of Labor*, 245, 288; Niehuis, *Landjahr*, 283–4.
295. Cf. Raphael Gross, *Anständig geblieben. Nationalsozialistische Moral* (Frankfurt am Main, 2010), 10; Stefan Kühl, *Ganz normale Organisationen. Zur Soziologie des Holocaust* (Berlin, 2014), 318.
296. Cf. Schneider, *Die höhere Schule*, Teil III and ch. III.4.2; also Konrad Jarausch, *The Unfree Professions: German Lawyers, Teachers, and Engineers, 1900–1950* (Oxford, 1990).
297. Cf. H. W. Koch, *The Hitler Youth. Origins and Development 1922–1945* (New York, 1975), 203; see also the Introduction and Conclusion.
298. Kühne, *Comradeship*, 93–4.
299. Kühne, *Comradeship*, 194, 201; cf. Kühl, *Organisationen*, 147–74.
300. Kühne, *Comradeship*, 193–5.

3
'Missions' and Extracurricular Activities

One of the most ostensibly attractive features of the education which the Napolas provided, both for current pupils and for prospective pupils and outsiders, was the all-encompassing and holistic nature of the pedagogical experience which the schools offered.[1] Although, as we have seen in the preceding chapter, the NPEA not only provided a comprehensive—if thoroughly politicized and ideologically saturated—academic curriculum, and an above-average training in physical and sporting activities of all kinds, this was only the tip of the iceberg. In addition, the schools also offered a wide variety of extracurricular experiences and activities for pupils to pursue, ranging from semi-pagan ceremonies accoutred with all of the most virulent trappings of Nazism's 'political religion', to the provision of frequent opportunities for the *Jungmannen* to realize their artistic ambitions through music, art and design, and amateur dramatics. Pupils would routinely embark upon school trips and exchanges to countries as far-flung as Finland, the Baltic States, or even South America, and, as they matured, they would also undertake annual labour 'missions' (*Einsätze*), during which they were sent to live and work with farmers, miners, or industrial labourers for months at a time, in order to experience the workers' way of life at first hand.

All of these aspects of education at the NPEA possessed specifically political—and politicizing—intentions; indeed, they were a crucial ingredient in sustaining the schools' overall ideological effectiveness, as well as bolstering the Napola authorities' claim to be genuinely furthering social progress in terms of the equalizing ideology of the *Volksgemeinschaft*. As we shall see, the NPEA were arguably much more successful in this regard than were other, more ubiquitous institutions of education and recreation during the Third Reich, including civilian schools, the Hitler Youth, the Reich Labour Service, and the Strength through Joy organization; from this perspective, the Napolas also offered their adherents far greater scope for the cultivation of individual self-fulfilment.[2] Put simply, the sheer scale of the financial and practical resources allotted to the NPEA, as well as their relatively exalted political standing, allowed them to grant their pupils almost unheard-of opportunities for travel, cultural endeavour, and personal development, whilst simultaneously siting these ostensible opportunities within the framework of the schools' comprehensive ideological programme of 'total education' (*Gesamterziehung*), so that, in effect, none of these activities would strictly have been considered 'extracurricular' in the schools' own parlance.

The Third Reich's Elite Schools: A History of the Napolas. Helen Roche, Oxford University Press. © Helen Roche 2021.
DOI: 10.1093/oso/9780198726128.003.0004

However, although the NPEA programme partially drew upon the principles and practices of the reform-pedagogy movement, its ultimate aim was scarcely to foster an educational culture of child-centred learning, but rather to instil pupils with the whole gamut of National Socialist values, ranging from the internalization of National Socialism's more 'socialist' tenets, to the inculcation of avowedly chauvinist attitudes to Germany's foreign neighbours. All in all, it was the '*schöner Schein*', the seductive glitter, of these cultural activities which made their politicization so dangerous—and so difficult for former pupils to discern with hindsight. Rarely was a school play at a Napola just a school play, or a school trip just a school trip, insulated from any ideological valency. Rather, some form of Nazified political agenda would have been integrated within almost every one of these activities, encoded either explicitly or implicitly.

This chapter will now go on to explore these aspects of the Napolas' 'total education' in detail, analysing the extent to which the theory of these initiatives measured up to their realization in practice. How far were the schools' cultural endeavours entirely saturated with Nazi ideology, and to what effect did pupils act as proselytizers of the National Socialist *Weltanschauung* on their travels abroad, or on their 'missions' to the working classes? We shall begin by examining the role of political religion at the NPEA, before turning to the schools' cultural and charitable endeavours, focusing in particular on art, music, and the theatre. We will then consider the Napolas' varied programme of school trips and exchanges, highlighting especially the schools' so-called 'borderland missions', and those exchanges which took place with preparatory schools in the United States, and public schools in Great Britain. Finally, we will examine the schools' 'missions' on the farm, in the factory, and down the mineshaft, using the latter (the so-called *Bergwerkseinsatz* or 'mining mission') as a case study of the effectiveness or otherwise of the schools' drive to foster social equality and undermine class tensions and divisions, in accordance with the rhetoric of the *Volksgemeinschaft*. Did either side gain anything from the exercise, or was this merely a veiled attempt to infiltrate milieux with a suspected penchant for Communism with regime-loyal teenage spies, or an economic scheme to ameliorate some of the grave problems prevalent in the Reich's industrial labour market via a periodic influx of youthful workers? In conclusion, we will close by briefly contextualizing these endeavours and practices with reference to existing scholarship on relevant social trends under the Nazi regime more generally.

The NPEA and National Socialist 'Political Religion'

In 1935–6, John Weekes Tate spent a year as an English exchange teacher at NPEA Naumburg; upon his return, he published a number of sympathetic accounts of his experiences in pedagogical periodicals and the media.[3] One of the aspects of school life which he described in most telling detail were those 'politico-religious' festivities which took place throughout the school year at the NPEA, effectively replacing the Christian assemblies, prayers, and feast-days of the pre-Nazi calendar:

> The semi-religious aspect of the political education is expressed in the '*Feier*'. In one school a short '*Morgenfeier*' [morning celebration] is held every Monday in the school chapel. Frequently a large swastika flag is hung across the chancel. In front of this a '*Sprechchor*' [speech choir] of boys is assembled, and one of them begins a patriotic recitation which is taken up by the others in unison, this being followed by a song in which the 'congregation' joins. Both recitation and song make a liberal use of militaristic terms.... The '*Morgenfeier*' may consist solely of a reading illustrating some act of heroism in the Great War or in the early days of the National Socialist movement, or a short recital of German music.... A ceremony occurring on Confirmation Day ['*Waffenleite*'], further illustrates the curious superposition of the National Socialist faith on the Christian. Just after dark the school was drawn up on the parade ground with lighted torches; a central flame was kindled, and the boys of confirmation age were admitted into the first hundred, or upper school. The Headmaster gave an address [...and] then presented each boy with the sidearm...and a text.... Typical examples are 'Only he can be free who daily masters himself'; and 'One does not beg for justice, one must fight for justice'. Another example of a National Socialist service is the '*Sonnenwendfeier*', held both at the winter and at the summer solstice. After dark the school gathers on the top of a neighbouring hill—with the inevitable lighted torches—and a huge bonfire is lit. Over the flames an address is given on the National Socialist Faith, which, 'like the sun continues its unshakable course'.[4]

Tate was far from the only adherent of the Napolas to highlight the schools' attempts to replace traditional forms of Christian worship with elements of political religion, however.[5] In an account entitled 'The Ceremony of 9 November and the Yule Celebration in 1937', published in NPEA Spandau's newsletter in early 1938, the author admitted that, in the search for a more truly *völkisch* ceremonial form, the NPEA had been forced to borrow from Christianity, even as staff and pupils attempted to replace the traditional trappings of Christmastide with a Germanic 'Yuletide festival', celebrating the joys of the winter solstice. Christmas carols were to be replaced by Nazi alternatives such as '*Volk will zu Volk*' ('Race calls to Race'), or the canon '*Lewer dod als Slav!*' ('Better dead than a Slav!'), and the message of the Gospels was to be supplanted by a celebration of comradeship and community which made no reference whatsoever to the Christian religion.[6] Meanwhile, in commemoration of 9 November (the anniversary of those National Socialist 'martyrs' who had died in Hitler's abortive Bavarian Beer-Hall Putsch in

1923), the ceremonies at Spandau featured a massive laurel wreath and swastika banner flanked by bowls of fire atop two columns, as well as massed brass fanfares, torch-bearers, orators, and choirs, concluding with a silent march to the memorial of the Nazi martyr and Berlin SA-man Gerhard Schlemminger.[7]

In similar vein, in an article published in 1940 in the periodical *Völkische Musikerziehung*, Eckhard Loge, a Napola music-*Erzieher*, documented in exhaustive detail the choreography for a '*Waffenleite*' ceremony which he had devised for the charges at his NPEA, making explicit the ceremony's link with ancient Germanic masculine initiation rituals. Often, the timing of this rite was not only deliberately correlated with the age at which boys from Christian backgrounds would usually have undergone the sacrament of Confirmation, in their mid-teens, but it also conveniently coincided with pupils' graduation from the junior branch of the Hitler Youth, the *Deutsches Jungvolk*, to become fully fledged members of the HJ.[8] Indeed, at some schools, such as NPEA Naumburg, the two rituals, the *Waffenleite* or *Schwertleite* and the ceremony of '*Verpflichtung*' ('Commitment') to the Hitler Youth, were subsumed into a single occasion.[9] As alluded to above, such ceremonies usually took place at either the summer or the winter solstice, in a bid to fuse the pseudo-religious pageantry of National Socialist rituals with older, allegedly 'Germanic' pagan rites. At NPEA Köslin in 1943, for instance, the *Jungmannen* were encouraged not only to remember all those Germans who had fallen in battle, but also to fan their hatred of their enemies as high as the flames of the solstice fire were leaping.[10] Preparation for this form of secular confirmation would include learning the relevant parts of the speech choirs, marches, fanfares, and Nazi hymns by heart, as well as choosing one's 'sword motto' (*Schwertspruch*), a task which some *Jungmannen* took extremely seriously.[11] Former pupils, even in old age, often recalled what a resounding impression the 'mystical' aspects of the ceremony had made upon them, and the thrill of being entrusted with a weapon of one's very own (even if it was only a small dagger, rather than an actual sword or fire-arm—see Figure 3.1).[12] The *Jungmannen* were frequently attracted to the pomp and solemnity of the occasion, without fully realizing the true meaning of the oaths they were taking—swearing to fight, die, and ultimately immolate themselves in the name of their National Socialist political convictions.[13] However, the fact that pupils' parents were invited, just as they would have been to a religious confirmation rite (see Figure 3.2), and that a knees-up and series of amateur dramatic entertainments would often follow, was also undoubtedly part of the ceremony's widespread appeal—even if parents had to bring their own ration coupons in order to facilitate the provision of an acceptably celebratory meal during the war years.[14]

In more lighthearted vein, pupils might also take part in wedding or (non-Christian) christening celebrations for members of the school community, and many schools also held regular open days (*Gästetage*), speech days, or '*Volk*

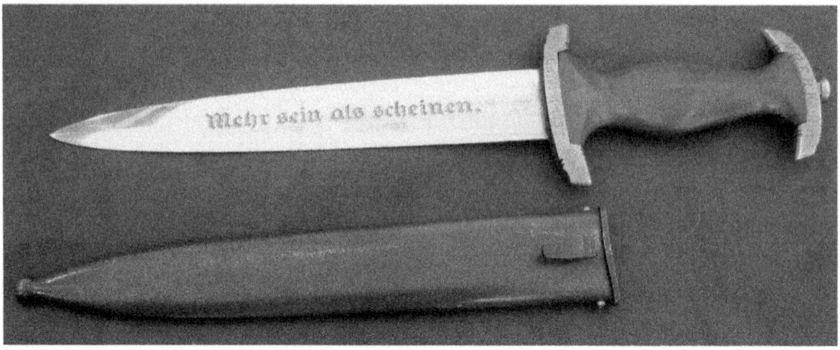

Figure 3.1 The ceremonial dagger bearing the schools' motto, 'Be more than you seem', with which all NPEA pupils were presented at the '*Waffenleite*' or '*Schwertleite*' initiation ritual.

Figure 3.2 Parents, staff, and pupils pose for a photograph, following the '*Waffenleite*' at NPEA Ballenstedt in 1940.

festivals' (*Volksfeste*), at which their sporting, academic, and artistic accomplishments could be suitably displayed and enjoyed by parents, dignitaries, and members of the local community alike.[15] On such occasions, certain schools also betrayed some form of attachment to their pre-Napola roots, with pupils at NPEA Schulpforta continuing to uphold the school's time-honoured custom of celebrating *Martinitag* (St. Martin's Day), while pupils at NPEA Ilfeld retained '*Neandertag*' (Neander Day), a celebration honouring the original monastic founder of the *Klosterschule* Ilfeld, in accordance with both schools' previous Christian traditions.[16] Many NPEA in Austria were also wont to retain local religiously connoted traditions such as St. Nicholas' Day (*Niklausfest*) and

Krampusfest, even well into the war years.[17] Meanwhile, NPEA Plön tended to display an unusual predilection for midnight rituals commemorating the martyrs of the Nazi movement or celebrating Hitler's birthday, presumably due to *Anstaltsleiter* Hermann Brunk's evident penchant for the more sacralized, quasi-occult elements of the National Socialist 'faith'.[18] Thus, even within the Napola system, there still existed some scope for the expression of local or ideological differences—differences which can also be discerned in individual schools' attitudes towards the arts.[19]

A Cultural 'Total Education'? Art, Music, and Drama at the NPEA

The provision of a varied spectrum of cultural activities was considered crucial to the broader NPEA curriculum, whether within or outside lessons—and, of course, musical and dramatic attainments were also key to the preparation of effective ceremonies (*Feiergestaltung*), as may be inferred from some of the descriptions above. A surviving programme for a conference of Napola art- and music-*Erzieher* which took place at Schulpforta in May 1937 gives the reader a good sense of the sheer range of activities on offer at the NPEA, with the scheduled presentations featuring a broad variety of topics and techniques. Aside from *Feiergestaltung*, these included drawing, clay modelling, sculpture in wood and metal, photography, art appreciation, amateur dramatics (including folk theatre, puppetry, and shadow plays), singing, choirs, instrumental teaching, and bands, as well as 'the political task of cultural education' (*die politische Aufgabe der musischen Erziehung*).[20] As boarding schools, the NPEA were generally able to allocate far more time to artistic pursuits than any civilian day-school, and staff could also support voluntary groups which would meet in their free time in order to work on musical, dramatic, or artistic projects.[21] Whenever possible, pupils were encouraged to put on performances in their local communities; however, in addition, they were also taken on frequent school trips to the theatre, the opera, or classical concerts—although such excursions were inevitably easier to arrange at schools such as Spandau, Potsdam, Schulpforta, Bensberg, and Backnang, which were all situated within relatively easy reach of theatres and concert-halls in nearby towns and cities.[22] This was the first time that many of the *Jungmannen* had ever had the opportunity to hear chamber musicians or a symphony orchestra perform, or attend a live performance of a play or an opera at the theatre. For some, these were fascinating and unforgettable experiences, and ones which could potentially lead to a lasting appreciation of high culture.[23]

In lessons, *Erzieher* would often take a holistic view of pupils' artistic activities, stressing the importance of providing the *Jungmannen* with projects which would allow them to pursue complementary spheres of arts and crafts according to their skills, whilst still contributing to the overall result. For instance, if a class were given the task of creating the theatre for a Punch and Judy show, those with an aptitude for sculpture might be assigned to carve the puppets; those with more technical interests might build the stage, and the more artistically talented would paint the backdrops.[24] The finished product would then showcase pupils' musical and dramatic talents. *Jungmannen* were also often encouraged to use their new-found skills in art and design to decorate their *Stuben* with murals and slogans—at NPEA Klotzsche, for instance, pupils dedicated one room to Rommel and his Africa Korps, featuring murals of a map of Africa, palm trees, and Stukas flying over the desert, while another was dedicated to SS-*Obergruppenführer* Sepp Dietrich, his tanks, and his 'courageous' SS-men.[25]

This choice of subject-matter was perhaps unsurprising, given teachers' insistence that even art lessons had to possess a political mission beyond the merely creative, and their belief that 'art always serves the *Weltanschauung* of its era, whether as its herald or its trailblazer'.[26] The extent of the ideological indoctrination inculcated through art lessons at the NPEA may be aptly illustrated by the stark contrast between the lower years' depictions of farmers and princesses, sailing ships, and space-travel futurist phantasmagoria, compared with the upper years' portrayals of unending ranks of Nazi hoplites, tanks, and Stukas on the attack, or blueprints for the decoration of festal halls, replete with Nazi symbology.[27] The *Jungmannen* might have been provided with state-of-the-art equipment and materials, but the rationale behind this provision was fundamentally ideological, rather than fostering the promotion of free-ranging creativity and individual expression—as Eugen K. of NPEA Wartheland found to his cost when, having previously garnered fulsome praise for his clay bust of a bald-headed, thick-lipped Mussolini, he received a less than rapturous reception for an (otherwise realistic) portrait of the Sudetenland forest-spirit Rübezahl sporting a new-fangled wrist-watch.[28]

Woodwork was also a particularly fertile source of propagandistic themes. This might merely apply to the choice of political subjects—for example, building models of stone-age settlements in celebration of prehistoric Germanic 'farming culture', or creating an almost man-sized sculpture of the NSDAP Party eagle clutching a swastika wreath in its claws, perched atop a rock-like podium, as did *Jungmannen* at NPEA Wahlstatt and NPEA Schulpforta respectively.[29] However, pupils were also frequently encouraged to create models with a more militaristic purpose, such as miniature gliders with which they might learn the physics of flight, or scale-models of destroyers and torpedo-boats.[30] Thus, although from July 1937 onwards, art-teachers at the NPEA were no longer required to register with the Reich Chamber of Fine Arts, since their artistic endeavours were deemed to be merely 'incidental or insignificant', their influence on their youthful charges in ideological terms was nevertheless unparalleled.[31]

*

The Napolas' musical education frequently performed a similarly propagandistic function—the description of the Third Reich as a '*Singediktatur*' ('singing dictatorship') which operated via 'collectivization through music' was certainly applicable to the spectrum of musical activities at the NPEA.[32] Every *Jungmann* was expected to learn a musical instrument as a matter of course—preferably one with which it was possible to march whilst playing—and those with a talent for composition were encouraged to perform their pieces with school ensembles and choirs.[33] Every Napola was equipped as a matter of course with a full complement of instruments, practice rooms, and an extensive sheet-music library, and the pupils' singing and marching bands formed an unmistakeable addition to the local soundscape wherever they went.[34] Even when planning for *Manöver* and camping trips (*Zeltlager*), the schools received detailed instructions from the Inspectorate about which songs were to be learnt beforehand, or which instruments would need to be transported to the location in question (for instance, at the camp attached to the headmasters' conference at NPEA Stuhm in 1937, bugles, accordions, recorders, and fiddles were *de rigueur*).[35]

Meanwhile, NPEA Bensberg and NPEA Potsdam also possessed a reputation for being particularly 'musical' Napolas, and, according to one former music-*Erzieher*, Paul Nitsche, Bensberg was even slated to become a specialist 'Musik-NPEA.' Indeed, in a post-war interview with a former pupil, Nitsche went so far as to claim that Reich Education Minister Bernhard Rust had used Bensberg as the initial model for the Third Reich's ultimate specialist music school, the '*Musisches Gymnasium*' in Frankfurt am Main.[36] Meanwhile, NPEA Plön was also instrumental in the publication of a new anthology of marching songs for National Socialist youth—a far cry from the school's Weimar-era reputation as a bastion of the musical avant-garde.[37]

All in all, *Erzieher* at the Napolas frequently claimed that there could be no better place for a music-teacher to work than at an NPEA, where one could cultivate the art of political song in the service of the national community, and the art of folksong as a source of German racial awareness, as well as working with the many bands and ensembles typically found at every school, such as the *Spielmannszug* (brass band), *Fanfarenzug* (fanfare band), and *Musikzug* (marching band).[38] After all, as Eugen Mayer-Rosa, a music-teacher at NPEA Schulpforta, put it, at the Napolas, music was by no means confined to a few weekly music-lessons; rather, it was inextricably entwined with the life and experiences of the entire school community (see Figures 3.3 and 3.4).[39]

Still, whether the *Jungmannen* were taking part in the 'Day of German Chamber Music' (*Tag der deutschen Hausmusik*), performing for local audiences with their school choirs and orchestras, participating in festal celebrations, or parading through local towns and villages with their marching bands, they were always encouraged to conceive of music in suitably 'Germanic' terms, only

Figure 3.3 Orchestra practice at NPEA Rügen, 1943; every pupil was required to learn a musical instrument.

performing works by a closed canon of 'ethnically' acceptable composers. At school concerts, Bach, Beethoven, Handel, Haydn and Mozart, and even Praetorius, featured prominently, not to mention less well-known, but equally 'Teutonic' composers, such as Karl Ditters von Dittersdorf, or even Frederick the Great. It was only in secret that some of the *Jungmannen* might dare to joke about their undimmed enthusiasm for rather more modern forms of music, not least those very jazz artists whom the Nazi regime had deemed most 'degenerate'.[40]

*

Theatrical activities (often politicized) were also ubiquitous at the NPEA—whether entertaining the local inhabitants of those villages in borderland areas where the *Jungmannen* aimed to drum up support for the National Socialist cause; performing for the mining communities where they spent time on their 'missions', or simply putting on a comic afternoon or evening variety show for the wider school community.[41]

Particularly popular choices for amateur dramatic performance included Martin Luserke's *Blut und Liebe* and *Peter Squenz*, as well as his *Rüpelkomedie*, a satirical adaptation of the rude mechanicals scene from Shakespeare's *Midsummer Night's Dream*. Even in much later life, Manfred B., a former pupil of NPEA Rottweil, vividly remembered having to play the role of Demetrius and speaking the single line: 'Well roared, lion!'[42] At NPEA Neuzelle, the playwright himself even came to visit for a few days in order to coach the performers in readiness for a triple-bill production of his work. However, those who remembered this

Figure 3.4 Members of one of the school marching bands at NPEA Rügen, 1943.

occasion were more interested in the manifold special effects which they had managed to rig up, including 'heaps of corpses', a large half-moon which exploded noisily, with a strong smell of gunpowder, at the line '... *And I'll still shoot the moon down as well...!*', and a severed skull with glowing red eyes which could light up on electrical command, appropriated from the skeleton which was usually to be found in the biology lab.[43]

Meanwhile, for boys in the older year-groups, Kleist's *Hermannsschlacht* and Schiller's *Die Räuber* and *Wallensteins Lager* might feature, as well as the Germanic *Thingspiel* 'The Frankenburg Dice Game' (*Das Frankenburger Würfelspiel*).[44] However, a production at NPEA Oranienstein of Peter Martin Lampel's play *Wir werden ummontiert, Leute*, coached by Lampel himself, almost caused the school to fall foul of the Amt Rosenberg's edicts on propaganda and *Weltanschauung*. As the author of an ostensibly anti-authoritarian play entitled *Die Revolte im Erziehungshaus* (Revolt in the Reformatory), which was adapted for the cinema as a silent film in 1929, Lampel was persona non grata with the regime, and a request was made that the production at Oranienstein be banned by the Amt Rosenberg, even though permission for the performance had already been granted by the NPEA central administration in Berlin.[45] The play was performed twice on 20 February 1935, but the only surviving indication of its reception, gleaned from the diary of Oranienstein's house-matron Emmy Spornhauer, was the laconic comment 'it was crap'.[46]

More common—and far more acceptable to the Nazi authorities—were comedic skits which poked fun or opprobrium at Germany's enemies. Thus, at NPEA

Stuhm's *Winterfest* in 1942, *Jungmannen* from the third class were lionized for their performance of a skit entitled '*Jungmannen* conquer the North Pole', which mocked Churchill and Roosevelt, while in 1939, a comedic performance by pupils from NPEA Bensberg on *Kreisbauerntag* (a Party celebration for the local farming community) depicted Chamberlain, Eden, Hore-Belisha, and Churchill hiding in Berlin, plotting to divide Germany between them. Their nefarious plan being interrupted by air raid sirens, the British dignitaries fled in cowardly disarray, leaving their signature umbrella, gloves, top-hat, and cigar to be stolen as booty by a brave band of comic German country-dwellers.[47]

Nevertheless, differences in theatrical practice at individual schools were still discernible. For example, NPEA Potsdam lived up to its artistic reputation by encouraging every *Stube* to found their own theatre-group, while the Napolas in the occupied Eastern territories placed a particular premium on influencing 'ethnic German' settlers through theatrical propaganda.[48] Meanwhile, NPEA Schulpforta retained its age-old custom of St. Martin's Day plays (*Martinispiele*), and, given its humanistic tradition and curriculum, was much more likely to put on productions with a classical theme, such as improvised skits or plays based on the *Iliad* or the *Odyssey* (sometimes performed in a makeshift amphitheatre).[49] All in all, however, whilst the surviving photographs of teenage boys on stage in theatrical costume, smiling into the camera to immortalize the cast at show's end, might suggest that the Napolas cultivated an innocent and untainted form of dramatic entertainment (see Figure 3.5), the plays in which the *Jungmannen* were performing had in fact, for the most part, been selected or produced with ideological ends in mind.

*

Finally, all of these cultural accomplishments could ultimately be combined in the form of the 'voluntary' charitable activities undertaken by the *Jungmannen*—most commonly under the aegis of the *Winterhilfswerk* or 'Winter-Help' programme (WHW) organized by the National Socialist Peoples' Welfare organization (NSV). As an example of the schools' charitable productivity in one month alone, in December 1936, NPEA Bensberg, NPEA Stuhm, and NPEA Köslin organized Christmas parties and distributed presents to local children in need; NPEA Ilfeld assisted the National Socialist Women's Organization to raise money for the WHW by putting on a musical, as well as helping out the local party administration by collecting secondhand clothes for the NSV; NPEA Potsdam-Neuzelle put on numerous musical and theatrical performances to raise money for the Winter-Help campaign, while NPEA Schulpforta undertook street-collections in Naumburg and Bad Kösen. Finally, NPEA Stuhm and NPEA Plön raised money for the WHW via a sponsored cross-country relay race, and NPEA Köslin's 'Circus N. Apolani' put on a street-performance in Köslin entitled 'In the Magic Kingdom of Princess Wihiwe', which raised 263 RM within three hours.[50]

Figure 3.5 Members of the cast of a production of Martin Luserke's *Blut und Liebe* at NPEA Spandau.

However, as well as more mundane activities such as collecting monetary contributions in the street, sorting charitable donations of clothes and books, disseminating propaganda door-to-door, or dishing out 'one-pot meals' at the WHW soup-kitchens, *Jungmannen* would frequently devote their wood-working skills to the cause, carving numerous toys for children from disadvantaged families, war orphans, or those whose families had been bombed out.[51] Hobby-horses, building sets, pull-along toys, dollshouses and furniture, and model cars, trains, ships, and animals were all popular (see Figure 3.6), as well as more militaristic gifts, such as cannons, submarines, and toy guns painted with genuine camouflage colours.[52] The schools would also put on plays and shows to raise money from the local community, such as NPEA Spandau's 'Winter-Help shooting show', which raised 1,540 RM, or NPEA Ilfeld's 'Colourful Afternoon' variety show, which raised a grand total of 2,146.10 RM for the WHW in donations and ticket-sales.[53]

Such activities, linked even more closely with propagandistic activism in the run-up to Nazi rallies and election campaigns, essentially formed a perfect fusion

Figure 3.6 Woodwork at NPEA Rügen, 1943. Toy boats such as the ones in the image were often used in charity drives for the National Socialist Welfare Organisation, the NSV.

of the cultural and the political.[54] The Nazi regime was only ever willing to offer charity to those who were considered 'worthy' members of the racial community, and the constant demands on citizens to give up their hard-earned cash in donations to an organization of the Nazi state masquerading as a charitable institution were seen by many Germans as an unreasonable extra tax, even as the scheme appealed to the less fortunate recipients of the NSV's largesse, implying the regime's continuing commitment to its promises of social renewal.[55] However, for the *Jungmannen*, the idea that they were ministering to the needs of the *Volksgemeinschaft* often served a crucial socializatory function.[56] The system allowed pupils to bask in the pleasurable glow of altruism and caritative artistic fulfilment, whilst simultaneously instrumentalizing them in the interests of the Nazi state. This strategy of pursuing a fundamentally political mission via social and cultural means would become even more marked in the context of the Napolas' trips and exchanges within Germany and in foreign lands—it is to these that we shall now turn.

Travels within Germany: Educational Excursions

Even within the borders of the Third Reich prior to World War II, pupils at the NPEA were given plenty of opportunities to travel. Camps and exchanges with other Napolas, such as the 'class swap' which took place between NPEA Ilfeld and NPEA Stuhm in 1936, were common, as were educational excursions (*Studienfahrten*) to museums and other sites of cultural or academic interest.[57] Thus, pupils in the final two years at NPEA Spandau might be taken to visit the Freemasonry Museum in Wilmersdorf, while the younger year-groups at NPEA Potsdam might visit the local planetarium, or Berlin zoo.[58] For pupils at NPEA Naumburg and NPEA Ilfeld, the Zeiss optical engineering works and planetarium at Jena were favoured destinations, as well as Jena University, where professors could sometimes be prevailed upon to give the *Jungmannen* tours of their scientific institutes.[59] Meanwhile, on a trip designed to teach pupils about the political, economic, and cultural institutions of their provincial capital, *Jungmannen* from NPEA Köslin were taken to Stettin, where they visited the harbour and dockyards, a mental asylum, a chemical plant, a blast furnace, a printing works, two local museums, and various political offices, finishing off by attending a performance at the town theatre by the Berlin State Opera's dance troupe.[60] In the ensuing report, published in the next issue of the Köslin school newsletter, *Jungmann* Winter waxed lyrical on the amazing dedication of the nurses and doctors whom he had seen at work at the Kükenmühle asylum, but concluded that ultimately, anyone who had seen the sorry state of the asylum's inmates could scarcely fail to agree with the measures that the National Socialist state was taking 'to lessen and hinder this misery'. A concluding editorial comment coyly noted that readers might be interested to learn that *Jungmann* Winter intended to pursue a career as a naval medic.[61]

Trips to nationalist memorials or political pilgrimage sites, such as the Tannenberg Memorial, or the many shrines to the Nazi movement in Munich and Nuremberg, also made a particular impression—especially for those *Jungmannen* who were schoolmates of the son of Dachau Commandant Oswald Pohl at NPEA Plön. A group of pupils from Plön, who had been selected to take part in the ceremonies and march-past celebrating the forging of the Rome-Berlin Axis alliance in September 1937, were invited to stay at Dachau's SS training-camp, which was part of the overall concentration camp complex there.[62] Pohl was delighted to offer the *Jungmannen* free board and lodging, even meeting the group at the station before giving them a tour of the camp at what the Plöner later described as 'guest-friendly Dachau'.[63] Whilst visiting Munich, the 'Degenerate Art' exhibition and the House of German Art were also popular destinations—one group from the Plön contingent was thrilled when they encountered Hitler himself within the halls of the latter, and one of the *Jungmannen* was even permitted to shake the Führer's hand.[64] However, despite being overwhelmed by the gigantic sculptures by Arno Breker displayed in the House of German Art, Kurt Meyer of NPEA Potsdam claimed to have been most interested in checking out Picasso's allegedly degenerate portrayal of 'Women Bathing', because it was the first time he had ever seen a depiction of a woman in the nude.[65] Meanwhile, older *Jungmannen* were also given the opportunity to help out as volunteers at the Berlin Olympics in

1936—Claus Cordsen of NPEA Bensberg even maintained that he had had the opportunity to assist Leni Riefenstahl by holding an umbrella to keep her dry during a rainstorm.[66]

However, perhaps one of the most eagerly-anticipated excursions of all was NPEA Plön's visit to the Holstein Brewery in Kiel, the thought of which aroused in all of the pupils' minds 'a certain idea, which does not need to be expressed'. The *Jungmannen* were delighted to be able to circumvent the warnings and fulminations of their Director of Studies (who had instructed them to spit out the beer that they would be given to try as soon as they had tasted it), since the laboratory director subsequently invited them all to drink a bottle of beer with him after the tour. At the same time, even during a beer-tasting session, political considerations inevitably still intruded: the author of the report in the Plön school newsletter was keen to attribute the clean and salubrious state of the plant to the endeavours of the German Workers' Front (DAF) 'Beauty through Labour' scheme, as well as remarking upon a sign which proudly stated that all of the workers there were members of the DAF.[67]

The NPEA authorities also owned two retreats; a 'seaside hostel' (*Seeheim*) in the town of Wyk on the North Frisian island of Föhr, and a smallholding on the coast east of Kolberg which was known simply as 'Vineta' (see further below).[68] *Jungmannen* from several Napolas were routinely given the opportunity to spend three to four weeks at Wyk or Vineta each year, spending a few hours a day on lessons, whilst also getting involved with local charitable campaigns and political initiatives (including facilitating the expulsion of the Jewish population on the island of Föhr, as discussed in detail in Chapter 2), relaxing, and enjoying the delights of sun, sea, and sand.[69]

'Borderland Missions' and Travels beyond the Borders of the Reich

As recent research on tourism under Nazism has shown, leisure travel outside Germany performed a significant ideological function during the Third Reich, allowing citizens to draw negative comparisons with the standard of living in other countries, and hence causing them to appreciate their own fatherland all the more.[70] Furthermore, as Kristin Semmens has noted, international tourism also played a particular role in foreign policy terms: 'to convey the "truth" about Germany to guests from abroad. Through tourism, Nazi Germany would persuade the international community of its peaceful intentions.'[71]

The Napolas' school trips also performed precisely these functions from a political and propagandistic viewpoint, whilst also presenting pupils with a whole new spectrum of sights, ideas, and experiences.[72] As one *Erzieher* at NPEA Ilfeld put it: 'Just as the perspectives of English youth were broadened through constantly looking to their colonies and their associated challenges, so can this experience abroad give our own youth new strength and breadth'.[73] Indeed, in a collection of CVs prepared by *Jungmannen* graduating from NPEA Schulpforta in 1938–9, the programme of trips and exchanges abroad was frequently presented as one of the highlights of each pupil's school career.[74]

In theory, every *Jungmann* was supposed to spend at least three months in a foreign country, and to have embarked upon at least one extended trip abroad before leaving the school.[75] At the discretion of the Inspectorate, and under the direction of each school's *Fahrtenobmann* (Director of School Trips), every Napola would take on a suite of European countries as its 'main travel area' (*Hauptfahrtengebiet*); trips within Germany would be led by the *Jungmannen* themselves, while those beyond the borders of the Reich would have an *Erzieher* in charge.[76] Although the programme did not reach its full extent during the schools' first couple of years, by 1937, Eduard Wolff, the *Fahrtenobmann* at NPEA Köslin, could proudly announce that 630 *Jungmannen* from all of the NPEA had visited twenty different foreign countries in that year alone.[77] In the following year, Wolff was able to boast that *Jungmannen* and *Erzieher* solely from NPEA Köslin had spanned the globe 'from Petsamo on the Arctic Ocean to Rio de Janeiro; from the Russian border to New York. A token of the expansiveness with which we desire to form our *Jungmannen* for their lives to come'.[78] In similar vein, during a speech given in 1941, Education Minister Rust declared that, in 1939, multiple groups of Napola-pupils had visited the Balkans, the Baltic States, Belgium, Denmark, Finland, Holland, Hungary, Iceland, Italy, Luxembourg, Romania, Slovakia, Sweden, Yugoslavia, the United Kingdom, and the United States.[79] Even in wartime, the Inspectorate of the NPEA was constantly pressing for the amount of funding allocated annually for trips at each school to be doubled from 10 to 20 RM per head, which would have come to a staggering total of 120,000 RM in 1944—an exponential increase on the 42,000 RM allocation for the 1942 budget, and the 80,000 RM total for 1943.[80]

To facilitate these endeavours, the NPEA collaborated enthusiastically with the *Deutsches Auslands-Institut* (Institute for German Foreign Affairs) and the *Haus für das Deutschtum im Ausland* (House for Germandom Abroad) in Stuttgart, as well as liaising with the German Foreign Office (*Auswärtiges Amt*) on potential points of interest or conflict.[81] For instance, problems could arise when individual schools took matters too much into their own hands, as did NPEA Stuhm on a trip to make contact with 'ethnic Germans' (*Volksdeutsche*) in Latvia in 1939, which had not been properly registered with the relevant authorities. The *Jungmannen* in question were arrested for giving the Heil Hitler salute in front of the Latvian Freedom Memorial, which led to an awkward diplomatic incident, since the Latvian government was convinced that these actions constituted proof positive of German machinations against Latvian rule. The German Embassy's only option was to request that the German-Baltic *Volksgemeinschaft* gain retroactive permission for the visit from the Latvian government, in order to smooth things over.[82]

The fundamental aim behind the majority of these trips, however, was not to 'wander haphazardly into the blue yonder', as one *Erzieher* at NPEA Naumburg put it, but to teach the *Jungmannen* at first hand about the hardships of the alleged ethnic German struggle for economic, cultural, and racial existence.[83] Before every trip, pupils were supposed to be thoroughly prepared by their teachers, studying the relevant 'national political' circumstances in the areas which they were visiting, as well as learning a sufficient number of regionally appropriate folksongs with which to regale their ethnic German listeners. A crucial pedagogical aspect of each trip included the creation of an academic report, compiled for the most part by the *Jungmannen* unaided, which allowed pupils to choose to write up those parts of the project which they were most interested in.[84] One of these reports, preserved at the Political Archive of the German Foreign Office, investigated the theme of Transylvanian Saxon settlements in Romania, and contained chapters on topics such as local population figures, the ethnic German villagers' origins, German organizations, and leading German personages in the area, integrating geographical, historical, racial, and antisemitic perspectives on the subject in hand.[85]

Even on shorter trips within Germany, *Jungmannen* were still routinely encouraged to keep official communal diaries or '*Fahrtenbücher*' to record their activities and impressions.[86] Suitably edited and proofread, since the writing of some of the *Jungmannen* could often lack syntactical (or even orthographical) finesse, such reports and journals were then used to provide rich fodder for the rather more polished accounts which were later published in the school newsletters.[87]

Such revanchist propensities were even more marked when it came to the Napolas' travels in 'borderland regions' of the Reich, especially those which were deemed to have been wrongly wrested from German control in the aftermath of the Treaty of Versailles. As Vanessa Conze has demonstrated in her seminal article on German borderland-discourse between the wars, during this period, areas such as Alsace, the Danzig corridor, Eupen-Malmedy, Memelland, North Schleswig, the Rhineland, Upper and Lower Silesia, and West Prussia, became the focus of a wave of so-called 'borderland mania' (*Grenzmanie*). This 'border-syndrome' fixated above all on the alleged shame and injustice of the post-Versailles European order, and the necessity of pursuing nationalistic policies which could further German aspirations towards territorial revisionism.[88] Metaphors depicting a mutilated, war-wounded Germany, bleeding from a thousand lacerations and amputations, and desperately needing to be healed, appeared in every conceivable literary forum, from novels to incendiary pamphlets and tendentious works of (pseudo-)scholarship—such images apparently appealed to almost every political camp, as well as crossing every class divide.[89] Academic works were frequently commissioned to delegitimize the current status quo, bringing historical, cultural, linguistic, and (increasingly) racialized arguments to bear in the attempt to prove millennia of continuous 'German' settlement in contested territories in both the West and the East, including those which lay well beyond Germany's traditional 'national' borders. 'Ethnic and Cultural Territory researchers' would collect pertinent works of literature, document ethnic German architectural and religious forms, analyse proportional ethnicities among relevant populations, and compare their dialects, in order to demonstrate that the regions in question had always been subject to enduring German influence. These activities also linked currently perceived threats to the integrity of Germany's 'ethnic territory' with a long-standing historical narrative of continual depredations by inimical foreign powers, engaging wider audiences with public lectures and conferences on 'borderland politics' (*Grenzlandpolitik*) or the perpetual 'Struggle for Germandom' (*Deutschtumskampf*).[90]

The regions listed above could easily have been drawn from a catalogue of areas in which the Napolas routinely conducted their own '*Grenzlandeinsätze*' or 'borderland missions', and the related academic projects which the *Jungmannen* undertook also emulated this precise brand of politicized pseudo-scholarship.[91] Meanwhile, pupils' interactions with local ethnic German populations arguably performed a similarly 'educative' function, which was intended to bring the inhabitants round to the National Socialist way of thinking, and encourage them to support Hitler's expansionist foreign policy objective of bringing all ethnic Germans 'home to the Reich'.[92] This attitude was particularly palpable at new Napolas such as Stuhm or Neuzelle, which had been deliberately founded in borderland areas.[93] However, even at institutions with a venerable pre-Napola past, such as Köslin, Bensberg, Wahlstatt, and Plön, much was made of the schools' need to bolster German claims to neighbouring contested territories in East and West Prussia, Eupen-Malmedy, Upper Silesia, and North Schleswig respectively.

As an example, we might take NPEA Plön's virulently propagandistic efforts to drum up revanchist support among German communities in North Schleswig, the only contested territory to possess a Versailles-created border abutting Germany's heartland.[94] This activity went far beyond pupils' giving up their monthly 'North Schleswig groschen' to sponsor their 'adopted' German school (*Patenschule*) in Norderseiersleff, or mentoring North Schleswig's Nazi youth group, the *Deutsche Jungenschaft*—although these were also considered important aspects of the school's anti-Danish mission.[95] Rather, pupils' illegal activity propagandizing for the pro-German party in more than thirty-five separate constituencies in the run-up to the 1938 election, wearing white shirts as a '*Verbotsuniform*' (a plainclothes uniform to circumvent the Danish National Socialist ban), led to their being followed by the Danish secret police; several *Jungmannen* were forcibly transported back over the German border, while two *Erzieher* were fined and briefly detained in police custody. The school's extensive dissemination of leaflets and posters, as well as using marching bands, songs, and speech choirs to spread further propagandistic messages, led to the Napola being dubbed the Plön 'propaganda school' in the Danish media, and the pupils' unwelcome appearance was allegedly mentioned in radio reportage as far afield as New York and Moscow.[96]

Meanwhile, NPEA Köslin and NPEA Stuhm were most likely to turn their attention to fostering revanchism in those formerly German territories in Eastern Europe which had come under Polish rule after World War I.[97] This tendency is exemplified in particular by a 1937 special issue of the Köslin school newsletter, focusing on Danzig, entitled '*Nach Ostland geht unsere Fahrt*'—an adaptation of the first line of the medieval Flemish folksong '*Nach Ostland geht unsere Ritt*' ('To the Ostland Goes Our Ride'), which was frequently used to abet the National Socialist drive to emulate the Teutonic Knights' Eastern crusades.[98] Articles contained within included 'The Bleeding Border', an inflammatory tract illustrated with pictures of the despised 'three-country marker-stone' (*Dreiländerstein*) that marked the Versailles-imposed national boundary. The author decried the evils of needing a permit to cross into what had until so recently been German territory, arguing for the necessity of a swift resolution to this untenable situation: 'There, we all felt that this drawing of the borders cannot remain a permanent condition.'[99] Meanwhile, other articles in the special issue took a more *longue-durée* historical perspective, such as 'The Threefold Betrayal of the Germans in the East', and 'The Polish Corridor (Countering Polish Historical Lies)'.[100] The author of the latter article described the Versailles Treaty as 'the most shameful piece of horse-trading in world history', asserting that, historically, Poland could claim no right to the Danzig Corridor whatsoever, since Germanic tribes had populated the region thousands of years before the Slavs' arrival, and avowing that in any case the Poles had utterly destroyed the culture which had flourished under German rule in West Prussia, without ever replacing it with a Polish culture of their own. Another article described the thrill of visiting the *Ordensburg* in Marienburg (now Malbork, Poland), the erstwhile fortress of the Order of the Teutonic Knights, treading in the footsteps of the 'brothers of the order' and visiting their monastic cells, while yet another detailed the findings of relevant archaeological excavations which could be used to serve the Third Reich's revanchist agenda.[101]

However, the contested territories in the West were by no means exempt from such propagandistic 'missions' either; for instance, pupils at NPEA Bensberg devoted their habitual 'Pentecost Trip' (*Pfingstfahrt*) in 1938 to heightening German 'racial awareness' in the newly Belgian Eupen-Malmedy region of Belgium.[102] The *Erzieher* in charge, Rudolf Wasmann, prepared his charges for the trip by having them collect newspaper and journal articles about the region, and getting them to read relevant publications by the Association for Germandom Abroad (*Verein für das Deutschtum im Ausland*).[103] All Wasmann's best-laid plans were cast awry, however, by the fact that the dates allotted for the trip unexpectedly ended up coinciding with the aftermath of the Austrian Anschluss, which had made the Belgian government extremely paranoid (in this instance, rightly so) about the intentions of groups of visitors from Germany. All travel from the Reich to the Belgian region of Eupen-Malmedy was instantly banned, and Wasmann was only able to obtain visas from the Belgian consulate by 'disguising' the trip as a harmless touristic jaunt to the Ardennes. The visas were finally granted by the consul only after a lengthy and hostile interrogation process, and on the strict understanding that the group were not to spend the night in the 'New Belgian territories'—if they disobeyed, they would run the risk of immediate arrest and imprisonment.[104] Despite the revanchist protestations of the branch office of the Cologne Students' Organization, which had helped to organize the trip, the Gestapo in Aachen ordered Wasmann and his charges to obey the visa prescription inscribed in their passports to the letter. They were instructed to avoid arousing any suspicion among the locals, to refrain from creating any written material (such as diaries) concerning the trip's true intentions which might incriminate them if they were imprisoned and their effects confiscated, and only to liaise with a list of trusted interlocutors who were sympathetic to the German cause. Some of the *Jungmannen* were rather excited by all of this cloak-and-dagger secrecy, and told Wasmann afterwards that they had secretly longed for the 'adventure' of being arrested.[105]

The sense of danger was made even more palpable by the fact that, only a few days earlier, the 'harmless' members of a German rambling club from the Eifel region, who had been driving through the Ardennes in a minibus, had been arrested in the middle of eating their lunch, and deported back over the German border. All sports matches between Belgian and German teams were being cancelled left, right, and centre, and violent skirmishes had also taken place between ethnic German citizens in the region and the Belgian police. Thus, on their arrival in Sankt Vith, Wasmann impressed upon the *Jungmannen* the importance of not letting 'the mask of the harmless wanderer' slip as they strolled through the streets, Baedeker guides in hand. Having finally managed to enter the designated 'safe tavern' despite the presence of Belgian gendarmes outside, the group were taken under the wing of the representatives of the local German minority, and instructed in the minutiae of the 'ethnic guerrilla war' in the region. At times, their very presence apparently led the German population to demonstrate open support for the Reich, calling out 'Heil Hitler' to the *Jungmannen* in the street, and expressing gratitude that Germany had not wholly forgotten them or left them behind.[106] In describing the trip, the *Jungmannen* often used highly militaristic language to describe their activity in the interests of their 'ethnic mission', whilst also stressing how 'German' Sankt Vith had seemed, both in terms of the appearance and pro-Nazi sentiments of the local population, and the fact that there were hardly any French-speakers in residence there.[107]

Such agitation was also common in Austria where, both before and after the Anschluss, the *Jungmannen* were keen to awaken pro-German and pro-Nazi feeling, particularly among ethnic Germans in Slovene Carinthia and the South Tirol. Once again, pupils would have to doff their uniforms in favour of more harmless-seeming attire, and disguise themselves as 'the most harmless of central Europeans'—until the 'joyful' moment at which Austria was united with the Reich.[108] On one expedition led by *Zugführer* Uplegger of NPEA Plön in spring 1938, which had long been planned even before the Anschluss, the *Jungmannen* were delighted that the trip could now be designated a 'domestic' one, and that they could now wear their HJ uniforms without a care. However, as well as climbing Alpine peaks and rejoicing in the beauties of the mountainscape which Hitler had 'given them back', their travels also revealed a far darker side: 'In Graz, we gained our first impressions of the ruthless eradication of Jewry from the business world in the German "Ostmark"... [Meanwhile,] in Burgenland, in contrast to the Croats, we learned utterly to despise the dirty gypsies living in their foul and overcrowded huts; there are supposed to be over 13,000 of them in Burgenland.'[109] In the wake of the Anschluss, *Jungmannen* were also highly active in disseminating pro-German propaganda before the plebiscites about whether certain regions of Austria should secede, since the Reich was concerned at all costs to forestall any risk of the Slovene Carinthians voting to join Yugoslavia.[110]

Trips to the Balkans, Romania, Hungary, and the Baltic States followed a similar pattern; on one trip to the Batschka in 1939, a group of Plöner fell foul of police measures to keep Reich Germans and ethnic Germans apart, and were thrown out of six different locations.[111] Meanwhile, during NPEA Schulpforta's aforementioned trip to Romania in 1939, the local police intervened to put a stop to a 'village evening's entertainment' put on by the *Jungmannen*, and the group was also banned from staying overnight in the vicinity of Nösen, the heartland of the Transylvanian Saxon *Volksdeutsche*.[112] Antisemitic and denigratory quasi-colonialist remarks concerning the inhabitants of these regions were often a feature of pupils' and teachers' accounts—as in the case of NPEA Oranienstein's report on a trip to Bosnia in the same year, which took issue with the local Slav population's belief that their homeland must be a paradise compared to Germany, and described the habits of Bosnian Muslims in orientalizing terms. When accosted in the street by a local hawker, one of the *Jungmannen* aggressively responded 'Hey, how do you say "Jew" in Croatian?' to scare their interlocutor away.[113]

Meanwhile, as far as trips to the Mediterranean were concerned, establishing connections with the Fascist regime in Italy was considered particularly important.[114] The programme which these expeditions followed varied: elements of sight-seeing and cultural edification might predominate at times—for instance, in 1937, pupils from NPEA Berlin-Spandau travelled to Verona, where they attended a performance of Verdi's *Turandot* in the amphitheatre, experienced the delights of Rome, Florence, Ischia, Vesuvius, and Naples—and also visited a Fascist youth camp in Siena.[115] On other occasions, there might be a more dedicated commitment to attending camps run by the Fascist youth organization, the *Gioventù Italiana del Littorio* or GIL.[116] In each case, a key motivation behind the trips was 'to get to know the land of Fascism', even if encountering local wine, girls, and exploring the Italian landscape were at least equally significant for a number of the *Jungmannen*. Establishing contact with members of the Fascist administration and Party functionaries, as well as with military institutions, was often considered crucial to the success of the Napolas' Italian 'missions', and the extant accounts abound with descriptions of heartfelt welcomes by local Fascist dignitaries and GIL-groups.[117] Trips to Greece, on the other hand, seem to have been reserved for pupils at the 'humanistic' Napolas, Ilfeld and Schulpforta, and were designed to stress above all the supposed racial kinship between the ancient Greeks and the modern-day Germans, encouraging the *Jungmannen* to see themselves as the heirs of the Greeks in general, and the 'Aryan' warrior race of the ancient Spartans in particular.[118]

Finally, pupils also made frequent trips to those countries which they considered most 'racially' acceptable: including Sweden, Finland, and Iceland. Here, revanchist tendencies were scarcely in evidence; instead, the *Jungmannen* tended to rue the Scandinavians' alleged 'passivity' and susceptibility to anti-German propaganda, despite their shared Nordic heritage.[119] For instance, on a trip to Sweden in 1935, pupils from NPEA Spandau were unable to understand why the Swedes they encountered would habitually describe the Night of the Long Knives in 1934 as a 'civil war', or why they insisted in making what the *Jungmannen* deemed to be a completely unnecessary fuss about Nazi antisemitism or anti-Christian attitudes. They came to the conclusion that the Swedes would need a Führer of their own within fifty to a hundred years' time, once they had been cured of their current inanity.[120] The Napola groups also made common cause with Swedish and Finnish fascist youth groups, and cultivated contacts with Finnish dignitaries and artists, including the President of Finland, Pehr Evind Svinhufvud. On one occasion, the President even invited a group of *Jungmannen* to his country estate, where he regaled them with stories of the Finnish War of Independence and his preceding exile in Siberia.[121] However, when it came to fostering the strongest links of all with supposedly racially related peoples, two countries above all led the field—namely, England and the United States.

The NPEA Exchange Programmes with American Preparatory Schools and British Public Schools

As early as 1935, only two years after the Napolas' foundation, the school authorities had begun to request as much as 15,000 RM per year from the Prussian Finance Ministry simply to cover the costs of their exchange programmes.[122] However, while NPEA Plön and NPEA Spandau did indeed establish a series of brief reciprocal visits with pupils from two historic schools in Stockholm, Norra Latin, and Södra Latin, and a few pupils even had the opportunity to take part in exchanges with Mexico, Argentina, and German South-West Africa (modern-day Namibia), the majority of the Napola exchanges took place with preparatory schools in the United States, and public schools in England.[123] The aim of these visits, extending in the case of the Americas for the better part of the academic year, was threefold: to enable pupils fully to comprehend the racial differences between peoples (and hence to understand their own nation better); to confirm them in their 'unshakeable' National Socialist faith, giving them the chance to prove themselves ideologically, and, finally, to bring them into contact with their global adversaries' favoured methods of political conflict.[124] Britain and America were considered particularly significant exchange partners, not only because their fates were politically bound up with Germany's, whether as allies or as foes, but also since, along with the Third Reich, it was believed that these nations must inevitably stand together in the fight against racial chaos, as 'the three mighty bulwarks of the Nordic race, whose achievements alone are responsible for the fact that today's world is that of the white man.'[125]

As a prerequisite, those *Jungmannen* who took part in these exchanges were given a thorough grounding in the history, culture, national mindset, and political and economic circumstances of the country which they were visiting, and on their return, they might well be judged upon how successfully they had pursued National Socialist aims.[126] Particularly in the United States, but often in England as well, pupils and *Erzieher* were charged with a vital propagandistic mission: namely, to counteract and neutralize the effect of anti-Nazi accounts in the media, and to form opinion and influence future foreign views of the Third Reich.[127] Most Trojan-horse-like of all, perhaps, was the inclusion of Reinhard Pfundtner, the son of State Secretary Hans Pfundtner, on the roster of *Jungmannen* selected to participate in the first US exchange in 1935. Pfundtner senior, who was also a member of the Olympic Committee, used this opportunity to persuade Reinhard's American headmaster, Walter Huston Lillard of Tabor Academy, Massachusetts, to lobby in favour of US participation at the upcoming 1936 German Winter Olympic Games in Garmisch-Partenkirchen.[128] Lillard subsequently assured Pfundtner that his 'excellent letter replying to...questions about the Olympic Games' had been 'quoted by several of our good newspapers, and was included in the Associated Press service throughout the country....Undoubtedly, this message of yours will be very helpful in submerging some of the false propaganda.'[129]

In fact, Lillard was very much the leading light behind the American exchange programme, due to his creation of the 'International Schoolboy Fellowship' (ISF) in 1927—an organization which aimed to foster better relations between all nations through the medium of schoolboy exchange. Although the ISF's ambitions became ever more wideranging as its success increased, the organization's initial initiatives focused on promoting exchanges between the United States, England, France, and Germany; the *Klosterschule* (later NPEA) Ilfeld had already become involved with the ISF programme by the beginning of the 1930s.[130]

On the German side of the Atlantic, practicalities were arranged by the German Academic Exchange Service (DAAD).[131] The ISF Annual Report for 1935 suggests that the ISF was presented with a National Socialist *fait accompli* in terms of the German exchanges being limited solely to the Napolas from this point onwards, and it is also unclear whether Lillard and the ISF committee were fully aware of the elite-school status of the NPEA, or their fundamental political aims:

> Contrary to expectations..., arrangements were completed in Germany and announced to us on February 12th for inviting ten of our boys to visit in their schools as guests in exchange for ten of their best boys—the time to extend from June until Christmas. This permits both groups to use the summer weeks for orientation and recreation before trying out the other fellow's school program during the fall term. By returning at Christmas time there will be sufficient opportunity during the winter and spring terms to get back into stride.[132]

The selection criteria on the German side included pupils' possessing sufficient command of English, being especially well suited to this 'task of great responsibility', and ideally coming from families which were deemed 'suitable' to offer hospitality to an American guest—though it is uncertain whether the criteria were based primarily on families' financial stability or political reliability.[133]

An article chronicling the beginnings of the American exchange programme, which was published in 1937 in the Nazi educational periodical *Weltanschauung und Schule*, proudly reported that, although very few US academies had been prepared to participate in the Napola exchange in 1935, by the following year, so many had signed up that fourteen Napola-pupils could be sent to spend the summer months in America, often living with local families to perfect their English language skills before being thrown into the deep end of American school life. The *Jungmannen* were also given opportunities to visit Mount Washington, the Niagara Falls, New York, and other quintessentially American sites or attractions. The article praised the attention given to sport at the US academies, and reported gleefully that many of the German pupils had successfully achieved their goal of being selected for the first teams of their host schools, as well as 'winning many friends for Germany'. It was also noted that in some of the schools, 'in honour of their German guests, the flag of the German Reich was flown' alongside the star-spangled banner, and that they had met many Americans with 'good German names', whose parents and grandparents still spoke German at home, although they themselves were learning it as a 'foreign language'.[134]

In practical terms, following the first (experimental) year of exchanges in 1935, when ten boys and a member of staff from each side of the Atlantic spent July–December in their respective exchange-countries, it was decided that from 1936 onwards, fifteen US pupils would stay in Germany for the full ten months, while two groups of around fifteen *Jungmannen* would cross the Atlantic at a five-month interval. Further plans to extend the length of the German boys' visits to match those of their American counterparts did not have a chance to come to full fruition before the programme petered out in 1938–9.[135] Even as late as 1938, however, Lillard was still urging the headmasters of the eighteen American preparatory schools involved with the Napola-ISF exchange to continue the programme into the 1939–40 academic year, urging them to reconsider their tendency 'to sidestep the German exchange in order to register protest' at 'recent cruelties' in Nazi Germany, just because the boys' adult leaders were 'misbehaving':

> If we continue to bring the boys together, something constructive may be accomplished; whereas, if we abandon all efforts in the direction of Germany, we are closing the opportunity for the future leaders to be enlightened, and we are retreating back toward the condition of ill-will which prevailed after the World War. It has been clearly demonstrated that there is no danger of having our boys import Nazi ideas of government when they return from Germany. Not a single one of our boys has come ready to trade democracy for a dictatorship. But German boys have certainly returned to their country with a knowledge of conditions in a free land and with some questions in their minds even though they are loyal to their home government. One boy in last year's group wanted to remain here.[136]

To a present-day reader, these protestations, along with Lillard's more or less contemporaneous claim that 'German and American boys have come to a profound realization of their mutual problems[,] and have gone home with a deep respect for the people of countries whose national ideologies are at variance' might seem naïve in the extreme.[137] However, Lillard's attitude to Nazi Germany does not appear to have been fundamentally out of kilter with that of many other educated Americans during this period—trusting in German good faith, and for the most part happy to downplay or disregard reports of National Socialist atrocities, at least until the November pogrom (*Kristallnacht*).[138]

All in all, then, the US exchanges were clearly successful from a propagandistic perspective, inasmuch as the Napola-pupils were often able to convince their American hosts that matters in Germany were not nearly as dire as press reports might lead them to believe; they were also frequently given the chance to put their own political point of view across—which, as we have seen, was one of the key aims of the exchange as far as the Nazi authorities were concerned.[139] Moreover, many of the accounts by *Jungmannen* and *Erzieher* stress the friendly reception with which the Germans were welcomed. For instance, two pupils from NPEA Ilfeld who went on an exchange with Tabor Academy asserted that they had never been treated with enmity, but rather with protestations that the American people had never wanted to enter the First World War against Germany, and had been forced into fighting by President Woodrow Wilson's personal politics and mendacious propaganda.[140] At the same time, if the *Jungmannen* waxed too lyrical about the advantages of Hitler's Germany, they risked being tarnished as propagandists themselves. Hence, less complimentary comments were often made about the American press and its tendency to report on the Third Reich unfavourably (which was ascribed to 'Jewish' influence). In similar vein, the *Jungmannen* also often expressed surprise or horror that apartheid had not, from a National Socialist standpoint, been fully put into practice, and rued the prevalence of make-up and nail varnish among the females of the American species—a fashion which did not chime with Nazi Germany's patriarchal sensibilities.[141]

Although the American pupils who came to attend the Napolas and stay with their exchange-partners' families rarely spoke very much German, reports in school newsletters suggest that they also enjoyed getting to know the 'new Germany', and could often quite easily be swayed into displaying some sympathy for their hosts' political perspective.[142] One American pupil who had attended NPEA Plön even claimed that the year he had spent there was the 'greatest experience of his life', while another was alleged to have been surprisingly fond of 'Nazi superficialities', since he had once been discovered practising the 'German greeting' in front of his mirror.[143] Meanwhile, many staff and pupils at the US academies kept in touch with their German partner-schools even after the outbreak of war; indeed, the propagandistic success of the exchange programme can in some measure be demonstrated by the following letter from Walden Pell, the headmaster of St. Andrew's School, Delaware, to the Director of Studies at NPEA Spandau, dated 9 November 1939:

My dear Herr Brandenburg,

Your good letter of October 14th has just come, and Oliver van Petten [the pupil from St. Andrew's who had been staying at NPEA Spandau the previous year] has translated it for me. Some day I hope to learn the German language.

Thank you very much for the two copies of Herr Hitler's speech. It was a shock to hear this morning of the attempt to kill him. I have given one copy to Oliver and the other to our Library. I had already read the speech in our papers. I agree that it is time the British and French should tell us exactly what they are fighting for.

You may be sure that this regrettable war will never destroy the friendship we have for the German people and our great gratitude to you and your School for all you did for our boy.

I am going to have the German class at St. Andrews translate this letter into German.

With best wishes and hoping for a speedy peace.[144]

After the war, Pell continued to correspond with the parents of Horst Roloff, an exchange student from NPEA Neuzelle, for decades, assisting the Roloff family in their search for their missing son, sending them food parcels and care packages, and donating a large sum of money to enable Frau Roloff to make a pilgrimage to Horst's war grave in Italy, once his final whereabouts were known.[145] Even today, a photograph of Horst Roloff still hangs in the school's memorial gallery, alongside those of all the genuine St. Andrew's alumni who died in World War II, and upper-level pupils currently studying history at the school are encouraged to undertake an elective project investigating Roloff's military career, before debating whether his portrait should be permanently removed from public view.

*

Meanwhile, closer to home, plans were afoot to develop an exchange programme with schools in Britain as early as January 1934—from this perspective, it was no coincidence that English had always been the most common modern foreign language at the NPEA.[146] Exchanges of pupils and British exchange teachers were common at most of the Napolas throughout the 1930s, and, while the programme was not always an unqualified success, it still enjoyed a broad appeal.[147] On the NPEA side, great care was taken to send *Jungmannen* and *Erzieher* who would make the best possible impression upon their English hosts, bearing in mind both the extent of pupils' sporting ability, and the suitability of their character and deportment, especially their capacity for tact, sincerity, and urbanity.[148] Individual *Erzieher* might also take their own initiative to organize exchanges, in collaboration with the NPEA *Landesverwaltung*, who could advise on likely partnerships and provide lists of relevant school addresses. Thus, Rudolf Wasmann's collected papers contain drafts of numerous letters attempting to convince schools such as Southlea Preparatory School in Malvern and Lancing House Prep School in Lowestoft to engage in exchanges with NPEA Bensberg. As a paradigmatic example of this genre, we might take the letter which Wasmann wrote on 18 March 1937 to John L. Andrewes, the headmaster of Exeter School:[149]

> Dear Sir,
>
> By the kindness of Mr. Riley I received your address. Our school, one of Germany's new Public Schools, likes to get into touch with an English school, and I myself as an old Student of Exeter University College should feel extremely happy if I could arrange an exchange with a school so well-known in my old university town and in glorious Devon.
>
> What we are thinking of is a visit in form of a holiday party. We are sending over a group of about twelve boys for a period of about three weeks. And we should like you to do the same. The boys will be accompanied by one of their masters.
>
> My plans are like this: You send us a group of boys who are keen on getting to know Germany and German institutions. As all our boys know English, there will be hardly any language trouble; if your boys can speak German, all the better for them. Those who like to cultivate their knowledge of the German language will attend a class according to their age with their German comrades. The others will be asked to go to the English lessons. In the afternoon they will engage in sports together. Of course your boys will often go to Köln, a culture centre of Western Germany. As we have for transports a lorry provided with seats a great part of the time will be devoted to seeing the countryside. In this connection I think of a Rhine tour together with a group of our boys. They will

find sleeping accommodation in the fine German youth hostels (e.g. the famous castle now serving as a youth hostel Burg Stahleck). They will go down as far as Heidelberg. They will go over the new German motor roads, on their way back they will ascend the famous Loreley. Another tour will take them to the Siebengebirge with the famous ruin of Drachenfels.

When the time is up our boys who are picked out, will go to England with their English friends, where they will be your guests, they stay either as boarders at your school or with the parents of the boys. Here they are to attend the classes and to live the life of an English schoolboy. If our exchange visit turns out to be a success—and I fell [*sic*] quite sure it will—and some of the boys express the wihs [*sic*] for a longer stay, we might arrange this too. As we are a state owned school the fees are arranged according to the income of the parents. The selection of our boys is strictly on merit. Of course this is quite a different thing with a guest. Again I think it would be the best that we send you a German boy for the English one who likes to stay for a longer period. I think then there will be no question of cost at all. The only thing to be paid for ist [*sic*] the journey.

As to the date of an exchange visit, I propose this. You send us your boys let us say towards the middle of April. They will be here with us till the 8th or 9th of May. And then our boys will stay with you towards the end of May. An arrangement like this would give your boys the experiences of the National Labour Day or they would witness the birthday celebration of our Führer, whereas our boys will have the thrill of experiencing the spell of Coronation tide [*sic*].

As to the age of the boys concerned I am thinking of sending you a group of boys aged about 17. Exchange visits as described by me have been successfully carried out by some of our 'Nationalpolitischen Erziehungsanstalten'. We ourselves have been visited by the combined fencing team of Eton and Harrow; and a football team of Shrewsbury will call on us the 14th and 15th of April.

I shall be pleased to answer you any questions you may put.

Yours truly,
Rudolf Wasmann

Few documents reveal so clearly the Napolas' habitual mode of approach, concealing their manifold propagandistic aims behind a façade of fostering international cooperation, whilst simultaneously highlighting the prospect of enticing sight-seeing trips and new experiences galore, in order to appeal as much as possible to the British schools in question, and encouraging them to send their pupils to be effectively indoctrinated at the NPEA.

Although Wasmann's efforts bore no fruit in this particular instance, NPEA Naumburg's exchange with Lancing House in 1936 was so successful that the headmaster, E. K. Milliken, waxed dubiously lyrical in his report to the *Anstaltsleiter* at Naumburg, declaring that 'I have never, in all my experience of School Mastering, handled two more attractive boys than G. Kühlewind and W. Tönhardt'. Milliken praised the two German boys' achievements in lessons to the skies, and stressed that everyone whom they met had commended their 'intense enthusiasm, constant alertness, and their natural courtesy'. In his conviction that promoting further exchanges between the younger year-groups of the Napolas and British prep schools could bring 'considerable benefit to the promotion of friendship between our two countries', Milliken even offered to put this proposition before the Association of Prep Schools, if the idea found favour with the NPEA authorities.[150] Visits to the Napolas by headmasters, teachers, and sports teams from England were also common—the British guests would frequently be greeted with fulsome speeches, emphasizing the commonalities between the NPEA and the public schools, stressing the bonds of racial kinship which bound England and Germany and their shared struggles at the time of Frederick the Great or the Napoleonic Wars, and stating that these two 'white nations' must never again take up arms against each other.[151]

British impressions of the Napolas and their *Jungmannen* seem to have been for the most part extremely favourable, implying that the German pretence of disinterested friendship was being taken largely at face value. For instance, English school newsletters tended to comment positively on the sporting prowess and remarkably muscular build of the German boys, while an exchange pupil at NPEA Spandau summed up his observations of the *Jungmannen* there as follows:[152]

> Some things that strike me about the boys here are: that they all have about the same opinions in the most important of matters, that they believe a soldier or army officer is about the best thing one could hope to become, that they are always so sure that German people and German things are far superior to the rest of the world, that they all seem healthy and happy, that they are always willing and glad to help, that they sing very well in harmony, that they have in most cases an extravagant selfconfidence, a tendency to be critical in usual matters, and are all so frank with one another....[153]

Meanwhile, a group from NPEA Oranienstein on an exchange with Westminster School discovered that, whilst wearing swastika belt-buckles in Belgium could get one into a great deal of trouble, in Britain, everybody just assumed that the *Jungmannen* were boy scouts, and thought nothing of their attire.[154]

German views of the British were more mixed, however, especially when it came to their perceived lack of susceptibility to Nazi propaganda. *Zugführer* Hildebrandt of NPEA Stuhm, who spent a year as an exchange teacher at Bromley in Kent in 1938, became increasingly frustrated both by the general hostility of British public opinion towards the Nazi annexation of the Sudetenland, and his colleagues' constant charitable collections for Czech refugees, blaming liberal 'press freedom' for creating a climate hostile to Chamberlain and his pro-appeasement cabinet policy. On one occasion, in the context of a lecture series entitled 'My Country's Problems in Relation to the Preservation of Peace', featuring speakers from Czechoslovakia, France, Germany, Yugoslavia, Russia, and

Poland, Hildebrandt even attempted to no-platform Dr. Schauroth, the German lecturer chosen by the relevant committee, since he was a former Reichstag representative for the Social Democratic Party: 'I tried first to speak about this matter with a few people from the committee and make it clear to them that a political refugee could scarcely present a fair judgment. It is impossible to find sympathy among the English, though. "But he's still German", was the response, or "But we can't present someone who peddles propaganda for National Socialism". Where is the "fair play" there?'[155] Eventually, the headmaster intervened in the matter, forcing the chairman of the committee to agree that a more pro-regime talk on Germany could be added to the programme, if a sufficiently famous German personage could be found who would not attempt to disseminate Nazi propaganda.[156] Meanwhile, Friedrich Dubslaff of NPEA Bensberg, who spent a year as an exchange-teacher at Grange High School for Boys in Bradford in 1937, remembered being treated by the headmaster with a certain 'mistrust', while a visit to Bradfield by a group of *Jungmannen* from NPEA Schulpforta was apparently disrupted by the protestations of a German émigré, although a Napola-friendly teacher, Mr Cartwright, still managed to provide the group with a place to pitch their tents on the school grounds.[157]

More detailed analysis of the gradually changing relationships between long-standing partner-schools, such as NPEA Ilfeld and Kingswood School in Bath, has revealed that Anglo-German political tensions were continually increasing during the course of the 1930s, in line with broader trends in international relations.[158] However, for the most part, the English participants in the exchange programme were ready to give the Germans the benefit of the doubt and listen to their version of events, hoping against hope that their national differences could ultimately be cast aside in the name of international cooperation.[159] After all, for many adherents of the public schools, Communism and Socialism would have appeared to present a far greater threat to the European world order than Hitler's methods of supposedly 'putting Germany to rights', and, even leaving appeasement aside, there existed a genuine will to foster peace and mutual understanding between the two nations. It is perhaps ironic, then, that the Napolas' final type of 'mission' would have appeared to outside observers to be the most socialist initiative of all.

Farm, Factory, and Mining 'Missions': Realizing the 'Socialist' Aspects of National Socialism?

In her survey of mechanisms of inclusion within the Nazi *Volksgemeinschaft*, Jill Stephenson has noted that, despite the manual worker being 'exalted in propaganda as a hero of National Socialist labour', the mobility promised by Nazi social engineering was 'for the most part either transient or illusory'—a widely prevalent view when considering Nazi attempts to engage blue-collar workers and labourers.[160] Nevertheless, the regime consistently took care to align itself with workers in symbolic terms, whilst also attempting to engage young men from working-class backgrounds in the Hitler Youth, providing them with apprenticeships, and fostering career-oriented enterprises such as the 'Reich Youth Vocational Contest' (*Reichsjugendberufswettkampf*).[161] Indeed, at first glance, it might seem that the Napola programmes went even further in this regard than initiatives such as the Reich Labour Service (RAD) or the Reich Education Ministry's 'Year on the Land' (*Landjahr*) programme, since the *Jungmannen* in question were compelled to spend several months not merely living in self-contained labour camps, but actually living with the families of miners and labourers, and getting to know their way of life intimately at first hand.[162]

In an internal memo describing the overall aims of the NPEA, Inspector August Heißmeyer explained the motivations behind this programme of labour 'missions' as follows:

> Every *Jungmann* in the 6th *Zug* works for a six-to-eight-week period in the land service (*Landdienst*) alongside a farmer or settler. He undertakes all of the requisite labours exactly as if he were dependent on the farmer for his wages and his daily bread. The following year, he works as an apprentice in a mine or a factory for eight to ten weeks; he lives with the family of the miner or labourer, and has to support himself on his apprentice's wage. Farmers and labourers make up the majority of the German people; their nature, desires, and actions form a key part of the make-up of the German body politic. One day, the *Jungmann* may well have to provide an example for farmers and labourers; he may have to lead them, and therefore he must know them and their way of life better than he would do merely from his official position. With youthful impressionability, he must grow into their world and their way of life, perceive the harshness of their vocation the hard way, and also learn from them that one demands and expects more from men in decisive and leading positions than mere book-learning.[163]

However, this did not mean that the *Jungmannen* waited until their late teens to begin the process of 'labour appreciation'. Even the youngest boys at the NPEA were routinely enspanned into helping on the land near their schools—assisting local farmers with the rye or potato harvest, for instance.[164] In this context, too, it is worth noting that differences between the varieties of land service employed at the various schools were still discernible. For instance, 'borderland' Napolas such as NPEA Stuhm, and those in the occupied Eastern territories, would stress above all the political nature of their work supporting 'ethnic German' farmers and settlers against alleged Slavic depredations by local Poles or Czechs, while schools in predominantly Catholic areas such as NPEA Emsland in Haselünne or NPEA Saarland in St. Wendel might instead use harvest assistance as a means to ingratiate the Napola and its inhabitants with the local community, despite their initial misgivings.[165] Meanwhile, trips to Vineta, the schools' clifftop smallholding near Kolberg, also led to boys' gaining extensive experience of animal husbandry, with groups of pupils taking it in turns for three days at a time to muck out the cattle (*Viehdienst*), take care of the pigs (*Schweinedienst*), and look after all of the rest of the miscellaneous livestock, including hens, doves, lambs, rabbits, and baby ducklings (*Kleintierdienst*).[166] Hans Lindenberg of NPEA Potsdam remembered there being fierce competition to see which group could get the best 'egglaying record', leading to consternation and monkeyhouse when some of the less experienced 'city kids' attempted to tackle the cockerels by mistake.[167] However, if you were tired, the round of constant farmwork could make life at Vineta seem less like a paradise, and more like a trial.[168]

Still, this was all (literally) child's play compared to the labour which the older pupils were routinely expected to accomplish—Heißmeyer noted in one official report that 3,500 *Jungmannen* and *Jungmädel* and their *Erzieher* had accomplished 65,000 days' labour in 1939 alone.[169] Once again, the explicitly political nature of the 'mission' was seen as paramount, and the work itself was described as a mere 'means to an end'—hence, the 'land service missions' (*Landeinsätze*) were always located either in borderland areas, or in areas with a significant population of ethnic German inhabitants or migrants.[170] One article in the NPEA Plön newsletter succinctly laid out the ideological and propagandistic aims of the school's *Landeinsatz* near Danzig in 1936 as follows: Firstly, pupils would assist farmers financially by providing them with cheap labour. Secondly, the *Jungmannen* would seek to influence the farmers politically, countering their complaints against Party or government officials, whilst inflaming their desire to 'return to the Reich'. Thirdly, they must demonstrate how closely bound Reich Germans and ethnic Germans truly were, whilst simultaneously proving that class and caste differences had entirely vanished from the new Germany. Finally, they should support local Party offices in fostering the village community, in opposition to Jews, Poles, Communists, Social Democrats, and other alleged enemies of the regime who might be working against German interests in the region.[171]

At first, when it came to 'missions' beyond Germany's borders, the NPEA had merely contracted to send *Jungmannen* as volunteers to join in with initiatives which had already been set up by the Reich Student Leadership's 'Student Land Service' (*Studentischer Landdienst*) in Pomerania, Silesia, East Prussia, and Danzig; organizing *Landeinsätze* within Germany's heartland still remained the remit of each individual Napola.[172] However, when it became clear that the Reich Youth Leadership wished to use this connection to attempt to gain greater influence over the NPEA, and the Reich Student Leadership seemed overly concerned to prevent the schools from taking their own initiative, the two organizations parted company.[173] This rift seems to have occurred not least because the *Jungmannen*, who were not as physically mature as university students, were being regularly overtaxed by the demands of their employers.[174] Moreover, all too often, they were being placed in highly problematic situations, due to the incompetence of the Student Land Service administration.[175] Most egregiously, on one occasion, a group of *Jungmannen* were 'accidentally' sent to Austria instead of

Silesia, and when they finally arrived at their Silesian quarters, none of the farmers were even willing to claim that they had made a request for extra labour; to add insult to injury, the family to which one of the *Jungmannen* was ostensibly registered did not appear to exist at all.[176]

As one might expect, the accounts of the Napola land service in school newsletters tended to be overwhelmingly positive, although they might readily reveal somewhat patronizing attitudes towards the farmers in question.[177] Pupils might report back on how 'good' a National Socialist 'their' farmer was, or stress the enduring relationships which they had managed to cultivate, as did *Jungmann* Recksieck from Schulpforta: 'In farewell, [my farmer] gave me his hand and said: "Now, just when you can cope with every type of work on your own, you have to leave. That's really a shame. If at any point you don't know where to go, then come to me! You'll always have a place here!"'[178] The newsletters might also quote correspondence between the farming families and 'their' *Jungmannen*, such as this letter to a pupil from NPEA Spandau: 'We only managed to get around to thanking you for your greetings card today! It arrived at lunchtime, there was great joy.... Otherwise, we still always miss you, you will never be forgotten. Resel and Agele keep asking why oh why is Hermann gone, he should have stayed with us forever. Where we would once have laughed, on Sunday when we were eating we wept; parting from you was specially hard for Resel and Mannwar....'[179]

However, pupils' experiences could also be chaotic, abusive, or even horrific, depending on the character and circumstances of the farming families to whom they were assigned. For instance, one surviving file from the *Kreisleitung* Trier-Westland describes an altercation between the *Erzieher* in charge of NPEA Oranienstein's *Landdienst* and a local farmer and his wife, who hysterically shrieked that *Jungmann* K., who had been allotted to them, had been forced on them as a spy, had done no work at all, and was too stupid to do anything except sleep and eat breakfast for hours at a time. When K. was suffering from diarrhoea, apparently the farmer and his wife had kept sneaking up on him to check how often he was visiting the privy, and then used this gastric affliction as an excuse to accuse him of congenital laziness.[180] Former pupils also recollected being forced to sleep alongside other farm labourers in the same cramped quarters, which might lead to resentment even at the best of times—Helmuth Junghans of NPEA Klotzsche recalled that at his billet in the Sudetenland, the surly farmboy, Jan, had put snails in the bed in retaliation for being forced to sleep elsewhere.[181] More worryingly, Hans Lindenberg recalled that a soldier who had also been enspanned to help with the potato harvest had almost come close to perpetrating an indecent assault upon him, deliberately getting under the covers with him naked while he was lying ill abed.[182] Even the presence of alluringly buxom farmers' daughters or BDM land-girls nearby could not always make up for the 'ginormous swarms of flies' or generally primitive conditions and ill-treatment, and some pupils later claimed that they had bitterly resented being forced to write subsequent saccharine accounts of 'romantic village life' by their teachers.[183]

Once World War II had begun, however, the crowning moment of each *Jungmann*'s career on the land was being sent on the annual 'Wartheland mission' (*Warthelandeinsatz*) to assist ethnic German farmers in the newly conquered 'Warthegau' region of Poland with the harvest, along with massed ranks of students, Adolf-Hitler-School pupils, and members of the Norwegian, Danish, and Dutch HJ.[184] Riding in the splendidly upholstered carriages of a 'special train' from Berlin, the *Jungmannen* would routinely be greeted by Gauleiter Arthur Greiser with great pomp and circumstance upon their arrival, and subjected to numerous speeches about the 'ethnic importance' of their work in the region.[185]

As we might expect from such an explicitly politicized 'mission', the *Jungmannen* were encouraged to display virulently anti-Polish attitudes, as exemplified by one pupil from NPEA Wien-Breitensee, who had started giving his Polish fellow-labourers a 'resounding box on the ears' for not working hard enough: 'Now some people might say that this way of carrying on wasn't right, that the Poles are treated too harshly; they are human beings too after all; they need a rest from their labours. There is only one answer to that! Think of the Bloody Sunday at Bromberg![186] Are they still human beings, those who can commit such atrocities; are they still human beings, those who slaughtered so many Germans in the most horrific ways? The farmers in Ebenhausen told us that they had found a 16-year-old boy whom they knew horribly mutilated with his eyes put out.... I heard of dozens of such cases from the lips of those who suffered them. And now one should treat these people as delicately as possible?'[187]

The *Jungmannen* might also enforce Nazi racial politics in a less physically violent, but no less insidious fashion, insisting that the ethnic German farming families treat their Polish labourers 'rightly' by never engaging them in conversation or allowing them to dine with the family, making them sleep outside, and generally treating them as contemptible serfs.[188] The Polish inhabitants were also mocked in the theatrical evenings put on by the *Jungmannen* in local villages, and pupils would constantly complain about the dirt and insufficiency of the formerly Polish farms which had been forcibly expropriated for use by ethnic German settlers.[189] From this perspective, Arthur Greiser's instruction that the *Jungmannen* should act as masters (*Herren*) towards the Poles seemed in many instances to have been fully realized.[190] At the same time, the *Jungmannen* also seem to have been more likely to patronize, and to some extent disdain, the ethnic Germans from Volhynia and Bessarabia with whom they were now working than they were to feel wholehearted solidarity with them.[191] How far, then, did these experiences in the Napola land service compare with the 'industrial missions'?

*

The Napolas' programme of industrial work experience seems to have developed more gradually, with the very first attempts to give pupils insight into the life of the working man taking place at NPEA Spandau. In October 1934, *Anstaltsleiter* Bernhard Pein approached AEG, a multinational electrical engineering firm based in Berlin, and set up an agreement with the company's training division that the *Jungmannen* would undertake a six-day training programme in the metal industry, during which pupils in the final two years would work at the firm's training workshop in Reinickendorf (whilst still living at the NPEA). Older apprentices would show the Napola-pupils how things were done, although they would not be permitted to work on their own at any point. The company's training division representative, Dr.-Ing. Heiland, commented that the *Jungmannen* were 'particularly fascinated by forging the red-hot iron', ignoring the blisters on their hands and the frequent small injuries which were unavoidable in this line of work.[192] Thereafter, the school at Spandau developed a friendly relationship with the firm over the next couple of years, playing matches with the apprentices' handball team, reciprocally inviting apprentices to the NPEA, and generally engaging in dialogue with them.[193] Care was taken that the *Jungmannen* should not gain too rosy a view of such forms of labour, however—once the programme of 'industrial missions' got going properly, the factories selected were intentionally not those 'model firms' which might give pupils a misleading impression of most workers' normal standard of living.[194] In addition, 'racial' and 'socialist' imperatives were frequently linked—for instance, *Jungmannen* from NPEA Bensberg would often be sent on 'missions' to work alongside ethnic Germans in factories in the Eupen-Malmedy region of Belgium.[195]

However, it was the 'mining mission' (*Bergwerkseinsatz*) which not only marked the pinnacle of each *Jungmann*'s industrial labour service, but which also garnered most attention from the outside world—indeed, very often, newspaper articles on the NPEA might begin with an eye-catching headline such as '*Die "Obersekunda" im Bergwerk*' ('Fifth-formers down the Mine'), before launching into a much more generalized appraisal of the schools' programme, only a small proportion of which would be devoted to the *Einsätze* per se.[196] This type of 'mission' officially took place for the first time in 1937, and the programme was confirmed by ministerial edict in 1938, although NPEA Spandau already appears to have experimented with the format in 1936.[197] Representatives from the mining companies and the NPEA authorities met in conference at the headquarters of Hibernia AG to arrange the eight-week-long programme, since a whole host of preparatory arrangements had to be put in place before the *Jungmannen* arrived at their billets, including acquiring the requisite insurance, and liaising with local Party offices.[198] Often, the Napola-pupils would be paid as little as 30 Pfennigs a day—the average amount that an apprentice miner would have left over once he had paid for the necessities of life. The ensuing savings in personnel costs could then be used to pay for those miners whom the *Jungmannen* were replacing to take a holiday at the firm's expense.[199]

Once again, pupils were very carefully selected and prepared for their 'mission' beforehand; boys generally had to be deemed sufficiently intellectually mature, morally sound, and physically fit in order to take part.[200] The *Jungmannen* would usually be employed in all of the different parts of the mine, both above and below ground, to get a sense of the different tasks involved in the firm's work; their *Erzieher* would also be expected to join in, not least when it came to the hard graft at the coalface—a fact which astonished some members of the mining communities.[201] One of the English exchange-teachers at NPEA Spandau described his experiences in the Ruhr in 1938 as follows, joking that he had previously been attempting to get into a forced labour company in order to spy on the German mines by criticizing National Socialist policy and failing to give the Hitler salute in large public assemblies, yet all to no avail:

> Before it became necessary to commit more grave offences, I was given the opportunity to go with a group of boys from the N.P.E.A. Spandau on a visit to Bochum-Hoerdel in the Ruhr district. Among them I soon discovered that they did not think of their work in the mines as a hardship. They looked forward eagerly to the adventure and considered themselves lucky to be able to meet and to live with the miners whose work is so essential to Germany's economic prosperity.... In order that we should gradually get used to working conditions, we began work above ground, in the washing department, at the sorting benches, in the woodyard, and on the '*Kratzbühne*' scraping out empty trucks on their way back to the pit. My apprenticeship began with an eight-hour shift at the '*Kratzbühne*'. It seemed to me about the longest eight hours I had ever spent. Standing made one's feet ache: the constant stooping to scoop up a shovelful of coal from the bottom of each passing truck, made one's back ache, and the clash and bang of the iron trucks made one's head ache. However, after a hot shower, a square meal and a sound sleep one felt fit again. As one got used to the work it became less tiring and time passed more quickly. Soon came the great day when we were to put in the first shift below ground. Well primed with horrid stories of previous disasters, we walked towards the shaft. Once again our work-mates reminded us that a year ago all four lift cages had crashed down this very shaft—two thousand feet into the sump below: it had taken four weeks to disentangle the wreckage! By comparison with such grim expectations the descent was a tame affair with very little 'sinking feeling'....[202]

Accounts by pupils themselves also demonstrate how far they were assimilated into this brave new world of backbreaking labour. Thus, in 1937, one *Jungmann* from NPEA Oranienstein claimed: 'We've fully settled in. We can't be distinguished any more from the other *Kumpels* (miners); our togs filthy, hands square and chapped, we don't burn our trousers any more on the mining lamps or bang our heads any more on every spur of rock. Above all, we replace a labourer, and they recognize our labour.'[203]

Sometimes, however, this could involve suffering minor injuries—or even witnessing horrific accidents—at first hand. A report from an *Erzieher* at NPEA Spandau describes the various health problems from which his *Jungmannen* suffered during a stint in the Ruhrgebiet in 1937, including gastric troubles, furunculosis, and anaemia or 'pit sickness'; he swiftly dismissed two 'lighter injuries' (a crushed finger and a broken arm) as 'harmless'.[204] Meanwhile, another, more dramatic eyewitness account from NPEA Oranienstein by the then 17-year-old Horst Ueberhorst describes the carnage caused by an exploding pump which sent countless gallons of water hurtling down the mineshaft, killing two men more or less instantly, and endangering the lives of many others; no one could be sure if the cables would withstand the weight of the cascade as the lift struggled to haul the survivors to safety.[205]

Nevertheless, a recurring theme throughout these accounts—whether by the pupils themselves, their *Erzieher*, the '*Kumpels*' alongside whom they worked, or the firms employing them—is the respect which the *Jungmannen* quickly earned, due to their willing and disciplined demeanour, and their exceptional ability as *Jungarbeiter* (apprentices). As one manager at the Grube Neue Haardt bei Weidenau an der Sieg put it in a letter of thanks to NPEA Oranienstein:

> I...could note to my satisfaction that the lads mastered their work deftly, diligently, and efficiently. This was...the greatest surprise for me as a trained miner. They treated all of their labours not as an imposition, but took pleasure and a keen interest in the mining work too. My colleagues and I took quiet pleasure in the lads, and were unanimous in the opinion that our remaining lads could really take a leaf out of their book.[206]

Whether the families with whom the *Jungmannen* stayed would have been as impressed with their constant attempts to discuss the thornier facets of the National Socialist *Weltanschauung*—which was considered an equally important aspect of their 'mission'—is harder to judge. As ever, pupils had to report on their accomplishments and the political views of the families and communities with whom they were staying, in order to complete a social science project relating to their experiences thereafter.[207] Themes of these reports (and the accompanying accounts in school newsletters) often included 'the miner's social situation' (*Die soziale Lage des Bergmanns*), accounts of 'my miner' (*Mein Kumpel*), and miners' attitudes towards the Party and the regime, or commentaries on the mining communities' manners and *mores*, which could often betray more than a tinge of moral superiority. Thus, pupils from NPEA Plön on their 'mission' in 1942 complained of the ways that the miners' children were being brought up (either being spoilt, or treated as a 'plague' and left to play in the street), and commented adversely on the teenagers' moral laxity, which might include playing with each others' genitals in the shower, or addiction to nicotine and alcohol. They also remarked uneasily on unwanted attempts by older miners to give them ill-meant or teasing tips as a form of 'sex education'.[208]

At the same time, far deeper and more meaningful relationships with mining families could still be forged: Hans Hinrich Zornig, a pupil on the same Plön 'mission', reported that when he had caught scarlet fever, his 'lodging parents' (*Quartierseltern*) had insisted on looking after him at their own risk rather than sending him to hospital, and their own parents had also come to visit him during his illness.[209] The miner's wife even went so far as to offer to adopt him if anything should happen to his widowed mother; she claimed that, by the end of the eight-week *Einsatz*, she already thought of him as a son. Zornig commented astonishedly in his report that, on the day that he first met his host, he would never have anticipated such a warm reception in his wildest dreams.[210]

That the schools' relationship with the mining communities was not wholly onesided may also be suggested by the frequent invitations extended to the miners and their families to attend celebrations at the NPEA, and the genuine penfriendships which seem to have been forged between *Jungmannen* and *Arbeiter*.[211] Indeed, the *Jungmannen* from NPEA Oranienstein who undertook their *Einsätze* in wartime, this time working alongside French, Italian, Russian, and Ukrainian PoWs as well as their compatriots, discovered that the latter still remembered the *Jungmannen* from Oranienstein who had worked there three or four years before with great fondness. They were delighted to hear that some of the Oraniensteiner were already highly decorated soldiers at the front, though they were devastated to learn that others had already been killed.[212]

Some *Anstaltsleiter* even saw these connections as providing a golden opportunity for recruiting more pupils from the working-classes, including Friedrich Lübbert, headmaster of NPEA Oranienstein. Speaking at a celebration to which all of the miners connected with the school had been invited in 1937, he announced that '"It would be a particular pleasure for me to see one or another [of the miners] here again next year. Perhaps he will come with a *Jungmann* who has worked alongside him, but perhaps he will also bring his son to the entrance exam here."'[213]

However, although the programme of *Einsätze* was explicitly designed to acquaint the *Jungmannen* most forcibly with 'how the other half lives', in a sense, it also presupposed that this was by no means the kind of life they would otherwise have experienced at first hand. Thus, the programme assumed—or even enhanced—the idea of class distinctions, except that the distinction this time was drawn according to a perceived paucity of political rather than financial capital. Even as the Napola authorities trumpeted the annihilation of all such class-based stratifications, ideas of 'them' and 'us' were being reinforced once again, only this time with the notion that these workers were not only poor, but less politically enlightened, and therefore needed 'help'.[214]

Thus, we may conclude that, although the programme of 'missions' did certainly give the *Jungmannen* a newfound respect for the unending toil of the labourers and miners, and a certain sympathy for some of their plaints, they still served a primarily indoctrinatory function, rather than effecting a fundamental change to existing class structures.[215] The most successful aspect of the 'missions' seems to have been the strong and often long-lasting connections which were forged between individuals and families, which led some *Jungmannen* and their 'lodging parents' to engage in extended correspondence, and which even encouraged one 'lodging mother' (*Quartiersmutter*) to raise the possibility of adoption with the pupil in question. From this perspective, the NPEA did at least succeed to some extent in diluting class prejudices, even as they simultaneously risked replacing these with political prejudices of a very similar ilk.

Conclusions

In her recent investigation of 'joy production' in the National Socialist 'Strength through Joy' (*Kraft durch Freude*/KdF) recreational programme, Julia Timpe has remarked that:

> Much of what KdF did and wanted to do—as well as much of what it propagandized—made appeal to ideas and aspirations that, [at] face value, could be considered positive or good: what, after all, is bad about building pleasant break rooms, or encouraging fun physical fitness? In fact, many aspects of [this] 'joy production'...might still sound appealing to us today. But crucially, of course, KdF's goals were always embedded in the overall goals of the Third Reich. This point goes beyond the simple observation that KdF was an organization set up and run by the Nazis. In fact, rather than noticing that KdF's goals were embedded in those of the Third Reich, we might almost assert that the goals of the Third Reich were embedded in those of KdF. *The interest in 'joy production' was not unique to KdF because ensuring German (Aryan) happiness was the core agenda of the Nazi regime.*[216]

An analogous disclaimer could similarly be made for all of the (ostensibly pleasant or pedagogically valuable) activities described in the pages above. Just like the recreational activities provided by 'Strength through Joy', the extracurricular activities which were on offer for pupils at the NPEA also testified to the Nazi regime's 'desire to convince its racially "valuable" citizens that it enhanced their wellbeing'.[217] From this perspective, the Napolas offered many of the same opportunities as the KdF programmes (whether high-cultural, low-cultural, sporting, or touristic), but at a more elite level—allowing for the development of pupils' individual talents, yet always employing and instrumentalizing them in the service of the national collective. Moreover, just like 'Strength through Joy', the Napolas also formed part of a broader propagandistic initiative to widen working-class participation in activities which had previously been the sole preserve of ruling elites or the middle classes.[218]

The same claim could also apply, *mutatis mutandis*, to the Hitler Youth. While the HJ and the BDM did provide a variety of analogous opportunities for their members, such as the pre-military branches of the Hitler Youth, the HJ-Music

Corps, and the HJ-Theatre Troupes (*Spielscharen*), as well as the possibility to travel within and (occasionally) outside Germany, such opportunities for self-fulfilment were only ever available to a tiny minority of boys and girls within the entirety of the mass organization.[219] Thus, as discussed in the Conclusion, it is hardly surprising that the NPEA were able to provide their adherents with a more varied and wide-ranging suite of activities than that offered by most other Nazi educational and recreational institutions, including the labour service and land service programmes, the HJ, and KdF—despite their many commonalities.

Nevertheless, as the schools' first Inspector, Joachim Haupt, asserted, the meaning and aims of such activities at the NPEA were wholly opposed to previous, liberal notions concerning the value of cross-cultural exchange and cultural edification for its own sake.[220] Rather, in all of these spheres, whether the celebration of school festivals, the fostering of artistic talent, the granting of opportunities for foreign travel, or the requirement to undergo various forms of labour service, the Napolas' extracurricular programmes and 'missions' served the revanchist, racist, and pseudo-socialist policy objectives of the National Socialist regime *in toto*. Whether labouring alongside farmers, factory-workers, or miners, performing theatrical entertainments for ethnic Germans in the 'borderlands', raising money or carving toys for the NSV 'Winter-Help' campaign, or acting as preachers of the Nazi gospel in lands afar, the *Jungmannen* were (wittingly or unwittingly) serving the purposes of the regime; in all of these activities, we can see the ideology and aspirations of the Nazi state revealed in microcosm.

Finally, we can also observe that, despite ever-greater efforts to homogenize the schools within the NPEA system as the war years drew on, individual Napolas' traditions and preoccupations could still play an important differentiating role. In the following section, we will therefore explore these variations between the schools—whether determined by long-standing historical tradition or geographical location—in greater detail.

Notes

1. On the importance of taking contemporaries' positive impressions of Nazi programmes seriously in the context of their appeal to and reinforcement of the propagandistic concept of *Volksgemeinschaft*, see e.g. Norbert Frei, '"Volksgemeinschaft". Erfahrungsgeschichte und Lebenswirklichkeit der Hitler-Zeit', in Norbert Frei, *1945 und wir. Das Dritte Reich im Bewußtsein der Deutschen* (Munich, 2009), 121–42, 123. However, as Julia Timpe has noted in her recent study of the National Socialist 'Strength through Joy' (*Kraft durch Freude*/KdF) leisure organization, acknowledging the superficial attractiveness of these programmes should never be taken uncomplicatedly to imply that they were a 'good thing' in and of themselves. Rather, all of these activities were fundamentally implicated in and entwined with the ideology of the National Socialist regime, and with its politics of racism and exclusion; as such, they

were scarcely neutral—cf. Julia Timpe, *Nazi-Organized Recreation and Entertainment in the Third Reich* (London, 2017), 214 (cited in the conclusion to this chapter).

2. See further the Conclusion. On the scope for cultivation of individuality and personal fulfilment which the Nazi regime offered its 'Aryan' citizens in more general terms, see Moritz Föllmer, *Individuality and Modernity in Berlin: Self and Society from Weimar to the Wall* (Cambridge, 2013).
3. 'Austausch mit England und Amerika', *10 Jahre Nationalpolitische Erziehungsanstalt Naumburg an der Saale* (1944), 46–7.
4. J. W. Tate, 'The German *Nationalpolitische Erziehungsanstalt* and the English Public School: II. The Public Schools of Germany', *Internationale Zeitschrift für Erziehung* 6 (1937), 165–70, 167–8.
5. Alternative favoured feast-days included 9 November (see further below), and the Führer's birthday. On the widespread sacralization of such anniversaries under National Socialism, see e.g. Sarah Thieme, *Nationalsozialistischer Märtyrerkult. Sakralisierte Politik und Christentum im westfälischen Ruhrgebiet (1929–1939)* (Frankfurt am Main, 2017); on National Socialist political religion and the aestheticization of politics more generally, see also Peter Reichel, *Der schöne Schein des Dritten Reiches. Gewalt und Faszination des deutschen Faschismus* (Hamburg, 2006); Klaus Vondung, *Deutsche Wege zur Erlösung. Formen des Religiösen im Nationalsozialismus* (Munich, 2013); Thomas Rohkrämer, *Die fatale Attraktion des Nationalsozialismus. Zur Popularität eines Unrechtsregimes* (Paderborn, 2013), 31–2, 37–9.
6. Zugführer Dr. Greve, 'Die Feier des 9. November und die Julfeier 1937', *Spandauer Blätter* 12 (3 February 1938), 7–9. On the de-Christianization of Christmas under Nazism more generally, see Joe Perry, 'Christmas as Nazi Holiday: Colonising the Christmas Mood', in Lisa Pine, ed., *Life and Times in Nazi Germany* (London, 2016), 263–89. On anti-religious sentiment at the Napolas, see further Chapter 6.
7. '9. November', 7–9.
8. Eckhard Loge, 'Das Fest der Waffenleite. Bericht über den Versuch einer Neugestaltung in einer Nationalpolitischen Erziehungsanstalt', *Völkische Musikerziehung* 6 (1940), 61–3, 61.
9. Cf. 'Aufbau im Frieden', *10 Jahre Naumburg*, 10–27, 20–1.
10. Winfried Roeske, 'Unsere Sommersonnenwende', *Die Brücke: Nachrichten von der Nationalpolitischen Erziehungsanstalt Köslin* 15, no. 2 (October 1943), 157.
11. For an example, see von Hidessen, 'Verleihung der Seitengewehre an die Obertertianer', *Wahlstatt-blätter: Blätter der Nationalpolitischen Erziehungsanstalt Wahlstatt* (Christmas 1936), 10–11.
12. E.g. Hans Schoenecker, *Lebenserinnerungen 1928–1960* (2007), 22–3; Rüdiger Bauer, private correspondence, 1 December 2012. These daggers, inscribed with the NPEA motto '*Mehr sein als scheinen*' (be more than you seem), are now treated as prime collectors' items with their own *catalogues raisonnés*; cf. e.g. Ron Weinand, *Waffenleite: Presenting NPEA Daggers of the Third Reich* (n.d.).
13. Peter Gerlach, *Lebenserinnerungen* (2007), 60. During the war years, similar ceremonies also took place more and more frequently in order to honour the schools' ever-mounting numbers of war-dead, and to fan the flames of pupils' desire to follow their sacrificial example (see further Chapter 10).

14. Cf. Gerlach, *Lebenserinnerungen*, 60; Klaus Kleinau, *Im Gleichschritt, marsch! Der Versuch einer Antwort, warum ich von Auschwitz nichts wusste. Lebenserinnerungen eines NS-Eliteschülers der Napola Ballenstedt* (Hamburg, 2000), 33–5.
15. Cf. e.g. Heise, 'Hochzeitsfeier', and Schoenecker, 'Geburtsfeier', *Die Brücke* 16, no. 2 (May 1944), 51–2; 'Kindergeburtsfeier im Führerkreise', *Nationalpolitische Erziehungsanstalt Sudetenland: Blätter*, 2. Folge (New Year [*Jahreswende*] 1941–2), 22–5; '4. Anstaltsfest', *Spandauer Blätter* 10 (1 July 1937), 5–13; Staf., *10 Jahre NPEA Plön. Sonderheft der Kameradschaft* (Kiel, 1943), 71–2; Reinhard Wagner, *Mehr sein als scheinen. Vier Jahre Jungmann in der NPEA Rottweil* (Ditzingen, 1998), 137–8.
16. On Schulpforta and Ilfeld, see further Chapter 6; also Helen Roche, '"Wanderer, kommst du nach Pforta...": The Tension between Classical Tradition and the Demands of a Nazi Elite-School Education at Schulpforta and Ilfeld, 1934–45', *European Review of History/revue européenne d'histoire* 20, no. 4 (2013), 581–609; Helen Roche, 'Die Klosterschule Ilfeld als Nationalpolitische Erziehungsanstalt', in Detlef Schmiechen-Ackermann et al., eds, *Die Klosterkammer Hannover 1931–1955. Eine Mittelbehörde zwischen wirtschaftlicher Rationalität und Politisierung* (Göttingen, 2018), 605–26.
17. E.g. *Nationalpolitische Erziehungsanstalt Wien-Breitensee*, 3. Rundbrief (31 March 1942), 4; Walter Knoglinger, *Stift Göttweig. Heimstätte einer 'Nationalpolitischen Erziehungsanstalt' in der Zeit von Jänner 1943 bis April 1945* (2000), 27. On the Austrian NPEA in general, see further Chapter 7.
18. E.g. 'Heldengedenkfeier', *Die Kameradschaft. Blätter der Nationalpolitischen Erziehungsanstalt Plön* 1, no. 1 (May 1935), 27–8; 'Chronik der Anstalt vom 31. März bis 15. Mai 1938', *Die Kameradschaft* 4, no. 1 (June 1938), 9–12.
19. On regional differences within the Napola system more generally, see Chapter 5.
20. Staatsarchiv Ludwigsburg (StAL), E 202 Bü 1746, advance programme dated 24 April 1937. N.B. The adjective '*musisch*' in this context was often used to denote the cultural sphere of the 'muses' in general, rather than 'music' in particular.
21. Cf. e.g. Franke, 'Gespräch über Kunsterziehung', *Die Brücke* 12, no. 1 (April 1939), 4–7.
22. For examples, see the lists of activities and excursions chronicled in the relevant school newsletters; for a glowing account of a trip to the theatre in Berlin and its political implications, see Leipelt, 'Unser Theaterbesuch', *Spandauer Blätter* 15 (May 1939), 29.
23. E.g. *Die Brücke* 11, no. 4/5 (February 1939), 88; Dieter Pfeiffer, 'Jungmann in vier Nationalpolitischen Erziehungsanstalten—Wahlstatt, Bensberg, Traiskirchen, Spanheim—1936–1943', *Der Freiwillige* 39, no. 9 (1993), 22–4, 24; Schoenecker, *Lebenserinnerungen*, 17. For more on the ways in which the NPEA facilitated a broader appreciation of activities which had previously been more or less exclusively the province of the middle and upper classes, see Helen Roche, 'Schulische Erziehung und Entbürgerlichung', in Norbert Frei, ed., *Wie bürgerlich war der Nationalsozialismus?* (Göttingen, 2018), 154–72. Comparisons might be drawn here with the cultural excursions of a similar kind offered by the KdF; see especially Timpe, *Recreation*, ch. 3; also Shelley Baranowski, *Strength through Joy: Consumerism and Mass Tourism in the Third Reich* (Cambridge, 2004).
24. Franke, 'Gespräch', 5.

25. Siegfried Oehme, 'Wir helfen uns selbst', *NPEA Klotzsche*, 13. Folge (Christmas 1942), 23. Sepp Dietrich was responsible both for extra-judicial murders perpetrated during the Night of the Long Knives, and for the Malmedy Massacre; he was tried and convicted of war crimes by a US military tribunal in 1946.
26. Cf. e.g. Riedel, 'Kunsterziehung', *Ballenstedt: Schriftenfolge der Nationalpolitischen Bildungsanstalt in Ballenstedt am Harz* 5 (Christmas 1938), 14–17.
27. See, for example, the illustrations accompanying Riedel, 'Kunsterziehung'; also the illustrations in *Nationalpolitische Erziehungsanstalt/Reichsschule für Volksdeutsche Rufach-Achern* (December 1941).
28. Eugen K., private correspondence, 28 April 2017. On the provision of equipment and materials, see e.g. 'Im neuen Schulpforta. Das alte Gymnasium als Nationalpolitische Erziehungsanstalt', *Frankfurter Zeitung*, 20 May 1943; 'Kunst- und Werkerziehung', *Pflug und Schwert* 1 (1943), 23.
29. Entzian, 'Neues aus unserem Heimatmuseum', *Wahlstatt-blätter* (Christmas 1935), 15–17; *Pförtner Blätter* 1, no. 3 (December 1936), frontispiece.
30. E.g. Karl Fetzer, 'Werkunterricht an der NPEA. Rottweil', *Der Deutsche Erzieher* (1935), 248–9; *Die Brücke* 14, no. 2 (November 1941), 44; 'Die Marine-Traditionsstuben in Potsdam', *Nationalpolitische Erziehungsanstalt Potsdam-Neuzelle: Arbeitsbericht* (March 1938), 23–6.
31. Cf. StAL, E 202 Bü 1746, letter from Trepte dated 13 July 1937. On the deliberately militaristic application of woodwork in this fashion in order to develop youthful interest in the armed forces, see Charles Lansing, *From Nazism to Communism: German Schoolteachers under Two Dictatorships* (Cambridge, MA, 2010), 119. Such activities were even given the status of '*wehrgeistige Erziehung*' (education in a warlike spirit) by the National Socialist Teachers' League, the NSLB.
32. Cf. Heidi Rosenbaum, *'Und trotzdem war's 'ne schöne Zeit': Kinderalltag im Nationalsozialismus* (Frankfurt am Main, 2014), 168–70, who attributes the term to Carola Stern.
33. On a talented violinist at NPEA Köslin being forced to take up the tuba instead, since 'one couldn't march with a violin or cello', see Bernhard von Gélieu, *1890—1990. Culm—Köslin. Kadettenhaus/Stabila/NPEA* (Butzbach-Maibach, 1990), 51; for examples of compositions by *Jungmannen*, see e.g. Paul Rohkst, 'Unser Glaube', *4. Rundbrief der Nationalpolitischen Erziehungsanstalt Bensberg* (*c.* March/April 1940); Silz, 'Aufbruch in den Tag', *Die Brücke* 13, no. 1 (June 1940), 1.
34. Cf. e.g. Geheimes Staatsarchiv Preußischer Kulturbesitz (GStAPK), I. HA Rep. 151, Nr. 1093, Bl. 53–65; Bundesarchiv Lichterfelde (BArch), R 2/19991, 'Erläuterungen zu dem Muster eines Kassenanschlages für eine Nationalpolitische Erziehungsanstalt'; StAL, FL410–4 Bü 109, 'Arbeitstagung im Reichsfinanzministerium Berlin und in der Nat.polit. Erziehungsanstalt in Ballenstedt vom 15.-18.7.1941'; on the Napolas' effect on the streetscape, see e.g. Günther Windschild and Helmut Schmid, eds, *Mit dem Finger vor dem Mund. Ballenstedter Tagebuch des Pfarrers Karl Fr. E. Windschild 1931–1944* (Dessau, 1999), 337.
35. StAL, E 202 Bü 1746, letter from Brunk dated 31 May 1937, letter from Sowade dated 19 June 1937; Österreichisches Staatsarchiv (ÖStA), BEA 7, letter from Calliebe dated 29 May 1939.

36. Arne Heinich, interview with Paul Nitsche (*c.* June 1981), 24; on the *Musisches Gymnasium*, see Anne C. Nagel, *Hitlers Bildungsreformer. Das Reichsministerium für Wissenschaft, Erziehung und Volksbildung, 1934–1945* (Frankfurt am Main, 2012), 199–203.
37. Otto Spreckelsen, *Plöner Liederbuch für die marschierende Jugend. Im Auftrage der Nationalpolitischen Erziehungsanstalt Plön von deutschen Jungen gesammelt und für den Schulgebrauch zusammengestellt* (Itzehoe, 1933), with a foreword by Joachim Haupt (Kreisarchiv Plön, L 18.4); cf. Staf., *10 Jahre Plön*, 9. On Plön's musical reputation during the Weimar Republic, see Chapter 4.
38. Zgf. Karneboge, 'Fest- und Feiergestaltung', *Die Brücke* 11, no. 4/5 (February 1939), 76–8.
39. Eugen Mayer-Rosa, 'Musikerziehung und Musik im Gemeinschaftsleben in einer NPEA', *Die deutsche höhere Schule* 5, no. 21 (1938), 702–10, 702–3.
40. Cf. e.g. 'Musik (Vor allem moderne Musik)', *Vurchtbare Begebenheiten. Abiturzeitung der NPEA 'Böhmen I' im Jahre 1944 in Raudnitz an der Elbe* (1944), 7.
41. Cf. e.g. 'Kunst- und Werkerziehung'; BArch, R 43-II/956b, Hempel, 'Bericht über den Bergwerkseinsatz des Zuges "Walter Clausen" (6. Zug) der Nationalpolitischen Erziehungsanstalt Plön im Jahre 1942' (24 June 1942); 'Drei Stimmungsberichte vom Elternnachmittag der 1. Hundertschaft. Drei Mitwirkende erzählen', *Die Fackel*, 18. Kriegsfolge (July 1944), 29–31. For more on propagandistic amateur dramatics beyond the NPEA, see Niehuis, *Landjahr*, ch. 9.3.5; Michael Buddrus, *Totale Erziehung für den totalen Krieg: Hitlerjugend und nationalsozialistische Jugendpolitik* (Munich, 2003), ch. 2; Kiran Klaus Patel, *Soldiers of Labor: Labor Service in Nazi Germany and New Deal America, 1933–1945* (Cambridge, 2005), ch. 3.3.2; Anne Keller, 'Das Deutsche Volksspiel. Jugendliche Propagandisten im Visier und Dienst der "Volksgemeinschaft"', in Detlef Schmiechen-Ackermann et al., eds, *Der Ort der 'Volksgemeinschaft' in der deutschen Gesellschaftsgeschichte* (Paderborn, 2018), 375–83.
42. Manfred B., 'Antworten zu den Nationalpolitischen Erziehungsanstalten im Nazi-Deutschland. Nationalpolitische Erziehungsanstalt Rottweil', private correspondence, 5 March 2015.
43. Helmut-Albrecht Kraas, ed., *Napola Neuzelle (ehem. Kreis Guben/Mark Brandenburg)—eine Dokumentation*, Bd. 2 (1993–4), 80–1.
44. E.g. '"Wallensteins Lager" in Ilfeld aufgeführt. Jungmannen der Napola spielen für das Winterhilfswerk', *Thüringer Gauzeitung*, 12 March 1941 [Kreisarchiv Nordhausen]; Schoenecker, *Lebenserinnerungen*, 17; Wolfgang Kögel, 'Aufführung der "Hermannsschlacht" von Kleist vom Zuge "Walter Clausen"', *Nationalpolitische Erziehungsanstalt Plön*, 22. Rundbrief (August 1942), 45–7; *Die Brücke* 16, no. 2 (May 1944), 56–60.
45. BArch, NS 15/51, Der Gauschulungsleiter, Frankfurt, an den Beauftragten des Führers für die gesamte geistige und weltanschauliche Erziehung der NSDAP, Pg. Rosenberg, letter dated 11 March 1935; [Emilie] Spornhauer, *Tagebuch* (Landeshauptarchiv Koblenz, Bestand 662,008 Nr. 13), entry dated 2 February 1935.
46. Spornhauer, *Tagebuch*, entry dated 20 February 1935.
47. W. Zentgraf, 'Kreisbauerntag', *Rundbrief der Nationalpolitischen Erziehungsanstalt Bensberg* (Spring 1940), reprinted in Dieter Pfeiffer, ed., *So war es. NPEA Bensberg: Nationalpolitische Erziehungsanstalt Bensberg 1935–1945*, Vol. 1 (1998), 122.

48. See further Chapter 8; also Helen Roche, '*Herrschaft durch Schulung*: The *Nationalpolitische Erziehungsanstalten im Osten* and the Third Reich's Germanising Mission', in Burkhard Olschowsky and Ingo Loose, eds, *Nationalsozialismus und Regionalbewusstsein im östlichen Europa: Ideologie, Machtausbau, Beharrung* (Berlin, 2016), 127–51, esp. 143–4; on such uses of propagandistic theatre in more general terms, see Elizabeth Harvey, *Women and the Nazi East: Agents and Witnesses of Germanization* (New Haven, 2003), 73; Caroline Mezger, 'Entangled Utopias: The Nazi Mobilization of Ethnic German Youths in the Batschka, 1930s–1944', *The Journal of the History of Childhood and Youth* 9 (2016), 87–117, 93.
49. On Potsdam, see Hans Lindenberg, *Montagskind. Erinnerungen*, Vol. 1 (1990), 68; on Schulpforta, see Hugo Selke, *Auch eine Jugend in Deutschland. Meine Schulzeit in Ilfeld und Schulpforte 1935–1939* (1990), 31; also Schorling, 'Unsere Taufe', *Pförtner Blätter* 1, no. 4 (March 1937), 93–4.
50. Sächsisches Hauptstaatsarchiv Dresden (SHStAD), 11125 Nr. 21351, Bl. 25–37: *Mitteilungsblätter der Nationalpolitischen Erziehungsanstalten* 2 (December 1936).
51. *Die Kameradschaft* 2, no. 2 (December 1936), 5–7, 26–8; *Spandauer Blätter* 15 (May 1939), 8; 'Eine Propagandaaktion', *Mitteilungen der Nationalpolitischen Erziehungsanstalt Naumburg/Saale*, 19. Kriegsnummer (December 1943), 8.
52. Wilhelm Braun, 'Winterhilfsarbeit im Zeichen- und Werkunterricht', *Der Deutsche Erzieher* (1935), 249; 'Wir basteln für's WHW', *Die Brücke* 14, no. 4 (December 1942), 99–100. Michael Buddrus has noted that, during World War II, such woodworking activities by members of the Hitler Youth more or less replaced the German toy industry, with over 12 million toys being made during Winter 1943–4 (Buddrus, *Totale Erziehung*, 152).
53. *Spandauer Blätter*, Kriegsausgabe 11 (December 1941), 20; 'Leute, bleibt stehen…', *Ilfelder Blätter*, 33. Kriegsheft (April 1944), [284–5].
54. E.g. G. Westphalen, 'Die N.P.E.A. im Wahlkampf', *Die Kameradschaft* 2, no. 1 (May 1936), 38–40.
55. Dietmar Süß, '*Ein Volk, ein Reich, ein Führer*'. *Die deutsche Gesellschaft im Dritten Reich* (Munich, 2017), ch. 2; cf. Peter Fritzsche, *Life and Death in the Third Reich* (Cambridge, MA, 2008), 49, 53; Ian Kershaw, '*Volksgemeinschaft*: Potential and Limitations of the Concept', in Martina Steber and Bernhard Gotto, eds, *Visions of Community in Nazi Germany: Social Engineering and Private Lives* (Oxford, 2014), 29–42, 34.
56. On the socializatory function of charitable work in the context of the SS, see Bastian Hein, 'Eine "Tat-Elite" in der "Volksgemeinschaft". Vergemeinschaftung im Rahmen der Auslese und Praxis der Allgemeinen SS', in David Reinicke et al., eds, *Gemeinschaft als Erfahrung. Kulturelle Inszenierungen und soziale Praxis 1930–1960* (Paderborn, 2014), 113–28, especially 122–3; more generally, see Thomas Kühne, *Belonging and Genocide: Hitler's Community, 1918–1945* (New Haven, 2010), 35–6.
57. Cf. e.g. 'Der Stuhmer Austauschzug erzählt von seinen Eindrücken' and 'Im Austausch mit der NPEA. Stuhm (Westpr.)', *Ilfelder Blätter* 5 (Christmas 1937), [115–17]. Occasional exchanges also took place with the 'National Socialist German High School' in Feldafing—cf. e.g. 'Feldafing', *Spandauer Blätter* 2 (1 April 1935), 11–17; Hundertschaftsführer Holst, 'Austausch der 6. Zug nach Feldafing', *Die Kameradschaft* 4, no. 2/3 (April 1939), 17–19. In general, the '*Chronik*' sections of many school

newsletters give a broad impression of the variety of camps and excursions on offer at most of the NPEA; however, prior to the centralization of the Napola administration in April 1941, financial and practical problems in this regard might often be experienced by non-Prussian NPEA in federal states such as Saxony and Württemberg (see further Chapter 5).

58. E.g. *Spandauer Blätter* 9 (1 May 1937), 8; *Potsdamer Kameradschaft. Blätter der Nationalpolitischen Erziehungsanstalt Potsdam* 3, no. 1 (May 1942), 39. On the prevalence of touristic visits to political museums and sites during this period more generally, see Kristin Semmens, *Seeing Hitler's Germany: Tourism in the Third Reich* (Basingstoke, 2005), 55–6, 66–7.
59. Wimmer, 'Fahrt des Zuges 7t nach Weimar und Jena', *Mitteilungen der Nationalpolitischen Erziehungsanstalt Naumburg/Saale*, 7. Kriegsnummer (Yule 1940), 10–12; *Ilfelder Blätter*, 20. Kriegsheft (November 1941), [389].
60. *Die Brücke* 11, no. 3 (November 1938), 63.
61. Winter, 'Kückenmühle', *Die Brücke* 11, no. 4/5 (February 1939), 70.
62. On Tannenberg, see G. Drescher, *Erinnerungen—Napola Neuzelle* (n.d., Institut für Zeitgeschichte, München [IfZ], ED 735-5), 12; on Munich and Nuremberg, see e.g. *Die Brücke* 9, no. 1 (June 1936), 3–9; on the visit to Dachau and the march-past, see 'Unsere Anstaltsfahrten nach Bayern', *Die Kameradschaft* 3, no. 3 (March 1938), 27–37; cf. Harald R., interview with the author, 22 August 2011. On the SS-training camp in general, see Christopher Dillon, *Dachau and the SS: A Schooling in Violence* (Oxford, 2015).
63. 'Bayern', 28; interview with Harald R., 22 August 2011.
64. Staf., *10 Jahre Plön*, 114.
65. Kurt Meyer, *Gelobt sei, was hart macht! Fröhliche, unbeschwerte, aber harte Jahre auf der NPEA* (2003), 34.
66. Claus Cordsen, *Meine Erinnerungen an Bensberg. Nationalpolitische Erziehungsanstalt in den Jahren 1935–1939* (1998), 33–4; for another former pupil's eyewitness account of the Olympics and his time as a volunteer, see Selke, *Schulzeit*, 26–7.
67. Hans Nitzsche, 'Wir besichtigen die Holsteinbrauerei in Kiel', *Die Kameradschaft* 4, no. 2/3 (April 1939), 26.
68. On practicalities concerning which schools were scheduled to send classes to Wyk and Vineta in which months, see ÖStA, BEA 51, 'Belegplan für die Lager Vineta und Wyk auf Föhr im Jahre 1939'.
69. For a timetable of lessons at Wyk, see 'Wykfahrt vom 20.6. bis 18.7.1937', *Tagebuch der 2. Zug II. Hundertschaft* (Bensberg, 1937), reprinted in Pfeiffer, *So war es*, Vol. 1, 261; also 'Als wir nach Wyk in's Seeheim führen', *Der Jungmann. Nationalpolitische Erziehungsanstalt Oranienstein/Lahn* 4, no. 6–7 (December 1938), 69–71; on antisemitic agitation in Wyk, see Trübenbach, 'Unsere politische Tätigkeit in Wyk a. Föhr', *Spandauer Blätter* 3 (20 August 1935), 11–12; also Dirk Warkus-Thomsen, '"Jüdische Kinder gehören in jüdische Heime." Von einem jüdischen Kinderheim und einer "Judenaustreibung" in Wyk auf Föhr', in Gerhard Paul and Miriam Gillis-Carlebach, eds, *Menora und Hakenkreuz. Zur Geschichte der Juden in und aus Schleswig-Holstein, Lübeck und Altona 1918–1998* (Neumünster, 1998), 387–96; Helen Roche, '"*Der Versuch einer Antwort, warum ich von Auschwitz nichts wußte*": The Evolution of

Napola-pupils' Responses to the Holocaust', in A. S. Sarhangi and Alina Bothe, eds, *Früher/später: Zeugnisse in der Zeit* (Berlin, forthcoming).

70. Semmens, *Seeing Hitler's Germany*, 132; Timpe, *Recreation*, 10, n. 51; Baranowski, *Strength through Joy*.
71. Semmens, *Seeing Hitler's Germany*, 12. For a comparison with Hitler Youth travel and propagandistic activity in foreign lands, see Buddrus, *Totale Erziehung*, ch. 9.
72. On the rationale behind the trips, see e.g. August Heißmeyer, *Die Nationalpolitischen Erziehungsanstalten* (BArch, NS 31/121); BArch, NS 45/35, 'Vom Wesen der Nationalpolitischen Erziehungsanstalten', 5. N.B. Juliane Tiffert is currently completing a doctoral thesis at the University of Kiel analysing the 'experiential' nature of Napola trips, provisionally entitled 'Auslandsfahrten der Nationalpolitischen Erziehungsanstalten—konstruierte Erlebniswelten in der Zeit des Nationalsozialismus'.
73. *Ilfelder Blätter* 4 (Christmas 1936), [96].
74. Landeshauptarchiv Sachsen-Anhalt, Abteilung Merseburg, C 23 Nr. 1–2.
75. *Nationalpolitische Erziehungsanstalt Stuhm im Aufbau* (Königsberg, 1938), 70–2; *Die Brücke* 10, no. 6 (March 1938), 58.
76. *Die Brücke* 10, no. 6 (March 1938), 58; *Die Brücke* 11, no. 3 (November 1938), 44. Köslin's *Hauptfahrtengebiet* was oriented towards North-Eastern Europe, comprising Poland, the Baltic States, and Finland. Such decisions were made at the annual conference of NPEA *Fahrtenobmänner*, the first of which took place in January 1938 under the chairmanship of Dr. Trepte (StAL, E 202 Bü 1746, letter dated 2 December 1937).
77. *Die Brücke* 10, no. 6 (March 1938), 58.
78. *Die Brücke* 11, no. 3 (November 1938), 44.
79. BArch, R 5/3362, 'Rede des Reichsministers Rust' (21 April 1941), 11. For further confirmation of the breadth of the Napolas' travels, see also the annual section of the *Internationale Zeitschrift für Erziehung* (sometimes excerpted as a separate pamphlet) entitled 'Der Schüleraustausch mit dem Auslande'; the NPEA were often the only schools in Germany to visit Yugoslavia and the Baltic States, in accordance with their ethnic 'mission'. As the international political situation began to worsen in the late 1930s, it was also noticeable that the Napolas were still far more willing to undertake foreign travel than were most other schools during this period.
80. BArch, R 2/12711, letter dated 17 July 1943. Although the response to this demand was predictably cool, the Prussian Finance Ministry had already agreed to the proposal, which narrowed the Reich Finance Ministry's scope for manoeuvre.
81. Cf. e.g. 'Die Anstaltsleiter der NPEA. tagten', *NS-Kurier*, 18 November 1937 [StAL, E 202 Bü 1746]; Politisches Archiv des Auswärtigen Amts (PAAA), R 98927, R 99018, R 27030. The *Haus des Deutschtums* in Stuttgart had been the seat of the *Deutsches Ausland-Institut* (DAI) since 1925; cf. Ernst Ritter, *Das Deutsche Ausland-Institut in Stuttgart 1917–1945. Ein Beispiel deutscher Volkstumsarbeit zwischen den Weltkriegen* (Wiesbaden, 1976).
82. PAAA, R 99018, letter from the German Embassy in Latvia to the Foreign Office dated 24 April 1939. N.B. Hereafter, the term 'ethnic German' will be used without scare-quotes, despite its problematic connotations, since this usage best reflects the language of the contemporary sources.
83. 'Fahrten, Grenzland und Volkstumsarbeit', *10 Jahre Naumburg*, 47–9, 47; cf. e.g. Warnke, 'Unsere Großfahrten', *Spandauer Blätter* 15 (May 1939), 22–3.

84. Karl-Heinz Liebich, 'Beobachtungen an Jungmannen während einer Grossfahrt 1936' (Prüfungsarbeit, 1936), 6–7, 23, Bibliothek für Bildungsgeschichtliche Forschung (DIPF), GUT ASS 851.
85. PAAA, R 27030, 'Bericht "Rumänienfahrt 1939" des 8. Zuges der NPEA Schulpforta über eine Fahrt nach Rumänien vom 22. Juli bis 27. August 1939' (1939).
86. E.g. Paul Steck, 'Ein Fahrtenbuch entsteht', *Der Deutsche Erzieher* (1935), 247; on the prevalence of such collective diaries in Nazi pedagogy and self-fashioning more generally, see Janosch Steuwer, *'Ein Drittes Reich, wie ich es auffasse'. Politik, Gesellschaft und privates Leben in Tagebüchern 1933–1939* (Göttingen, 2017), 253.
87. For example, extracts from the report on the trip to Romania mentioned above (n. 85) were published almost verbatim in *Pförtner Blätter* 4, no. 3 (March 1940). On the idiosyncrasies and imperfections of some pupils' writing style, see e.g. Liebich, 'Beobachtungen', 23.
88. Vanessa Conze, '"Unverheilte Brandwunden in der Außenhaut des Volkskörpers". Der deutsche Grenz-Diskurs der Zwischenkriegszeit (1919–1939)', in Wolfgang Hardtwig, ed., *Ordnungen in der Krise. Zur politischen Kulturgeschichte Deutschlands 1900–1933* (Munich, 2007), 21–48.
89. Conze, 'Brandwunden', 21–2.
90. Conze, 'Brandwunden', 43; see also Michael Burleigh, *Germany Turns Eastwards: A Study of* Ostforschung *in the Third Reich* (Cambridge, 1988); Burkhard Dietz, Helmut Gabel, and Ulrich Tiedau, eds, *Griff nach dem Westen. Die 'Westforschung' der völkisch-nationalen Wissenschaften zum nordwesteuropäischen Raum (1919–1960)*, Vol. 1 (Münster, 2003).
91. On the theory behind the 'borderland missions', see Alfred Männich, 'Die Bedeutung des Grenzlanddienstes für die Erziehungsarbeit der Nationalpolitischen Erziehungsanstalten' (DIPF, GUT ASS 876, 1936).
92. It should be noted here that ethnic proselytization of this kind was by no means exclusive to the NPEA—for similar borderland activities in the context of other National Socialist educational institutions, see Harvey, *Women and the Nazi East*; also Edith Niehuis, *Das Landjahr. Eine Jugenderziehungseinrichtung in der Zeit des Nationalsozialismus* (Nörten-Hardenberg, 1984); Kathrin Stern, 'Vom Volksschullehrer zum Volkserzieher—Ostfriesische Lehrkräfte im Einsatz für die nationalsozialistische "Volksgemeinschaft"?', in Dietmar von Reeken and Malte Thießen, eds, *'Volksgemeinschaft' als soziale Praxis. Neue Forschungen zur NS-Gesellschaft vor Ort* (Paderborn, 2013), 225–39. However, due to their relative lack of resources, these institutions' efforts could scarcely compare with the propagandistic potential of the Napolas' 'missions'.
93. Cf. e.g. *Potsdam-Neuzelle: Arbeitsbericht* (March 1938), 19–20; Bolzmann, 'Austausch nach Stuhm', *Die Kameradschaft* 3, no. 1/2 (September 1937), 22–5; *Nationalpolitische Erziehungsanstalt Stuhm im Aufbau* (Königsberg, 1938), as well as the preponderance of relevant articles in NPEA Stuhm's school newsletter, the *Stuhmer Altkameradschaft*; on the genesis of the school at Stuhm, see Roche, *'Herrschaft durch Schulung'*, 131–3.
94. On the 'Struggle for Germandom' in North Schleswig in general, see e.g. Steffen Werther, '"Volksgemeinschaft" vs. "Rassengemeinschaft". Nationalsozialisten in der dänischen Grenzregion Nordschleswig/Sønderjylland 1933–39', in Reinicke, *Gemeinschaft als Erfahrung*, 35–61.

95. Cf. e.g. Abel Feig, 'Das Grenz- und Auslandsdeutschtum und wir', *Die Kameradschaft* 1, no. 1 (May 1935), 24–5; A. Hintze, 'Nordschleswig', *Die Kameradschaft* 1, no. 2/3 (November 1935), 13–14; 'Nordschleswig—Ostern 1936', *Die Kameradschaft* 2, no. 1 (May 1936), 30–2; Zugführer Brandt, 'Am 12. März in Nordschleswig', *Die Kameradschaft* 4, no. 1 (June 1938), 25–6; *10 Jahre Plön*, 129, 133, 136.
96. *10 Jahre Plön*, 156–7; cf. interview with Harald R., 22 August 2011.
97. On the roots of such revanchist activity at Köslin in the Weimar period, see Chapter 4.
98. *Die Brücke* 10, no. 4/5 (October/November 1937); cf. Horst Fuhrmann, *Einladung ins Mittelalter* (Munich, 1997), 266–7. On the instrumentalization of such medievalizing imagery under Nazism to facilitate the Third Reich's revanchist agenda and, eventually, its war of conquest, see Vejas Gabriel Liulevicius, *War Land on the Eastern Front: Culture, National Identity, and German Occupation in World War I* (Cambridge, 2000), 262–4; Vejas Gabriel Liulevicius, *The German Myth of the East: 1800 to the Present* (Oxford, 2009), 178–80.
99. Hohmuth, 'Die blutende Grenze', *Die Brücke* 10, no. 4/5 (October/November 1937), 43–4.
100. Schröder, 'Der dreifache Treubruch der Germanen im Osten', *Die Brücke* 10, no. 4/5 (October/November 1937), 44–5; Kunde, 'Der polnische Korridor (Wider die polnischen Geschichtslügen)', 45–7.
101. von Schlicht, 'Marienburg', *Die Brücke* 10, no. 4/5 (October/November 1937), 48; Oehlmann, 'Ausgrabungen auf dem Schloßberg bei Alt-Christburg', 47.
102. N.B. It was common for many of the Napolas to undertake trips, often within Germany, around Pentecost—perhaps in part because this would have prevented *Jungmannen* with a religious background from attending church services at this key point in the cycle of Christian festivals. On German revanchism in the Eupen-Malmedy region more generally, see Carlo Lejeune, '"Des Deutschtums fernster Westen". Eupen-Malmedy, die deutschen Dialekt redenden Gemeinden um Arlon und Montzen und die "Westforschung"', in Dietz, *Griff nach dem Westen*, 493–538; Thomas Müller, 'Der Gau Köln-Aachen und Grenzlandpolitik im Nordwesten des Deutschen Reiches', in Jürgen John, Horst Möller, and Thomas Schaarschmidt, eds, *Die NS-Gaue. Regionale Mittelinstanzen im zentralistischen 'Führerstaat'* (Munich, 2007), 318–33. On Bensberg's role in furthering the Napolas' educational expansionism in Holland and Belgium once these countries had been occupied by Nazi Germany during World War II, see Chapter 8.
103. Rudolf Wasmann, *Bericht über die Eupen-Malmedy Fahrt Pfingsten 1938. Durchgeführt mit 11 Jungmannen des 5. Zuges der Nationalpolitischen Erziehungsanstalt Bensberg (Alter: 14–15 Jahre) von Studienassessor Wasmann* (1938). For more information on the VDA, see Chapter 4.
104. Wasmann, *Bericht*, 2–3. For an example of the passport-related bureaucracy related to such expeditions, see Brandenburgisches Landeshauptarchiv, Rep. 41 Amtsbezirk Neuzelle Nr. 15, Wehrmeldeamt Guben, which not only gives a sense of the number of countries which a group of pupils from NPEA Neuzelle visited in summer 1937 (Austria, Hungary, Poland, and Yugoslavia), but also gives an indication of the sheer amount of behind-the-scenes bureaucracy which constantly had to be dealt with by individual teachers and the school authorities merely to enable the trips to take place

at all—a historical fact of life which, in the era of the Schengen Agreement, is relatively easy to overlook.

105. Wasmann, *Bericht*, 2–3.
106. Wasmann, *Bericht*, 4–5.
107. E.g. Zentgraf, 'Der belgische Staat verhindert unsere Volkstumsarbeit', and Schäpe, 'Das Deutschtum in Eupen-Malmedy', in Wasmann, *Bericht*, 6–8.
108. Cf. e.g. 'Als die alten Grenzen fielen: In der Ostmark', *Der Jungmann* 4, no. 6–7, 6–37.
109. Zugführer Uplegger, 'Ostmarkenfahrt', *Die Kameradschaft* 4, no. 2/3 (April 1939), 27–30, 29.
110. Matern, in 'Als die alten Grenzen fielen', 19.
111. H. Godtknecht, 'Batschkafahrt', *Die Kameradschaft* 4, no. 2/3 (April 1939), 31. For an analysis of the Napolas' 'mission' in South-Eastern Europe, see Juliane Tiffert, '"Wer mit hinübergeht, muß ein Jungmann mit guter innerer Haltung sein". Über die Fahrten Nationalpolitischer Erziehungsanstalten zu den "Auslandsdeutschen" in Südosteuropa', in Daniel Drascek, ed., *Kulturvergleichende Perspektiven auf das östliche Europa. Fragestellungen, Forschungsansätze und Methoden* (Münster, 2017), 113–28; also Juliane Tiffert, 'Der "volksdeutsche Bildgedanke". Über den Einsatz von Fotografien bei den Fahrtenberichten der Nationalpolitischen Erziehungsanstalten', in Markus Tauschek, ed., *Handlungsmacht, Widerständigkeit und kulturelle Ordnungen. Potenziale kulturwissenschaftlichen Denkens* (Münster, 2017), 249–60. On Germanizing efforts by Nazi youth groups in the Batschka more generally, see Mezger, 'Entangled Utopias'; also Caroline Mezger, '"Denn du bist die Zukunft deines Volkes": Youth, Nation, and the Nazi Mobilization of Southeastern Europe's *Donauschwaben*, 1930s–1944', in Olschowsky and Loose, *Nationalsozialismus und Regionalbewusstsein*, 105–26.
112. 'Rumänienfahrt 1939', 9–11.
113. BArch, R 57 NEU/660, *Fahrtengruppe der Nationalpolitischen Erziehungsanstalt Oranienstein: Fahrt nach Bosnien. 10. Juli 1939 bis 11. August 1939* (1939), 11, 18. On antisemitic attitudes at the NPEA more generally, see Chapter 2.
114. On Italy as a particularly favoured destination for tourists from the Third Reich, see Semmens, *Seeing Hitler's Germany*, 135, 138.
115. Graßberger, 'Italienfahrt', *Spandauer Blätter* 11 (10 October 1937), 18–20.
116. On the GIL, see e.g. Alessio Ponzio, *Shaping the New Man: Youth Training Regimes in Fascist Italy and Nazi Germany* (Madison, 2015); Luca la Rovere, 'Totalitarian Pedagogy and the Italian Youth', in Jorge Dagnino, Matthew Feldman, and Paul Stocker, eds, *The 'New Man' in Radical Right Ideology and Practice, 1919–45* (London, 2018), 19–38.
117. For an in-depth study of the Napolas' connections with Fascist Italy and Fascist youth-groups, see Helen Roche, 'Nazi Elite-School Pupils as Youth Ambassadors between Fascist Italy and the Third Reich', forthcoming in a special issue of *JCH*, edited by Christian Goeschel and Hannah Malone.
118. Cf. e.g. Selke, *Schulzeit*, 39–48, and the relevant accounts in *Pförtner Blätter* 1, no. 3 (December 1936); *Pförtner Blätter* 3, no. 2 (November 1938); Gauß, 'Sparta. Aus dem Griechenlandbericht unserer Jungmannen', *Ilfelder Blätter* 4 (Christmas 1936), [104–5]. Since I have discussed this phenomenon at great length in my first monograph,

I have decided not to treat it again in any detail here—interested readers are advised to consult my previous work on Nazi philhellenism and phillaconism, especially Helen Roche, *Sparta's German Children: The Ideal of Ancient Sparta in the Royal Prussian Cadet Corps, 1818–1920, and in National Socialist Elite Schools (the Napolas), 1933–1945* (Swansea, 2013), 203–37.

119. E.g. 'Segelfahrt der Nationalpolitischen Erziehungsanstalt Köslin nach Schweden und Dänemark vom 15. bis 29. August 1937', *Weltanschauung und Schule* 1, no. 12 (1937), 710–17.

120. Gerhard Spree, 'Gedanken zu unserer Schwedenfahrt', *Spandauer Blätter* 3 (20 August 1935), 18–20, 19.

121. Fritz Traugott Müller, *Potsdamin Pojat (Potsdamer Jungens). Ein Finnland-Fahrt von Jungens der Nationalpolitischen Erziehungsanstalt in Potsdam* (Nürnberg, 1943), 8, 21–5. See also the relevant accounts in 'Finnlandfahrt', *Die Brücke* 11, no. 3 (November 1938), 50–2, especially Rolf d'Angelo, 'Unsere jungen Freunde im Kampf um Finnlands Freiheit', 52; also 'Finnlandfahrt', *Die Brücke* 10, no. 6 (March 1938), 67–9; Kreisarchiv Plön, F 9.8.2., Bericht über die Fahrt einer Gruppe von Jungmannen der N.P.E.A. Plön nach Finnland von 13.7.-11.8.1936 (1936); Anon., *Erlebnisse als [Erzieher] der NPEA Potsdam* (IfZ, ED 735–3), 154–9.

122. GStAPK, I. HA Rep. 151, Nr. 1093, Bl. 208; cf. GStAPK, I. HA Rep. 151, Nr. 1094, Bd. 2, Bl. 142–3.

123. N.B. A note on terminology: in British English, the term 'preparatory school' usually denotes a fee-paying independent junior school, educating pupils up to the age of 13 or so. However, in American English, 'preparatory school' is an abbreviation of the term 'college-preparatory school'; i.e., a form of secondary school which prepares pupils for university entrance from the age of about 13 upwards. In similar vein, 'public schools' in British English denote a select group of privately funded, fee-paying secondary boarding schools, often possessing a certain elite status. Meanwhile, the term 'public school' in American English denotes a *non*-fee-paying school supported by public funds. Hence, many of the more elite American preparatory boarding schools can be considered somewhat analogous in nature to the British public schools. On the Swedish exchanges, see the relevant issues of *Die Kameradschaft* and the *Spandauer Blätter*, especially *Die Kameradschaft* 4, no. 2/3 (April 1939), and *Spandauer Blätter* 6 (10 August 1936), 9 (1 May 1937), and 10 (1 July 1937). On South American and African exchanges, see e.g. *Ilfelder Blätter*, 2. Reihe, no. 2 (November 1935), [25]; *Die Kameradschaft* 1, no. 2/3 (November 1935) and 2, no. 1 (May 1936); *Die Brücke* 10, no. 6 (March 1938), 73; 'Seit Juni befinden sich zwei Jungmannen zum Austausch in Mexiko', *Der Jungmann* 1, no. 1 (December 1935), 24–6; Eisenlohr, 'Als Austauschschüler in Südwestafrika', *Spandauer Blätter* 8 (16 December 1936), 31–2. NPEA Spandau also cultivated an exchange partnership with St. Columba's College in Dublin—cf. Scheffler, 'Irlandfahrt', *Spandauer Blätter* 11 (10 October 1937), 5–6; 'Zweite Austauschfahrt nach Irland', *Spandauer Blätter* 14 (15 October 1938), 15–18; M. H. Meredith, 'The German Trip', *The Columban* 2, Vol. LVII (July 1936), 21; L. G. L. Watkinson, 'Columban Visit to Hitler Youth School Germany, 1936', *Old Columban Society Bulletin* (May 2002), 28–9. Some Napolas,

including Schulpforta, Plön, and Köslin, also welcomed the occasional visiting student from Turkey—though Hugo Selke recalled, drawing on prevalent stereotypes, that the Turkish exchange student at Schulpforta was allegedly expelled for '*Rassenschande*' (racial defilement) after he was caught sating his newfound taste for fairhaired Germanic women by indulging in some hanky-panky with a 'blonde bombshell' behind the altar in the school chapel (Selke, *Schulzeit*, 31).

124. Winfrid [Haupt], *Sinnwandel der formalen Bildung* (Leipzig, 1935), 94–5; Helmut Trepte, 'USA-Austausch der Nationalpolitischen Erziehungsanstalten', *Weltanschauung und Schule* 1, no. 13 (1937), 54–61; Droste, 'Schüleraustausch', *Spandauer Blätter* 15 (May 1939), 25–7.
125. Droste, 'Schüleraustausch', 25–6. See Semmens, *Seeing Hitler's Germany*, ch. 6, for Nazi foreign policy imperatives in relation to cultivating cultural and touristic connections between Britain and the United States.
126. Droste, 'Schüleraustausch', 26; Trepte, 'USA-Austausch', 58–9.
127. Droste, 'Schüleraustausch', 27; Trepte, 'USA-Austausch'.
128. Cf. BArch, R 1501/5656, letters dated 14 November 1935, 23 November 1935, 13 December 1935.
129. BArch, R 1501/5656, Lillard to Pfundtner, letter dated 23 November 1935.
130. For material on the ISF, see Niedersächsisches Landesarchiv, Hauptstaatsarchiv Hannover, Dep. 90, Nr. 2; Phillips Academy, Andover, Mass., Archives and Special Collections, Box 15, Head Fuess Records, Tabor Academy Folder (hereafter abbreviated as PAASC); also '"Schoolboy Ambassadors" About to Return to Germany: Eleven Have Been Spending Six Months at New England Preparatory Schools', *Boston Globe*, 9 December 1935. N.B. I am deeply indebted to John Stephan of the University of Hawaii for discussing his insights into the US exchange programme with me, and for sharing some relevant material. Stephan's own work on the exchanges, focusing on his alma mater, Lawrenceville (provisionally entitled *An Affair to Forget: Lawrenceville and the Third Reich*) is still forthcoming.
131. SHStAD, 11125 Nr. 21361, DAAD letter dated 31 March 1936. The DAAD organized the exchange programme via the Carl Schurz Foundation, an association set up in memory of German émigré politician Carl Schurz in order to foster American-German relations and cultural exchange. Hence, receptions for participants in Berlin were always held at the 'Carl-Schurz-Haus', and the programme was officially known as the 'Carl-Schurz-Student-Exchange of the National Political Educational Institutes' (*Carl-Schurz-Schüleraustausch der nationalpolitischen Erziehungsanstalten*)—cf. 'Austausch-Schüler im Carl-Schurz-Haus empfangen', *Berliner Tageblatt*, 1 August 1936 [Bundesarchiv Koblenz, ZSg. 117 Nr. 286]; SHStAD, 11125 Nr. 21351, *Mitteilungsblätter der Nationalpolitischen Erziehungsanstalten* 2 (December 1936), Bl. 28. However, the Foundation's involvement in promoting Nazi Germany led to controversy in the United States, as revealed by the title of the following article in the *New York Times*: 'Schurz Relatives Fight Nazi Link: His Nieces and Old Friends Protest Use of the Name by Groups Friendly to Hitler—Call Him Foe of Despots—Patriot, if Living Today, would Denounce "Tyrants" of Reich, Statement Declares', *New York Times*, 21 January 1935 [PAAA, R 80328].

132. *ISF Annual Report*, 28 February 1935, 3 (PAASC).
133. SHStAD, 11125 Nr. 21361, DAAD letter dated 31 March 1936; SHStAD, 11125 Nr. 21351, Bl. 223–5.
134. Erwin Kreitz, 'Austausch der Nationalpolitischen Erziehungsanstalten mit Nordamerikanischen Academies', *Weltanschauung und Schule* 1, no. 4 (1937), 222–5.
135. SHStAD, 11125 Nr. 21351, Bl. 223–5; *ISF Annual Report 1936–37* (PAASC). Details of the financial practicalities of the exchange can also be found in these files. Broadly speaking, Napola-pupils' parents or guardians still had to pay their usual school fees and supply them with 20 RM pocket money for the duration of the exchange, but the Prussian *Landesverwaltung* (or non-Prussian federal states, in the case of Saxony, Anhalt, and Württemberg) would undertake to pay their travel costs and any other associated expenses.
136. Lillard to Fuess, letter dated 8 December 1938 (PAASC). The 'recent cruelties' to which Lillard alludes presumably refer to the November pogrom.
137. *The International Schoolboy Fellowship. Ten Years: 1928–1938* (PAASC), 12.
138. On American attitudes and sympathies towards Nazi Germany more generally during the 1930s, especially in educational circles, see e.g. Stephen H. Norwood, *The Third Reich in the Ivory Tower: Complicity and Conflict on American Campuses* (Cambridge, 2009); Bradley W. Hart, *Hitler's American Friends: The Third Reich's Supporters in the United States* (New York, 2018), esp. 140–59.
139. For an example of this tendency in practice, see Wolfgang Korten, 'Wolfgang Korten Emphasizes Values of Exchange Programme', *The Tabor Log* (10 June 1939), 3, 8 (I am deeply indebted to Sophie Arnsfield, the Tabor Academy archivist, for this reference). On similar propagandistic drives by Nazi exchange students at American universities, see Norwood, *Ivory Tower*, 107–8, 131; Hart, *Hitler's American Friends*, 158–9.
140. 'Zwei Ilfelder Jungmannen in Amerika. Austausch mit der Tabor Academy', *Ilfelder Blätter* 3 (Easter 1936), [72–7].
141. E.g. 'Plöner Jungmannen in den Vereinigten Staaten von Nordamerika', *Die Kameradschaft* 1, no. 4 (March 1936), 19–25.
142. E.g. 'Ilfelder Bericht der amerikanischen Austauschschüler', *Ilfelder Blätter* 3 (Easter 1936), [77–9].
143. 'Brief aus Amerika', *Die Kameradschaft* 3, no. 3 (March 1938), 46–7; Wolfgang Vormbrock, *Miniaturen. Wahllos niedergeschriebene Erinnerungen, Geschichten und Anekdoten aus meinem Leben*, Vol. 1 (Norderstedt, 2011), 32–3.
144. 'Nachlese vom Schüleraustausch mit Amerika', *Spandauer Blätter* 20, Kriegsausgabe 5 (June 1940), 8. According to Matt Edmonds, the resident historian at St. Andrew's School, there is no reason to doubt that the letter is genuine, since it corresponds with Pell's style in similar correspondence held in the St. Andrew's School Archive.
145. See the relevant documents from the St. Andrew's School Archive, available online at https://standrews-de.libguides.com/20th-century_horst-roloff. N.B. I am extremely grateful to Matt Edmonds and the archivist at St. Andrew's School for making this material available to me, and for their assistance with my research.
146. PAAA, R 62972, Foreign Office report on a visit to NPEA Potsdam on 19 January 1934, dated 23 January 1934. N.B. For a far more detailed account of the Napola exchange programmes with British public schools, focusing in particular on

the Oranienstein-Dauntsey's and Ilfeld-Kingswood exchanges, see Helen Roche, '*Zwischen Freundschaft und Feindschaft*: Exploring Relationships between Pupils at the Napolas (*Nationalpolitische Erziehungsanstalten*) and British Public Schoolboys', *Angermion: Yearbook for Anglo-German Literary Criticism, Intellectual History and Cultural Transfers/Jahrbuch für britisch-deutsche Kulturbeziehungen* 6 (2013), 101–26.

147. Cf. G. A. Rowan-Robinson, 'The Training of the Nazi Leaders of the Future', *International Affairs* 17 (1938), 233–50: 'MR. A. G. DICKSON said that in 1933 he had visited the leaders' school at Potsdam and had arranged subsequently an exchange with boys from his own Public School, Rugby. As far as he could see the whole thing had been an unqualified failure. The English boys had not been specially selected. They had been told that those possessing the means might go to Germany after Christmas, and so quite the wrong type of boy had gone, the type who thought it would be a good idea to spend some of the Christmas holidays in Germany and get out of the first week of term's work. *The Germans on their side chose boys who they thought would be completely impervious to any influence or impressions they might receive*' (247, my emphasis).

148. Selke, *Schulzeit*, 48–9, citing a report by *Hundertschaftsführer* Horst Rußland; see also SHStAD, 11125, Nr. 21351, Bl. 188; 'Gerhard Kühlewind', *Mitteilungen der Nationalpolitischen Erziehungsanstalt Naumburg/Saale*, 23. Kriegsfolge (Yulemoon [December] 1944), 4.

149. Wasmann Nachlass, letter from Wasmann to Andrewes dated 18 March 1937 (copy courtesy of Arne Heinich).

150. IfZ, MA 1438, 'Report on G. Kühlewind and W. Tönhardt, Lancing House Prep School', from E. K. Milliken, Headmaster, to the *Anstaltsleiter* of NPEA Naumburg, 20 June 1936. In a letter to Milliken dated 12 March 1937, Wasmann implied that the report had been distributed to all of the *Erzieher* in charge of the exchange programme, and had met with widespread approval. He deemed the idea of engaging with younger pupils a fruitful one, since 'boys of this age not having so many prejudices more easily make friends with one another [*sic*]' (Wasmann Nachlass, copy courtesy of Arne Heinich). An article by Milliken presenting the proposal to members of the Incorporated Association of Preparatory Schools was subsequently included in the organization's inhouse review that autumn, alongside a highly positive depiction of Lancing House School's return visit to Naumburg: E. K. Milliken, 'Freundschaft', *The Preparatory Schools Review* (November 1936), 270–2.

151. E.g. 'A summary of the adress [*sic*] of the Anstaltsleiter Oberregierungsrat Dr. med Schieffer, SS-Standartenführer, Bensberg', Shrewsbury School Archive; cf. M. B. Charlesworth, 'Football against the Nazis', *Old Salopian Newsletter* (May 1987). For a detailed account of one of the sports trips, see 'Deutsche Jungen in England', *Weltanschauung und Schule* 1, no. 6 (1937), 372–3; for an eyewitness perspective on the sports tour which NPEA Schulpforta undertook in 1938, see also Selke, *Schulzeit*, 48–55—section entitled 'Our peaceful invasion of Great Britain'.

152. E.g. 'Visit of Schloss Oranienstein', *Bradfield College Chronicle* (March 1937), 1779; 'Schulpforta Visit', *Bradfield College Chronicle* (July 1938), 1961; '1st VIII v. Oranienstein School, Germany', *The Pauline* (?Summer 1936?), 132; cf. ÖStA, BEA 7, *Der deutsche Schulaustausch mit dem Ausland 1938* (1939), 4; Roche, '*Zwischen*

Freundschaft und Feindschaft'. On British visitors' opinions of the Third Reich more generally, see Angela Schwarz, *Die Reise ins Dritte Reich. Britische Augenzeugen im nationalsozialistischen Deutschland 1933–1939* (Göttingen, 1993); Julia Boyd, *Travellers in the Third Reich: The Rise of Fascism through the Eyes of Everyday People* (London, 2017).

153. 'Eindrücke eines Austausch-Schülers', *Spandauer Blätter* 6 (10 August 1936), 19.
154. Wehrhan, 'Vom 28. Juni bis 15. Juli 1935 fand ein Austausch Oraniensteiner Jungmannen mit einer Gruppe der Westminster-Schule in London statt', *Der Jungmann* 1, no. 1 (December 1935), 12–14.
155. *Stuhmer Kameradschaft*, 2. Rundbrief (1938), 11–12.
156. *Stuhmer Kameradschaft*, 2. Rundbrief (1938), 11.
157. Friedrich Dubslaff, *Erinnerungen* (n.d.), 14–15; Hundertschaftsführer Dr. Rußland, 'Englandreise der Nationalpolitischen Erziehungsanstalt Schulpforta (4.-25.6.1938)', *Pförtner Blätter* 3, no. 2 (November 1938), 55–60, 57. For a rather different account of the visit from the English perspective, see 'Schulpforta Visit', *Bradfield College Chronicle* (July 1938), 1961.
158. For an in-depth discussion of these issues, see Roche, '*Zwischen Freundschaft und Feindschaft*'; on pre-war attitudes to Nazism in Britain more generally, see e.g. Richard Griffiths, *Fellow Travellers of the Right: British Enthusiasts for Nazi Germany, 1933–1939* (London, 1980); Petra Rau, *English Modernism, National Identity and the Germans, 1890–1950* (Farnham, 2009); and Dan Stone, *Responses to Nazism in Britain, 1933–1939: Before War and Holocaust* (Basingstoke, 2012).
159. Roche, '*Zwischen Freundschaft und Feindschaft*', 123–6.
160. Jill Stephenson, 'Inclusion: Building the National Community in Propaganda and Practice', in Jane Caplan, ed., *Nazi Germany* (Oxford, 2008), 99–121, 102. See also Peter Fritzsche, 'The NSDAP 1919–1934: From Fringe Politics to the Seizure of Power', in the same volume, 48–72; Frank Bajohr, 'Dynamik und Disparität. Die nationalsozialistische Rüstungsmobilisierung und die "Volksgemeinschaft"', in Frank Bajohr and Michael Wildt, eds, *Volksgemeinschaft. Neue Forschungen zur Gesellschaft des Nationalsozialismus* (Frankfurt am Main, 2009), 78–93; cf. Mark Buggeln and Michael Wildt, eds, *Arbeit im Nationalsozialismus* (Munich, 2014).
161. Fritzsche, *Life and Death*, 48; Martin Kipp, 'Militarisierung der Lehrlingsausbildung in der "Ordensburg der Arbeit"', in Ulrich Herrmann and Ulrich Nassen, eds, *Formative Ästhetik im Nationalsozialismus. Intentionen, Medien und Praxisformen totalitärer ästhetischer Herrschaft und Beherrschung* (Weinheim, 1994), 209–19; Buddrus, *Totale Erziehung*, ch. 7.
162. On the *Landjahr*, see Niehuis, *Landjahr*; on the RAD, see Patel, *Soldiers of Labor*.
163. BArch, NS 45/35, 'Vom Wesen der Nationalpolitischen Erziehungsanstalten', 5.
164. E.g. 'Nationalpolitische Erziehung: Wir helfen dem Bauern!', *Ilfelder Blätter* 5 (Christmas 1937), [118]; 'Jungmannen helfen in der Hackfruchternte', *Die Brücke* 15, no. 3 (December 1943), 189–93; Dieter Eschenhagen, 'Auch ich war ein Eliteschüler Hitlers' (Oldenburg, 2000), 30.
165. E.g. *Stuhm im Aufbau*, 66–7; 'Landdienst', *Pflug und Schwert* 1 (1943), 17–19; Helmut Pophanken, *'Jungmann' 1942–1945. Erinnerungen eines ehemaligen Schülers an die Nationalpolitische Erziehungsanstalt Emsland (Napola)* (n.d.), 150 (see further Chapter 6 and Chapter 8).

166. 'Wyk und Vineta', *Spandauer Blätter* 13 (15 June 1938), 28–31. For more on life at Vineta in general, see the relevant special issue of *Die Brücke* 8, no. 4/5 (October/November 1935). The smallholding was originally bought by the *Landesverwaltung* for NPEA Wahlstatt and NPEA Naumburg to use as a retreat, but soon became a favoured destination for all of the schools: cf. Or-Wei, 'Erlebnisse aus "Vineta"', *Die Brücke* 8, no. 1 (May 1935), 10–11.
167. Lindenberg, *Montagskind*, 83.
168. Eberhard Vogel, *Wanderungen in Deutschland. Lebensstationen 1935–1948* (Berlin, 2007), 75–80, 96–7. N.B. The name 'Vineta' is probably an allusion to the mythical sunken city of Vineta which local legend locates somewhere off the Baltic coast, as immortalized by the lyric poet Wilhelm Müller (1794–1827) in his eponymous poem.
169. BArch, R 43-II/956b, Heißmeyer, 'Bericht', Bl. 62.
170. 'Landdienst', *10 Jahre Naumburg*, 60–3; Heißmeyer, 'Bericht', Bl. 62.
171. H. Rohardt, 'Landdiensteinsatz Sommer 1936', *Die Kameradschaft* 2, no. 2 (December 1936), 25–6.
172. BArch, NS 38/3913; StAL, E 202 Bü 1746, 'Bericht des Anstaltsleiters der Nationalpolitischen Erziehungsanstalt Backnang über die Teilnahme bei der Anstaltsleiterbesprechung am 2.12.1936 in der Nationalpolitischen Erziehungsanstalt in Berlin-Spandau'; SHStAD, 11125 Nr. 21351, 'Bericht über die Anstaltsleiterbesprechung in der Nationalpolitischen Erziehungsanstalt Spandau und im SS-Hauptamt am 2. und 3. Dezember 1936', Bl. 14–20, Bl. 14; cf. Männich, 'Grenzlanddienst', *Spandauer Blätter* 11 (10 October 1937), 10–12.
173. Cf. BArch, NS 38/3913.
174. BArch, NS 38/3917, 'Bericht über den Einsatz der NPEA Backnang (Württemberg) im Kreise Rosenberg/Guttentag'.
175. BArch, NS 38/3917, NS 38/3886.
176. BArch, NS 38/3886, Gräter to Reichsstudentenführung, complaint dated 21 July 1937.
177. For similar experiences undergone by girls working in the occupied Eastern territories, see Harvey, *Women and the Nazi East*.
178. Recksieck, 'Mein Bauer und sein Hof', *Pförtner Blätter* 3, no. 2 (November 1938), 64–6, 66.
179. 'Auszüge aus Briefen oberschlesischer Bauern', *Spandauer Blätter* 8 (16 December 1936), 14–15.
180. Landeshauptarchiv Koblenz, Bestand 662,003, Nr. 21, Bl. 131–3.
181. Helmuth Junghans, *Dawaj. Ein Echo der Vergangenheit: Tagebuchszenen aus russischer Gefangenschaft 1942–1945* (Rheine, 2010), 156–8. At a later juncture, Jan also allegedly attempted to attack Helmuth with his penknife while they were out binding corn stooks together.
182. Lindenberg, *Montagskind*, 102.
183. Heinz Winkler and Hans Worpitz, *Die Nationalpolitischen Erziehungsanstalten (NPEA) und ihre Jungmannen. Berichte, Entwicklungen und Erlebnisse von Jungmannen der NPEA Loben/Annaberg* (2003), 118–19. It should be noted, however, that plaints concerning 'dirt', 'infestation', and the 'unsanitary' nature of Eastern European habitations had long been a key *topos* in German accounts of these regions—cf. Nancy R. Reagin, *Sweeping the German Nation: Domesticity and*

National Identity in Germany, 1870–1945 (Cambridge, 2007); Harvey, *Women and the Nazi East*; Michaela Kipp, 'Großreinemachen im Osten'. Feindbilder in deutschen Feldpostbriefen im Zweiten Weltkrieg (Frankfurt am Main, 2014), esp. 19–20. Hence, pupils' reports and recollections can also be easily interpreted within the framework of this longstanding tradition of orientalizing, quasi-colonialist discourse.

184. *Nationalpolitische Erziehungsanstalt Plön*, Kriegsbrief Nr. 23 (April 1943), 40; cf. 'Landdienst', 62–3. On Hitler Youth land service in the East more generally, see also Buddrus, *Totale Erziehung*, ch. 8.5; also Gerhard Rempel, *Hitler's Children: The Hitler Youth and the SS* (Chapel Hill, 1989), ch. 5; Michael H. Kater, *Hitler Youth* (Cambridge, MA, 2004), 34–5.

185. *Zugschronik Jahrgang 1943, NPEA Rottweil* (1943); Fritz Oerter, 'Jungmannen packen zu. Jugend schlägt Brücken ins Grenzland—Der Grenzlandeinsatz der Nationalpolitischen Erziehungsanstalten—Jungmannen im Land- und Fabrikdienst—Briefe berichten von großem Erleben', *Die Innere Front N.S.K.*, 10 September 1941 [BArch, NS 5/VI/18842]; cf. Roche, '*Herrschaft durch Schulung*', esp. 127–8. For more on Greiser and the Napolas' aims in the occupied East more generally, see Chapter 8.

186. The so-called 'Bloody Sunday' at Bromberg (present-day Bydgoszcz) was the Nazi propaganda term for the violent resistance which took place against the ethnic German minority in the city after snipers from the *Volksdeutscher Selbstschutz* (an ethnic German paramilitary organization) killed a number of Polish civilians. The exact numbers of victims on either side were hotly disputed, and those on the German side were hugely inflated to serve Goebbels' propagandistic purposes. After the city had fallen, the Wehrmacht and the *Selbstschutz* enacted a series of extremely harsh retaliatory reprisals against the local Polish population, during which thousands more Polish civilians were killed or imprisoned; cf. Markus Krzoska, 'Bromberger Blutsonntag. Unklare Fakten, klare Interpretationen', in Hans Henning Hahn and Robert Traba, eds, *Deutsch-Polnische Erinnerungsorte. Bd. 2. Geteilt/Gemeinsam* (Paderborn, 2014), 351–63; also Christian Jansen and Arno Weckbecker, eds, *Der 'Volksdeutsche Selbstschutz' in Polen 1939/40* (Munich, 1992).

187. *Nationalpolitische Erziehungsanstalt Wien-Breitensee*, 5. Rundbrief (November 1942), 27; Reinhard Wagner of NPEA Rottweil also reported acting violently towards a Polish labourer during his *Warthelandeinsatz*—cf. Wagner, *Mehr sein als scheinen*, 150. For more on such anti-Polish attitudes and their genesis, see e.g. Hans-Christian Harten, *De-Kulturation und Germanisierung. Die nationalsozialistische Rassen- und Erziehungspolitik in Polen 1939–1945* (Frankfurt am Main, 1996); Winson Chu, *The German Minority in Interwar Poland* (Cambridge, 2012); Gerhard Wolf, *Ideologie und Herrschaftsrationalität. Nationalsozialistische Germanisierungspolitik in Polen* (Hamburg, 2012), as well as the relevant literature cited in Chapter 8. For similarly anti-Czech sentiments expressed in relation to *Landeinsätze* in the conquered Czech lands, see e.g. 'Erntehilfe 1939. Vom Volkstumskampf in der Sprachinsel Iglau', *Alte Kameradschaft. Mitteilungen der Nationalpolitischen Erziehungsanstalt Backnang* (Christmas 1939), 11–18.

188. 'Ernteeinsatz des 6. Zuges in Wartheland', *NPEA Neuzelle*, 12. Kriegsbrief (October 1942), 18–19; cf. 'Landdienst des 5. Zuges im Warthegau', *Der Jungmann*, 8. Kriegsnummer (Summer 1942), 86: 'My task is to oversee the Poles at their labour and work alongside them. I must goad the Poles on and watch out that they don't

steal. They are mostly illiterate and not very intelligent. Their dwellings, compared with Oranienstein, are indescribable. They are simply Poles and they are inferior. That's all there is to be said.'

189. E.g. v. Tippelskirch, 'Zwei Dorfnachmittage im Wartheland', *Potsdamer Kameradschaft* 4, no. 1 (April 1943), 29–31; 'Landdienst 1941', *Spandauer Blätter*, Kriegsausgabe 11 (December 1941), 10–14.
190. Lothar Steinbach, *Ein Volk, ein Reich, ein Glaube? Ehemalige Nationalsozialisten und Zeitzeugen berichten über ihr Leben im Dritten Reich* (Bonn, 1995), interview with Klaus E., 131–2.
191. On such sentiments more generally, see Harvey, *Women in the Nazi East*.
192. Dr.-Ing. A. Heilandt, 'Primaner als Arbeiter', *Spandauer Blätter* 2 (1 April 1935), 24–6.
193. Cf. e.g. 'Besuch bei der A.E.G.', *Spandauer Blätter* 4 (10 December 1935), 18–20. Meanwhile, at Plön, younger boys were sent once a week to visit local craftsmen's workshops, where they were trained to assist with trades such as smithing, carpentry, saddlery, plumbing, glaziery, locksmithing, and car repairs—cf. e.g. Zugführer Jakobsen, 'Werkstättenbesuch der Jungmannen', *Die Kameradschaft* 1, no. 1 (May 1935), 31; 'Beim Handwerkerdienst', *Die Kameradschaft* 4, no. 1 (June 1938), 15–16.
194. 'Industrie-Einsatz', *10 Jahre NPEA Naumburg*, 49–60, 56.
195. BArch, R 43-II/956b, Bl. 95–8; 'Fabrikdienst 1942 in Herbesthal-Welkenraedt', *Rundbrief der NPEA Bensberg*, 15. Kriegsfolge (15 November 1942), 14–16.
196. E.g. 'Die "Obersekunda" im Bergwerk. Aus einer Nationalpolitischen Erziehungsanstalt', *Frankfurter Zeitung*, 21 June 1939 [BArch, NS 5/VI/18842].
197. 'Gesamtbericht', *Spandauer Blätter* 8 (16 December 1936), 7–9; StAL, E 202 Bü 1746, letter from Sowade dated 11 June 1937; letter from Gräter dated 9 February 1938.
198. StAL, E 202 Bü 1746, letter from Sowade dated 11 June 1937; 'Gesamtbericht', 7–8; on the technicalities of health and safety preparation, see the relevant files relating to NPEA Klotzsche at the Bergwerkarchiv Freiberg.
199. Karl Drechsler, 'Napola-Jungmannen als Kumpel in der Grube', *Weltanschauung und Schule* 1, no. 11 (1937), 663–9, 664–5. However, the miners were still selected for this privilege along ideological lines—in this case, 'forty-five deserving fathers of families with many children'.
200. StAL, E 202 Bü 1746, letter from Gräter dated 9 February 1938.
201. Hellmann, 'Jungmannen im Bergwerk', *Weltanschauung und Schule* 1, no. 3 (1937), 179–82; cf. Drechsler, 'Kumpel'; BArch, NS 26/349, 'Bergwerkseinsatz des Zuges "Walter Clausen" der Nationalpolitischen Erziehungsanstalt Plön' (1942).
202. 'Werkspionage in Deutschland (Eindrücke eines Austauschlehrers)', *Spandauer Blätter* 13 (15 June 1938), 26–7 (N.B. obvious English transcription errors in the original have been corrected).
203. Brenner, '73 Oraniensteiner Jungmannen im Arbeitseinsatz 1937', *Der Jungmann* 3, no. 5 (December 1937), 6–15, 10–11.
204. Zugführer Selitsch, '7a und 7b im Ruhrgebiet', *Spandauer Blätter* 10 (1 July 1937), 17–19.
205. Ueberhorst, 'Bergwerkseinsatz 1942', *Der Jungmann*, 8. Kriegsnummer (Summer 1942), 80–1.
206. Betriebsführer Bruck, 'An die Ehemaligen der Grube Neue Haardt [21 November 1937]', *Der Jungmann* 3, no. 5 (December 1937), 30–1.

207. Cf. e.g. 'Zum Bergwerkseinsatz!' special issue, *Die Brücke* 10, no. 3 (July 1937).
208. Cf. 'Bergwerkseinsatz des Zuges "Walter Clausen"'.
209. 'Bergwerkseinsatz des Zuges "Walter Clausen"', 14.
210. 'Bergwerkseinsatz des Zuges "Walter Clausen"', 15.
211. E.g. Heißmeyer, 'Bericht', Bl. 63.
212. 'Ein Tag im Bergwerk', *Der Jungmann*, 8. Kriegsnummer (Summer 1942), 81–4.
213. 'Betriebsappell Oranienstein—Die Kumpels als Gäste unserer Anstalt!', *Der Jungmann* 3, no. 5 (December 1937), 53–4.
214. For a full elaboration of this argument, see Roche, 'Erziehung und Entbürgerlichung'.
215. For a similar judgement on the effects of the Reich Labour Service, see Patel, *Soldiers of Labor*, 260: 'The shared labour and the shared life of Germans of the most diverse backgrounds constituted an intense form of contact, which at least put the existing notions about other social classes under the microscope... no small number of labor men emphasized that the social interaction with others expanded their own horizon.' However, Patel concludes that, despite effecting a reduction in social prejudices and class preconceptions, the RAD was nevertheless still linked to a rigid sense of inclusion and exclusion, and hence could not be deemed to have brought about a 'modernizing accomplishment in this respect' (396–7).
216. Timpe, *Recreation*, 214 (emphasis mine).
217. Baranowski, *Strength through Joy*, 2.
218. Baranowski, *Strength through Joy*, 6–12; cf. Roche, 'Erziehung durch Entbürgerlichung'.
219. Cf. Armin Nolzen, 'Inklusion und Exklusion im "Dritten Reich". Das Beispiel der NSDAP', in Bajohr and Wildt, *Volksgemeinschaft*, 60–77, 66; Katrin Kollmeier, 'Erziehungsziel "Volksgemeinschaft"—Kinder und Jugendliche in der Hitler-Jugend', in Klaus-Peter Horn and Jörg-W. Link, eds, *Erziehungsverhältnisse im Nationalsozialismus. Totaler Anspruch und Erziehungswirklichkeit* (Bad Heilbrunn, 2011), 59–76, 65; Rohkrämer, *Fatale Attraktion*, 121; Keller, 'Das Deutsche Volksspiel'; Buddrus, *Totale Erziehung*, ch. 9.
220. Winfrid [Haupt], *Sinnwandel der formalen Bildung* (Leipzig, 1935) 94: 'School exchanges in the National Socialist educational system, despite their apparent superficial similarity with liberal school exchanges, are derived from opposite assumptions and pursue a completely different goal, namely, to teach comprehension of the races in all of their differences and their peculiarity, whereas the proponents of the Enlightenment, through school exchanges and the teaching of foreign languages, had hoped to light upon a universally identical nature for the whole of humanity.'

PART II

VARIETY WITHIN UNITY

4

The Prussian Paradigm?

Resurrecting Cadet-School Traditions at the Former *Staatliche Bildungsanstalten*

Only half a year or so after the founding of NPEA Köslin, on 12 December 1933, a solemn ceremony took place which commemorated the Napola's past incarnation as a Royal Prussian Cadet School. *Oberleutnant* Erich Reuter, adjutant to the Second Jäger-Battalion infantry regiment, and the last ever cadet-corporal to serve at Köslin during his school-days, had returned the cadet school's hallowed military ensign to the authorities at the NPEA, with the request that it be honoured in an appropriate fashion:

> This flag flew over the former Royal Prussian Cadet School at Köslin from 1890 until 10 January 1920. Under this eagle, generations of young soldiers were trained and laid down their lives in the Prussian spirit. It is that same spirit which has allowed the National Socialist movement to grow great for the good of Germany. Both during the decades of peace, and during Germany's hardest and greatest battle, this flag flew over the institute which is called today to train the young generation with high German ideals in the spirit of our Führer Adolf Hitler. After the ignominious revolution, former cadets divided this flag amongst themselves with ceremonial gravity, before it could be burnt by the new Marxist authorities. This flag shone before us, as the cadet school closed its gates on 10 January 1920, and we left the institute with a 'Hurrah' and faced a new, uncertain future. But above all, the flag gave us an inner stability and faith that a new era would dawn; the era of the swastika.[1]

In honour of this request and its historical significance, *Anstaltsleiter* Dr. Adolf Schieffer presented the flag to his assembled *Jungmannen* with a stern admonition to emulate that self-same spirit.[2] For a few months, the ensign hung in pride of place in the armoury, before being ceremonially ensconced in a new glass case at the entrance to the dining hall. Once again, the *Jungmannen* were exhorted, this time by Otto Calliebe, to 'emulate that Prussian spirit which the cadets demonstrated as they rescued their flag'.[3]

Of all the Napolas, NPEA Köslin was perhaps the most sedulously attached to its historical roots as a former Prussian cadet school—more than one special issue of the school newsletter was devoted to exploring the institution's cadet-corps

The Third Reich's Elite Schools: A History of the Napolas. Helen Roche, Oxford University Press. © Helen Roche 2021.
DOI: 10.1093/oso/9780198726128.003.0005

past, and Dr. Schieffer and his successor as *Anstaltsleiter*, Lothar Dankleff, were equally diligent in their attempts to cultivate an enduring relationship with the former cadets and their old boys' networks.[4] However, Köslin was far from the only Prussian NPEA to celebrate and hark back to the militaristic traditions of the cadet-school past. For instance, NPEA Bensberg and NPEA Oranienstein possessed miniature cadet-museums or *Kadettenerinnerungszimmer* (cadet tradition rooms), while *Jungmannen* at both NPEA Plön and NPEA Oranienstein created lovingly crafted and beautifully presented *Ehrenbücher* (honour books) to commemorate the cadets at each school who had gone on to fall in the Great War.[5]

For *Jungmannen* who attended the seven former preparatory Prussian cadet schools (*Voranstalten*) at Potsdam, Plön, Köslin, Naumburg, Oranienstein, Bensberg, and Wahlstatt, then, the ex-cadets represented not only an abstract model for emulation, but also a real (if sporadic) presence in school life, attending ceremonies at their war memorials on the school grounds, or celebrating significant cadet-school anniversaries, such as the hundredth anniversary of Bensberg's foundation in 1940.[6] In the eyes of many observers both within the Napola-system and without, not least the former cadets themselves, the NPEA seemed to represent a resurrection of the cadet schools; an often longed-for manifestation of *Borussia rediviva*. After all, many elements of the Napolas' praxis seemed to mirror that of the cadet corps substantially, not least in terms of the preternatural emphasis placed on physical and pre-military training, and the analogous institutional hierarchies, ranging from the identical positions of *Stubenältester* (room-captain) and *Jungmann vom Dienst* (equivalent to *Kadett vom Dienst*), or *Jungmann-Gruppenführer* (equivalent to the cadet-corps rank of *Kadettengefreiter*/cadet-NCO), to *Jungmann-Zugführer* (equivalent to the cadet-corps rank of *Klassenältester*), and *Jungmann-Hundertschaftsführer* (equivalent to the cadet-corps rank of *Kompagnieführer*).[7] Some of the forms of hazing practised both by *Jungmannen* and *Erzieher*, such as the much-detested 'masked ball' or *Kostümfest*, were also obvious relics of the cadet-school tradition.[8] At the Napolas themselves, the notion that the schools represented a symbolic reincarnation of the Prussian spirit was not only frequently welcomed, but eagerly embraced—most visibly in the case of NPEA Potsdam and NPEA Spandau (the successor of the former Central Cadet School or *Hauptkadettenanstalt* in Berlin-Lichterfelde; now the site of the German Federal Archives). Both schools adopted a logo comprising the Prussian heraldic eagle and '*Gott mit uns*' (God with us) motto to grace the covers of their school newsletters; however, in keeping with the political tenor of the times, a swastika was expediently branded on the Prussian eagle's breast.[9]

Yet, at the same time, the attitudes displayed towards the cadet-corps tradition by the NPEA authorities appear to have been markedly Janus-faced. On the one hand, Bernhard Rust and, somewhat less whole-heartedly, August Heißmeyer, seem to have approved of the idea of the cadet schools and their heroic alumni as potential exemplars of 'total education' and 'Prussian virtue'. On the other hand (as we have seen in the Introduction), they simultaneously wished to stress the Napolas' innovative qualities or *Neuartigkeit*, and their lack of subservience to any previous pedagogical paradigm—especially one which reeked as strongly of caste arrogance and anti-egalitarianism as the Royal Prussian Cadet Corps.[10] This led to the cadet-school tradition being frequently disowned in programmatic statements about the Napolas, sometimes by the very personages (including Heißmeyer himself) who elsewhere had hymned that same tradition's virtues. Like cultural magpies, the Napola authorities appropriated those aspects of the Prussian military heritage which gleamed most brightly and enticingly by their current lights, whilst discarding any aspects which seemed politically or ideologically inopportune. From this perspective, then, we can see the Napolas as representative of broader trends in the National Socialist espousal of Prussianism more generally—an opportunistic appropriation which was, as Christopher Clark has put it, 'selective, talismanic, and instrumental'.[11]

In this context, the aims of the following chapter are threefold. Firstly, I give a brief account of the demise of the Prussian cadet schools during the aftermath of the Treaty of Versailles, and their troubled transition into civilian state boarding schools (*Staatliche Bildungsanstalten* or Stabilas), dedicated to upholding the Weimar Republic. Although the educational reformers who aimed to transform the Stabilas into liberal centres of pedagogical experimentation were stymied in part by a chronic lack of funds, by the mid- to late 1920s, they had nevertheless managed to create a new culture at the schools which avoided overt militarization or politicization, and which may fairly be considered to represent a significant contribution to the educational and cultural achievements of the Weimar Republic. Thus, the triumph of Nazification and Napolisation at the Stabilas should by no means be treated as an ultimately foregone conclusion.[12]

However, by the beginning of the 1930s, as the political situation in Germany began to radicalize, we can begin to discern increasing evidence of revanchist sentiments and proto-National-Socialist leanings among the student body at the Stabilas, which led to illegal Hitler Youth activity becoming prevalent at some of the schools in the run-up to 1933. The ever-worsening political climate meant that, by the time of the Nazi seizure of power, little protest was elicited when Bernhard Rust and Joachim Haupt first proposed, and then swiftly put into practice, their plan to turn Potsdam, Plön, and Köslin into the first three Napolas (as briefly described in Chapter 1).[13] Secondly, we will therefore consider these political developments and the process of Napolisation at the Stabilas in greater detail, before returning to the question of how far the Napolas in fact represented a resurrection of the pre-Stabila cadet-school tradition (and, indeed, whether elements of that tradition had managed to survive unscathed throughout the Weimar era).

Finally, we will situate this enquiry within the context of broader discussions concerning continuity and change in the wake of the Nazi seizure of power, and the existing affinities (or otherwise) between Prussianism and National Socialism, as alluded to above. Were the Napolas merely cadet schools in a new, brown-shirted guise, and did the militaristic spirit of an idealized 'Prussia' inevitably infuse all of the NPEA—or merely those which were founded as successor-institutions to the Royal Prussian Cadet Corps? Or ultimately, in truth, did the Napolas and the Stabilas, despite their political differences, have much more in common than either their contemporary adherents, or later historians of education, would ideally have wished to concede?

*

In the immediate aftermath of the signing of the Treaty of Versailles, civilian staff at the Royal Prussian Cadet Corps were concerned at all costs to safeguard their institution and the livelihoods of the *c.*2,000 pupils and 500 teachers, administrators, and other workers (most with dependants to provide for) whose futures were completely reliant upon its fate. Yet, in order to survive, all of the cadet schools had to be fully demilitarized within eight weeks of the treaty coming into force.[14] Despite desperate attempts on the part of the military authorities to find a loophole and retain control of the schools, however, it soon became apparent that the only way forward would be to turn the Central Cadet School in Berlin-Lichterfelde and all of the preparatory cadet schools into civilian boarding schools.[15] The cadets who were currently *in situ* would continue their education there, so that they could gain the requisite academic qualifications for a civilian future; otherwise, the schools would prioritize admission in the first instance for war orphans and the children of disabled veterans, Germans living abroad, or inhabitants of those parts of the Reich which had been lost due to the post-Versailles border settlement. Whatever places remained would be allocated to children from less well-off families, who could also benefit from the schools' generous allocation of means-tested bursaries and scholarships (between 10 to 15 per cent of places at the Stabilas were fully paid for by the state during the mid-1920s).[16]

All of the former cadet schools (apart from Oranienstein and Bensberg, which had both been occupied by French troops, and Karlsruhe) officially opened their doors as *Staatliche Bildungsanstalten* at the beginning of the new academic year, at Easter 1920—much to the chagrin of the cadet schools' adherents.[17] Most virulently opposed were the former cadets who were forced to remain at or return to the former Central Cadet School at Lichterfelde in order to complete their studies. At the opening ceremony on 5 May 1920, it was reported that pupils wearing swastikas in their buttonholes had tried to pull down the black, red, and gold flag (symbolizing the new Republic) which adorned the building.[18] They also distributed flyers which decried all of the new *Erzieher* as 'filthy Jews' who would never be worthy of Germany, and encouraged all pupils to fight back against their new teachers with 'passive aggression'.[19] Many of the ex-cadets had been sent back to the school to gain some qualifications after having spent time in the *Freikorps*, and had thus been instilled with an anti-republican spirit—including a strong element of antisemitism. They felt betrayed by the socialist government which would not allow them all to be enrolled in the new (dramatically reduced) German army, the *Reichswehr*, and were determined not to lose the role of 'active fighters' which they had gained in the *Freikorps*, battling the 'reds' alongside much older military men. As the oldest pupils at the school (all aged between 16 and 20) it was easy for the former cadets to organize resistance to the new Social Democratic school authorities, especially the freshly appointed Jewish Director Friedrich Karsen.[20]

In 1921, anarchy erupted at Lichterfelde in the form of the 'cadet revolts' (*Kadettenrevolte*), in which one of the new house-matrons was attacked and subjected to extreme verbal abuse because she had denounced another matron for inviting boys to tea on the Kaiser's birthday and allowing them to sing patriotic songs. Needless to say, the 'revolts' were raked over in the press, and discussions raged in parliament regarding suitable punishments for the cadets involved, and the ways in which the Education Ministry should diffuse the dangerous influence of the older cadets' anti-republican, monarchist convictions.[21] The cadets were branded '*Hurrabengel*' (jingoistic whippersnappers) and '*Arbeitertöter*' (worker-killers), while the school at Lichterfelde was presented as a reactionary hotbed, stirring up hatred against civilians.[22]

Even at the preparatory cadet schools, similar incidents also took place; for instance, at Plön, a group of ex-cadets burnt the black, red, and gold republican flag before an official visit; some of the offenders were transferred to other Stabilas, while others were expelled.[23] Meanwhile, at Köslin, the aforementioned Erich Reuter and his comrades played frequent monarchist pranks on the new school authorities, such as decking out the Kaiser's bust with the Prussian flag on the formerly celebrated festival of his birthday, and holding their own secret midnight celebrations, or hoisting the cadet-corps ensign clandestinely on the eve of certain Prussian feast-days, so that the astonished inhabitants of the town were greeted in the morning by the Prussian flag flying overhead, to the great chagrin and vexation of the Stabila leadership.[24]

For a time, the only uniforms available were those which the cadets had worn; only gradually did the newly minted Stabila-pupils begin to resemble the civilians whom they would now have to become, wearing what they derisively dubbed the '*Kutscherfrack*' (coachman's coat) as their new uniform.[25] During the first few years, the unchecked power of the ex-cadets who acted as *Stubenältester* remained a terror for the younger pupils, who were often forced by the older boys to spend their free time on military-style drills, or to participate in former cadet-school hazing rituals.[26] The gradual turnover, both of cadet-corps staff and pupils, meant that the *Aufbau* process at the Stabilas, and in particular at the preparatory cadet schools, which had never previously educated pupils all the way up to the school-leaving exam (*Reifeprüfung*), was not fully complete until the mid-1920s. By then, the last cadets had finally left the schools, and were no longer able to exercise their baneful anti-republican influence over their younger counterparts at first hand.[27] At least at Lichterfelde, the advent of the educational reformer Hans Richert as Director in 1922 seems to have exerted a decisive influence, leading to the so-called 'reforms of 1924'—a thorough-going reinvention and reinvigoration of the Stabila ethos.[28] By the late 1920s, the only ostensible relics of the cadet-school tradition were the continuing prevalence of corps slang and rituals, and the visits paid by former cadets to their war memorials in the school grounds.[29] Now, it was only in sporting terms that a Stabila might legitimately claim to have 'taken on the mantle of the cadet corps'.[30] And, while sport does seem to have held a particularly privileged position at many of the Stabilas—especially those, such as Lichterfelde/Spandau, which were later renowned for their sporting prowess as Napolas too—reports in school newsletters recounting pupils' athletic feats or championship victories rarely eclipsed their accounts of all the other many and varied activities which the *Staatliche Bildungsanstalten* had to offer.[31]

In cultural and artistic terms, the Stabilas appear to have embraced many of the new developments which took shape under the Weimar Republic. The schools held art exhibitions featuring potentially controversial 'modern masters' such as Käthe Kollwitz or Heinrich Zille, and encouraged pupils to emulate the Bauhaus style in their lino-cuts, or debate the stylistic merits of the 'New Objectivity' (*Neue Sachlichkeit*).[32] Many pupils also eagerly embraced the delights of jazz, and founded their own school jazz-bands.[33] In the case of Plön, the Stabila's music groups regularly featured on radio broadcasts, as well as premiering avant-garde works by the contemporary composer Paul Hindemith, and hosting the celebrated Schleswig-Holstein Youth Music Week (*Schleswig-Holsteinische Jugendmusikwoche*).[34]

Some of the *Staatliche Bildungsanstalten* also deliberately adopted a more homely mode of boarding-school life, taking Hermann Lietz's *Landerziehungsheime* (country boarding schools) as a model. Pupils lived in small groups (*Erziehungsgemeinschaften*) with a responsible *Erzieher* who would play an avuncular rather than an authoritarian role—reading aloud to his charges, for instance, or saying goodnight to each pupil individually.[35] On occasion, the schools' directors travelled to conferences inspired by reform-pedagogy, and were also ready to allow for experiments in allowing pupils autonomy to participate in school decision-making (*Schülerselbstverwaltung*), as well as founding their own clubs and societies—so long as these possessed no political bent.[36] Given the absence of the constant '*Dienst*'—physical exercises and other duties—which had so characterized life at the cadet schools (and which would do so again at the Napolas), Stabila-pupils had far more free time at their disposal to devote to the many extracurricular activities on offer.[37] These might be musical, dramatic, artistic, or practical—many of the schools possessed clubs or voluntary working groups (*Arbeitsgemeinschaften*) which expressly cultivated vocational skills such as gardening, book-binding, amateur radio, animal husbandry, or stenography. Although, in the interests of stability, pupils were expressly forbidden from engaging in any form of overt political activity, many of the *Arbeitsgemeinschaften* run by the *Erzieher* would engage in ostensibly even-handed discussion of current affairs—the 'English debating-club style' deliberations at the so-called 'political evenings' held at the *Staatliche Bildungsanstalt* in Plön appear to have been particularly popular in this regard.[38]

Yet, ultimately, all of the school authorities' asseverations that 'politics must halt at the gates of our institution!', as the first director of Stabila Köslin, Dr. Tominski, had asserted during his inaugural speech in May 1920, were to no avail.[39] Despite the prevalence of festivities at the schools invoking Republican sentiment, such as the annual celebrations of Constitution Day (*Verfassungsfeier*), we find clear evidence of right-wing radicalism taking hold among some members of the student body at the Stabilas by the beginning of the 1930s, although the degree of susceptibility seems to have differed from school to school.[40]

It is difficult to discern with absolute certainty how strongly infused with German-nationalist spirit the teaching at the *Staatliche Bildungsanstalten* may or may not have been. The lists of essay themes printed in the schools' official annual reports suggest that the Stabilas at Potsdam and Plön were more likely to promote questions which highlighted Germany's political and territorial losses in World War I, or which engaged specifically with right-wing issues and texts, than was the case at, say, Stabila Wahlstatt. For example, themes for the *Oberprima* (final year) at Potsdam in 1927–8 included 'The settlement of the East: Germany's salvation', 'Why does Germany need her colonies?', and 'The Greater-German idea'; themes for the *Reifeprüfung* at Plön in 1929–30 included 'The damage caused to Germany by the loss of territories after the Versailles Treaty'. Meanwhile, a similarly colonial theme at Wahlstatt in 1928–9 was phrased somewhat less tendentiously: 'Do you believe that the Germans' striving for colonies is justified?'[41]

However, one fairly reliable indication of the existence or extent of revanchist sentiment among the student body at large is evident in the foundation, and subsequent popularity, of school chapters of the *Verein für das Deutschtum im Ausland* or VDA (Association for Germandom Abroad). For instance, at the Stabilas in Köslin, Lichterfelde, and Plön, VDA groups were founded in 1926, 1927, and 1928 respectively, and each soon boasted an active and numerous following.[42] In 1930, the members of the VDA chapter at the school in Lichterfelde, which was now known as the 'Hans Richert-Schule', reported that they had been allocated a room of their own in which to keep books, articles, and pictures relating to Germandom abroad, as well as a 'VDA-board' which was used to display relevant notices and pictures in front of the school. That same year, the VDA group's chairman went on to be elected to the chairmanship of the entire Lichterfelde district of the VDA.[43] By 1932–3, the group at the Hans Richert-Schule had gone from strength to strength, and its members' fixation with Germany's 'borderland troubles' became ever shriller and more heated as time progressed. That same year, the group went so far as to put on a play about murderous Polish insurgents entitled '*Volk ohne Heimat*' ('People without a Homeland'), in the hope that it would not only entertain the audience, but also focus their minds on those 'terrible days when German land was stolen from us'. According to the author of the group's annual report, the play was performed with 'love'.[44]

'Borderland' schools such as Stabila Köslin appear to have felt this imperative still more keenly, as an issue of the Köslin school newsletter from August 1930 well demonstrates.[45] Accounts of a final-year field trip to Upper Silesia featured prominently, in which the youthful contributors touched upon many of the tropes which would later become familiar in analogous accounts of the Napolas' own 'borderland missions' a few years later: for instance, the countless anti-German atrocities allegedly committed by dastardly Poles or evil Czechs, and the penury, inequality, and universal misery purportedly caused by the hideously unfair post-Versailles border settlement.

Perhaps it was no coincidence, then, that at the end of April 1932, at a meeting of the library committee, the director of Stabila Köslin, Dr. Tominski, had to refuse the pupils' unanimous request to order a National Socialist newspaper for the reading-room.[46] Six months or so later, the more-or-less republican Tominski left his position, to be replaced by *Oberstudiendirektor* Dr. Höpken. In contrast to Tominski's staunchly anti-political stance in his own inauguration speech, Höpken instead betrayed his rather more reactionary sympathies by praising the school's 'ancient Prussian' sense of duty.[47] In similar vein, at Plön, some of the *Arbeitsgemeinschaften* run by the *Erzieher* (a few of whom later went on to work at the Napolas) began to include voluntary classes on themes such as eugenics and heredity.[48] Joachim Haupt, the future founder and Inspector of the NPEA, who was then a trainee teacher at the Stabila, also led a group on 'Philosophy of German Idealism and Modern Psychology'.[49] Of course, it was still possible for some boys to be aware that heated discussions concerning the merits and demerits of Nazism were taking place among the *Primaner* (sixth-formers) without themselves engaging with political questions. However, by this point, other pupils' potential for fanaticism had already begun to fundamentally alter the fabric of school life.[50]

At some of the Stabilas, the process of radicalization advanced so far that groups of pupils began to found secret cells of the National Socialist Pupils' League (NSS) or the Hitler Youth (the two organizations were amalgamated in 1932); they soon began to disseminate Nazi propaganda among their peers.[51] One pupil at Köslin, Erich Andrée, fell foul of this practice, risking expulsion from the Stabila under false pretences after the school authorities discovered Hitler Youth advertising material in his wardrobe, hidden behind his underwear; he had unwisely promised to hide it on behalf of a friend who had recently come under suspicion.[52] Despite his lack of affiliation to the Hitler Youth cell, Andrée refused to betray his classmate and confess where the material had come from.[53]

When, on polling day in March 1933, the swastika ended up being flown instead of the black, red, and gold republican flag, Andrée was treated as the most obvious culprit for the flag-swapping, and thereafter left the Stabila voluntarily.[54] At Naumburg, meanwhile, two pupils named Rudi Jork and Fips Jahn also risked expulsion when, with the surreptitious blessing of one of the female teachers, they founded an NSS cell whose activity was subsequently uncovered by the authorities. Instead of disbanding, however, the group moved underground, holding covert ideological education sessions in the evenings, and delivering Nazi propaganda material from the local NSDAP office to neighbouring villages on their bicycles in their free time during the day.[55] Similar groups also appear to have sprung up with more or less alacrity at the Stabilas in Potsdam and Lichterfelde during this period.[56]

Great was the rejoicing, then, when these clandestine Nazi youth groups were finally able to reveal themselves without fear of penalty or censure, after the National Socialists had seized power. At Potsdam, the director, Dr. Neuhaus, expressed solidarity with those members of the school's NSS-group who were now able to stand proudly with their banner beneath the main portal singing the Horst-Wessel-Lied, as the black, white, and red imperial flag and the swastika were hoisted side by side to celebrate the 'Victory of the National Movement' on 8 March 1933.[57] By contrast, at Plön, Dr. Teichert's role as headmaster was destined to be short-lived, after he protested against the group of local SA-men who had taken it upon themselves to celebrate the Nazi Party's victory by flying the swastika from the tower of Schloss Plön.[58]

Meanwhile, at Köslin, it was announced in the May/June edition of the school newsletter that the Stabila would soon be turned into an 'Adolf-Hitler-School', and that the director, Dr. Höpken, and several other members of staff would compulsorily be furloughed. The former trappings of the cadet school—rolls of honour, portraits, and weapons in the armoury—were swiftly returned to their former privileged places. All in all, it seemed that the new school authorities were determined to resurrect the cadet-corps tradition as quickly as possible, and treat the Stabila era as if it had been just a bad dream.[59] By August 1933, Dr. Schieffer, the NPEA *Anstaltsleiter*, and his deputy, *Unterrichtsleiter* Otto Calliebe, had arrived to oversee the Napolisation process, even though, as far as the school newsletter was concerned, the new institution was still called the 'Adolf-Hitler-School'.[60]

At the *Staatliche Bildungsanstalt* in Naumburg, where the Hitler Youth cell had now gleefully emerged from hiding, the hated republican flag was burnt at the main gate, allegedly in the director's presence, and with his permission. In his capacity as the official leader of Hitler-Youth Squad 28, the former renegade Rudi Jork, full of regret that Naumburg had not been chosen to become one of the three flagship Napolas, sent a telegram to Bernhard Rust pleading for his Stabila to be permitted to join the ranks of the NPEA too. Rust's laconic reply read '*Abwarten, aushalten*' ('Wait, persevere'), and Jork's dream was finally realized a year later when Naumburg, along with Wahlstatt and the Hans Richert-Schule, which had moved to Spandau in late 1933 in order to make room for the *Leibstandarte Adolf Hitler* at Lichterfelde, were the next three Napolas to be founded.[61]

The turnover of directors and teachers during the Napolisation phase at the Stabilas was deliberately swift and ruthless; Heinrich Rieper, one of the teachers at Plön, suggested that Rust ideally wanted all staff at the *Staatliche Bildungsanstalten* to be 'purged' by 1 April 1934.[62] Meanwhile, any Stabila-pupils who did not accord with the new regime's ideals physically, ethnically, or ideologically were also summarily dismissed, especially those with any hint of Jewish ancestry—for example, at Spandau, 120 pupils were slated to leave, in order to get the numbers down to the mandatory strength.[63] At Plön, those day-pupils who initially had to remain at the Napola because there was no other school which they could immediately attend posed a particular problem; they quite naturally objected to being treated both by the Napola leadership, and by their new fellow-students, as second-class citizens.[64]

However, despite odd administrative teething troubles, such as the dilapidated state of the horsehair mattresses in the dormitories at Potsdam, or the fact that many of the beds at Köslin were too small—not to mention what the NPEA administration deemed to be a lamentable lack of National Socialist literature in the schools' libraries, or Führer-portraits on their walls—the former Stabilas soon began to find their initial, experimental feet.[65] And, as we shall see, a significant part of this process of Napolisation was undoubtedly a deliberate and concerted effort by the school authorities to return to the 'Prussian' virtues of the cadet-corps era, whilst simultaneously attempting to efface all memory of the Stabilas' detested liberalism and left-wing idealism.

*

The idea that the NPEA represented a resurrection of the Prussian cadet schools was widely prevalent throughout the Third Reich, whether among conservative or aristocratic families who were keen to send their sons to be educated in the cadet-corps tradition, military men and former cadets who were delighted to see that the educational clauses of the 'shackles of Versailles' had finally been riven asunder—or merely among the inhabitants of those towns which lay immediately beyond the former cadet-school gates.[66] For instance, readers of Beyer's *Modezeitschrift* were proudly informed that:

> In the afternoon, in Potsdam, one often sees lads in the Hitler Youth uniform out and about, who are wearing a black-white-and-black armband with a red swastika, instead of the HJ's red-white-and-red version. Every Potsdamer knows that these are the 'cadets'; lads who are being trained…in a location steeped in Prussian-German tradition. The present-day National Political Education

> Institute is Prussia's oldest cadet school. Here, the greatest men in Prussian history learnt everything which later enabled their great achievements. In recognition of this tradition, the Prussian Government granted the lads at the Potsdam Institute this special armband, in the Prussian colours, with the red swastika.[67]

Once a year, *Jungmannen* from the Napola would also march through the streets of Potsdam garbed in the historic uniform that Prussian cadets would have worn at the time of Frederick the Great, including authentic-looking wigs and cocked hats.[68] During World War II, this cadet-school collocation was made even more explicit when pupils from NPEA Potsdam were used as extras in Karl Ritter's anti-Soviet propaganda-film, *Kadetten* (*Cadets*). The film, based on a screenplay by Felix Lützkendorf, depicted an episode from the Seven Years War when cadets from the Prussian cadet school in Berlin were imprisoned and deported by Russian soldiers. The film was originally shot in 1939, with the premiere due to take place at the Reich Party Rally in Nuremberg the following September.[69] However, the premiere was postponed for diplomatic reasons after the signing of the Molotov-Ribbentrop pact, so that *Kadetten* was only screened for the first time in 1941, once Hitler had finally broken his alliance with Soviet Russia.[70]

In more general terms, the ways in which links with the cadet-school tradition were preserved and cultivated varied from school to school. While all of the Prussian NPEA had adopted the cadets' uniform insignia to demarcate rankings such as *Jungmann-Zugführer* and *Jungmann-Gruppenführer*, as well as inheriting the colour of their schools' respective cadet-corps epaulettes (this sometimes led to violent confusion during the annual manoeuvres, given that Potsdam's epaulettes were brick-red, and Naumburg's crimson), there existed many other differences—less official, perhaps, but none the less noticeable.[71] Thus, at Plön, commemoration would tend to focus most frequently upon Erich Ludendorff, 'the greatest Plön cadet' of all, and on the idea that the *Jungmannen*, as the cadets' heirs, should uncomplainingly be able to bear all of the hardships which their martinettish *Anstaltsleiter* Hermann Brunk chose to inflict upon them.[72] That these exhortations had an effect on at least some of the *Jungmannen* may be inferred from the last letter which former pupil Franz Mordcj, who died in battle in 1942, sent to his mother—a rousing encomium both to Ludendorff and Brunk, and to the spirit of Plön.[73]

Meanwhile, the denizens of Napola Köslin were far more interested in commemorating Frederick the Great; there, no opportunity was ever lost to reprint and disseminate reproductions of the first ever budget of the cadet school in Culm (Köslin's predecessor), which bore the King's signature, as proof of the Napola's noble Prussian heritage.[74] Indeed, one such reproduction was even gratuitously included in *Anstaltsleiter* Schieffer's birthday present to Education Minister Rust in 1934—a bound volume containing a collection of essays written by the *Jungmannen*.[75] Meanwhile, Frederick's 225th anniversary, which took place in 1936, was also celebrated with all due pomp and circumstance. As part of the commemoration, *Anstaltsleiter* Dankleff exhorted Köslin's *Jungmannen* to follow the warrior king's example and cultivate the iron will, strict discipline, order, austerity, and obedience which had made Prussia great, deliberately comparing Frederick's achievements with Hitler's own struggle for German unity.[76]

Accounts by former cadets or potted histories of the cadet-school era also featured prominently in the Köslin school newsletters; the daring flag-saving exploits of Erich Reuter (who subsequently reached the rank of General in the Wehrmacht High Command) were rehearsed frequently; in general, no effort was spared to ensure that the cadet-school tradition would live on in the minds of the *Jungmannen*.[77] The effectiveness of this strategy may be suggested by the fact that, even in later decades, former pupils of NPEA Köslin would frequently still identify themselves as 'cadets of the new era' (*Kadetten der neuen Zeit*).[78] Meanwhile, nothing could exemplify Köslin's desire to revivify a Nazified version of Prussianism better than *Anstaltsleiter* Schieffer's first appeal to all Köslin ex-cadets to renew contact with their old school:

> For two years now, the Red Building in Köslin has housed a National Political Education Institute. Once again, as in the decades prior to 1919, ancient Prussian masculine discipline and a Frederician sense of duty hold sway at our school. As an earnest of our intent, the side-arms of our *Jungmannen* bear Schlieffen's motto, 'Be more than you seem'. The 'swottish spirit' of the intervening era has vanished. *N.P.E.A. Köslin consciously conceives of itself as the heir and steward of the former cadet school, to which it is connected by the ties of our selfsame will and striving.* With the help of our newsletter, the 'Bridge', we wish to make contact with all 'old boys'; we wish to bring them all together into one great comradely collective![79]

Many of the other Prussian Napolas also attempted to cultivate such relationships with 'their' ex-cadets—for instance, the 'political evenings' at Plön were now recast as a prime opportunity to involve former members of the school community in a similarly comradely fashion. These relationships could also allow for propagandistic interventions by members of the armed forces who had known the schools of old (see Chapter 10).[80] Thus, *Jungmannen* at NPEA Oranienstein were granted the opportunity to visit a tank regiment at Wünsdorf solely due to the school's prior connection with the colonel, who had been a member of the cadet corps there, while the highly decorated general August von Hellermann, a former cadet at Naumburg, visited the Napola in 1944, primarily in order to encourage pupils to join the Wehrmacht and follow in his footsteps.[81]

For the *Jungmannen* themselves, the idea of emulating the Prussian cadets who had once strode their corridors, or the supposition that, as members of these historic institutions, they represented a living embodiment of the cadet-corps tradition, could be intoxicating. For instance, reflecting on his time at NPEA

Spandau many decades later, the Bundeswehr general Günter Kießling recalled his overwhelming pride whenever he beheld the school soup bowls, which were still emblazoned with the inscription '*kgl. preuß. Kadettenkorps*' (even though the bowls' contents were not always wholly to his taste).[82] Arne Heinich, who attended NPEA Bensberg, similarly stressed the power which the idea of the cadet-school heritage exerted on pupils there.[83]

Meanwhile, even *Jungmannen* who had never experienced life at a former cadet school at first hand could still begin to take pride in cadet-corps traditions, as did those pupils at NPEA Loben (Lubliniec) in occupied Silesia who were initially shown the ropes by a group of *Jungmannen* from NPEA Naumburg in 1941:

> [Under the *Erzieher* and 5th *Zug* from Naumburg,] an extremely strict regime held sway..., which we later simply considered as normal. We took over many [cadet-school] customs and practices, right up to certain habits at table (*Dixi*—I have spoken, i.e., that piece of bread belongs to me!). These customs and practices comprised the majority of our school culture later on. We were proud to be the successors of the cadet schools, and so we also had to accept the drilling with which the Naumburger so unstintingly provided us.[84]

*

But how far did all of this outright glorification of the cadet-school past at the Prussian NPEA chime with the original intentions of the Napolas' founders and administrators? Ironically, Joachim Haupt, the first Inspector of the NPEA, seems to have been far more interested in promoting an ethos derived from the post-war youth movement (*Jugendbewegung*) than that of the cadet schools, despite having attended the Royal Prussian Cadet Corps himself.[85]

However, Haupt's co-founder, Education Minister Bernhard Rust, was generally extremely positive in his assessment of the cadet-corps tradition and its significance for the NPEA, declaring that:

> In these Prussian Cadet Schools, timeless German values were once nurtured and trained which must live once again; the soldierly spirit with its traits: courage, consciousness of duty, and frugality. For this reason, I have also effectively given all National Political Education Institutes the words of a great Prussian soldier [Moltke] as the legacy which they will carry with them on their journey: '*Mehr sein als scheinen*' (be more than you seem).[86]

The only major difference between the two institutions, in Rust's view, was that the Napolas should aim to educate the future elite in all walks of life, not just the military.[87]

Similar caveats were also raised by the second Inspector of the NPEA, August Heißmeyer, who made it clear that the cadet schools' spirit of caste arrogance and one-sidedly military orientation should be strictly avoided at the Napolas, although, during World War II, he was still keen enough to boast to his superiors that the schools were more than equalling the cadet corps' achievements in supplying the armed forces with first-class officer-fodder.[88] At the same time, Heißmeyer repeatedly hailed the Prussian cadet corps as the only true manifestation in German history of that type of anti-individualistic education which he most desired the Napolas to embody.[89] By contrast, the idea that the NPEA might ever have possessed anything in common with the Stabilas, those institutions of the hated Weimar era or '*Systemzeit*', would have seemed anathema not only to Rust and Heißmeyer, but also to most of the Napola directors and administrators at large.

And yet, we can nevertheless discern continuities between the Stabilas and the Napolas which existed beyond the level of merely superficial similarities. Rather, elements such as a new emphasis on companionship, especially between younger *Erzieher* and pupils, the fostering of quasi-socialist principles, especially via the system of free places and a sliding scale of means-tested bursaries, and even the paramount importance accorded to the selection process (including a long-drawn-out trial period), as well as the privileging of certain categories of applicant, were all aspects of the Stabilas' organization which were taken over, sometimes more or less wholesale, by the NPEA administration.[90] Thus, we might agree with Walter Becker's contention that 'the cleft between Stabilas and NPEA was not nearly so deep as one would have liked to think'.[91] While such continuities might have been sedulously denied by the NPEA authorities, in part because of their desire to stress above all the pedagogical novelty of the schools' approach, significant aspects of the culture which existed at the Napolas had already been prefigured at the *Staatliche Bildungsanstalten*. Thus, while many of the organizational and pre-military aspects of the Napolas could easily be adapted from the cadet-school model, as we have seen, the more reformist elements of the Napola programme were at least partially indebted to developments which had taken place subsequently, under the Stabilas' republican star.

In conclusion, then, we can ultimately discern two impulses at work here which are fundamentally indicative of Nazi attitudes to the 'pre-revolutionary' past in general. Firstly, we can identify the tendency to appropriate positive developments (whether social, political, or economic) which had already begun to come to fruition under the Weimar state, whilst simultaneously recasting these prior achievements as purely National Socialist triumphs.[92] Examples of this tendency more generally might include Hitler's propagandistic appropriation of Chancellor Kurt von Schleicher's twenty-million Reichsmark job creation scheme, the *Sofortprogramm*, to further his aims of reducing unemployment, or the Nazi regime's claiming the *Autobahn* as a National Socialist invention, when in fact the first stretch of motorway had already been ceremonially inaugurated by none other than Konrad Adenauer, then the Mayor of Cologne, in 1932.

Secondly, we also find a key instance of that widespread desire to associate Nazism with all of the much-bruited virtues of the Prussian 'spirit' which was prevalent even among the leaders of the Third Reich, yet which nevertheless existed alongside a conspicuous contempt for notions of Prussian aristocratic exclusivity.[93] In this context, wittingly or unwittingly, the Napolas and their pupils played a significant part in that drive to choreograph the Prussian past for propagandistic purposes which had first motivated Hitler's hagiographic treatment of Hindenburg at the Garrison Church on the so-called 'Day of Potsdam' on 21 March 1933, and which subsequently inspired the filming of a whole series of Prussian-themed 'Fredericus-flicks'. These titles not only included *The Old and the Young King* (*Der alte und der junge König*, 1935), *The Higher Command* (*Der höhere Befehl*, 1935), and *Kolberg* (1945), but also that very same propaganda film, *Kadetten* (1941), which had explicitly and deliberately featured Napola-pupils in the guise of historical cadets.[94]

What the NPEA authorities desired, in truth, was to fuse Prussianism and National Socialism in such a way that 'what the cadet schools once achieved for the Prusso-German officer-corps, what other schools have achieved in the nurturing of intellectual education, we must now combine in order to train the type of the political soldier as the backbone of the Reich'.[95] Or, as Graf Knyphausen put it in an article on NPEA Spandau and its *Jungmannen* which was published in the *Deutsche Allgemeine Zeitung* on 19 October 1937, 'the "ideal Napola-pupil"... is a National Socialist through and through (just as the cadet was a Prussian through and through), since from the outset, given his entire way of life and the entire scope of his task, he can be nothing other than a National Socialist'.[96]

And yet, in the end, perhaps the most apt image of all for the Napolas' constant appeal to the Prussian paradigm has to be a depiction of *Fastnacht* (Mardi Gras) at NPEA Naumburg: as part of the festivities, a *Jungmann* who had been appointed as the 'Mardi Gras General' (*Faschingsgeneral*) would take control of the entire school in true Saturnalian fashion, garbed in an old cadet-school uniform which now represented just one of the many outfits used on occasion to supplement the Napola's theatrical wardrobe.[97] The symbolism of the Prussian cadet-school past may have been powerful, but it was still a mere disguise; an insubstantial costume nonetheless. No matter how attractive the collocation of Prussianism and National Socialism in the educational sphere might initially have appeared to both ex-cadets and *Jungmannen* alike, and despite their evident affinities, ultimately, the revolutionary ideological core of Nazism could never be adequately clothed in the monarchist trappings of the Prussian military establishment.

Notes

1. Reuter, 'Die Fahne hoch!', *Die Brücke: Nachrichten von der Nationalpolitischen Erziehungsanstalt Köslin* 6, no. 6 (December 1933), 97.
2. *Die Brücke* 6, no. 6 (December 1933), 98.
3. *Die Brücke* 7, no. 1 (April/May 1934), 14.

4. *Die Brücke* 8, no. 7 (March 1935); *Die Brücke* 9, no. 7 (February 1937); Schieffer, 'Ehemalige Kösliner Kadetten!', *Reichskadettenblatt* 33 (May 1935), 526; Dankleff, 'Aufruf!', *Reichskadettenblatt* 38 (October 1936), 599.
5. See Stadtarchiv Bergisch Gladbach (StABG), S 1/92, for photographs of Bensberg's *Kadettenerinnerungszimmer*, which was later completely destroyed in the fire that devastated one wing of Schloss Bensberg in 1942 (cf. K. R. Moritz, 'Das Kadettenzimmer im Bensberger Schloß. Wertvolle Erinnerungsstücke gingen mit dem Brand verloren', *Westdeutscher Beobachter*, 4 April 1942); *Reichskadettenblatt* 37 (July 1936), 579; 'Ehrenbuch der gefallenen ehemaligen Oraniensteiner Kadetten', *Reichskadettenblatt* 45 (March 1938), 712–13.
6. E.g. Geheimes Staatsarchiv Preußischer Kulturbesitz (GStAPK), IV. HA Rep. 13, Nr. 83, Bl. 85, Richard Feiber to Reichsbund ehemaliger Kadetten Gau West, letter dated 21 September 1940.
7. Helen Roche, *Sparta's German Children: The Ideal of Ancient Sparta in the Royal Prussian Cadet Corps, 1818–1920, and in National Socialist Elite Schools (the Napolas), 1933–1945* (Swansea, 2013), 184.
8. Roche, *Sparta's German Children*, 185; see also Chapter 2.
9. *Potsdamer Kameradschaft: Blätter der Nationalpolitischen Erziehungsanstalt Potsdam; Blätter der Nationalpolitischen Erziehungsanstalt Berlin-Spandau.*
10. On the history of the cadet schools more generally, see Roche, *Sparta's German Children*; also John Moncure, *Forging the King's Sword: Military Education between Tradition and Modernization—The Case of the Royal Prussian Cadet Corps, 1871–1918* (New York, 1993); and Klaus Schmitz, *Militärische Jugenderziehung. Preußische Kadettenhäuser und Nationalpolitische Erziehungsanstalten zwischen 1807 und 1936* (Frankfurt am Main, 1997).
11. Christopher Clark, *Iron Kingdom: The Rise and Downfall of Prussia, 1600–1947* (London, 2006), 662, 670; cf. Brendan Simms, 'Prussia, Prussianism and National Socialism, 1933–1947', in Philip G. Dwyer, ed., *Modern Prussian History 1830–1947* (Harlow, 2001), 253–73. See further the conclusion of this chapter.
12. Overall, I therefore take a rather more positive view of the Stabilas' political achievements than that suggested by Klaus Schmitz in his monograph, *Militärische Jugenderziehung*. On recent scholarly developments which stress the contingency of the Weimar Republic more generally, and which resist narratives that present the Weimar state as being inevitably doomed to Nazism, see e.g. Peter Fritzsche, 'Did Weimar Fail?', *Journal of Modern History* 68, no. 3 (1996), 629–56; Anthony McElligott, ed., *Weimar Germany* (Oxford, 2009); Kathleen Canning et al., eds, *Weimar Publics/Weimar Subjects: Rethinking the Political Culture of Germany in the 1920s* (New York, 2010); Jochen Hung et al., eds, *Beyond Glitter and Doom: The Contingency of the Weimar Republic* (Munich, 2012), especially the chapters by Jochen Hung and Moritz Föllmer; Anthony McElligott, *Rethinking the Weimar Republic: Authority and Authoritarianism 1916–1936* (London, 2014).
13. Cf. Schmitz, *Militärische Jugenderziehung*, 273.
14. 'Umwandlung der Kadettenanstalten in Zivil-Erziehungsanstalten für befähigte Kinder, deren Väter im Kriege gefallen oder schwer beschädigt sind, sowie für befähigte Volksschüler. An die Reichsregierung und die Preußische Staatsregierung'

(11 August 1919), Niedersächsisches Landesarchiv—Staatsarchiv Wolfenbüttel, 12 Neu Präs 13 Nr. 15960.

15. On the political wrangling involved, see Schmitz, *Militärische Jugenderziehung*, 167–85; Roche, *Sparta's German Children*, 157–8; also GStAPK, I. HA Rep. 76 VI. Sekt. I aa, Nr. 19, Bd. VI.
16. 'Umwandlung der Kadettenanstalten', 2–3; Bundesarchiv Lichterfelde (BArch), R 3901/9909; GStAPK, I. HA Rep. 151 IC, Nr. 7430; Landesarchiv Nordrhein-Westfalen, Abteilung Rheinland, Duisburg (LNRW-D), BR 5 Nr. 20251.
17. Although plans were set in train to turn Bensberg into a *Staatliche Bildungsanstalt* at a later date, none of these ultimately came to fruition, partly due to the intense confessional tensions in the area—see further GStAPK, I. HA Rep. 151 Finanzministerium IV Nr. 2728, and further files at the Archiv der Evangelischen Kirche im Rheinland, Düsseldorf, and Stadtarchiv Bergisch Gladbach; also Klaus Schmitz, 'Gründung und Aufbau der "Nationalpolitischen Erziehungsanstalt" in Bensberg im Rahmen der NS-Schulpolitik in Preußen (1933–1940)', *Zeitschrift des Bergischen Geschichtsvereins* 93 (1987/8), 133–69; Max Morsches, 'Nutzungsgeschichte des Neuen Schlosses Bensberg. Vom Tod des Erbauers 1716 bis zum Kauf durch die Aachener und Münchener Lebensversicherung 1997', in Albert Eßer and Wolfgang Vomm, eds, *Bürgerburg und Musenvilla. Zugänge zu historischen Herrschaftsbauten in Bergisch Gladbach* (Bergisch Gladbach, 2006), 91–115. Meanwhile, Oranienstein was converted into a private *Landerziehungsheim* which opened its doors in December 1927—see further the prospectus by the director in GStAPK, I. HA Rep. 76. VI. Sekt. I aa, Nr. 19, Bd. VI, Bl. 368–86: Hanns Riess, *Erziehungsheim 'Schloß Oranienstein'* (Diez an der Lahn, 1928).
18. This paragraph and the one following are adapted from Roche, *Sparta's German Children*, 159. N.B. At this time, the swastika was still a general symbol of German *völkisch* nationalism, not yet primarily linked with the Nazi Party.
19. Schmitz, *Militärische Jugenderziehung*, 197.
20. Schmitz, *Militärische Jugenderziehung*, 204–5.
21. E.g. *Sitzungsberichte des preußischen Landtages* 1922, 126.–27. Sitzung (3–4 April 1922), 8961–9056.
22. For more on the cadet-revolts, see e.g. GStAPK, I. HA Rep. 151 IC, Nr. 7331; GStAPK, I. HA Rep. 76 VI. Sekt. 1 Gen.aa Nr. 19 Bd. VI.
23. Hans Kasdorff and Erwin Schmidt, eds, *100 Jahre Erziehung der Jugend auf Schloss Plön: 1868–1968* (Plön, 1968), 97.
24. Erich Reuter, 'Vom Kadettenhaus zur Stabila', *Die Brücke: Nachrichten von der Stabila Köslin* 5, no. 6 (December 1932), 133–5.
25. Axel Burggaller, 'Brief eines ehemaligen Wahlstätters', *Wahlstatt: Blätter der Staatlichen Bildungsanstalt Wahlstatt* 1, no. 1 (Easter 1931), 6; Walter Becker, *Erinnerungen an die NAPOLA Naumburg. Ein über die 'Kadette Naumburg' hinausgehender Beitrag zur Geschichte der NPEA* (Neustrelitz, 2000), 22; *Ehemalige kgl. preußischer Kösliner Kadetten, Rundbrief* 5 (December 1974), 7 (GStAPK, IV. HA Rep. 13, Nr. 109, Bl. 103).
26. Wilhelm Rutzen, 'Neun Jahre Stabila. Rückblick, Eindrücke und Erfahrungen', *Die Brücke: Nachrichten von der Stabila Köslin* 3, no. 7 (January 1931), 132–4; Wilhelm Rutzen, '1921–1930', *Die Brücke: Nachrichten von der Stabila Köslin* 6, no. 5 (November 1933), 79–82; '*Der letzte Kadett*', *Reichskadettenblatt* 33 (May 1935), 524–6; '10 Jahre

NPEA. Naumburg—ein Überblick. Von der "Stabila" zur "Napola"', *10 Jahre Nationalpolitische Erziehungsanstalt Naumburg an der Saale* (1944), 7–9.

27. Cf. Schmitz, *Militärische Jugenderziehung*, 225–8.
28. Cf. Dieter Margies, *Das höhere Schulwesen zwischen Reform und Restauration. Die Biographie Hans Richerts als Beitrag zur Bildungspolitik in der Weimarer Republik* (Rheinstetten, 1972), 84.
29. Gerd Herbig, 'Mein Lebensgeschichte. Plön' (1983); Günter S. (former pupil of Stabila Wahlstatt), private correspondence, 8 January 2013; *10 Jahre Naumburg*, 7; on former cadets' visits, see e.g. *Staatliche Bildungsanstalt Berlin-Lichterfelde—Bericht über das Schuljahr 1927/28*, 23; Friedrich Kaldenbach, 'Das Ehrenmal auf der Südfront', *Blätter der Hans Richert-Schule—Staatliche Bildungsanstalt Berlin Lichterfelde* 6 (1 October 1930), 14–15. Stabila Wahlstatt considered itself especially fortunate to be able to welcome not only an ageing General Field Marshal (August von Mackensen), but even Reich President Paul von Hindenburg himself, who had been a pupil at the cadet school there in the early 1860s—cf. Conrad-Dieter Freiherr von Zedlitz und Neukirch and Hans Heinrich Weske, *Wahlstatt. Einstige Propstei der Benediktiner—Das Kadettenhaus (1838–1920)—Die Staatliche Bildungsanstalt (1920–1934)* (Lorch, 1989), 81–9.
30. *Zehn Jahre Staatliche Bildungsanstalt Potsdam* (1930), 2.
31. For examples of the Stabilas' sporting prowess, see e.g. Hans-Günter Cnotka, ed., *Chronik der Anstalt am Gollen. Teil 2: Staatliche Bildungsanstalt/Stabila—Köslin 1920–1933* (Kiel, 2002); also the official annual 'Berichte über das Schuljahr' for Potsdam and Lichterfelde during the late 1920s. An outsider's perspective can be found in Viktor Belohoubek's 'Bericht über meine Reise nach Deutschland zur Besichtigung der staatlichen Bildungsanstalten in Berlin und Dresden am 2.–4. Juli 1924' (Österreichisches Staatsarchiv, BEA 1).
32. *Die Brücke: Nachrichten von der Stabila Köslin* 2, no. 8 (February 1930), 91; 'Kunstausstellung', *Die Brücke: Nachrichten von der Stabila Köslin* 2, no. 9 (March 1930), 101–6; von Zedlitz und Neukirch and Weske, *Wahlstatt*, 79; Kappelbusch, 'Etwas über die neue Sachlichkeit', *Die Brücke: Nachrichten von der Stabila Köslin* 3, no. 4 (September 1930), 53–4; *Die Brücke: Nachrichten von der Stabila Köslin* 3, no. 8 (February 1931), 144.
33. Cf. e.g. Majewski, 'Etwas vom Jazz!', *Die Brücke: Nachrichten von der Stabila Köslin* 2, no. 5 (November 1929), 47–8.
34. Cf. Schleswig-Holsteinische Bildungsanstalt Plön i. Holst. (Kaiserin Auguste-Viktoria-Gymnasium und Staatliche Bildungsanstalt), *Bericht über das Schuljahr 1926–27*, 14; *Bericht über das Schuljahr 1927–28*, 12; *Bericht über das Schuljahr 1931/32*, 23–8. Schmidt and Kasdorff, *100 Jahre Erziehung*, 110–14, also depict the 'Plöner Musiktage' and the school's close relationship with Hindemith in great detail.
35. Cf. Möller, 'Erziehungsgemeinschaft', *Wahlstatt: Blätter der Staatlichen Bildungsanstalt Wahlstatt* 2, no. 2 (Christmas 1932), 4–5. See also Felix Taubitz, 'Wahlstatt: Wechselvolle Vergangenheit—Das Kadettenkorps, dem Hindenburg entstammt. Die Staatliche Bildungsanstalt', *Kölnische Volkszeitung*, 3 August 1931; Felix Taubitz, 'Die Staatliche Bildungsanstalt Wahlstatt', *Wahlstatt* 3, no. 2 (Christmas 1933), 2–6.
36. E.g. *Blätter der Hans Richert-Schule* 5 (1 July 1930), 20–1; Cnotka, *Chronik*, 13; *Schleswig-Holsteinische Bildungsanstalt Plön, Bericht über das Schuljahr 1924/25*, 21.

37. Cf. Becker, *Naumburg*, 18.
38. Cf. e.g. *Schleswig-Holsteinische Bildungsanstalt Plön, Bericht über das Schuljahr 1928/29*, 27.
39. Excerpt from the inaugural speech made on 4 May 1920 by Dr. Tominski, quoted in *Die Brücke: Nachrichten von der Stabila Köslin* 5, no. 6 (December 1932), 117–18.
40. On the strenuous attempts made (especially by Social Democrat-led states such as Prussia) to model citizens for the Weimar Republic effectively through schooling, see Richard Evans, *The Coming of the Third Reich* (London, 2003), 131; McElligott, *Rethinking the Weimar Republic*, 145, and in particular Marjorie Lamberti, *The Politics of Education: Teachers and School Reform in Weimar Germany* (New York, 2002).
41. *Staatliche Bildungsanstalt Potsdam (Realgymnasium mit Alumnat), Bericht über das Schuljahr 1927/28*, 9; *Schleswig-Holsteinische Bildungsanstalt Plön, Bericht über das Schuljahr 1929/30*, 15; *Staatliche Bildungsanstalt Wahlstatt bei Liegnitz—Bericht über das Schuljahr 1928/29*, 8.
42. Cnotka, *Chronik*, 15; *Staatliche Bildungsanstalt Berlin-Lichterfelde—Bericht über das Schuljahr 1927/28*, 24; *Schleswig-Holsteinische Bildungsanstalt Plön, Bericht über das Schuljahr 1928/29*, 25. There is evidence that VDA groups existed at Wahlstatt and Naumburg also; cf. *Staatliche Bildungsanstalt Wahlstatt bei Liegnitz—Bericht über das Schuljahr 1928/29*, 39–40; *10 Jahre Naumburg*, 8. For further historical context on the association, see Gerhard Weidenfeller, *VDA—Verein für das Deutschtum im Ausland. Allgemeiner deutscher Schulverein (1881–1918): Ein Beitrag zur Geschichte des deutschen Nationalismus und Imperialismus im Kaiserreich* (Frankfurt am Main, 1976), which focuses on the organization's roots in the Wilhelmine era; for more on the VDA's development during the Weimar Republic, see Kurt Poßekel, 'Verein für das Deutschtum im Ausland (VDA) 1881–1945', in Dieter Fricke, ed., *Die bürgerlichen und kleinbürgerlichen Parteien und Verbände in Deutschland (Band 4)* (Leipzig, 1986), 282–97.
43. Johannes Schröter, 'Jahresbericht der VDA-Schulgruppe an der Hans Richert-Schule 1929/30', *Blätter der Hans Richert-Schule* 5 (1 July 1930), 9. The association's popularity was undoubtedly assisted by the fact that many of the pupils at the Stabila were in fact the sons of Germans living in the contested territories (see above).
44. Kurt Bremer, 'Jahresbericht 1932/33 des Vereins für das Deutschtum im Ausland. Schulgruppe Stabila', *Blätter der Hans Richert-Schule* 13 (3 April 1933), 14–16. For a broader contextualization of this type of revanchist sentiment during this period, see the opening chapters of Elizabeth Harvey's *Women and the Nazi East: Agents and Witnesses of Germanization* (New Haven, 2003).
45. Cf. 'Studienfahrt der Oberprima vom 11. bis 21. Juni—Von Köslin nach Hindenburg (O.S.). Oberschlesien—das äußerste Bollwerk des Deutschtums', *Die Brücke: Nachrichten von der Stabila Köslin* 3, no. 3 (August 1930), 29–38. For similar accounts a year or so later, see also *Die Brücke: Nachrichten von der Stabila Köslin* 4, no. 6 (December 1931). On VDA-activity at Köslin more specifically, see e.g. 'V.D.A. und Grenzkampfbund an unserer Schule', *Die Brücke: Nachrichten von der Stabila Köslin* 5, no. 5 (November 1932), 101–3.

46. *Die Brücke: Nachrichten von der Stabila Köslin* 5, no. 1 (May 1932), 17. Right-wing periodicals of this type had already been banned from all of the schools in the area a few years earlier by the regional school board (*Provinzialschulkollegium*).
47. Dr. Höpken, 'Von drei Grundlagen einer rechten Schule', *Die Brücke: Nachrichten von der Stabila Köslin* 5, no. 6 (December 1932), 119–20.
48. Cf. e.g. *Schleswig-Holsteinische Bildungsanstalt Plön, Bericht über das Schuljahr 1928/29*, 23–4.
49. *Schleswig-Holsteinische Bildungsanstalt Plön, Bericht über das Schuljahr 1929/30*, 23.
50. On political ignorance or apathy among pupils during this period, cf. e.g. 'Auch ein Jahrgang', *Die Brücke: Nachrichten von der Nationalpolitischen Erziehungsanstalt Köslin* 6, no. 6 (December 1933), 108–10; Rolf Diercks, *Lebenserinnerungen—überschattet vom Irrweg im 'Dritten Reich'. Autobiographische Schilderung von den Anfängen der Weimarer Republik bis zum Beginn des 21. Jahrhunderts* (Munich, 2010), 40–1. On the susceptibility of youth in the Weimar Republic to the lure of Nazism more generally, see e.g. Peter Stachura, *Nazi Youth in the Weimar Republic* (Santa Barbara, 1975); Daniel Horn, 'The National Socialist *Schülerbund* and the Hitler Youth, 1929–1933', *Central European History* 11, no. 4 (1978), 355–75; Elizabeth Harvey, *Youth and the Welfare State in Weimar Germany* (Oxford, 1993), 266–73; Mark Roseman, 'Introduction: Generation Conflict and German History 1770–1968', in Mark Roseman, ed., *Generations in Conflict: Youth Revolt and Generation Formation in Germany 1770–1968* (Cambridge, 1995), 1–46.
51. For a detailed account of the relationship between the NSS and the Hitler Youth, see Horn, 'Schülerbund'.
52. Dr. Erich Andrée, private correspondence, January 2013.
53. Hans-Georg Schulze, 'Kadettengeist in der Stabila', *Die Brücke: Nachrichten von der Nationalpolitischen Erziehungsanstalt Köslin* 8, no. 7 (March 1936), 105–7. Here, the culprit in the whole affair gives the other side of the story, as part of a detailed and highly self-congratulatory account of the scope of illegal Hitler Youth activity at Köslin.
54. Dr. Erich Andrée, private correspondence, January 2013.
55. *10. Jahre Naumburg*, 7–8.
56. Cf. Heinz Goerke, *Am Puls der Medizin: Arzt im 20. Jahrhundert. Eine Autobiographie* (Hildesheim, 1996), 22; Weber, 'Unterbann V/150 Stabila', *Blätter der Hans Richert-Schule* 14 (20 December 1933), 14–15.
57. Karl Friedrich Casper, 'Flaggenhissung', *Stimmen aus der Stabila Potsdam* 3, no. 1 (March 1933), 8. Of all the Stabilas, Potsdam initially seems to have greeted the National Socialist 'revolution' most enthusiastically. Since Klaus Schmitz uses Stabila Potsdam as his case study for the Nazification of the Stabilas, it is perhaps for this reason that his assessment of the Stabilas' potential for perpetuating the educational ideals of the Weimar Republic is less than sanguine (*Militärische Jugenderziehung*, 273). However, a more nuanced view can undoubtedly be gained when one also considers the state of affairs at other Stabilas—Wahlstatt, for instance, appears to have taken a rather more distanced perspective on the Nazi seizure of power.
58. Kasdorff and Schmidt, *100 Jahre Erziehung*, 115–16; cf. Herbig, 'Meine Lebensgeschichte', 20–1.
59. *Die Brücke: Nachrichten von der Stabila Köslin* 6, no. 1/2 (May/June 1933), 14.

60. *Die Brücke: Nachrichten von der Stabila Köslin* 6, no. 3 (August 1933), 38.
61. *10. Jahre Naumburg*, 8–9. On the practicalities of the Hans Richert-Schule's move from Lichterfelde to Spandau, see Landesarchiv Berlin, A. Pr. Br. Rep. 042, Nr. 1624 and Nr. 1625.
62. Cf. GStAPK, I. HA Rep. 151, Nr. 1093, especially Bl. 7, 25, 27; also GStAPK, I. HA Rep. 90 A, Nr. 1765, Bl. 46–7; Heinrich Rieper, *Meine Tätigkeit an der N.P.E.A. Plön, meine Beziehungen zu ihr und meine Erinnerungen an Sie* (*c.*1948 [Kreisarchiv Plön, F 9 2.2]), 6.
63. Matthias Paustian, *Die Nationalpolitische Erziehungsanstalt Plön 1933–1945* (Rostock, 1995), 10; Breidenbach, 'Ein paar Zahlen...für unsere Schüler und Eltern', *Spandauer Blätter* 2 (1 April 1935), 6. On the transformation process in general, see also Schmitz, *Militärische Jugenderziehung*, 278–9.
64. Kasdorff and Schmidt, *100 Jahre Erziehung*, 126, 132.
65. On these teething troubles, see e.g. GStAPK, I. HA Rep. 151, Nr. 1093, especially Bl. 40, 44, 51.
66. Cf. Hans Lindenberg, *Montagskind. Erinnerungen*, Vol. 1 (1990), 39; Hans Günther Zempelin, *Des Teufels Kadett: Napola-Schüler von 1936 bis 1943. Gespräch mit einem Freund* (Frankfurt am Main, 2000), 39; Dietrich Schulz, private correspondence, 21 January 2010; Gustav Seitz, 'Das Jugend Regiment', *Kyffhäuser*, 22 December 1935, reprinted in *Reichskadettenblatt* 36 (April 1936), 569–72; 'Reichserziehungsminister Dr. Rust über die Kadettenanstalten', *Nachrichten für alte Kadetten* 3 (10 May 1941), 27. On aristocratic attitudes towards National Socialism more generally, see Stephan Malinowski, *Vom König zum Führer. Deutscher Adel und Nationalsozialismus* (Frankfurt am Main, 2004).
67. 'Nationalpolitische Erziehungsanstalt Potsdam', *Beyer's Modezeitschrift* (Summer 1933). For similar sentiments, see also 'Vom Kadettenhaus zur Nationalpolitischen Erziehungsanstalt. 1840 wurde als erste preußische Offizierserziehungsstätte im Westen die Kadettenanstalt Bensberg eröffnet', *Kölnische Zeitung/Stadtanzeiger*, 29 September 1940.
68. Christian Gellinek, *Deutsches Elternland—Eine geographisch-historische Untersuchung. Essays* (Münster, 2013), 43; cf. private correspondence, 9 January 2013. In 1936, pupils at NPEA Potsdam-Neuzelle also performed one of Frederick the Great's own symphonies; cf. *Nationalpolitische Erziehungsanstalt Potsdam-Neuzelle: Arbeitsbericht* (March 1937), 28.
69. For a lively and extremely detailed depiction of the Potsdam pupils' experience of filming, see Lindenberg, *Montagskind*, 71–3.
70. For further contextualization of the film and its genesis, see Kurt Abels, *Kadetten: Preußenfilm, Jugendbuch und Kriegslied im 'Dritten Reich'* (Bielefeld, 2002).
71. Harald Schäfer, *NAPOLA: Die letzten vier Jahre der Nationalpolitischen Erziehungsanstalt Oranienstein bei Diez an der Lahn 1941–1945. Eine Erlebnis-Dokumentation* (Frankfurt am Main, 1997), 11; Becker, *Naumburg*, 59. Zempelin also notes that, when Heißmeyer suggested that individual schools' coloured epaulettes should be replaced by a catch-all monochrome design bearing the legend 'NPEA', there was an outcry—the cadet-school colours were seen as a paramount part of each school's identity (*Des Teufels Kadett*, 51).

72. Cf. e.g. *Die Kameradschaft. Blätter der Nationalpolitischen Erziehungsanstalt Plön* 3, no. 3 (March 1938), 6; 'Der Feldherr Ludendorff', *Die Kameradschaft* 4, no. 1 (June 1938), 6–7; Eckhard R., private correspondence, 25 February 2012. Ludendorff's non-aristocratic background, which had still been unusual at the cadet corps during his time there, might perhaps have provided an additional reason for Brunk, an ardent National Socialist, to lionize him with particular fervour.
73. *Nationalpolitische Erziehungsanstalt Plön, Rundbrief* 22 (August 1942), 10.
74. E.g. *Die Brücke* 8, no. 7 (March 1936), 100. For more on Culm/Köslin's cadet-school history, see Bernhard von Gélieu, *1890—1990. Culm—Köslin. Kadettenhaus/Stabila/NPEA* (Butzbach-Maibach, 1990); also Roche, *Sparta's German Children*.
75. Wolf, 'Besichtigung', *Die Brücke* 7, no. 5/6 (October/November 1934), 74–7.
76. 'Großes verpflichtet!', *Die Brücke* 9, no. 7 (February 1937), 114. This entire issue of the school newsletter was devoted to Frederick the Great's anniversary and the history of the cadet school at Culm.
77. E.g. Unterrichtsleiter Propp, '1890–1940: Kadettenhaus—Staatliche Bildungsanstalt—Nationalpolitische Erziehungsanstalt', *Die Brücke* 13, no. 2 (October 1940), 44–8; *Die Brücke* 16, no. 2 (May 1944), 74.
78. E.g. Gélieu, *Culm—Köslin*, 51; Henning Lenthe, *Lenthe Familiengeschichte Teil 2—Henning mit Eltern und Geschwistern von 1934–1955* (1997), 27ff.
79. Schieffer, 'Ehemalige Kösliner Kadetten!', 526 (all emphasis original); this seemingly random ascription of the NPEA motto to Schlieffen rather than Moltke was not uncommon.
80. On the expanded scope of the 'political evenings', see Zugführer Prinz, 'Der politische Abend', *Die Kameradschaft* 1, no. 1 (May 1935), 22–4; on the formation of a network comprising all '*Buten- und Binnenplöner*' (Plöner within and without) which was intended to include all former *Jungmannen*, former Stabila-pupils and ex-cadets, see pp. 32–5 of the same issue.
81. Rumbler, 'Besuch bei der Tankwaffe in Wünsdorf', *Der Jungmann* 1, no. 3–4 (December 1936), 28–9; 'Rede des Ritterkreuzträgers Oberst von Hellermann (OKH.) am 20. April', *Mitteilungen der Nationalpolitischen Erziehungsanstalt Naumburg/Saale*, 22. Kriegsnummer (July 1944), 14–16.
82. Gerd-Bruno Ludwig and Ernst-Christian Gädtke, ed., *Jahrgang '45. 1937 bis 1944 und 60 Jahre danach. Erlebt, berichtet und reflektiert von Überlebenden eines Jahrgangs der NPEA Spandau* (2004), 30.
83. Arne Heinich, *'Niemand entgeht seiner Zeit': Erziehung, Lernen und Leben in der Nationalpolitischen Erziehungsanstalt (Napola) Bensberg bei Köln. September 1942 bis April 1945* (Norderstedt, 2007), 42.
84. Heinz Winkler and Hans Worpitz, eds, *Die Nationalpolitischen Erziehungsanstalten (NPEA) und ihre Jungmannen. Berichte, Entwicklungen und Erlebnisse von Jungmannen der NPEA Loben/Annaberg* (2003), 73. For more on NPEA Loben and the other Napolas in the occupied territories in Eastern Europe, see Chapter 8.
85. See Schmitz, *Militärische Jugenderziehung*, 253–4, for further biographical information on Haupt and his adjutant Reinhard Sunkel, including their shared cadet-school background; on Haupt's interest in ideas culled from the youth movement, see pp. 286–7.

86. Bernhard Rust, 'Erziehung zur Tat', *Deutsche Schulerziehung* 1941/2, 3–12, 6. Rust expatiated along these lines at even greater length in 'Die Grundlagen der nationalsozialistischen Erziehung', *Hochschule und Ausland*, 13/1 (1935), 1–18. For similar sentiments expressed by Rust during a speech at one of the schools, see also 'Ab Ostern 1935: Die neue Deutsche Schule. Bedeutsame Ankündigungen des Reichserziehungsministers: Wert der Gemeinschaftserziehung' [BArch, N 12/90, Bl. 35].
87. Roche, *Sparta's German Children*, 182.
88. BArch, R 43-II/956b, Heißmeyer to Lammers, 'Bericht über die Arbeit der Nationalpolitischen Erziehungsanstalten', Bl. 51–78, Bl. 68–9; see further Chapter 10. Although other members of the Inspectorate of the NPEA also wished to emphasize discontinuities with the 'one-sided' education provided by the Prussian Cadet Corps (in particular Helmut Trepte, an aide of Reinhard Sunkel's who swiftly fell from grace after Sunkel's dismissal from the Education Ministry), the positive aspects of the cadet-school tradition were still frequently acknowledged by the majority of administrators and *Anstaltsleiter*; cf. Helmut Trepte, 'Die Nationalpolitische Erziehungsanstalt', *Internationale Zeitschrift für Erziehung* 3, no. 4 (1934), 489–92; Schmitz, *Militärische Jugenderziehung*, 245.
89. Such sentiments are to be found in many of Heißmeyer's speeches, pamphlets, and bureaucratic reports and memos; cf. e.g. August Heißmeyer, *Die Nationalpolitischen Erziehungsanstalten* (1938); August Heißmeyer, *Die Nationalpolitischen Erziehungsanstalten* (BArch, NS 31/121); BArch, NS 45/35, 'Vom Wesen der Nationalpolitischen Erziehungsanstalten'.
90. Cf. BArch, N 2203/441, 'Denkschrift des Reichsministeriums des Innern betreffend: Die staatlichen Bildungsanstalten (ehemaligen Kadettenanstalten)'; BArch, R 4701/10474; LNRW-D, BR 5 Nr. 20251, letters from Richert to the relevant *Landräte* dated 10 December 1923, January 1926; *Staatliche Bildungsanstalt Potsdam—Bericht über das Schuljahr 1924/25*, 18; Fritz-Hartwig von Plüskow, 'Erzieher und Schüler in der Stabila', *Die Brücke: Nachrichten von der Stabila Köslin* 3, no. 8 (February 1931), 147–9.
91. Becker, *Naumburg*, 20.
92. Cf. Tim Schanetzky, *'Kanonen statt Butter': Wirtschaft und Konsum im Dritten Reich* (Munich, 2015), ch. 2. In this context, it is perhaps rather telling that NPEA Plön continued to carry out extensions and renovations which had already been planned for the Stabila in the early 1930s (GStAPK, I. HA Rep. 151 IV, Nr. 2735).
93. Cf. Simms, 'Prussianism'; Clark, *Iron Kingdom*, 655–70; Philip G. Dwyer, 'Introduction: Modern Prussia—Continuity and Change', in Philip G. Dwyer, ed., *Modern Prussian History 1830–1947* (Harlow, 2001), 1–20; see also Stefan Berger's contribution in the same volume: 'Prussia in History and Historiography from the Nineteenth to the Twentieth Centuries', pp. 21–40.
94. See above. Cf. Simms, 'Prussianism', 255–6; Clark, *Iron Kingdom*, 660–1; also the contributions by Gerhard Schoenberner and Friedrich P. Kahlenberg in Axel Marquardt and Heinz Rathsack, eds, *Preußen im Film. Eine Retrospektive der Stiftung Deutsche Kinemathek* (Rheinbek bei Hamburg, 1981), entitled 'Das Preußenbild im deutschen Film. Geschichte und Ideologie' and 'Preußen als Filmsujet in der Propagandasprache der NS-Zeit' respectively.

95. *Die Fackel* (*Blätter der Nationalpolitischen Erziehungsanstalt Bensberg*), 18. Kriegsfolge (July 1944), 15. For similar sentiments, see also *Die Brücke: Nachrichten von der Nationalpolitischen Erziehungsanstalt Köslin* 6, no. 9 (March 1934), 159, which describes the *Jungmannen* as 'cadets of the people' (*Volkskadetten*).
96. Graf Knyphausen, 'Moderne Erziehung durch die Napola. Ein Besuch bei der Nationalpolitischen Erziehungsanstalt Spandau', *Deutsche Allgemeine Zeitung*, 19 October 1937 [BArch, NS 5/VI/18841].
97. *10. Jahre Naumburg*, 12.

5

Centralism versus Particularism

Harnessing Regional Ambitions and Negotiating Federal Tensions at the NPEA in Saxony, Anhalt, and Württemberg

On 12 December 1934, Education Minister Bernhard Rust sent out a disgruntled circular to the education ministries of the German federal states (*Länder*) outside Prussia, demanding that regional governments desist from founding their own local 'National Political Education Institutes' without his prior permission. Acknowledging that in the case of the home-grown Napola at Klotzsche, on the outskirts of Dresden, he had been presented with a *fait accompli*, Rust concluded with a request that the Saxon administration provide him with a report on the school's progress.[1]

Yet, by April 1941, the four original *Länder-NPEA*—Klotzsche in Saxony, Ballenstedt in Anhalt, and Backnang and Rottweil in Württemberg—had been entirely disconnected from their respective federal states, and subsumed under the aegis of the Reich-wide Inspectorate of the NPEA. Needless to say, Inspector August Heißmeyer's triumphalist speech at the ceremonial festivities which marked the schools' full transfer into the custody of the Reich, which took place in Backnang on 22 April 1941, gave no indication of the particularist tensions and frictions which had flared along the way. Instead, he presented the increasing centralization or '*Verreichlichung*' of the Napola system as the product of a seamless and logically inevitable progression.[2]

In this context, then, the Napolas can be seen as a bellwether for the type of fully centralized 'reformation of the Reich' (*Reichsreform*) which the National Socialist regime desired to effect not only in the realm of education, but in all spheres of government, devolving power and autonomy from the periphery to the centre; from the *Länder* to Berlin. Although it is a commonplace for scholarship on the much-bruited plans for *Reichsreform* to assert that such tenets were far more a matter of propaganda than praxis—not least because of the federal governments' strong desire to retain their independence and capacity for political decision-making—the NPEA system arguably represented a sphere in which the Nazi state did in fact achieve its centralizing aims.[3]

Despite the numerous tensions which arose in this connection between the Inspectorate and the federal education ministries, as well as the Reich Finance

The Third Reich's Elite Schools: A History of the Napolas. Helen Roche, Oxford University Press. © Helen Roche 2021.
DOI: 10.1093/oso/9780198726128.003.0006

Ministry, Rust and Heißmeyer were ultimately able to consolidate the Napola system so successfully that the regional differences at the *Länder-NPEA*, which had initially seemed so marked, were almost completely effaced—an effect which also found expression in the attitudes of the schools' alumni. Being a graduate of any Napola began to matter far more than which NPEA one had actually attended—a phenomenon which not only seems to have bolstered morale and fostered camaraderie among former pupils serving at the front during the war years, but which also effectively laid the foundations for the post-war fellowship of self-styled 'Napolaner', and their cultivation of a specific group identity later in life.[4]

However, this aim of constructing a pan-German Napola-community did not merely lead the Inspectorate to attempt to cultivate a sense of cohesion among former pupils. While creating a comprehensive old boys' network which encompassed graduates from all of the schools was seen as an important goal, there were further long-term plans afoot to ensure that pupils would, as a matter of course, be educated at NPEA in regions other than those in which they had grown up.[5] Staff were also regularly posted to schools in different areas in order to cultivate a Reich-wide Napola spirit—diluting local pedagogical influences, rather than allowing them to flourish.[6] For example, Klotzsche in Saxony was allegedly inundated with a flood of so-called Prussian and Swabian 'invaders' during the early 1940s, led by *Erzieher* Eugen Wittmann, formerly of NPEA Backnang.[7]

This chapter therefore begins by delineating the general process of *Verreichlichung* within the Napola system, before moving on to examine in detail the cases of the NPEA in the three afore-mentioned *Länder*. In conclusion, the Inspectorate's efforts to create a Reich-wide educational system are considered within the context of broader scholarship on impulses towards centralization within the Nazi state.

*

According to Gustav Skroblin, one of the officials employed by the Inspectorate, writing in an article published in the periodical *Deutsche Schulerziehung* in 1943, it had always been the NPEA authorities' intention to consolidate the schools' administration under a unified Reich leadership. He concluded his summary of the Napolas' development with the following peroration:

> With the subsumption of all of the National Political Education Institutes outside Prussia under the direct leadership of the Reich, a step of particular significance has been achieved within the constitution and administration of the German Reich: For the first time in the history of the German Reich, institutions of youth education have been treated as a direct concern of the Reich because of their particular pedagogical aims, and not...as a concern of the *Länder*.[8]

However, the path towards centralization or '*Weg zur Verreichlichung*' during the pre-war years was gradual, and far from straightforward. Right from the outset, the Reich Finance Ministry noted that there were considerable discrepancies in financial outlay and provision of scholarships and assisted places between the various *Länder-NPEA* and those in Prussia. The Saxon Napola, Klotzsche, which possessed a notably high incidence of pupils from extremely poor backgrounds who were unable to afford to pay any school fees at all, provided a salutary example of this tendency.[9]

In September 1935, at Rust's behest, NPEA-Inspector Joachim Haupt sent all of the federal ministries a sample budget and blueprint for room-size and -allocation, so that the Napolas in the different federal states could begin to work towards a unified organizational and financial structure.[10] This practice was also bolstered by regular meetings of *Anstaltsleiter* from all of the schools, so that they could combine their individual experiences in every sphere of pedagogy and administration into '*unified guidelines* for the future work in hand'.[11] As *Ministerialrat* Richter of the Finance Ministry put it, not only would it be a highly undesirable state of affairs if the schools were to develop differently in different regions, but this might also lead to the *Länder* proposing measures for all of the schools which would end up being 'better, but costlier'.[12] It was therefore envisaged that the *Länder-NPEA* should be fully aligned with Prussian practice by 1937.[13] This plan was successful, inasmuch as from 1 April of that year, the *Landesverwaltung der Nationalpolitischen Erziehungsanstalten in Preußen* (State Administration of the National Political Education Institutes in Prussia) gained full responsibility for all educational questions and matters of personnel at the non-Prussian Napolas, although other administrative and financial affairs still lay with the federal states.[14]

As discussed in Chapter 1, it was only Hitler's increasingly aggressive foreign policy, which brought about the necessity of administrating new NPEA in Austria (and, later, the Sudetenland) without federal-state financial backing, that provided the catalyst for the *Landesverwaltung* to take on a fully Reich-wide identity, and to be renamed accordingly as the *Inspektion der Nationalpolitischen Erziehungsanstalten* (Inspectorate of the National Political Education Institutes).[15] From this point onwards, the Inspectorate's centralizing drive grew ever stronger, despite objections from the Reich Finance Ministry whenever Heißmeyer urged that all of the NPEA, including those in the *Länder*, should be funded from the Reich budget.[16] The Inspector insisted that the NPEA were 'unequivocally a matter for the Reich', and that establishing a special allocation for the Napolas within the state budget was a necessary part of the *Reichsreform*, especially as the schools' reach swiftly expanded to include the newly founded 'Reich Gaus' beyond Germany's borders.[17] Heißmeyer also pressed that the Inspectorate's relationship with the *Länder* be urgently reconsidered, in order to consolidate his authority:

> Although I am personally appointed as Inspector of each of these individual NPEA-schools by the Minister-Presidents of the federal states, this can only lead

> to a superficial form of administration and organization. The basis of all uniformity in the leadership of the schools, the uniform management of finances, is still missing, and thus a decisive means of exerting influence over these schools is ultimately still lacking.[18]

However, Heißmeyer's urgings only gained weight once he was able to mobilize the Reich Chancellery's support for his centralizing aims.[19] Unable to gainsay the Führer's express desire, the Reich Finance Ministry had to capitulate. From 1 April 1941, all of the NPEA, excepting the ten Napolas in Prussia, were to be financed through the Reich budget; all aspects of finance and administration would henceforward devolve from the *Länder* to the Inspectorate.[20] Plans to complete the process of *Verreichlichung* fully, and finance the Prussian Napolas through the Reich as well, were still being discussed in February 1945, but were prevented from coming to fruition due to the failing fortunes of war.[21]

However, the Reich Finance Ministry's recalcitrance was not the only obstacle to *Verreichlichung* with which the Inspectorate had to deal. Powerful interests within the federal state administrations, particularly those politicians such as the Minister-President of Württemberg, Christian Mergenthaler, who had been keen to develop their own visions of what a Napola should be, working towards Rust in their own fashion, were loth to see their beloved brainchildren snatched from their eager embrace. In a letter to the Backnang *Anstaltsleiter* Reinhold Gräter written on 5 December 1940, Eugen Wittmann, who had recently taken on a new role in the Inspectorate as adjutant to Heißmeyer, reported on the tricky diplomacy needed to act as a broker between the Inspector and Mergenthaler as regional satrap:

> Last week, *Obergruppenführer* Heißmeyer was in Stuttgart.... He brought me along to the negotiations with Minister-President Mergenthaler and *Reichsstatthalter* Murr with the words: 'You speak the language of the *Land*.' The result: both are agreeable to the schools in Württemberg being taken into the Reich budget.... The question of how far the schools would then still remain under Mergenthaler's control was handled very carefully. Mergenthaler expressed his great personal interest in being able to continue to be involved in the setting-up of the schools! The Inspector consented. The limits of his involvement were not discussed.... The tone which Mergenthaler struck was heartfelt. It emerged from the whole discussion that he acknowledged Heißmeyer as the leader of the schools.[22]

This unwillingness to let go of the NPEA in Württemberg completely was also expressed in Mergenthaler's speech at the Napola-*Verreichlichung* festivities in Backnang on 22 April 1941. The Minister-President referred repeatedly to the achievements and will to power of men of 'Swabian stock', eloquently demonstrating his attachment to the state's strong spirit of federal particularism.[23] As

Zugführer Braun of NPEA Rottweil remarked in his account of the celebrations for the school newsletter, it was only fitting that the left-hand flag should have got stuck at half-mast during the ceremonial hoisting of the flags—'a gesture of fate towards the representatives of Württemberg, who in any event did not perform the handing over of our two NPEA with entirely light hearts'.[24] For, although there was a sense in which all of the *Länder* had taken the Prussian Napolas as a model, first freely, and then under the duress of ever-increasing regulation from the *Landesverwaltung* and subsequently the Inspectorate, Prussia could also serve as an antitype; a model of militarism and top-down leadership whose hold might be resented rather than welcomed.[25] It is in this context that we shall now turn to the three case-studies represented by the individual *Länder*, elucidating both the variation in their regional specificities and the different paths to *Verreichlichung* which they pursued, beginning with the Saxon NPEA, Klotzsche.

*

As one of the 'brownest' of all the *Länder* prior to Hitler's seizure of power, and one of the regions which embraced Nazism most enthusiastically thereafter, it was hardly surprising that National Socialist educational innovations in Prussia should have been imitated with particular enthusiasm in Saxony.[26] On 1 April 1934, the *Landesschule* Dresden (successor of the Saxon cadet school in Dresden, and hence a form of Saxon Stabila) was officially re-named the 'State National Political Education Institute Klotzsche: Rudolf-Schröter-Schule', after a youthful local Nazi martyr who had allegedly been shot by Communists after joining an SA parade in Leipzig in 1931.[27]

The headship of the school was taken over initially by Walter Kleint, a leading light of the Saxon youth movement and a high-ranking civil servant in the Saxon Education Ministry, who wished to experiment with creating a Hitler Youth-oriented boarding school. Fearing that attempts to take over one of the long-established *Fürstenschulen* (ducal schools) in Grimma and Meißen might prove counterproductive, Kleint settled on the *Landesschule* Dresden, in part because its tradition seemed to be less strongly anchored, and the current headmaster could easily be persuaded into early retirement.[28] However, Kleint's sway over the new institution was to be short-lived. During what has been termed the 'second seizure of power' in Saxony, Gauleiter and *Reichsstatthalter* Martin Mutschmann ('King Mu') used the fall-out from the Night of the Long Knives in July 1934 as a means to sideline his SA-affiliated rival Minister-President Manfred von Killinger and his cabinet, especially the Education Minister Wilhelm Hartnacke and all of his aides.[29] As one of Hartnacke's confidants, Kleint was immediately dismissed both from his post in the Education Ministry, and from his role as director of the Rudolf-Schröter-Schule.[30]

The annexation of the *Landesschule* itself also led to certain frictions between the new leadership and existing pupils and members of staff. Kleint rued the fact that the *Landesschule* had recruited on the basis of academic potential rather than fanatical adherence to Nazism, and decried many of his new charges as 'intensely literary, brooding, partly snobbish, partly restlessly ambitious types' who displayed a vexing scepticism towards the benefits of the new order.[31] On *Fastnacht* (Mardi Gras) 1935, this hostile attitude among the student body allegedly led to a series of regrettable incidents, including brawling, choruses chanting threats directed at the new teachers, and the shooting of popguns, the releasing of frogs, and the lighting of flares during the evening meal. These experiences left Kleint even more determined to 'eradicate' the culprits at the first available opportunity.[32]

Nor were the teachers immune to Kleint's castigatory criticism: he fulminated against the 'leaden weight' of staff incompetence which the Prussian Napolas had already been able to banish: 'The Rudolf-Schröter-Schule must not lag behind in this matter. Otherwise it will only be able painstakingly to imitate the other National Political Education Institutes, instead of leading them!' He fulminated against the 'unheroic, weak' freemason, the anti-ideological Latin teacher whose lessons contradicted those of his colleague, the 'National-Socialistically immature' modern-languages teacher who was desperate to become a reserve-lieutenant, but unwilling to do SA duties, and the 'liberal' philologist who still refused completely to disown literature by Jewish authors. Even one of the newly appointed, more politically engaged *Erzieher* appeared to be unhealthily obsessed with propagandizing for the pro-Nazi German Christian movement, a pastime of which Kleint heartily disapproved.[33]

However, there were three factors above all which set Klotzsche's initial development apart from that of the other Napolas, both within Prussia and without: firstly, its special relationship with the Hitler Youth; secondly, its fundamental mission to educate the children of the underprivileged; and thirdly (and relatedly), its chronic lack of funds, which led to constant fears that the school might ultimately be banished from the ranks of the NPEA.[34]

From its inception, the Rudolf-Schröter-Schule's regulations, as set out by the Saxon Education Ministry, made its Hitler Youth affiliation glaringly obvious:

> Every pupil is a Hitler Youth; the uniform of the HJ is always worn by every boy. The divisions of the boarding school are simultaneously formations of the HJ (Comradeship Units, Squads, Cadre Units [*Kameradschaften*, *Scharen*, *Gefolgschaften*]); the school community forms an independent unit (*Unterbann*).... The director of the school leads the *Unterbann*; the *Erzieher* are simultaneously the *Scharführer* (Squad Leaders). Life at the boarding school in everyday activities, service, and festivities takes place in the spirit and in the forms of the HJ; the *Erzieher* live alongside their boys as comrades and leaders.... The *Erzieher* are specially selected young, unmarried trainee teachers, who should have been

trained in the HJ and who belong to the organization; they are usually appointed for three years.[35]

In many ways, given its explicit organization on Hitler Youth lines, the Rudolf-Schröter-Schule seems to have been far closer to a proto-form of Adolf-Hitler-School (AHS) than to a Napola—a point which Kleint himself made when recalling the school's foundation nearly a decade later.[36] Certainly, the school's ethos of 'youth being led by youth', the role of the unmarried *Erzieher*, and the 'comradely' relationship between pupils and staff, including use of the informal '*Du*' mode of address, was much closer to that found at an AHS.[37] However, this ethos of comradeship did not always impress Nazi grandees; Gauleiter Mutschmann, who never paid a great deal of attention to the Rudolf-Schröter-Schule despite his residence being situated relatively close by, allegedly dismissed the school with the Saxon-inflected comment, '*Ach ja, das is ja die gomische Schule, wo se ihre Lährer duzn*' ('Oh yes, that's that funny school where they call their teachers "*Du*"').[38] Still, it was hardly an accident that *Stabsführer* Lauterbacher of the Reich Youth Leadership (*Reichsjugendführung*), and *Bannführer* Kurt Petter, the future Inspector of the Adolf-Hitler-Schools, both expressed considerable interest in the Rudolf-Schröter-Schule's organization and educational methods.[39] It was only in 1938, when a new set of regulations codifying the Napolas' relationship with the Hitler Youth came into force, that new teachers joining the Rudolf-Schröter-Schule were no longer permitted to be members of the Hitler Youth, and the old HJ-designations '*Schar*' and '*Scharführer*' were replaced by '*Zug*' and '*Zugführer*'.[40]

Perhaps the most damaging specificity for the Rudolf-Schröter-Schule, however, was the school's relative poverty—partly due to its long-established tradition, dating back to *Landesschule* days, of providing numerous free places for pupils from less well-off backgrounds.[41] As Herbert Barth, Kleint's successor as *Anstaltsleiter*, put it in a letter to the Saxon Education Ministry in January 1939, 'In contrast with the rest of the National Political Education Institutes, and indeed with other secondary schools *in toto*, the sons of parents with high standards of living are almost completely absent from the National Political Education Institute in Klotzsche.'[42] As Hanke Blesse has noted, in 1936, 79 per cent of Klotzsche pupils' fathers earned as little as 60–200 RM per month—substantially less than the 225 RM monthly salary allotted even to a lowly machinist employed by the school.[43] The sixty-five state-sponsored free places which the Rudolf-Schröter-Schule had at its disposal proved wholly insufficient to satisfy demand, so that the school was regularly forced to solicit sponsorship from other sources, such as local municipalities (*Gemeinden*), to fund further assisted places.[44]

From this perspective, it certainly did not help matters that the Saxon Education Ministry itself was chronically underfunded, and was therefore unable to provide the Rudolf-Schröter-Schule with all of the trappings—swimming pools, assault courses, motor vehicles, horses, and trips abroad—which were considered *de rigueur* at the Prussian NPEA.[45] A large proportion of the Klotzsche *Anstaltsleiters'* correspondence with their superiors in the Saxon government during the mid- to late 1930s can adequately be summed up in Kleint's despairing phrase: 'The Rudolf-Schröter-Schule simply lacks absolutely everything in this regard.' Kleint was incensed that NPEA Plön was able to spend 2,000 RM a year solely on cross-country war-games, while Klotzsche was reduced to borrowing tents and rucksacks from the SA and begging for financial handouts in order to fund any school trips at all.[46] Often, staff ended up subsidizing pupils when their families were unable to supply them with sufficient pocket money to cover their expenses, and there were far too few scholarships to ensure that all worthy applicants were able to attend the school.[47]

To add insult to injury, the available uniforms at Klotzsche initially comprised only one brown shirt and one pair of trousers, which potentially had to be worn in all weathers, rain or shine, and could rarely be washed. Barth therefore warned that it was highly probable that Klotzsche would be the only Napola in the Reich which would be unable to send its graduands to the first ever NPEA-graduation ceremony presided over by Rust and Göring, since the school could not even afford to provide them with a decent suit.[48] The regular conferences which all of the *Anstaltsleiter* attended merely rubbed salt into the wound, since they made it painfully obvious how much better-equipped and -funded all of the other Napolas were, even those situated beyond Prussia.[49] All in all, the spectre of Klotzsche's being cast out of the charmed circle of the NPEA due to lack of funds was never far away.[50]

This desire to keep up at all costs with the Prussian Joneses arguably contributed to the Saxon authorities' willingness to adopt the path of centralization set out for the *Länder-NPEA* by Heißmeyer and the *Landesverwaltung*. Despite the fact that, in October 1937, the Saxon Education Ministry had denied Barth's request to change the school's official name to 'NPEA Klotzsche', ultimately, the financial advantages involved with the school's *Verreichlichung* were too great to dismiss out of hand.[51] By throwing in their lot with the Reich, the authorities at Klotzsche could finally be assured that the school would have the resources necessary to ensure its status as a true NPEA in perpetuity.

Perhaps it was for this reason that Klotzsche, out of all of the *Länder-NPEA*, betrayed the least regret at having been entrusted to the tender mercies of the Reich. Even though Barth had been transferred to another position as director of the Lessingschule in Kamenz shortly before the *Verreichlichung* took place, he was clearly in favour of the idea in principle.[52] Moreover, reports from former pupils at the front profess an ever-increasing dedication to Heißmeyer's designation of the Napola alumni as an 'Order', a unified community with a single *esprit de corps*, while celebrations of Klotzsche's Saxon heritage are scarcely to be found.[53] More than former pupils of any other non-Prussian Napola, then, Klotzsche alumni appear to have welcomed their initiation into an overarching comradeship of Napola-graduates, divorced from any particularist tradition. But how far was this pattern of *Verreichlichung* followed at the other non-Prussian NPEA?

*

In neighbouring Anhalt, which had also been a stronghold of National Socialism even before the Nazi seizure of power, similar plans were set in train by the *Staatsministerium* (State Ministry) to establish a '*Nationalpolitische Bildungsanstalt*' (National Political Learning Institute) or 'Napobi' in the town of Ballenstedt am Harz.[54] In the beginning, this had partly been an emergency measure to offset the fact that the town budget was insufficient to continue funding the local *Realgymnasium*, but the project soon took on a life of its own.[55] The authorities declared that the founding of the Napobi was a crucial development in the Nazification of Anhalt's educational landscape, following the lead of the school's Prussian 'sister institutes', and announced proudly that Reich Minister Rust himself had given the Napobi his blessing.[56] The school also boasted the dubious honour of educating Heinz Hitler, the Führer's own nephew.[57]

At first, the school itself was ensconced in the buildings of the former Woltersdorff Gymnasium in Ballenstedt, with the pupils' accommodation situated in three boarding-houses elsewhere in the town.[58] However, for pressing reasons of space, Haupt and Rust suggested that the Reich should collaborate with Anhalt in the construction of a brand new building for the school on the nearby Ziegenberg.[59] Ultimately, Ballenstedt was the only Napola ever to inhabit a building which had been constructed from scratch, although the building work was only completed in late 1940, and Vice-Inspector Calliebe and other Prussian observers critically deemed the monumental structure too reminiscent of a barracks and unwelcoming (see Figure 5.1).[60] Prior to this point, the school's classes had been briefly divided, with a separate *Aufbauzug* ('Napobi II') residing in the neighbouring town of Köthen.[61] The edifice on the Ziegenberg still stands today, though in a semi-abandoned state, having been put to use during the German Democratic Republic as a school for local Socialist Party leaders.[62]

The Minister-President of Anhalt, Albert Freyberg, was extremely keen to foster this new pedagogical prestige project. Freyberg made regular visits to the Napobi, attended the school's musical and theatrical performances, donated instruments to its brass band, and played a leading role in the foundation-stone laying ceremony for the new building in autumn 1936, as well as funding the construction works most generously (the State Ministry in Anhalt expended 650,000 RM to this end in 1936 alone).[63] The Minister-President also officiated at separate graduation ceremonies for pupils leaving the school until the late 1930s.[64] The Napobi additionally fostered certain Anhaltinian traditions, taking the 'Dessauer' march as its official anthem, bearing the colours of Sachsen-Anhalt on the

Figure 5.1 The monumental architecture of the 'Napobi' at Ballenstedt, the only school to be purpose-built during the Third Reich. The complex was also used as a school for Socialist Party leaders during the German Democratic Republic, and still survives today, as the following aerial photograph shows.

armbands of the school uniform, and emphasizing Ballenstedt's connections with Albert the Bear, the first Margrave of Brandenburg, a local Crusader hero who was lionized in Nazi colonizing mythology.[65]

Moreover, although the first *Anstaltsleiter*, Friedrich Hiller, who combined his directorial role with a senior civil service position in the State Ministry in Dessau, ostensibly welcomed closer collaboration with the Prussian 'sister schools', he was also hopeful that 'each individual school will retain a certain freedom of manoeuvre in expressing its particular nature'.[66]

But what form did Ballenstedt's professed individuality take? Prior to the *Verreichlichung*, we can distinguish three singular ways in which the school in Anhalt differed markedly from its counterparts in Prussia. Firstly, as at Klotzsche, the Napobi's mission was fundamentally defined by its relationship with the Hitler Youth.[67] Secondly, the school was also instrumental in promoting innovative initiatives to combat social inequality. Finally, the authorities at Ballenstedt unabashedly prioritized military-style drills and physical training over academic education, sometimes to the detriment of pupils' health, to an extent which few other Napolas seem to have shared.

As Hiller put it in his preface to the Napobi's first ever school newsletter, the school's educational principles aimed towards a 'harmonious and meaningful collaboration between schooling and the Hitler Youth'.[68] Hermann Maenicke, one of the *Erzieher*, framed the contours of this relationship even more forcefully:

> While the Prussian Education Institutes were founded without any connection to the HJ, and are only now carrying out an adjustment, and the National Socialist German High School Starnberger See [Feldafing] is a Party school as such, at Ballenstedt, right from the beginning, a *close connection was cultivated with the Hitler Youth*. It is not always easy to separate the three pedagogical powers of school, Hitler Youth, and parental home from each other. In Ballenstedt, we are attempting to follow a new path. With us, school and Hitler Youth are one and the same. The teaching is part of the duties. We always wear the brown uniform with the green armband 'NA. PO. BI. Ballenstedt'. The *Anstaltsleiter* is simultaneously the leader of the section, which, being 350 in number, forms its own *Unterbann* in *Gebiet* 23 (Mittelelbe). The leaders of the three *Gefolgschaften*, that is, the three boarding-houses in which the boys are accommodated according to their age, are under his command. The *Scharführer* follow. These are all young teachers from the HJ itself, or those who have transferred from the SA and SS. Deputies stand ready to hand, who, like the *Kameradschaftsführer*, are boys of appropriate ability.[69]

As at Klotzsche, leading dignitaries in the *Reichsjugendführung*, including future AHS-Inspector Kurt Petter, took a keen interest in the Napobi's development—indeed, Baldur von Schirach, the Reich Youth Leader himself, sent a congratulatory telegram to the school on the occasion of the foundation-laying ceremony on the Ziegenberg.[70] The Napobi II at Köthen was also run by *Oberbannführer* Schulze of the *Reichsjugendführung* from Easter 1938 onwards.[71]

Teacher-training at Ballenstedt was closely modelled on Hitler Youth principles, too; all new members of staff were supposed to lead a '*Schar*' as soon as they arrived, even if they had never held a leadership position before. The idea was that they must learn what it meant to be a '*Kamerad*' (comrade) before they could become a true '*Kameradschaftsführer*'. In practice, this meant sleeping in the same dormitory as their charges and undertaking exactly the same activities, from making one's own bed and keeping one's bedside locker in order to participating in early-morning sport, or wargames.[72] Meanwhile, the school's extracurricular activities also placed a strong emphasis on attending Hitler Youth camps, and on keeping up with the HJ 'outside'.[73] Even when the Ballenstedter embarked on trips and excursions, they did so for the most part explicitly in their capacity as Hitler Youths, rather than as pupils of the Napobi.[74]

While Ballenstedt also encouraged local councils (*Kreisen*) to sponsor free places and bursaries, and used the full fees paid by better-off parents to subsidize those families (approximately 50 per cent) who could not afford to pay the necessary 50 RM per month, the school's most novel form of outreach had a rather different focus.[75] Following a successful series of 'missions' in local industry, the

Napobi invited thirty apprentices from the Gau Magdeburg-Anhalt who had done exceptionally well in the *Reichsberufswettkampf* (National Vocational Competition) to join in with school life at the Napobi II. The apprentices would subsequently take up places at the technical college in Köthen.[76]

However, perhaps the most noticeable difference in everyday life at the Napobi was the intense focus on militaristic drills and physical education, as well as an unashamedly anti-intellectual attitude towards academic studies. Thus, in the school newsletter's first edition, Hiller assured his readers that the curriculum had been devised so that 'everything has been left out which is not completely necessary for attaining the academic goal. In deciding upon the academic level of achievement of our boys, we have consciously taken the perspective that anything excessive is to be cast aside.'[77] This attitude found its most explicit expression in an article by one of the *Erzieher*, Walter Gollhardt, who decried the mere learning of facts as alien to the Napobi's mission. German scholarship might have depended on specialist knowledge, perhaps even that cultivated by bookish swots, but Gollhardt did not perceive this as sufficient reason to relent in his stance:

> As in the past, we will need these special achievements, and must guard against judging a mathematical, physical or technical genius or an artist by his biceps or his achievements in the long jump. Perhaps we might not even expect them fully to take part in HJ- or SA-duties. But we must not adjust the foundations of our entire curriculum to take account of these special cases. Our school does not desire to impart specialist knowledge, but rather general knowledge. However, that does not mean that one should know something about everything and therefore know nothing properly; rather, it means to know what is necessary for a thorough formation of the mental powers and for the development of a unified *Weltanschauung*, namely that of National Socialism.[78]

By contrast, any pupil who failed to attain the requisite sporting achievement for his year-group, such as the HJ-Achievement Award (*HJ-Leistungsabzeichen*) for the 6th class, or the Reich Sport Award (*Reichssportabzeichen*) for pupils in the final year, risked expulsion.[79] Former pupil Klaus Kleinau recalled in his memoirs the fanatical eagerness with which he and his comrades would train in their free time, hoping to be selected for the Reich Youth Sport Championships (*Reichsjugendwettkämpfe*).[80] The recollections of another Ballenstedt alumnus, Heinz V., also confirm that the Napobi was particularly sport-focused, whilst additionally highlighting the teachers' extreme emphasis on obsessive order and cleanliness, and on performing Prussian-style military drills perfectly. This regularly included practising the Heil Hitler salute whilst marching; one had to be sure to raise one's arm at precisely three metres from the personage whom one was greeting in order to achieve the desired effect.[81] He recalled feeling very envious of the *Jungmannen* from NPEA Potsdam and NPEA Spandau whom he met on a trip in the Harz mountains, not only because, as former cadet schools, the Prussian Napolas had their 'own' uniforms (rather than the Hitler Youth uniform which was *de rigueur* at Ballenstedt), but also because their belts had clearly never been polished, whereas at the Napobi, the boys' black leather belts constantly had to be cleaned to eradicate any scuffs, or severe chastisement would ensue.[82]

This emphasis on physical exertion could have perilous consequences, however. Local pastor Karl Windschild noted in his diary on 20 May 1936 that the authorities at the Napobi had just received a dressing-down from the local *Reichswehr* general, since twenty-one pupils had been diagnosed as suffering from heart conditions due to 'sporting over-exertion'.[83] Indeed, since pupils were always too exhausted by their manifold physical exertions to complete their homework adequately in the afternoons, Hiller was even moved to implement a novel form of school timetable, in which each morning was taken up with six lessons in related disciplines, such as German, History, and Geography (giving a total of thirty-six lessons per week); each lesson of classroom teaching was then immediately followed by a period in which the homework for that lesson would be carried out.[84]

However, by 1940, the Napobi's freedom of manoeuvre had clearly been somewhat curtailed. On 9 September of that year, the school's name was officially changed from '*Nationalpolitische Bildungsanstalt*' to '*Nationalpolitische Erziehungsanstalt*', and further steps along the road to *Verreichlichung* were soon to follow.[85] Reporting on the hand-over ceremony which took place in Backnang on 22 April 1941, the Ballenstedt school newsletter laconically commented: 'For us, that also signalled a farewell to Anhalt, and being taken over by the Reich. With that, the special position of individual schools was over and done with. We're delighted about it.'[86] Indeed, *Zugführer* Walter Heine, writing in a newsletter published in March 1942, decried the name 'Napobi' as 'hideous'; 'a verbal monstrosity which we still can't get rid of; even today it leads a spectral existence, when it should have disappeared long ago!'[87]

Nevertheless, former pupils of Ballenstedt who sent letters schoolward from the front do not seem to have been quite so preoccupied with the idea of becoming part of a pan-German Napola 'Order' as were the former pupils from Klotzsche (or, at the very least, messages emphasizing this point were printed far less regularly in the school newsletters). The former 'Napobi' ultimately appears to have been more self-contained, and far more concerned with competing with the other Napolas on the sportsfield, than it was eager to revel in its new, Reich-defined identity. Indeed, some alumni even seem to have been relieved that the school had not completely lost its individuality when they returned on furlough. As Harro Leisenberg put it, 'When I visited the school recently, true, the Napobi might have been turned into an NPEA, but the spirit was as of old'.[88]

*

The state of affairs in Württemberg, meanwhile, was determined more than in any of the other *Länder* by the vision and whims of one man above all—Minister-President Christian Mergenthaler.[89] As Jürgen Finger has compellingly delineated in his magisterial study of educational politics in Alsace, Baden, and Württemberg during the Third Reich, Mergenthaler styled himself as a pedagogical pioneer whose innovations would assure Württemberg's exalted position in the avant-garde of educational Nazification.[90] In service of these ideological aims, the former schoolmaster turned head of state deliberately imitated the innovations of other *Länder*. He regularly anticipated Reich-wide legislation, presenting Education Minister Rust with numerous *faits accomplis*, and concertedly pushed forward his own particularist programme of education policies, even when this brought him into conflict with the Party or the Reich.[91] This tendency towards educational experimentation not only informed his decision to found a homegrown NPEA in the town of Backnang on his own initiative—the school opened its doors on 2 May 1934—but also led to his early adoption of the Prussian '*Landjahr*' agricultural service scheme for school leavers (a development which pleased Rust greatly).[92]

Two driving forces above all seem to have motivated Mergenthaler's creation of novel educational policies. Firstly, he had extremely strong views on the importance of selective education (*Auslese*), and was highly committed to providing subsidized schooling for children with talent (*Begabtenförderung*).[93] This not only informed his personal conception of what an NPEA should be, but also led to his founding a specific type of selective SA-run boarding school unique to Württemberg: the *Aufbauschule*, which allowed children with a non-traditional background or a somewhat chequered school career to continue unproblematically in secondary education.[94]

Secondly, like many leading Nazis in Württemberg, Mergenthaler was extremely hostile towards Christianity in general, and Catholicism in particular.[95] He therefore saw the foundation of both the NPEA and the *Aufbauschulen* as providing an excellent opportunity to expropriate the former Protestant seminaries in Backnang, Nagold, Nürtingen, Saulgau, Markgröningen, Schwäbisch Gmünd, and Kunzelsau.[96] In speeches, Mergenthaler explicitly hailed the NPEA as 'standing in direct opposition to the theological seminaries', and it was almost certainly no accident that the second NPEA site to be selected, situated in the overwhelmingly Catholic town of Rottweil, was a former Catholic seminary.[97] That this anti-religious gambit was at least partially successful may be inferred merely by a cursory glance at the relevant reports in Stuttgart's *Landeskirchliches Archiv* (regional church archives), which detail the Protestant authorities' ever-vainer attempts to secure some form of religious instruction for pupils at NPEA Backnang and NPEA Rottweil. The attitude towards Christianity at both schools was uniformly hostile.[98]

At first, Backnang and Rottweil functioned as two independently run outposts of a single school: Backnang was founded initially to house the top three secondary-school year-groups (*Oberstufe*), while the lower three year-groups (*Mittelstufe*) were added at Rottweil from February 1936 onwards.[99] However, this somewhat anomalous method of organization vis-à-vis the other NPEA was to lead to significant tensions, as Max Hoffmann, the director of NPEA Rottweil, made plain to his superiors in a report on the conference of Napola *Anstaltsleiter* which had taken place in December 1936. Hoffmann complained that he could not rid himself of the impression that 'the non-Prussian *Anstaltsleiter* were being observed particularly carefully' in the post-prandial small-group discussions, and claimed that the Spandau *Anstaltsleiter* had attempted to get him to speak ill of his colleague in Backnang; he remarked laconically that 'similar attempts were probably made in the reverse direction'.[100]

More worryingly still, Hoffmann was constantly bombarded by Heißmeyer, Vice-Inspector Brunk, and the other *Anstaltsleiter* with queries as to why Württemberg should think it necessary to use two separate sites for what was, in effect, a single school. His defence of the advantages of the split-location method were heard out in silence, but he was left with the impression that his response had labelled him indelibly as a 'particularist' in his listeners' eyes.[101] As if this were not bad enough, Heißmeyer repeatedly spoke only of 'three non-Prussian National Political Education Institutes' throughout the conference. Moreover, he only invited the 'three non-Prussian *Anstaltsleiter*' to join him in his car, treating Reinhold Gräter, the Backnang *Anstaltsleiter*, as head of both Backnang and Rottweil; Hoffmann was clearly considered surplus to his requirements. Hoffmann therefore requested that his position be clarified as a matter of urgency, since attending further Prussian conferences as the *Anstaltsleiter* of an NPEA which was not fully recognized by Berlin clearly put him in an impossible position. He concluded that:

> The State Administration of the NPEA in Prussia is working towards unifying the two schools in Württemberg, and since they do not possess the external instruments of power to effect this so long as Württemberg has its own cultural administration, they seek to do so through a certain 'moral' pressure, i.e., through sidelining and disregarding NPEA Rottweil, and through gaining the support of the Backnang *Anstaltsleiter* by winning him over on a personal level, since he takes the side of the Prussian State Administration in this question. From other remarks by *Obergruppenführer* Heißmeyer and Vice-Inspector Brunk, it further emerged that, as an interim measure, collaboration with the non-Prussian *Anstaltsleiter* in questions of education, selection of pupils, timetabling, and possibly also selection of *Erzieher* is intended, so long as the administration cannot be amalgamated.... Prior to our schools in Württemberg continuing to take part in these regular conferences, I deem it an urgent necessity that the relationship of our schools with each other and with the Prussian state organization (*Landesverband*) be more precisely defined, since otherwise, as *Anstaltsleiter* of a Württembergisch NPEA, I am unclear as to the nature of my duties and the substantial competencies relevant to my role.[102]

Financial tensions between the NPEA in Württemberg and those in Prussia were also in evidence, though not in such a drastic form as at Klotzsche. For example, in March 1939, Hoffmann complained to his superiors that Rottweil possessed insufficient motor vehicles to transport its pupils to the Napola manoeuvres, remarking acerbically that it would not have been necessary to use the headmaster's personal car on school business if the state's Finance Ministry had only allowed him to purchase vehicles for school use the previous year.[103]

What other characteristics marked out the NPEA in Württemberg from those in the other *Länder*? On a superficial level, the slang terms used for the schools by their denizens and by locals differed from the norm, in accordance with Swabian dialect—'Napo' was often used instead of 'Napola', '*Napolitaner*' instead of '*Napolaner*', and '*Astl*' (an alternative variant of '*Alei*') for '*Anstaltsleiter*'. Secondly, the schools in Württemberg also adhered to a Hitler-Youth oriented mode of organization, although this appears to have been less ideologically emphasized than at Klotzsche and Ballenstedt. Thus, the school uniform resembled the Hitler Youth uniform; the school was organized into three 'squads' or '*Scharen*' (this model was still in place at Easter 1941, as the Backnang school newsletter demonstrates), and the names of ranks within the schools followed HJ terminology in similar fashion; '*duzen*' was also *de rigueur*.[104]

In addition, the NPEA in Württemberg appear to have been especially dedicated to teaching local history and geography, and celebrating regional culture—learning Swabian folksongs, for example.[105] Indeed, at Rottweil, pupils created a whole Swabian medieval model town in their woodwork lessons, complete with walls, gates, towers, churches, and long streets of half-timbered houses—each *Jungmann* constructed a small part of the model, leaving his contribution behind as a lasting memento.[106]

Finally, as might perhaps have been expected given Minister-President Mergenthaler's own schoolmasterly background, high academic achievement appears to have been a *sine qua non* at the NPEA in Württemberg (in stark contrast to the state of affairs at the Napobi in Ballenstedt). For instance, a surviving report on candidates' performance at an NPEA entrance examination which took place early in 1941 reveals—sometimes very explicitly—that applicants were often rejected solely on academic grounds, even when their physical and sporting capabilities were highly developed, their 'racial fitness' had been approved by SS 'experts', or when their fathers had been Party members since the very beginning of the 1930s.[107]

Outside observers also seem to have noticed differences between the ethos at the NPEA in Württemberg and that of other Napolas. For instance, Dieter Eschenhagen, a former pupil of NPEA Loben who was transferred to NPEA Rottweil, found it much harder to keep up in lessons there, ascribing this to the fact that an inordinate amount of time had been spent on pre-military training at Loben. He also remarked that the duties at Rottweil were far more 'relaxed'; the harvest 'missions' were much less demanding, and pupils were generally allowed much more free time.[108]

This particularist spirit becomes even more noticeable when we consider old boys' dispatches from the front. Despite Eugen Wittmann's attempts to foster communal fellow-feeling for alumni of all the schools, his correspondents seemed to be much more interested in narrating their serendipitous meetings with other Backnanger than waxing lyrical over encounters with ex-pupils from the 'Prussian' or 'North German' NPEA.[109] It was a commonplace for former pupils of Backnang or Rottweil to note that they were 'the only Swabian' among the other Napolaner whom they encountered in their companies or squadrons.[110] One alumnus named Brecht from NPEA Rottweil even felt the need repeatedly to excuse his getting first engaged, and then married, to a sweetheart from Brandenburg, of all places: 'As I already wrote after my betrothal, she is thoroughly "Swabian-friendly!" (*schwabenfreundlich*). So I haven't been disloyal to my Swabian blood!'[111]

In the Backnang school newsletter, the *Verreichlichung* itself was explained away in terms of the financial and material advantages which it would bring to the school; *Anstaltsleiter* Gräter attempted to reassure those alumni who had posed 'countless questions' about the process by asserting that: 'as long as the war lasts, no appreciable effects will be visible from this change. Later on..., we have various hopes in connection with the outward arrangement of our life here.... [But] what we will achieve, building from our innermost core, should in future also be of the same form as that which you old hands grew up with here....'[112] As one might therefore expect, given the state's robust history of particularist sovereignty (*Eigenstaatsgedanke*), out of all the *Länder-NPEA*, the Napolas in Württemberg were least ready and willing to be wholly subsumed by the Reich.[113]

*

'What the *Fürstenschulen* once were for the *Länder*, the National Political Education Institutes will become for the whole Reich', declared the *Unterrichtsleiter* of NPEA Klotzsche at the school's tenth anniversary celebrations in 1944.[114] And yet, when the Reich had first attempted to mobilize a top-down effort to turn all of the former cadet schools in Germany into '*Reichsschulen*' in the aftermath of the Great War, Saxony and Prussia had both point-blank refused—such an expensive endeavour was perceived as a purposeful and unconscionable attack on the educational autonomy of the *Länder*.[115] Only just over a decade later, however, the eagerness with which individual federal states began to 'work towards the Reich Education Ministry' by establishing copy-cat Napolas told a very different story.

Jürgen Finger has used the term '*reichsfreundlicher Eigensinn*' (a Reich-friendly striving for autonomy) to describe this phenomenon—a desire on the part of the *Länder* to act swiftly and boldly, asserting their National Socialist legitimacy through revolutionary acts of educational legislation.[116] While, in this sphere of education as in many others, Prussia remained a key point of orientation, the ministers and civil servants in the federal states had no desire to lose their positions of power entirely, or to allow their state administrations simply to be dismantled in the interests of a Prussian-led *Reichsreform*.[117]

However, by summer 1941, the Napolas had already been freed from the confines of particularist interests, local interference, or financial or war-related problems which primarily affected the federal state governments. Thus, they necessarily form an exception to what Finger has defined as the final wartime phase of educational 'decentralization', which largely derailed the planned National Socialist unification process.[118] The NPEA can therefore be regarded as a bellwether institution for that form of total state control over the *Länder* which Rust (and his Prussian predecessors) had long desired to effect in all spheres of education—a triumph of 'law-bound centralism' (*gesetzlicher Zentralismus*) over 'practical particularism' (*praktischer Partikularismus*), to use Alfred Rosenberg's terminology.[119]

As Thomas Schaarschmidt has noted, educational maps of Germany in the 1930s attempted cartographically to represent a National Socialist geopolitical vision which in many respects remained forever wishful thinking—obscuring the boundaries of the *Länder*, while displaying the 'Greater German Reich' as a unified and uniform pink-toned expanse.[120] Yet, in the case of the Napolas, the process of *Verreichlichung* and increased control by the Inspectorate soon began to erase the individuality and regional distinctiveness of schools in the different federal states within the Reich. Thus, we might well conjecture that, given the passage of sufficient time, and further centralizing measures such as regular exchanges of *Erzieher* and *Jungmannen*, the *Länder-NPEA* would soon have discarded any remaining vestiges of particularist specificity. For the Napolaner, then, the Reich-centric worldview depicted by these Nazi school atlases was well on the way to becoming a reality.

Notes

1. Geheimes Staatsarchiv Preußischer Kulturbesitz, I. HA Rep. 151 IC Nr. 7308, Bl. 18. On Rust's visit to Klotzsche soon after the school's foundation, see Walter Kleint, 'Die Rudolf-Schröter-Schule Sachsen, Staatliche Nationalpolitische Erziehungsanstalt—Unterbann Rudolf Schröter im Gebiet 16 HJ. 1934/1935' (1943), Sächsisches Hauptstaatsarchiv Dresden (SHStAD), 13771 Nr. 19, 38–9.
2. 'Die Nationalpolitischen Erziehungsanstalten. Ansprache des SS-Obergruppenführers Heißmeyer in Backnang', *Völkischer Wille*, May 1941 [Bundesarchiv Lichterfelde (BArch), NS 5/VI/18842].
3. For such sceptical comments on the '*Verreichlichung*' process, see e.g. Ulrich von Hehl, 'Nationalsozialismus und Region. Bedeutung und Probleme einer regionalen

und lokalen Erforschung des Dritten Reiches', *Zeitschrift für bayerische Landesgeschichte* 56, no. 1 (1993), 111–29, 111; Michael Ruck, 'Zentralismus und Regionalgewalten im Herrschaftsgefüge des NS-Staates', in Horst Möller, Andreas Wirsching, and Walter Ziegler, eds, *Nationalsozialismus in der Region. Beiträge zur regionalen und lokalen Forschung und zum internationalen Vergleich* (Munich, 1996), 99–122, 108; Andreas Wirsching, 'Nationalsozialismus in der Region. Tendenzen der Forschung und methodische Probleme', in the same volume, 25–46, 43; Michael Kißener and Joachim Scholtyseck, 'Nationalsozialismus in der Provinz: Zur Einführung', in Michael Kißener and Joachim Scholtyseck, eds, *Die Führer der Provinz. NS-Biographien aus Baden und Württemberg* (Konstanz, 1997), 11–29, 12; Michael Grüttner, 'Hochschulpolitik zwischen Gau und Reich', in Jürgen John, Horst Möller, and Thomas Schaarschmidt, eds, *Die NS-Gaue. Regionale Mittelinstanzen im zentralistischen 'Führerstaat'* (Munich, 2007), 177–93, 177. On the incomplete state of *Verreichlichung* in education more specifically, see Anne C. Nagel, *Hitlers Bildungsreformer. Das Reichsministerium für Wissenschaft, Erziehung und Volksbildung, 1934–1945* (Frankfurt am Main, 2012).

4. See further Chapters 10 and 12.
5. For one example of this old boys' network initiative, as promulgated by the *Anstaltsleiter* of NPEA Rottweil during an old boys' reunion, see *Im Gleichschritt* 2, no. 3 (February 1941), 96.
6. For examples of such *Erzieher*-swaps, see e.g. *Nationalpolitische Erziehungsanstalt Klotzsche in Sachsen*, 13. Folge (Christmas 1942), 20.
7. Cf. Eberhard Schilde on what the older members of staff termed the 'South-German SS invasion', *Rundklotz*, Nr. 25, 1 (SHStAD, 13771 Nr. 2). N.B. Accusing Napolas in other regions of 'Prussianism' in such a fashion became a key trope in post-war exculpatory strategies—for more on this tendency, see Chapter 12.
8. Gustav Skroblin, 'Die Nationalpolitischen Erziehungsanstalten', *Deutsche Schulerziehung* 1941/42 (1943), 211–18, 216. For more on the Inspectorate's desire to vanquish any remaining 'federal consciousness' in the *Länder* and to consolidate the administration of the NPEA wholly under the aegis of the Reich Education Ministry, see also Otto Calliebe, 'Gedanken zur Entwicklung der Nationalpolitischen Erziehungsanstalten (NPEA)' (unpublished typescript, 1969), 10.
9. BArch, R 2/12710, Bl. 1, 3.
10. Niedersächsisches Landesarchiv, Staatsarchiv Oldenburg, Best. 134 Nr. 2353, Bl. 3, letter from Haupt dated 5 September 1935; see also Chapter 1.
11. SHStAD, 11125, Nr. 23151, *Mitteilungsblätter der Nationalpolitischen Erziehungsanstalten* 2 (December 1936), Bl. 30 (emphasis original).
12. BArch, R 2/19991, letter from Richter to Kluge dated 28 October 1935; see also BArch, R 4901/8, Bl. 48–9.
13. BArch, R 2/19991, letters dated 16 June 1936, 1 July 1936.
14. BArch, R 4901/5272, Bl. 3, Rust, decree dated 24 October 1936.
15. BArch, R 4901/8, Bl. 67, Rust, decree dated 23 May 1938; Bl. 70, letter from Heißmeyer to Zschintzsch dated 7 November 1938; Bl. 71, Rust, decree dated 26 October 1938; cf. Skroblin, 'Nationalpolitische Erziehungsanstalten', 216.
16. BArch, R 2/19991, letter from Richter dated 26 January 1939; letter dated 25 June 1940. Richter thought it unwise to allow the Inspectorate to act as a free agent and be

treated as an equal partner in negotiation—previous experiences with the SS- and police-leadership had led him to believe that allowing the *Landesverwaltung* its own budgetary allocation could constitute a dangerous precedent.

17. BArch, R 2/19991, letter from Heißmeyer dated 27 October 1939.
18. BArch, R 2/19991, letter from Heißmeyer to Reinhardt dated 25 May 1940.
19. Cf. BArch, R 43-II/956b, Bl. 47–50, 80, 85, 88.
20. BArch, R 43-II/956b, Bl. 88, letter from Heißmeyer to Lammers dated 27 January 1941.
21. BArch, R 2/12712, letter dated 12 February 1945.
22. Staatsarchiv Ludwigsburg (StAL), F 455 Nr. 1, letter from Wittmann to Gräter dated 5 December 1940.
23. 'Ansprache von Ministerpräsident SA.-Obergruppenführer Mergenthaler in Backnang', *Regierungs-Anzeiger für Württemberg*, Nr. 31 (April 1941), 3 [StAL, E 202 Bü 1745]. For an instance of somewhat analogous particularist recalcitrance on the part of the Saxon authorities, see e.g. SHStAD, 11125 Nr. 21351, letter from the head of the Saxon Ministry of Education to Rust, letter dated 29 January 1937.
24. Zugführer Braun, 'Feier in Backnang', *Im Gleichschritt* 2, no. 4 (May 1941), 112–13.
25. On Prussia as model, see e.g. Max Hoffmann, 'Bericht des Anstaltsleiters über die Einführung eines Aufbauzuges an der NPEA Rottweil' (14 November 1937), StAL, E 202 Bü 1746; Herbert Barth, 'Bericht über meinen Besuch der Nationalpolitischen Erziehungsanstalten Ballenstedt, Ilfeld, Naumburg und Schulpforta vom 19.-22. Oktober 1936', SHStAD, 11125, Nr. 21351, Bl. 43–9. On Prussia as antitype, see Kleint, 'Rudolf-Schröter-Schule', 6–7; Anlage 28.
26. On the rise of Nazism in Saxony, see e.g. Clemens Vollnhals, 'Der gespaltene Freistaat. Der Aufstieg der NSDAP in Sachsen', in Clemens Vollnhals, ed., *Sachsen in der NS-Zeit* (Leipzig, 2002), 9–40; Günther Heydemann, Jan Erik Schulte, and Francesca Weil, 'Sachsen und der Nationalsozialismus. Zur Vielfalt gesellschaftlicher Teilhabe—Einführung', in Günther Heydemann, Jan Erik Schulte, and Francesca Weil, eds, *Sachsen und der Nationalsozialismus* (Göttingen, 2014), 9–19; also more broadly Benjamin Lapp, *Revolution from the Right: Politics, Class, and the Rise of Nazism in Saxony, 1919–1933* (Boston, 1997); Claus-Christian W. Szejnmann, *Nazism in Central Germany: The Brownshirts in 'Red' Saxony* (New York, 1999); Andreas Wagner, *'Machtergreifung' in Sachsen. NSDAP und staatliche Verwaltung 1930–1935* (Cologne, 2004).
27. On the genesis of the *Landesschule*, see e.g. SHStAD, 10736, Nr. 17745; Stadtarchiv Dresden, Hauptkanzlei 2.3.1. II. A.b. Nr. 30; on the school's subsequent development and transfer to a specially built campus in Klotzsche, designed by the prominent Weimar architect Heinrich Tessenow, see SHStAD, 12506, Nr. 38, 'Zur Einweihung der Landesschule Dresden in Klotzsche am 15. Oktober 1927'. On the institution's history, see also Hauptverband der gewerblichen Berufsgenossenschaften, *Zur Geschichte des Standortes der Berufsgenossenschaftlichen Akademie für Arbeitssicherheit und Gesundheitsschutz: Landesschule Dresden in Klotzsche (1927–1933)* (Dresden, 2001); Ulrich Amlung, 'Landesschule Dresden—Entstehung, Konzeption und Praxis (1920–1933)', in DGUV, ed., *Lernräume. Von der Landesschule Dresden zur Akademie* (Dresden, 2009), 24–49. On Rudolf Schröter and his demise, see *Die junge Front. Kameradschaftsblätter der Staatlichen Nationalpolitischen Erziehungsanstalt Klotzsche, Rudolf-Schröter-Schule* 1, no. 1 (1938), 1.

28. Kleint, 'Rudolf-Schröter-Schule', 6–8; Anlage 1. On the Saxon youth movement more generally, see Friederike Hövelmanns, 'Zwischen Weimarer Republik und Zweitem Weltkrieg. Die Bürgerliche Jugend in Sachsen am Beispiel der Sächsischen Jungenschaft', in Heydemann et al., *Sachsen und der Nationalsozialismus*, 335–48.
29. Andreas Wagner, 'Partei und Staat. Das Verhältnis von NSDAP und innerer Verwaltung im Freistaat Sachsen 1933–1945', in Vollnhals, *Sachsen*, 41–56; Andreas Wagner, *Mutschmann gegen von Killinger. Konfliktlinien zwischen Gauleiter und SA-Führer während des Aufstiegs der NSDAP und der 'Machtergreifung' im Freistaat Sachsen* (Beucha, 2001); Mike Schmeitzner, 'Dresden: Landtag und Staatskanzlei', in Konstantin Herrmann, ed., *Führerschule, Thingplatz, 'Judenhaus'. Topografien der NS-Herrschaft in Sachsen* (Dresden, 2014), 58–61.
30. Cf. Hanka Blesse, 'Rudolf-Schröter-Schule—Die Staatliche Nationalpolitische Erziehungsanstalt (1934–1945)', in *Lernräume*, 94–113, 104; Hanka Blesse, 'Die Anfänge der Rudolf-Schröter-Schule, Staatliche Nationalpolitische Erziehungsanstalt Klotzsche', *Dresdner Hefte: Beiträge zur Kulturgeschichte* 97, no. 1 (2009), 54–63, 58; Hanka Blesse, 'Die Anstaltsleiter der sächsischen Napola Dresden-Klotzsche', in Christine Pieper, Mike Schmeitzner, and Gerhard Naser, eds, *Braune Karrieren. Dresdner Täter und Akteure im Nationalsozialismus* (Dresden, 2012), 238–45.
31. SHStAD, 11125, Nr. 21361, Bl. 244–5, Bl. 250.
32. Kleint, 'Zur Anzeige über die Vorfälle am Fastnachtsdienstag 1935' (14 March 1935), SHStAD, 11125, Nr. 21350, Bl. 76–7.
33. Kleint, 'Die weitere Entwicklung der Staatlichen Nationalpolitischen Erziehungsanstalt Rudolf-Schröter-Schule, Klotzsche', SHStAD, 11125, Nr. 21352, Bl. 12–16.
34. Cf. e.g. SHStAD, 11125, Nr. 21352, Bl. 1–2.
35. 'Nationalpolitische Erziehungsanstalt Klotzsche', *Verordnungsblatt des Sächsischen Ministeriums für Volksbildung* Nr. 8 (9 April 1934) [BArch, R 3903/2249].
36. Kleint, 'Rudolf-Schröter-Schule', 103; see also Anlage 1, 'Umwandlung der Landesschule in eine nationalpolitischen Erziehungsanstalt (Hitlerjugend-Schule)'. Interestingly, at a conference of Napola-*Anstaltsleiter* which took place in early December 1936, Kleint's successor as headmaster, Herbert Barth, reported favourably on a lecture given by *Stabsführer* Lauterbacher of the Reich Youth Leadership (*Reichsjugendführung*), who saw the future of the NPEA very much in these terms, hailing the Rudolf-Schröter-Schule as a potential paradigm for the future relationship which the *Reichsjugendführung* hoped to cultivate between the Napolas and the Hitler Youth (Barth, 'Bericht über die Anstaltsleiterbesprechung in der Nationalpolitischen Erziehungsanstalt Spandau und im SS-Hauptamt am 2. und 3. Dezember 1936', 6–7, SHStAD, 11125, Nr. 21351, Bl. 14–20). Barth also made unfavourable comparisons with the state of relations between the Hitler Youth and the Prussian Napolas when he made a tour of a number of NPEA earlier in 1936; only Ballenstedt came close to having a similarly HJ-inspired mode of organization (Barth, 'Besuch', 1–3).
37. Cf. Kleint, 'Rudolf-Schröter-Schule', 15–16. For more on the AHS, see Barbara Feller and Wolfgang Feller, *Die Adolf-Hitler-Schulen. Pädagogische Provinz versus ideologische Zuchtanstalt* (Weinheim, 2001); also the Conclusion.
38. Manfred Klotz, *Trotzdem groß geworden! Jugenderfahrungen eines kleinen Mannes* (Norderstedt, 2000), 117.

39. Barth, 'Anstaltsleiterbesprechung', Bl. 19.
40. SHStAD, 11125, Nr. 21351, Bl. 286–7.
41. SHStAD, 11125, Nr. 21350, Bl. 233; cf. Kleint, 'Rudolf-Schröter-Schule', 34. Klotzsche therefore provides an interesting example of the ways in which a Napola's previous incarnation could potentially have an adverse effect on its subsequent development.
42. SHStAD, 11125, Nr. 21350, Bl. 233.
43. Hanka Blesse, 'Die Nationalpolitische Erziehungsanstalt Klotzsche, Rudolf-Schröter-Schule. Versuch der Rekonstruktion der Schulgeschichte einer sächsischen NS-Eliteschule in den Jahren 1934–1945' (MA dissertation, Universität Leipzig, 2001), 90; cf. Barth, 'Besuch', 3. For statistics on pupils' family background, see Kleint, 'Rudolf-Schröter-Schule', 135 (relating to school leavers at Easter 1935); SHStAD, 11125, Nr. 21361, Bl. 385 (relating to pupils joining the school at Easter 1937).
44. BArch, R 2/12710, Bl. 3; SHStAD, 10717, Nr. 9063, Bl. 2.
45. SHStAD, 10717, Nr. 9063, letter dated 2 December 1935.
46. Kleint, 'An das Finanzministerium. Betr. Aufbau der Staatlichen Nationalpolitischen Erziehungsanstalt (Rudolf-Schröter-Schule) in Klotzsche' (August 1934), SHStAD, 11125, Nr. 21354, Bl. 327–9.
47. Kleint, 'Aufbau', Anlage 1, Bl. 330.
48. SHStAD, 11125, Nr. 21352, Bl. 25, 61–2.
49. Cf. SHStAD, 11125, Nr. 21352, Bl. 155–6, 161.
50. Cf. e.g. SHStAD, 11125, Nr. 21352, Bl. 9–10.
51. On the proposed name-change and the reasons behind it, see SHStAD, 11125, Nr. 21350, Bl. 182–5.
52. *Die junge Front* 2 (February 1940), 3. Barth's services in bringing the Napola up to a 'Prussian standard' were also hymned to the skies at the school's tenth anniversary celebrations in 1944—cf. 'Aus der Rede des Unterrichtsleiters zur Zehnjahresfeier', *Nationalpolitische Erziehungsanstalt Klotzsche in Sachsen*, 18. Folge (Autumn 1944), 37–8.
53. For examples of this tendency, see e.g. *Die junge Front, Rudolf-Schröter-Schule* 2 (February 1940), 11, 23; *Nationalpolitische Erziehungsanstalt Klotzsche in Sachsen*, 18. Folge (Autumn 1944), 18, 29–30.
54. On the rise of Nazism in Anhalt in general, see e.g. Torsten Kupfer, 'Umfeldbedingungen des Aufstieges der anhaltischen NSDAP zur Regierungspartei (1918–1932)', in Werner Freitag, Klaus Erich Pollmann, and Matthias Puhle, eds, *Politische, soziale und kulturelle Konflikte in der Geschichte von Sachsen-Anhalt. Beiträge des landesgeschichtlichen Kolloquiums am 4./5. September 1998 in Vockerode* (Halle am Saale, 1999), 175–94; Alexander Bastian and Christiane Stagge, 'Forschungsbericht zur Geschichte des heutigen Bundeslandes Sachsen-Anhalt im Nationalsozialismus', in Detlef Schmiechen-Ackermann and Steffi Kaltenborn, eds, *Stadtgeschichte in der NS-Zeit. Fallstudien aus Sachsen-Anhalt und vergleichende Perspektiven* (Münster, 2005), 150–79; Detlef Schmiechen-Ackermann and Steffi Kaltenborn, 'Stadtgeschichte und NS-Zeit in Sachsen-Anhalt und im regionalen Vergleich. Forschungsstand, Fragen und Perspektiven' in the same volume, 7–38. On the state of affairs in Ballenstedt in particular, see Günther Windschild and Helmut Schmid, eds, *Mit dem Finger vor dem Mund. Ballenstedter Tagebuch des Pfarrers Karl*

Fr. E. Windschild 1931–1944 (Dessau, 1999). Kupfer also notes that Köthen, the site of Ballenstedt's temporary additional campus, was 'where the National Socialists disported themselves most barbarously'. Prior to the *Machtergreifung*, 76 per cent of Köthen's inhabitants voted for the NSDAP and other nationalist parties, compared with 73 per cent in Ballenstedt (Kupfer, 'Umfeldbedingungen', 187, table 2).

55. Cf. Karl-Heinz Meyer, 'Eine Schule—zwei Geschichten. Von der Nationalpolitischen Bildungsanstalt Ballenstedt zur Bezirksparteischule der SED "Wilhelm Liebknecht"', in Justus H. Ulbricht, ed., *Schwierige Orte. Regionale Erinnerung, Gedenkstätten, Museen* (Halle am Saale, 2013), 153–70, 161.
56. BArch, R 2/19991, Bl. 204–6.
57. Cf. BArch, R 43-II/956b, Bl. 13–14; 'Vom Kameradschaftsbund', *Ballenstedt: Schriftenfolge der Nationalpolitischen Bildungsanstalt in Ballenstedt am Harz* 5 (Christmas 1938), 67–8.
58. Cf. Brinck, 'Zur Geschichte der höheren Knabenschule in Ballenstedt', *Anhalter Harz-Zeitung*, 24 April 1934; Friedrich Dietert, 'Das Werden der Na-Po-Bi Ballenstedt' (1935); Landeshauptarchiv Sachsen-Anhalt, Abteilung Dessau (LHASA-D), Z 111, Nr. 104, Bl. 208–9, 244.
59. BArch, R 2/19991, Bl. 25–7; cf. BArch, R 2/27767; BArch, R 2/12715.
60. Calliebe, 'Gedanken', 2; Kurt Rischmann et al., '"Wie Ilfelder Jungmannen das Ende des Krieges erlebten"—Ballenstedt November 1944 bis April 1945', in Rudolf Marggraf, ed., *Die Nationalpolitische Erziehungsanstalt Ilfeld. Sammlung der von 1934 bis 1944 herausgegebenen Ilfeld-Blätter—Ein Beitrag zur Zeitgeschichte. Band II: Januar 1943 bis April 1944/45* (1998), 433–62, 438.
61. Cf. Maenicke, 'Napobi Ballenstedt II', *Ballenstedt* 5 (Christmas 1938), 7–8.
62. Cf. Meyer, 'Ballenstedt'.
63. Harro Leisenberg, 'Grundsteinlegung', *Ballenstedt* 2 (Christmas 1936), 23–5; 'Chronik', *Ballenstedt* 3 (Summer 1937), 41–4; 'Chronik', *Ballenstedt* 4 (Easter 1938), 42–5; BArch, R 2/19988, letter dated 2 May 1936; 'Vermerk über die Prüfung des ersten Entwurfs zu einem Haushaltsgesetz und Haushaltsplan des Landes Anhalt für das Rechnungsjahr 1936'.
64. Cf. Hiller, 'Geleitwort des Anstaltsleiters', *Ballenstedt* 4 (Easter 1938), 5–6.
65. Heinz V., 'Meine Jugendjahre. 1. Bericht NAPOBI Ballenstedt' (2000), 5, 10; Klaus Kleinau, *Im Gleichschritt, marsch! Der Versuch einer Antwort, warum ich von Auschwitz nichts wusste. Lebenserinnerungen eines NS-Eliteschülers der Napola Ballenstedt* (Hamburg, 2000), 35–6; cf. Gollhardt, 'Nach Osten geht unser Ritt', *Ballenstedt* 3 (Summer 1937), 24–40.
66. Hiller, 'Von unserer Arbeit', *Ballenstedt* 2 (Christmas 1936), 5–9, 9.
67. This similarity led Herbert Barth to remark, in his report on a visit to Ballenstedt in October 1936, that the school had been established 'in the same style as the Rudolf-Schröter-Schule, i.e., not according to the model of the Prussian National Political Education Institutes' (Barth, 'Besuch', 1).
68. Hiller, 'Zum Geleit', *Die Nationalpolitische Bildungsanstalt. Ballenstedt/Harz* 1 (July 1936), 3–4.
69. Hermann Maenicke, 'Wir sind der Zukunft Soldaten: Die Nationalpolitische Bildungsanstalt Ballenstedt—Keine Standesschule, sondern Weg zur Leistung über

die Gemeinschaft', *Mitteldeutsche Zeitung* (LHASA-D, E 144, Nr. 200, n.d., *c.*1935); emphasis original.

70. Leisenberg, 'Grundsteinlegung'.
71. Maenicke, 'Napobi II', 8.
72. Wilhelm Bischoff, 'Die "Kameraden" (Die Anwärterzeit der neuen Scharführer.)', *Die Nationalpolitische Bildungsanstalt. Ballenstedt/Harz* 1 (July 1936), 26–7.
73. Gollhardt, 'Unsere Heimdienst-Sommerarbeit 1937', *Ballenstedt* 4 (Easter 1938), 22–3.
74. Cf. e.g. Gollhardt, 'Die Heimdienst-Sommerarbeit der Napobi Ballenstedt I', *Ballenstedt* 5 (Christmas 1938), 33–4.
75. Cf. e.g. LHASA-D, Z 140, Nr. 1495, Bl. 22; LHASA-D, K 13 Ballenstedt, Nr. 401, Bl. 283–4.
76. Maenicke, 'Napobi Ballenstedt II', 8; cf. Häußler, 'Unsere "jüngste" Schar', *Ballenstedt* 5 (Christmas 1938), 57–8.
77. Hiller, 'Arbeit', 6.
78. Gollhardt, 'Lernschule?', *Die Nationalpolitische Bildungsanstalt. Ballenstedt/Harz*, 1. Heft (July 1936), 5–8, 8.
79. Klauß, 'Bericht über die Leibesübungen im Schuljahr 1936/37', *Ballenstedt* 3 (Summer 1937), 6–12, 6.
80. Kleinau, *Im Gleichschritt*, 23.
81. Heinz V., 'Jugendjahre', 6–7, 9–10.
82. Heinz V., 'Jugendjahre', 15–16.
83. Windschild, *Ballenstedter Tagebuch*, 343.
84. Hiller, 'Arbeitsstunde', *Die Nationalpolitische Bildungsanstalt. Ballenstedt/Harz* 1 (July 1936), 9–12. Barth ('Besuch', 3), criticized this 'most radical' model as 'going too far'.
85. LHASA-D, Z 111, Nr. 567, Bl. 88.
86. Burkhard Laas, 'Unsere Anstalt von April bis Juli 1941', *Nationalpolitische Erziehungsanstalt Anhalt in Ballenstedt*, 9. *Rundbrief* (12 October 1941), 4–7, 4.
87. *Nationalpolitische Erziehungsanstalt in Ballenstedt*, 10. *Rundbrief* (10 March 1942), 7.
88. *Nationalpolitische Erziehungsanstalt Ballenstedt*, 8. *Rundbrief* (4 April 1941), 5.
89. On Mergenthaler's biography, see Michael Stolle, 'Der schwäbische Schulmeister. Christian Mergenthaler, Württembergischer Ministerpräsident, Justiz- und Kultminister', in Kißener and Scholtyseck, *Führer der Provinz*, 445–75.
90. Jürgen Finger, *Eigensinn im Einheitsstaat. NS-Schulpolitik in Württemberg, Baden und im Elsass 1933–1945* (Baden-Baden, 2016), 65–6, 81.
91. Finger, *Eigensinn*, 86–7.
92. Finger, *Eigensinn*, 88; cf. Stolle, 'Schulmeister', 466.
93. Cf. Finger, *Eigensinn*, 85–7.
94. On Mergenthaler's conception of the NPEA, see e.g. 'Deutsche Jungen in der nationalpolitischen Erziehung. Ministerpräsident Mergenthaler in Backnang', *Völkischer Beobachter*, 2 November 1936 [BArch, NS 5/VI/18840]; on the *Aufbauschulen*, see StAL, E 202 Bü 1749, 'Die Aufbauschulen für Jungen und für Mädchen in Württemberg'; Finger, *Eigensinn*, 90–1.
95. Kißener and Scholtysek, 'Einführung', 15–16. On Mergenthaler's mission to deconfessionalize education in Württemberg as extensively as possible, see Finger, *Eigensinn*, 94–114; Stolle, 'Schulmeister', 466–9; also Jill Stephenson, *Hitler's Home Front: Württemberg under the Nazis* (London, 2006), 248–56.

96. 'Ansprache von Ministerpräsident SA.-Obergruppenführer Mergenthaler in Backnang am 22. April 1941', *Regierungs-Anzeiger für Württemberg* (April 1941). The remaining former seminary in Esslingen was repurposed as a teacher-training college (*Hochschule für Lehrerbildung*).
97. 'Ministerpräsident Mergenthaler eröffnet die Nationalpolitische Erziehungsanstalt', *Murrtalbote*, 4 May 1934; Hauptstaatsarchiv Stuttgart (HStAS), E 130 b Bü 1464, 'Auszug aus der Niederschrift über die Sitzung des Staatsministeriums am 4. Mai 1934; 3. Nachtrag zum Staatshaushaltsplan 1933 und Nachtrag zum Staatshaushaltsplan 1934'. On Rottweil and Catholicism, see Marieluise Conradt, *Vom Königlichen Württembergischen Lehrerseminar zum Staatlichen Aufbaugymnasium des Landes Baden-Württemberg. 1912 bis 1994 in Rottweil: eine Schulchronik* (Rottweil, 1994), 5; Reinhard Wagner, *Mehr sein als scheinen. Vier Jahre Jungmann in der NPEA Rottweil* (1998), 24; Katrin Heinrichs, 'Die Nationalpolitische Erziehungsanstalt in Rottweil am Neckar 1936–1945' (Hausarbeit, Schwäbisch Gmünd, 1991), 51–4. The Catholic seminary in Rottweil was only the third ever to have been founded in the state of Württemberg.
98. Cf. e.g. Landeskirchliches Archiv Stuttgart, A126 Nr. 1497; A126 Nr. 1501; Altreg. Gen. Nr. 204 IV; Dekanatsamt Backnang Nr. 442. For more on anti-Christian sentiment at the NPEA, see Chapter 6.
99. Andreas Förschler, 'Die Nationalpolitische Erziehungsanstalt Backnang. Eine Eliteschule im Dritten Reich' (MA thesis, Stuttgart, 2002), 62–3 (N.B. Förschler's thesis provides the most illuminating and comprehensive account of life at NPEA Backnang, and the genesis of the NPEA in Württemberg, to date). Of all the *Länder-NPEA*, Ballenstedt was the only school to admit boys from the age of 10 upwards, in accordance with the Prussian model; the authorities in Saxony and Württemberg disapproved strongly of such a measure on pastoral grounds (cf. Barth, 'Besuch', 4; HStAS, E 130 b Bü 1464, 'Auszug aus der Niederschrift über die Sitzung des Staatsministeriums am 5. Februar 1936'). It was only during the process of *Verreichlichung* that all of the schools began to admit boys of the youngest age-group (Sexta and Quinta in the old gymnasial designation).
100. Max Hoffmann, 'Bericht des Studienrats Dr. Max Hoffmann über die Tagung der Anstaltsleiter der Nationalpolitischen Erziehungsanstalten in Berlin-Spandau am 1. und 2. Dezember 1936', StAL, E 202 Bü 1746.
101. Hoffmann, 'Bericht', 6.
102. Hoffmann, 'Bericht', 7, 9.
103. StAL, E 202 Bü 1747, letter dated 13 March 1939; for further plaints, see e.g. StAL, E 202 Bü 94.
104. Wilhelm Preuß, 'Die Aufgaben des Gefolgschaftsführers an der Nationalpolitischen Erziehungsanstalt', *Der Deutsche Erzieher* (1937), 238; *Alte Kameradschaft. Mitteilungen der Nationalpolitischen Erziehungsanstalt Backnang* (Easter 1941), 24–6; Willi Merkel, 'Ein Wahlspruch der Jungmannen in den nationalpolitischen Erziehungsanstalten Backnang und Rottweil' (21–2 October 1938).
105. Cf. e.g. the Rottweil school prospectus, 'Nationalpolitische Erziehungsanstalt Rottweil am Neckar' (n.d.), which devoted significant space to discussing the ways in which the school engaged with *Heimatkunde*; on folksongs, see e.g. Zugführer

Christoph Hoffmann, 'Die Musik im Winterhalbjahr 1940/41', *Im Gleichschritt. Rundbrief der NPEA Rottweil* 2, no. 3 (February 1941), 91–2.

106. Merkel, 'Wahlspruch'.
107. StAL, PL 501 Bü 77.
108. Dieter Eschenhagen, 'Auch ich war ein Eliteschüler Hitlers' (Oldenbourg, 2000), 27–30. Pupils at NPEA Plön remarked on this difference much more unfavourably when describing a visit to Backnang in their tenth anniversary school newsletter—cf. *10 Jahre NPEA Plön. Sonderheft der Kameradschaft* (1943), 118, 120–1.
109. Eugen Wittmann, 'Altkameraden!', *Alte Kameradschaft* (Christmas 1940), 27; cf. *Alte Kameradschaft* (Easter 1941), 2, 23.
110. Cf. e.g. *Alte Kameradschaft* (Summer 1942), 18. I have (somewhat facetiously) dubbed this phenomenon of former pupils expressing particular joy at meeting fellow-Swabian NPEA-comrades, to the exclusion of all others, '*Schwabenfreude*'.
111. *Im Gleichschritt* 5, no. 15A (June 1944), 380; cf. *Im Gleichschritt* 4, no. 13 (November 1943), 307: 'Sadly it wasn't possible for me to visit the NPEA during my last furlough in May/June, as I have got engaged to Miss Elisabeth Zehlke from Mark Brandenburg. That she isn't a Swabian lass may well be a shame; still, I couldn't be happier!'
112. Gräter, 'Lieber Kameraden!', *Notausgabe der Alten Kameradschaft* (1 September 1941), 2.
113. Cf. Kißener and Scholtyseck, 'Einführung', 20–1.
114. 'Aus der Rede des Unterrichtsleiters zur Zehnjahresfeier', *Nationalpolitische Erziehungsanstalt Klotzsche in Sachsen*, 18. Folge (Autumn 1944), 43.
115. 'Zur Einweihung der Landesschule Dresden in Klotzsche am 15. Oktober 1927', 6.
116. Finger, *Eigensinn*, 55. N.B. Finger notes that he is explicitly *not* using the term '*Eigensinn*' as defined by Alf Lüdtke; rather, he takes the term to mean 'a combination of persistency and wilfulness' (71, n. 49).
117. Finger, *Eigensinn*, 59, 473.
118. Finger, *Eigensinn*, 471–81; cf. Jürgen Finger, 'Gaue und Länder als Akteure der nationalsozialistischen Schulpolitik. Württemberg als Sonderfall und Musterbeispiel im Altreich', in John et al., *NS-Gaue*, 159–76, esp. 166.
119. Cf. Nagel, *Hitlers Bildungsreformer*, on the Prussian Cultural Ministry's centralizing aims during the Weimar Republic; Alfred Rosenberg, *Letzte Aufzeichnungen* (Göttingen, 1955), 260, cited and discussed in Kißener and Scholtyseck, 'Einführung', 20, and in Ruck, 'Zentralismus', 99.
120. Thomas Schaarschmidt, 'Regionalität im Nationalsozialismus—Kategorien, Begriffe, Forschungsstand', in John et al., *NS-Gaue*, 13–21, 13.

6

The Annihilation of Tradition?

The 'Napolisation' of Humanistic and Religious Foundations

In 1938, a group of *Jungmannen* from NPEA Schulpforta visited an (unnamed) English public school, as part of an itinerary of sporting fixtures intended to foster and promote Anglo-German relations.[1] Recalling the trip in 1942, Gustav Skroblin, a senior official from the Inspectorate of the NPEA, described the pride of the English boys and masters in the antiquity of their institution, and their arrogant assumption that no German school could possibly have such a long-standing tradition. They were shocked by the Napola-teacher's put-down: 'Oh, that's nice. Then your institution is almost as old as ours.... Schulpforta's been around for 800 years.'[2]

While this claim was somewhat disingenuous, inasmuch as the school at Schulpforta, previously a Cistercian monastery, had only been founded by Duke Moritz of Saxony in 1543, it does reflect the Napola authorities' widespread strategy of laying claim to educational institutions with venerable traditions and transforming these for their own ends, Nazifying and 'Napolising' them in the process. This might take the form of appropriating and taking over schools which were already in existence, such as Schulpforta, which was well-known throughout Germany as the intellectual hothouse which had produced such illustrious alumni as Nietzsche, Ranke, Fichte, and Klopstock, or the *Klosterschule* in Ilfeld (Thuringia), whose former pupils included the colonialist and explorer Carl Peters, the poet Börries Freiherr von Münchhausen, and the educational reformer Gustav Wyneken.

However, in accordance with the National Socialist regime's deep hostility towards Catholic foundations, the Inspectorate also appropriated the property of former monastic schools which had been closed by diktat, such as the Ursuline convent school in Haselünne, or the Missionary School of the Society of the Divine Word (*Steyler Orden*) in St. Wendel, which became NPEA Emsland and NPEA Saarland respectively. Expropriation could also be a convenient way of dealing with potentially oppositional non-religious schools—a strategy which the Inspectorate employed in the case of the aristocratic *Landschulheim* Neubeuern in Bavaria.

The Third Reich's Elite Schools: A History of the Napolas. Helen Roche, Oxford University Press.
DOI: 10.1093/oso/9780198726128.003.0007

Although all of these schools (except St. Wendel) fully retained the curriculum of a humanistic *Gymnasium*, teaching both Latin and ancient Greek, by the end of the Second World War their existing humanistic traditions and religious character had not only been diluted; they had been more or less completely expunged. In cases where the schools in question were Protestant rather than Catholic, the Napola authorities attempted to find some kind of accommodation with the institutions' existing leadership, whether via threats (as in the case of the *Landesschule zu* Pforta) or persuasion (as at Ilfeld). The schools were taken over as a going concern, and existing pupils who passed the Napola entrance test, which often prioritized rather different (and less intellectual) skills than those which had been privileged in the schools' previous incarnation, were allowed to stay on. Meanwhile, Neubeuern and the Catholic monastic foundations were simply closed down and reopened with a completely different clientele—a distinction which reflects the prevailing contention that Protestant institutions were often readier to cooperate with the Nazi regime, and that their collaboration was more readily accepted.[3]

We can also see these forms of expropriation and Napolisation as part of a more general movement towards the de-Christianization of education during the Third Reich. Once again, the Napolas formed the vanguard of this antireligious crusade: banishing services, graces, prayers, and other religious observances; marginalizing and then banning all forms of religious instruction; and replacing these with ideological indoctrination, or secular rituals and festivals in the service of the new National Socialist 'political religion' (see Chapter 3).[4] From this perspective, the NPEA acted as a kind of bellwether for the suppression and marginalization of Christianity in education—not only did they immediately seek to rid former school chapels of all the trappings of Christianity, converting them into secular 'festal halls', but in some cases they also demolished (or planned to demolish) any church buildings which still existed on school sites.[5] Given that the drive to suppress Catholicism in Austria after the Anschluss was particularly strong, this tendency was even more marked at those Napolas which were founded on Austrian soil, the majority of which were established in expropriated monastic buildings (see Chapter 7).[6] Thus, following Annette Mertens' exhaustive study of 'Himmler's *Klostersturm*', that is, the deliberate dissolution and appropriation of Catholic monastic foundations by the SS,[7] we could also usefully speak in this context of 'Heißmeyer's *Klostersturm*'—for on numerous occasions, the Inspector of the NPEA used the security services' expropriation initiative to gain control of monastic building complexes for his own Napolising ends.

This chapter is therefore divided into three main sections. The first section considers the 'Napolisation' of Schulpforta and Ilfeld, and the Nazification of their humanistic traditions, as well as the marginalization of their Protestant background.[8] The second section treats antireligious tendencies at the Napolas in more detail, using the expropriation of the Ursuline convent school at Haselünne and the Missionary School at St. Wendel as case studies for the destruction of religious educational traditions in the context of the Napolas' virulent anti-Catholicism. The final section uses the case of *Landschulheim* Neubeuern to demonstrate that schools with other traditions, such as that of a private country boarding school for scions of the aristocracy, could also face closure and Napolisation if they were perceived as a threat to the regime. The chapter concludes with a brief consideration of NPEA Weierhof, a former Mennonite school which, despite its adherents' post-war protestations, was both favourably treated by and collaborated with the regime, such that we should not take all claims concerning the annihilation of tradition (or otherwise) at the Napolas with equal seriousness.

*

The first school with a long-standing non-military tradition to be Napolised, in 1934, was the *Klosterschule* in Ilfeld. The headmaster, Dr. Marcus Ites, was persuaded by Education Minister Bernhard Rust to allow the school to be turned into a Napola, while Ites himself was transferred to a senior teaching position in Münster (following a brief period of gardening leave). Some commentators speculated that Rust had been inspired to take this step because his own son, Hans-Bernhard, was a graduating pupil at the *Klosterschule*. In any case, as a Hanoverian born and bred, Rust was keen to establish a Napola in his home territory.[9]

Despite the fact that the old boys' association and other concerned parties had been assured that the school would retain its religious and humanistic character, most Christian observances, such as grace and 'morning prayers', were abolished by 1938, when a more fanatical *Anstaltsleiter*, Hans Eckardt, was appointed.[10] The teaching of Latin and Greek texts was also refocused along racial lines—as the first Napola headmaster, Professor Steche, put it:

> Within the circle of the [NPEA], Ilfeld has been given a special task, according to its age-old humanistic tradition: cultivating the study of the ancient world. Not, however, so that we can take joy in a culture that is dead and past, though it be ever so exalted, but in order to unlock a source of power for our own race. We do not want to advance philological meticulousness.... We do not seek the form, but the spirit and the soul of Rome and Greece, born out of identical Nordic blood, which is deeply akin to ours and lives within us.[11]

The period of Napolisation itself unfolded fairly unproblematically, given that the *Klosterschule* had already boasted a thriving chapter of the National Socialist Pupils' League (NSS) even before the Nazi seizure of power, and that the majority of the student body had what former pupil Wilhelm Rautenberg terms a 'black-white-red conservative disposition', boasting an affinity with right-wing parties such as the *Stahlhelm*.[12] Since the mid-1920s, the school had already become an active participant in the revanchist activities of the *Verein für das Deutschtum im Ausland* (Association for Germandom Abroad), and had also established its own local *Arbeitsdienst* (Labour Service); by the 1930s, pupils had become fully engaged in pre-military training and sporting activities of the kind which the Napolas would have considered *de rigueur*, often alongside local chapters of right-wing youth groups, such as the *Jungdeutscher Orden* and the *Adler und Falken*.[13] Immediately after the seizure of power in 1933, the *Klosterschule* became heavily involved with local Hitler Youth activities, and former pupils even remarked upon how well-attuned Ilfeld seemed to be to the new political currents, and how aptly the school's ethos fulfilled both the Nationalist and Socialist tenets of National Socialism.[14] On 30 January 1934, the announcement that Ilfeld would become a Napola on Hitler's birthday (20 April) was greeted at the school with rejoicing, and on 15 August, Rust himself came to speak to staff and pupils and spur them on. The 'Chief' of the NPEA hailed the religious tradition of the *Klosterschule* and the military tradition of the former cadet schools as the newly founded Napola's most important exemplars: these older forms of education would now animate Ilfeld's 'new spirit of ruthless readiness to serve, and dedication to the German people and Hitler's state'.[15]

Soon, there remained few reminders of Ilfeld's pre-Napola past, apart from odd survivals such as the school's annual festival being called 'Neander Day' after Michael Neander, the first headmaster of the *Klosterschule*, or the fact that one of the more gruesome initiation rituals for new boys was named 'Thomas Stange', after the last abbot of the Cistercian monastery, who had founded the school in 1546.[16] While old boys serving in the Mediterranean theatre of war during World War II might fondly recall their Greek lessons at Ilfeld as they stood on the steps of the Acropolis, flew over Marathon, or sailed the Dodecanese 'on similar voyages to Odysseus', their loyalty to the 'Ilfeld spirit' (*Ilfelder Geist*) was firmly rooted in the ideological assumptions of their Napola education, rather than having any connection with the *Klosterschule*'s past.[17] Most damningly, in a post-war tract responding to a plan by the old boys' association to refound the *Klosterschule* in some form following German reunification, former *Jungmann* Gerhart Voigt summed up his impression of NPEA Ilfeld's true educational values:

> ...as far as the [younger] generation was concerned who, like me, were only at Ilfeld during the war, [the school] had scarcely any connection to Christian humanism, and Greece was most worthily represented by Leonidas the Spartan....[18]

Unsurprisingly, the *Jungmannen* at Ilfeld were overjoyed when it was announced that Schulpforta would be joining the ranks of the humanistic Napolas on 1 July 1935.[19] Using the pretext of inappropriate relationships between pupils and staff at the *Landesschule zu* Pforta, Rust and the Napola authorities had issued the school and its league of former pupils (the *Pförtner Bund*) with a stark ultimatum: Napolisation, or the closure of a renowned educational institution of almost four hundred years' standing.[20] As one might expect, the old boys fell into line, attempting to make the best of a bad business by claiming that Pforta's values had always been compatible with National Socialism, so that it was only right that the entire student body should now be educated according to the principles of the Hitler Youth.[21]

Once again, both Bernhard Rust and the new leadership, in the guise of gynaecologist and SS-officer Adolf Schieffer, claimed repeatedly that the school's Christian and humanistic character would be retained.[22] However, by 1936, the requirement that pupils be practising Christians had been removed from the selection criteria, while Schieffer's successor as *Anstaltsleiter*, the classicist Kurt Person, made repeated requests for the adjective 'humanistic' to be removed forthwith from the school's description in advertisements and application materials for government bursaries, asserting that such an appellation did not accurately reflect the Napola's new orientation and aims.[23] In his oration at the first speech day after Schulpforta's transformation into an NPEA, Person laid out his programme for classical education in the new Germany, reinterpreting Plato as anticipating the Nazi state's law legitimizing the sterilization of the hereditarily ill (*Gesetz zur Verhütung erbkranken Nachwuchses*), and upholding the ancient Spartans as the ultimate paradigm of patriotic courage.[24]

Meanwhile, a collection of CVs written by those *Jungmannen* who graduated in 1939, preserved in the regional archives in Merseburg, demonstrates a prevailing tendency among pupils to lambast the school's previous incarnation, denigrating the education which they had received at the *Landesschule* in comparison with that offered at the Napola.[25] The verdict of *Jungmann-Gruppenführer* Heinrich Z. is representative of this trend; he writes: 'After the transformation [into a Napola], things were no longer oriented towards the greatest possible heaping up of useless knowledge, but more attention was given to the idea that the *Jungmann* who left the school should be able to stand his ground.'[26] By the early 1940s, former pupils who had only ever attended the Napola wanted no more truck with the long-standing old boys' league, the *Pförtner Bund*, and rejoiced when the NPEA founded its own alumni association (*Altkameradschaft*) in 1941. As one former *Jungmann* who had graduated in 1937 put it, 'we wish singleheartedly to strive to give the new Pforta a tradition; a tradition in accordance with the principles by which we ourselves have been educated'.[27]

As at Ilfeld, religious instruction, rituals, and services had completely disappeared by 1938; during the war, the younger boys habitually used the chapel as a clandestine hide-out rather than as a place of worship.[28] Ultimately, *Zugführer* Bussow's contention that the younger year-groups would come to embody the spirit of the Napola more and more, since 'a new type of school can't be stamped out of the ground by official decree. It grows gradually from within, and gains its own expression, inasmuch as it rejects traditions that are alien to its nature', had been realized.[29] By the end of the war, the stock epithet for Latin and Greek lessons among the *Jungmannen* was 'cussed' (*stur*); Latin was known as 'balderdash' (*Stuß*), and the relevant textbook was dubbed the 'balderdash book' (*Stuß-Buch*).[30] Learning classical vocabulary or the vagaries of the ablative absolute were seen as the most pointless of tortures—a far cry from the travails of those nineteenth-century pupils who deliberately arose each morning at four a.m. in order to fit in another hour of Latin or Greek reading before breakfast, or composed epics in Greek hexameters in their spare time.[31] Apart from the fact that ancient Greek still formed part of the schools' curriculum, then, there was now little to differentiate Schulpforta and Ilfeld from those Napolas which had never possessed a notable humanistic or religious tradition.

*

The appropriation and transformation of these two Protestant foundations, however, was relatively benign in comparison with the treatment meted out to Catholic foundations with scholastic or monastic buildings which the NPEA authorities deemed an appropriate setting for a Napola. Two distinct impulses were at play here: firstly, a pragmatic need to find suitable accommodation for new schools, in order to expand Heißmeyer's educational empire as expeditiously as possible; secondly, an ideological desire to quench the influence of Catholicism, and especially Catholic religious orders, in what were termed 'confessionally endangered areas'—that is, regions where the counter-influence of Christianity against Nazism was perceived to be especially strong and pernicious.[32] From this perspective, the authorities were seeking to oust what they saw as the 'elite troop and vital nerve' of the Catholic Church,[33] replacing them with their own troop of elite-school pupils, who could then use their influence to win over the population at large.

Nowhere was this twofold strategy more apparent than in the foundation of NPEA Emsland at Haselünne, a 'daughter institution' (*Tochteranstalt*) of NPEA Ilfeld, and NPEA Saarland at St. Wendel, which was a nominal dependency of NPEA Oranienstein. Both of these schools were deliberately established in areas with a large and predominantly devout Catholic population, where it was assumed that the presence of a Napola (and its corollary, the banishment of the Catholic religious and the pupils whom they had brought up in the Christian faith) would have a salutary politicizing effect. We will therefore move on to consider these two case studies as representative of the much broader programme of expropriation and de-Christianization which can be discerned wherever Napolas were founded, whether in the *Altreich*, in Austria, or in the Eastern and Western territories which the Third Reich conquered during World War II.[34]

NPEA Emsland was not the first Catholic foundation in Gau Weser-Ems to be put forward as a potential Napola—other possible locations, including a seminary in Füchtel and a girls' convent school in Vechta, had previously been suggested, partly at Gauleiter Röver's behest.[35] However, the prospect afforded by the seizure of the Ursuline Convent in Haselünne by the Gestapo on 9–10 July 1941 seemed too good an opportunity to let slip. Founded in 1652 by the Poor Clares, the convent had been sold to the Ursuline order in 1854, and a girls' convent school was opened there soon afterwards.[36] Although the school had fallen foul of Rust's edict of 2 October 1939 that all confessional secondary schools must close their doors by Easter 1940,[37] around seventy nuns still remained in residence. The sisters were forced by the police to pack their bags and leave the convent within twenty-four hours, with a stern admonition not to return within 100 kilometres of the town. The pretext for the nuns' exile was their supposed involvement in subversive activities, including the possession of English propaganda leaflets.[38]

During August and early September 1941, Rust and the Prussian Finance Minister Johannes Popitz negotiated that the school and convent buildings should be taken over and refashioned as a Napola, and at the end of September, *Anstaltsleiter* Hans Eckardt of Ilfeld was given the task of founding NPEA Emsland *im Aufbau*, beginning with just two year-groups.[39] On 17 October 1941, a sixteen-strong group of *Jungmannen* marched into Haselünne, 'ready to take on any assailant, but nothing hostile was to be seen. So we took the former Ursuline convent by storm.'[40] By September 1942, there were 114 *Jungmannen* ensconced at Haselünne, under the tutelage of acting *Anstaltsleiter* Derk de Haan—taking on leadership roles in the Hitler Youth, helping local farmers on the land, and volunteering with the town fire service.[41] However, the road to cooperation with the residents of Haselünne had not been an easy one; former pupil Helmut Pophanken recalled that the nuns' treatment, and their swift and brutal banishment at the hands of the Nazi state, had led locals to greet the Napola with extreme hostility; stones were thrown at the *Jungmannen* over the courtyard walls, and they were routinely insulted in the street.[42]

In a report to Heißmeyer from 21 June 1943, Eckardt describes the newly fledged Napola's endeavours to reduce the unseemly and threateningly powerful influence of Catholicism in the area, winning over the residents through a combination of football and folk-dancing; battling with the priesthood for the hearts and minds of the local youth.[43] In fact, Heißmeyer was so impressed by this proof of NPEA Emsland's salutary political impact that he passed the report on to Hans Lammers, Chief of the Reich Chancellery, as part of his bid to convince the Führer that more Napolas should be founded even in wartime.[44]

In his report, Eckardt presents a clear portrait of Haselünne as a 'centre of Catholic faith', its benighted rural population constricted by the bonds of the strictest Catholicism. Despite the fact that the local NSDAP and its subsidiary organizations boasted a normal level of membership, the power of the Church was such that no Party member would dare to gainsay the demands of their faith. Nazi officials such as the *Ortsgruppenleiter* would still attend Mass, even if only at dead of night, and the Hitler Youth would routinely appear to celebrate the installation of a new priest, even if they formed a rear guard slightly distanced from the rest of the procession.[45] This combination of credulousness and mistrust towards National Socialism therefore had to be vanquished and transformed by the Napola's 'political efficacy'.[46] The fact that the first contingent of *Jungmannen* had been greeted with insults such as 'SS-swine' by local youths was simply a spur to win them over by more subtle means:

> With boys, physical capability is decisive and convincing. A nearby anti-aircraft battery challenged our lads to a football match, and had to content themselves with a draw. All of the young people in Haselünne had watched the game, and were more than astonished by this result. Then Haselünne demanded that they play.... Haselünne was beaten two-nil. That broke the ice. A combined team was formed and regular training began. Shared battles forged comradeship, and hence the basis for future partnership in the H.J....
>
> The zenith of the school's political work came about with the shared organization of a parents' evening for the League of German Girls. Our lads had been practising folk dances with the lasses for weeks beforehand. A varied programme of singing, music, dancing, gymnastics, and poetry reading was on offer.... Now we saw whether the mothers would set foot on the convent's 'desecrated' ground. And they came. The evening was a great success. Since then, the school has been a hub, transforming the political will of the entire population. All social circles and classes have been penetrated.[47]

Eckardt then depicts the attempts made by the local priests to vilify the Napola and its denizens in detail; defamation campaigns intended to portray the *Jungmannen* and their *Erzieher* as ravening wolves foundered upon the fact that the residents were already clearly convinced of their diligence and clean living. Clerical prohibitions against Catholic girls attending dances with the *Jungmannen*, and even a plot to have two *Erzieher* falsely sent away on active service, also failed.[48] Eckardt concludes:

> We are convinced that victory can only be achieved through
>
> 1. every single one of us living an exemplarily scrupulous life,
> 2. admittance and training of Catholic boys at our school,
> 3. political influencing of individual Catholic comrades,
> 4. untiring continuation of our political work in public within the most effective parameters....

> Our strength is insufficient to destroy the might of the enemy. As National Socialists, we can only live out and promulgate...our *Weltanschauung* and contribute with constructive activity to the annihilation of ecclesiastical power which will one day become necessary....The National Socialist idea must blaze through the life of our young institution like a flame. We have become grim and determined in a long battle, and will faithfully bear onward the flag which we have unfurled, until it has become the symbol of salvation for all Germans.[49]

The expropriation and expulsion of the priests, brothers, and ordinands at the *Missionshaus* in St. Wendel, which had initially been founded by the Order of the Divine Word in 1898–9, was also carried out by the Gestapo.[50] This was not the first time that the '*patres*' had fallen foul of the Nazi authorities; in 1937, the *Missionshaus* had already been the victim of a viciously defamatory press campaign, which had ended with three priests being arrested on trumped-up charges of treason, trafficking subversive texts, and so forth.[51] In 1938, in the wake of the remilitarization of the Rhineland, the house had been requisitioned for use by Wehrmacht troops and, as at Haselünne, the school had been closed at Easter 1940; the pupils still lived there, but were forced to attend the *Gymnasium* in St. Wendel instead.[52] On 10 January 1941, the Gestapo arrived to seal the fate of the *Missionshaus*, and expropriated all of the order's property by government decree.[53] Apart from the few who were permitted to remain on site in order to serve the new institution's needs as workers on the estate or as handymen, the brothers and ordinands were given just one hour to pack a suitcase each with all of their belongings; former pupils could only watch as they were loaded onto waiting omnibuses and driven away to St. Augustin (see Figure 6.1).[54]

Only a month later, on 12 February 1941, an advance guard of *Jungmannen* from Oranienstein under the leadership of *Hundertschaftsführer* Weber were sent to make the buildings ready for the Napola which was to be founded there.[55] The entrance tests for the new cohort of *Jungmannen* took place after Easter, and NPEA Saarland officially opened its doors on 1 September of that year.[56] According to the new headmaster, *Anstaltsleiter* Westermann, Gauleiter Bürckel considered the confiscation of the *Missionshaus* to be of particular political significance because of the strong religious influence which the *Steyler Orden* had exerted on the surrounding area:

> As successors of the religious order in the same house, the previous significance of the house could only sharpen our conscience. Two worlds were destroying each other. The term 'mission' had to be conceived in a National Socialist sense. Now it was no longer the business of this house to bend German youths into delivering heathen peoples in far-flung parts of the world; rather, it would train the best German youths for the tasks of the Führer in the battle for the freedom of our race. Instead of thinking saturated with alien spirituality, the will had to

Figure 6.1 St. Wendel, 10 January 1941: Pupils watch from the windows of the *Missionshaus* as the brothers and ordinands of the Society of the Divine Word are forced to board the waiting omnibuses by the Gestapo.

> arise to transform this house into a fortress of National Socialist thinking and a corresponding way of life....[57]

As at Haselünne, there were also plans afoot to deconsecrate and convert the church, dividing it into two floors and creating a festal hall; all religious trappings were removed and destroyed.[58] Former pupil Franz Speicher, who attended the Napola from 1942 onwards, confirmed that the church doors were kept locked at all times, so that none of the *Jungmannen* had any idea what it looked like inside. From 1944 onwards, the interior was apparently used as a storage depot for Obenauer, a logistics firm based in Saarbrücken.[59]

Speicher's account also confirms the covert hostility towards religion which now reigned at the NPEA:

> The one thing that was quite hard for me and for my parents was that at home we were a good Catholic family. I was supposed to be a server after communion, as was usual back then. Then school got in the way. I told my pastor about that and he said that I should always go to church and to confession in the holidays, and so I did that too. At school there was no direct ban on going to church, but it was the way of things that on Sunday mornings we got up quite a bit later, so that one was practically too late for Mass.... We were pretty happy that we didn't have to go.[60]

Meanwhile, the remaining brothers of the order were now known to the *Jungmannen* only as occasional fellow workers on the school estate, the Langefelder Hof.[61] Thus, until the arrival of American troops in St. Wendel and the return of the *Steyler Orden* in March 1945, the religious tradition of the *Missionshaus* had been radically—and effectively—erased.

*

Despite being situated in the staunchly Catholic state of Bavaria, the case of *Landschulheim* Neubeuern differed from that of Haselünne and St. Wendel, inasmuch as the impetus for expropriation was driven by political rather than religious motives. The school had been founded in 1925 by Baroness Wendelstadt, a former lady-in-waiting at the Württemberg Court, in order to make ends meet and prevent her home, Schloss Neubeuern, from being sold to cover outstanding debts in the wake of the Great Inflation. The school's clientele was primarily made up of the scions of noble families and the sons of industrialists and the upper-middle classes, and the *Landschulheim* routinely received patronage from such exalted personages as General-Fieldmarshal Keitel, Ribbentrop, and the Prince of Hessen.[62]

The *Landschulheim* cultivated a religious and fundamentally liberal ethos even after the Nazi seizure of power, holding itself as far as possible aloof from the National Socialist state.[63] The headmaster, Josef Rieder, was decried by the Nazi authorities as an educator whose ideas were still steeped in the darkest liberalism, unforgivably seeking to instil pupils with a politically neutral sense of civic responsibility (*staatsbürgerliche Gesinnung*). Moreover, local state officials, such as the *Kreisleiter*, were scandalized when pupils habitually returned the 'Heil Hitler' greeting with a simple '*Guten Tag*' or '*Grüß Gott*'.[64] However, further outrages were to follow: the few members of staff who were sympathetic to Nazism reported that one pupil, Prince von Hatzfeld, had stated that it would be a good thing if Germany lost the war if this would ensure the restoration of the monarchy, while another pupil, Wilfried von Stumm, was overheard remarking that 'really there are a whole lot of swine sitting up top in the government'. After

Georg Elser's attempt on Hitler's life in Munich in November 1939, pupils had also allegedly greeted the reading out of the names of dead SS-men with approbation: 'Thank God, another seven less of these SS-swine'.[65] To add insult to injury, before the official investigations which followed these incidents, the *Landschulheim* had not possessed a single portrait of the Führer. Even in 1942, when the school had been forced by ministerial intervention to acquire a number of Führer-portraits, a painting of the Madonna still held centre stage in the assembly hall, flanked by far smaller pictures of Hitler on the left and Hindenburg on the right—a state of affairs which was deemed wholly unacceptable.[66]

Since the National Socialist state was effectively 'still only tapping occasionally and very lightly at the *Landschulheim*'s feudal gates', Gauleiter Wagner decided to take matters into his own hands and force Baroness Wendelstadt to sell up, so that he could use the Schloss for his own ends—perhaps as a Gauleiters' conference centre.[67] On 13 February 1941, Wagner ordered the school to be closed and the castle emptied; however, the Baroness elected to sell the Schloss to the Reich instead, considering this to be the slightly lesser evil.[68] By May 1941, the NPEA Inspectorate was already showing a keen interest in purchasing the Schloss, despite the cavilling of the Reich Finance Ministry; this was partly the fruit of an initiative to ensure that a Napola would soon be founded in Bavaria, since it was considered an egregious oversight that such a large region should not yet possess a single NPEA.[69] Heißmeyer apparently attached 'particular political importance to the idea that a National Political Education Institute should be established in Neubeuern if at all possible. Namely, until this point, the ancient nobility of Bavaria were educated in Neubeuern, and so it hardly seems beside the point that our youth should be educated on precisely this spot from henceforward.'[70] On 11 March 1942, it was decided that the Reich would buy the Schloss for 2.8 million Reichsmarks, in order to forestall its purchase by other interested parties, including the Bavarian State, and the buildings were officially taken over by the Reich on 1 April 1942.[71] The school's fine baroque chapel was deliberately earmarked for secular purposes, initially as a chamber music room and assembly hall; later in the war, it was merely used as a storage space for skis.[72] The new NPEA began its work on 1 September of that year, under the direction of Schulpforta's *Anstaltsleiter* Kurt Person.[73] Once again, the rich cultural life of the *Landschulheim*, as well as its fundamentally oppositional ethos, had been utterly eradicated by the machinations of the Inspectorate and the Nazi authorities. Very little, if anything, now remained to link NPEA Neubeuern with the tradition of the erstwhile *Landschulheim* Neubeuern.[74]

*

As a final, counter-case study, we will consider NPEA Weierhof/am Donnersberg, a former Mennonite school which had been turned into a National Socialist Gau High School (*Gau-Oberschule*) by Gauleiter Bürckel in 1936.[75] The headmaster,

Fritz Pfaller, and the predominantly Mennonite *Schulverein* (School Association) cooperated willingly with the Nazi authorities in this regard; even before the school's transformation, there had been relatively little conflict between Nazi values and the school's pre-existing nationalist tradition, which also betrayed certain racist and antisemitic tendencies.[76]

While Bürckel was keen to keep the school under his aegis, at least in the first instance, he saw the Prussian Napolas as the ultimate model for his *Gau-Oberschule*, and so representatives were sent to NPEA Oranienstein in order to take note of similarities, differences, and aspects ripe for emulation.[77] Cordial relations between the NPEA authorities and the second headmaster of the *Gau-Oberschule*, Kaspar, deepened from 1938 onwards, so that Kaspar was regularly invited to the Napolas' annual *Anstaltsleiter* conferences, and to the summer manoeuvres in Carinthia in 1939.[78] Kaspar also gradually Napolised the school's sporting curriculum and selection criteria, so that soon the *Gau-Oberschule* was a Napola in all but name—a fact which the Bavarian Culture Ministry had acknowledged as early as May 1939.[79] Once the *Gau-Oberschule* became too expensive for the *Kreis* to run—it had cost the local authorities 2 million Reichsmarks by 1941—and Bürckel had to some extent lost interest in the project, it was a fairly simple matter for the NPEA Inspectorate to take over.[80] There was a relatively low turnover of staff and pupils, and the *Schulverein* made little substantial protest at the school's Napolisation, despite their post-war avowals to the contrary.[81] From this perspective, despite its erstwhile Mennonite tradition, the case of NPEA Weierhof bears far more resemblance to that of NPEA Klotzsche, inasmuch as the school had already been turned from a pre-existing National Socialist educational institution into a Napola, than it does to any of the other foundations described in this chapter.

At the same time, Weierhof was also the school which most sedulously crafted its own martyr narrative after the war had ended, and its successor, the *Gymnasium* Weierhof, continued to do so well into the new millennium. Historians working on the school's history in the 1990s and early 2000s might encounter reactions ranging from refusal by Weierhof's Mennonite Research Institute (*Mennonitische Forschungsstelle*) to distribute published work on the history of the *Gau-Oberschule*, to the suspicious disappearance of relevant Napola-related documents from the school archives.[82] In the view of Steffen Wagner, the school's foremost historian, the myth of Weierhof—that it was 'the only Napola which still remained a completely normal school'—has a dynamic all its own.[83] Yet such exculpatory narratives can also be discerned in the discourse of former pupils from NPEA Schulpforta and NPEA Ilfeld; Valerie Giesen, a pupil at Schulpforta who was spurred by the school's official silences and taboos about the Nazi past to undertake an extended project on the Napola's history in 2009, was informed by former *Jungmannen* that Schulpforta 'had only ever been an NPEA as a sideline'.[84] Former *Jungmannen* at Ilfeld similarly stressed the benign influence of the school's Christian tradition and humanistic ethos, dubbing the Napola an 'isle of the blessed' in contrast with other Napolas or the outside world.[85] It is therefore crucial to differentiate between existing evidence of genuine (if only partial) retention or annihilation of former religious and humanistic traditions, and claims to this effect by institutions and former pupils which are fundamentally self-seeking, and which aim above all at post-factum justification (see Chapter 12).

Hence, it is important to make a clear distinction between those schools which were shut down completely, because their religious or political ethos was deemed to be fundamentally hostile to the Nazi state, and those institutions which were taken over as going concerns. In the former cases, the schools' existing traditions were completely destroyed, with no continuities to speak of, either in terms of pupils or of personnel. Catholic foundations which could offer a competing confessional model of 'total education' were seen by the National Socialist authorities as an existential threat which must be annihilated at all costs, and the case of Neubeuern, the only non-monastic school which preserved an avowedly anti-Nazi ethos, showed that genuine political resistance or non-conformity could just as easily lead to closure and expropriation. Meanwhile, Schulpforta swiftly capitulated to the Napolisation process after being threatened with closure, while the unproblematic course of Napolisation at Ilfeld demonstrates the fundamental accommodability of the *Klosterschule*'s existing ethos with the Nazi *Weltanschauung*. Weierhof followed a somewhat similar trajectory to Ilfeld upon its transformation into a *Gau-Oberschule*—such National Socialist developments could draw sustenance from both schools' pre-existing nationalist propensities. The contrast between the real cases of expropriation—or even to some extent the case of Schulpforta, where Napolisation was at least greeted with some measure of resistance—is salutary.

At the same time, it is perhaps these very ruptures (or alleged ruptures) in a far longer educational tradition which allowed all of the schools discussed here, apart from Ilfeld, to continue their existence, and even prosper, after the war's end—as a GDR elite school, in Schulpforta's case. These institutions' ability to construct a narrative of a non-Nazified, untainted tradition which they could fall back on suggests that the question posed in the chapter heading can ultimately be answered in the negative—the traditions in question were not wholly annihilated, only temporarily effaced, and then salved and revivified through a combination of relative good fortune and post-war selective amnesia.

Notes

1. Cf. August Heißmeyer, *Die Nationalpolitischen Erziehungsanstalten*, 10 (Bundesarchiv Lichterfelde [BArch], NS 31/121); *Pförtner Blätter* 3, no. 2 (November 1938), 36–7, 55–60; on the exchange programme more generally, see Chapter 3.

2. Gustav Skroblin, 'Tradition und Zukunft. Aufgabe der Nationalpolitischen Erziehungsanstalten', *Die Pforte. Neue Folge des 'Alten Pförtners'; Zeitschrift des Pförtner-Bundes* 19, no. 1 (1942), 3–6, 3.
3. Cf. e.g. Lothar Kettenacker, 'Hitler und die Kirchen. Eine Obsession mit Folgen', in Günther Heydemann and Lothar Kettenacker, eds, *Kirchen in der Diktatur. Drittes Reich und SED-Staat* (Göttingen, 1993), 67–87, 74; also more generally Manfred Gailus, *Protestantismus und Nationalsozialismus. Studien zur nationalsozialistischen Durchdringung des protestantischen Sozialmilieus in Berlin* (Cologne, 2001); and Manfred Gailus and Armin Nolzen, eds, *Zerstrittene 'Volksgemeinschaft'. Glaube, Konfession und Religion im Nationalsozialismus* (Göttingen, 2011). On the relationship between Nazism and Catholicism, see e.g. Karl-Joseph Hummel and Michael Kißener, eds, *Die Katholiken und das Dritte Reich. Kontroversen und Debatten* (Paderborn, 2009), especially the contribution by Michael Kißener, 'Katholiken im Dritten Reich: eine historische Einführung', 13–35; also Gerhard Besier, *Die Kirchen und das Dritte Reich. Spaltungen und Abwehrkämpfe 1934–1937* (Berlin, 2001); Rainer Bendel, ed., *Die katholische Schuld? Katholizismus im Dritten Reich—Zwischen Arrangement und Widerstand* (Münster, 2002); Thomas Brodie, *German Catholicism at War, 1939–1945* (Oxford, 2018).
4. On education and de-Christianization, see Eva-Maria Kleinöder, 'Der Kampf um die katholische Schule in Bayern in der NS-Zeit', in Georg Schwaiger, ed., *Das Erzbistum München und Freising in der Zeit der nationalsozialistischen Herrschaft* (Vol. 1; Munich, 1984), 596–638; on Nazism as political religion, see e.g. Klaus Vondung, *Deutsche Wege zur Erlösung. Formen des Religiösen im Nationalsozialismus* (Munich, 2013).
5. At the *Reichsschule* in Valkenburg (Holland), the church of the former Jesuit College of St. Ignatius was demolished to make room for a new sports hall—cf. David Barnouw, *Van NIVO tot Reichsschule. Nationaal-socialistische onderwijsinstellingen in Nederland* ('s-Gravenhage, 1981), 29. Plans were also afoot to demolish the church in the abbey complex at Göttweig (BArch, R 2/27772, letter dated 28 November 1941).
6. Cf. Annette Mertens, *Himmlers Klostersturm. Der Angriff auf katholische Einrichtungen im Zweiten Weltkrieg und die Wiedergutmachung nach 1945* (Paderborn, 2006), 272–3: 'National Political Education Institutes were established in a series of expropriated monasteries (Göttweig, Lambach, St. Paul, Vorau, and Seckau); their placement in monastic buildings palpably demonstrated the National Socialists' claim to total control over education, and the expulsion of the Church from this sector.'
7. Mertens, *Klostersturm*; see also Wolfgang Dierker, *Himmlers Glaubenskrieger. Der Sicherheitsdienst der SS und seine Religionspolitik 1933–1941* (Paderborn, 2002).
8. For a much more detailed account of the 'Napolisation' process at Schulpforta and Ilfeld respectively, see Helen Roche, '"*Wanderer, kommst du nach Pforta*...": The Tension between Classical Tradition and the Demands of a Nazi Elite-School Education at Schulpforta and Ilfeld, 1934–45', *European Review of History/revue européenne d'histoire* 20, no. 4 (2013), 581–609; and Helen Roche, 'Die Klosterschule Ilfeld als Nationalpolitische Erziehungsanstalt', in Detlef Schmiechen-Ackermann et al., eds, *Die Klosterkammer Hannover 1931–1955. Eine Mittelbehörde zwischen wirtschaftlicher Rationalität und Politisierung* (Göttingen, 2018), 605–26.

9. Although Ilfeld lay just beyond the border of Rust's Gau, in Thuringia, the *Klosterschule* was funded and supported by the *Klosterkammer* in Hanover, an organization with which Rust had a long-standing relationship (for more on the history of the institution, see Schmiechen-Ackermann, *Klosterkammer*).
10. Roche, 'Klosterschule', 614–19; cf. Rudolf Marggraf, ed., *Die Nationalpolitische Erziehungsanstalt Ilfeld. Sammlung der von 1934 bis 1944 herausgegebenen Ilfeld-Blätter—Ein Beitrag zur Zeitgeschichte* (1998), Vol. 2, especially the foreword and contributions by Herbert Bessel, Wilhelm Rautenberg, Erwin Ocker, and Harry Bolte. Page numbers in brackets refer to the editions of the newsletters contained in these volumes, which use continuous numbering.
11. Steche, 'Das neue Ilfeld im neuen Jahre', *Ilfeld. Nachrichtenblatt für ehemalige Angehörige der Klosterschule und der jetzigen Nationalpolitischen Erziehungsanstalt Ilfeld*, 2. Reihe, no. 1 (1934), 1–3; Steche also expressed similar sentiments in person to the old boys' league on 29 June 1934—cf. 'Das Alt-Herren-Fest 1934' in the same issue, 6–7.
12. Wilhelm Rautenberg, 'Von der Klosterschule zur Nationalpolitischen Erziehungsanstalt. Ilfeld April 1932–April 1935', in Marggraf, *Ilfeld*, Vol. 2, 487–517, 494–7.
13. Cf. e.g. 'Kriegsspiel des Falken-Kreises', *Ilfelder Blätter* 19 (Michaelmas 1931), 8–9; *Ilfelder Blätter* 21/22 (Christmas 1932), 10–12; on the *Arbeitsdienst* see also Rautenberg, 'Klosterschule', 495.
14. See for example the effusions by Otto H. v. Markard, '2. September', *Ilfelder Blätter* 24 (Michaelmas 1933), 8–9. On the school's involvement with the Hitler Youth, see e.g. Hans Bernhard Schuldt, 'Hitler-Jugend', *Ilfelder Blätter* 23 (Summer 1933), 10–11.
15. *Ilfeld*, 2. Reihe, no. 1 (1934), 3.
16. Cf. Hugo Selke, *Auch eine Jugend in Deutschland. Meine Schulzeit in Ilfeld und Schulpforte 1935–1939* (1990), 10–11.
17. *Ilfelder Blätter*, 19. Kriegsheft (August 1941), [314]; *Ilfelder Blätter*, 27. Kriegsheft (January 1943), [6]; *Ilfelder Blätter*, 33. Kriegsheft (April 1944), [277].
18. Gerhart Voigt, 'Anmerkungen zur Idee einer Wiederbegründung', Niedersächsisches Landesarchiv—Hauptstaatsarchiv Hannover (NLA-HStAH), Dep. 90, Nr. 123.
19. Indeed, a small group of Ilfeld pupils were sent to Schulpforta in perpetuity to facilitate the Napolisation process, along with a group of Köslin *Jungmannen* who only stayed a few months, and with whom the Ilfeld boys cultivated a lively enmity (Selke, *Schulzeit*, 15). All in all, the relevant section of Selke's memoir provides an excellent case study of the 'colonization' of a new foundation by its '*Stammanstalt*'—a Napolisation strategy which was to become increasingly common in later years.
20. For further literature on Schulpforta in general, see Roche, '*Wanderer, kommst du nach Pforta*'; the most relevant works on the school's history in the twentieth century include Marianne Doerfel, 'Der Griff des NS-Regimes nach Elite-Schulen. Stätten klassischer Bildungstradition zwischen Anpassung und Widerstand', *Vierteljahrshefte für Zeitgeschichte* 37, no. 3 (1989), 401–55; Hans Heumann, ed., *Schulpforta. Tradition und Wandel einer Eliteschule* (Erfurt, 1994), especially the chapter by Justus Weihe, 'Die Nationalpolitische Erziehungsanstalt Schulpforta 1935 bis 1945', 231–58; Barbara Schneider, 'Die sächsischen Fürstenschulen unter dem Einfluß nationalsozialistischer Bildungspolitik: Ein Beitrag zum Verhältnis von Schulkultur und Politik', in Jonas

Flöter and Günther Wartenberg, eds, *Die sächsischen Fürsten- und Landesschulen. Interaktion von lutherisch-humanistischem Erziehungsideal und Eliten-Bildung* (Leipzig, 2004), 141–63; and Jonas Flöter, *Eliten-Bildung in Sachsen und Preußen. Die Fürsten- und Landesschulen Grimma, Meißen, Joachimsthal und Pforta (1868–1933)* (Cologne, 2009).

21. 'Die Pforte als nationalpolitische Erziehungsanstalt. Bericht des Vorstandes des Pförtner Bundes', *Die Pforte* 12, no. 4 (1935), 222.
22. 'Die Pforte als nationalpolitische Erziehungsanstalt. Bericht des Leiters der Nationalpolitischen Erziehungsanstalt Schulpforta, Oberregierungsrat Dr. Schieffer vom 5. September 1935', *Die Pforte* 12, no. 4 (1935), 223; 'Erziehungsziele der Nationalpolitischen Erziehungsanstalt Schulpforta. Rede des Anstaltsleiters, SS.-Standartenführers Dr. Schieffer, zum Schulfest am 21. Mai 1936', *Pförtner Blätter* 1, no. 1/2 (June 1936), 3–12; Landeshauptarchiv Sachsen-Anhalt, Abteilung Merseburg (LHASA-M), C 48 II b, Nr. 1656 II, Bl. 292, decree by Rust dated 19 July 1935: 'The particular, humanistic character of the school... will be preserved.'
23. On the selection criteria, see BArch, R 2/19991, letter dated 30 June 1936. On Person's anti-humanism, see Geheimes Staatsarchiv Preußischer Kulturbesitz (GStAPK), I. HA Rep. 151 IC, Nr. 7422/1, letters from Person to the Prussian Finance Minister, dated 18 January 1938 and 22 January 1941.
24. Kurt Person, 'Was bedeuten uns die Griechen und Römer? Rede des Unterrichtsleiters Dr. Person zum Schulfest am 21. Mai 1936', *Pförtner Blätter* 1, no. 1/2 (June 1936), 12–24. For a more detailed analysis of both Person's and Schieffer's speeches, see Roche, '*Wanderer, kommst du nach Pforta*', 591–3. On the significance of Sparta in National Socialist educational ideology in general, and at the NPEA in particular, see Helen Roche, *Sparta's German Children: The Ideal of Ancient Sparta in the Royal Prussian Cadet Corps, 1818–1920, and in National Socialist Elite Schools (the Napolas), 1933–1945* (Swansea, 2013).
25. LHASA-M, C 23, Nr. 1–2.
26. LHASA-M, C 23, Nr. 2, Bl. 5–6.
27. *Pförtner Blätter* 5, no. 3 (April 1941), 112.
28. Cf. Jonas Flöter, 'Von der Landesschule zur Nationalpolitischen Erziehungsanstalt—Transformationsprozesse in Schulpforte und deren Rückwirkungen auf den Religionsunterricht', in Michael Wermke, ed., *Transformation und religiöse Erziehung. Kontinuitäten und Brüche der Religionspädagogik 1933 und 1945* (Jena, 2011), 35–52; on pupils' use of the chapel, see Hartmut Vahl, *Napola Schulpforta 1943–1945. Erinnerungen eines Schülers* (Hamburg, 2000), 42–3.
29. *Pförtner Blätter* 2, no. 3/4 (March 1938), 63.
30. Vahl, *Schulpforta*, 18; Jochen Männig et al., eds, *Das Tagebuch. Aufzeichnungen des 2. Zuges der N.P.E.A. Schulpforta 1943–1945* (1997).
31. On Schulpforta in the nineteenth century, see Flöter, *Eliten-Bildung*, 167; Heumann, *Schulpforta*, 179–82; Gerhard Arnhardt and Gerd-Bodo Reinert, *Die Fürsten- und Landesschulen Meißen, Schulpforte und Grimma: Lebensweise und Unterricht über Jahrhunderte* (Weinheim, 2002), 162. The father of one of Hugo Selke's classmates confirmed that standards had declined even since his own time at Schulpforta; compared with his in-depth knowledge of classical literature, the Napola-pupils barely knew the first ten lines of the *Iliad* and the *Odyssey* (Selke, *Schulzeit*, 63).

32. Cf. Mertens, *Klostersturm*, 119, citing a document from the Central Historical Archives in Moscow (500 1/615, Bl. 7) from a copy contained in Wolfgang Dierker's private archive.
33. Mertens, *Klostersturm*, 21, see also 46–52; also Alfred Rinnerthaler, 'Die Orden als Feindbilder des NS-Staates', in Maximilian Liebmann et al., *Staat und Kirche in der 'Ostmark'* (Frankfurt am Main, 1998), 351–94.
34. For examples, see e.g. GStAPK, I. HA Rep. 151 IC Nr. 7309/1; BArch, R 2/12711; BArch, R 2/27762; BArch, R 58/5764r; also Mertens, *Klostersturm*, 95–6, 108–9, 119–20, 205, 272–4, 278, 280–1; and Johannes Koll, *Arthur Seyß-Inquart und die deutsche Besatzungspolitik in den Niederlanden (1940–1945)* (Vienna, 2015), 161.
35. Niedersächsisches Landesarchiv—Staatsarchiv Oldenburg (NLA-StAOL), Rep. 410 Akz. 162 Nr. 561, letter from Heißmeyer to Gauleiter Röver dated 27 January 1941; NLA-StAOL, Best. 134 Nr. 2353, Bl. 92–6.
36. Daniel Fischer, 'Die Napola Emsland und ihre Gegner—Die Nationalpolitische Erziehungsanstalt Emsland als Instrument nationalsozialistischer Einflussnahme im katholischen Milieu des Emslandes in Haselünne 1941–1945' (Qualifikationsarbeit, Universität Osnabrück, 2002).
37. Niedersächsisches Landesarchiv—Staatsarchiv Osnabrück (NLA-StAOS), Dep 75b Nr. 527, letter to the Bürgermeister of Haselünne dated 19 October 1939.
38. Fischer, 'Emsland'.
39. GStAPK, I. HA Rep. 151 IC Nr. 7309/1, letters and memos dated 6 August 1941, 20 August 1941, 22 August 1941; Eckardt, 'Die NPEA. Emsland (im Aufbau) in Haselünne (Emsland)', *Ilfelder Blätter*, 20. Kriegsheft (November 1941), [383–5].
40. von Hornborstell, 'Wir ziehen ein', *Nationalpolitische Erziehungsanstalt Emsland* 1 (March 1943), in Marggraf, *Ilfeld* 2, 73.
41. NLA-HStAH, Hann.122a Nr. 5140, letter from Eckardt to Gauleiter Lauterbacher, 25 September 1942.
42. Helmut Pophanken, *'Jungmann' 1942–1945. Erinnerungen eines ehemaligen Schülers an die Nationalpolitische Erziehungsanstalt Emsland (Napola)* (n.d.), 150. There later arose quarrels between the Bishop of Osnabrück, Wilhelm Berning, and the Nazi authorities, over the population's being barred from using the church in the grounds of the former convent, and de Haan's plans to 'profane' it by converting it into an accommodation block (NLA-StAOS, Rep 430 Dez 400 Nr. 397). The authorities' response to Berning's complaints was cutting; they retorted that the term 'profanation' was wholly unsuitable in the context of accommodating the cream of German youth according to National Socialist principles, which was clearly far more important than pleasing a few dismal Catholic churchgoers, who could just as easily use the larger church in the town (report dated 24 January 1944; cf. letters dated 16 July 1943, 17 September 1943, 5 January 1944). However, no complaints seem to have been made about the Napola's expropriation of Jewish property to house the *Anstaltsleiter*, or about de Haan's proposal to buy the Jewish cemetery and turn it into a playground for the younger pupils (cf. NLA-StAOS, Dep. 75b Nr. 78; NLA-StAOS, Dep. 75b Nr. 522; NLA-StAOS, Rep 430 Dez 209 Akz. 61/1987 Nr. 57; see further Helen Roche, 'Antisemitismus und Eliteerziehung in den Nationalpolitischen Erziehungsanstalten', *Stiftung Niedersächsischer Gedenkstätten, Jahresbericht 2017. Schwerpunktthema: Kindheit im Nationalsozialismus* (2018), 12–17, 13; also Chapter 10.

43. Eckardt, 'Die politische Auswirkung des Aufbaus der Nationalpolitischen Erziehungsanstalt Emsland in Haselünne', BArch, R 43-II/956c, Bl. 24–8.
44. BArch, R 43-II/956c, Bl. 23, letter fom Heißmeyer to Lammers dated 13 October 1943. It was noted on 26 October that Lammers had read the report with interest (Bl. 29).
45. Eckart, 'Auswirkung', Bl. 24.
46. Eckart, 'Auswirkung', Bl. 25.
47. Eckart, 'Auswirkung', Bl. 25–6.
48. Eckart, 'Auswirkung', Bl. 26–7. Eckardt clearly suspected that Bishop von Galen might have been behind this plot.
49. Eckart, 'Auswirkung', Bl. 27. Note the appropriation of religious language for political ends in his peroration.
50. On the history of the *Missionshaus* and its Napolisation, see P. Elmar Stier, 'Das Missionshaus St. Wendel zur NS-Zeit', *Heimatbuch des Landkreises St. Wendel* 19 (1981/2), 181–6. N.B. I am extremely grateful to the video club of the Arnold-Janssen-Gymnasium (Florian Hagenbourger, Marie Hagenbourger, Julia Kümmel, Johannes Burgard, and Karsten Mayer) for giving me access to material from the school archives in St. Wendel, as well as other relevant documents.
51. For an example of the hostile newspaper coverage orchestrated by the *Gauleitung*, see 'Gemeinheiten des politischen Katholizismus. Gauleiter Bürckel enthüllt das verbrecherische Komplott geistlicher Staatsfeinde in St. Wendel. Katholische Seelsorger und Jungfrauenkongregation, Ordenspriester und Ordensschwestern in trauriger Verschwörung gegen den Staat. Die Lügenfabrik im St. Wendeler Missionshaus', *Saarbrücker Zeitung*, 31 July 1937; on the contrary protestations of the *Steyler Orden*, see also Archiv Missionshaus St. Wendel (AMSW), letter from Pater Ruschel to Gauleiter Bürckel dated 7 August 1937; letter to the Reich Education Minister dated 2 November 1937.
52. Viktoria Franz, 'Die Nationalpolitische Erziehungsanstalt St. Wendel. Eine privilegierte oder indoktrinierte Elite?' (MA-Hausarbeit, Universität Trier, 2014), 32.
53. AMSW, Verfügung der Gestapo über die Beschlagnahme des Missionshauses, 7 January 1941.
54. AMSW, Pater Breuer, 'Bericht über die Beschlagnahme des Missionshauses St. Wendel' (15 April 1941); AMSW, Hermann-Josef Gräf, 'Die Auflösung des Missionshauses St. Wendel (10. Januar 1941)'; AMSW, 'Aktennotiz die Beschlagnahme des Missionshauses St. Wendel betreffend'; AMSW, 'Bericht über das Missionshaus St. Wendel' (1 March 1947); AMSW, Bruno Schmitt, 'Die Beschlagnahme des Missionshauses St. Wendel heute vor 50 Jahren' (1991).
55. 'Bericht über das Missionshaus', 3; 'Jungmannen des 5. Zuges erzählen von der Aufbauarbeiten in St. Wendel. Vom Missionshaus zur NPEA', *Der Jungmann*, 6. Kriegsnummer (Summer 1941), 15–16; Karl Heinz, 'Mannschaftsformende Erziehung. Nationalpolitische Erziehungsanstalt ersteht aus dem Missionshaus St. Wendel / Erzieher und Jungmannen in Feldgrau', *Saarbrücker Zeitung*, 7 June 1941.
56. 'Erste Nationalpolitische Erziehungsanstalt der Westmark. Eröffnung am 1. September in St. Wendel', *Deutsche Allgemeine Zeitung*, 7 June 1941 [BArch, R 3903/2249].
57. 'Bericht über das Missionshaus', 3, citing a report by Westermann. The *Anstaltsleiter* expressed similar sentiments in 'Die Nationalpolitische Erziehungsanstalt St. Wendel',

Der Jungmann, 8. Kriegsnummer (Summer 1942), 90–2. Pages 90–5 of this issue give an account of the beginning of St. Wendel's life as an NPEA, including reports by staff and pupils.

58. Stier, 'Missionshaus', 185.
59. Franz Speicher, interview with Viktoria Franz, in Franz, 'St. Wendel', 78.
60. Speicher in Franz, 'St. Wendel', 76, 78.
61. Speicher in Franz, 'St. Wendel', 78; cf. 'Jungmannen des 6. Zuges waren zum Landdienst in St. Wendel eingesetzt', *Der Jungmann*, 6. Kriegsnummer (Summer 1941), 16–17.
62. For a detailed (if somewhat encomiastic) history of the school from its foundation onwards, see Alwin Müller, *Geschichte und Geschichten der Jahre 1925–1950. 50 Jahre Landschulheim Neubeuern 1925–1975* (Fischbach, 1975); for a contemporary and fundamentally hostile account by the National Socialist authorities, see Bayerisches Hauptstaatsarchiv (BayHStA), MK53973, report entitled 'Das Landschulheim Neubeuern. Seine wirtschaftliche Lage, seine soziale Struktur und seine politische Haltung'.
63. BayHStA, MK53973, 'Betreff: Landschulheim Neubeuern' (n.d.). Although the school did have its own branch of the Hitler Youth, it appears to have kept this activity separate from other aspects of school life as far as possible—for relevant reports, see the school newsletters from this period (*Landschulheim Neubeuern—Schulzeitung*, 1935–9). N.B. I am very grateful to Reinhard Käsinger for showing me round the school in Schloss Neubeuern, and for giving me access to these school newsletters and other relevant documents from the school archive.
64. 'Das Landschulheim Neubeuern', 6–7.
65. 'Betreff: Landschulheim Neubeuern'; 'Das Landschulheim Neubeuern', 15.
66. 'Das Landschulheim Neubeuern', 6.
67. 'Das Landschulheim Neubeuern', 9; BayStHA, MK53972, Antrag auf Rückerstattung des Landschulheims Schloss Neubeuern, 14 July 1945.
68. BayStHA, MK53972, Antrag; cf. Arnulf Moser, 'Die Nationalpolitische Erziehungsanstalt (Napola) Neubeuern im Zweiten Weltkrieg', *Das bayerische Inn-Oberland. Zeitschrift des Historischen Vereins Rosenheim* 57 (2004), 130–9.
69. BArch, R 2/12722, letter from Sowade to Reich Finance Ministry dated 9 May 1941.
70. BArch, R 2/12722, letter from Sowade to Reich Finance Ministry dated 15 July 1941.
71. BArch, R 2/12722, letters dated 11 March 1942 and 1 April 1942.
72. BArch, R 2/27781, letter dated 6 November 1942; Frieder Loeffler, *Betrachtungen zu meiner Schulzeit in Neubeuern 1944/1945* (2000).
73. 'Die erste Nationalpolitische Erziehungsanstalt im Gau München-Oberbayern. Beginn des Lehrbetriebes am 1. September', *Völkischer Beobachter (Münchener Ausgabe)*, 8 May 1942.
74. For accounts of life at the Napola, see e.g. Michael Klaes, 'Die Napola Neubeuern 1942–1945', and Josef Taubeneder, '"Napola"-Schüler in Neubeuern', in *Landschulheim Neubeuern—Jahrbuch* (1995), 42–3; Reinhard Käsinger, ed., *Napola Schloss Neubeuern* (n.d.); also Moser, 'Neubeuern'.
75. On the school's history, see in particular Steffen Wagner, '"Aus weltanschaulichen Gründen besonders bekämpft und gehaßt"? Die Weierhöfer Schule und ihre

Umwandlung in eine NS-Eliteanstalt im Jahr 1936', *Mennonitische Geschichtsblätter* 68 (2011), 89–160; also more generally Gerhard Bugiel et al., eds, *150 Jahre Weierhof—(mindestens) 150 Facetten. Festschrift des Gymnasiums Weierhof am Donnersberg zum 150. Jubiläum 1867–2017* (Göllheim, 2017). N.B. I am extremely grateful to Steffen Wagner for showing me around the school, and for providing access to numerous relevant documents.

76. On the school's translation into the *Gau-Oberschule* Donnersberg, see Landesarchiv Speyer, H3 Nr. 9469; Zentralarchiv des Bezirksverbands Pfalz (ZABVP), T 21 Nr. 15 and T 21 Nr. 30. On the school's tradition and its compatibility with National Socialism, see Wagner, 'Weierhöfer Schule'; on the relationship between the Mennonite community and Nazism more generally, see Benjamin W. Goossen, *Chosen Nation: Mennonites and Germany in a Global Era* (Princeton, 2017), 121–46.
77. ZABVP, T 21 Nr. 27, 'Bericht über die Besichtigung der nationalpolitischen Erziehungsanstalt Oranienstein bei Diez an der Lahn am 15. und 16. Oktober 1936'.
78. ZABVP, T 21 Nr. 17, letters from Kaspar to Regierungspräsident der Pfalz dated 9 November 1938, 29 June 1939.
79. ZABVP, T 21 Nr. 15, letter from Boeppler to the Directorate of the Gau-Oberschule Donnersberg in Weierhof dated 9 May 1939; BArch, R 2/12717, letter from Calliebe dated 5 September 1941; cf. Arnulf Moser, 'Von der Mennoniten-Schule zur Nationalpolitischen Erziehungsanstalt. Weierhof am Donnersberg im Dritten Reich', *Pfälzer Heimat* 53, no. 2 (2002), 55–61, 58.
80. BArch, R 2/12717 and R 2/29664; cf. Moser, 'Weierhof', 59.
81. ZABVP, T 21 Nr. 367; Moser, 'Weierhof', 60; personal communication with Steffen Wagner, 15 March 2014, 25 May 2019. The School Association's only protest was a lukewarm complaint from Ernst Goebel that Mennonite religious instruction had been taken off the curriculum, despite its retention being one of the conditions made when the school had been given over to Bürckel.
82. Cf. Thomas Behnke, '"Es ist höchste Zeit, darüber zu reden". Podiumsdiskussion im Weierhof-Gymnasium beleuchtet die Zeit der Schule als "Nationalpolitische Lehranstalt" (Napola) und ihre Aufarbeitung', *Mannheimer Morgen*, 29 April 2017.
83. Personal communication with Steffen Wagner, 15 March 2014. Tim Müller has also recently undertaken a study of the school's denazification, which partially led to the creation and fostering of this myth, in his PhD dissertation 'From Racial Selection to Postwar Deception: The Napolas and Denazification' (McMaster University, 2016).
84. Valerie Giesen, 'Nur im Nebenberuf Napola? Ein Beitrag zur Aufarbeitung der NS-Zeit in Schulpforta' (Valediktionsarbeit, Schulpforta, 2009).
85. Roche, 'Ilfeld', 625.

7
Ostmark
The Annexation of the Viennese *Bundeserziehungsanstalten* and Heißmeyer's 'Dissolution of the Monasteries'

On 6 October 1938, a visitor observing the staff-meeting of the Theresianum state boarding school in Vienna might have evinced some surprise when the headmaster not only opened the session with the Heil Hitler greeting, but also compelled all staff present to sing the first verse of the SS anthem 'The Mouldering Bones Are Trembling' (*Es zittern die morschen Knochen*), before launching into discussion of the school's potential future as a Napola.[1] However, such moments were arguably symptomatic of the wholesale Nazification of the Austrian educational system which had been taking place in the wake of the Anschluss—a process which also led to the Napolisation of the Viennese *Bundeserziehungsanstalten* (BEA) or *Staatserziehungsanstalten* (state boarding schools), the Austrian equivalent of the Weimar Republic's *Staatliche Bildungsanstalten*.[2] In contrast with most of the case studies considered in the previous chapter, however, the cooperation with the process of Nazification by the Central Directorate (*Zentraldirektion*) of the BEA and its director, *Hofrat* Adolf Watzke, was entirely unproblematic. The Austrian authorities complied readily with the Napola Inspectorate's seizure of power, continuing their work under Vice-Inspector Otto Calliebe's direction, and facilitating a gradual process of Napolisation which continued for over a year.[3]

However, the transformation of Vienna's *Bundeserziehungsanstalten* was far from the only way in which the Inspectorate was able to gain a fast foothold in the '*Ostmark*'. Beyond the capital, several Napolas were also founded in the buildings of monastic foundations which had been requisitioned and expropriated by the security services, using measures similar to those employed at Haselünne and St. Wendel (as discussed in the previous chapter). This chapter therefore explores the genesis of these two types of Napola in the newly acquired territory of the '*Ostmark*', before concluding with a consideration of the ways in which these processes of Napolisation conformed to patterns of Nazification policy in post-Anschluss Austria more broadly.

Firstly, we will consider the background of the *Bundeserziehungsanstalten*, which shared their genesis with the Weimar Republic's *Staatliche Bildungsanstalten* in the aftermath of World War I. The BEA and the Stabilas also followed a

The Third Reich's Elite Schools: A History of the Napolas. Helen Roche, Oxford University Press.
DOI: 10.1093/oso/9780198726128.003.0008

somewhat similar political trajectory, not least because they represented their respective states' endeavours fundamentally to refashion imperial officer-training institutions with long-standing military traditions.[4] In the Austrian case, the socialist educational reformer and politician Otto Glöckel (1874–1935) had created the BEA out of the former Habsburg imperial and royal (*k.u.k.*) cadet schools at Graz-Liebenau, Wien-Breitensee, Traiskirchen, and the Theresian Military Academy in Wiener Neustadt, as well as the former school for officers' daughters (*Officierstöchter-Erziehungs-Institut*) in Wien-Hernals.[5] These erstwhile military schools were ostensibly transformed with lightning swiftness into centres of experimental pedagogy imbued with a new and radical left-wing ethos, putting into practice a fresh vision for education in post-war Austrian society which focused on child-centred learning, pupils' self-governance, integral vocational training, the prioritization of arts and handicrafts, and other key reform-pedagogical principles.[6]

Despite stiff opposition from conservatives both within the educational system and without, the *Bundeserziehungsanstalten* were able to forge a new pedagogical paradigm which swiftly became the envy of reformers throughout the world, welcoming visitors from all over Europe, or even as far afield as the United States and Australia.[7] Nevertheless, military mindsets and conservative codes of conduct proved harder to eradicate from these institutions than Glöckel and his acolytes might ideally have wished, and the schools' transformation into tools of, first, the Dollfuß-Schuschnigg regime, and then the National Socialist regime, took place far less problematically than the only extant chronicles of these institutions—hagiographic histories by former pupils and teachers—might imply.[8]

From the outset, the *k.u.k.* cadet schools were embroiled in wrangling over who should take ultimate control of the former military education institutions, with the military and civilian administrations competing unsuccessfully to divide responsibilities, until a law passed on 28 November 1919 finally gave the schools a firm legal foundation.[9] The future Austrian Chancellor Bruno Kreisky, who attended one of the schools during this initial period, was cutting in his criticism; he claimed to have despised the whole set-up so much that he started aiming deliberately to get the worst possible marks in order to facilitate his being thrown out, as well as running away into the bargain, 'to speed up the process':[10]

> Everything in that establishment still reeked of the emperor. Those who wished could wear the old cadet uniforms, tall shakos, light blue coats, and dark gray uniform jackets. I did not wear a uniform. In the dormitory the black and yellow blankets with the emblem of the double eagle always had to be perfectly centred on the beds, otherwise the prefect would come and pull the blanket right off and one would have to start all over again. It was an awful struggle to get the eagles exactly in the middle, because the beds stood very close together. Occasionally, too, a particularly annoying prefect would empty out your locker completely,

> claiming that it was not neat. At 6 o'clock we had to get up and report for early morning drill in the courtyard. Up on the first floor the prefect, wearing the short fur jacket of the Dragoons, stood and barked out orders. Another survival of the cadet school tradition was 'weekend leave'. They had not even bothered to find a new name for it; it was like that with everything there, it was all old wine in [ostensibly] new bottles. Many children, especially those from poorer families, were perfectly happy, but for me it was hell.[11]

Even once this initial period of chaos had been superseded, and despite their deep opposition to the previously prevailing social and pedagogical order, in their writings, Glöckel and his acolytes did not only stress the importance of providing an education which led pupils to respect all forms of work, including manual labour.[12] They also emphasized the necessity of toughening their charges up in the service of severely 'spartan' virtues—they should be inured to heat, cold, and be able to bear any pain without flinching, in accordance with the example of a pupil who had found a shard of glass embedded in his foot right at the start of the cross-town '*Quer durch Wien*' race, yet still went on to win.[13] In general, however, Glöckel's plans for the BEA were modelled on Hermann Lietz's *Landerziehungsheime* (country boarding schools), with a very explicit mission to provide a first-rate education for talented children from disadvantaged backgrounds. To this end, a generous system of bursaries and full scholarships was established, in order to ensure that any pupil who passed the entrance examination would be able to attend, regardless of parental income.[14]

In a pamphlet on the schools' aims and ethos published in 1924, Viktor Belohoubek, an inspector in the Education Ministry and one of the key architects of the *Bundeserziehungsanstalten*, gives a taste of some of the pupil-centred activities which were prioritized at the schools. As well as developing a broad focus on music, theatre, and the arts, specific study groups or *Arbeitsgemeinschaften* were also cultivated—small groups of pupils who would meet regularly over a long period of time, carrying out productive activities such as providing braille books for the blind, offering free shoe repairs to their fellow pupils in order to save the state money, or looking after the school gardens, pets, and so forth.[15]

Pupils were also given the opportunity to contribute to the governing of their 'school state'—they were allotted small tasks and offices at first, such as the role of book monitor; in the older year-groups, offices with much more serious responsibilities were introduced, such as the role of *Klassenführer*. This 'form prefect' was given the wherewithal to arrange trips, organize the class library, and even deal with disciplinary matters—although the incumbents often still left such grave matters up to the staff.[16] Belohoubek also mentions the 'University game', in which some of the best pupils in the school would be permitted to take on designated roles as 'Vice-Chancellors', 'Pro-Vice-Chancellors', and 'Professors'—titles which then gave them licence to help pupils who were struggling in class by offering them extra tuition. According to Belohoubek, the reports given out by the pupils who acted as ersatz staff in this way almost always matched the marks given out by the 'real' professors at the year's end.[17]

On one level, the experiment which was being carried out at the *Bundeserziehungsanstalten* during this period was evidently very successful. The institutions provided a varied programme, giving many talented children from disadvantaged backgrounds access to a wide-ranging education which they would never otherwise have had the opportunity to enjoy. The schools were constantly visited and hailed as an inspiration by educationalists from as far afield as the United States and the Far East, and their artistic and cultural endeavours were widely exhibited and reported in pedagogical periodicals—not least the innovative artworks fostered by Karl Grütschnig, one of the art professors.[18]

And yet, when it came to openness towards political radicalization, the *Bundeserziehungsanstalten* were wholly unable to protect all of their charges from being infected by the fever of political unrest. During the early 1930s (and beyond), Nazism took root in the minds of many pupils; attempts were made to found illegal Hitler Youth cells, or to spread National Socialist propaganda literature. Even more shockingly, it was discovered that pupils from the *Bundeserziehungsanstalt* in Traiskirchen had been involved with numerous Nazi terrorist activities, most notoriously an attack on the Wien-Baden electric railway (*Badener Elektrische*) on 26 June 1933. Some of the newspapers' more outlandish claims regarding this scandal—that the police had led pupils from the school in chains, or that caches of explosive had been found in their dormitories—proved to be unfounded.[19] Nevertheless, the underlying tendency towards radicalization among the student body was a problem which the authorities tried to battle with increasing desperation during the reign of the Austrofascist Christian Corporatist State (*Christliche Ständestaat*).[20]

During this period (1934–8), pupils were routinely threatened with permanent exclusion for such seemingly innocuous activities as referring to the 'German greeting', while more serious involvement with the underground Nazi movement—for example, smuggling weapons to the illegal SA in the neighbouring towns, planning gas attacks on the local *Schutzkorps* (auxiliary militia), or self-publishing Hitler Youth propaganda, could lead to immediate expulsion and police involvement.[21] However, as might be claimed for the broader culture of Austrofascism more generally, the narrowing of intellectual horizons at the *Bundeserziehungsanstalten*, and the interminable flood of propaganda in support of the Dollfuß-Schuschnigg regime (the *Bundeserziehungsanstalt* in Traiskirchen was even renamed the 'Dollfuß-Kolleg') did not succeed in endearing its recipients' hearts and minds to the Austrofascist state.[22]

After the Anschluss, the advent of the 'Greater German Reich' was welcomed with untold rejoicing by many pupils at the *Bundeserziehungsanstalten*. One group at the school in Wien-Breitensee even published a special issue of the school newsletter, entitled 'Hitler Youths' (*Hitler-Jungen*), documenting all of their illegal travails, and their tireless and undaunted striving to put their greater-German political principles into practice. Nazi-inspired doggerel, illustrations of burly SA-men, and the tunes and lyrics of National Socialist battle-songs were interspersed with accounts of the risks which the illegal Hitler Youths of Breitensee had run during the hated '*Systemzeit*'. This might have involved a night in prison being interrogated by the police, attending a clandestine meeting of local youth leaders, or merely the danger of singing the Horst-Wessel-Lied on a mountain hike. The volume then triumphantly concluded with joyful depictions of the final 'revolution', during which Hitler Youths and BDM functionaries had taken over the school from without.[23]

But how exactly did the full transformation from *Bundeserziehungsanstalten* to National Socialist-oriented *Staatserziehungsanstalten* to *Nationalpolitische Erziehungsanstalten* come about?[24] The evidence suggests that Reich Education Minister Rust was swift to see the advantages, power, and prestige which would accrue to him as 'Chief' of the NPEA if he were able to extend the reach of the (nominally still Prussian) Napola *Landesverwaltung* into the Reich's new Austrian territories.[25] Just as the power of the Reich was growing and its grasp ever-extending, so too did the power of the NPEA authorities and the extent of the Napola system grow; first in Austria, and then in the Sudetenland.[26] On 29 July 1938, Rust decreed that the Theresianum academy in Vienna, along with the former BEA at Wien-Breitensee, Traiskirchen, and Wien-Boerhavegasse (soon to be the first ever Napola for girls), would become the first four NPEA on Austrian soil.[27]

As soon as Vice-Inspector Calliebe arrived in Vienna in August 1938, the BEA *Zentraldirektion* began to collaborate enthusiastically with all of the Inspectorate's demands, in order to ensure that the transition process could be effected as efficiently and expeditiously as possible—including the immediate expulsion of all Jewish pupils, and all pupils with disabilities.[28] Not only were the Austrian bureaucrats cooperative to a fault; they even seem to have been prepared to risk censure from their masters in the Interior Ministry when it came to winning the Inspectorate's approbation; for instance, claiming that it was wholly unreasonable to expect the *Zentraldirektion* to await timely approval for official business trips to the schools at such a crucial time, when they needed to be in 'the most lively contact' with them.[29] Indeed, in February 1939, when Heißmeyer himself had announced a personal inspection to see if the schools were truly worthy of being placed under the Inspectorate's aegis, the *Zentraldirektion*'s desperation to impress led them to declare that workers' overtime was no object, for one thing above all was paramount: '*Everything must run smoothly!*'[30]

And yet, despite such eager cooperation, the *Zentraldirektion* were to find their strenuous efforts wholly unrewarded. On 9 March 1939, in response to an anxious query about the bureau's future, Heißmeyer declared that there was no place for the *Zentraldirektion* or any other intermediary authority when it came to administrating the Napolas; the Inspectorate must be in sole control.[31] On 31 March 1939, the schools were removed from the *Zentraldirektion*'s jurisdiction, and on 30 July 1939, the bureau's affairs were brought to a definitive close.[32]

Nevertheless, the encomia which Watzke and the *Zentraldirektion* heaped upon the new Napolas betray no bitterness, simply glowing devotion to the National Socialist cause.[33] Perhaps this level of commitment to Nazism should not surprise us, given the fervent greater-German nationalist sentiments which Watzke had been airing as early as April 1929, over a decade earlier: 'If we really want the Anschluss, then once and for all, we must seek to act here as the Germans do. Who laughs at German orderliness? Let us cleave to it here also. Who thinks himself above German devotion to duty? We too can fulfil our highest duty by paying the most painstaking attention to detail. Then we shall be working practically towards Anschluss with Germany.'[34] In this context, the dedication which Watzke and his subordinates were prepared to expend on the gradual dismantling of the previous traditions which had held sway at the former *Bundeserziehungsanstalten* and the Theresianum, including their forcible de-Christianization and the ideologically motivated purging of their libraries, as well as the racially motivated purging of their staff and student body, appear more comprehensible, if no less reprehensible.[35]

However, it was the biological selection process to which Calliebe and the Inspectorate paid most attention—it was considered crucial that all remaining pupils, staff, and personnel should be deemed both capable and worthy of continuing their careers at an NPEA. Even before Calliebe had taken over the leadership of the *Zentraldirektion* on 15 August 1938, Heißmeyer demanded that a fitness test (*Tauglichkeitsprüfung*) be put in place to determine the physical and racial suitability of all potential future *Jungmannen*.[36] On 1 October 1938, the *Zentraldirektion* was instructed to draw up a dossier on every individual teacher, *Jungmann*, and *Jungmädel* in preparation for the coming tests, which placed a much greater emphasis on character and physical aptitude than the more academically oriented entrance examinations at the BEA had done.[37] Yet in the end, the number of pupils excluded on these grounds was fairly small: for example, there were only twenty expulsions at Traiskirchen (an average of three per class), and eleven at the Theresianum.[38]

The grand denouement of the schools' transformation took place on 13 March 1939, the first anniversary of Austria's incorporation into the Reich. A varied programme of festivities was held at the Theresianum, including speeches by Rust, Heißmeyer, *Staatskommissar* Friedrich Plattner, and *Reichsstatthalter* Arthur Seyß-Inquart, as well as fanfares, singing, and massed speech choirs performed by the *Jungmannen* and the first ever *Jungmädel*, hymning the long-awaited fulfilment of Austria's greater-German fate (see Figures 7.1 and 7.2). Copies of these texts were liberally distributed by the *Zentraldirektion* to every single teacher and pupil at the former BEA, as 'a memento to commemorate this red-letter day'.[39]

Figure 7.1 Vienna, 13 March 1939: Pupils and staff from the former Austrian *Bundeserziehungsanstalten* attend the ceremony at the Theresianum which incorporated the schools into the NPEA system.

Figure 7.2 Reich Education Minister Bernhard Rust speaks at the ceremony which celebrated the transformation of the former Austrian *Bundeserziehungsanstalten* into Napolas.

Ultimately, most of the pupils who were deemed physically and racially suitable had few qualms about continuing their studies *in situ* once the *Bundeserziehungsanstalten* had been taken over by the NPEA. After the intellectual and political depredations of two fascist regimes in succession had taken their toll, there were next to no reminders left of Otto Glöckel's reformist vision. Indeed, the militaristic education on offer at the Napolas ultimately had far more in common with the cadet-school training which had taken place within the schools' walls before 1918 than with the vibrant reform-pedagogical experimentation which had taken place there during the 1920s.

*

However, the former *Bundeserziehungsanstalten* only formed the vanguard of the Napolas in the '*Ostmark*'. Although there were a number of planned NPEA which never got beyond the drawing board—including putative Napolas at Zell am See and the Faaker See, which were suggested in part at the behest of the Gauleiter of Salzburg and Carinthia respectively, a further seven Napolas were still founded in Austria during the 1940s.[40]

Based on the reckoning that there should be at least one Napola for every 80,000 members of the general population, and on the fact that Gau Salzburg and Gau Tirol-Vorarlberg still did not possess a single NPEA, Heißmeyer was adamant that at least ten schools overall should be established in Austria's seven new 'Danubian and Alpine Reich Gaus', not including the girls' school at Hubertendorf-Türnitz, which 'as the only National Political Education Institute for Girls, possesses significance for the entire Reich, and therefore cannot be included in the regional total'.[41] All of these new foundations, excepting Mokritz on the Croatian border (now Mokrice, Slovenia), and Burg Strechau, which operated as a retreat-, training- and conference-centre rather than as a fully functioning Napola in its own right, were also the fruit of Heißmeyer's *Klostersturm*; that is, the Inspectorate's wholesale and widespread appropriation of former monasteries.[42] These included the abbeys at Vorau, Seckau, Lambach (where Hitler himself had sung as a choirboy), Göttweig, and St. Paul in Lavanttal/Spanheim, as well as the former Catholic seminary at St. Veit in Southern Carinthia (now Šentvid, Slovenia).[43] The priests and monks who inhabited these religious foundations were expropriated and expelled using a similar mélange of false accusations of treason, mismanagement, and sexual impropriety as those detailed in the cases of St. Wendel and Haselünne (see Chapter 6).[44] Once again, even when the monastic buildings in question had not explicitly been requisitioned in order to house an NPEA, the Inspectorate hastened to take advantage of their becoming available. Meanwhile, in some instances, such as the requisitioning of Vorau and Seckau, the expropriation process had apparently been carried out entirely for Heißmeyer's benefit, on the orders of the Chief of the Security Service, Reinhard Heydrich himself.[45] In the case of St. Paul/Spanheim, the Carinthian *Reichsstatthalter* explicitly delineated the fundamentally anti-religious ideological motivation behind these measures:

> The expropriated monasteries were designed in the first instance to be cultural transmitters of the dogma of the Catholic Church.... Therefore, it is first and foremost my concern...to place cultural transmitters in these properties, with the sole difference that from this point onwards it should no longer be the teachings of the Catholic Church, but the *Weltanschauung* of National Socialism, which should be absorbed in an appropriate form by the people. I therefore immediately thought of the foundation of National Socialist educational institutions.[46]

In the case of the abbey at Göttweig, which was only considered as a suitable location for a Napola some time after its original expropriation, the Inspectorate became especially keen to secure the site 'against the depredations of other authorities' by deploying two classes from NPEA Ballenstedt to take over the building complex, until NPEA Vorau could be moved there in its entirety.[47]

Ultimately, however, many of these monastic jewels of baroque architecture seem to have proved almost more trouble than they were worth from the Inspectorate's perspective, particularly when it came to minimizing the dominating influence of their ecclesiastical edifices. Heißmeyer's subordinates appear to have been constantly involved in wrangling with heritage conservation professionals over the preservation of these sites of historic interest, since the conservators were understandably loth to see the church in Vorau converted into an indoor swimming pool, or the church at Lambach denuded of its two distinctive onion-dome steeples.[48] One particularly iconoclastic architect's plan suggested that the church at Göttweig (now part of a UNESCO world heritage site) should be completely demolished, and its ruins used to provide further building material.[49] Yet Göttweig had originally been considered especially suitable as a potential location for a Napola precisely because it did not give off a particularly 'monastic' impression.[50] Conversely, the eventual translation of NPEA Vorau to Göttweig had been deemed necessary because 'the central position of the church [at Vorau] must on all counts exert a disturbing effect on the operation of the school'.[51] Often, a vigorous sense of mistrust was also sown between the denizens of the Napola and the local inhabitants, who had frequently been denied access to their habitual place of worship, as had occurred at Spanheim.[52] On at least one occasion, this led staff at the Napola to instruct their charges to attend the market town's parish Mass incognito in civilian clothing, to check 'whether National Socialism was being inveighed against from the pulpit'.[53]

We will now turn to one case study in particular—that of the former seminary for Catholic priests at St. Veit an der Sawe (present-day Ljubljana-Šentvid, Slovenia), which was founded as a dependency of NPEA Traiskirchen in October

1942.[54] A series of reports to the Inspectorate by the acting *Anstaltsleiter*, *Hundertschaftsführer* Günther Büttler, reveal in detail not only how far the former seminary had been de-Christianized, since part of the renovation process predictably involved remodelling and repurposing the church buildings. In addition, the reports also demonstrate the sheer tenacity with which Büttler pushed the Napola's foundation and his particular conception of Nazi Germanizing ideology forward, despite constant threats from Communist partisans in the area, and increasingly troubled relations with the local, largely Slovene, population.

From 3 September 1942, Büttler set in train the complete refurbishment of the seminary in time for the school's opening at the beginning of the following month, using Slovenian prisoners as construction workers.[55] These had been cooperatively supplied by the relevant Higher SS and Police Leader (*Höherer SS- und Polizeiführer*) Erwin Rösener, and the High Commissioner in the Operational Zone of the Adriatic Littoral (*Oberste Kommissar, Operationszone Adriatisches Küstenland*), Gauleiter Friedrich Rainer, who were both entirely supportive of Büttler's endeavours.[56]

Büttler's key aim was to prove 'that an NPEA is not an island remote from political events, but rather that it constitutes a political centre, from which powerful forces stream forth into the surrounding area'.[57] The acting *Anstaltsleiter* harboured grandiose dreams of turning the school into NPEA Laibach (Ljubljana), a regional powerhouse which could prove crucial in winning 'racially suitable' ethnic German Slovenes back to the Reich, thereby making 'a contribution to the realization of our pan-European responsibilities in the sphere of education'.[58] Büttler's steadfast faith in the tenets of National Socialist racial ideology evidently saturated his conception of his mission, as well as giving the education of the *Jungmannen* at this 'borderland' NPEA a particular charge:

> First of all, our *Jungmannen* gain a genuine enthusiasm for Carinthia from their trips and camps, in that they learn to appreciate the region not only for its mountains and lakes, but above all as the location of a grim battle for the borderlands which is scarcely recognized in the Reich. It is also valuable that here, our North German *Jungmannen* learn about the struggle of the NSDAP in the *Ostmark* during the illegal time from the lips of the combatants themselves.... And it is particularly valuable for our Prussians to get to know the methods by which pioneers from the *Ostmark* have tolerantly and cannily ruled the people in this region, as well as, on the other hand, recognizing their further mistakes, which then led to the collapse of German rule. The racial struggle, the de-Germanization appeared visibly before the eyes of the *Jungmannen* in the many German names of people who are now dyed-in-the-wool Slovenes and want nothing more to do with Germany; gravestones in the cemeteries, shop fascias in Laibach, which today is wholly Slovene, eloquently bespeak this region's German past, and the names of the bandits who have been shot in reprisals

> (on the wall-placards listing the names of those shot, up to 30 per cent of the names we read were German) allow the *Jungmannen* to grasp the eternal tragedy of our race, which allowed the best German blood to flow into alien nations, [those which now] engage us in armed combat.[59]

Despite all manner of practical problems, from the absence of sufficient furniture, bedclothes, crockery, and cutlery (for instance, the *Jungmannen* initially had to drink their coffee out of water glasses) to the parlous lack of horses for riding lessons—the solution being to appropriate some from the fleeing Italian army after Mussolini's capitulation—Büttler ostensibly managed to get NPEA St. Veit up and running to the expected academic and extra-curricular standard within a year.[60] Until the end of the war, the school welcomed a succession of classes from Napolas beyond the '*Ostmark*', including Naumburg, Loben, Spandau, and Ilfeld, as well as pupils from Traiskirchen and Spanheim.[61]

However, the most significant challenge was presented by the persistent hostile activity of alleged Communist partisans in the area, which necessitated all of the *Jungmannen* being fully trained in armed combat in the interests of self-defence:

> The danger from partisan bands has also given our school life a particular tone. The building stands under military and police surveillance.... SS-*Gruppenführer* Rösener arranged that the *Jungmannen* be supplied with carbine rifles, so that in case of an emergency we are capable of defending ourselves. The weapons-training, above all with live ammunition, took centre-stage in our afternoon activities. Naturally this delighted the *Jungmannen* no end. The student body took on their own night patrols and an armed guard over the dormitories, since, what with the [Slovene] personnel and the prisoners, we effectively already have the enemy within our gates.... Only a year ago, we could still march out into the outstandingly beautiful countryside roundabout. Now, due to the increased danger of partisan attacks, we can no longer do so responsibly.[62]

As the military situation in the region worsened, the NPEA was even harder hit; during spring and summer 1944, the gardener was forcibly recruited by the partisans; the coachman was hi-jacked and abducted and the school's best horse stolen; one of the cooks and one of the handymen voluntarily went 'into the forest' to join the 'bandits', and one of the worker-prisoners also absconded without leave.[63]

Nevertheless, even as World War II neared its end, and more and more of the school's local personnel fled to join the partisans, Büttler continued to devise yet more hubristic plans for the Napola's future.[64] Having secured special permission from Gauleiter Rainer to flout the ever-tightening restrictions on wartime building work, Büttler continued to oversee the construction of the NPEA's new festal hall, 'precisely in order to demonstrate to the Slovene race that we have no plans to evacuate, but on the contrary intend to retain this region under the sovereignty of the Reich with unbroken confidence'.[65] Indeed, Büttler was still so convinced of the Reich's final victory that he even recommended that Heißmeyer should employ the architect who had designed the hall's new stained-glass windows, replete with National Socialist symbology, for similar projects at other NPEA in the 'post-war period' (*Nachkriegszeit*).[66]

In this case study, then, we can see many of the ramifications of the Napolas' Germanizing ideology on Austrian soil at play—and, as we shall see in the following chapter, such use of the NPEA as tools of Germanization policy would be both mirrored, and radically expanded, as the Third Reich extended its grasp still further over the European continent, both East and West.

*

For now, however, it remains to determine to what extent the forms of Napolisation depicted here conformed with broader patterns of Nazification policy and praxis in post-Anschluss Austria—are wider trends illuminated here in microcosm? And how far did the experience of the NPEA in the '*Ostmark*' remain distinctively 'Austrian', or did daily life at these schools merely mirror that found at Napolas back in Germany, in the *Altreich*?

As we have seen in the case of St. Veit, the school authorities attempted to make the local setting of each NPEA specifically relevant to the *Jungmannen* in question, whether they had arrived from elsewhere in Austria, or from Germany. Pupils were expected to learn to appreciate both the regional beauties of their school's setting, and its regional particularities in terms of the pre-Anschluss battle for National Socialist hegemony, or the 'struggle' with ethnic minorities, especially in borderland areas.[67] Nevertheless, perhaps in part due to the authorities' deliberate intent to intermingle pupils from the new 'Danubian and Alpine Reich Gaus' and the Reich itself, extant contemporary accounts, school newsletters, and memoirs betray very little to suggest that life at an Austrian NPEA differed fundamentally from that at an NPEA in Germany, save for local peculiarities, or divergences in tradition which might have varied just as substantially between different Napolas within Germany.[68] Indeed, at least initially, schools such as Wien-Breitensee or Traiskirchen, with their former cadet-school and *Bundeserziehungsanstalt* tradition, might well have felt more similar in ethos to the former Prussian cadet schools and Stabilas than to schools which possessed a more humanistic and academic tradition, such as Schulpforta. However, we might reasonably claim, as Sebastian Pumberger has suggested, that the Napolas for girls ended up bearing a more distinctively 'Austrian imprint', given that the former BEA-Boerhavegasse, NPEA Hubertendorf-Türnitz, set the tone for all of the *Mädchen-Napolas* which came after (see further Chapter 9).[69]

In general terms, the processes of Napolisation at play here appear to reflect broader post-Anschluss developments in the '*Ostmark*', both in the case of the former *Bundeserziehungsanstalten*, and that of the former monasteries. Firstly, the initial phase of consolidating the former BEA as *Staatserziehungsanstalten* and subsequently effecting their transformation into Napolas, including the eager collaboration of the *Zentraldirektion* to this end, was symptomatic of the fundamental transformation and Nazification of the Austrian political administration which took place during this initial phase of annexation.[70] The NPEA Inspectorate's frictionless takeover of the *Zentraldirektion*, and its bureaucrats' willingness to subordinate themselves instantaneously to the National Socialist agenda, also reflect processes found more specifically in the Nazification of the Austrian state education system. For example, we find a very similar process of *Gleichschaltung* or coordination taking place at the Austrian universities, ranging from the immediate removal and ostracism of all Jewish students and professors, to the favouring of former illegal National Socialists and their elevation to new positions of power, in order to ensure the hegemony of regime-loyal staff—one might compare the case of German-teacher Karl Schön, a former illegal Nazi who was subsequently promoted to become *Anstaltsleiter* of the school at Traiskirchen.[71] The parallels in the sphere of primary and secondary education are also immediately apparent—not only the policies of ethnic cleansing and privileging previously 'illegal' pupils, which were enthusiastically supported by administrators and staff at schools throughout the former Austrian Republic as well as at the former *Bundeserziehungsanstalten*, but also the jubilant greeting of the Anschluss by a youthful generation who had to a large extent already been radicalized both to accept and to promote National Socialism.[72]

Secondly, since National Socialism had always seen the Catholic Church as its true opponent in Austria, the obliteration of clerical power and the requisition of ecclesiastical property led to a whole raft of opportunities for expropriation which benefited any Nazi institutions that were able and willing to take advantage of the situation.[73] The wave of secularization and explicit de-Catholicization which overtook Austria's 'concordat-free space' after the Anschluss, and which also led to the wholesale deconfessionalization of Austria's educational landscape, enabled the swift establishment of a wide range of National Socialist institutions in the '*Ostmark*', of which the NPEA formed just one fraction.[74]

Ultimately, as Evan Burr Bukey has suggested, Hitler's Austria became 'a laboratory for...pagan and pseudo-scientific theories...a site for the realization of visionary projects that ranged from the separation of church and state, to the extermination of social and racial undesirables....For those who profited...it was an exhilarating experience. For others, the Anschluss left a legacy of unbearable emotional and physical suffering.'[75] From this perspective, the NPEA in the '*Ostmark*' can arguably be seen not only as one of the first of these visionary projects in the sphere of education, but also as a key experiment in the Nazi social and cultural 'laboratory' *tout court*. As such, the schools' development and expansion in Austria would soon pave the way for still more wide-ranging endeavours of Napolisation and Germanization in further Eastern and Western European territories as yet unconquered.

Notes

1. Österreichisches Staatsarchiv (ÖStA), BEA 87, Verhandlungsschrift der Lehrerberatung, 6 October 1938.
2. The terminology used for these institutions changed more than once between 1919 and 1939: initially, the schools were known as *Staatserziehungsanstalten*; from 1920 onwards, the official designation was *Bundeserziehungsanstalten*, but after the Anschluss, in April 1938, they were once more renamed *Staatserziehungsanstalten*. To avoid confusion, the term *Bundeserziehungsanstalt* (BEA) will be used throughout. For more on the general background of educational Nazification, see e.g. ÖStA, BEA 236; also Helmut Engelbrecht, 'Die Eingriffe des Dritten Reiches in das österreichische Schulwesen', in Manfred Heinemann, ed., *Erziehung und Schulung im Dritten Reich. Teil 1: Kindergarten, Schule, Jugend, Berufserziehung* (Stuttgart, 1980), 113–59; Herbert Dachs, *Schule und Politik. Politische Erziehung an den österreichischen Schulen 1918–1938* (Vienna, 1982); Helmut Engelbrecht, *Geschichte des österreichischen Bildungswesens. Erziehung und Unterricht auf dem Boden Österreichs Band 5: Von 1918 bis zur Gegenwart* (Vienna, 1988); Herbert Dachs, 'Schule in der "Ostmark"', in Emmerich Tálos et al., eds, *NS-Herrschaft in Österreich. Ein Handbuch* (Vienna, 2002), 446–66.
3. See further the relevant documents in ÖStA, BEA 1, BEA 7, and BEA 172 (II).
4. For example, one could argue that, after suffering teething troubles due to the negative influence of ex-cadets, followed by a period of relative stability in the mid-1920s, pupils and some teachers at both the BEA and the Stabilas began to fall prey to the lure of National Socialism, despite the schools' strivings to preserve some form of apolitical neutrality. The BEA, the Hans Richert-Schule in Lichterfelde, and the *Landesschule* Dresden also participated in joint exchanges and pedagogical visits; see for example Viktor Belohoubek, 'Bericht über meine Reise nach Deutschland zur Besichtigung der staatlichen Bildungsanstalten in Berlin und Dresden am 2.-4. Juli 1924' (ÖStA, BEA 1; see also ÖStA, BEA 115 and BEA 146 for information on exchanges which took place in 1930 and 1931).
5. N.B. BEA Graz-Liebenau and BEA Wiener Neustadt were never considered as potential Napolas, and will not be mentioned further. In 1934, a second *Bundeserziehungsanstalt* for girls was founded at Wien-Boerhavegasse—shortly thereafter, BEA Wien-Hernals was closed and amalgamated with BEA Wien-Boerhavegasse, which would later form the basis of the first ever Napola for girls at Hubertendorf-Türnitz (see Chapter 9).
6. For more on Glöckel and his reforms, see e.g. Ernst Papanek, *The Austrian School Reform: Its Bases, Principles and Development—The Twenty Years between the Two World Wars* (New York, 1962); Oskar Achs and Albert Krassnigg, *Drillschule—Lernschule—Arbeitsschule. Otto Glöckel und die österreichische Schulreform in der Ersten Republik* (Vienna, 1974); Erik Adam, 'Austromarxismus und Schulreform', in Erik Adam and Primus-Heinz Kucher, eds, *Die Schul- und Bildungspolitik der österreichischen Sozialdemokratie in der Ersten Republik. Entwicklung und Vorgeschichte* (Vienna, 1983), 271–416; Engelbrecht, *Geschichte*; also Otto Glöckel, *Drillschule—Lernschule—Arbeitsschule* (Vienna, 1928); Otto Glöckel, *Aus dem Leben eines großen*

Schulmannes—Otto Glöckel—Selbstbiographie. Sein Lebenswerk: Die Wiener Schulreform (Zürich, 1939); Otto Glöckel, *Ausgewählte Schriften und Reden* (Vienna, 1985). On the flowering of left-wing political, social, and cultural projects in Vienna during this period more generally, see e.g. Helmut Gruber, *Red Vienna: Experiment in Working-Class Culture, 1919–1934* (Oxford, 1991); Judith Beniston and Robert Vilain, eds, *Culture and Politics in Red Vienna* (Leeds, 2006); Janek Wassermann, *Black Vienna: The Radical Right in the Red City, 1918–1938* (Ithaca, 2014).

7. See, for example, the relevant correspondence and newspaper cuttings contained in ÖStA, BEA 6, BEA 7, and BEA 95.
8. For post-war accounts of the BEA, see Franz Thaller, ed., *50 Jahre österreichische Bundeserziehungsanstalt* (Saalfelden, 1969); Friedrich Schlager, 'Die Entwicklung der österreichischen Bundeserziehungsanstalten' (Dissertation, University of Salzburg, 1978); Felix F. Strauss, *Bilder von der Wiener Neustädter Burg zwischen zwei Weltkriegen. Ansichten von fünfzehnjährigen Augenzeugen in den Jahren 1932/1933, ergänzt durch Darstellungen aus dem Jahre 1923. Ein Beispiel der Schulreform von Otto Glöckel an der Bundeserziehungsanstalt 'Schule am Turm'* (Vienna, 1985); Agnes Rudda, ed., *Später Dank: Erinnerungen an die österreichischen Bundeserziehungsanstalten. Ein Beitrag zur Geschichte und Entwicklung des Bildungswesens von 1919 bis zur Gegenwart* (Heidenreichstein, 2007).
9. Charles A. Gulick, *Austria from Habsburg to Hitler. Volume I: Labor's Workshop of Democracy* (Berkeley, 1948), 556–7.
10. Matthew Paul Berg, ed., *The Struggle for a Democratic Austria: Bruno Kreisky on Peace and Social Justice* (New York, 2000), 8.
11. Berg, *Kreisky*, 7.
12. Cf. e.g. Viktor Belohoubek, *Die österreichischen Bundeserziehungsanstalten. Ein Werk kulturellen Aufbaues der Republik Österreich* (Vienna, 1924); Viktor Fadrus, ed., *Die österreichischen Bundeserziehungsanstalten* (Vienna, 1924); Hans Fischl, *Schulreform, Demokratie und Österreich 1918–1950* (Vienna, 1950).
13. Belohoubek, *Bundeserziehungsanstalten*, 40.
14. Engelbrecht, *Geschichte*, 67–8, 132–9; Belohoubek, *Bundeserziehungsanstalten*, 13.
15. Belohoubek, *Bundeserziehungsanstalten*, 55.
16. Belohoubek, *Bundeserziehungsanstalten*, 54.
17. Belohoubek, *Bundeserziehungsanstalten*, 53.
18. See for example the article by Karl Grütschnig, 'What Craftwork Means to Me', *Teacher's World*, 11 September 1935, 18 September 1935, 25 September 1935, which also contains numerous illustrations featuring pupils' artwork (ÖStA, BEA 6); also n. 7 in this chapter.
19. Reports on the terrorist incident include: 'In der Bundeserziehungsanstalt Traiskirchen: Vier Gymnasiasten als Bombenverschwörer. Sensationelle Untersuchungsergebnisse über das Badener Sprengstoffattentat', *Wiener Mittags-Zeitung*, 3 July 1933; 'Mittelschulprofessor als Bombenwerfer verhaftet. Nazi-Sprengstofflager in einer Mittelschule—Sensationelle Verhaftung von Gymnasiasten—Siebzehnjährige rüsten zum Bürgerkrieg—In Ketten aus der Schule abgeführt—Neue Anschläge in Baden', *Wiener Mittagsblatt*, 3 July 1933; 'Die Schülerverhaftungen in der Bundeserziehungsanstalt Traiskirchen. Auch die Verhaftung von Professoren im Bereiche der Möglichkeit', *Wiener Allgemeine Zeitung*, 4 July 1933; 'Wie die Nazibombenverbrecher entlarvt wurden.

Polizei verteilt die Prämien an die Anzeiger. Anzeiger, die ihre Namen nicht nennen', *Der Abend*, 4 July 1933; 'Das Nazi-Nest von Traiskirchen. Strengstes Stillschweigen über die Ergebnisse der Untersuchung', *Die Stunde*, 5 July 1933 [ÖStA, BEA 234].

20. For more on youth radicalization during this period, see Johanna Gehmacher, *Jugend ohne Zukunft. Hitler-Jugend und Bund Deutscher Mädel in Österreich vor 1938* (Vienna, 1994), esp. 321–5, and, on Nazi radicalization in Austria more generally, Francis L. Carsten, *Fascist Movements in Austria: From Schönerer to Hitler* (London, 1977), esp. 189; also Martin Kitchen, *The Coming of Austrian Fascism* (London, 1980); Bruce F. Pauley, *Hitler and the Forgotten Nazis: A History of Austrian National Socialism* (London, 1981); John T. Lauridsen, *Nazism and the Radical Right in Austria, 1918–1934* (Copenhagen, 2007).
21. See for example the relevant material in ÖStA, BEA 107, BEA 114, BEA 115, BEA 171, and BEA 236.
22. Cf. Emmerich Tálos, *Das austrofaschistische Herrschaftssystem: Österreich 1933–1938* (Vienna, 2013). On Austrofascist education in particular, see R. John Rath, 'Training for Citizenship, "Authoritarian" Austrian Style', *Journal of Central European Affairs* 3, no. 2 (1943), 121–46; R. John Rath, 'History and Citizenship Training: An Austrian Example', *The Journal of Modern History* 21, no. 3 (1949), 227–38; Wolfgang Sorgo, 'Autoritärer "Ständestaat" und Schulpolitik 1933–1938' (Dissertation, University of Vienna, 1978); Dachs, *Schule und Politik*, 225–369; Engelbrecht, *Geschichte*, 262–74; Carla Esden-Tempska, 'Civic Education in Authoritarian Austria', *History of Education Quarterly* 30, no. 2 (1990), 187–211; Thomas Pammer, 'Austrofaschismus und Jugend: gescheiterte Beziehung und lohnendes Forschungsfeld?', in Florian Wenninger and Lucile Dreidemy, eds, *Das Dollfuß/Schuschnigg-Regime 1933–1938. Vermessung eines Forschungsfeldes* (Vienna, 2013), 395–410, and Julie Thorpe, 'Education and the Austrofascist State', in the same volume, 381–93. For a programmatic text from the period, see Josef A. Tzöbl, *Vaterländische Erziehung. Mit einem Geleitwort von Bundesminister Dr. Kurt v. Schuschnigg* (2nd edn; Vienna, 1933).
23. *Hitler-Jungen. Sonderheft der 'Blätter der Staatserziehungsanstalt Wien-Breitensee'* (1938).
24. On the change in nomenclature, see n. 2 in this chapter.
25. Cf. Geheimes Staatsarchiv Preußischer Kulturbesitz, I. HA Rep. 151 IC, Nr. 7308, Bl. 17, letter from Rust dated 23 May 1938.
26. On NPEA Sudetenland, see the following chapter; also Helen Roche, '*Herrschaft durch Schulung*: The *Nationalpolitische Erziehungsanstalten im Osten* and the Third Reich's Germanising Mission', in Burkhard Olschowsky and Ingo Loose, eds, *Nationalsozialismus und Regionalbewusstsein im östlichen Europa. Ideologie, Machtausbau, Beharrung* (Berlin, 2016), 127–51.
27. ÖStA, BEA 7, decree by Rust dated 29 July 1938.
28. The *Zentraldirektion* was a subsidiary of the Austrian Ministry for Interior and Cultural Affairs (*Ministerium für innere und kulturelle Angelegenheiten*). On racially motivated expulsion policy, see ÖStA, BEA 172 (II), letters from Watzke dated 29 August 1938 and 9 September 1938.
29. ÖStA, BEA 25, correspondence from September 1938.
30. ÖStA, BEA 7, *Zentraldirektion* to the directors of all *Anstalten*, letter dated 1 February 1939 (emphasis original).

31. ÖStA, BEA 7, *Zentraldirektion* to Heißmeyer, letter dated 14 February 1939; Heißmeyer to *Zentraldirektion*, letter dated 9 March 1939.
32. ÖStA, BEA 7, 'NPEA—Abschied der Zentraldirektion', 31 March 1939; ÖStA, BEA 1, letter dated 15 July 1939.
33. Cf. e.g. ÖStA, BEA 7, 'NPEA—Abschied der Zentraldirektion', 31 March 1939; ÖStA, BEA 1, Watzke to Regierungsrat Wilhelm Tietze, letter dated 22 June 1939.
34. ÖStA, BEA 165, 'Verhandlungsschrift Nr. 1, aufgenommen in der Beratung des Lehr- und Erziehungskörpers der BEA Traiskirchen am 4. September 1929'. During World War II, Watzke went on to be instrumental in putting Nazi educational policy into effect in the Polish General Government, including involvement in plans for setting up further NPEA, as well as the putative 'Copernicus University' in Krakow—cf. Michael Burleigh, *Germany Turns Eastwards: A Study of* Ostforschung *in the Third Reich* (Cambridge, 1988), 288–9. See further Chapter 8.
35. On de-Christianization, see e.g. ÖStA, BEA 25, letter dated 5 September 1938; ÖStA, BEA 95, letter dated 4 October 1938 (on the removal of religious artefacts); ÖStA, BEA 7, letter dated 18 October 1938 (on the banning of the titles of Christian holidays as a replacement for date designations); ÖStA, BEA 1, Watzke to Professor Ernst Schwarzinger, letter dated 13 April 1939 (thanking him for his deconfessionalization initiatives). On the removal of Communist, Marxist, Jewish, pacifist, atheist, and religious literature from the school libraries, and the provision of a grant of 3,000 RM for each school to replace these with relevant National Socialist literature, see ÖStA, BEA 7, letters dated 10 May 1938, 9 June 1938, 20 October 1938. On antisemitic policies during the handover period, see n. 28 in this chapter; also ÖStA, BEA 71, protocol dated 30 June 1938; ÖStA, BEA 7, letter dated 2 July 1938; ÖStA, BEA 178, letter dated 13 September 1938; ÖStA, BEA 172 (II), letter dated 20 September 1938, and personnel documents in ÖStA, BEA 58 and BEA 101.
36. ÖStA, BEA 7, letter from Heißmeyer dated 10 August 1938.
37. ÖStA, BEA 7, letter dated 1 October 1938; ÖStA, BEA 49, letter dated 4 September 1938. On BEA examination practice, see more generally ÖStA, BEA 47 and BEA 49.
38. ÖStA, BEA 172 (II), letter dated 25 October 1938 (cf. ÖStA, BEA 164, letter dated 9 December 1938); ÖStA, BEA 92, letter dated 26 January 1939 (cf. ÖStA, BEA 116, letter dated 2 February 1939). In addition, Heißmeyer and Calliebe had no qualms about dismissing staff whom they deemed unsuitable (even in the face of protest from outraged *Jungmannen*), or poaching likely candidates from schools elsewhere in Austria (cf. ÖStA, BEA 164, letters dated 31 May 1938, 20 July 1938, 28 September 1938; ÖStA, BEA 87, letter dated 24 September 1938; letter dated 2 November 1938).
39. ÖStA, BEA 52 contains relevant invitations, programmes, and press releases. See also 'Nationalpolitische Erziehungsanstalten in der Ostmark. Übernahme der österreichischen Staatserziehungsanstalten in Obhut des Reiches', *Völkischer Beobachter*, 14 March 1939 [BArch, R 8034-II/9296]; 'Unser Erziehungsziel: Wille und Ausdauer. Übernahme der österreichischen Staatserziehungsanstalten', *Völkischer Beobachter*, 14 March 1939 [BArch, NS 5/VI/18842].
40. ÖStA, BEA 25, letter from Plattner dated 24 October 1938; letter from Sowade dated 21 December 1938, which also mentions potential plans for a Napola on the Achensee; for further discussion of a purpose-built NPEA at the Faaker See, see Bundesarchiv

Lichterfelde (BArch), R 2/27771, Heißmeyer to Gauleiter Rainer, letter dated 17 February 1943. On plans to found an NPEA at Thumersbach, Zell am See, see e.g. ÖStA, BEA 7, 'Denkschrift zur Errichtung einer nationalpolitischen Erziehungsanstalt in Zell am See, Gau Salzburg', 21 January 1939 (the motivation behind the proposal included a desire to reduce Catholic influence in the Gau); for discussion of further potential sites, see BArch, R 2/27762, letter dated 10 May 1941 ('Unterkunft Nationalpolitischer Erziehungsanstalten in der Ostmark'); excerpt from travel report dated 12–22 November 1941; also BArch, R 2/12742, Sowade, 'Reisebericht', 17–21 March 1941; BArch, R 58/5764r.

41. BArch, R 2/27780, letter dated 9 October 1941.
42. On the varied uses of Burg Strechau, see e.g. BArch, R 2/12741, letters dated 26 September 1944, 12 November 1944; also ÖStA, BEA 49, letter dated 27 September 1938.
43. N.B. The Nazi authorities had deliberately renamed the town and the monastery complex 'Spanheim' after the noble dynasty which had founded the monastery, in order to erase the Christian connotations of 'St. Paul'. For a table of expropriation- and Napola foundation-dates for each of these schools, see Sebastian Pumberger, 'Führen und gehorchen. Die Nationalpolitischen Erziehungsanstalten in Österreich 1938–1945' (MA-thesis, Universität Wien, 2013), 119. On Lambach, see Johann Großruck, *Benediktinerstift Lambach im Dritten Reich 1938–1945. Ein Kloster im Fokus von Hitlermythos und Hakenkreuzlegende* (Linz, 2011); Franz Niedermair-Auer, 'Das Stift Lambach als Nationalpolitische Erziehungsanstalt. Arbeit aus Kirchengeschichte zur Erlangung des theologischen Diploms' (Linz, n.d.); the Führer had explicitly stated that he wished a Napola to be established there, rather than an Adolf-Hitler-School (cf. BArch, R 2/12737, Bormann to Reinhardt, letter dated 7 May 1941).
44. On the expropriations and expulsions, see Pumberger, 'Führen', 110–16; cf. BArch, R 5101/21735; BArch, R 5101/21736; also Peter Gretzel, *'Klostersturm' im Gau 'Niederdonau'. Die Geschicke des nicht enteigneten Zisterzienserstiftes Zwettl* (St. Pölten, 2017); Annette Mertens, *Himmlers Klostersturm. Der Angriff auf katholische Einrichtungen im Zweiten Weltkrieg und die Wiedergutmachung nach 1945* (Paderborn, 2006), 266–75.
45. BArch, R 2/12735, Heißmeyer to Reinhardt, letter dated 13 June 1940.
46. Landesarchiv Kärnten, Landesregierung Präsidium, Sch. 713, Reichsttatthalter Kärnten to Reichsinnenministerium, letter dated 23 January 1941, cited in Pumberger, 'Führen', 114.
47. BArch, R 2/12735, letter dated 25 March 1943.
48. On Vorau, see Ferdinand Hutz, 'Die Vorauer Stiftskirche als Hallenbad. Ein geplanter Umbau aus dem Jahre 1941', *Blätter für Heimatkunde* 71 (1997), 81–4; on Lambach, see BArch, R 2/27778, letter dated 27 April 1942, and correspondence following.
49. BArch, R 2/27772, letter from Dr. Ing. Kammler dated 28 November 1941, citing a plan by architect Christl.
50. BArch, R 2/12734, letter from Schikore dated 26 September 1941 (Reisebericht, 4 August 1941).
51. BArch, R 2/27762, letter dated 10 May 1941. For similar disagreements over the church at Seckau, see also BArch, R 2/12735; BArch, R 2/12742; BArch, R 2/27785.

52. BArch, R 2/12740, letter from Calliebe dated 15 October 1940; cf. Gerfried Sitar, 'Das Stift St. Paul unter der Herrschaft der Nationalsozialisten und der Wiederaufbau nach 1945. Mit einer Transkription der Tagebücher von P. Thiemo Raschl (STA St. Paul, P 567) und P. Hartwig Labi (STA St. Paul, P 563)' (Thesis, University of Salzburg, 2011).
53. Hans-Dieter Pfeiffer, ed., *Nationalpolitische Erziehungsanstalt Spanheim in Lavanttal, Kärnten, Österreich, 1941–1945. Persönliche Niederschriften als eine Brücke des Verstehens* (n.d.), 34, diary entry from 21 March 1943.
54. On the initial expropriation of the seminary, see BArch, R 2/12711, letter dated 10 November 1941; BArch, R 2/12738.
55. Günther Büttler (henceforward abbreviated as G.B.), 'Gesamtbericht über den Aufbau der NPEA. St. Veit/Sawe', 23 June 1944. See also G.B., 'Bericht über die Nationalpolitische Erziehungsanstalt in St. Veit', 16 February 1943, and 'Ereignisbericht für April 1944' for Büttler's plaints concerning the havoc which the Gauleiter's amnesties and politics of reconciliation had played with his supply of worker-prisoners. N.B. Political prisoners had also been used to supplement Croatian workers during the refurbishment of NPEA Mokritz; cf. BArch, R 2/27780.
56. On cooperation with the Gauleiter and local Party organizations, see Büttler's reports to Heißmeyer dated 20 November 1942, 23 June 1944, 19 July 1944, 25 July 1944, and 13 November 1944. On Gauleiter Rainer, see further Maurice Williams, *Gau, Volk and Reich: Friedrich Rainer and the Paradox of Austrian National Socialism* (Klagenfurt, 2005). For more on ethnic strife in the Slovenian borderlands, see Martin Moll, 'Der Reichsgau Steiermark 1938–1945', in Jürgen John, Horst Möller, and Thomas Schaarschmidt, eds, *Die NS-Gaue. Regionale Mittelinstanzen im zentralistischen 'Führerstaat'* (Munich, 2007), 364–77, 373.
57. G.B., 'Gesamtbericht', 8.
58. G.B., 'Musterung von Oberkrainer Slowenen und Ausleselehrgang in St. Veit', 19 July 1944.
59. G.B., 'Gesamtbericht', 11; for similar sentiments, see also G.B., 'Ansprache zur ersten Feierstunde in der Festhalle der NPEA. St. Veit', 8 November 1944; on the role played by such Germanizing ideology at the other Napola in present-day Slovenia, NPEA Mokritz, see also *Hauptzugführer* Henninger's report in the *Ilfelder Blätter*, 28. Kriegsheft (March 1943), [61–3].
60. Cf. reports to Heißmeyer dated 20 November 1942, 16 February 1943; also G.B., 'Familienbericht', December 1943.
61. G.B., 'Gesamtbericht'; further reports of school life at St. Veit by pupils and staff can be found in the *Ilfelder Blätter, Kriegshefte* 31 and 32.
62. G.B., 'Gesamtbericht', 10. For more on former pupils' perceptions of their encounters with partisan activity, see e.g. Kurt Jäger, 'Erinnerung an die Zeit in der Nationalpolitischen Erziehungsanstalt Spanheim—St. Paul in Lavanttal' (n.d.); Manfred F., private correspondence, 4 September 2011. On partisan problems in Mokritz, see also BArch, NS 19/2741, Bl. 55–6.
63. G.B., 'Ereignisbericht April 1944'; 'Ereignisbericht für Juni 1944'.
64. Cf. reports to Heißmeyer dated 2 October 1944, 9 November 1944.
65. G.B. to Heißmeyer, 9 November 1944.

66. G.B. to Heißmeyer, 9 November 1944; for a detailed description of the design of the stained-glass windows and their symbolism, see G.B., 'Ansprache'.
67. For a further example of this tendency in the schools' official ideology, see the leaflet 'Was will die Nationalpolitische Erziehungsanstalt Wien-Breitensee, was verlangt sie, was bietet sie?', which emphasizes the importance of extended trips to Carinthia and the southern Austrian borderlands for pupils' political education (a copy is reprinted in Pumberger, 'Führen', 31–2).
68. The only possible exception to this rule seems to have been the retention of more traditional Christmas festivities at some of the Austrian NPEA, including the *Niklausfeier* and *Krampusfest*—cf. e.g. Pfeiffer, *Spanheim*, 21, diary entry from 29 November 1942, and Hansjörg Weber, 'Auszüge aus meinem Tagebuch', diary entry from 14 December 1944; Water Knoglinger, *Stift Göttweig. Heimstätte einer 'Nationalpolitischen Erziehungsanstalt' in der Zeit von Jänner 1943 bis April 1945* (2000), 27–8; Helga Jörns, 'Mokritz—Praktikumsbericht, 1. Januar 1944', 5 January 1944.
69. Cf. Pumberger, 'Führen', 11.
70. Cf. e.g. Gerhard Botz, *Die Eingliederung Österreichs in das Deutsche Reich. Planung und Verwirklichung des politisch-administrativen Anschlusses (1938–1940)* (Vienna, 1972); Emmerich Tálos, *NS-Herrschaft in Österreich. Ein Handbuch* (Vienna, 2002); Steven Beller, *A Concise History of Austria* (Cambridge, 2006), 231–47.
71. Cf. Brigitte Lichtenberger-Fenz, '"Es läuft alles in geordneten Bahnen". Österreichs Hochschulen und Universitäten und das NS-Regime', in Tálos, *NS-Herrschaft*, 549–69. On Schön's illegal activities as a teacher at BEA Traiskirchen under the Austrofascist regime, see e.g. ÖStA, BEA 162, Bundes-Polizeidirektion in Wien to Präsidialbüro des Bundesministeriums für Unterricht, letter dated 14 July 1933; on Schön's alleged involvement with the Traiskirchen bomb plot, see also 'Die Schülerverhaftungen in der Bundeserziehungsanstalt Traiskirchen. Auch die Verhaftung von Professoren im Bereiche der Möglichkeit', *Wiener Allgemeine Zeitung*, 4 July 1933 [ÖStA, BEA 234].
72. Engelbrecht, *Geschichte*, 304–33; Dachs, *Schule und Politik*, 316; Dachs, 'Ostmark'.
73. Evan Burr Bukey, *Hitler's Austria: Popular Sentiment in the Nazi Era, 1938–1945* (Chapel Hill, 2000), 100–11.
74. Walter Sauer, 'Loyalität, Konkurrenz oder Widerstand? Nationalsozialistische Kultuspolitik und kirchliche Reaktionen in Österreich 1938–1945', in Tálos, *NS-Herrschaft*, 159–86, especially 167–73; cf. Engelbrecht, *Geschichte*, 307. From this perspective, it is also worth noting that many *Deutsche Heimschulen* were also founded in Austria from 1941 onwards—see further the Conclusion.
75. Bukey, *Hitler's Austria*, 227.

8

The *Reichsschulen* and the Napolas' Germanizing Mission in Eastern and Western Europe

On 10 October 1944, NPEA-Inspector August Heißmeyer wrote to the Reich Finance Minister with urgent concerns regarding the future financing of the increasingly transnational network of Napolas and *Reichsschulen* which had, by this point, been founded throughout the occupied territories which lay beyond the borders of the *Altreich*. The *Reichsschulen* (Imperial Schools) in the Netherlands and Flanders should, in the Inspector's view, henceforward be subsidized entirely via his own personal bureau in the SS Central Office (*SS-Hauptamt, Dienststelle SS-Obergruppenführer Heißmeyer*), since the schools which were soon to be founded in the Polish General Government, in Denmark, and in Norway, could all then be financed in a suitably unified fashion. In particular, Heißmeyer stressed that the development of these institutions must remain free of any threat of external interference: 'The political situation is different in all of the countries in question here, so that the tackling of this task cannot be carried out schematically, but must be adjusted to suit the state of affairs in each region.' He concluded his observations with the resounding claim that 'the work of these schools is really exclusively directed towards the safeguarding of our empire'.[1]

This communiqué reveals very acutely a number of elements which are of cardinal importance when considering the genesis and role of the Napolas and *Reichsschulen* which were established during World War II in the Eastern and Western occupied territories respectively.[2] First and foremost, these institutions were considered crucial, if not irreplaceable, to the Third Reich's Germanizing mission. As such, their aims and praxis both mirrored and directly contributed to broader Nazi occupation and Germanization policies in Eastern and Western Europe.[3] On the one hand, the schools in Holland, Flanders, and Luxembourg promoted a positive engagement with their 'Germanic' pupils, whose allegedly Aryan bloodline supposedly made them suitable guarantors of the future National Socialist 'Greater Germanic Reich'.[4] Had the schools which were planned in Norway, Denmark, and Switzerland ever got off the ground, these would have served the same function.[5] On the other hand, the schools in the Czech and

The Third Reich's Elite Schools: A History of the Napolas. Helen Roche, Oxford University Press. © Helen Roche 2021.
DOI: 10.1093/oso/9780198726128.003.0009

Polish occupied territories were far more preoccupied with 'rescuing' Eastern European children of supposedly 'ethnic German' (*volksdeutsch*) heritage, in order to 're-Germanize' them and incorporate them into the 'Greater German Reich' or *Volksgemeinschaft*.[6] Nor were these ambitions merely propagandistic; the Napola authorities and their counterparts in regional and local government, both East and West, appear to have genuinely believed in their institutions' capacity to instil the requisite imperial ambition and loyalty in their charges.[7] That the schools were also at least partially successful in this mission may be inferred from the number of graduands of the *Reichsschulen* and the Eastern Napolas who eagerly volunteered for the Waffen-SS—even if some were less than keen to be condemned to the pioneering life of an SS warrior-farmer somewhere beyond the Urals.[8]

Furthermore, it was this extreme preponderance of SS influence and tutelage which marked out the Eastern NPEA and the *Reichsschulen* most particularly—indeed, the *Reichsschulen* in the 'Germanic' lands were ultimately subordinated to Heißmeyer in his capacity as head of the SS Central Office (*SS-Hauptamt*), rather than in his role as Inspector of the NPEA, reporting to Bernhard Rust and the Reich Education Ministry.[9] Just as the Waffen-SS recruited 'Germanic' collaborators in the Western occupied territories and selected willing '*Volksdeutsche*' (ethnic Germans) in the conquered Eastern borderlands, in the hope of gaining broader political influence and creating a 'catalyst for an organic alignment of the Germanic countries and...the seed for a new Europe[, forming] the core of its elites and leaders',[10] the *Reichsschulen* and the Eastern Napolas also provided the SS with a means of gaining political control over the children of those whom they had conquered. Thus, the Third Reich's imperial SS legions now potentially possessed an ever-renewable source of fresh manpower which could fuel Himmler's insatiable ambition to secure yet further *Lebensraum* in the wild East, training future officers as loyal National Socialist cannon fodder from their earliest youth.

Indeed, this parallel between the imperial role of the Waffen-SS and the *Reichsschulen* was one which was made frequently, not only by Dutch critics of the regime and by the Nazi occupation authorities, but also by 'Germanic' collaborators and officials, as exemplified by this extract from the protocol of a meeting between NPEA representative Dr. Wilhelm Kemper and the Dutch collaborationist education tsar Robert van Genechten:

> In the SS, as at the NPEA, there are no Württembergers, Bavarians, Austrians, and Prussians, but solely Germans; yes, more than that, here, from one Germanic wellspring, *Jungmannen* live and grow together as the guarantors of Greater Germania. We feel ourselves to be the Führer's long Germanic arm, which trains and leads a Germanic youth in tried and tested collective education for the new

Europe. It is within this framework that I view the significance of the NPEA in the Netherlands.[11]

This chapter therefore explores the ways in which the various facets of the Third Reich's racist colonial project were mirrored at the level of Napola policy. In the West, Nazi imperial praxis was premised on the fundamental assumption of racial (quasi-)equality and 'Germanic' brotherhood. Meanwhile, in the East, the emphasis lay rather on 'saving' those ethnic Germans and Slavs who were deemed to possess suitably 'German' blood. The cases of the *Reichsschulen* and the Eastern NPEA will hence be used to parse and analyse the varying styles of colonization policy which shaped these two very different spheres of Nazi-occupied Europe.

In so doing, the chapter aims to compare and contrast the relevant aspects of National Socialist Eastern and Western Germanization policy *tout court*, treating the Napola project as a genuinely pan-European enterprise which deserves to be considered in a fully transnational context.[12] As Bernd Wegner has put it, 'Himmler regarded the integration of the "Germanic West" as a necessary complement to the subjugation of the Slavic East. Both goals were... two sides of the same coin.'[13] Arguably, NPEA policy in different areas of the 'Greater German Reich' mirrored the varying occupation strategies, attitudes towards conquered populations, and prevalent styles of rule in each region (whether these were determined by local Gauleiter, SS officials, or the Dutch Reich Commissariat).[14] And, while the Eastern Napolas and the *Reichsschulen* may only have made a symbolic contribution to swelling the ranks of dedicated National Socialists working towards the realization of an SS-led Greater-German or Greater-Germanic empire in numerical terms, the schools were still highly significant in exhibiting and putting into practice their political and racial aims, serving as a bellwether for further planned political, social, and educational reforms in the occupied territories more broadly.[15]

In this way, the NPEA in the occupied territories, even more than in Austria (see Chapter 7) represented what Hans-Christian Harten has termed an 'experimental site for the realization of the National Socialist utopia'.[16] This putative *tabula rasa* allowed SS and NPEA officials to dream of a Greater Germanic Reich led by dedicated graduates of the *Reichsschulen*, or of a version of the *Generalplan Ost* which gave pride of place to former Napola-pupils turned warrior-farmers, whatever costs this might impose upon those deemed to be racially 'less valuable'.[17]

The body of this chapter is therefore divided into three main sections. The first section explores the genesis and praxis of the *Reichsschulen* in the West, with a particular focus on the schools in the Netherlands, where Nazi and NPEA education policy was most fully developed.[18] The second section then turns eastwards to consider the Napolas' role in the conquered Czech and Polish lands.[19] Finally, the conclusion draws these two strands together, reflecting on the schools' function in the Third Reich's Eastern and Western Germanization programmes more generally, and the ways in which regional differences in policy were held in constant tension with broader Reich and SS centralization initiatives.

*

In July 1942, Heißmeyer's extensive plans to establish a transnational network of *Reichsschulen* were only just getting under way—a concerted power grab which brought him into severe conflict with SS-*Obergruppenführer* ('the Almighty') Gottlob Berger, his chief rival for Himmler's favour.[20] Berger was now Chief of the SS Central Office and head of the *Germanische Leitstelle*, a sub-department with particular responsibility for SS affairs in the Germanic lands, and thus he was extremely keen to include the *Reichsschulen* under his sway.[21]

Heißmeyer explained the reasoning behind the *Reichsschule* project as follows:

> The objective of the National Political Education Institutes is the safeguarding and consolidation of Adolf Hitler's Reich through the selection of the best German youth, and their education in an explicitly National Socialist stance. When Holland, Denmark, Norway, and Flanders were occupied, I immediately took in hand the expansion of the National Political Education Institutes in these territories also. These Germanic peoples must be tightly bound to the Germanic heartland—and that means Germany. I see the best opportunity of this if in these countries too, a selection of youth is carried out, and they in turn are educated and strengthened in the idea of the Reich. At that time, the task of developing the National Political Education Institutes in the Nordic lands was intended for the National Political Education Institute Plön, and National Political Education Institute Bensberg would be assigned the same task for Holland, Flanders, and Luxembourg, while Oranienstein would later be employed in Switzerland. I have had numerous discussions in Norway with Reich Commissioner Terboven, and in particular with SS-*Obergruppenführer* Redieß in this regard.[22]

The Inspector of the Napolas was far from the only official to be convinced of the importance of the *Reichsschulen* for the endeavour of Germanizing Western Europe, however. Arthur Seyß-Inquart, the Reich Commissioner of the Netherlands, was also fully supportive of Heißmeyer's ambitions:

> The connection with the Reich's National Political Education Institutes appears to me to be of particular importance. Otherwise we would be giving the Germanic countries a peculiar role model; that in the very first area in which we are beginning to work with Greater Germanic politics, we are incapable of creating or sustaining a unified organization for the entire Greater Germanic realm.[23]

If, as Johannes Koll has argued, the occupation authorities in the Netherlands were keen to cultivate a 'policy of the outstretched hand' (though it was nevertheless an iron hand in a silken glove), tolerating a certain amount of national self-sufficiency so long as the conquered population were prepared to exhibit a genuine commitment to National Socialism, then the *Reichsschulen* undoubtedly reflected this Janus-faced policy of ostensible imperial cooperation combined with forcible colonializing *Gleichsschaltung*.[24] The schools promised equality between the German and Dutch boys who were being educated alongside each other as *Jungmannen*, whilst still ultimately aiming to Germanize and indoctrinate their Dutch pupils. It is within this context that scholars have often deemed the *Reichsschulen* to be one of the most insidious and potentially dangerous means of Nazification in the Netherlands—as opposed to the rest of the Dutch education system, which largely retained its previous structure and administration.[25]

But how were the schools established in the first place? While the *Reichsschule* at Quatrecht in Flanders was directly funded by Himmler's *Germanische Leitstelle*, given the absence of a Reich Commissar in the territory, the Dutch *Reichsschulen* were funded by Seyß-Inquart's Reich Commissariat.[26] The wheels had been set in motion for the creation of Napolas in the Netherlands as early as autumn 1940, with the close cooperation of Seyß-Inquart, his immediate subordinate Friedrich Wimmer, General Commissar for Administration and Justice, and the Higher SS and Police Leader (HSSPF) for the Netherlands, Hanns Albin Rauter; the aim being to establish a school which would educate Dutch boys in the spirit of the NPEA.[27] The new collaborationist General Secretary in the Dutch Education Ministry, Professor Jan van Dam, then incorporated these ideas into his own plans for a '*Nederlandsche Instelling voor Volksche Opvoeding*' or NIVO (Dutch Institute for *Völkisch* Education). The names of promising Dutch *Erzieher* with National Socialist sympathies were put forward as potential members of staff, and six of these were then invited to spend two months at NPEA Bensberg and NPEA Oranienstein, so that they could get the requisite sense of the Napolas' ethos.[28] Van Dam announced the NIVO's founding on 12 August 1941, when he gave a widely reported speech on the radio defining the broader outlines of his new, Nazified educational programme.[29] The school opened on the same date at the former sanatorium in Koningsheide, which had previously been requisitioned by the Wehrmacht.[30]

However, the German occupation authorities very quickly came to consider the NIVO experiment as a mere stopgap; both Himmler and Seyß-Inquart were adamant that if the *Reichsschulen* were to succeed in their mission, they must under no circumstances continue under joint German and Dutch leadership; rather, they must become wholly 'schools of the Reich'.[31] Particular concerns were raised about the quality of the Dutch teachers—since the institution was financed by the Dutch government, German *Erzieher* could only be seconded to positions there, and the Dutch staff apparently resented their presence bitterly.[32] Seyß-Inquart was of the opinion that only around 50 per cent of the current staff could unproblematically be reassigned to the *Reichsschule*, and therefore recommended that the NIVO should be closed, and its pupils either transferred to the *Reichsschule* in due course, or sent home.[33] NPEA Bensberg, which had already taken on a mentoring role at Koningsheide, and had regularly exchanged classes with the NIVO, took on the relevant cohorts while the first *Reichsschule* at Valkenburg, near Maastricht, was still under construction. Classes of German boys from Bensberg then continued to make up the numbers at Valkenburg after the school opened in September 1942.[34]

In financial and practical terms, Seyß-Inquart was wholly supportive of Himmler and Heißmeyer's efforts to establish the *Reichsschule*, pledging 5 million Reichsmarks to assist with building costs, as well as undertaking to cover half of the annual running costs, which would come to approximately 500,000 RM per year.[35] Moreover, Seyß-Inquart was keen to facilitate the founding of two new Dutch NPEA in the near future: a second *Reichsschule* for boys in Soestdijk Palace, a former possession of the Dutch Royal Family, and a *Reichsschule* for girls in Heythuysen. Once again, the Reich Commissioner generously offered to pay half of the costs for these two schools also—coming to a grand total of 7–8 million RM out of the total 15 million RM projected expenditure over the next two to three years.[36] Although the local SS leaders were unsure whether it was desirable for the Reich Commissariat to be so extensively involved in the project, they were aware that if they attempted to curtail Seyß-Inquart's influence completely, there might be unfavourable consequences.[37] Thus, Seyß-Inquart was able to ensure that this Germanic prestige project bore his mark, whilst simultaneously strengthening his standing within the SS hierarchy.

The two Dutch *Reichsschulen* at Valkenburg and Heythuysen both appropriated sites belonging to Catholic religious orders—a familiar *modus operandi* for Heißmeyer and the Inspectorate (see Chapters 6 and 7); both campuses were requisitioned in July 1942. The Franciscan nuns who ran the St. Elisabeth girls' boarding school in Heythuysen were forced to leave the building within three days, while the Jesuits in charge of the St. Ignatius College in Valkenburg were given less than one and a half hours to leave the premises.[38]

In the end, only two of the original NIVO teachers were kept on at Valkenburg after the school's opening, and Himmler's express desire to have the Dutch boys educated alongside German *Jungmannen* in a ratio of 1:2 was impossible to realize in practice. The school began its life with fifty-seven Dutch pupils and sixty-six German pupils; a state of affairs which Kemper blamed on German parents' reluctance to send their sons to the *Reichsschule*, despite a concerted propaganda campaign via the German press in Holland.[39] At times, this dearth of German applicants appears to have led the authorities at NPEA Bensberg to send boys with poor academic records to Valkenburg, rather than expelling them *tout court*.[40] Nevertheless, Kemper's deputy, acting *Anstaltsleiter* Debusmann, was able to ensure that German remained the primary language of instruction at the *Reichsschule*, although the Dutch and German pupils had to have separate German classes. The girls at Heythuysen were taught in Dutch, but also underwent a year of intensive coaching (around ten hours a week) to improve their facility in the German language.[41]

The fortunes of the girls' school in Heythuysen, which opened its doors on 1 September 1942, appear to have been fundamentally shaped by the whims and pedagogical incompetence of its headmistress, Baroness Julia op ten Noort, who had no previous experience working in the education sector, nor any professional qualifications (save three years' secondary schooling at a *Gymnasium*).[42] Nevertheless, as one of the founding members of the Dutch National Socialist Movement's women's organization, the *Nationaal-Socialistische Vrouwenorganisatie* (NSVO), as an aficionado of Moral Rearmament, and an active member of the clique of Dutch fascists around Meinoud Marinus Rost van Tonningen, she had become a particular favourite of Himmler's.[43] As early as 1941, the *Reichsführer* had already earmarked her as the future headmistress of a putative NIVO for girls.[44] However, Op ten Noort's lack of experience, as well as problems with underqualified teachers, poor hygiene, and outbreaks of diphtheria, meant that the school was never fully able to realize its academic potential.[45] Tensions also ran high between Op ten Noort and Debusmann over which school could claim to be the best; apparently the teachers at Heythuysen styled their charges as 'diminutive goddesses', and generally behaved with offensive arrogance towards the boys from Valkenburg.[46]

However, Valkenburg was not immune from serious teething troubles either. The number of applications from Dutch families was extremely low, and many Dutch parents were unhappy not only with the lack of religious instruction at the *Reichsschule*, but also with German being the school's official language. Apparently this fact had gone (conveniently) unmentioned in the initial prospectus, so that many of the Dutch *Jungmannen* were faced with severe linguistic difficulties when they first arrived.[47] General Commissar Wimmer also complained that the Dutch staff were of thoroughly inferior quality, lacking in empathy and 'any sympathy for the soldierly mindset', while some of the German *Erzieher* similarly lacked understanding for the *Reichsschule*'s sense of *Volk*; in his view, the only true solution to this problem would be for all of the *Erzieher*, Dutch and German, to serve at the front together.[48] Furthermore, the racial selection of pupils had, in Wimmer's opinion, been based far too much on superficial physical criteria, rather than on a true assessment of the applicants' intellectual talents and capabilities.[49] Finally, to add insult to injury, the uniforms which had been ordered for the *Reichsschule* were simply too small, so that *Anstaltsleiter* Debusmann had to confess to the clothing manufacturers that 'we must conclude that the Dutch lad is consistently taller and broader than the German lads from whom the measurements of the uniform have been taken (*Jungmannen* from NPEA Bensberg)'.[50]

In general, pupils and staff had to contend with constant disruption from the Allied bombing campaign, with the resulting chaos, lack of heating, and deficient sanitation leading to an epidemic of scarlet fever, as well as giving rise to numerous opportunities for petty theft by the Dutch personnel. During the Christmas holidays in 1942, every easily removable object, including lightbulbs and door handles, apparently disappeared, while urine and faeces (allegedly belonging to the kitchen maids) were discovered on the floor of the building's third storey.[51] Tensions also arose between the Hitler Youth at the *Reichsschule* and the local branch of the Dutch fascist youth organization, the *Jeugdstorm*.[52] According to Debusmann and Kemper, the *Jeugdstorm*'s influence on the *Jungmannen* was potentially 'catastrophic', since the Dutch group merely promoted 'running riot, brawling, dancing, and cheap pop hits'.[53]

Nevertheless, life at Valkenburg seems to have settled on a fairly even keel by mid-1943, air raids notwithstanding. And, as accounts by pupils on an exchange visit from NPEA Ballenstedt show, the *Reichsschule*'s joint propaganda campaign with the Germanic SS in Leeuwarden and Groningen the following year also proved extremely efficacious:

> In the presence of the most high-ranking guests, including Reich Commissar Dr. Seyß-Inquart, the *Reichsschule* sings, speaks, and plays, and *Standartenführer* Feldmeier speaks on 'Youth and the Reich'. The influx of the population is vast, the biggest halls are only just sufficient for the thousands of people in the audience, and the success can be perceived by the applications to the *Reichsschule*. The editors of the Dutch newspapers seek the *Reichsschule* out and reinforce the idea of the Greater Germanic Reich in the public eye.[54]

This glowing account is borne out by Kemper's official report from 19 May 1944, which mentions that 1,300 spectators attended the demonstration in Leeuwarden, while 950 attended the event in Groningen. All visitors were given a copy of the school prospectus, while the *Jungmannen* sang propagandistic songs such as '*Germaniens junge Mannschaft*' ('Germania's Youthful Rank and File'), and chanted speech choirs with refrains such as 'We, the youth of the Netherlands, we, the youth of the German Reich, we proudly greet the Führer of all Germanic people'.[55] However, further demonstrations which were supposed to take place shortly thereafter in Amsterdam and The Hague had to be cancelled due to the D-Day landings.[56] By September 1944, the *Jungmannen* from Valkenburg had had to be evacuated to Bensberg, partially on foot, while only nine of the girls from Heythuysen, most of whom had recently returned from a holiday trip to Austria and were spending a few days at home with their parents, could be brought to safety in Reichenau (see Chapter 11).[57]

In sum, one might consider journalist Dr. P. H. Keuler's contention that the *Reichsschulen* had truly succeeded in their aim of eliminating differences between German and Dutch youth, and moulding them into future bearers of the Greater Germanic Reich, to be somewhat premature.[58] Nevertheless, scholars of Nazi occupation policy in the West have tended to agree on the potential Nazificatory power of the *Reichsschulen*—indeed, J. C. H. Pater has dubbed them one of the most dangerous institutions involved in the annexation of the Netherlands *tout court*.[59] By contrast, the significance of the Germanizing potential of the Napolas in the Eastern occupied territories—which performed an analogous, if complementary, function—has rarely been considered; scholars have largely been oblivious or indifferent to their role, perhaps because those *Volksdeutsche* who were specifically targeted for inclusion in the NPEA formed a lesser (and scarcely marginalized) proportion of the occupied population *in toto*.[60] In the service of comparison and contrast, then, it is to these institutions which we shall now turn.

*

It is not for nothing that Mark Mazower has termed the SS in the Eastern territories 'a motor of Germanization'.[61] Whether in his capacity as Reich Commissioner for the Strengthening of Germandom (RKfDV), through subsidiary bureaus such as the *Volksdeutsche Mittelstelle* (Ethnic German Liaison Office), or through the network of 'racial experts' employed by the SS Race and Resettlement Office (RuSHA), Himmler aimed to seek out two constituencies within local populations in particular, and win them back to the Reich.[62] Firstly, there were the *Volksdeutsche* or 'ethnic Germans', who were believed to possess largely German blood; secondly, there were those native Czechs, Poles, and members of other Eastern European nationalities who were supposedly 'racially sound' enough to be 'Germanizable' (*eindeutschungsfähig*).[63] These sectors of the population of Eastern Europe would then form the core of a new Greater German Reich based predominantly on racial criteria.[64]

In this constant battle to rescue 'racially valuable' elements within the conquered nations, the role of education was considered paramount. Those children who passed through the SS' process of 'racial sieving' would be educated and indoctrinated accordingly—in the most extreme cases, through kidnapping and forced relocation to German families and boarding schools.[65] Meanwhile, those children who were deemed racially 'unworthy' could expect to be condemned to an education so limited that they would only possess levels of literacy and numeracy sufficient to enable them to serve their German masters as enslaved helots.[66]

As Isabel Heinemann has noted, such policies (which were inextricably linked with longer-term plans for Slavic genocide) were deliberately aimed at children, 'in order to weaken what, according to Himmler's logic, were the "blood foundations" of the peoples under German occupation'.[67] Thus, in the Polish General Government, Himmler aimed to institute 'an annual sorting of all children... aged between 6 to 10 into those with good blood and those with valueless blood'; the former would be sent to Germany, where either their parents would accompany them and become loyal citizens of the state, or their children would be taken away from them.[68] The Eastern Napolas were therefore one more cog in this apparatus of effective Germanization—though arguably a crucial one, since they deliberately set out to estrange the most capable future leaders from their own peoples, putting their talents instead at the service of the Greater German Reich.[69] In a speech to SS-leaders given in Zhitomir on 16 September 1942, Himmler expressed this sentiment more forcefully, with reference to future plans for the Napola network to extend into occupied Ukraine:[70]

> Our task is to seek out what is racially valuable. We will take it to Germany, send it to a German school, and those who are even better qualified will come to a *Heimschule* or a Napola, so that the boy grows up from the beginning as a conscious bearer of his blood and as a conscious citizen of the greater Germanic Reich, and is not brought up as a Ukrainian national. No one need have any concerns that in carrying out this selection the SS might taint the blood of the German race.[71]

This, then, was the context within which the Napolas in the East came into being. As with Seyß-Inquart in the Netherlands, the local authorities, in the form of the Gauleiter, were extremely keen to cooperate with Heißmeyer and the Inspectorate, and to push for further NPEA to be established within their sphere of influence.[72] In fact, the Gauleiter and *Reichsstatthalter* of the Sudetenland, Konrad Henlein, had long been so intrigued by the work of the Napolas that in 1935 he had even sat in on classes at NPEA Plön incognito, and had maintained contact with the school's headmaster, Hermann Brunk, ever since.[73] In a preface to the second edition of the NPEA Sudetenland school newsletter, Henlein also declared that he would always dedicate his full attention to the Napola's development and triumphs.[74]

Founded in April 1939, NPEA Sudetenland in Ploschkowitz (Ploskovice) was the first non-German or Austrian Napola to be established, in Ploschkowitz Castle near Leitmeritz (Litoměřice), which had formerly been the property of the Czech Government. The focus of the school's Germanizing endeavours lay above all on the 'restoration' of Sudeten ethnic Germans to their supposedly rightful heritage. Indeed, August Hellmann, *Anstaltsleiter* at NPEA Naumburg (the *Stammanstalt* charged with mentoring the new Napola), was so committed to furthering this cause that he instituted a special class at Naumburg for those boys from the Sudetenland who were too old for the official entrance exam; lessons were taught in Czech by Sudeten-German *Erzieher* who were learning the ropes at Naumburg, who would then go on to teach at Ploschkowitz.[75] NPEA Sudetenland also made a point of having pupils work on the land in the Sudeten region, in order to instil in them a suitable connection with their native soil—indeed, during their 'harvest mission' in August 1940, *Jungmannen* from the Napola completed a total of 2,118 working days bringing in the harvest for local farmers.[76]

The first Eastern Napola to be founded in wartime, meanwhile, was NPEA Wartheland, which was located in Schloss Reisen (Rydzyna) near Lissa (Leszno). Formerly the property of the noble Sułkowski family, following the Great War, the palace had become a state boarding school run by the Polish provincial school board in Poznań.[77] Here, under Gauleiter Arthur Greiser's tutelage, the school aimed to educate the most promising ethnic German children not only from the Warthegau and Danzig-Westpreußen, but also from Upper Silesia and the General Government. However, among the *c.*110-strong group of boys aged 12–16 who comprised the school's first cohort, there could also be found the children of ethnic German resettlers who had been uprooted from the Baltic States, Volhynia, and elsewhere, and brought to the Warthegau between October 1939 and January 1940.[78] The school's brand of *Volkstumspolitik* was particularly bellicose; at times, at the *Anstaltsleiter*'s behest, *Jungmannen* even participated in the expulsion and forced resettlement of ethnic Poles who were living in the region.[79] The school authorities and Gauleiter Greiser were also keen to encourage families from the *Altreich* to send their sons to NPEA Wartheland, in the hope that they would then be inspired to settle and make their careers in the Eastern territories.[80]

NPEA Loben (Lubliniec), founded in April 1941 in a building which had formerly housed a school for deaf Polish children, saw recruiting in the Polish rump state as an important part of its mission too.[81] A report from *Deutschlanddienst* celebrating the school's foundation waxed lyrical about the life of the *Jungmannen* there, and their future potential for the Third Reich's Germanization project:

> Today, 'Bubi' and the 'Professor'—those are their nicknames—are still on the school bench, bickering with each other at their ballgames and creeping around through the former borderland forests of Upper Silesia in their cross-country war-games as Winnetou once did; who knows if in ten or fifteen years' time they may not be holding some leading position in political life? Or whether in the meantime the '*Jungmann*' will have become a Wehrmacht officer or a warrior-farmer, and important manoeuvres will have replaced the war-game? At any rate, the world lies wider open to these lads here... than to any youth before them.[82]

However, former pupils could testify that the attrition rates at NPEA Loben were extremely high; of the seventy successful candidates (out of 350 applicants) who were selected to form *Zug* 3 and *Zug* 4, only thirty-five remained after the probationary first six months (*Probehalbjahr*).[83] From this perspective, it scarcely helped matters that the class from Naumburg which had been assigned to help the new pupils settle in to life at the Napola considered them to be 'barbarians from the East', who self-evidently needed to be exposed to all of the drills and hazing which the former cadet school particularly favoured, in order to be fully 'confronted with German culture'.[84]

Meanwhile, presumably not wishing to be outdone by his fellow Nazi satraps, Governor General Hans Frank was immediately willing to cooperate with Heißmeyer's suggestion, made only a couple of weeks after Loben's opening, that the General Government should be furnished with an NPEA of its own—the suggested 'object' in this instance being the secondary school in Zakopane. Frank instructed his subordinate, *Hofrat* Adolf Watzke (the former chief of the Central

Directorate of the Austrian *Bundeserziehungsanstalten*, who was now serving as one of the heads of the General Government's education department), to get in touch with Heißmeyer directly in order to hasten the building's procurement.[85]

As Michal Šimůnek has amply demonstrated, Karl Hermann Frank (whose own son attended NPEA Sudetenland) was also equally keen to kick-start the establishment of a number of NPEA in his own sphere of influence, the Protectorate of Bohemia and Moravia.[86] The first potential location, Iglau (Jihlava), suggested in May 1939, was favoured in part because of the consolidating effect which this would have on the ethnic German population in this German 'language island' (*Sprachinsel*).[87] This strategy appears to have been part of a conscious effort by the Inspectorate and the local authorities to use the Napolas as tools in their policy of forming German-speaking 'land-bridges' (*Landbrücken*) across the Czech lands, which would gradually be broadened and extended until the Protectorate had become 'fully German'.[88] However, due to the difficulty of finding a suitable property to appropriate (since the Order Police had already managed to secure the former lunatic asylum in Iglau), it was eventually an Adolf-Hitler-School which had the dubious honour of making its mark upon the area, rather than an NPEA.[89]

The scheme to open NPEA Moravia in the former seminary in Brünn (Brno) also foundered due to escalating building costs; nevertheless, the Lobkowicz family residence at Raudnitz (Roudnice na Labem) was considered suitable by the Inspectorate, and was later opened as a 'branch' of NPEA Sudetenland. Getting permission for the use of this building had caused significant difficulties, however, for although Karl Hermann Frank and Heißmeyer both favoured the establishment of a Napola, Reich Protector Konstantin von Neurath wished to turn the residence into a 'Baroque Museum' which could showcase the substantial—and highly valuable—Lobkowicz collections. From this perspective, Heißmeyer's task was eased considerably with the advent of Reinhard Heydrich as von Neurath's successor in September 1941, since Heydrich was happy to treat the establishment of new Napolas as a priority, and presumably agreed with the Inspector's own estimation of the schools' 'beautiful political task'.[90]

Indeed, at this point, the unholy trinity of Himmler, Heydrich, and Heißmeyer seem to have been collaborating very closely in order to realize a shared vision of the Napolas' role in the Protectorate—Himmler envisaged that, eventually, two NPEA for boys and one for girls would also be established, which would mainly take children from the *Altreich*, whilst 'racially suitable' Bohemian, Moravian, and *volksdeutsch* children from the Protectorate would be educated at Napolas in Germany in their stead.[91] Although this wholesale Germanization programme was never fully realized, with the first intake of 'racially suitable' Czech boys being scheduled for September 1945,[92] it may be significant that the initial selection of pupils for NPEA Bohemia in Kuttenberg (which, despite Heißmeyer's best efforts during the preceding years, only opened in 1944) contained only pupils from the

Sudetenland (67 per cent) and the *Altreich* (33 per cent), but none from the Protectorate itself.[93]

In the early 1940s, Himmler had even envisaged that the NPEA should extend their reach into Slovakia; a first phase was suggested in June 1941—alongside other measures which would help to ensure Nazi control over the Slovakian puppet state—in which one hundred Slovakian boys and fifty Slovakian girls would be sent to Napolas in Germany.[94] In January 1942, SS-*Obergruppenführer* Werner Lorenz of the *Volksdeutsche Mittelstelle* then became heavily involved in plans for the establishment of an NPEA for Slovakian *Volksdeutsche* in Bojnice Castle. However, the final decision on whether to go ahead with the idea was shelved until after the war, since it was doubted whether enough 'suitable' pupils could currently be found to fill an entire school. Himmler seems to have been the driving force behind both suggestions; the very real nature of his desire to see a Slovakian NPEA in action may be inferred by the number of times that he requested an update on the current state of affairs between February 1942 and April 1943.[95]

*

While the exhaustive process of racial selection of supposedly ethnically irreproachable human 'material' for the Napolas had always been deemed crucial even for children from the *Altreich*, in the Eastern territories, this process took on a new and wholly sinister tenor—the selection was now merely part of a whole raft of racial measures which, at their most inhumane, could include the kidnapping of thousands of children whose blood was deemed sufficiently 'valuable'.[96] And, just as organizations such as the Waffen-SS and the Polish paramilitary *Sonderdienst* (Special Service) deliberately aimed to recruit the racial and ideological 'cream' of the ethnic German population of Eastern Europe, in order to 'recapture' German blood and bind the scattered ethnic German inhabitants to the fortunes of their Nazi rulers, instilling them with the requisite 'racial consciousness', the Napolas also formed a key component in Himmler's concerted attempts to return erring *Volksdeutsche* to Germandom.[97]

In a sense, then, the Napola selection process can be seen as the peak of the pyramid of all of the 'racial sieving' processes which ethnic Germans, Czechs, and Poles had to undergo at the Nazi state's behest—inextricably bound up with the Third Reich's wider race, resettlement, and extermination policies. Thus, the Napolas in the Eastern territories were part of the other side of the coin of the Nazi programme of '*Säuberung*' or ethnic cleansing; privileging mechanisms of racial inclusion rather than exclusion.[98] In so doing, they also represented a genuine attempt to mitigate the ever-present tensions between *Reichsdeutsche* and *Volksdeutsche*—even if, in practice, the Napolas sometimes fell short of the ideal (as when *Jungmannen* from Naumburg treated the ethnic German pupils at Loben as lesser breeds without the law). However, in theory, Himmler and the

Napola authorities genuinely desired that the most 'valuable' *volksdeutsch* pupils should go on to become future leaders of the Greater German Reich, on a par with their *Reichsdeutsch* counterparts—even if it was envisaged that their careers would largely be forged in the Eastern marches of the Nazi empire.[99]

So, what comparative conclusions can we draw from this analysis? Scholars such as Gerhard Hirschfeld and Konrad Kwiet have tended to draw stark contrasts between the extremely harsh measures undertaken by the Nazi imperial administration in the colonized 'settlement territories' in the East, and the more lenient and accommodating treatment of the 'Germanic' populations of the West.[100] While this distinction can indeed be fully justified, given the far more extreme levels of violence directed at those elements of the populations of Eastern Europe which were deemed 'racially inferior', there are certain similarities on the level of Germanization policy at the Napolas and *Reichsschulen* which may usefully be noted here.

Firstly, although the Eastern NPEA and the *Reichsschulen* were aiming, on the one hand, to unite Germandom (*Deutschtum*) into a Greater *German* Reich and, on the other, to forge a Greater *Germanic* Reich, the boundaries between these two imperial conceptions were inherently fluid in practice, given that graduates of the *Reichsschulen* would also have been expected to play their part in the Germanization and resettlement of Eastern Europe. Secondly, while it is true that the various nations within this putative empire operated within a hierarchy of racial esteem, with the 'Germanic' inhabitants of the Dutch and Flemish nations at one end of the spectrum, gradating down through Czechs and Poles to Baltic and, eventually, Ukrainian or Russian 'ethnic Germans', the authorities' interest in the Germanization of potential Napola candidates of all nationalities seems to have been genuine. In fact, *more* sympathy appears to have been extended to *Jungmannen* from the Eastern territories who struggled with linguistic competence in German due to enforced estrangement from their cultural heritage, than to the 'Germanic' *Jungmannen* of the Netherlands, who were ostensibly expected to gain instant fluency through some form of racially tinted osmosis.[101]

We also find similar initiatives for expediting the Germanization process by mingling Reich German and ethnic German or Germanic *Jungmannen*, educating the two groups alongside each other, with the ultimate aim of creating a unified cohort of future leaders of a Nazi empire spanning the European continent in its entirety, all moulded into fanatical bearers of a truly National Socialist attitude. From this perspective, once again, we can see the obsession with homogenizing *Jungmannen* of all backgrounds into a unified political fighting force as representative not only of broader centralization aims within the SS, but also of more fundamental de-regionalization initiatives which had long lain at the heart of Napola policy even in the *Altreich* (see Chapter 5)—aiming to secure the ultimate triumph of the centre over the periphery.

In sum, then, the inextricable entanglement of educational and racial policy which we find here fundamentally reflects broader patterns of Germanization policy in each region. Despite the varying nature of collaboration with authorities on the ground, and the very different conditions of occupation in Eastern and Western Europe, the Inspectorate's programme followed a unified pattern which was then shaped to fit local circumstances, as Heißmeyer had envisaged—in line with broader SS racial and imperial policy. The differences which did then emerge were largely due to the differing nature of the populations in the regions in question, and, in particular, the varying positions which those populations occupied within the Nazi racial hierarchy of empire.

Notes

1. Bundesarchiv Lichterfelde (BArch), R 2/12767, Heißmeyer to Graf Schwerin von Krosigk, letter dated 10 January 1944. Heißmeyer had been planning this strategy for over a year, as part of a broader pattern of educational empire-building; see also NIOD Institute for War, Holocaust and Genocide Studies Archives, Amsterdam (NIOD), 020 586, Kemper, 'Führung der Reichsschulen, Besprechung mit Obergrüppenführer Heißmeyer am 21.8.', 25 August 1943: '[It is necessary] not to isolate the *Reichsschulen* in the Netherlands from the NPEA in the core of Germany and Alsace, Luxembourg etc., further that the *Reichsschulen* in the Netherlands, Flanders, Norway, Denmark etc. and the *Heimschulen* in the Reich, in the General Government, in the occupied territories etc., and the schools for ethnic Germans in the Reich, in Slovakia, in Transylvania, in the Balkans etc., must be led from *one* central SS bureau.' N.B. I am extremely grateful to Nathaniël Kunkeler for acting as my research assistant and obtaining material for this chapter from the relevant Dutch archives.
2. On Himmler's deliberate choice of the name '*Reichsschulen*' (rather than NPEA) for the schools established in the 'Germanic' lands, in recognition of their avowed aim to mould their Dutch, Flemish, and Luxembourgish pupils into 'forceful and unquestioning supporters of the idea of the Reich', see BArch, R 43-II/956b, Bl. 111. Apparently, the *Reichsführer* had also extracted an order from Hitler that no other institutions should now be permitted to bear the title '*Reichsschule*'; however, due to the extensive amount of bureaucratic upheaval and expense which would have been necessary to effect this measure in wartime, including the creation of new signs, letterheads, stamps, etc. for the many other institutions which currently bore this title, the Chancellery vetoed this suggestion, citing the Führer's previous order on 'Administrative Simplification' (*Vereinfachung der Verwaltung*) dated 25 January 1942 (Bl. 112–13; see further BArch, NS 19/1563).
3. For a general overview of Nazi imperial policy, see Mark Mazower, *Hitler's Empire: Nazi Rule in Occupied Europe* (London, 2008); also Shelley Baranowski, *Nazi Empire: German Colonialism and Imperialism from Bismarck to Hitler* (Cambridge, 2011), 233–95.

4. See Isabel Gallin, 'Machtstrukturen im Reichskommissariat Niederlande', in Robert Bohn, ed., *Die deutsche Herrschaft in den 'germanischen' Ländern 1940–1945* (Stuttgart, 1997), 145–57, for more on such ideas of 'racial brotherhood'; also Konrad Kwiet, *Reichskommissariat Niederlande. Versuch und Scheitern nationalsozialistischer Neuordnung* (Stuttgart, 1968), 152.
5. Cf. BArch, NS 19/2741, Bl. 28–30 (Heißmeyer to Berger, letter dated 24 July 1942).
6. For more on Nazi Germanization policies in the East, see e.g. Doris Bergen, 'The "Volksdeutschen" of Eastern Europe, World War II and the Holocaust: Constructed Ethnicity, Real Genocide', *Yearbook of European Studies* 13 (1999), 70–93; Elizabeth Harvey, *Women and the Nazi East: Agents and Witnesses of Germanization* (New Haven, 2003); Markus Leniger, *Nationalsozialistische 'Volkstumsarbeit' und Umsiedlungspolitik 1933–1945. Von der Minderheitenbetreuung zur Siedlerauslese* (Berlin, 2006); Jerzy Kochanowski and Maike Sach, eds, *Die Volksdeutschen in Polen, Frankreich, Ungarn und der Tschechoslowakei. Mythos und Realität* (Osnabrück, 2006); Tara Zahra, *Kidnapped Souls: National Indifference and the Battle for Children in the Bohemian Lands, 1900–1948* (Ithaca, 2008), 169–251; Andreas Strippel, *NS-Volkstumspolitik und die Neuordnung Europas. Rassenpolitische Selektion der Einwandererzentralstelle des Chefs der Sicherheitspolizei und des SD 1939–1945* (Paderborn, 2011); Alexa Stiller, 'On the Margins of the *Volksgemeinschaft*: Criteria for Belonging to the Volk within the Nazi Germanization Policy in the Annexed Territories, 1939–1945', in Claus-Christian W. Szejnmann and Maiken Umbach, eds, *Heimat, Region and Empire. Spatial Identities under National Socialism* (Basingstoke, 2012), 235–51; Gerhard Wolf, *Ideologie und Herrschaftsrationalität. Nationalsozialistische Germanisierungspolitik in Polen* (Hamburg, 2012); Detlef Brandes, *'Umvolkung, Umsiedlung, rassische Bestandsaufnahme'. NS-'Volkstumspolitik' in den böhmischen Ländern* (Munich, 2012).
7. From this perspective, at least as far as the *Reichsschulen* are concerned, we might go so far as to qualify Dietrich Orlow's contention that the Nazi 'conquerors' had no interest in treating the occupied Dutch and Flemish populations as partners in any meaningful sense; cf. Dietrich Orlow, *The Lure of Fascism in Western Europe: German Nazis, Dutch and French Fascists, 1933–1939* (Basingstoke, 2009), 153.
8. Cf. e.g. NIOD, 020 586, Kemper, 'Bericht zu dem Erlass vom 30.9.1942, der am 17.10. einging', 17 October 1942, 10: 'When the older *Jungmannen* are already naming their hard and fast career choices as: Waffen-SS leader; Luftwaffe officer; engineer in the East; farmer in the Ukraine, then this shows that the *Reichsschule* is... on the right track, and that here a germ cell is growing which will one day prove its worth in consolidating the idea of the Greater Germanic Reich'; see also the statistics on the military career choices of graduating *Jungmannen* from NPEA Sudetenland (*Notabitur* 1942/43) in Bruno Treitl, ed., *Ploschkowitz: NPEA 'Sudetenland' 1939–1943* (n.d.), 27, which show that a plurality (42 per cent) chose the Waffen-SS over any other branch of the armed forces (the next most popular branch was the Luftwaffe, with 24 per cent). For a former pupil who professed a marked disinclination towards the apparent expectation that graduates of NPEA in the Eastern territories would pursue an SS-warrior-farmer lifestyle, see Rüdiger Bauer, *Wie und warum wir so waren? Erinnerungen an Damals—Schicksalsjahre 1925–1945* (Gelnhausen, 2009), 57.
9. Cf. BArch, NS 19/2741, Bl. 39, Heißmeyer to Himmler, letter dated 5 September 1942.

10. Martin R. Gutmann, *Building a Nazi Europe: The SS's Germanic Volunteers* (Cambridge, 2017), 4; cf. Claus Bundgård Christensen, Niels Bo Poulsen, and Peter Scharff Smith, 'Germanic Volunteers from Northern Europe', in Jochen Böhler and Robert Gerwarth, eds, *The Waffen SS: A European History* (Oxford, 2017), 42–75, 44; also Bernd Wegner, *The Waffen-SS: Organisation, Ideology and Function* (Oxford, 1990); Jan Erik Schulte, Peter Lieb, and Bernd Wegner, eds, *Die Waffen-SS. Neue Forschungen* (Paderborn, 2014); Jochen Böhler and Robert Gerwarth, 'Non-Germans in the Waffen-SS: An Introduction', in Böhler and Gerwarth, *Waffen-SS*, 1–15.
11. NIOD, 020 431, Kemper, 'Abschrift [Besprechung mit van Genechten]', 12 February 1942, 4; cf. also NIOD, 020 586, 'Abschrift eines Berichtes von Zugführer Debusmann' (report on visit by Henk Feldmeyer, 31 March 1944). On ideas of the Greater Germanic Reich in Holland, see N.K.C.A. In't Veld, ed., *De SS en Nederland. Documenten uit SS-archieven 1935–1942* ('s-Gravenhage, 1976), Vol. 2, 1508; Kwiet, *Reichskommissariat Niederlande*, 9; Gerhard Hirschfeld, *Nazi Rule and Dutch Collaboration: The Netherlands under German Occupation 1940–1945* (Oxford, 1988), 18–19; also more generally Paul Kluke, 'Nationalsozialistische Europaideologie', *Vierteljahrshefte für Zeitgeschichte* 3, no. 3 (1955), 240–75; Hans-Dietrich Loock, 'Zur "Großgermanischen Politik" des Dritten Reiches', *Vierteljahrshefte für Zeitgeschichte* 8, no. 1 (1960), 37–63; Jürgen Elvert, *Mitteleuropa! Deutsche Pläne zur europäischen Neuordnung (1918–1945)* (Stuttgart, 1999); Birgit Kletzin, *Europa aus Rasse und Raum. Die nationalsozialistische Idee der neuen Ordnung* (Münster, 2002); Hans-Christian Harten, *Himmlers Lehrer. Die Weltanschauliche Schulung in der SS 1933–1945* (Paderborn, 2014); Benjamin Martin, *The Nazi-Fascist New Order for European Culture* (Cambridge, MA, 2016).
12. See Böhler and Gerwarth, 'Introduction', 4, for similar recent approaches to researching the Waffen-SS in transnational context.
13. Wegner, *Waffen-SS*, 337–8.
14. For example, the defining influence of Gauleiter Arthur Greiser, who instituted very specific measures of racial categorization in the service of Germanizing the inhabitants of his Gau, Wartheland, in the form of the *Deutsche Volksliste* (DVL/German People's List), is apparent from the fact that the entrance requirements for NPEA Wartheland were calibrated to include DVL criteria—cf. Brandenburgisches Landeshauptarchiv, Rep. 32A Nr. 96, Bl. 11, 'Merkblatt für die Aufnahme in die Nationalpolitische Erziehungsanstalt Wartheland (Schloß Reisen und Schloß Wollstein)'; for more on Greiser's efforts to turn the Wartheland into a '*Mustergau*' (model Gau), see Catherine Epstein, *Model Nazi: Arthur Greiser and the Occupation of Western Poland* (Oxford, 2010).
15. See Brandes, *NS-'Volkstumspolitik'*, 53; Georg Hansen, 'Schulpolitik im besetzten Polen 1939–1945', *bildungsforschung* 3, no. 1 (2006); David Barnouw, *Van NIVO tot Reichsschule. Nationaal-socialistische onderwijsinstellingen in Nederland* ('s-Gravenhage, 1981), 19; Johannes Koll, *Arthur Seyß-Inquart und die deutsche Besatzungspolitik in den Niederlanden (1940–1945)* (Vienna, 2015), 509–14, for discussion of broader education policy in Czechoslovakia, Poland, and Holland respectively.
16. Harten is speaking here primarily of the Polish context, but I would argue that the term can be applied more broadly: Hans-Christian Harten, *De-Kulturation und Germanisierung. Die nationalsozialistische Rassen- und Erziehungspolitik in Polen*

1939–1945 (Frankfurt am Main, 1996), 8. Interestingly, Hirschfeld expresses a somewhat similar sentiment with regard to the Netherlands (*Nazi Rule*, 18): 'The Reich Commissariat was an interregnum between military occupation…and *völkisch* Utopia.'

17. See Gutmann, *Nazi Europe*, 205, on the need to take Nazi plans for a Greater Germanic Europe seriously.
18. For the purposes of this analysis, I will not be treating the NPEA/*Reichsschule für Volksdeutsche* (Reich Schools for Ethnic Germans) at Rufach and Achern, since the type of education offered there was not identical to that of the Dutch and Flemish *Reichsschulen*, and the ethnic German pupils accepted there hailed almost exclusively from the South Tirol. However, it is worth noting that the schools' deliberate engagement with South Tiroleans who had chosen to 'return to the Reich' (following the German-Italian option agreement in 1939) represents yet another aspect of the Third Reich's foreign policy which both mirrored and was fostered by the NPEA Germanization programme. For detailed information on the schools' praxis, see the relevant school newsletters; on education at the *NPEA für Mädchen* at Achern and Colmar-Berg, Luxembourg, see also the following chapter.
19. Elsewhere, I have covered themes relating to the Eastern NPEA in greater detail, namely, in my article entitled '*Herrschaft durch Schulung*: The *Nationalpolitische Erziehungsanstalten im Osten* and the Third Reich's Germanising Mission', in Burkhard Olschowsky and Ingo Loose, eds, *Nationalsozialismus und Regionalbewusstsein im östlichen Europa: Ideologie, Machtausbau, Beharrung* (Berlin, 2016), 127–51. In this chapter, I will therefore primarily draw on material *not* covered in the aforementioned publication; readers are encouraged to consult the article for a fuller and more extensive account.
20. On Berger's background, including his nickname, 'the Almighty Gottlob', see Gutmann, *Nazi Europe*, 32.
21. On the resulting battle of wills, including Berger's repeated attempts to gain control of the *Reichsschulen* for his own ends by badmouthing Heißmeyer to the *Reichsführer*, and calling the Inspector's loyalty to the SS into question, see BArch, NS 19/2741, especially Bl. 26–30, 36, 39, 47–8 (as well as Chapter 1).
22. BArch, NS 19/2741, Bl. 28 (Heißmeyer to Berger, letter dated 24 July 1942).
23. NIOD, 020 586, Seyß-Inquart to Wimmer, letter dated 17 May 1943. Seyß-Inquart took Heißmeyer's side in the quarrel with Berger, as the remainder of the letter makes clear.
24. Cf. Koll, *Seyß-Inquart*, 195–8, 202, 204–8, 525–6.
25. E.g. J. C. H. Pater, *Notities voor het Geschiedwerk—Valkenburg* (NIOD, 785 148), 118; Barnouw, *Reichsschule*, 57; Veld, *SS en Nederland*, Vol. 1, 143–5; on the Nazification of the education system more generally, see Koll, *Seyß-Inquart*, 509–14. Koll also uses the establishment of the *Reichsschulen* as a case study of the Reich Commissar's canny ability to harness the colonial ambitions of the SS in order to extend and enhance his own sphere of influence (*Seyß-Inquart*, 146ff.).
26. BArch, NS 19/2741, Bl. 50 (Heißmeyer to Kemper, letter dated 5 December 1942); BArch, R 2/12767, Heißmeyer to Kluge, letter dated 8 May 1944. Plans to start financing the Dutch *Reichsschulen* through the *Germanische Leitstelle* in addition ground to a halt due to war-related shortages of personnel; cf. Veld, *SS en Nederland*, Vol. 2,

Documents 114, 468, 515, 528; NIOD, 020 586, letter from Rauter dated 18 August 1943, and accompanying remarks by Kemper. For more on the role of the *Germanische Leitstelle* more generally, see Harten, *Himmlers Lehrer*, 351–409; Gutmann, *Nazi Europe*, 42–7. The school in Quatrecht will not be considered in detail here; for more information, see e.g. 'Eine Reichsschule in Flandern. Nach dem Vorbild der Nationalpolitischen Erziehungsanstalten in Deutschland', *Brüsseler Zeitung*, 18 April 1943 [BArch, R 4902/1490]; Niedersächsisches Landesarchiv—Hauptstaatsarchiv Hannover (NLA-HStAH), Hann. 180 Lüneburg Acc. 3/88 Nr. 26, letters dated 27 March 1944, 1 May 1944; Niedersächsisches Landesarchiv—Staatsarchiv Oldenburg, Best. 134 Nr. 2353, Bl. 175–90, *Reichsschule Flandern* (undated prospectus). Unlike the *Jungmannen* at the *Reichsschule* in Valkenburg, the Flemish boys appear to have been taught in the Dutch language. For more on Nazi occupation policy in Flanders in general, see Werner Warmbrunn, *The German Occupation of Belgium, 1940–1944* (New York, 1993).

27. BArch, NS 19/2741, Bl. 29 (Heißmeyer to Berger, letter dated 24 July 1942); NIOD, 020 586, Jacobs, 'Zusammenfassender Bericht über meine Tätigkeit beim Reichskommissar für die besetzten niederländischen Gebiete, Hauptabteilung Erziehung und Kirchen, vom 29.7. bis 30.11.1941', 30 November 1941, 2.
28. Jacobs, 'Bericht', 1–2.
29. Jacobs, 'Bericht', 6–7; cf. Nationaal Archief Den Haag, O&W/Kabinet, 1940–5 (2.14.37) 00598, Bl. 2–9.
30. Barnouw, *Reichsschule*, 24.
31. BArch, NS 19/1558, Bl. 29 (Himmler to Seyß-Inquart, letter dated 5 March 1942); Bl. 32 (Seyß-Inquart to Himmler, letter dated 16 March 1942).
32. Jacobs, 'Bericht', 8–9; Barnouw, *Reichsschule*, 26. Memoranda detailing the content of discussions between SS-*Hauptsturmführer* Kemper and van Genechten which took place on 12 and 20 February 1942 (NIOD, 020 431) also reveal deep-running tensions over whether the NIVO should be run by German or Dutch staff, and what the primary language of instruction should be—reinforcing the decision that the NIVO was ultimately an untenable vehicle for furthering Himmler and Heißmeyer's interests.
33. BArch, NS 19/1558, Bl. 32 (Seyß-Inquart to Himmler, letter dated 16 March 1942).
34. On Bensberg's long-established relationship with Flanders and Holland, especially through the school's frequent trips and industrial missions to Eupen-Malmedy, see e.g. *Rundbrief der NPEA Bensberg*, 12. Kriegsfolge (15 December 1941). On tensions which later arose between Bensberg pupils and Dutch pupils at Vineta, see e.g. Arne Heinich, *'Niemand entgeht seiner Zeit': Erziehung, Lernen und Leben in der Nationalpolitischen Erziehungsanstalt (Napola) Bensberg bei Köln. September 1942 bis April 1945* (Norderstedt, 2007), 148.
35. BArch, NS 19/1558, 'Dienstreise Den Haag, 29. März 1942—31. März 1942)', report to Himmler dated 31 March 1942, Bl. 2–3; Bl. 33 (Seyß-Inquart to Himmler, letter dated 16 March 1942).
36. BArch, NS 19/1558, Bl. 32–4 (Seyß-Inquart to Himmler, letter dated 16 March 1942).
37. Cf. Koll, *Seyß-Inquart*, 158, citing HSSPF Rauter.
38. Koll, *Seyß-Inquart*, 162; cf. Gerd Siegel, *Wechselvolle Vergangenheit* (Göttingen, 1980), 134, for the perspective of an *Erzieher* with anti-Catholic tendencies. On nuns habitually

being treated slightly better than monks and priests during the eviction process, see Annette Mertens, *Himmlers Klostersturm. Der Angriff auf katholische Einrichtungen im Zweiten Weltkrieg und die Wiedergutmachung nach 1945* (Paderborn, 2006).

39. Kemper, 'Bericht', 3–4; Pater, *Valkenburg*, 36–7. Promotional materials for the *Reichsschule* Quatrecht went one step further, attempting to convince parents that the number one reason they should send their sons to Flanders was because their education would then no longer be disrupted by evacuations and air raids. Training for 'the European mission of the German people' only came in at second place (NLA-HStAH, letter to *Schulräte* dated 1 May 1944).
40. See the relevant correspondence in Landesarchiv Nordrhein-Westfalen, Abteilung Rheinland, Duisburg, RW 0023 Nr. 279, RW 0023 Nr. 281, RW 0023 Nr. 282.
41. Kemper, 'Bericht', 5. On life and the curriculum at the girls' Napolas more generally, see Chapter 9; also Stefanie Jodda-Flintrop, *'Wir sollten intelligente Mütter werden'. Nationalpolitische Erziehungsanstalten für Mädchen* (Norderstedt, 2010).
42. J. C. H. Pater, *Notities voor het Geschiedwerk—Heythuysen* (NIOD, 785 149), 3; cf. BArch, NS 19/1556, Bl. 1.
43. Barnouw, *Reichsschule*, 48–9. Rumours that the illegitimate son whom Op ten Noort bore in early 1944 was in fact Himmler's own child have never been substantiated, despite his being named 'Heinrich' (cf. BArch, NS 19/795).
44. Barnouw, *Reichsschule*, 49.
45. Barnouw, *Reichsschule*, 52.
46. Barnouw, *Reichsschule*, 55.
47. Barnouw, *Reichsschule*, 30.
48. NIOD, 020 586, Wimmer, 'Bericht über die Reichsschule Valkenburg', 23 July 1943.
49. Wimmer, 'Bericht'.
50. NIOD, 088 386, Debusmann to the clothing firm Tolke and Zimmer, letter dated 17 January 194[3].
51. Gerd Siegel, 'Ein ehemaliger Erzieher der NPEA Bensberg schrieb an seine Frau (Auszüge aus einem intensiven Briefwechsel)', letters dated 6 October 1942, 8 October 1942, 18 October 1942, 23 November 1942, 14 January 1943.
52. NIOD, 020 586, 'Abschrift eines Berichtes von Zugführer Debusmann'; cf. also relevant correspondence in NIOD, 123 1145. N.B. As a daughter organization of the NSB, the *Jeugdstorm* was ideologically in direct conflict with the NPEA ethos, since it explicitly promoted the idea of Greater-Dutch sovereignty within a Germanic Europe (my thanks to Nathaniël Kunkeler for this point).
53. Kemper, 'Bericht', 7. For more on the *Jeugdstorm*, see J. M. Damsma, 'Nazis in the Netherlands: A Social History of National Socialist Collaborators, 1940–1945' (Thesis, University of Amsterdam, 2013), 98–100.
54. Paul Rückert, 'Bericht über den Aufenthalt des 4. Zuges in der Reichsschule Valkenburg', *Ballenstedt: Schriftenfolge der Nationalpolitischen Bildungsanstalt in Ballenstedt am Harz* 20/21 (September 1944), 40–1.
55. NIOD, 020 586, Kemper, report dated 19 May 1944; *De Jeugd en het Rijk*; NIOD, 088 388, *Die Jugend und das Reich. Zur Feierstunde der germanischen SS in Gemeinschaft mit der Reichsschule in Valkenburg*, Bl. 7–10. Armin Eise, a former pupil of NPEA Bensberg who spent some time at the *Reichsschule*, remembers participating in

similar events in Valkenburg and Maastricht alongside the Dutch youth organizations (private correspondence, 26 September 2013).

56. Barnouw, *Reichsschule*, 46.
57. BArch, NS 19/2741, Bl. 55 (Heißmeyer to Himmler, letter dated 19 September 1944). The *Jungmannen* from Quatrecht had also had to be evacuated post-haste, partly by lorry and partly on foot, in order to avoid encirclement by enemy tank troops.
58. P. H. Keulers, 'Wir wollen ein hartes Geschlecht. In den Nationalpolitischen Erziehungsanstalten der Niederlande werden deutsche und niederländische Jungen und Mädel nach den Grundsätzen soldatischer Moral erzogen', *Deutsche Zeitung in den Niederlanden*, 23 May 1943 [BArch, R 4902/1490].
59. Pater, *Valkenburg*, 118; see also n. 25 in this chapter.
60. Cf. Roche, '*Herrschaft durch Schulung*'.
61. Mazower, *Hitler's Empire*, 184.
62. Cf. e.g. Valdis O. Lumans, *Himmler's Auxiliaries: The* Volksdeutsche Mittelstelle *and the German National Minorities of Europe, 1933–1945* (Chapel Hill, 1993); Isabel Heinemann, *'Rasse, Siedlung, deutsches Blut'. Das Rasse- und Siedlungshauptamt der SS und die rassenpolitische Neuordnung Europas* (Göttingen, 2003); Alexa Stiller, 'Gewalt und Alltag der Volkstumspolitik. Der Apparat des Reichskommissars für die Festigung deutschen Volkstums und andere gesellschaftliche Akteure der veralltäglichten Gewalt', in Jochen Böhler and Stephan Lehnstaedt, eds, *Gewalt und Alltag im besetzten Polen 1939–1945* (Osnabrück, 2012), 45–66; Andreas Strippel, 'Race, Regional Identity and *Volksgemeinschaft*: Naturalization of Ethnic German Resettlers in the Second World War by the Einwandererzentralstelle/Central Immigration Office of the SS', in Szejnmann and Umbach, *Heimat, Region and Empire*, 184–98.
63. Brandes, *NS-'Volkstumspolitik'*, 52; Heinemann, *'Rasse'*, 195ff.; Lumans, *Himmler's Auxiliaries*, 185; Mazower, *Hitler's Empire*, 188, 209.
64. Brandes, *NS-'Volkstumspolitik'*, 235; Heinemann, *'Rasse'*, 189.
65. Cf. Isabel Heinemann, '"Until the Last Drop of Good Blood": The Kidnapping of "Racially Valuable" Children and Nazi Racial Policy in Occupied Eastern Europe', in A. Dirk Moses, ed., *Genocide and Settler Society: Frontier Violence and Stolen Indigenous Children in Australian History* (New York, 2004), 244–66; Ines Hopfer, *Geraubte Identität. Die gewaltsame 'Eindeutschung' von polnischen Kindern in der NS-Zeit* (Vienna, 2010). For more on the '*Lebensborn*' programme in general, see e.g. Georg Lilienthal, *Der 'Lebensborn e.V.': Ein Instrument nationalsozialistischer Rassenpolitik* (Frankfurt am Main, 2003); Volker Koop, *Dem Führer ein Kind schenken. Die SS-Organisation Lebensborn* (Cologne, 2007).
66. Georg Hansen, *Ethnische Schulpolitik im besetzten Polen: der Mustergau Wartheland* (Münster, 1995).
67. Heinemann, 'Kidnapping', 246.
68. Himmler, 'Einige Gedanken über die Behandlung der Fremdvölkischen im Osten', 28 May 1940, reprinted in Hansen, *Ethnische Schulpolitik*, 24–7.
69. Himmler, 'Gedanken', in Hansen, *Ethnische Schulpolitik*, 26: 'The training should take place in a pre-school, after four classes of which one can then decide whether the children should be allowed to continue in the German primary school, or whether they should be conveyed to a National Political Education Institute.'

70. BArch, NS 19/4009, Bl. 128–78.
71. Quoted in Heinemann, 'Kidnapping', 250. Interestingly, some former pupils who served on the Eastern front seem to have been inspired to keep an active look-out for sites for a putative 'NPEA Ukraine' or 'NPEA Osteuropa' (e.g. *Ilfelder Blätter*, 27. Kriegsheft (January 1943), [3]; *Ilfelder Blätter*, 29. Kriegsheft (June 1943), [117]).
72. Cf. Roche, '*Herrschaft durch Schulung*'.
73. *Die Kameradschaft. Blätter der Nationalpolitischen Erziehungsanstalt Plön* 4, no. 2/3, April 1939, 7. For more on Henlein and Sudeten politics, see Ralf Gebel, *'Heim ins Reich!' Konrad Henlein und der Reichsgau Sudetenland (1938–1945)* (Munich, 2000).
74. 'Geleitwort des Gauleiters und Reichsstatthalters Konrad Henlein', *Nationalpolitische Erziehungsanstalt Sudetenland*, 2. Folge (Jahreswende [New Year] 1941–2), 17. On Henlein's commitment to the Napola in the hope of furthering the cause of a specifically Sudeten *Volkstum* (a theme which he develops here in some detail), see also Otto Jank, 'Nur aus der Gemeinschaft wächst die deutsche Kraft—Der Dank des Gauleiters / Errichtung einer zweiten Napola im Gau', *Die Zeit*, 11 October 1940 [Bundesarchiv Koblenz, ZSg. 117 Nr. 290].
75. 10. *Jahre Nationalpolitische Erziehungsanstalt Naumburg a. d. Saale* (1944), 23.
76. 'Patendörfer, Jungmann und Bauer', *Nationalpolitische Erziehungsanstalt Sudetenland*, 2. Folge (Jahreswende [New Year] 1941–2), 49. For more on NPEA Sudetenland, see Roche, '*Herrschaft durch Schulung*', 133–9.
77. BArch, R 2/12726, especially the letter dated 28 June 1940.
78. 'Zwei neue nationalpolitische Erziehungsanstalten. "Wartheland" und "Sudetenland" beginnen ihre Arbeit', *Deutsche Allgemeine Zeitung*, 8 October 1940 [BArch, NS 5/VI/18842]; W. J., 'Schloß Reisen bei Lissa: Die Nationalpolitische Erziehungsanstalt für den deutschen Osten', *Deutsche Allgemeine Zeitung*, 26 April 1940 [BArch, R 8034-II/9296]. On the Warthegau resettlement programme for ethnic Germans more generally, see Harvey, *Women and the Nazi* East, 152–7, and Stiller, 'Gewalt und Alltag'.
79. Roche, '*Herrschaft durch Schulung*', 144–5.
80. Cf. 'Merkblatt für die Aufnahme in die Nationalpolitische Erziehungsanstalt Wartheland'. For more on NPEA Wartheland, see Roche, '*Herrschaft durch Schulung*', 139–45.
81. Georg Hansen, ed., *Schulpolitik als Volkstumspolitik. Quellen zur Schulpolitik der Besatzer in Polen 1939–1945* (Münster, 1994), Documents 180–2, 184. Loben's initial recruitment drive had focused on Silesia and those parts of the Sudetenland which abutted it.
82. 'Hier wächst die kommende Führergeneration heran', *Deutschlanddienst*, 9 December [1941] [BArch, R 8034-II/9296].
83. Heinz Winkler and Hans Worpitz, *Die Nationalpolitischen Erziehungsanstalten (NPEA) und ihre Jungmannen. Berichte, Entwicklungen und Erlebnisse von Jungmannen der NPEA Loben/Annaberg* (2003).
84. Hans Worpitz, *Roter und schwarzer Moloch. Erkenntnisse des Napola-Schülers Benjamin—Russische Kriegsgefangenschaft 1945–1950* (Norderstedt, 2005), 27. N.B. The next five paragraphs are largely drawn from Roche, '*Herrschaft durch Schulung*', 145–8.
85. Hansen, *Schulpolitik als Volkstumspolitik*, Document 183.

86. One of the Naumburg *Erzieher*, Friedrich Dubslaff, confirms in his private memoirs that Frank's son did in fact attend the Napola in Ploschkowitz (cf. Friedrich Dubslaff, *Erinnerungen*, n.d., 16).
87. Šimůnek, Michal, 'Poslední "vůdcovska škola" nacistické diktatury: tzv. Nacionálně politický výchovný ústav Čechy (Nationalpolitische Erziehungsanstalt Böhmen) v Kutné Hoře, 1943–1945 [Die "NPEA Böhmen" in Kuttenberg 1943–1945: Letzte "Führerschule" der national-sozialistischen Diktatur]', *Acta Universitatis Carolinae* 51, no. 1 (2011), 59–81, 66.
88. See BArch, R 2/27767, letter from Heißmeyer dated 4 August 1941, on the expropriation of the *Erzbischöfliches Knabenseminar* in Brno: 'The political situation is the most favourable possible for a National Political Education Institute, since it lies within the German language island of Brno and is suitable for giving Germandom in the Protectorate...strong cultural backing'; cf. Brandes, *NS-'Volkstumspolitik'*, 76ff., 237ff.
89. Šimůnek, 'Böhmen', 66, 75. The AHS was founded on 26 April 1944.
90. Šimůnek, 'Böhmen', 71 (quoting a letter from Heißmeyer to Heydrich dated 31 October 1942).
91. BArch, NS 19/2741, particularly the letter from Himmler to Heydrich dated 19 February 1942.
92. BArch, NS 19/605. The son of the Czech puppet education minister, Emanuel Moravec, was sent to NPEA Reichenau in 1942, where he gained a prize in July 1943 for good work in academic subjects and art (Staatsarchiv Freiburg, B 715/1 Nr. 765, letter from Anstaltsleiter to Bürgermeister Maier, Reichenau, dated 9 July 1943). However, he appears to have died of poliomyelitis in NPEA Klotzsche in 1944—cf. *Nationalpolitische Erziehungsanstalt Klotzsche in Sachsen*, 18. Folge (Autumn 1944), 11.
93. Šimůnek, 'Böhmen', 75. Apparently, Heißmeyer had suggested that pupils from the Protectorate should gather in Raudnitz, and only be transferred to Kuttenberg at a later date. For a detailed account of the events leading up to the founding of NPEA Bohemia, and its short-lived existence, see pp. 65–77.
94. BArch, NS 19/1846, particularly Bl. 28–30.
95. BArch, NS 19/1394, *passim*. For more on the *Volksdeutsche Mittelstelle*, see Lumans, *Himmler's Auxiliaries*.
96. Tara Zahra, 'Reclaiming Children for the Nation: Germanization, National Ascription, and Democracy in the Bohemian Lands, 1900–1945', *Central European History* 37, no. 4 (2004), 501–43, 540; Hopfer, *Identität*.
97. Peter Black, 'Indigenous Collaboration in the Government General: The Case of the *Sonderdienst*', in Pieter M. Judson and Marsha L. Rozenblit, eds, *Constructing Nationalities in East Central Europe* (New York, 2005), 243–66, cf. 243–4, 248; Thomas Casagrande et al., 'The *Volksdeutsche*: A Case Study from South-Eastern Europe', in Böhler and Gerwarth, *Waffen-SS*, 209–51.
98. Cf. Roche, '*Herrschaft durch Schulung*'.
99. From this perspective, the Napola authorities' attitude towards ethnic Germans seems to have been rather more positive than those described by Mirna Zakić in her recent monograph, *Ethnic Germans and National Socialism in Yugoslavia in World War II* (Cambridge, 2017).

100. Gerhard Hirschfeld, 'Formen nationalsozialistischer Besatzungspolitik im Zweiten Weltkrieg', in Joachim Tauber, ed., *'Kollaboration' in Nordosteuropa. Erscheinungsformen und Deutungen im 20. Jahrhundert* (Wiesbaden, 2006), 40–55, 43; cf. Kwiet, *Reichskommissariat Niederlande*, 11. Johannes Koll has also noted that the contrasts in Germanization policy between Austria, Poland, and the Netherlands can usefully be explored through the lens of Seyß-Inquart's political career, since he had been active at some point in each of these three colonial administrations (Koll, *Seyß-Inquart*, 15, 18).
101. Cf. Roche, *'Herrschaft durch Schulung'*, 143.

9
For Girls Only
The *NPEA für Mädchen*

The so-called *Mädchen-Napolas* (Napolas for girls) still represent the most obscure and least well-understood component of the Napola system. Suggested explanations of their aims and function have ranged from the prosaic (training 'intelligent mothers' to serve the state) to the somewhat scandalous (grooming concubines or brides-to-be for future SS elites).[1] Even during the Third Reich, government officials seem to have been at a loss when attempting to calculate how many Napolas for girls actually existed at any given time—and scholars in subsequent decades have fared little better.[2] The girls' schools are rarely mentioned in mainstream scholarship on women in the Third Reich, and the connections between their origins and programme and the policy of other Nazi womens' and girls' organizations have seldom been analysed in detail, if at all.[3]

This chapter begins by giving an account of how the *NPEA für Mädchen* came into being, their purported aims, and the heated intra-ministerial debates which dogged their foundation, before going on to describe everyday life at the schools, and the similarities and differences between the education which they offered and that of the boys' Napolas. It then suggests, with reference to recent historiography, that the political infighting which the *Mädchen-Napolas* provoked, the nebulousness surrounding their programme, and the piecemeal and contested nature of their development, reflect the fundamental flexibility (or incoherence) inherent in the Nazi state's attitude towards the 'woman question' more generally.

At the same time, the *NPEA für Mädchen* shared many of the characteristics and programmatic assumptions which had already been established at the *NPEA für Jungen* (NPEA for boys). The sense of comradeship, elitism, and assumed capacity for leadership which the girls' schools instilled in their alumnae seem to have been broadly analogous—even if the girls' education focused far more on training for traditionally 'feminine' vocations, rather than following the highly militaristic bent of the boys' schools. Both boys' and girls' Napolas drew upon previous models, including reform pedagogy and the turn-of-the-century youth movements, whilst sedulously attempting to present themselves as divorced from all previous archetypes.[4] In the case of the *Mädchen-Napolas*, this led to a strenuous disavowal of 'outdated' female antitypes, such as the privileged bourgeois or upper-class daughter (*höhere Tochter*), the pale, wilting finishing-school pupil

The Third Reich's Elite Schools: A History of the Napolas. Helen Roche, Oxford University Press. © Helen Roche 2021.
DOI: 10.1093/oso/9780198726128.003.0010

(*blasse Pensionspflanze*), the dreaded bluestocking (*gefürchteter Blaustrumpftyp*), or the unfeminine tomboy marching around in hobnailed boots.[5]

So, how did the *NPEA für Mädchen* come into being? The idea of introducing Napolas for girls had first been suggested by Potsdam *Erzieher* Fritz Kloppe, author of a programmatic tract on the Napolas, who feared that sexual irregularities might ensue at the boys' schools if pupils had no opportunities to meet girls of the right sort.[6] However, no more was heard of the idea until autumn 1936, when Trude Bürkner, then Reich Leader of the League of German Girls (*Bund deutscher Mädel*/BDM), was revealed to have had a series of discussions with the then recently appointed Napola-Inspector August Heißmeyer.[7] In an article published in the Nazi periodical *Wille und Macht* on 1 November 1936, Bürkner had apparently declared that:

> National Political Education Institutes for Girls must be founded, in which those girls who are considered particularly valuable from the perspective of race and character can be granted the same opportunities for education and training that the boys already possess. The demand for an equal schooling and training for boys and girls has been raised not only by the leaders of the National Socialist youth movement, but also accords with the views of the leading men in the Party and State.[8]

Heißmeyer then voiced his support for Bürkner's proposals publicly during a lecture at the *Obergauführerinnenschule* in Potsdam on 24 November 1936, suggesting that a number of Napolas for girls would soon be founded in collaboration with Bürkner and the BDM.[9] However, this proposed institutional alliance did not bear any fruit either.

It was only with the incorporation of Austria into the Reich, and the Napolas' corresponding annexation of the former *Bundeserziehungsanstalten*, including the existing state boarding school for girls in Wien-Boerhavegasse, that Heißmeyer's ostensible desire to further the cause of female elite education found an outlet (see Chapter 7). The first ever *NPEA für Mädchen* finally came into being on 13 March 1939—the seniors (*Oberstufe*) immediately moved into the confiscated former estate of the Starhemberg family in Hubertendorf, while the juniors (*Unterstufe*) remained in Vienna initially, before eventually settling in Türnitz.[10]

Heißmeyer's moment of triumph was to be shortlived, however. Officials in the Reich Finance Ministry and the Party Chancellery (including *Reichsleiter* Martin Bormann) soon began to make it clear that they disapproved entirely of this endeavour, and that they would oppose the founding of future Napolas for girls with all the powers at their disposal. As early as March 1939, in a letter giving permission for all of the former *Bundeserziehungsanstalten* to be turned into

NPEA, *Ministerialdirigent* von Manteuffel displayed resistance to the idea of any further expansion, stating that just because the school in Wien-Boerhavegasse had been given permission to continue its life as a *Mädchen-Napola*, that should not be taken to imply that any plans to found further Napolas for girls were in the offing.[11] The Prussian Finance Ministry also refused point-blank to appoint a full-time female bureaucrat (*hauptamtliche Sachbearbeiterin*) to the NPEA-Inspectorate's administrative staff to deal with *Mädchen-Napola*-related questions, claiming that it should be perfectly sufficient if the *Anstaltsleiterin* (headmistress) were to liaise with the Inspectorate herself.[12]

This was only the tip of the oppositional iceberg, however. For at every point at which Heißmeyer and the Inspectorate sought to found new *Mädchen-Napolas*, officials in the Reich Finance Ministry and the Chancellery proved virulently hostile to the idea, arguing that there was no reason or necessity whatsoever to educate girls selectively, or to prepare them for leadership roles. This response was repeated time and again, with Bormann arguing emphatically that '*Napolas should be elite schools,* and *that* isn't essential for *lasses*', while *Ministerialrat* Richter of the Reich Finance Ministry went so far as to suggest that 'the *character* and *reputation* of the National Political Education Institutes would be *damaged*, if National Political Education Institutes for *Girls* were created'.[13]

In fact, Heißmeyer seems only to have been able to push through the establishment of a *Mädchen-Napola* in the former Grand-Ducal summer residence at Colmar-Berg in Luxembourg because it lay under the jurisdiction of the *Chef der Zivilverwaltung* (head of civil occupation administration), meaning that the Inspectorate could go ahead with the foundation without consulting the ministry in Berlin, thus presenting the Reich authorities with a *fait accompli*. In an ironic twist, it appears that the decision to turn the palace into an *NPEA für Mädchen* rather than an *NPEA für Jungen* had been made on the spot when Himmler, Heißmeyer, and Gauleiter Simon inspected the building in September 1940, ostensibly out of concern for the grand-ducal soft furnishings therein:

> The entire structural set-up of the house and its furnishings forbid its use for the rigorous and rough life of a boys' school. Marble floors with valuable carpets, sumptuous furniture and parquet flooring would soon have lost all their beauty, if they were constantly being trodden by hobnailed boots.[14]

Nevertheless, as soon as this decision had been made, Heißmeyer vowed to 'extract' a written order from Hitler to safeguard the development of the Napola in Colmar-Berg.[15] Richter's chagrin-filled response, in which he rued the day that he had ever permitted the first Napola for girls to be founded, demanded in return that both Colmar-Berg and Hubertendorf-Türnitz, the initial *Mädchen-Napola*, be turned into common-or-garden girls' boarding schools

(*Heimoberschulen für Mädchen*) as soon as possible, since the Napolas' aim of preparing their alumni for various leading positions, especially in the military, could have no counterpart in the feminine sphere.[16] At this point, Heißmeyer fought back fiercely, outlining his own programme and ambitions for the girls' schools:

> The task of the National Political Education Institutes lies explicitly in the *political* sphere, of which communal education forms a significant part. This holds true at least as much for girls as it does for boys. That the communal education for boys takes place in the spirit of military fitness is in accordance with the later tasks which the *Jungmannen* will take up.... The training in the spirit of comradeship should apply equally to boys and girls. The security of our Reich will be decided in the first instance by the training of our youth, girls as well as boys. Women are bestowed with no less important political tasks than men—the formation, preservation, and heightening of a clearly formed National Socialist *attitude*. The girls' educational path is naturally determined differently from the boys' in some subjects, in accordance with their later *völkisch* tasks as *housewives* and *mothers*.... I know from history, that sometimes the stance of women was decisive for the outcome of a battle or for the purity and preservation of our race. I believe that now, and in the near future, women will help to decide the eternal life of our *Volk* more than ever before. And, inasmuch as the destructive influence of the international politicizing Church is removed from our *Volk*, the woman will also take on the position of custodian of our race and our customs, as befits her status as a woman of Germanic blood.[17]

In later correspondence with State Secretary Reinhardt, Heißmeyer also used the putative foundation of an Adolf-Hitler-School for girls as another cast-iron reason to secure the status of the *NPEA für Mädchen*. If the Party planned to provide an elite education for the 'fairer sex', and the two types of elite school were supposed to develop in tandem, according to the Führer's will, then 'it must be our ambition...not only to survive the coming battle for supremacy [with the AHS] in good shape, but to win it'.[18]

Nevertheless, the opposition to every single foundation was unrelenting, and it was only when Himmler took the *Mädchen-Napola* project under his wing, and extracted a concrete statement of approval from Hitler himself, that Bormann and the Finance Ministry were forced (with very bad grace) to capitulate and allow the functioning of the girls' schools to continue unhindered.[19] From this standpoint, it is perhaps unsurprising that all of the *NPEA für Mädchen* which were able to flourish—Hubertendorf-Türnitz, Colmar-Berg, and the *Reichsschule für Mädchen* in Heythuysen in the Netherlands—were all situated beyond the German border.[20] The one *Mädchen-Napola* in Germany itself, Achern, had a chequered and transitory career, ending its life as a *Deutsche Heimschule* (as the Finance Ministry officials might have wished).[21] The schools were also situated in areas where they could easily contribute to the Germanization of the surrounding population—indeed, the school in Achern was initially founded as a *Reichsschule für Volksdeutsche* (Reich School for Ethnic Germans) in order to Germanize girls from the South Tirol whose parents had opted for Germany in the recent referendum on nationality in the region.

Oddly, we are left with the distinct impression that, in comparison with the sheer chauvinistic intransigence of the openly misogynistic bureaucrats with whom he had to deal, Heißmeyer—whether due to pragmatic, power-political considerations, or to the putative influence of his second wife, Reich Women's Leader Gertrud Scholtz-Klink—was fighting hard to provide a form of elite education for young women which would at least allow them a modicum of social mobility and career progression in National Socialist terms, even if its promise could never begin to measure up to the progressive standards of a liberal democracy. By contrast with those Ministry officials who believed that selective or elite education and femininity were completely mutually exclusive, and who desired at all costs to relegate girls to an avowedly anti-careerist form of schooling, Heißmeyer appears as the unlikely champion of some form of gender equality, albeit in a highly distorted, ideological form (a point to which we shall return).

Yet the aims of the *NPEA für Mädchen*, despite Heißmeyer's own statements on the matter, remain somewhat opaque. Articles in the media, eyewitness accounts by pupils and teachers, and contemporary documentation from the schools all give the impression that the programme vacillated constantly between promoting the National Socialist holy grail of motherhood and family life as the only true calling for women, and fostering the expectation that alumnae would take up a range of careers—even if these did focus largely on the caring professions, or on leadership of Nazi womens' organizations.[22] Teachers at the girls' Napolas seem to have regularly taken part in conferences and discussions promoting women's higher education, and it appears that a substantial proportion of those alumnae who graduated during the Third Reich went on to study at university and gain professional qualifications in medicine, teaching, or other professions (including chartered surveying and the book trade) as a matter of course.[23] Even the industrial *Einsätze* in which the girls took part—working in spinning mills and textile factories rather than in steelworks and coal mines—instilled pupils with the idea that many German women, if not the majority, would have to go out and work, and that experience of this way of life was therefore paramount for future female leaders. There was certainly an explicit expectation that every pupil at a *Mädchen-Napola* would be capable of taking on leadership roles (in the BDM, for example), and numerous alumnae seem to have put these skills into practice even after graduation, working in leadership positions in the Reich Labour Service or the

Party administration, or taking on educative or colonial roles in the occupied Eastern territories.[24] Even after the war, many of those former pupils who were permitted to continue in higher education despite their Napola credentials appear to have excelled in fields such as medicine and law; six of the sixteen university graduates whom Stefanie Flintrop interviewed for her dissertation on the *Mädchen-Napolas* went on to complete a doctorate.[25]

*

But what did life at a *Mädchen-Napola* actually entail, and how did its demands measure up to those at the boys' schools? And, first of all, what were the motivations behind parents sending their daughters there? Some former pupils have stressed the seductive power of the richly illustrated prospectuses and reports on the *NPEA für Mädchen* in periodicals for schoolchildren such as *Hilf mit!*, which pictured joyful groups of girls in dirndls undertaking exciting activities in an idyllic landscape. The allure of comradeship, twinned with a modicum of independence from parental supervision, could prove intoxicating, leading girls to pester their parents to allow them to attend the school in question.[26] Other girls who already had brothers at a Napola might also desire to experience a similar life for themselves.[27] In some areas which lacked local day schools, sending a daughter to a boarding school might appear to be the only way to ensure that she received a suitably academic education. In other cases, families on low incomes might simply be keen to have their daughters educated largely at state expense, or, during the war years, to remove them from the urban perils of Allied air raids.[28]

In many ways, day-to-day life seems to have unfolded along similar lines to that at the boys' schools, beginning with early-morning sport in all weathers, and continuing with the daily honouring of the flag—one of Stefanie Flintrop's interviewees remembered being castigated by a comrade when she dared to hoist the flag wearing gloves on a cold day; this was interpreted as a heinous sign of disrespect.[29] The same regard for extreme orderliness in dormitories and in the organization of one's personal effects was considered paramount, with ill-tempered *Erzieherinnen* ready to dash all one's clothes to the floor if they had not been folded neatly enough, or to inflict punishment if any stray hair were found still caught in the girls' brushes or combs.[30] One pupil at NPEA Achern reflected, however, on the observable differences in discipline which still existed between the girls' and boys' schools:

> We often have visitors. Really high-ranking men often come here. Then, sometimes, I wish we were lads. I must admit that to you. You should see how the Rufach boys march! They've really learnt something. When we came to Rufach, we were simply astounded when we saw what order and discipline ruled there. But girls simply can't do it like that. But I must say that the lining up is now

> going as well with us as it does with the boys. In the dining room it's got a lot quieter, not to mention the beds, especially in *Zug* 3a; they're radiant. There's not a crease to be seen...I must say that the lads keep their beds neat, but ours are simply a treasure, they ought to just put them in the museum, Miss Keit [the headmistress] said so herself.[31]

Lessons at the girls' Napolas followed the normal curriculum of a *Deutsche Oberschule für Mädchen*; however, they differed from 'civilian' girls' schools inasmuch as the girls did not have to choose between pursuing an academic education and the so-called '*Pudding-Abitur*', which focused on 'domestic' subjects.[32] Instead, pupils at the *NPEA für Mädchen* routinely spent a few hours a week alongside their academic lessons on subjects such as cookery, housework, nursing, and the care of infants and livestock, along with less explicitly gendered activities, including sport, theatre, and music.[33] Some former pupils described their schooling as characterized by a 'hysterical upholding of the ancient Germanic'—giving the example of art lessons in which the girls were required to model runes out of clay. However, the general impression given is of an academic education which matched the average standards of the time, even if it did not necessarily surpass them.[34]

In terms of school trips and extracurricular activities, the girls do not seem to have ranged as widely as the boys—probably because the girls' schools only really found their feet during the war years. Pupils at Hubertendorf-Türnitz were often taken to the Alps and the Bodensee, and, on one memorable occasion, voyaged down the Danube in a paddle steamer; however, the highlight of the school's early years appears to have been a visit to Munich, where the graduating class had the honour of being received by Gauleiter Adolf Wagner, and even managed to catch a glimpse of Hitler himself.[35] Girls from Hubertendorf also provided an *Aufbauzug* to get the new NPEA at Colmar-Berg in Luxembourg off the ground, which led to effusive expressions of wonder in the school newsletter at the luxury of the palace's rococo furnishings, marble staircases, and the like.[36] Another experience which many former pupils remembered fondly, or even with tears of nostalgia, was the Napolas' summer camp and manoeuvres at the Faaker See in 1939.[37] Hubertendorf-Türnitz was represented alongside all of the boys' schools, which led to much mutual curiosity, and some fast friendships being forged on both sides.[38] Visits to the boys' schools did also take place—the girls from Hubertendorf spent some time at Stuhm, Reisen, and Plön, as well as taking part in an inspirational joint study week at Traiskirchen in 1941, in which the girls had the opportunity to try out small-bore shooting and riding and take a trip to the opera, as well as dancing, attending lectures, taking part in heated discussions in lessons about the nature of poetry, and listening to Beethoven symphonies in the *Anstaltsleiter*'s study.[39]

During their day-to-day existence, girls were encouraged to take part in artistic, musical, and thespian activities—like their male counterparts, they might carve toys for the Winter Help Scheme (WHW), or write and put on plays, such as a version of Snow White which was produced in order to entertain wounded soldiers (entertaining the war-wounded is an ever-recurring theme in the school newsletters).[40] Christiane K. also remembered that at Hubertendorf, there was an annual 'music week', which featured instrumental music, singing, and dancing.[41] Musical visitors also included the celebrated pianist Elly Ney, famed for her interpretations of Beethoven, and Professor Georg Götsch, whose inspiring sessions on folk-dance and folk-music were a regular feature at the schools.

In general, analysis of the girls' school newsletters suggests that the tenor of the curriculum was artistically oriented, and betrayed a marked emphasis on preparing pupils for the caring professions and for family life: for instance, older girls would be expected to train for the German Red Cross examination, or to undertake work experience in a kindergarten. Instead of having external speakers who were soldiers on leave or high-ranking military men, the girls might be given lectures by child psychologists, or visit a local clinic for a talk by the head doctor on the care of infants. Nevertheless, the emphasis on physical activities and sporting prowess seems to have been roughly similar, even if its purported end (encouraging potential fitness in childbearing, rather than military fitness) was somewhat different.

Some of the *Einsätze* which the girls had to undergo were clearly gendered, such as the 'industrial missions'. Liese Pöllhuber described her experiences working in a woollen mill in Leiben in summer 1941 as follows:

> The general work of the factory began early, at six o'clock. Engineer Ruckensteiner showed us the factory, especially the machines which we would have to work with. For the first time, we saw what a long road there lies between the wool fibre and the finished article of clothing, how much work hides in every piece.... I found my place at a bobbin-winding machine. Twenty-four bobbins have to be rewound onto bigger bobbins so that they fit the knitting machines. At the beginning, I felt like a madwoman, because I was always running from one end of the machine to the other, and as soon as I'd happily tied the thread back on again there, here a bobbin had run out and I had to insert a new one. But after the first day, I'd learnt various tricks, and could soon lean on a nearby crate, like my admiring opposite-number, and take things as they came.
>
> The attitude of the women in the factory was exemplary. I had simply boundless admiration for these ordinary women. I never saw a woman in despair or bemoaning the fate that had given her no better position, and had led her husband or son to war. All were identical in their steadfast belief in the Führer and in victory.[42]

However, the fundamental ideas behind the *Einsätze* do not seem to have differed substantially—including the requirement to inculcate one's temporary co-workers as far as possible with National Socialist doctrine. Meanwhile, the recurring work on farms, and opportunities to take up leadership roles in the children's evacuation programme (KLV), were experiences which pupils at both the girls' and boys' Napolas shared.[43]

On one level, the schools were dedicated to promoting the idea that women could perform an equal, though different, function to men in helping the Third Reich achieve its ends. In an editorial for the Hubertendorf-Türnitz school newsletter, *Alles für Deutschland!*, Martha Rheina-Wolbeck, the *Anstaltsleiterin*, spurred her charges to reflect upon this theme, making an explicit comparison with the *NPEA für Jungen*:

> In the middle of a time of great decisions and the hardest, most sacrificial missions in all theatres of war, our own school life appears to roll on undisturbed and peacefully, far more peacefully than at the schools of the *Jungmannen*, in whose ranks the heroes' death of many comrades constantly tears new rents which can no longer be filled. We are seemingly forced to lose time doing our old accustomed work, without directly being able to help in the great struggle. And yet, there are work and tasks enough, even in the *Heimat*, that the sacrifices of our soldiers never lose their deep meaning. And there we women and girls can help a great deal. If our girls see small successes in their work with farmers, in factories, in their BDM work and in their collaboration with the local Party organization; if those people who are often enough extremely mistrustful notice that we work and that we want to help and can help, then we are thankful that we too are able to contribute a very little to the solution of the great, ever-growing tasks of our time.[44]

In similar vein, in the seventh edition of the newsletter, the headmistress printed a poem on the virtues of self-sacrifice which emphasized the particular nature of the girls' tasks, explicitly equating the girls' duty in standing their ground on the home front with that of the former *Jungmannen* who were holding fast on the battle front:

> We are standing fast! ...
> No! And a thousand times no!
> We battle with daily want
> Our joyful courage is undying!
> No smaller, no poorer do we wish to be
> than those in the field for the Fatherland bleeding;
> At home we are battling, and we are standing fast!

No! And a thousand times no!
Now of all times, *do not stand aside!*
Only see your duty and your task!...[45]

Nevertheless, other aspects of life at the *Mädchen-Napolas* seemed to mirror the life of the boys' schools more directly. Even accounts of the younger girls' *Geländespiele* sometimes seem as if they could have been written by boys in the youngest year-groups at a *Jungen-Napola*:

> Quickly I ran into the forest.... We hid in thick shrubbery, but that didn't seem to me to be safe enough.... Scarcely had I run a step or two, than I saw the white belts of the policemen shining.... 'Adi'. 'What?'...'Come, I've found a hidey-hole!' Then we both crept back into the cave. Scarcely were we below, than steps sounded.... Suddenly I'd made a careless movement. Already a stone had rolled with a loud clatter into the valley. 'What was that there?' 'There's no one here, we don't need to look there any longer.' 'Come on, we'll go round the back there', slowly the voices of the two girls speaking, which had given us such a shock, died away. Suddenly we heard three whistles, the sign for the end [of the game].... We ran to the muster point. Now we could march back singing proudly to the Burg, where the maths lesson awaited us.[46]

In sum, then, Stefanie Flintrop's contention that there were ultimately far more similarities than differences between the *NPEA für Mädchen* and the *NPEA für Jungen* seems highly convincing.[47] In the first instance (as she makes clear), this was due to the schools' shared administration and identical hierarchies. Both *Mädchen-* and *Jungen-Napolas* possessed *Anstaltsleiter/innen* and *Erzieher/innen*, *Mädel* or *Jungmannen vom Dienst*, divided their year-groups into *Züge* (platoons), and performed similar functions in leading local Hitler Youth groups. Both types of school enabled their graduands to take the *Abitur* and proceed to further education, and the academic and ideological content of their academic lessons was more or less identical. The processes by which staff and pupils were recruited followed similar lines, and the tasks and ideological activities which constituted *Dienst* at a Napola (including flag parades, celebration of National Socialist festivals, and the recitation of daily political slogans) were also broadly the same. The desired character traits which the schools aimed to foster—comradeship, honour, discipline, responsibility, and the like—were the same too. As the programmatic description below from an information brochure distributed by the school in Achern demonstrates, even many aspects of the selection process, including the academic standards demanded of applicants, do not appear to have differed substantially between the boys' and girls' schools:

Only girls will be accepted who are hereditarily sound, valuable in character, and particularly capable physically and intellectually. They are to be trained into German women who are conscious of their aims and take joy in responsibility; in them, a secure political stance, sound knowledge, and readiness for action in all spheres of female creation will be combined in a steadfast singularity, so that they can later fulfil the leadership tasks which the Greater German Reich poses women in political life, and which the German people poses women in family life.

The focus of the educational aim lies in the training to a personality bound to the community. It encompasses the young person in its entirety.

1. Through a multifaceted sporting training in light athletics, games, gymnastics, swimming, and winter sports, the girls will consistently be thoroughly physically trained and toughened, and brought up to the spirit of comradeship, exertion of the will, courage, endurance, and graceful mastery of their bodies.
2. The artistic and musical training includes all girls together in communal singing, folk-dancing, and in pictorial design, and prepares them in this way for practical *Volkstumsarbeit.*
3. All girls learn the foundations of housewifery in working groups; this includes care of the household, cooking, care of infants and the sick, sewing and mending, weaving and horticulture.
4. Through political work in the framework of the BDM, through helping in harvest kindergartens, through work on the land for several weeks at a time (with farmers in border regions where possible) and through trips within and outside Germany, the girls are led to an active engagement with the political tasks of the German people.

Through their lessons, they receive a thorough academic education in accordance with the curriculum of the *Deutsche Oberschule*, so that a transfer is possible at any time. The education concludes with the *Abitur* certificate, which confers the right to any course of study at university.[48]

Even the '*Mutprobe*' aspect of the entrance examination seems to have been taken over directly from the boys' schools, although it was not always explicitly described as such.[49] However, interestingly, when it came to the 'racial' selection of girls, the examiners from the SS Race and Resettlement Head Office (RuSHA) were instructed to disguise themselves as doctors (wearing a white coat, with civilian clothes rather than a uniform underneath), conducting their inspection under the pretext of checking the girls' hearing and vision.[50]

Where the two types of Napola did differ most fundamentally, however, was in the orientation of the more vocational aspects of the education which they provided. As one journalist put it in a report for the *Völkische Frauenzeitung* in 1941, 'the same girl who may have "sparkled" in art history or a foreign language in the morning must soon prove that she knows how to use a cooking spoon or a sewing machine in the afternoon'.[51] While the *NPEA für Jungen* privileged paramilitary training and cross-country wargames, as we have seen, the *NPEA für Mädchen* promoted the acquiring of housewifely skills—cooking and baking, sewing, gardening, looking after children, and tending to the sick. Alongside their *Einsätze* on farms and in suitably female-oriented industries such as the textile trade, the girls were also expected to take it in turns to help with preparing meals and doing the washing up and clearing away afterwards, or even with cleaning the lavatories—tasks which the *Jungmannen* were expected to perform more rarely.[52] All in all, the girls and their teachers were supposed to embody the conservative German ideal of womanhood: long (preferably blonde) hair neatly plaited, bereft of any hint of makeup, and usually clad in the traditional dirndl, rather than an official uniform.[53] Meanwhile, the ultimate aim of the domestic elements of the girls' education, as Flintrop suggests, seems to have been to prepare the girls for an autarchic, petit bourgeois familial existence which could enable them to live off their own smallholding.[54]

*

How far, then, did this dual orientation mirror prevailing trends in policy towards women and girls under National Socialism? Were the *NPEA für Mädchen* strange outliers, preparing women for roles and careers which Nazi ideology would necessarily deny them, in favour of their unambiguous relegation to the avowedly feminine sphere of the three Ks (*Kinder, Küche, Krankenpflege*—children, cooking, and care of the sick), as the Finance Ministry officials would have wished? Or did the girls' schools in fact represent the underappreciated vanguard of a specifically (and constrictingly) National Socialist form of [pseudo-]feminism?

The apparently contradictory nature of the *Mädchen-Napolas'* mission can to some extent be explained if, as Dagmar Reese, Franka Maubach, and others have done, we distinguish a separate category of female youth (*Jugend*) lying somewhere in between the realms of childhood and womanhood under Nazism. As Reese has noted with reference to the BDM, 'despite the rhetoric of gender segregation, the National Socialist youth organization subordinated male and female youth, and in particular their leading elites, to fundamentally the same maxims—duty, loyalty, unconditional action and discretion'[55]—an observation which could pertain equally well to the similarities between the *NPEA für Mädchen* and the *NPEA für Jungen*. Within this self-contained sphere of youth, then, it was not only permissible, but even demanded, that girls in later adolescence and early adulthood should postpone the advent of motherhood, and devote themselves instead to tasks which would aid the Reich.[56] Often, these were war- or occupation-related, as in the case of those female auxiliaries who served in air-raid defence batteries and in administrative roles alongside the armed forces and the SS, or those young women who went out to teach in the conquered Eastern territories—but it also applied to those who took on leading positions in the female Reich Labour Service or the BDM, which was often left chronically short of properly qualified leaders.[57] Hence, there already existed a specifically female paradigm of comradeship, leadership, and agency, which was eagerly embraced by many young women under Nazism.[58]

In this context, the continuing dominance of the perception of National Socialist women as baby-making machines, initially propagated by Nazi iconography and by the programmatically misogynistic statements put forward by Hitler in *Mein Kampf*, can in part be explained by the prevalence of a post-war desire to cast German women as purely passive, suffering mothers, victimized by the regime, and therefore guiltless.[59] Yet, as Jill Stephenson has argued, the 'organizational apartheid' to which the Nazi women's movement was condemned by National Socialism's severely chauvinist character, whilst inevitably leading to the 'separate development' of the Nazi women's organizations, did nevertheless allow these a significant degree of autonomy in determining their own role and function.[60] Later on, former *NPEA-Erzieherinnen* and *Anstaltsleiterinnen* would claim that they had also enjoyed precisely such freedoms when deciding upon the direction which the *Mädchen-Napolas* were to take.[61] In this sense, Hitler's views on women and the family arguably limped nostalgically behind some of his own cadres' far more radical policies.[62]

From this perspective, recent scholarship has stressed the inherent 'flexibility' of National Socialist ideology with regard to the 'woman question', whether in accordance with the dictates of the labour market, or the demands of total war.[63] This ability to compromise, or at least to admit the validity of female political activity in certain spheres beyond the merely familial, was shaped and conditioned by the notion that women were fundamentally '*gleichwertig, aber nicht gleichartig*' (of equal worth, but of a different type); that is, they could perform equally useful functions in different yet complementary spheres of public life, focusing in particular on 'healing, helping, and education' (*Heilen, Helfen und Erziehen*).[64] This doctrine formed the core of the ideology peddled by female leaders of the Nazi women's organizations, including Heißmeyer's second wife, Gertrud Scholtz-Klink,[65] and, as we have seen, it was also fundamental to Heißmeyer's vision of the mission of the *NPEA für Mädchen*. In the context of National Socialist elite education, the *Mädchen-Napolas*, too, would form a separate but complementary sphere, within which women capable of performing future political tasks could be trained, whilst also being educated to perform the familial functions which were defined as suitable for their gender. In this sense, the *Mädchen-Napolas* can be seen as broadly analogous to elite schools such as the *SS-Helferinnenschule* or the *BDM-Führerinnenschulen*, or even to the elite *Reichsschulen* and leadership courses founded by Scholtz-Klink's *Nationalsozialistische Frauenschaft*.[66] The fact that the Napola-girls were being trained up to domesticity, as well as to more public or political tasks, need not surprise us unduly, since (as Nancy Reagin has shown), this was a sphere which had long been considered of crucial significance to notions of German imperialism and the cultivation of the greater-German *Volksgemeinschaft* since long before the advent of the Third Reich.[67]

All in all, then, we can suggest that the *NPEA für Mädchen* provided a significant space for female socialization and the development of female comradeship within the context of the *Volksgemeinschaft*. Recent scholarship on women and gender in Nazi Germany has stressed the wealth of new opportunities which the 'racial state' promised to its female *Volksgenossinnen*, providing women with a sense of freedom, recognition, and (albeit circumscribed) opportunities for participation in public life.[68] The *Mädchen-Napolas* arguably represented one end of this spectrum in the educational sphere, potentially to a greater degree even than the BDM, given the total separation from the encumbrance of family responsibilities and ties which life at a Napola entailed—indeed, some of the former pupils whom Stefanie Flintrop interviewed remembered being completely freed from looking after their numerous younger siblings as a true liberation.[69] In contrast with the training and extracurricular activities offered by the BDM (which also became more focused on training for motherhood and housewifery from around 1936 onwards),[70] the *NPEA für Mädchen* might also have appeared to possess a lustre and an exoticism which the massed ranks of the state youth group could no longer quite match, both in terms of what Franka Maubach has dubbed mechanisms of 'playful integration',[71] opportunities to take part in sporting activities, cultural work and artistic fulfilment,[72] and in terms of the augmented self-importance which former adherents could go on to enjoy.[73] Just like the *Jungen-Napolas*, the *Mädchen-Napolas* were arguably better able to attain their indoctrinatory, physical, and cultural aims than the BDM, given the nature of the Napolas' all-encompassing boarding-school education.[74]

Finally, although the girls at the *Mädchen-Napolas* were no more prepared for specific leadership positions than were the boys at the *Jungen-Napolas*, the education which they received still readied them for any form of service in the *Volksgemeinschaft* which might necessitate their taking on such a role, not least because it provided them with the requisite elite consciousness and experience of taking responsibility for younger pupils. Indeed, the very similarity in attitudes and habitus displayed by Napola-graduates of both genders, as revealed in post-war interviews and correspondence, is striking—whether in terms of their sense of having been selected to accomplish significant future tasks, their attitudes towards current affairs, or their modes of engagement with the Nazi past.

In conclusion, it can be argued that the *NPEA für Mädchen* demonstrate, in microcosm, *both* the scope *and* the totalitarian restrictions engendered by Nazi attitudes towards young women. On the one hand, the girls who attended the *Mädchen-Napolas* were educated to believe that growing up female in Nazi Germany need be no bar to experiencing comradeship, leadership, and even having a successful career, and they were given an education broadly analogous to that of their male counterparts. On the other hand, the girls were still trained to see taking care of a husband and family as an ultimate good; moreover, any public or political roles which they might later have taken on would still have been largely limited to the state-sanctioned female spheres of the National Socialist women's and girls' organizations, and the caring professions. Nevertheless, both at the time, and after the war, former pupils often praised the varied tenor of their schooling, and the future promise which it seemed to offer.

These contradictions are perhaps most aptly revealed in the following excerpt from a gushing letter by former pupil Gretl Hornek, which was sent in to the Hubertendorf-Türnitz school newsletter in December 1943. Gretl hoped soon to marry her beloved SS-officer fiancé (possibly a former *Jungmann*), whom she had first encountered at Hubertendorf in autumnal sunshine under deep blue skies, while her fellow-pupils were playing netball in the field by the nearby stream:

> Now my future lies ahead, and seems to me to be as glowing as that autumn day. After this war we want to have a farm; we want to settle on our own piece of German land, which through the work of our own hands will become truly German for the first time! I'm glad that neither of us own property, and so we will first have to begin and build everything from the ground up. I believe that much of what I have learnt in Hubertendorf will be of benefit to me. I will think of the horticulture and homemaking lessons with Frau Ingenieur, the unforgettable chemistry lessons with Fräulein Junker 'Chemical Fertilizer', the hours in the kindergarten with Frau Walluschek—the music and the sport, and all the many things which we experienced in our school, and which we are only now fully learning to understand and appreciate![75]

Notes

1. Cf. the only comprehensive study of the Napolas for girls to date, Stefanie Flintrop's groundbreaking PhD dissertation: Stefanie Jodda-Flintrop, *'Wir sollten intelligente Mütter werden'. Nationalpolitische Erziehungsanstalten für Mädchen* (Norderstedt, 2010). N.B. I am deeply indebted to Stefanie Flintrop for her invaluable assistance in allowing me to view material from her private archive (PASF) whilst researching this chapter. More dated and cursory treatments of the *Mädchen-Napolas* include two

articles by Ursula Aumüller-Roske, 'Weibliche Elite für die Diktatur? Zur Rolle der Nationalpolitischen Erziehungsanstalten für Mädchen im Dritten Reich', in Ursula Aumüller-Roske, ed., *Frauenleben—Frauenbilder—Frauengeschichte* (Pfaffenweiler, 1988), 17–44; and Ursula Aumüller-Roske, 'Die Nationalpolitischen Erziehungsanstalten für Mädchen im "Großdeutschen Reich": Kleine Karrieren für Frauen?', in Lerke Gravenhorst and Carmen Tatschmurat, eds, *Töchter-Fragen. NS-Frauengeschichte* (2nd edn, Freiburg im Breisgau, 1995), 211–36, as well as Gregory Paul Wegner, 'Mothers of the Race: The Elite Schools for German Girls under the Nazi Dictatorship', *Journal of Curriculum and Supervision* 19, no. 2 (2004), 169–88. On the under-researched nature of female elites under Nazism more generally, see e.g. Andrea Böltken, *Führerinnen im 'Führerstaat'. Gertrud Scholtz-Klink, Trude Mohr, Jutta Rüdiger und Inge Viermetz* (Pfaffenweiler, 1995), 9; Franka Maubach, 'Führerinnen-Generationen? Überlegungen zur Vergesellschaftung von Frauen im Nationalsozialismus', *H-Soz-Kult* (2003): www.hsozkult.de/debate/id/diskussionen-331; Anette Michel, '"Führerinnen" im Dritten Reich. Die Gaufrauenschaftsleiterinnen der NSDAP', in Sybille Steinbacher, ed., *Volksgenossinnen. Frauen in der NS-Volksgemeinschaft* (2007), 115–37; Massimiliano Livi, *Führerinnen del Terzo Reich. Nascita, sviluppo, funzione e struttura dell'élite politica femminile nazionalsocialista (1918–1939)* (Münster, 2012); also more generally Barbara Vogel, 'Eliten—Ein Thema der Frauenforschung?', in Günther Schulz, ed., *Frauen auf dem Wege zur Elite* (Munich, 2000), 15–40.

2. Cf. Bundesarchiv Lichterfelde (BArch), R 2/12711 (note dated 24 June 1943).
3. On the few occasions where the *Mädchen-Napolas* are mentioned in more mainstream works, the information given may simply be wrong, as in Jill Stephenson's *Women in Nazi Germany* (London, 2001), 74, which misnames the schools as 'Napoleas', and gives further erroneous details regarding their numbers and function.
4. On the continuities between the female *Jugendbewegung* and Nazi pedagogy more generally, see Irmgard Klönne, *'Ich spring' in diesem Ringe'. Mädchen und Frauen in der deutschen Jugendbewegung* (Pfaffenweiler, 1990), 267–73; and Irmgard Klönne, 'Kontinuitäten und Brüche: Weibliche Jugendbewegung und Bund Deutscher Mädel', in Dagmar Reese, ed., *Die BDM-Generation. Weibliche Jugendliche in Deutschland und Österreich im Nationalsozialismus* (Berlin, 2007), 41–85; also Maubach, 'Führerinnen-Generationen', and Marion E. P. De Ras, *Body, Femininity and Nationalism: Girls in the German Youth Movement 1900–1934* (London, 2008), 11–12, 193.
5. Cf. e.g. Johannes Otto, 'Schule des Lebens. Hubertendorf, die erste Nationalpolitische-Erziehungsanstalt für Mädel', *Reichselternwarte* (July 1941), Nr. 14 [BArch, R 3903/2249]; Ursel Wilke, 'Nationalpolitische Erziehungsanstalt auch für Mädel', *Die Bewegung. Zentralorgan des NSD-Studentenbundes*, 18 June 1940 [BArch, R 3903/2248]. This rhetorical strategy was also regularly deployed in defence of the League of German Girls (BDM), which felt the need to reassure parents that its adherents were 'neither "Gretchens" nor "Valkyries"', using antitypes of this kind as a form of advertisement by contrast—cf. Sabine Hering and Kurt Schilde, *Das BDM-Werk 'Glaube und Schönheit'. Die Organisation junger Frauen im Nationalsozialismus* (Berlin, 2000), 21, 54; Birgit Jürgens, *Zur Geschichte des BDM (Bund Deutscher Mädel) von 1923 bis 1939* (Frankfurt am Main, 1994), 81, 203; Louise Willmot, 'Zur Geschichte des Bundes Deutscher Mädel', in Reese, *BDM-Generation*, 89–154, 135.

6. Fritz Kloppe, *Nationalpolitische Erziehungsanstalten* (Leipzig, n.d.), 7–8.
7. For more on Trude Bürkner-Mohr and her work in the BDM, see Böltken, *Führerinnen*.
8. 'Nationalpolitische Erziehungsanstalten für Mädchen? Ein Vorschlag der Reichsleiterin Trude Bürkner', *Frankfurter Zeitung*, 1 November 1936 [BArch, NS 5/VI/18840].
9. 'Nationalpolitische Erziehungsanstalten auch für Mädel', *Reichsjugendpressedienst*, 25 November 1936 [BArch, NS 5/VI/18840].
10. *Berufskundliche Mitteilungen* Nr. 9, 19 April 1939, Hauptabteilung V des Reichsarbeitsministeriums [BArch, R 3903/2249].
11. BArch, R 2/12719, Manteuffel to Rust, 11 March 1939; see further BArch, R 2/12711, Reichsfinanzministerium to Rust, letter dated 20 May 1941.
12. Geheimes Staatsarchiv Preußischer Kulturbesitz, I. HA Rep. 151 IC, Nr. 7308, Bl. 48, letter dated 29 April 1939.
13. BArch, R 2/31684, note from Bormann dated 14 November 1942; BArch, R 2/12719, letter dated 7 November 1942 (emphasis original).
14. BArch, R 2/12719, letter from Regierungspräsident Siekmeier, Ständiger Vertreter des Chefs der Zivilverwaltung in Luxemburg to Kluge, Reichsfinanzministerium, 18 June 1942.
15. BArch, R 2/12711, Richter (Abschrift), note dated 9 June 1941.
16. BArch, R 2/12719, Richter, letter dated 2 August 1942.
17. BArch, R 2/12719, Heißmeyer to Richter, letter dated 3 September 1942.
18. BArch, R 2/12719, Heißmeyer to Reinhardt, letter dated 27 January 1943. Reinhardt claimed in his reply that Bormann had no knowledge of these plans, nor did he endorse them (letter dated 24 March 1943); Heißmeyer averred that his information had come directly from Kurt Petter, the Chief Inspector of the Adolf-Hitler-Schools (letter dated 30 March 1943).
19. BArch, R 2/12719, letter dated 24 June 1943; cf. R 2/31684, Vorlage für Herrn Reichsleiter, Betr. Heimschulen und Nationalpolitische Erziehungsanstalten, Heißmeyer/Reinhardt Besprechung, 5 November 1942; Vermerk, Gündel, dated 24 May 1943.
20. On Heythuysen, see further Chapter 8; also David Barnouw, *Van NIVO tot Reichsschule. Nationaal-socialistische onderwijsinstellingen in Nederland* ('s-Gravenhage, 1981); on Colmar-Berg, see also Robert Krantz's pamphlet '*...Auf ausdrücklichen Befehl des Führers als kriegsentscheidende Erziehungseinrichtung...*': *Materialien zur 'Nationalpolitischen Erziehungsanstalt Kolmar-Berg' vom Einzug in das ehemalige großherzogliche Schloss (1941) bis zur Auflösung in Reichenau (1945)* (Luxembourg, 2007). Himmler also planned to set up a female NPEA in the Protectorate of Bohemia and Moravia—cf. BArch, NS 19/2741.
21. On the substantial opposition to founding an *NPEA für Mädchen* in Achern, see BArch, R 2/12728. For an account of the school's various peregrinations (it moved at various points to Hegne and Schweiklberg, as well as being evacuated to Reichenau at the war's end), see Flintrop, *Nationalpolitische Erziehungsanstalten*, ch. 3.3; also Arnulf Moser, 'Die Illenau im 2. Weltkrieg. Quellen zur nationalsozialistischen Schul- und Volkstumspolitik', *Acherner Rückblicke* 2 (2002), 70–7; Arnulf Moser, 'Die Reichsschule für Volksdeutsche in Achern/Illenau 1940–44', *Die Ortenau. Veröffentlichungen des Historischen Vereins für Mittelbaden* (2003), 107–16.

22. 'Unser Erziehungsziel: Wille und Ausdauer. Übernahme der österreichischen Staatserziehungsanstalten', *Völkischer Beobachter*, 14 March 1939 [BArch, NS 5/VI/18842]; 'Vorbilder deutschen Frauentums. Nationalpolitische Erziehungsanstalt für Mädchen', *Münchener Neueste Nachrichten*, 28 March 1939 [Bundesarchiv Koblenz, ZSg. 117 Nr. 222]; *Das Reich*, Nr. 31, 30 July 1944 [BArch, R 4902/10646]; Wilke, 'Nationalpolitische Erziehungsanstalt'; Otto, 'Schule des Lebens'. See also the speech-choir of massed boys and girls which took place at the official ceremony in Vienna which accompanied the transformation of the *Staatserziehungsanstalten* into NPEA, in which the boys' role as future fighters was equated with the girls' role as future mothers (Österreichisches Staatsarchiv, BEA 52, 'Gelobnis der Jugend', 13 March 1939).
23. Cf. the announcements and sections featuring news from alumnae (*Altkameradinnen*) in the Hubertendorf-Türnitz school newsletter, *Alles für Deutschland! Mitteilungen der Nationalpolitischen Erziehungsanstalt Hubertendorf-Türnitz*. However, one might suggest that the intellectual nature of the career paths chosen by some of these alumnae might also reflect the stringent academic selection criteria of the *Bundeserziehungsanstalten*, since many of those pupils who graduated in the early 1940s would have started their secondary-school careers in Vienna under the old regime.
24. E.g. *Alles für Deutschland!* 2 (January 1942), 14–16; see also 'Mädchen werden Leiterinnen', *Werkend Volk* (August 1943). One might compare the trajectories of the BDM functionaries analysed in Elizabeth Harvey's *Women and the Nazi East: Agents and Witnesses of Germanization* (New Haven, 2003).
25. Flintrop, *Nationalpolitische Erziehungsanstalten*, 158.
26. E.g. private correspondence with Christiane K. (Hubertendorf-Türnitz), 9 October 2013. For examples of media reports of this type, see e.g. BArch, NS 5/VI/18842.
27. E.g. private correspondence with Hannelore B. (Hubertendorf-Türnitz), 12 October 2013.
28. Flintrop, *Nationalpolitische Erziehungsanstalten*, 155–6.
29. Flintrop, *Nationalpolitische Erziehungsanstalten*, 110.
30. PASF, Interview Nr. 15.
31. 'Daß Du einmal das alles sehen könntest, liebe Mutter', *Reichsschule für Volksdeutsche Rufach-Achern* (April 1941), 42–3.
32. Flintrop, *Nationalpolitische Erziehungsanstalten*, 127. On female education in Nazi Germany more generally, see Claudia Huerkamp, *Bildungsbürgerinnen. Frauen im Studium und in akademischen Berufen 1900–1945* (Göttingen, 1996), esp. 61–3.
33. Flintrop, *Nationalpolitische Erziehungsanstalten*, 120–1.
34. PASF, Interview Nr. 15.
35. 'Hubertendorfer Mädeln erzählen: Die Fahrt des 8. Zuges der Abschlussprüfung nach München', *Alles für Deutschland!* 1 (June 1941), 6–11.
36. 'Der 7. Zug berichtet aus Colmarberg', *Alles für Deutschland!* 2 (January 1942), 9–13.
37. Flintrop, *Nationalpolitische Erziehungsanstalten*, 103–4.
38. Cf. e.g. Helmuth J., *Klotzsche: Unser Weg zum Erwachsenwerden... Erzogen als 'Elite für die Diktatur'?* (*c.*2002), 55: 'The girls from Hubertendorf soon became our favourite subjects for photographs.'
39. Ena Seutter von Loetzen, 'Die Arbeitswoche Hubertendorf-Traiskirchen', *Alles für Deutschland!* 2 (January 1942), 5–8.

40. The script of Snow White can be found in *Alles für Deutschland!* 7 (December 1943), 7–8. On the toy-carving, see also Ilse Breit, 'Wir machen ein Spielzeugrößlein!', 9–11, in the same issue. On the prevalence of such activities at the boys' schools, see Chapter 3.
41. Christiane K., private correspondence, 9 October 2013.
42. Liese Pöllhuber, 'Unser Fabrikeinsatz in der Wollspinnerei Leiben (Sommer 1941)', *Alles für Deutschland!* 2 (January 1942), 4–5.
43. On these activities at the boys' schools, see Chapter 3 and Chapter 10.
44. Rheina-Wolbeck, 'Aus dem Anstaltsleben', *Alles für Deutschland!* 2 (January 1942), 1.
45. 'Wir halten stand!', *Alles für Deutschland!* 7 (December 1943), 3 (emphasis original).
46. Gerda Heinig, 'Aus dem Lagertagebuch des 2. und 3. Zuges auf Burg Strechau', *Alles für Deutschland!* 2 (January 1942), 8–9.
47. Flintrop, *Nationalpolitische Erziehungsanstalten*, 144–5.
48. 'Merkblatt für die Aufnahme in die Nationalpolitische Auslesezüge für Mädchen der Reichsschule für Volksdeutsche in Achern (Baden)' (Generallandesarchiv Karlsruhe, Bestand 235, Nr. 35344). See also an earlier brochure applying to the schools in Austria and Luxembourg, the 'Merkblatt für Eltern und Erziehungsberechtigte über die Aufnahme von Mädel in Nationalpolitischen Erziehungsanstalten für Mädel' (Niedersächsisches Landesarchiv—Staatsarchiv Oldenburg, Best. 134 Nr. 2353, Bl. 160–1), which remarks more laconically and obfuscatorily that 'as a place of National Socialist communal education, the National Political Education Institute for Girls has the task, through a multifaceted education, of training women for the German people, who to a high degree embody the stance which will be demanded of the coming generation of German women.'
49. Cf. Flintrop, *Nationalpolitische Erziehungsanstalten*, 59–60; see also Chapter 2.
50. BArch, NS 47/40, Chef des RuSHA to SS-Führer in Rasse- und Siedlungswesen, Betr: Eignungsuntersuchung für die NPEA-Bewerber, letter dated 17 April 1939.
51. Ingeborg Altgelt, 'NPEA? Buchstaben füllen sich mit Leben', *Völkische Frauenzeitung* 35 (November 1941) [BArch, NS 5/VI/18842].
52. PASF, *Meine Geschichte*, quoted in Flintrop, *Nationalpolitische Erziehungsanstalten*, 185. For examples of *Jungmannen* at various *Jungen-Napolas* having to perform kitchen duties or clean the lavatories, see e.g. Walter Becker, *Erinnerungen an die NAPOLA Naumburg. Ein über die 'Kadette Naumburg' hinausgehender Beitrag zur Geschichte der NPEA* (Neustrelitz, 2000), 182–3, Klaus Kleinau, *Im Gleichschritt, marsch! Der Versuch einer Antwort, warum ich von Auschwitz nichts wusste. Lebenserinnerungen eines NS-Eliteschülers der Napola Ballenstedt* (Hamburg, 2000), 26; Harald Schäfer, *NAPOLA: Die letzten vier Jahre der Nationalpolitischen Erziehungsanstalt Oranienstein bei Diez an der Lahn 1941–1945. Eine Erlebnis-Dokumentation* (Frankfurt am Main, 1997), 88.
53. BDM uniforms were generally only worn on official occasions, or during BDM service.
54. Flintrop, *Nationalpolitische Erziehungsanstalten*, 87, 122. Perhaps it was envisaged that these smallholdings would have been situated in the conquered Eastern territories, given the emphasis placed on these as a crucial site of 'missions' for the girls, both during and after their time at the schools.
55. Reese, *BDM-Generation*, 12.

56. Maubach, 'Führerinnen-Generationen'; Dagmar Reese, *Growing Up Female in Nazi Germany* (Ann Arbor, 2006), 44–5, 58–9, 100.
57. Cf. Harvey, *Women and the Nazi East*; Franka Maubach, *Die Stellung halten. Kriegserfahrungen und Lebensgeschichten von Wehrmachthelferinnen* (Göttingen, 2009); Jutta Mühlenberg, *Das SS-Helferinnenkorps. Ausbildung, Einsatz und Entnazifizierung der weiblichen Angehörigen der Waffen-SS 1942–1949* (Hamburg, 2010); Nicole Kramer, *Volksgenossinnen an der Heimatfront. Mobilisierung, Verhalten, Erinnerung* (Göttingen, 2011); Rachel Century, *Female Administrators of the Third Reich* (Basingstoke, 2017). On the lack of qualified leaders in the BDM, see Dagmar Reese, 'Verstrickung und Verantwortung. Weibliche Jugendliche in der Führung des Bundes Deutscher Mädel', in Kirsten Heinsohn, Barbara Vogel, and Ulrike Weckel, eds, *Zwischen Karriere und Verfolgung. Handlungsräume von Frauen im nationalsozialistischen Deutschland* (Frankfurt am Main, 1997), 206–22, 209–10; Reese, *Growing up Female*, 75ff.; also Elizabeth D. Heineman, *What Difference Does a Husband Make? Women and Marital Status in Nazi and Postwar Germany* (Berkeley, 1999), 39–41.
58. Cf. Maubach, 'Führerinnen-Generationen'. For insight into some of the more dated scholarly debates over women's role in the Third Reich, catalysed in part by the so-called *Historikerinnenstreit* (featuring Claudia Koonz and Gisela Bock as protagonists) over the extent to which women under Nazism should be considered to be victims or perpetrators, see e.g. Gisela Bock, 'Nazi Gender Politics and Women's History', in Françoise Thébaud, ed., *A History of Women in the West. V. Toward a Cultural Identity in the Twentieth Century* (Cambridge, MA, 1994), 149–76; Renate Bridenthal, Atina Grossmann, and Marion Kaplan, eds, *When Biology Became Destiny: Women in Weimar and Nazi Germany* (New York, 1984); Ute Frevert, *Women in German History: From Bourgeois Emancipation to Sexual Liberation* (New York, 1990); Claudia Koonz, *Mothers in the Fatherland: Women, the Family and Nazi Politics* (New York, 1987); Dagmar Reese and Carola Sachse, 'Frauenforschung zum Nationalsozialismus: Eine Bilanz', in Gravenhorst and Tatschmurat, *Töchter-Fragen*, 73–106; and Adelheid von Saldern, 'Victims or Perpetrators? Controversies about the Role of Women in the Nazi State', in David F. Crew, ed., *Nazism and German Society, 1933–1945* (London, 1994), 141–65.
59. Maubach, 'Führerinnen-Generationen'.
60. Jill Stephenson, *The Nazi Organisation of Women* (London, 1981), 14.
61. E.g. PASF, Interviews 3 and 4.
62. Maubach, 'Führerinnen-Generationen', quoting Barbara Vinken.
63. Steinbacher, *Volksgenossinnen*, 20; Kirsten Heinsohn, 'Germany', in Kevin Passmore, ed., *Women, Gender and Fascism in Europe, 1919–45* (Manchester, 2003), 33–56, 52; Kathrin Kompisch, *Täterinnen. Frauen im Nationalsozialismus* (Cologne, 2008), 14; Sybille Steinbacher, 'Differenz der Geschlechter? Chancen und Schranken für die "Volksgenossinnen"', in Frank Bajohr and Michael Wildt, eds, *Volksgemeinschaft. Neue Forschungen zur Gesellschaft des Nationalsozialismus* (Frankfurt am Main, 2009), 94–104, 98–9; Massimiliano Livi, *Gertrud Scholtz-Klink: Die Reichsfrauenführerin. Politische Handlungsräume und Identitätsprobleme der Frauen im Nationalsozialismus am Beispiel der 'Führerin aller deutschen Frauen'* (Münster, 2005); cf. Annemarie Tröger, 'Die Frau im wesensgemäßen Einsatz', in Frauengruppe Faschismusforschung,

ed., *Mutterkreuz und Arbeitsbuch. Zur Geschichte der Frauen in der Weimarer Republik und im Nationalsozialismus* (Frankfurt am Main, 1981), 246–72; Lore Kleiber, '"Wo ihr seid, da soll die Sonne scheinen!"—Der Frauenarbeitsdienst am Ende der Weimarer Republik und im Nationalsozialismus', in Frauengruppe Faschismusforschung, *Mutterkreuz und Arbeitsbuch*, 188–214.

64. Stephenson, *Women in Nazi Germany*, 19; Jürgens, *Geschichte*, 204; Steinbacher, 'Differenz'; cf. Gabriele Kinz, *Der Bund Deutscher Mädel: Ein Beitrag über die außerschulische Mädchenerziehung im Nationalsozialismus* (Frankfurt am Main, 1991), 123, on varying National Socialist paradigms for boys and girls—broadly speaking, boys were expected to focus on struggle, conquest, rationality, and action, while girls were supposed to focus on feeling, experience, devotion, and service.
65. Cf. Leonie Wagner, *Nationalsozialistische Frauenansichten. Vorstellungen von Weiblichkeit und Politik führender Frauen im Nationalsozialismus* (Frankfurt am Main, 1996); Böltken, *Führerinnen*; Livi, *Gertrud Scholtz-Klink*, 147–79, 234.
66. Cf. Mühlenberg, *SS-Helferinnenkorps*; Stephenson, *Organisation*.
67. Nancy R. Reagin, *Sweeping the German Nation: Domesticity and National Identity in Germany, 1870–1945* (Cambridge, 2007).
68. Cf. Steinbacher, *Volksgenossinnen*, 12; Steinbacher, 'Differenz'; also Kompisch, *Täterinnen*, 14; Kramer, *Volksgenossinnen*, 18.
69. PASF, Interviews 17 and 21.
70. Jürgens, *Geschichte*, 92–3.
71. Maubach, *Stellung*, 54–61.
72. Cf. Michaela Czech, *Frauen und Sport im nationalsozialistischen Deutschland. Eine Untersuchung zur weiblichen Sportrealität in einem patriarchalen Herrschaftssystem* (Berlin, 1994); Kinz, *Bund Deutscher Mädel*.
73. Cf. Franka Maubach, 'Expansionen weiblicher Hilfe: Zur Erfahrungsgeschichte von Frauen im Kriegsdienst', in Steinbacher, *Volksgenossinnen*, 93–111, 110; also more generally Nori Möding, '"Ich muß irgendwo engagiert sein—fragen Sie mich bloß nicht, warum." Überlegungen zu Sozialisationserfahrungen von Mädchen in NS-Organisationen', in Lutz Niethammer and Alexander von Plato, eds, *'Wir kriegen jetzt andere Zeiten'. Auf der Suche nach der Erfahrung des Volkes in nachfaschistischen Ländern* (*Lebensgeschichte und Sozialkultur im Ruhrgebiet 1930 bis 1960*, Bd. 3; Bonn, 1985), 256–304.
74. Though it is perhaps worth noting that the premises at Hubertendorf and Türnitz were often castigated for their 'primitive' nature (cf. e.g. BArch, R 2/27773; R 2/27762)—one might surmise that providing the funds for the requisite redecoration might have been considered less important because the school was not performing a specifically war-oriented goal.
75. *Alles für Deutschland!* 7 (December 1943), 22.

PART III

NEMESIS

10
The Demands of Total War

When *Jungmann* Hans Schoenecker returned to NPEA Köslin after the summer holidays in autumn 1939, the theme of the school's first 'flag parade' was, unsurprisingly, 'War'. A bugler played the tattoo, the flag was hoisted, and one of the *Jungmannen* read the week's watchword: 'It is sweet and honourable to die for the Fatherland.' The *Anstaltsleiter* then spoke of the fateful struggle of the German people, and of the new order which was in the making, both for Europe, and for the world:

> He proclaimed the first great victories of the German soldiers in Poland and emphasized that...the long-overdue redemption of all the shame which had been heaped upon us was just beginning. The plutocrats on the Thames and in Paris would soon perceive that....The words of our *Anstaltsleiter* didn't just move me to a state of quasi-intoxication. The impassionedly proclaimed slogans about sweet and honourable death caused me to thrill inwardly...at the thought of the endeavour of proving myself on the battle front, just as, by this time, former pupils of the school at Köslin were already proving themselves as young officers.[1]

The outbreak of war in September 1939 had brought a brief surge of chaos in its wake; some Napola buildings had even been requisitioned by Wehrmacht units, while emergency measures were swiftly put in train for the registration of all the schools' available motor vehicles and horses with the Wehrmacht.[2] H. B. of NPEA Rottweil remembered being sent a postcard from the Napola authorities requesting *Jungmannen* to enrol at schools in the vicinity of their parental home for the time being; it was a great relief, however, when the order to return to Rottweil came a couple of weeks later.[3]

More than half of the *Erzieher* at many of the Napolas were called up immediately, leading to the necessity of introducing starkly reduced curricula; indeed, Vice-Inspector Otto Calliebe decreed that the only subjects whose survival could be guaranteed were German, History, Geography, Biology, and Physical Education; foreign languages and the humanities would have to take a back seat.[4] Both Calliebe and Inspector August Heißmeyer also suggested that, from henceforth, pupils' intellectual failings should not be counted against them: 'the expulsion of *Jungmannen* who are acceptable in character and in physical prowess, and who only demonstrate weaknesses in purely academic subjects, should now cease

The Third Reich's Elite Schools: A History of the Napolas. Helen Roche, Oxford University Press. © Helen Roche 2021.
DOI: 10.1093/oso/9780198726128.003.0011

as far as possible.'[5] By October 1939, according to a circular sent round by Heißmeyer, eleven out of nineteen *Anstaltsleiter*, and 295 out of 568 *Erzieher*, had been called up—statistics which the Inspector was convinced no other organization could better.[6] Furthermore, the Inspectorate was keen to seal a deal with the Wehrmacht for a rota system which would continually allow two-thirds of the staff to be on active service, with one-third remaining at the schools during term-time; all teachers and personnel would then serve at the front in the school holidays.[7]

This initial period of disruption would only be the beginning of the Napolas' wartime travails, however. As Germany's military position vis-à-vis the Allies worsened between 1940 and 1945, life at the schools slowly but surely became ever more circumscribed. However, the privations undergone by the NPEA were arguably never so severe as those experienced at many civilian schools, in no small measure due to the Napolas' privileged position as unofficial preparatory officer-training academies.[8]

The structure of this chapter is broadly threefold. Firstly, I consider the great expectations placed on the Napolas by the Inspectorate and the armed forces, due to their purported '*Kriegswichtigkeit*' (vital nature for the war effort), as well as the increasing impediments to their effective functioning, both at an administrative and at a local level. Secondly, I explore daily life at the schools, including the 'war missions' (*Kriegseinsätze*) which pupils were expected to undertake, and the all-important connections between the Napola home-front and former pupils at the battle front, as exemplified by the school newsletters or *Altkameradenbriefe*, which were expressly designed to foster a transgenerational sense of comradeship among all who belonged to the Napolas' 'extended family' (*Großfamilie*). Finally, I briefly examine the ways in which the NPEA system profited from or abetted the wartime crimes of the Nazi regime, including the expropriation of asylums and Jewish property, and the use of forced labour (not least that of concentration-camp inmates). The conclusion then situates the experience of the Napolas more broadly within the context of existing scholarship on the state of German education and society during this turbulent period of total war.

*

Even before the outbreak of war, high-ranking generals in the Wehrmacht had taken a keen interest in the military 'material' which the NPEA were producing—they attended the schools' annual 'manoeuvres', and liked what they saw.[9] By 1940, the Wehrmacht High Command (*Oberkommando der Wehrmacht*/OKW) were stressing the fact that Hitler himself wanted as many prospective Wehrmacht officers as possible to be selected from the ranks of NPEA graduates.[10] However, a proposal mooted in early 1940 by General Johannes Frießner, the Inspector of Army Training and Education (*Inspekteur des Erziehungs- und Bildungswesens des Heeres*), that the Wehrmacht should establish special classes at the Napolas to provide the army with a long-term source of officer cadets was swiftly and viciously repudiated by Himmler: 'A division of educational authority is out of the question. I also made this clear to General Frießner yesterday before the beginning of the parade of 6,000 officer candidates in front of the Führer himself.... I must request that in future negotiations, it is made clear to these gentlemen that, with all due respect, *I* determine educational policy in the National Political Educational Institutes, and not the Army.'[11]

However, Hitler's privileging of the schools ultimately led to the promulgation of a 'Führer Order' (*Führerbefehl*) dated 7 December 1944, which decreed that all officer candidates for the Wehrmacht and Waffen-SS should undergo training at an NPEA, an Adolf-Hitler-School, or the NSDAP Reich School in Feldafing.[12] This decision had apparently come about following a protracted conversation between a Wehrmacht Divisional Commander, Himmler, and Hitler in October 1944, during which the officer's praise of his Napola-educated troop-leaders had allegedly brought a smile to the Führer's face for the first time that day.[13] Although problems with providing sufficient accommodation meant that the first training course for 1,500 officer cadets, scheduled to begin in February 1945, never got off the ground, this did not prevent the Inspectorate from using the Führer Order as a trump card in their negotiations and disputes with other state institutions almost from the moment that it had been promulgated.[14]

However, while Himmler and Heißmeyer were extremely concerned to avoid the Napolas becoming mere 'cadet schools' which would provide recruits for the army alone (as opposed to the SS), they could not prevent the NPEA becoming a battle-ground for the competing branches of the armed forces. Both the army and the navy were adamant that Napola graduates made the best possible recruits; in one case, the *Heerespersonalamt* (Army Personnel Office) reported that they had never needed to reject a single NPEA-applicant, while the Inspector of Naval Education (*Inspekteur des Bildungswesens der Marine*), Admiral Wilhelm Marschall, told the Inspectorate that the Napolas were the only schools in Germany whose applicants fully satisfied his requirements, whilst simultaneously making very unfavourable comparisons with the 'abysmal state' of the youthful population at large.[15]

In order to tempt such promising new recruits, all the branches of the armed forces sent representatives to the Napolas, each concerned to advertise their wing of the service in the most glowing terms possible; Karl Dürrschmidt, who attended NPEA Neubeuern, remembered that some of these military visitors would even bribe *Jungmannen* to join their units with chocolate which their men had allegedly 'saved up' for them.[16] More impressive 'treats' included the Wehrmacht High Command's organizing trips for the *Jungmannen* to visit the recently vacated battlefields of the Western Front, or arranging visits to see regiments at work—possibly with a free evening at the opera thrown in.[17] The following report by a *Jungmann* from NPEA Bensberg, writing to his mother in October

1942, demonstrates just how attractive such sanitized glimpses into the everyday life of the military could be for younger boys (though one wonders whether his anxious parent would have fully shared his enthusiasm, given some of the activities involved):

> Dear Mother! We've now arrived back in Bensberg. Please don't be cross that I haven't been in touch for so long. It was simply terrific in the Pioneers' barracks. We saw and learnt a lot. When we arrived, we immediately got given drill kit and a steel helmet. In the afternoon we saw how raiding patrols destroy bunkers. During the following days we blew things up, threw live hand grenades, shot with the machine gun and paddled on the Rhine in rubber dinghies. I liked the assault boat best. Everyone could have a turn at steering, and so we whizzed around on the Rhine for an hour. The food was better than here at Bensberg. Every day at midday there was meat. In the evenings everyone got a third of a loaf of army bread, 40g butter and 130g Leberwurst. 7am was when we had to get up. But mostly we were already awake at 6.15, since we had a loudspeaker in our dorm. On Friday afternoon we went to the opera 'Don Giovanni' by Mozart. We had very good seats, first row in the house.... The Pioneer Battalion had paid for the seats.[18]

Meanwhile, the Kriegsmarine might organize excursions to a conquered Baltic seaport, or offer *Jungmannen* free places on sailing courses at Glücksburg, or on the Chiemsee—all of which gained similarly glowing testimonials from the *Jungmannen* who attended them.[19]

However, while the navy did spend a significant amount of money on equipping Plön, Köslin, Spandau, Reichenau, and Putbus as '*Marineanstalten*' (naval schools), so that they could use their proximity to large bodies of water to best advantage, it was Reich Air Marshal Goering and the Luftwaffe who gained pole position in the competition for cadets, at least at the beginning of the war.[20] While an average of three hundred *Jungmannen* were slated to become army officers each year, Potsdam, Rottweil, and Köslin each instituted a '*Sonderzug*' (special class) for boys from all over the Reich who wished to pursue careers as Luftwaffe officers, turning out a total of 110 graduates each year in 1940 and 1941.[21] Rust and Göring had begun planning this fast-track programme in early 1939, and the first candidates began their training after Easter of that year. The more academic aspects of the course, which was intended for sixth-formers, focused on the theory and physics of flight, as well as building models and gliders, and all of the schools in question were fitted out with state-of-the-art workshops and equipment.[22] Although the so-called '*Fliegerzüge*' were dissolved in 1943, they evidently trained a significant proportion of future Luftwaffe officers during their brief existence.[23]

Needless to say, this privileging of the traditional branches of the armed forces infuriated Himmler, who desired that the schools should come fully under the sway of the SS. A confidential report on pupils' career choices prepared by Gottlob Berger in March 1942 claimed that, although the proportion of *Jungmannen* expressing a wish to take up military careers was far higher at the NPEA than at civilian schools, the number of SS applicants had fallen since 1940, undoubtedly because of the Wehrmacht's subsequent propaganda campaign. Popularity of the other services also appeared to rise in tandem with the number of propagandistic visits which they paid to the schools.[24] To counter this trend, the SS increased their promotional efforts too, leading to a 25 per cent increase in Waffen-SS applications by 1944.[25]

Small wonder, then, that the Inspectorate repeatedly used the Napolas' 'vital importance to the war effort' as a means to argue that the relevant authorities should release teachers from the front, provide the requisite administrative personnel, or allow building work on the schools to continue, even as the demands of total war increased. After all, how could one dare to gainsay an institution which, according to the Inspectorate, would singlehandedly be sending almost one thousand fresh-minted officers into the Wehrmacht in 1944 alone?[26]

Quite easily, it would seem: when it came to attempts to have teachers and administrators at the schools designated 'indispensable', debates became particularly heated. Files at the Bundesarchiv Lichterfelde reveal the constant disputes and frictions which arose between Reich Education Minister Rust and his Inspectorate and the Reich Interior Ministry, generally in response to increasingly imperious demands that properly qualified *Erzieher*, bursars, and administrators be transferred or released from active service, even as the need for soldiers on the battlefronts grew ever more pressing.[27] Heißmeyer and his colleagues were forced to consider training women or disabled Waffen-SS veterans to take on these roles; indeed, towards the end of the war, one of the Inspectorate's new spheres of responsibility involved contacting and visiting military hospitals in order to find potentially suitable *Erzieher* among the war-wounded—a far cry from the Napolas' pre-war emphasis on physical fitness as a *sine qua non* for all teaching staff.[28]

The number of employees running the Inspectorate itself had also dwindled catastrophically, even as the number of Napolas simultaneously rose in wartime from sixteen to forty; by autumn 1943, Vice-Inspector Calliebe had been forced to use female typists and secretaries to take on tasks which had previously been solely the preserve of male bureaucrats. One female clerk who had proved herself particularly capable, Frau Raddatz, was even allocated all of the duties which would otherwise have been undertaken by a *Regierungsoberinspektor* (senior civil service administrator).[29] In December 1943, *Anstaltsleiter* Eckardt of NPEA Ilfeld and two of his *Erzieher* colleagues, Rußland from NPEA Schulpforta and Drews from NPEA Potsdam, had to be seconded to the Inspectorate, simply to keep the central administration of the schools going at all.[30]

The most catastrophic lack, however, was the chronic shortage of qualified teaching staff, as ever more *Erzieher* were called up to the front, where they died, were seriously wounded, or went missing in action, in vast numbers—a problem which was exacerbated by the fact that Heißmeyer himself desired all members of staff to gain experience at the front at all costs.[31] Some *Erzieher* were so desperate to prove themselves in battle that they might even try and clandestinely report for service behind their *Anstaltsleiter*'s back, as did Gerd Siegel of NPEA Bensberg.[32] Moreover, despite constant demands that qualified substitutes must be provided for all *Erzieher* who had been called up, the Reich Interior Ministry ultimately refused to honour Rust's agreement with the OKW that this rule should apply to all teaching staff born after 1906.[33] At one point in August 1944, a panicked Calliebe even had to write to the Interior Ministry begging them to intervene, since all of the staff at NPEA Köslin were in imminent danger of being called up by the Army Recruitment Inspectorate (*Wehrersatzinspektion*), despite an explicit agreement having previously been made between the Inspectorate and the Reich Defence Commissioner (*Reichsverteidigungskommissar*) in Stettin that they should be allowed to remain *in situ*.[34] Perhaps unsurprisingly, such disputes about the exact status of the Napola *Erzieher*, and the 'indispensable' nature of their work on the home front, were still raging in early 1945.[35]

*

But what effect did all of this have on life at the schools themselves? From 1941 onwards, at Spandau, the 8th *Zug* was granted one day of self-directed study a week due to the lack of sufficient teachers, while written exams for the NPEA *Reifeprüfung* were replaced by a viva voce and four submitted essays in specified subjects.[36] Many former pupils still vividly recall the negative effects which the dearth of qualified *Erzieher* had on their academic education.[37] For example, Hans Lindenberg remembered a whole parade of odd and ineffectual substitute teachers arriving at NPEA Potsdam, such as the Latin professor from a Berlin university who treated the class as a lecture-theatre, and had ridiculously inflated notions of the pupils' actual level of knowledge.[38] Meanwhile, H. B. of NPEA Rottweil commented acidly that 'we raced from one exam to the next, or from test to test, without processing and consolidating what we'd learnt. By the time the answer was written down, we'd already forgotten the question. So the certificate with which we were issued when we were called up for military service very much deserved the designation "emergency *Abitur*".'[39]

Moreover, it became increasingly difficult to secure new cohorts for the Napolas' youngest year-groups; on the one hand, parents were becoming ever more wary of sending their children away from home; on the other hand, the evacuation of whole classes of local schools by the children's evacuation programme, the *Kinderlandverschickung* (KLV), made it harder to carry out the usual process of screening and selection systematically.[40] The shortage of *Erzieher* and the scarcity of petrol both made visits to all individual schools in each area an impossibility, at the same time that the sphere within which each Napola was permitted to canvass for applicants was shrinking, due to the dramatically increased number of NPEA.[41] Furthermore, even those candidates who were accepted lagged significantly behind academically, due to war-related lacunae in their previous schooling. This led the *Anstaltsleiter* at NPEA Potsdam to institute a summer programme to bring prospective *Jungmannen* up to scratch before the beginning of the school year in 1943, while NPEA Köslin sought to solve the same problem by setting up an entire new *Hundertschaft* of aspirants in 1944.[42]

In tandem, the Napolas' demographic range was also shrinking apace, what with the 18-year-olds already having been called up, the 17-year-olds doing their Reich Labour Service, and the 16-year-olds serving as anti-aircraft auxiliaries; to those left behind, the schools began to feel like 'kindergartens' or 'crèches', filled with the shrieks and laughter of 'tinies', rather than with the broken-voiced basses of the upper forms. One teacher at NPEA Rottweil described this phenomenon using an unusually alcoholic epic simile:

> Put simply, NPEA Rottweil has rejuvenated; the youthful hordes behave like foaming cider, which threatens to burst its cask unless wise coopers leave vents open for its excess energy, and thus *Erzieher* and *Jungmannführer* must muster all their strength, whether through patience or perseverance or thundering authority, gradually to bring order and consistency into this fermentation process.[43]

This '*Verjüngung*' process also had an effect on the quality of the Napolas' artistic activities. For instance, at Ballenstedt, the music teacher reported that all of the school's brass instruments were now lingering unused in their cupboard without any of the experienced older boys to play them (rather than having been donated to the scrap metal drive, as some had joked).[44] Meanwhile, at Bensberg, the music *Erzieher* could only rue the fact that the bottom had dropped out of his school choir—literally, since any pupils capable of singing the tenor and bass parts had long since departed on their 'missions', and only boys with piping trebles and half-broken voices remained.[45] War-related constraints also affected the schools' wider extracurricular programme. As well as the lack of horses and motor vehicles, jaunts overseas were now a thing of the past—and even trips to allied countries such as Italy, Hungary, and Slovakia eventually had to be put on hold.[46]

The provision of more fundamental prerequisites also began to suffer as the war situation worsened. Problems with finding sufficient coal to fuel the Napolas were less pressing than at those civilian schools which were forced to close due to lack of heating, but they were still scarcely negligible; Plön was plagued with burst pipes and flooded and then frozen lavatories, while at Oranienstein, lessons took place in the dormitories rather than in the classroom building in order to save fuel.[47] The Inspectorate was also extremely worried that pupils were not getting enough to eat in the face of the ever greater physical demands which were being placed upon them; by February 1944, Calliebe reported that *Jungmannen* were losing weight at an alarming rate. The Vice-Inspector was intensely concerned to have extra rations allocated to the Napolas, even though he admitted that the Waffen-SS were already supplying the schools with special allocations of fruit, eggs, oil, milk, and legumes.[48] Former pupils also reported that the food at the schools became increasingly monotonous, featuring swedes and beets ad nauseam, or even horseflesh.[49]

Most importantly, many of the *Anstalten* increasingly began to suffer disruption from air raids—particularly Potsdam and Spandau, given their location on the outskirts of the capital, but also Bensberg, given its proximity to Cologne, and Plön, given its propinquity to Hamburg and Kiel; even out-of-the-way Haselünne was struck by a stray unexploded bomb.[50] The *Jungmannen* began to spend ever more time stuck in make-shift air-raid shelters, the only silver lining being that they might be allowed to miss some morning lessons the following day in recompense. *Jungmann* Fuchs of NPEA Spandau described one such experience in a report for his school newsletter:

> The specialist says: 'The air-raid warning is a long-drawn-out, simultaneously fluctuating wailing noise of the air raid siren.' The layman says: 'The air-raid warning is a scurvy disturbance of the peace.' I for my part am in complete agreement with the opinion of the layman. For who doesn't spring in terror from his bed, when this long-drawn-out, simultaneously fluctuating wailing noise of the air raid sirens sounds? Swiftly, we run to our *Stuben* and pull on our clothes, which we've laid out ready the evening before. To protect my skiing trousers I pull my tracksuit bottoms over them. Now there's nothing to do but go down to the cellar, since the flak battery is already beginning to fire. Here below it's dusty and the air is bad. Breathing heavily, I struggle through to my spot. Finally I reach it. I sit down with a sigh. Now my neighbour's here too. We whisper a few fragments, for instance: 'No Latin tomorrow!' or 'We've had no Physics for a whole half-year!' but then we doze off. Until—yes, until a *Jungmann* knocks my head with his foot. Full of rage, I want to strike back, but as I hear the last notes of the All-Clear, I'm immediately reconciled. Now I take my blanket and gasmask and return the way I came about two hours before.... Immediately I go to sleep with the thought that Latin will be cancelled tomorrow. The next morning, the *Jungmannen* will have only one thought between them: 'Shrapnel!!!'[51]

Meanwhile, Gerd Siegel's correspondence with his wife from spring 1944 provides a striking impression of the stress caused by the air raids at Bensberg; he writes of constant attacks on Cologne, day and night, and hails two days without a raid as 'wonderful'. The effects of incessant insomnia and the unceasing tyranny of sirens and detonations are vividly depicted:[52]

> For two days I was Duty *Zugführer*, now I am pretty much finished; exhausted and morose. I didn't get any sleep last night. I had just lain down and was about

to go to sleep, then the early warning siren went, and I had to get dressed as quickly as possible. After the All-Clear, the same thing again: scarcely was I lying back in bed, when the same palaver kicked off once more. As if that weren't enough, after having lain down again I was wrenched from sleep by loud piano-playing from the *Kameradschaftsheim*. And who was playing at half past five in the morning? Two Polish women, who were supposed to be cleaning up there.[53]

Eventually, Spandau and some of the other schools, including the Dutch *Reichsschulen*, were evacuated to Napolas further north and east, while Ilfeld was forced to move to Ballenstedt in 1944, so that the administration of the concentration camp and V2 rocket-works at Mittelbau-Dora could take over the school buildings wholesale.[54]

*

So, how did all of this affect the *Jungmannen*? One source in particular, a 'class diary' (*Zugtagebuch*) which was kept turn and turn about by a group of *Jungmannen* at Schulpforta from 1943 until 1945, illustrates particularly well the ways in which the war shaped everyday life at the Napolas—while never curtailing it completely until the very end.[55] For instance, we regularly find the *Jungmannen* eagerly listening to the Wehrmacht Daily Bulletins on the radio, and taking their contents completely at face value—expressing undying hatred for the Italians after Badoglio's 'capitulation' to the Allies, cursing the 'Tommys' after an air raid which left Münster Cathedral in disrepair, or rejoicing when they heard that V1 rockets were being fired on London once more: 'hopefully they'll warm those guys up again sharpish.'[56] The *Jungmannen* also lapped up the excerpts from letters sent in by old boys serving at the front which were read out to them by *Hauptzugführer* Popp, and were fascinated by the talks and films presented by visiting officers from the armed forces.[57] When Inspector Heißmeyer paid the school a visit, the boys were incredibly excited to see him for the first time, and were evidently reassured by his telling them that they 'didn't need to have any worries about the progress of the war'.[58]

On one level, life at Schulpforta seemed to be carrying on just as normal for the *Jungamnnen* in question—including trips to attend piano or string quartet recitals in nearby Naumburg an der Saale, clandestine cherry-stealing excursions, or incitements to racial hatred during history lessons, when *Hauptzugführer* Rommel told them tall tales of the terrible travails undergone by ethnic Germans at Polish hands.[59] At the same time, it couldn't be ignored that, when it was their classmate Bößenroth's birthday, the *Jungmannen* had to sing to him in the air-raid shelter in the cellars; moreover, they were now forbidden to play football because their shoes were in too poor a state and could not be repaired due to lack of raw materials: 'We aren't exactly happy about it, but we can understand why, since we want to lend a hand with the victory of our fatherland.'[60] Moreover, a vicious circle caused both by the boys' inability to concentrate on lessons, and by the incapacity of a string of inadequate substitute teachers to teach them effectively, led to increasing demoralization and fraying tempers among pupils and masters alike:

> The Penguin waddled into our substitute lesson once again. One has to be on one's toes to make sure that one doesn't suddenly get dragged up by the neck. That is to say, at one point I was unlucky enough to be pulled up by the chin. After that we had Fissmann. He was beastly annoyed that we didn't understand any German any more, or rather didn't know it....A cuffed ear and a failing grade were the marks which that lesson left with me.[61]

Following the D-Day landings, this escalating discontentment with their situation led the *Jungmannen* to commit an act of such gross insubordination that it was censored from the original diary. Erwin Stöckeler writes:

> It was usual for us to sing a song together in the dining room after supper. Today the song was: 'We're trotting into the vastness, the flag flies in the wind; many thousands at our side, who've moved out to ride into enemy land, to fight for the Fatherland...' What the *Jungmannen* sang so cheerfully went like this:
>
> 'We're trotting into the vastness, the suitcase is in its store; the Napola goes bankrupt, because we're so bloody bored.' I think we were even a bit scared by our own daring.[62]

That night, the class were severely reprimanded, and then they were hazed within an inch of their lives—forced to march to a freshly ploughed field in the Knabenberg direction and do endless press-ups until they were so covered in mud that they looked 'like pigs'. Then a further telling-off, and an hour later, a command to present themselves with their uniforms completely clean—all of this in the middle of the night.[63]

While the particulars might change slightly at different Napolas, the overall pattern of increasing disruption and militarization of school life was broadly the same. Even the youngest year-groups' playtime was influenced by the military situation—for instance, at NPEA Plön, a visiting general gave the first-year boys an electric model railway; the games which they subsequently played with it involved soldiers standing on the platform longing to travel to the front.[64] Meanwhile, as *Geländespiele* began to merge with wartime realities, boys who were only a couple of years older might even find themselves taking real prisoners, as did a group of Ballenstedter who ended up being instrumental in catching the crew of a downed Russian aircraft.[65] Indeed, at Naumburg, the programme of cross-country war-games was deliberately adjusted to prepare pupils for service on the Eastern front, comprising activities which were expressly designed to accustom the *Jungmannen* to enduring the harsh cold of the Siberian winter, including handling food and building bivouacs and fires in sub-zero temperatures, and crossing frozen expanses of water.[66]

Those older *Jungmannen* who had not already been called up for military service or the Reich Labour Service generally found themselves deployed in one of three ways: as anti-aircraft auxiliaries (*Marinehelfer/Luftwaffenhelfer*) serving in coastal or land batteries, as under-age labourers building military defences such as the Pommernwall or the Westwall, or as camp youth-leaders overseeing the children's evacuation programme (KLV).

Although the *Luftwaffenhelfer* were often overjoyed to be doing their bit on the front line of civil defence, being treated as '*Altkameraden*' (comrades at the front) in their own right, and having their dispatches published in the school newsletters alongside those of former pupils who were already officers, the air-raid defence duties themselves could be alternately stultifying and terrifying.[67] In addition, although the *Erzieher* attempted to ensure that the *Luftwaffenhelfer* received sufficient teaching at their batteries that their schooling would not be completely disrupted, the toll on staff time could be inordinate, as in the case of Heinrich Rieper, a Latin teacher at NPEA Plön who had to walk the several-mile commute to the battery where his charges were stationed sixty-six times.[68]

However, the '*Kriegseinsätze*' which gave 16- or 17-year-old *Jungmannen* the greatest scope for exercising their own authority (and possibly pursuing a little romance with local girls or BDM-leaders into the bargain) were those which promoted pupils to leadership roles in KLV evacuee camps in the occupied Eastern territories. Many *Jungmannen* perceived their youthful charges as in dire need of licking into shape through Napola-style discipline. Thus, Dietrich Roessler of NPEA Wien-Breitensee proudly described in great detail how he had managed to turn his troop from an undisciplined rabble into a well-disciplined group of marchers, who took to *Geländespiele* like ducks to water.[69] However, sometimes, this led to *Jungmannen* overstepping the mark to quasi-sadistic levels, as when Klaus Kleinau of NPEA Ballenstedt forced a troop of evacuees to march for hours in the blazing sun, nearly causing one to expire from heat stroke.[70]

The Napola education also provided the camp leaders with paradigms for ideological as well as physical training. For instance, one *Jungmann* from NPEA Bensberg was equally keen to instil his charges with both a soldierly attitude and the right political stance, although he admitted that this task was much harder with the evacuees than it would have been with the younger classes at a Napola. However, he endeavoured to use 'examples from daily life' to explain politics to them in simple terms, and prepared a 'weekly political bulletin' for them using material from the available newspapers.[71] Meanwhile, *Jungmannen* from NPEA Neuzelle not only attempted to teach the children in their charge racial theory, but also endeavoured to counteract the influence of local representatives of the Catholic Church, condemning 'the slavish type of Christianity which, after receiving a box on the ears, still says thank you', and trying to prevent evacuees from churchgoing on Sundays.[72]

Not to be outdone, however, the younger *Jungmannen* who were left behind at the Napolas were also keen to pull their weight. Thus, NPEA Naumburg reported that pupils were taking on many roles previously allocated to personnel who had been called up, acting as porters, telephone operators, and air raid wardens around the school. The role of 'air-raid warning telephonist' was particularly popular, as Peter Gerlach recalled: 'Anyone who had received over fifty reports during his watch felt like a hero!'[73] At other schools, such as Plön, *Jungmannen* were trained to act as volunteer firefighters, or enlisted to clear up the debris which was left behind after air raids.[74] Other, less risky pursuits included gathering healing herbs, or silkworm husbandry (to produce parachute silk).[75]

The Napolas also considered it crucial to stimulate their pupils' enthusiasm for war—an aim which the sections of the school newsletters containing 'news from our *Altkameraden* at the front' were perfectly designed to achieve. These spurred on former pupils at the front by providing morale-boosting missives from their *alma mater*, whilst simultaneously firing the *Jungmannen* up with carefully chosen tales of derring-do excerpted from those same former pupils' letters. Reinhard Wagner describes the effect which these newsletters had on his year-group at NPEA Rottweil:

> [The boys] were deeply impressed by the first newsletter..., which contained so many reports from the front piled up together. That was all much closer to home than the novels about the First World War. One knew practically all of the people who were writing personally. One knew them well enough to know that this was the truth; that they weren't fibbing or boasting.[76]

The schools also instigated pen-pal schemes between *Jungmannen* and former pupils on the front line, in order to cultivate a still stronger sense of comradeship between the home and battle fronts.[77]

In tandem with this strategy, the schools also cultivated an obsessive glorification of heroic death; for instance, NPEA Potsdam-Neuzelle held a funeral flag parade (*Trauerflaggenparade*) for every single *Altkamerad* who died, while NPEA Plön and NPEA Naumburg named *Züge* after fallen *Erzieher* and *Altkameraden*, so that they could live on even without having passed on their genes, as well as keeping in touch with the relatives of the fallen comrade in question: 'Instead of one son, they should [now] have as many sons as the *Zug* has *Jungmannen*.'[78] 'Last Will and Testament' letters by former pupils thanking their schools for all that they had given them, and exhorting their loved ones and comrades not to weep for their heroic death, also became a subgenre in their own right (one example by a former *Jungmann* from Köslin became particularly popular), and some of the newsletters boasted entire subsections with titles such as 'How They Fell / *Wie sie fielen*' (Spandau), or 'How They Died / *Wie sie starben*' (Neuzelle).[79] Ultimately, all of the schools' newsletters were filled with a romanticization of war and sacrificial death which was completely divorced from the brutal and horrific reality.

Meanwhile, obituaries and lists of the fallen became ever more numerous as time went on, and lists of decorated *Altkameraden* and *Erzieher* also figured prominently. By the beginning of March 1944, Heißmeyer could boast to Himmler that 'this young cohort of commanders have already fully proved themselves before the enemy. Four have been awarded the Knight's Cross of the Iron Cross with Oak Leaves (*Eichenlaub*), one has even been awarded the Knight's Cross of the Iron Cross with Oak Leaves and Swords (*Schwerter zum Eichenlaub*), thirty-three the Knight's Cross, ninety-six the German Cross in Gold (*Deutsche Kreuz in Gold*), 1,226 have fallen, are missing etc.'[80] Indeed, at NPEA Naumburg alone, one hundred *Altkameraden* and seventeen *Erzieher* had been killed by the end of 1943.[81]

These sacrifices were also celebrated on the home front with elaborate 'commemoration ceremonies' (*Gedenkfeier*), orchestrating pupils' emotions using all of the tried and trusted trappings of National Socialist political religion. Torches flared; drums thundered; solemn hymns were sung; and the names of all the dead were called, row on row, before wreaths were laid or slogans chanted: 'They all fell for Germany and for the Führer. They gave their lives for Germany's future!'[82] The *Jungmannen* could not escape the conclusion that they, too, should be ready to make the ultimate sacrifice. Many schools also made plans to erect shrines to their war-dead, and to fully map out all of their final resting places, after the 'final victory'.[83] Even some of the parents of the fallen *Jungmannen* seem to have found comfort in these forms of communal mourning, encircled by the Napola 'extended family'—whilst remaining unable or unwilling to admit the fact that the schools' adherence to Nazi ideology and martial values had contributed to their sons' untimely death.[84]

*

However, the war did not only cause the Napola communities countless deaths or suffering. As we have seen in Chapters 6 and 7, the schools were able to benefit corporatively from wartime expropriations of property from the Catholic Church—yet the rapacity of the NPEA authorities did not end there. Appropriation of Jewish property was also par for the course, and some schools also profited directly from the Nazi state's antisemitic measures, as well as from the expropriations and mass-murder facilitated by the 'T4' state euthanasia programme.

For instance, with the connivance of the local authorities, NPEA Emsland in Haselünne was able to appropriate a nearby house which had belonged to a Jewish family in order to convert it into a more comfortable residence for the *Anstaltsleiter*, and also planned to turn the former Jewish cemetery into a playground for the younger Napola-pupils.[85] Furthermore, the acting *Anstaltsleiter*, Dirk de Haan, expressed a keen interest in acquiring a substantial amount of furniture which had been confiscated from Dutch Jews in 1943, in order to supplement the rather meagre accoutrements of the former Ursuline convent and girls' convent-school which the NPEA had forcibly seized in 1941 (see Chapter 6). De Haan's wish-list of Jewish property included carpets for visiting-rooms, guest-rooms, the house-matron's room and the maids' sitting-room, various desks and tables, armchairs for the reception room and headmaster's study, and pictures for the pupils' *Stuben* and common-rooms.[86] Although this request does not ultimately appear to have been granted, the relevant correspondence between de Haan and the local *Landrat* fully betrays the school authorities' willingness to benefit from the ill-gotten gains of the Holocaust.[87]

Furthermore, the Inspectorate also sought out asylums for the handicapped or the mentally ill (*Heil- und Pflegeanstalten*) as potential sites for new schools—the NPEA at Reichenau and Rufach being cases in point.[88] Klaus E., a pupil at NPEA Rottweil, remembered having to join a commando of *Jungmannen* who were given the task of cleaning the building at Rufach after the patients had 'left' (they were almost certainly then annihilated at one of the 'T4' killing centres): 'Clearing out a mental asylum isn't much fun, that I can tell you. It was really creepy, lots of filth and piss, but we pulled up our socks and got on with it.'[89]

At the opening ceremony of NPEA Reichenau, the *Anstaltsleiter* even explicitly alluded to the fate of the former inhabitants of the asylum, celebrating the fact that a place which had once been in the service of death was now serving youth and life: 'The sacrifice which the previous inmates of the institution had to make, in order to make room for the youth, is therefore the most deeply meaningful sacrifice, one which fosters the life and future of our *Volk*, and one to which we also pay full homage.' His speech was followed by songs and amusing theatrical skits performed by the *Jungmannen*.[90]

Finally, not only were forced labourers, including prisoners of war and concentration-camp prisoners, used extensively on the estates at Schulpforta, but they were also compelled to perform building or maintenance work at Stuhm, Naumburg, Ballenstedt, Heythuysen, and Bensberg.[91] Following a fire which broke out at Schloss Bensberg on the night of 2–3 March 1942, which destroyed the left-hand tower of the main building, and much of the roof of the north wing, the *Anstaltsleiter*, SA-*Brigadeführer* Paul Holthoff, requested with increasing urgency that he be granted the use of skilled forced labourers to help make good the damage. He had hoped for reinforcements from the nearest prison, but all the available prisoners there were needed for clearance operations after air raids in Cologne.[92] Eventually, following the intercession of various high-ranking officials, including Heißmeyer himeself, the Bensberg authorities were granted the use of a number of concentration-camp inmates—not Jews, but political prisoners. In this way, the '*Außenlager* Bensberg' was founded, in March 1944, using at least ten concentration-camp prisoners who had previously been transported from Buchenwald to Cologne.[93] Dieter Zühlke and Jan Erik Schulte, the authors of the most recent article on the *Außenlager*, aver that the living conditions were far from humane, with all of the prisoners being forced to sleep in a bike shed, and that the sanitary provisions were 'catastrophic'.[94] Holthoff himself was delighted with the arrangement, however, and was pleased to inform the relevant building firm in Cologne that the Reichsführer himself had made sufficient prisoners available for the work to go ahead expeditiously; numbers could then be made up if necessary by civilian prisoners from Cologne jail.[95] The Napolas' close connections to the SS and Himmler's brutal economy of exploitation could scarcely have proved more useful in the short term—or more damning in the long term.

*

On 19 November 1943, Günter Leopold, a pupil at NPEA Reichenau, wrote to his aunt Hedwig in Donaueschingen as follows:

> I just heard that your parents' house in Hannover is in ruins now; I'm very, very sorry. We've got it so good here in comparison, where until now no bombers have come over.... I'm no longer in Reichenau now, but in Rottweil am Neckar at the NPEA there.... It's also part of the Reichenau school, or rather the other way round. I like it there very much, we learn a lot and see a lot of the world. Ten weeks ago we went on a fourteen-day trip to the Vosges and Alsace on our bicycles.[96]

Unlike the civilian schools in Baden, Württemberg, Alsace, and Brandenburg described by Jürgen Finger and Charles Lansing in their respective monographs on local Nazi educational politics, the Napolas only began to suffer chronic disorientation and risk utter disintegration as the battle fronts finally approached (see Chapter 11).[97] The NPEA were allocated better rations, in many cases suffered less from bombing raids due to their isolated locations, and were generally far less constrained by the privations of the home front.[98] The Napolas might suffer shortages of coal or raw materials, but never closure, and rarely expropriation; they endured a dearth of qualified *Erzieher*, but were never forced to rely on totally unqualified people as lay-teachers, as did many civilian schools towards the end of the war.[99] Nor were they as constrained by the ever-increasing shortages suffered by the local authorities who had charge of the educational system in individual *Länder*, given their centralized administration.[100] Moreover, pupils' military socialization often seems to have made them better able to adapt to the adverse circumstances of war, both physically and psychologically.[101]

The *Jungmannen* had also been inoculated against defeatism to an extent that was rare among the general population. While recent scholarship on the German experience during World War II has highlighted the ways in which consecutive crises and defeats led to a 'defensive' mentality, resulting in a hardening of Germans' political and social attitudes, most *Jungmannen* still believed fanatically in the possibility of Germany's 'final victory' until the very end. Even after Stalingrad, most did not share the general population's gathering doubts and deepening depression.[102] They therefore exemplified, or even surpassed, that model of 'politicized youth' which Hitler had so desired to create, but had failed universally to find.[103]

As we shall see in the next chapter, many Napola-pupils represented a hard core of inveterate believers—simply unable to cease believing that the Third Reich would win out until it was far too late, and Allied or Russian troops were almost at their door. It is to this final catastrophic period of evacuation and re-evacuation, hazard and downfall, to which we shall now turn.

Notes

1. Hans Schoenecker, *Lebenserinnerungen 1928–1960* (2007), 19.
2. Cf. Goos, 'Rechenschaftsbericht der Heimat—Kriegsbeginn', *Der Jungmann. Feldpostbericht der Nationalpolitische Erziehungsanstalt Oranienstein*, 1. Kriegsnummer ([December] 1939), 23–5; NPEA Backnang, *Rundbrief*, 19 October 1939; Staatsarchiv Ludwigsburg (StAL), E 202 Bü 1747, letters dated 6 September 1939, 21 September 1939.
3. H. B., private correspondence, October 2013.
4. StAL, E 202 Bü 1747, letter from Calliebe dated 18 September 1939.
5. StAL, E 202 Bü 1747, letter from Heißmeyer dated 11 October 1939; cf. letter from Calliebe dated 18 September 1939.
6. StAL, E 202 Bü 1747, letter from Heißmeyer dated 11 October 1939.
7. Sächsisches Hauptstaatsarchiv Dresden (SHStAD), 11125 Nr. 21350, Bl. 257.
8. On the state of affairs at other schools, see Jürgen Finger, *Eigensinn im Einheitsstaat. NS-Schulpolitik in Württemberg, Baden und im Elsass 1933–1945* (Baden-Baden, 2016), 369–470. On the Napolas' privileged position even in wartime, see also Helen Roche, 'Sport, Leibeserziehung und vormilitärische Ausbildung in den Nationalpolitischen Erziehungsanstalten: Eine "radikale" Revolution der körperlichen Bildung im Rahmen der NS-"Gesamterziehung"?', *Beiträge zur Geschichte des Nationalsozialismus* 32 (2016), 173–96, 191–5.
9. Bundesarchiv Lichterfelde (BArch), R 5/3362, 'Rede des Reichsministers Rust' (21 April 1941), 6.
10. BArch, R 2/12735, letter from Frießner dated 5 March 1940; letter from Heißmeyer to Reinhardt dated 13 June 1940; BArch, R 43-II/956b, letter from Heißmeyer to Lammers dated 22 October 1940, Bl. 48; see also relevant correspondence in BArch, NS 19/1560.
11. BArch, NS 19/1560, Bl. 11, letter from Himmler to Heißmeyer dated 1 May 1940.
12. BArch, NS 6/142, Bl. 53–4. It is worth noting that this decree was part of a tranche of other measures designed to strengthen the development of political will in the army,

and that Hitler therefore presumably believed that those who had been educated at these schools would be unflinchingly loyal to the National Socialist *Weltanschauung*, and hence able to provide exactly the kind of politicized military leadership which he so strongly desired at this point in the war.

13. *Nationalpolitische Erziehungsanstalt Plön. Rundbrief*, no. 26 (October 1944), 19 (letter from Rolf Diercks dated 31 October 1944); cf. BArch, R 2/27763, letter from Himmler dated 12 November 1944, where Himmler takes the credit for the idea, while stressing that pupils at the schools should never feel that they have to take up a career in the Wehrmacht. The *Anstaltsleiter* at NPEA Stuhm, Wolf, had also reported to the Inspectorate as early as January 1943 that the school's army liaison officer had told him that the Führer's Adjutant, General Schmundt, could confirm that Hitler believed that the Napolas produced the best future officers, following a recent conversation (BArch, R 2/12711, letter from Wolf dated 14 January 1943).
14. On the proposed training courses, see BArch, NS 19/665; on the problems involved with finding 'massive barracks' to accommodate all of the prospective cadets, see BArch, NS 19/2741, Bl. 75; BArch, R 2/12743. On the *Führerbefehl* as trump card, see relevant correspondence in BArch, R 1501/624.
15. BArch, R 43-II/956c, Bl. 2, letter from Heerespersonalamt to Calliebe dated 14 January 1943; BArch, R 2/12711, letter from Admiral Marschall to Sowade. It was also a commonplace for former pupils undergoing military training, or already fighting at the front, to report that their military superiors were extraordinarily impressed with their martial prowess and leadership abilities, such that the NPEA began to achieve a broad reputation for military excellence among the armed forces in general.
16. Karl Dürrschmidt, *Mit 15 in den Krieg: Ein Napola-Schüler berichtet* (Graz, 2004), 20.
17. On the visits to the battlefields, see e.g. 'Bericht von der Schlachtfelderfahrt vom 23. bis 31. Oktober 1940', *Potsdamer Kameradschaft. Blätter der Nationalpolitischen Erziehungsanstalt Potsdam* 2, no. 1 (1941), 13–16; H. R., 'Jugend erlebt die Schlachtfelder. Jungmannen der Nationalpolitischen Erziehungsanstalten erzählen', *Völkischer Beobachter*, 6 November 1940 [Bundesarchiv Koblenz, ZSg. 117 Nr. 290].
18. Stadtarchiv Bergisch Gladbach (StABG), R 4/29/1, Bensberg *Jungmann* to his mother, letter dated 4 October 1942.
19. Dieter Rahn, 'Wir waren bei der Kriegsmarine in einem besetzten Ostseehafen zu Gast', *Die Brücke: Nachrichten von der Nationalpolitischen Erziehungsanstalt Köslin* 15, no. 2 (October 1943), 162; 'Segellager des 6. Zuges in Glücksburg', *Spandauer Blätter* 30 (September 1942), 10–11; Hans Günther Zempelin, *Des Teufels Kadett: Napola-Schüler von 1936 bis 1943. Gespräch mit einem Freund* (Frankfurt am Main, 2000), 138–9.
20. 'NPEA Berlin-Spandau—"Marineanstalt"?', *Spandauer Blätter*, Kriegsdoppelheft 16/17 (November 1942), 12–14; cf. BArch, R 2/12725, letters dated 18 January 1941, 29 November 1941, 21 May 1942.
21. BArch, R 43-II/956b, Heißmeyer, 'Bericht über die Arbeit der Nationalpolitischen Erziehungsanstalten', Bl. 68–9.
22. Niedersächsisches Landesarchiv—Staatsarchiv Oldenburg (NLA-StAOL), Best. 134 Nr. 2353, Bl. 72–4, Schnellbrief dated 4 December 1939; Hessisches Staatsarchiv Darmstadt (HStAD), G 53 Gymn. Dieburg Nr. 82; on life in the 'Fliegerzug', see *Die*

Brücke 12, no. 2 (June 1939), 'Wir fliegen' special issue, especially 27–9; 'Aus dem Leben der III. Hundertschaft', *Die Brücke* 14, no. 1 (June 1941), 9–11; also Gerd Stehle, *Fliegen—nichts als fliegen. Pilot in Krieg und Frieden* (Berg am Starnberger See, 2001), 40–51. H. B. reports that, at least at first, there were tensions between the '*Fliegerzügler*' and their coeval counterparts at NPEA Rottweil (private correspondence, October 2013).

23. *Die Brücke* 15, no. 3 (December 1943), 187.
24. BArch, NS 19/1531, Berger, 'Denkschrift an Reichsführer-SS. Erziehernachwuchs 1942' (March 1942); cf. also BArch, NS 2/68, Bl. 95.
25. Heißmeyer, 'Bericht über die Studien- und Berufsberatung an den NPEA der Donau und Alpenländer und Bayern', 10 January 1944 (BArch, NS 19/490). Heißmeyer suggested that further measures should include forming the old boys (*Altkameraden*) into a closed network which would be overseen by his department in the SS Central Office, and which would deliberately steer all former pupils in an SS-wards direction, both career-wise, and ideologically. For an account of Waffen-SS officers recruiting at the schools, see Reinhard Wagner, *Mehr sein als scheinen. Vier Jahre Jungmann in der NPEA Rottweil* (Ditzingen, 1998), 31, 156–7; for an account by a former Napola-pupil entrusted by Heißmeyer with the task of such recruitment, see Walter Flemming, 'Ehemalige Schüler der Nationalpolitischen Erziehungsanstalt Ilfeld/Südharz äußern sich über ihre Erlebnisse in der Anstalt. Walter Flemming—Interview durch eine Studentin' (1984), 38–9.
26. BArch, R 1501/131026, letter dated 25 May 1944. The author stresses the fact that this was three times as many officers as the Reich's cadet schools had managed to supply in one year during the Great War.
27. See the relevant correspondence in BArch, R 1501/131026 and BArch, R 1501/624. The fact that the Inspectorate were extremely choosy about whom they were prepared to employ in administrative positions of this kind did not make the negotiations with the Interior Ministry run any more smoothly.
28. Geheimes Staatsarchiv Preußischer Kulturbesitz (GStAPK), I. HA Rep. 151 C, Nr. 7308, Bl. 170, letter from Reich Education Ministry dated 16 March 1944; cf. BArch, R 1501/131026, letters dated 15 September 1942 (where the idea of using war-wounded Waffen-SS veterans was first mooted by Heißmeyer as a form of 'self-help'), 25 May 1944, 15 June 1944.
29. GStAPK, I. HA Rep. 151 C, Nr. 7308, Bl. 153, letter from Calliebe dated 15 October 1943.
30. GStAPK, I. HA Rep. 151 C, Nr. 7308, Bl. 167, letter from Fischer-Dorp dated 14 December 1943.
31. Cf. e.g. Institut für Zeitgeschichte, München (IfZ), MA 24/6, correspondence between Heißmeyer, SS-Obersturmbannführer With, and Staatssekretär Mussehl, March–April 1943.
32. Gerd Siegel, *Wechselvolle Vergangenheit* (Göttingen, 1980), 132–3.
33. See the relevant correspondence in BArch, R 1501/624, especially the letters dated 12 May 1943, 26 May 1943, 19 July 1943, 23 August 1944. For the Reich Education Ministry's requests for *Erzieher* more broadly, see e.g. NLA-StAOL, Best. 134 Nr. 2353, Bl. 112, Schnellbrief from Rust dated 24 February 1941; Bayerisches Hauptstaatsarchiv, MK53972, letter dated 12 October 1942.

34. BArch, R 1501/624, letter from Calliebe dated 26 August 1944.
35. BArch, R 1501/624, letter dated 5 January 1945.
36. *Spandauer Blätter* 26, Kriegsausgabe 11 (December 1941), 21; *Berufskundliche Mitteilungen* 20, 31 December 1941 [BArch, R 3903/2252].
37. Dietrich Schulz, *Meine Napolazeit in Putbus 1941–1945* (2013), 3.
38. Hans Lindenberg, *Montagskind. Erinnerungen*, Vol. 1 (1990), 91–2.
39. H. B., private correspondence, October 2013.
40. E.g. HStAD, G 15 Heppenheim 608, letter from Schulleitung, Volksschule Rimbach, dated 11 December 1944; Staatsarchiv Hamburg (StAH), 361–10 Nr. 30, Bl. 17, letter dated 17 March 1944; StAH, 361–2 VI Nr. 604, letter dated 16 November 1944.
41. Cf. e.g. Niedersächsisches Staatsarchiv—Hauptstaatsarchiv Hannover, Hann. 180 Lüneburg Acc. 3/88 Nr. 26, letter dated 25 April 1940; Brandenburgisches Landeshauptarchiv Potsdam (BLHA), Rep. 2A II Gen Nr. 1294, Bl. 60, letter dated 16 November 1942; Landeshauptarchiv Sachsen-Anhalt, Abteilung Magdeburg, Rep. C 28 II, Nr. 2361, 'Erfahrungsbericht, zusammengestellt von Hundertschaftsführer Brenner. Betr: Jungmannen-Auslese' (April 1944), Bl. 130–1.
42. Leiter der NPEA Potsdam an Erziehungsberechtigten aller Jungmannenanwärter, letter dated 12 April 1943; Hauptzugführer Liebich, 'Die Anwärterhundertschaft', *Die Brücke* 16, no. 3 (September 1944), 98–9.
43. *Im Gleichschritt: Rundbrief der NPEA Rottweil* 4, no. 13 (November 1943), 303; cf. NPEA Oranienstein, *Rundbrief* (10 December 1944), 7.
44. *Nationalpolitische Bildungsanstalt Ballenstedt*, 4. Rundbrief (30 May 1940), 3.
45. *Die Fackel*, 17. Kriegsfolge (March 1944), 34.
46. Wolff, 'Slowakeifahrt 1941', *Die Brücke* 14, no. 3 (April 1942), 68; 'Unsere Ungarnfahrt 1942', *Der Jungmann*, 10. Kriegsnummer (April 1943), 54–5; *Die Brücke* 16, no. 3 (September 1944), 98; cf. BArch, R 2/12711, letter dated 17 July 1943.
47. 'Aus Plön', *Plön: Rundbrief*, Nr. 9, 4–5; *Der Jungmann*, 3. Kriegsnummer (Summer 1940), 8.
48. BArch, R 2/12712, letter from Calliebe dated 4 February 1944.
49. Cf. e.g. Harald Schäfer, *NAPOLA: Die letzten vier Jahre der Nationalpolitischen Erziehungsanstalt Oranienstein bei Diez an der Lahn 1941–1945. Eine Erlebnis-Dokumentation* (Frankfurt am Main, 1997), 94; Walter Knoglinger, *Stift Göttweig. Heimstätte einer 'Nationalpolitischen Erziehungsanstalt' in der Zeit von Jänner 1943 bis April 1945* (2000), 14.
50. On bomb damage caused to the buildings at NPEA Spandau, see Landesarchiv Berlin, A Rep. 005–07–203, report dated 30 January 1944. On the bomb at Haselünne, see Niedersächsisches Landesarchiv—Staatsarchiv Osnabrück (NLA-StAOS), Rep 430 Dez 209 Akz. 61/1987 Nr. 7, letter dated 7 February 1945. Even the newest schools in the Eastern occupied territories might suffer from consignments of furniture being destroyed either in the warehouse or *en route* (see BArch, R 49/2880 for numerous examples of this phenomenon).
51. 'Fliegeralarm—Drei Stimmungsberichte', *Spandauer Blätter* 22, Kriegsausgabe 7 (November 1940), 9–10, 10. cf. *Spandauer Blätter* 34, Kriegsausgabe 19 (May 1943), 11: In one round-robin to parents, the Spandau *Anstaltsleiter* admonished boys' mothers severely for panicking and enquiring whether all was well with their sons,

following a heavy air raid in 1943. Lübbert castigated their attitude as 'not very valuable in national-political terms', since they were clearly lending credence to reports of city-wide 'pulverization' (*Pulverisierung*) which they could only have obtained from listening to illegal enemy broadcasts from London. He also remarked pointedly that mothers of soldiers could scarcely expect to call the regiment after every battle to find out whether they were all right. He tersely recommended that they take a good long walk round Berlin instead, to reassure themselves that the city was still standing—and that they confine themselves to listening to German broadcasts in future, 'in the interest of their nerves'.

52. Gerd Siegel, 'Ein ehemaliger Erzieher der NPEA Bensberg schrieb an seine Frau (Auszüge aus einem intensiven Briefwechsel'), letters dated 31 May 1944, 2 June 1944, 15 June 1944.
53. Siegel, 'Briefwechsel', letter dated 11 June 1944.
54. On Spandau's evacuation to Köslin, see Arnulf H. K. Putzar, *Im Schatten einer Zeit* (Schwerin, 1998), 56–64; on Ilfeld's move to Ballenstedt, see *Ilfelder Blätter*, 35. Kriegsheft (November 1944), [428]. On the further spate of evacuations which began as the war neared its end, see Chapter 11.
55. Jochen Männig et al., eds, *Das Tagebuch. Aufzeichnungen des 2. Zuges der N.P.E.A. Schulpforta 1943–1945* (1997).
56. *Tagebuch*, entries dated 18 September 1943, 19 September 1943, 11 October 1943, 16 September 1944.
57. *Tagebuch*, e.g. entries dated 19 January 1944, 20 October 1943, 26 January 1944. The presentation and accompanying film shown by the naval commander of a minesweeper seems to have exerted a particular fascination.
58. *Tagebuch*, entries dated 2 March 1944, 3 March 1944.
59. *Tagebuch*, entries dated 1 October 1943, 11 October 1943, 18 October 1943, 18 June 1944.
60. *Tagebuch*, entries dated 2 December 1943, 15 November 1943.
61. *Tagebuch*, entry dated 20 October 1944.
62. *Tagebuch*, gloss on torn-out pages from 11 June 1944.
63. *Tagebuch*, 31–2; cf. Hans-Joachim Männig, 'Schulpforta: NPEA im Krieg', *Die Pforte. Schulpforta-Nachrichten. Zeitschrift des Pförtner Bundes e.V.* 51 (1998), 15–19.
64. Plon, *Rundbrief* 21 (November 1941), 2.
65. Griethe, 'Wie man auch in der Heimat an Russen geraten kann', *Ballenstedt* 19 (July 1944), 54. See also Werner Suhr, 'Wir fangen einen Flüchtling! Eine aufregende Nachtübung', *Nationalpolitische Erziehungsanstalt Plön*, 22. Rundbrief (August 1942), 44, in which boys describe catching a Ukrainian.
66. 'Wehrsport in der dritten Hundertschaft', *Mitteilungen der Nationalpolitischen Erziehungsanstalt Naumburg/Saale*, 19. Kriegsnummer (December 1943), 20–2.
67. Cf. e.g. G. Drescher, *Erinnerungen—Napola Neuzelle* (IfZ, ED 735-5, n.d.), 31; H. W. Knobloch, 'Die Anstaltszeitung in Passade!', *Spandauer Blätter* 37, Kriegsausgabe 22 (1. Dezember 1943), 18–19; *Ilfelder Blätter*, 29. Kriegsheft (June 1943), [109].
68. Heinrich Rieper, *Meine Tätigkeit an der N.P.E.A. Plön, meine Beziehungen zu ihr und meine Erinnerungen an Sie* (*c.*1948 [Kreisarchiv Plön, F 9 2.2]), 9. For a contemporary account by a pupil at Plön who describes Rieper's teaching, see Harald R., *Tagebuch vom 18.07.1943–26.08.1944*, 13–22.

69. 'Jungmannen als Erzieher. Zwei Berichte von der Kinderlandverschickung', *Nationalpolitische Erziehungsanstalt Wien-Breitensee*, 4. Rundbrief (15 July 1942), 20–2.
70. Klaus Kleinau, *Im Gleichschritt, marsch! Der Versuch einer Antwort, warum ich von Auschwitz nichts wusste. Lebenserinnerungen eines NS-Eliteschülers der Napola Ballenstedt* (Hamburg, 2000), 50–1; for a further example, see Gerhard Kock, *'Der Führer sorgt für unsere Kinder...' Die Kinderlandverschickung im Zweiten Weltkrieg* (Paderborn, 1997), 163. However, while Kock argues that the KLV 'exported' the NPEA model to the whole of the youthful population, and that many camps came to resemble Napolas or Adolf-Hitler-Schools in miniature (144, 309, 328), he fails to draw the logical conclusion that this was presumably often due to the fact that many of the camps were largely run by elite-school pupils, who were merely trying to recreate the circumstances of their own education as faithfully as possible, rather than necessarily being a matter of explicit policy.
71. Paulheinz Fengler, 'Berichte und Erfahrungen aus meinem Dienst in der erweiterten Kinderlandverschickung', *Die Fackel*, 17. Kriegsfolge (March 1944), 37–41.
72. 'Einsatz des sechsten Zuges in Lagern der Kinder-Landverschickung', *NPEA Neuzelle*, 14. Kriegsbrief (March 1943), 21–7. On the deliberately deleterious effect of KLV camps on children's religious life in general, see Thomas Brodie, *German Catholicism at War, 1939–1945* (Oxford, 2018), 159–60.
73. *Mitteilungen der Nationalpolitischen Erziehungsanstalt Naumburg/Saale*, 18. Kriegsnummer (October 1943), 20–3; Peter Gerlach, *Lebenserinnerungen* (2007), 55.
74. When interviewed in January 2013, one former pupil, Uwe L., was still extremely proud of the medal which he had gained for his stalwart service clearing Plön's streets of rubble.
75. Oberzugführer Hempel, 'Heilkräutersammlung 1943', *Mitteilungen der Nationalpolitischen Erziehungsanstalt Naumburg/Saale*, 18. Kriegsnummer (October 1943), 23; Helmut-Albrecht Kraas, ed., *Napola Neuzelle (ehem. Kreis Guben/Mark Brandenburg)—eine Dokumentation*, Vol. 2 (1993–4), 74–5.
76. Wagner, *Mehr sein als scheinen*, 101. The *Spandauer Blätter* even encouraged former pupils to write accounts of their experience *while the battles in question were still going on*, in order to provide as vivid a depiction as possible for the younger year-groups (*Spandauer Blätter* 23, Kriegsausgabe 8, March 1941, 21).
77. Cf. e.g. *Nationalpolitische Erziehungsanstalt Wien-Breitensee*, 3. Rundbrief (31 March 1942), 3; *NPEA Neuzelle*, 9. Kriegsbrief (December 1941), 24; 'Kameradendienst der Oraniensteiner Jungmannen', *Der Jungmann*, 10. Kriegsnummer (April 1943), 33–4.
78. *NPEA Neuzelle*, 13. Kriegsbrief (December 1942); Plön, *Rundbrief* 17, 22; '"Ich will kämpfen bis zum Sieg!" Zur Feier des 9. November 1944', *Mitteilungen der Nationalpolitischen Erziehungsanstalt Naumburg/Saale*, 23. Kriegsfolge (Yulemoon [December] 1944), 12–14, 14.
79. 'Aus dem Testament eines unserer gefallenen Altkameraden, dessen Name auf eigenen Wunsch nicht erwähnt werden soll', *Die Brücke* 14, no. 4 (December 1942), 89; cf. *Potsdamer Kameradschaft* 4, no. 2 (November 1943), 31. One *Jungmann* from Spandau who had been expelled even asked that his death might make good the shame of his expulsion, and ensure his place on the Roll of Honour for the fallen—a request which was granted; cf. *Spandauer Blätter* 30, Kriegsausgabe 15 (September 1942), 13–14.

80. BArch, NS 19/3096, Bl. 2, letter from Heißmeyer to Himmler dated 9 March 1944.
81. 'Waffenleite am 9. November', *Mitteilungen der Nationalpolitischen Erziehungsanstalt Naumburg/Saale*, 19. Kriegsnummer (December 1943), 8–9, 9.
82. As an example, see Harring Cölln, 'Heldengedenktag 1943', *Nationalpolitische Erziehungsanstalt Plön*, 23. Kriegsbrief (April 1943), 46–7.
83. E.g. *Mitteilungen der Nationalpolitischen Erziehungsanstalt Naumburg/Saale*, 13. Kriegsnummer (August 1942), 8; 'Aufruf', *Potsdamer Kameradschaft* 5, no. 1 (April 1944), 41–2.
84. E.g. *NPEA Neuzelle*, 5. Kriegsbrief (December 1940), 6–8; *Potsdamer Kameradschaft* 5, no. 1 (April 1944), 7; *Spandauer Blätter* 43, Kriegsausgabe 28 (December 1944), 3.
85. NLA-StAOS, Rep 430 Dez 209 Akz 61/1987 Nr. 57; NLA-StAOS, Dep 75b Nr. 78 (on the NPEA's plans for the cemetery, see the letter from de Haan to the Bürgermeister of Haselünne dated 18 January 1945).
86. NLA-StAOS, Dep 75b Nr. 82, letter from de Haan dated 14 June 1943 (Betr: Judenmöbel aus Holland).
87. NLA-StAOS, Dep 75b Nr. 82, letter from the Landrat, Kreiswirtschaftsamt, Meppen, dated 18 June 1943 (Betr: Judenmöbel).
88. When Heißmeyer wanted to expropriate the asylum in Füchtel, however, he stumbled upon too much resistance from the local authorities to put his plan into practice (NLA-StAOL, Rep. 410 Akz. 162 Nr. 561). In a letter on this subject to Gauleiter Röver dated 27 January 1941, the Inspector made it clear that any concerns he might have about using former asylums as NPEA focused solely on the fact that it might not be very nice for *Jungmannen* to have to live in a building which had formerly been used for such a purpose, but that 'in many similar cases, we have already thrust such reservations aside'.
89. Lothar Steinbach, *Ein Volk, ein Reich, ein Glaube? Ehemalige Nationalsozialisten und Zeitzeugen berichten über ihr Leben im Dritten Reich* (Bonn, 1995), 158; Arnulf Moser, *Die Napola Reichenau. Von der Heil- und Pflegeanstalt zur nationalsozialistischen Eliteerziehung (1941–1945)* (Konstanz, 1997), 11–13, 18–20.
90. Zugführer Baumann, 'Zug 4 in Rufach und bei der Eröffnung der NPEA Reichenau', *Im Gleichschritt* 2, no. 4 (May 1941), 106–8.
91. This list is not intended to be exhaustive; it merely lists the schools for which incontrovertible evidence exists: on Schulpforta, see Landeshauptarchiv Anhalt, Abteilung Merseburg, C48IIIa Nr. 11967; on Stuhm, BArch, R 2/12730, letter dated 19 August 1940; on Naumburg, *Mitteilungen der Nationalpolitischen Erziehungsanstalt Naumburg/Saale*, 18. Kriegsnummer (October 1943), 21; on Ballenstedt, Bundesarchiv, Außenstelle Ludwigsburg (BAL), B162/27628; on Heythuysen, NIOD, 039 2259, memo dated 17 September 1942; on Bensberg, see below.
92. Dieter Zühlke and Jan Erik Schulte, 'Vom Rheinland nach Westfalen: KZ-Außenlager bei der "Nationalpolitischen Erziehungsanstalt" in Bensberg und Hardehausen', in Jan Erik Schulte, ed., *Konzentrationslager im Rheinland und in Westfalen 1933–1945. Zentrale Steuerung und regionale Initiative* (Paderborn, 2006), 113–30.
93. Cf. StABG, F2/1080, J16/3, S6/1, and S6/189; Landesarchiv Rheinland-Westfalen, Abteilung Rheinland, Duisburg (LNRW-D), RW0054 Nr. 92; BAL, B162/26786; NPEA Bensberg's Außenlager at Hardehausen is documented in BAL, B162/25766.

94. Zühlke and Schulte, 'KZ-Außenlager', 121.
95. LNRW-D, RW0054 Nr. 92, letter from Holthoff to GB-Bau Köln dated 11 December 1943.
96. BLHA, 116 Bollhagen Nr. 285, letter dated 19 November 1943.
97. Cf. Finger, *Eigensinn*, 369–470; Charles Lansing, *From Nazism to Communism: German Schoolteachers under Two Dictatorships* (Cambridge, MA, 2010), 101–28.
98. Jill Stephenson, *Hitler's Home Front: Württemberg under the Nazis* (London, 2006), 181; cf. Dietmar Süß, *Death from the Skies: How the British and Germans Survived Bombing in World War II* (Oxford, 2014) on the hugely chaotic nature of communal air-raid shelters and the privations of city life during the bombing war.
99. Cf. Finger, *Eigensinn*, 375–6; Lansing, *Schoolteachers*, 115–18, 127–8, 130–3.
100. Cf. Finger, *Eigensinn*, 461–3.
101. Cf. Helen Roche, 'Surviving "*Stunde Null*": Narrating the Fate of Nazi Elite-School Pupils during the Collapse of the Third Reich', *German History* 33, no. 4 (2015), 570–87. One might compare their reactions to those of the children described in Nicholas Stargardt, *Witnesses of War: Children's Lives under the Nazis* (London, 2006).
102. Nicholas Stargardt, *The German War: A Nation under Arms, 1939–45* (London, 2015).
103. Joachim Szodrzynski, 'Die "Heimatfront" zwischen Stalingrad und Kriegsende', in Forschungsstelle für Zeitgeschichte in Hamburg, ed., *Hamburg im 'Dritten Reich'* (Göttingen, 2005), 633–85, 634; cf. Marlis G. Steinert, *Hitler's War and the Germans: Public Mood and Attitude during the Second World War* (Athens, OH, 1977), 331.

11
The *Endkrieg* and the Last of the Napolas

For pupils at the Napolas, the last few months of the Second World War heralded an inexorable transition from 'total war' to total chaos.[1] Boys as young as 15 or 16 were called up into the armed forces, and many of the schools had to be evacuated wholesale in the face of the advancing Allied armies. The position of Napolas in the Eastern territories of the Reich, especially those in West Prussia and Pomerania, was particularly precarious. The startling speed of the Russian advance, alongside propaganda-inflamed fears of bestial Bolshevik brutality, led to an all-pervasive atmosphere of instability; '*Stunde X*', the hour of reckoning when the school would have to be abandoned and the harsh trek westwards begun, could potentially arrive at any hour of the day or night.[2] Although the Inspector of the Napolas, August Heißmeyer, had already suggested in October 1944 that pupils should be expected to defend their schools, which would then become 'permanent combat bases', and certain plans were later put into place instructing any school that was in danger of being overtaken by the enemy to retreat to another, 'safe' Napola, as the war situation worsened, the authorities at individual NPEA were frequently forced to improvise.[3]

This chapter will explore the experiences of pupils from a range of different Napolas throughout the Third Reich, as Germany's territories shrank around them, leaving some in imminent peril of imprisonment—or worse.[4] Some boys were forced to fight their 'liberators' to the last, having been drafted into makeshift units of the SS, the Wehrmacht, or the *Volkssturm* (the Third Reich's 'Home Guard'); others fought on willingly even after the armistice, unable to believe that the regime to which they had given their all had collapsed into utter ruin. Many were merely concerned to reunite themselves with their families, even if they were unsure whether any of their relatives remained alive, or if their homes would still be standing. Yet others simply wished to flee and avoid internment at all costs, once they knew that the war was truly lost.

In a sense, then, the fates of pupils at the Napolas in 1945 provide a fascinating cross-section of experiences of Nazi Germany's collapse, focusing not only on those refugees fleeing the advancing Eastern Front, but on those trapped in southern Germany and Austria, and those who witnessed—or even participated in—the fall of Berlin. Yet, at the same time, it could be argued that the Napolaner had more to lose than the average refugee. It was already widely suspected—if not yet officially known—that former pupils of any Nazi elite schools who found themselves in Soviet hands would be interned, and that their parents might well

The Third Reich's Elite Schools: A History of the Napolas. Helen Roche, Oxford University Press. © Helen Roche 2021.
DOI: 10.1093/oso/9780198726128.003.0012

lose their jobs, particularly if they worked in the public sector.[5] But even the Western Allies were highly unlikely to treat adherents of such institutions with any consideration; rather, they would be perceived as some of the most inveterate youthful supporters of the regime.[6] If their educational affiliation were discovered, then, the Napolaner could expect no quarter in their dealings with the enemy.

In the pages which follow, the last days of four different groups of Napolas will be charted: firstly, those in the extreme northeast of Germany—Stuhm, Köslin, and Rügen—which had most to fear from the encroaching Red Army (as well as Plön, the Napola to which Stuhm was evacuated); secondly, Rottweil and Reichenau in south-west Germany, which fell into French hands; thirdly, Göttweig, Traiskirchen, and Wien-Theresianum in eastern Austria, and finally, Berlin-Spandau and Potsdam, whose pupils were caught up in a series of desperate last stands as Hitler's capital was finally reduced to rubble. Such a selection can highlight the similarities of the experiences which pupils at many of the Napolas were compelled to undergo, whilst also illustrating the differing ways in which all four corners—and, finally, the centre—of the collapsing Greater German Reich were affected by the Allies' onslaught. The schools in question are highlighted in Figure 11.1.

Terror from the East: The Fates of NPEA Stuhm, Köslin, Rügen, and Plön

One of the very first Napolas to be affected by the Russian advance was NPEA Stuhm (now Sztum in northern Poland), which found itself in the path of the Red Army in early January 1945. Manfred-Peter Hein describes the chaotic departure of the younger year-groups which followed the first 'Soviet tank alarm':

> Go! The long-awaited moment has arrived; assembly in the *Appellhof*! There is no motor-driven transport; the fleet of cars is only sufficient for the wives and children of the *Erzieher*. Before us the Chaussee, northward-bound, the baggage, the packs laced on skis, three abreast.... Napola Stuhm, a long-drawn-out column in the nettle-sharp driving east wind, which sweeps the snow from the asphalt, snowdrifts built up on the slope of the road; we are left mere tatters.... Our ski-boards, more brake-blocks than skates, are left one by one along the way.... Night: food in tin bowls and sleeping on straw....[7]

The next day, the boys arrived at the railway station in Simonsdorf, and began the arduous journey westwards towards Plön in Schleswig-Holstein, on trains so packed with refugees that (Hein claims) some of them could only be accommodated by squashing into the luggage-nets suspended above the seats.[8] Their destination was Schloss Plön, home of the very first school to become a Napola; it

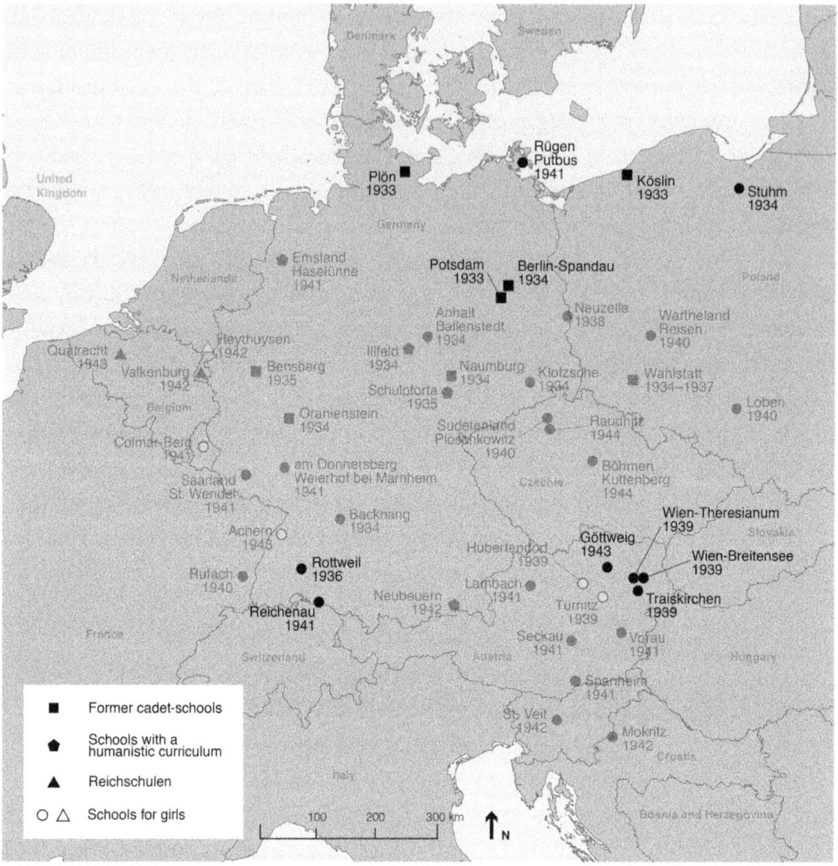

Figure 11.1 Map of the schools whose fates during 1945 are charted in detail in Chapter 11 (map by Tess McCann).

would now become their sanctuary until the war's end. The older year-groups stayed behind in Stuhm for two more days, burning all official documents and similar material which they could lay their hands on before the second 'tank alarm'. Around one o'clock in the morning of the third day, they also set off on foot towards Plön, heading for Dirschau (Tczeu), where one of the only bridges across the river Vistula remained passable; it had not yet been detonated to delay the Russian advance.[9]

However, even the Stuhmers' arrival at Plön could not guarantee their safety. Eckhard R., who was 15 at the time, remembers that here, air raids were much more common (Stuhm had been out of range of most British and American bombers), and one attack even left a 3-metre-wide crater in the castle courtyard. In April, in readiness for the Western Allies' invasion, the boys were set to work building tank traps and trenches throughout the surrounding countryside.

Eckhard R.'s group had to defend one particular spot on the way to Lütjenburg, about 10 kilometres north-east of Plön, where two lakes on either side caused the road to narrow suddenly. The boys had to chop down beech trees, make stakes from their branches, and plant them in holes in the road where the paving-stones had been removed; these were then piled elsewhere on the road to make it impassable. They then had to make crawl-spaces beneath the roadside hedges so that they could pass from the trenches on one side to those on the other. When the time came, it was intended that they would fire an anti-tank grenade (*Panzerfaust*) from one side of the road, then creep quickly under and fire a second grenade from the other side. Training with the *Panzerfäuste* had already begun while the boys were still in Stuhm, but they had never actually practised firing these 'mini-rockets'.[10]

Ultimately, however, the Napola pupils were never required to man these last-ditch positions. Those whose homes were still accessible, particularly among the younger boys, were dismissed at the end of March.[11] After the school buildings were requisitioned by the Wehrmacht High Command (OKW) at the end of April, those pupils who remained were quartered in two neighbouring villages, Kossau and Rathjensdorf.[12] Once it became clear that the war was lost, the boys themselves assumed that they would have to hide in the woods, perhaps even in holes under fallen trees, in order to escape the Allies' furious vengeance. The teachers proposed a more sensible plan: all school uniforms with recognizable insignia must be burnt, and farmers in the neighbourhood would take on those boys who could no longer safely reach home, friends, or relatives as 'labourers', whilst concealing their real identity.[13]

NPEA Plön was formally and finally dissolved on 8 May 1945, and the town was handed over to the British without any bloodshed.[14] However, the aftermath of the war would affect former pupils for many months to come. Eckhard R. describes his own experiences during this fraught time as follows:

> I found myself as an unskilled labourer on a farm in Kossau, about 8 kilometres north-east of Plön. I didn't feel happy there. I didn't understand the Holstein local dialect, and the farmer thought that I didn't want to understand.... Then a former soldier of the Wlassow Army, a Russian Wehrmacht brigade, turned up at the farm. He spoke good German and we chatted in the evenings in the stable about Soviet Russia and Nazi Germany. Apparently, he still had connections with former comrades, since he told me that he had to go into hiding, because otherwise the Western Allies would extradite him to the Soviet Union....
>
> In the last days of April 1945 I had visited my mother in Güstrow in Mecklenburg...where she had fled from Bromberg.... We had agreed that, if we were separated again by the ongoing war, we would leave our new address at the Post Office in Güstrow, where my mother was now employed—even if only

> rubble remained of it, then our new address would be written on a piece of rubble. That was how I arrived in the Soviet Occupation Zone in July 1945, after an adventurous crossing of the demarcation line. I was happy to be back with my mother again.[15]

Harald R., a former pupil of NPEA Plön who had already been called up in January at the age of 16 to fight in a parachute regiment, had a far more harrowing experience during his desperate quest to return to the non-Soviet side of the demarcation line. In fact, this was even to play a part in determining his later career path, as the following extract from an interview with the author shows:

> [I first knew that I wanted to be a pastor] when I understood that I was behind the Russian lines, alone, with my pistol.... I did not wish to be imprisoned, so I made for the demarcation line on the Störkanal, south of Schwerin and Ludwigslust.... On the one side, the Russians, on the other, the Americans. And I had to get over...so I swam across the canal during the night, and...on the other side, the discovery; I found an American cigarette packet...and I knew: 'Now I will not be a Russian prisoner of war.'...Then I fell to my knees, truth be told, so that I could thank God...[he weeps]...and wondered 'your life must still have some meaning, then'.... The others are dead...you live. [He weeps a little more]...And then the decision, after I did my *Abitur*, to study theology. That was precisely out of thankfulness.[16]

In diary entries and correspondence from 1946 recalling this period, Harald R. described his wanderings in more detail:

> The call of the cuckoo was hateful to me, the leaping deer and the boar breaking cover, the solitary cat and the baying of the dog filled me with terror. I dreaded the light of day and longed for the night; the radiant full moon did not fill me with gladness, far more the clouds, which covered her; only the lofty stars, they remained constant—and showed me the way homeward....[17]
>
> My comrades had let their courage dwindle, removed all their decorations and symbols of rank, and wanted to become honest citizens once again. I broke away from them. I wanted to avoid falling into Russian hands at any cost. I stuck my pistol into my boot, and night and loneliness were my travelling companions. I shunned the roads and sought the propinquity of men under the most extreme caution—only when hunger commanded.
>
> These were the hardest weeks of my life, these five weeks of being eternally on the run. As free game, robber and criminal, beggar and vagrant I pulled myself through the newly resurgent world of nature. But I could not appreciate it anymore; the instincts of an animal ruled me, and it was a long while before I woke again to myself.

> The worst, the most perilous day was the crossing of the border, the demarcation line between the Russians and Americans.... Here did I perceive God's guidance most clearly.... It was at home that I realized for the first time that, despite the collapse, life still went on. How thankfully did I take everything which the day offered me. Even the smallest piece of civilization was an uplifting gift.[18]

*

Less than a month after the evacuation of Stuhm, at the very end of January 1945, NPEA Köslin was one of the next Napolas to find itself in the path of the advancing Russian troops. Instead of heading straight for Holstein, however, the authorities decided that the younger year-groups should be transferred to the Napola at Putbus on the island of Rügen, some 300 kilometres away.[19] The older boys were to remain in Köslin until the last possible moment, performing tasks such as escorting evacuees from the railway station to their lodgings, helping with registration for the *Volkssturm*, assisting with the transportation of weapons, or simply guarding the school itself. Joachim Dettmann, a 17-year-old who stayed at the school right until the end, recalled that the hardest of these tasks was the so-called *Bahnhofsdienst* (station duty), where one often had to assist with the removal of refugees who had frozen to death.[20]

The first and second *Zug* (class) were evacuated by train on the 30th of January, a day after the decision to retreat to Putbus had been made; they reached the island of Rügen the next day. The third *Zug*, despite leaving on the same day, were supposed to go as far as Kolberg on foot—a distance of some 42 kilometres—and then continue their journey by ship. Martin Köhler describes the preparations which ensued:

> Before shutting our cupboards, we fooled around, decorating the inside of the lockers with Nazi ideology, pictures and texts from newspapers, Nazi emblems, and pamphlets castigating the Soviets and their 'helot character'. The invaders should have got a nice shock....
>
> The departure was scheduled for the small hours of 30 January. In the afternoon, bed rest was ordered, how awful, then we had our haversacks liberally filled, and a drink for our canteens into the bargain. Our luggage was left behind...to be brought to Kolberg on a lorry and then to Rügen on a fishing boat—and that happened too, in accordance with the schedule.
>
> We were instructed to go through the town not in a marching column, and without the usual singing, but as a loose formation, so as not to give the civilian population any call for agitation or fear.... Everything in the town seemed to be fast asleep....
>
> It was very cold, and deep snow was lying, as high as our boots, perhaps even higher. We were completely alone on the road, and cast about for a way where

> vehicles had driven through. A horse-drawn sleigh caught up with us; quickly I stood on the rear runner and let myself be carried along. Another *Jungmann* stood on the other side. Sadly, the farmer, who was well disposed towards us, soon turned off towards his homestead and asked us to dismount.... Soon I began to flag, perhaps even after the first 10 kilometres. I became unspeakably tired, and wanted to lie down to sleep in the beautifully soft snow.... Everything was very lonely, only a wide, deserted, very still snowy landscape all around us.[21]

However, relief was at hand, in the form of a military motorbus which picked the boys up and dropped them off at Kolberg quay, where the sailors of the hospital ship *Oberhausen* were waiting to welcome them aboard. After a few days of respite, they set off again, this time attempting to complete the journey by train (possibly because the Napola authorities had heard of the sinking of the *Wilhelm Gustloff*, a ship crammed with thousands of evacuees, which had just been torpedoed by a Soviet submarine on its way from Gotenhafen to Kiel).[22] The railway journey appears to have been even more chaotic than that experienced by the Stuhmer a month before, with passengers clinging to the buffers and the running-boards of the carriages, and an inordinate number of changes and stops being required before the boys finally reached their destination. By this time, it was mid-February.[23]

Three memories of the time at Putbus remained particularly vivid in Köhler's memory, firstly, the fact that there was an utter shortage of salt (a block of pink cattle-salt, carried round in a matchbox in his pocket, became one of his most prized possessions); secondly, the day that a *Panzerfaust* went wild in class and set off the school fire alarm; and, lastly, the fact that regular power cuts meant that the only sure way to light the dining hall during the frugal dinners was to have *Jungmannen* taking it in turns to pump a makeshift dynamo powered by half a dismembered bicycle.[24]

Meanwhile, the older year-groups, who had been left behind in Köslin, made ready to leave on 1 March. They each received a bar of chocolate and other rations, and were given a final send-off by the school's *Anstaltsleiter*, Lothar Dankleff, before setting off on the long march towards Kolberg and Putbus.[25] Joachim Dettmann, who had stayed behind to help Dankleff with some last-minute assignments, recounts what happened next:

> In the afternoon on 1 March, I had a job to do in town, when suddenly the sirens gave the signal for a tank alarm. I rode my bicycle back along the Danziger Straße and turned into the school. Shortly afterwards, three Russian tanks started firing their cannons into the Danziger Straße.... According to Dankleff junior, a grenade exploded in the *Anstaltsleiter*'s bathroom.... The soldiers [who were also quartered in the school buildings] didn't do anything against the tanks. *Zugführer* Ackermann, [three other *Jungmannen*] and I left the school grounds

> by the sickbay entrance, armed with some *Panzerfäuste*, rifles, and pistols. It was already getting dark, and we went by the hospital and the orphanage into the wood, then in the direction of the road, where about 5 metres above us the tanks were standing. We shot all the *Panzerfäuste*, but, probably because of the gloom, they all missed their mark. The Russian soldiers must still have noticed us, though, because we were shot at with machine guns. Sometime later, the tanks began to retreat in the direction of Zanow, and we were all lucky enough to get back to the school safely.[26]

Meanwhile, the whole town was being fully evacuated, and the remaining teachers and pupils at the school followed suit; trains were still leaving the station, but only towards Kolberg. Three of Dettmann's classmates escaped by bicycle to Vineta, the Napolas' seaside retreat, where they spent the night and were then led over the last passable bridge in the Kolberg direction by the Vineta caretaker Herr Heck, taking his two daughters along with them to Putbus. Dettmann and *Zugführer* Ackermann decided to stay behind and help the refugees, only leaving the school on 3 March, after the soldiers who were in residence had received the command to relocate to the centre of town.[27]

> Well-armed with *Panzerfaust*, rifle, and pistol, with fondant pralines as marching rations in our haversacks, we left the school on bicycles, via the bicycle shed. Here, unfortunately, a horse-drawn wagon with the luggage of the school administrators and employees was stuck, since the horses had been stolen from the stable shortly before the decampment. We rode down the Kadettenstraße, turned down Ziegelgraben, Lindenstraße, and Eliesenstraße. Here, both sides of the street were in blazing flames, and we had to carry our bicycles over the shards of glass which had exploded.... The town centre was completely ablaze. Unhindered, we reached the Buchwaldstraße, in order to carry on to Kolberg. On the Buchwaldstraße, a column of refugees had been gunned down...very systematically. Dead horses and men, remains of cars, everything lay in chaos....[28]

Eventually, they too managed to make their way to Putbus, which the rest of the school had already reached in safety. Yet NPEA Rügen was not to be the end of their journey, for on 18 March, the Kösliner were evacuated once more, this time to Heide in Holstein, where they occupied a boys' day school.[29]

In April, the youngest pupils were sent home 'until further notice', and on 3 May, the older pupils followed their lead. Many, whose native districts were now under Soviet occupation, had absolutely no idea where their families might be, or even if they were still alive. Even those with a particular destination to head for would only with difficulty be able to make their way on the last remaining trains, which moved only at a snail's pace, and were regularly strafed by enemy fighters.

As at Plön, many of the remaining *Jungmannen* were given civilian clothing and distributed among neighbouring farmers until such time as they might be able to return home. One Erich Zemke (who had been in the second *Zug*) spent a whole year with a farmer and his family, only later finding his parents via the German Red Cross search lists.[30] For Martin Köhler, however, there was a happy ending of sorts:

> I reached Lübeck, Schwerin, and Kröpelin safely. I marched the last few kilometres to Radegast [where my aunt and cousins were staying] along the lonely country road. I caught up with a milk float, and already from a long distance away I could see that behind, on the loading platform, a young woman with dangling legs was sitting. It was my sister Christel, who had just been released from the Labour Service, still in uniform, and striving as I was to reach the relations in Radegast, the Köhlers' collection point. It was a massive joy to see her again, which was repeated after a few kilometres in Radegast...where we found our parents, our little sister Marianne, an aunt and two of our housemaids, all from the little exiled group from Bublitz, and all hale and hearty.[31]

*

The evacuation of Napola Rügen itself was perhaps one of the most adventurous (or foolhardy) operations of all, since it was decided at the last moment that a group of older pupils, several of the masters, and the *Anstaltsleiter*, *Haupthundertschaftsführer* Lüders, should attempt to sail their way over the high seas to safety in Schleswig-Holstein, using the school's miniature fleet of yachts and cutters. Many of the boys were used to handling the boats in sailing lessons and on small excursions, but this journey through enemy-infested open waters would be a potentially fatal test of their skills, particularly since very few of the *Erzieher* had any nautical experience whatsoever.

Before the great escape could take place, however, Lüders wished to abdicate all responsibility for the younger year-groups.[32] Pupils in the first four classes and their *Erzieher* were dismissed on 23 April, with instructions to report back to the school 'after the final victory'. Those who had lost touch with their parents due to 'temporary' loss of territory to the enemy were to stay with friends or relatives on the island of Rügen. Jürgen Schach von Wittenau (and many other Putbusser) remember that Lüders concluded his farewell speech with the following words: '...those who have stayed away after the Easter holidays instead of resuming their tasks here have forfeited their right to return. We shall not re-admit them when after our victory they come knocking on our door!'[33] The flag was duly raised, and the command to 'dismiss' given for the final time. The boys were only allowed to take with them what they could carry; many squeezed themselves into multiple layers of undergarments in order to make space in their backpacks for personal treasures—everything else, even valuable musical instruments, would have to be left behind.[34]

The older boys, meanwhile, had been caught up in a whirlwind of clandestine activity—some of which could easily have cost them their lives. In mid-April, one group were sent all the way to Berlin, ostensibly in order to pick up a morale-boosting consignment of bonbons from a sweet factory; their real purpose (only fully determined decades later) was to deliver a top-secret message from Lüders to the Inspector of the Napolas, August Heißmeyer.[35] Others, without even Lüders' knowledge, had been set to work by *Zugführer* Wiers and *Zugführer* Knapp building hidden bunkers in the woods around Putbus, which could potentially have been used as hideouts for insurgent 'were-wolf' teenage fighting units after the invasion.[36]

Once the secret decision to leave by boat had been made, many of the older boys were sent to the fishing village of Lauterbach, where the school's flotilla resided, in order to make all the boats as seaworthy as possible.[37] The feverish activity was all-consuming, in part a reaction to the fact that the Red Army had already reached Stralsund, less than 30 kilometres away, and the gateway to the island of Rügen. The school buildings were now crammed with refugees, including the mother, sister, and blind grandmother of 17-year-old Dietrich Schulz, one of the last two pupils to leave the Napola behind.

Schulz and his friend Klaus Schikore (who had already been called up into the Waffen-SS 'Hitler Youth' Division, but had made the decision to return to Putbus after having survived the invasion of Stralsund, his home-town)[38] were completely shocked and disgusted by the Napola teachers' refusal to stand and fight to the last. They found it incomprehensible—and utterly abhorrent—that their elders and 'betters' were unwilling to put into practice the rhetoric of defending the fatherland at all costs which they had peddled for so long, and which Schulz and Schikore (and many other pupils) had believed without question. In his journal, Schulz described the bitter disappointment and desperation which he experienced on discovering the authorities' real plans:

> Now *Hauptzugführer* Berkowski [the sailing teacher from Köslin] comes to us and tells us with a heavy heart everything that has happened while we were away from Lauterbach.... 'And now we're just sitting around here', I say, 'We absolutely must join the *Volkssturm* and take whatever defensive measures we can!' Now Berkowski comes a bit closer to me and says, unhappily, 'Schulz, the war is over for us, the school leadership wants to relocate and try to reach Schleswig-Holstein with the rest of the *Jungmannen* in the yachts and cutters.' I can't digest all that at once at all. What am I hearing; the school wants to vamoose? These cowardly dogs! It's too much for me, on the way back to the cutter I can't hold back the tears....And here's the best thing, the cutters have to be brought to Wittower Fähre [ready to set off]. There are four of us and four cutters. Each one

> has to sail a cutter. I believe that's almost impossible. But one can hardly believe what one man can achieve when he has to!
>
> ...A yacht appears in front of us. I recognize it as the *Seevogel* [one of the school yachts], and am pleased when I see *Zugführer* Wiers. Hache and Hein are aboard too. I greet them and yell across, when are we going to attack Ivan? But I receive no reply. Wiers' gaze goes right through me, he doesn't answer! He goes right past us and doesn't turn back. What does all that mean? I can't fathom it all anymore....As I make the bowline fast [to the mooring at Wittower Fähre], I hear a roar of motors and seconds later a lorry comes into view, packed with *Jungmannen* and *Erzieher*. It's as if someone were choking me. I'm sure of one thing, I'm not going to join them!...Now Lüders and Steinmetz come up to us. We greet them coolly and full of contempt. Steinmetz gives me post, which is already weeks old. I put it away without a word and go to the *Jungmannen*. With tears in their eyes, they tell me about the last hours in Putbus. The 5th *Zug* had provided themselves with enough rations for almost a month, and wanted to disappear on their own initiative, but Lüders realized about the endeavour in time and forbade it.... Still, we parted from each other with the best hopes for the future.[39]

When Schulz returned to Putbus, an even greater shock awaited him, for when he decided to go and see how things stood with *Zugführer* Wiers, who had just married his fiancée Erna, he found his room filled with cigarette smoke and the stink of drunkenness, with a few boys lolling around in various stages of inebriation, and Wiers gazing emotionlessly out of the window. From the still sober Schikore, he found out that the island of Rügen had been completely cut off; the Russians had already pressed on from Stralsund to Rostock. Eagerly, Schulz and the other boys decided that the island must be defended to the last; Schulz asked Wiers, 'What shall we do next, *Zugführer*? We should definitely join a fighting unit and go to the Front?' Three times, he posed the question, and each time, Wiers ignored him. Filled with anger, Schulz demanded that the *Zugführer* at least give them the key to the sports hall, which was being used to store all the school's weaponry—Wiers handed him the key without a word and, after they had left, is supposed to have commented 'Those two are past helping'.[40]

Meanwhile, the self-appointed 'two last fighters' armed themselves to the teeth with guns and hand-grenades. When their Latin teacher, Dr. Pelkmann, attempted to stop them, Schikore raised his newly acquired pistol and threatened to shoot him, while Pelkmann pleaded with them to see reason: 'For God's sake, lads, the war is lost, don't court disaster, chuck away your weapons and take off your uniform. It can't be long before the Russians get here!' Deeply agitated, the boys left him and continued on their way, desperately trying to find out whether anyone was actually planning to defend the island or not—nobody seemed to know a thing.[41] In his journal, Schulz wrote:

> I have never felt so abandoned as I did today! [Wiers] could certainly have 'helped us' if he had thought for a moment about anything other than his own welfare. Precisely in times of danger, then for the first time it's revealed who is really a man and a comrade....How should we comprehend this, when we swore an oath on the flag of youth, which was and is more than death! The total war had made us so hard, that we couldn't cry at all, although we're still kids....[42]

The next day, Schulz bade farewell to his family (who were staying in the sick-bay at the time) with the words '*Alles für Deutschland!*' (Everything for Germany!), and he and Schikore set off to try and find soldiers with whom they could defend the area, in the knowledge that the Russians were already less than 10 kilometres away from Putbus, in the village of Garz. After sleeping the night in a barn, they pushed on to Binz, where they found what appeared to be a veritable treasure-trove of brand new firearms in a Waffen-SS administrative office. The SS-*Oberscharführer* in charge, however, was adamant that not a single weapon could leave the room without a suitable licence. When Schulz shouted at him 'That's nonsense, Ivan is 10 kilometres from Binz, no one's asking about licences anymore!', the *Oberscharführer* raved at them 'I don't give a s*** where Ivan is, nothing here is going to be given out, so long as I'm in charge! To hell with you, and now get out!'[43]

They then fell in with a group of soldiers, who told them that the only thing to do was get rid of their uniforms, and try to find a ship to Denmark or the West; two Waffen-SS soldiers had been beaten up by civilians in the nearby resort of Saßnitz, so they should avoid going there with their uniform on at all costs. Having struck off on their own once again without their uniform, however, in accordance with the soldiers' instructions, they found themselves in even greater danger—a group of Waffen-SS led by a young officer, who demanded why they were heading in the opposite direction from the front. Schulz knew that, if they were suspected of 'desertion', they might soon end up hanging from a lamppost with a placard round their necks reading 'I am a coward', killed by their own compatriots. Thinking quickly on his feet, he claimed that they were on their way to join another Waffen-SS unit in Stubnitz, whose task was to defend the rest of the peninsula. Luckily, the officer did not decide to waste time on a summary court-martial, but merely told them curtly to 'Hurry up and join your troop; the Soviet attack will begin any moment!' Finally, having seen that there was no way to board any ship at Saßnitz because of the hordes of refugees who were dangerously overweighting every vessel in sight, they made their way back to the school, leaving their arsenal of grenades and ammunition pouches by the side of a road.[44]

The following day, *Zugführer* Daerr, one of the last remaining members of staff, brought them each a suit of civilian clothes to put on (even the SS-eagle on the arm of their NPEA uniform would have been enough to ensure the boys a spell in a Russian work-camp), and they spent the morning making a bonfire of all the

Figure 11.2 One of NPEA Rügen's 'cutters'.

paperwork and photographs which remained in the school. Four years' worth of pictorial documentation was destroyed in as many minutes. At around 12.30, they heard the sound of horses' hooves below—the Russians had finally entered Putbus, and, despite all their yearning for a last-minute reprieve by Goebbels' 'wonder-weapons', Schulz and Schikore's war was over. It was 4 May 1945.[45]

Meanwhile, the remaining Putbusser had set off on their 250-mile voyage west, along with Lüders, his wife and children, and a few of the *Erzieher*.[46] The so-called 'torpedo-boat cutters' in which they were sailing were barely 6 metres long (see Figure 11.2), and each had to carry three 14- or 15-year-old boys, and three adults who had no experience of sailing; the only experienced seaman was *Zugführer* Berkowski, whom Lüders had put in charge of the expedition. Their sole navigation aid consisted of 'a small compass and a torn-out page from a school atlas which showed the land map of North Germany'.[47] By the end of the first day, one of the cutters was already out of commission, and when the others became beached on a sandbank within reach of Russian artillery fire, much of the luggage in the other three boats had to be dumped overboard (including one boy's piano accordion), in order to lighten the vessels enough to set them free.[48] The pupils themselves were still convinced that they would soon be rejoining the army in the West in order to help to turn the tide of the war, not realizing that the only thing '*Hufü*' Lüders had on his mind was to flee as far from any fighting as possible.[49]

Jürgen Schach von Wittenau, who was 12 years old at the time, recalled that, on the second day, a passing motor launch hailed them with the news of the Führer's death, which had just been received on their radio:

> We gasped. Hitler dead, the great leader on whom everything was centred.... So there was no miracle weapon, no secret reserve army (as Goebbels had implied) after all? Now what did Lüders think on hearing their news? The other teachers? Surprisingly, they said very little. Now I think that they must have guessed all along, perhaps even known, better then we, the boys, that the game was over. And that is why Lüders had decided to flee, and why he did not reveal his intention to us, knowing very well that it could have cost him his life if he had uttered a word about the inevitable German defeat.... I simply felt relief.... I never wanted to see any Napola again.[50]

On the next day, 3 May, however, the little flotilla was to be caught up in a far more dangerous situation. A whole fleet of vessels, including requisitioned merchant ships, torpedo boats, former ocean liners, and convoy vessels, had been ordered to make all speed for the Baltic peninsula of Hela, in order to clear out as many as possible of the prisoners and refugees who had been trapped there by the Soviets. This mass mustering of the Baltic fleet in its turn drew the attention of the Allied air force, who saw an opportunity for expeditious mastery of the seas if they acted quickly and picked off as many of the enemy ships as possible.[51] What Jürgen Schach von Wittenau was later to term the 'Staberhuk inferno' then ensued—his own account runs as follows:

> Three British fighter planes came towards us flying low and opening fire at the ships around us, but—well, we were in the line of fire. The attack took us entirely by surprise yet we reacted quickly. A sharp command from Berkowski: 'Haul down sail!', and we pulled the sail down as fast as we could to get out of the way. Accidentally we had been the bull's eye of the planes' target. Angry anti-aircraft fire from the ships ended the attack quickly, the planes turned away, and up went the sails again. But it was only a matter of minutes before the second wave of attackers appeared. Sails down again! This time the 'Typhoon' fighters flew lower still. Machine guns barked, the whining howl of bombs dropping made me panic. I ducked away automatically under my life vest—a useless reaction but my instincts blocked any reasonable behaviour. When I reappeared, I perceived fountains of water where the rockets had hit the sea. And I also saw a big hole in the side of the ship nearest to us before it began to capsize slowly. Lifeboats dashed away towards the beach. Another ship had caught fire. 'Heavens! They've loaded ammunition!' Berkowski cried. And so it was. We watched the crew scrambling for their lifeboats and trying to get them clear. Others just jumped overboard. More rockets hit the ships or the surface of the sea. The noise was indescribable, and never again in my life was I ever so terrified as I was then. I knew our lives were at stake. Would the thread be cut?
>
> One of our cutters still under sail ploughed along close by the bow of a big ship under attack. Glancing up they noticed a sailor trying to escape through a

> porthole. He was halfway out when a burst of machine gun fire finished him off. The cutter managed to get out of the way and eventually out of reach. In our boat, the sails went up and down as Berkowski commanded, I don't remember how often; our skipper skilfully manoeuvred our little boat away from the scene as much as possible, seemingly unperturbed. He had seen combat; we had not. Suddenly we saw a German seaplane coming towards us, flying lower and lower. I saw the pack hunting it down with persistent machinegun fire from astern until it caught fire. The German board gunner fired back incessantly oblivious of the predictable end. The seaplane hit the waves just a few yards away from our portside, its nose dived deep into the waves and the plane began to disappear with its tail up and the gunner still firing. Then there was silence....[52]

Finally, the cutters managed to get clear, and came to land on the island of Fehmarn, hard by the Staberhuk lighthouse, where, thankfully, the lighthouse keeper allowed them to stay the night.

Perhaps predictably, the remaining *Erzieher* and Lüders were far more concerned about their own potential fates under Allied occupation than with protecting the 14- and 15-year-old boys who had brought them to (at least partial) safety. On 4 May, Lüders told the pupils that their time at the Napola was at an end, and that he and his family were going to wait out the end of the war on Fehmarn. *Zugführer* Berkowski was instructed to take all the boys with him (except Jürgen Schach von Wittenau, who was considered too young to be left without an adult *in loco parentis*) to a navy camp in Puttgarden, on the other side of the island, where he assured them that they would be well looked after. All pieces of clothing and decorations which might have identified them as former pupils of a Napola, including their ceremonial daggers, were already buried along the rocky coast, or hidden down rabbit-holes.[53]

However, the day after Berkowski dropped the boys off at Puttgarden (before attempting to make his own way back to Thuringia), British troops took over the island, and all non-combatants were forced to leave the camp, which was now designated for prisoners of war only. The boys were left completely alone, with no responsible adults to turn to, no food, money, or even any official identity, since all their passes and identity-cards had been destroyed because they contained potentially incriminating evidence that they had been pupils at an NPEA.[54] After a few days wandering around the island without any real idea of what to do—during which they made the unpleasant discovery of a number of drowned corpses floating along the coastline, and endured a discomfiting encounter with a couple of English soldiers who accused them of having abetted the atrocities which had taken place in the concentration camps—hunger forced them to return to Staberhuk, where they knew that Lüders would still be in possession of all the rations which he had commandeered. Henner Menge describes the confrontation which followed:

> Our reception by Herr Lüders was cool; he seemed distrustful. He refused our plea that he give us some of the supplies which were stored. A quarrel developed, during which he repeatedly pointed out his family as the reason for his refusal. Finally, after one of us had pulled a pistol out of its holster, Herr Lüders cleared the way to the supplies with the words 'Do whatever you want!' We assured Frau Lüders, who was standing by crying and pointing to her small children, that we would not take any provisions which were needed for her children.... This was our last encounter with Herr Lüders.[55]

The hypocrisy and venality of the staff at NPEA Rügen can thus be seen to have reached their apogee in the utter selfishness of the school's former director. Lüders was not even prepared to share his food with the pupils who had sailed him to safety, until threatened to do so at gunpoint. In such a manner did the Putbussers' 'great adventure' reach its final and ignominious conclusion.[56]

Fighting the French in South-West Germany: Skirmishes around NPEA Reichenau and Rottweil

Although the pupils of NPEA Reichenau and Rottweil did not have to fear the advance of the Red Army, they did know that they would be among the first in the firing line if French troops were to cross the German border.

At NPEA Rottweil, events followed a familiar pattern, with the pupils in the first two year-groups being sent home, the third- and fourth-years being evacuated, and the older boys being volunteered (willingly or unwillingly) to defend the fatherland. Hans Binder, an older pupil who had already been called up, but had returned to Rottweil after being severely wounded, was put in charge of the pupils who were left. Binder remembered that Major Hans Bock (leader of the eponymous *Kampfgruppe* Bock, which now had responsibility for the defence of the whole local area) made a specific point of visiting the school in order to discuss the steadily worsening situation with the *Erzieher* at the NPEA. The result of the meeting was a unanimous agreement amongst the staff that the boys should be sent into battle. 'On the next day, 20 April, the NPEA taskforce set off: eight to ten adults...and around three-dozen *Jungmannen* aged between 15-and-a-half and 17.'[57]

Over the next couple of days, the unit split up into three groups, with the aim of defending the nearby villages of Balgheim, Dürbheim, and Rietheim. Each group contained two or three adults with experience of the front, and a dozen *Jungmannen*; their mission being 'to hold off the enemy, [and then] relocate after the first engagement with the foe'.[58] The only place where the *Jungmannen* experienced any serious fighting, however, was Balgheim, where they had the opportunity to attack the spearhead of a French tank battalion with their *Panzerfäuste*.

Four Frenchmen and one Balgheimer were killed, and the church and castle in Balgheim suffered damage from French artillery, before the inhabitants of the village were able to persuade the invaders that they themselves had no wish to engage in further resistance—one account in a local newspaper from April 1954 also claims that the inhabitants begged the Napola pupils to stop fighting, without any success.[59] Five of the *Jungmannen* were then taken into French custody as prisoners of war (the last of whom only returned home in 1946), and two days later, on 23 April, the remaining adults decided that, 'given the situation which had eventuated', the rest of the *Jungmannen* should be disarmed and sent home.[60]

Fritz D., who was 16 at the time, never managed to reach the unit with which he was supposed to be fighting, but ended up in French hands nevertheless:

> The 1928 year-group had already been called up, and also went into action with different units. I myself tried to reach my position by bicycle; however, on the way I was taken up by another unit and went into action against the French. I was also imprisoned; however, I was quickly discharged, because I pretended to have a serious illness. Things were mostly similar for the rest of my year-group. The younger boys from the 1929 year-group were still in Rottweil when the French marched in. They still went into action with the *Volkssturm* and shot up two tanks. One of them couldn't get away quickly enough, and had to do two years' hard labour in a mine in France.[61]

When the French arrived in Rottweil, however, the school's headmaster, *Anstaltsleiter* Dr. Max Hoffmann, had already gone into hiding. One pupil later declared bitterly that 'he had left them all in the lurch'.[62]

Meanwhile, even though Napola Reichenau had optimistically sent out leaflets in January 1945 encouraging applications to the school, with the new intake supposedly starting their studies on 1 May 1945, normal school routine had essentially fallen by the wayside as early as autumn 1944. All the older boys who had not yet been called up had been sent to Alsace in order to build earthworks—they also had to be provided with pistols by the local Hitler Youth organization which was organizing the fortification work, in order to protect the girls from the BDM, who were working alongside them, from assault by the hordes of German soldiers who were by now retreating from France with their morale in tatters. Those younger boys who were left behind in Reichenau were given basic infantry training, as well as having to undertake other tasks which were considered important for the war effort, such as gathering saplings to reinforce all the trenches in the area.[63]

One small silver lining, at least as far as the boys were concerned, was the fact that a number of girls' boarding schools had had to be evacuated to Reichenau, including two *Mädchen-Napolas* from Achern and Colmar-Berg in Luxembourg, the *Deutsche Heimschule* Hegne, and the *Reichsschule* from Heythuysen in Holland (they were also joined by some *Jungmannen* from NPEA Rufach and

NPEA Rottweil).[64] The schools regularly held dances at which the boys and girls could meet, and a former pupil from one of the girls' schools remembered with great fondness that 'it was a sport for us to climb out of the cellar window at night and meet up with [the *Jungmannen* from NPEA Reichenau].'[65] Although very little is known about what became of the girls after the war—most of those who had not already been collected by their parents were sent home in April 1945, and those who could not reach home were sent to work in the kitchens of the hospital in the nearby town of Konstanz—there is at least one report of a *Jungmann* from Reichenau and a Dutch girl from a *Mädchen-Napola* getting married after the war.[66]

All the younger pupils at NPEA Reichenau were sent home (as far as possible) towards the end of April, but the older boys were expected to join up and defend the area. Most were then captured by the French on the day of the invasion, 26 April, and brought as prisoners to Konstanz; apparently, no acts of violence actually took place on the school grounds.[67] Paul Sch., who had already been forced to join the armed forces in January at the age of 16, describes his own experiences during the last few days of the war as follows:

> After my basic infantry training, which I completed as a naval officer cadet at Saalfelden..., I received marching orders for Stralsund.... Because of the war situation, I was no longer able to get there, and quickly returned to Reichenau. There I received a massive dressing down, because I hadn't reported to the nearest Wehrmacht administrative office. But on the same day, my class was incorporated into an anti-tank commando, the *Kampfgruppe* Bock, and sent into battle. In steady retreat we came to Sonthofen, where we were surprised by American tanks and torn apart. While the majority of my comrades decided to make a break for home, we tried, in pairs, to make our way over the snow-covered mountains to the Bregenzerwald. Against the advice of experienced mountaineers, we managed it. There, we discovered that the *Kampfgruppe* Bock no longer existed. We were then taken over by the remainder of the 405th E.u.A. Division. One day later, the so-called 'Alpine Fortress Tirol-Vorarlberg' surrendered, and the war—and with it, the time at the Napola—was at an end. Still, I could demonstrate once again that everything that we had learned and practised had not been for nothing. The five youngest in the company, of which I was the second-youngest, joined forces in order to get home unchallenged, as far as possible. The remaining four spontaneously voted me as their leader. The skills and virtues which had been instilled in me at Reichenau helped us, despite many days without food, and under the greatest possible stresses and strains, to make it unmolested through thick forest and trackless countryside to Bregenz on the Bodensee, and to get over the German-Austrian border, which had been re-erected in the meantime. From there, we each set off homeward. As I found out long afterwards, we were the only five in the company who returned home without becoming prisoners of war.[68]

While these recollections—particularly the emphasis on their author's own preternaturally developed leadership qualities—may have been a little exaggerated for the sake of effect, Paul Sch.'s account does capture a genuine sense of the unholy chaos which reigned during these last days of the war in southern Germany. In particular, his depiction illustrates very clearly the way in which smaller and ever smaller groups of German fighters were being fragmented, reformed, and finally split asunder or imprisoned, until it had to be accepted that all was lost.

Austrian Experiences: Flight from NPEA Göttweig and NPEA Traiskirchen

On 29 March 1945, over 1 and a half million Russian troops crossed the Austrian border, effortlessly overwhelming the German positions, and began to march on Vienna; the attack on the Austrian capital began on 5 April. *Jungmannen* from NPEA Wien-Theresianum were immediately evacuated westwards before the situation could become any more precarious, and the youngest of them were sent to join NPEA Göttweig, which was situated in a former Benedictine monastery near Krems an der Donau in Lower Austria. At the same time, however, another Soviet force was marching south from Vienna towards St. Pölten, which was only 20 kilometres away from Göttweig. To the pupils at the monastery, it seemed inevitable that the Napola would lie directly within the Red Army's path.[69]

Nevertheless, the Göttweig authorities had hitherto seemed fairly optimistic about the future, providing the older year-groups with a special academic course which, after submission of their call-up documents 'in Autumn 1946', would allow them to proceed straight on to university after one more term of schooling. However, this course ended abruptly on the 6th of April, and the official documents entitling the pupils to special consideration were only typed up once the school had already fled to the Benedictine monastery at Lambach.[70]

It was clear to the boys that the situation was becoming ever more desperate; the only question was how best the schools might effect their escape. Apart from a couple of bicycles, the only transport available consisted of the headmaster's car, a three-wheeled pick-up truck, and a van driven by wood gas. Even the riding horses from the Theresianum, which had been quartered in Göttweig for some time, had already been evacuated to the west. It was decided that the first priority should be to send the 10- and 11-year-olds from the Theresianum to relative safety—by getting them onto the last passenger train to leave the nearby station at Stein an der Donau. The station forecourt was so tightly packed with refugees that it was all the older boys could do to clear a path for the first-years, but they managed in the end to ensure that their charges reached the train, which took them as far as the Tirol (where their class was finally disbanded).[71]

Those who remained at Göttweig had to live with constant fear of air raids by allied bombers, which were flying overhead in ever increasing numbers. There was a real fear that the monastery buildings, which were highly visible from the air, might be treated as a legitimate target (comparisons might be made with the monastery at Montecassino), yet the school had no air-raid shelters, only basement vaults, to provide shelter for the pupils. The event which really brought the dangers of the war home to the boys, however, was the bombing of Krems an der Donau on 1 April 1945, which many saw with their own eyes. Walter Knoglinger describes their experience as follows:

> On Easter Monday...there was another air raid warning in broad daylight, and we were ordered down to the cellar corridor. After not all that long a time, we heard the drone of bomber engines, and ran, out of curiosity...to the round barred windows in the wall which overlooked Krems. Already we could see the bombers above us, drawing white vapour trails behind them across the blue spring sky. Then, suddenly, there was a whooshing noise in the air, getting ever louder. Instantly, we feared that the bombs rushing down were aimed at the monastery, then we heard muffled explosions from the direction of Krems. We hurried to the openings in the wall and were eyewitnesses to the bombardment of the city...we saw the flashes of the fallen bombs flickering. Columns of smoke rushed heavenward, and clouds of smoke spread ever more thickly over the city. Now we knew that the war stood before our very gates, and that we too could become its victims.[72]

Shortly afterwards, a large group of soldiers from the Waffen-SS, SA, and Wehrmacht drove up to the monastery, claiming that they were the staff of Dr. Jury, *Gauleiter* of the Lower Danube, and that they needed fuel in order to reach their objective; this could probably only still be found at Moosbierbaum refinery, some 30 kilometres away. One of the *Erzieher* at Göttweig, *Hauptzugführer* Blauhut, decided to get some boys from the oldest class to volunteer to fetch what they could from the refinery:

> Of course the *Jungmannen* came forward for such an 'honourable' task, as we thought it to be then.... [We] were sent with a driver by lorry in the direction of Moosbierbaum, gawped at curiously by the *Volkssturm* men...and the civilian population. Soon we reached the refinery, where a pile of ruins presented itself; none of the petrol pumps which were still standing could be made to work. Through sheer coincidence we then found one, made out of two glass cylinders coupled to a handpump. Empty iron drums had to be found and rolled alongside, and then the painful pumping began. We filled the drums with five litres of petrol, while the fighter-planes chased eastwards overhead, and explosions could be heard in the distance.

> When, suddenly, there came a deafeningly loud crash…not very far from us, we felt we'd had enough of our pumping mission. We didn't know what had given rise to the explosions, so it seemed wiser to take to our heels. Additionally, at this point bridges were already being detonated in order to hinder the advancing enemy. With two drums of petrol, we drove safely back to Göttweig, and there delivered our dangerous consignment according to our orders.[73]

Fighting also broke out dangerously close to the monastery a few days later, due to the escape of some inmates from the prison in the nearby town of Stein. Not knowing what was happening, the boys were greatly alarmed when shooting and explosions began during dinner, and the school was put on alert, with a strengthened guard and night-long perimeter patrols, since it was believed that the Russians might already have broken through. Although nothing more came to pass, the next day, the pupils were appalled to find corpses lying in the ditches along the roadside.[74]

It was soon decided that the school must be evacuated in its entirety to the monastery at Lambach (about 45 kilometres from Linz) on the 10th of April, since the Red Army had already taken Vienna, and were advancing ever further westwards. The roads were packed with unending streams of refugees and fleeing soldiers, most of them Hungarian, and desperate not to fall into Russian hands. This provided the Göttweiger with the opportunity they needed to requisition some form of transport, particularly horses and carts. *Jungmannen* stationed themselves at the cross-roads at the foot of the Göttweiger Berg and halted the Hungarian troops at pistol-point. Walter Knoglinger believes that their intervention was the more effective because of their unknown uniform, which bore an SS-eagle—in any case, the Hungarians generally submitted to their request to stop quite meekly.[75]

Meanwhile, daily life at the school had become severely restricted, with lessons being reduced to an absolute minimum, and preparation for the evacuation being placed at a premium. Pupils had permission to rifle the uniform cupboard and take whatever they wanted in terms of underwear, clothes, and shoes, and the larders were laid open for all; their principal bounty seems to have consisted of 'great heaps of stewed fruit in jars, cocoa, and Emmental cheese'.[76] In the boys' quarters, an atmosphere of turmoil held sway, while the pupils listened with ever-increasing disquiet to the army reports on the radio.[77] Some of the boys decided to dedicate their lives to 'the flag of the Führer', and reported to the army registration office in the town of Gmunden in the hope of joining up. The young officer in charge dissuaded them, however, telling them that there was no point: 'the whole business couldn't last much longer anyway.'[78]

Finally, all was ready for the departure to Lambach, and then—who knew? Walter Knoglinger describes the last days of the school as follows:

> In the morning of 10 April 1945, the horses were yoked, the wood gas-driven vehicles properly warmed up, and anyone who had one to hand swung onto his

bicycle and out of the gate, down the Göttweiger Berg in the direction of Melk.... The bridges over the river Danube were already prepared for detonation. Along with us there rolled an interminable flood of refugees, westward bound.

Ultimately, we reached Lambach, where we rejoined [*Anstaltsleiter*] Dr. Kühnelt again, and he finally took his leave of us. We pushed onwards with Dr. Blauhut and Dr. Schliffer, in order to arrive at Burg Strechau. However, our class was divided on the way there. One group under the leadership of Dr. Blauhut reached Strechau, the other under Dr. Schliffer was surprised by the Americans in Kainisch....

Thus did NPEA Göttweig come to an end, on Burg Strechau, and in a barn in Kainisch in the first days of May in the year 1945.[79]

Meanwhile, NPEA Traiskirchen, not far from Vienna, had also suffered from the constant threat of bombing, not only because of its proximity to the capital, but also because some of the factories in the area were a prime target for Allied air raids. All morning lessons normally had to take place in the school cellars, since this was the usual time for bomber attacks.[80] Helmut Wigelbeyer, who was 11 at the time, remembered seeing a nearby munitions factory go up in flames during one of the tough night-time military exercises which had become an ever greater part of institutional life at Traiskirchen towards the end of the war. The night was lit up for several seconds as bright as day, and, even after two hours, individual grenades could still be heard exploding.[81]

The boys aged 14 and over had already been sent to affiliated schools in parts of Austria where Slovenian partisans held sway, such as southern Carinthia, where they were being deployed in military units. However, as the Front approached ever closer to Vienna, and the thunder of artillery could be heard even within the school itself, it was decided that the rest of the pupils would have to be sent home or evacuated.[82] Richard Picker recalled being dismissed on Good Friday with a sausage and some bread in his haversack, carrying marching orders from the *Anstaltsleiter* which instructed him to return home 'and wait in readiness for further instructions from the school authorities'.[83] Although he managed to catch one of the last trains from Vienna Westbahnhof going in the right direction, one of the problems which he remembered most clearly from his homeward journey was that of not having a clue what the significance of 'Good Friday' might be—when he managed to find his way to a National Socialist Peoples' Welfare office in order to rest before carrying on towards the Westbahnhof, the lady in charge forbade him to eat his snack: 'But my child, you can't eat sausage today! It's Good Friday!'[84]

Meanwhile, the rest of the boys were crammed into a couple of lorries and driven first to Türnitz, then Hubertendorf (both *Mädchen-Napolas* from which all the girls had already been evacuated), and on to the monastery at Lambach.[85]

At Türnitz, many pupils had had the opportunity to be picked up by their parents; others now decided to make their own way home. Harald Ofner remembers receiving his marching orders for the Sudetenland, 300 kilometres away, from the *Anstaltsleiter* ('typed with the "two-finger system"'), as he was cleaning the man's boots. He also recalled getting into trouble because, at some point during the chaotic journey to Lambach, he had lost his uniform cap:

> What a catastrophe: all is lost, and, to crown it all, this *Jungmann* loses his cap too! But..., with my map of the country torn out of my atlas, I still managed to reach the temporary quarters where my mother was staying within a few days, where she embraced me with tears in her eyes.[86]

For the boys who remained in Lambach for a little while, the monastery seemed a heavenly respite from the dirt, hunger, and fear which had been their constant companions on the eight-day journey from Türnitz. The young monks made them very welcome, and one of the teachers who was looking after them, an art professor, gave them lessons on the monastery's history and architecture. The boys also caught trout in a nearby brook, and even remember catching and roasting snails in order to supplement their (still fairly meagre) rations.[87]

At the end of April, however, it was decided that the small group of Traiskirchner who were left should make for Altaussee in the Salzkammergut. Along the way, they learned from soldiers who got onto their train that the Americans had already taken Salzburg, and would almost certainly soon reach the Salzkammergut. This went some way towards explaining the unfriendly reception which the group received when they finally reached Altaussee—the mayor told the teachers that the presence of a group of Nazi elite-school pupils in uniform could cause the Americans to treat the civilian population unfavourably when they invaded, as was expected any day.[88] Although he allowed them to stay in a nearby youth hostel, the mayor refused to take any responsibility for their welfare, or to allow them to use any food from the village's stocks—after all, they had no ration cards—and made it quite clear that he wished them to leave the area as soon as possible. As far as he was concerned, it was common knowledge that the Allies would make short work of any 'elite boys', and the *Erzieher* were almost certainly already on their hit list (*Todesliste*).[89] The staff were luckily able to circumvent the mayor, however, by enlisting the help of a kindly priest, and a local landlady who was so taken with the art professor's painting of her house that she bought it from him in return for provisions.[90]

In general terms, the boys were able to forget the war to a certain extent, still spending time on lessons (particularly those with a practical bent) and some physical exercise.[91] At one point, two resistance fighters attempted to take one of the *Erzieher* prisoner while he was giving an open-air lesson, but the art professor persuaded them that this would not be for the best. The *Erzieher* in question worried that they ought to leave the village before the Americans came, since he had heard of certain atrocities which US soldiers were supposed to have committed against Hitler Youths. Professor S. was not so sure.[92]

The Americans finally arrived early one Sunday morning (probably 6 May) in a colonnade of tanks, cars, and jeeps. The boys were terrified, and when the time came to open the door of the youth hostel to the invaders, they cowered back as their *Erzieher* was roughly manhandled and held against the wall at rifle-point. Helmut Wigelbeyer describes what then took place:

> As the officer gazed at the scene, he stopped short for a moment. Then he asked in a harsh voice:
>
> 'Are you Hitlerboys?'
>
> As some of the trembling boys nodded anxiously, he asked, putting his pistol away, in quite a different tone:
>
> 'You are hungry?'
>
> Doubtfully, as if they hadn't quite heard aright, the boys looked alternately at the Captain and the snarling Sergeant, who couldn't suppress his smile any longer. Then they all cried, as if on command:
>
> 'Yes!'
>
> 'Come on', the officer called and ordered the group outside with a hand gesture....
>
> The *Jungmannen* were received by the American soldiers with great curiosity. They felt the boys' uniforms and swapped their ties, badges, and sheath-knives for chocolate and chewing gum....During the meal [which followed], there arose an almost friendly rapport between the soldiers, who were mostly young, and the scoffing kids. Up until this point, members of German elite schools had been described to the American soldiers as murderous and wayward little devils. These ravenous children didn't make that impression at all.[93]

On the day of the armistice, the entire population of Altaussee and the Americans held a huge party, accompanied by fireworks and gunshots, and the Captain and his staff ate a hearty meal with the Traiskirchner at the youth-hostel, lubricated with whisky and copious culinary gifts. At the end of the evening, the boys sang folksongs round the campfire for the Americans' entertainment. The only thing that really seemed to matter was that the war was over, and, somehow, they had all survived.[94]

Desperate Days: Pupils from NPEA Spandau, Potsdam, and Neuzelle Experience the Battle for Berlin

On the orders of the *Anstaltsleiter*, SS-*Obersturmbannführer* Friedrich Lübbert, most pupils from NPEA Spandau had been evacuated either to Thuringia or to Schleswig-Holstein before the final struggle for mastery of Berlin had begun.

In April 1945, the Napola was disbanded at Burg in Dithmarschen, and each pupil was given discharge papers confirming his membership of an obscure civilian boarding school, as well as some vouchers for food and travel. As had happened at the other schools which ended their days in Schleswig-Holstein, many boys hired themselves out to local farmers until such time as it might be possible for them to return home.[95] However, one pupil, Mike M., was given a twofold special mission by *Anstaltsleiter* Lübbert, which would involve his travelling back to Berlin. Firstly, he was instructed to report to the Inspector of the Napolas, August Heißmeyer, at his headquarters on Unter den Linden, and deliver a dispatch to him (perhaps a complement to the message which the Putbusser had delivered under the pretext of their sweet-factory mercy mission). Secondly, he was to travel on to the school at Spandau and destroy a number of important documents which had been left there. Finally, since his grandfather had died in Berlin a few days before, he was allowed to take this opportunity to assist with the burial. Lübbert's parting words to him were: 'We will see each other again on 23 or 24 April, as circumstances allow, and when your parents let you travel.'[96]

Mike M. describes his expedition as resembling nothing more than a form of military examination; the train journey from Burg via Hamburg, much of which had been razed to the ground, could only take place at night due to attacks by British fighter-bombers which were operating all the way along the railway line. Frequently, the train would come to a halt, and all the passengers would have to disembark and find safety outside. Finally, the train reached the ruined Lehrter Bahnhof (Berlin's central station) with no more damage than a few bullet-holes, and Mike M. was able to continue his journey via the 'tireless' S-Bahn, Berlin's inner-city railway network, which was still functioning.[97] Yet his reception at Heißmeyer's headquarters was gravely disappointing, for all was in chaos:

> Everything was in a process of disintegration; luggage was being packed; on the street a giant heap of burning furniture and documents; in the middle of it all people from the SS, vehicles, and a wounded young SS-*Untersturmführer*, a son of Heißmeyer's (Heißmeyer was married to Gertrud Scholtz-Klink, the Reich Women's Leader. Both had dozens of children from their two marriages). Heißmeyer junior offered me the chance of driving to Bavaria on a Waffen-SS lorry. 'But you must decide quickly, we'll be off this afternoon....' At home, we decided that I should *not* go along, the reason being that my father had been called up into the *Volkssturm*: my mother and 10-year-old brother could definitely use some help. A few days later the Adlershof was under artillery fire; we looted a few grocers' shops. Then the Soviets came.[98]

The fate of the Napola pupils at Potsdam was not to be so peaceful as that of the Spandauer; indeed, they were among the only pupils to be caught up in actual combat and suffer serious losses. On 14 April 1945, Potsdam bore the brunt of a direct air attack by 490 Allied bombers, which destroyed whole swathes of the old town, including the famous Garrison Church. NPEA Potsdam, which lay only a few hundred metres from the railway station, found itself in the firing line, and the sickbay received a direct hit; the pupils in the cellars of the building felt utterly helpless as the walls swayed and quaked around them. After an exhausting remainder of the night spent helping to put out fires, digging graves for civilians who had been killed, and aiding those who had been bombed out of their homes, the *Jungmannen* returned to their rooms to find 'a chaos of soot, windows which had burst asunder, and shards of glass'. Lockers had been turned upside down, and underwear, uniforms, and books were scattered everywhere. The grounds of the school were a maze of craters, and the indoor swimming pool and other buildings in the grounds had been completely destroyed. The NPEA would have to move elsewhere in order to find habitable accommodation.[99]

During the next few days, a makeshift routine was established until the pupils could be moved on to NPEA Spandau. Otto Calliebe, the Vice-Inspector of the Napolas, but also the *Anstaltsleiter* of NPEA Potsdam, could be observed 'quartering the grounds, clambering over fallen trees and skirting craters, crowing from time to time in his light, always somewhat gravelly voice "Any looters will be shot! Any looters will be shot!"' The boys were given pistols, machine guns, and *Panzerfäuste*, and allowed to practise among the ruins. Many were delighted by the idea that they would soon be allowed to protect the Fatherland with their own weapons, and avenge the 'senseless destruction' of Potsdam and the 'terror attack' which had caused it.[100] They also believed that, once they had joined forces with pupils from NPEA Neuzelle (which had also been evacuated to Spandau) and the Spandauer themselves, they would form an even stronger troop, ready for anything. Before they left, Inspector Heißmeyer himself arrived, and gave a brief speech to them: 'The Führer has ordered me here to Potsdam for a special task; I will remain at my post! Let us remember in this final hour all comrades, who have fallen in this war. We think of our Führer and of Germany. *Sieg Heil*!'[101] Yet, when they reached Spandau, they found that all the pupils there had already been evacuated.[102] They were all then made to put on SS uniforms, although they were not forced to undergo the usual Waffen-SS procedure of being tattooed with their blood group.[103] Gerd-Ekkehard Lorenz describes their first evening in Spandau:

> We were sent down into the cellar of the main building to sleep. Straw had been heaped up there. Together with the *Erzieher*, we listened to the traditional speech of the Reich Propaganda Minister Dr. Goebbels on the eve of Hitler's birthday. With visionary powers, he magicked up an image formed of copious words. In Berlin, the turning-point of the war would come to pass, the Eastern onslaught would be broken.... The plans for the rebuilding of the city were already stored in cupboards in the Reich Chancellery. We listened, spellbound.

> The *Erzieher* made no comment. For five years and eleven days, I was a *Jungmann* of Napola Potsdam. Now, for the first time, I had to go to sleep as an SS-Panzergrenadier. That was hard for me....[104]

On around 21 April, some of the Potsdamer were put to work by the SS in a very alarming fashion which might have confirmed Lorenz's worst fears—guarding the route of what they later discovered to be a 'death march' of prisoners who were being removed from the concentration camp at Sachsenhausen.[105] One of the pupils involved, Siegfried Fischer, allegedly remembered stepping forward to give one of the 'poor fellows' a piece of nougat, when he felt a hand on his shoulder; one of the soldiers who was also standing by said to him 'You'd better leave that alone' and pulled him away.[106] Another pupil, Christian Gellinek, did not remember feeling any pity or solidarity with the prisoners at the time; in his recollection, they merely 'passed by like cattle'.[107]

From 22 April onwards, however, the Potsdamer, who were mostly only 14 or 15 years old, were caught up in engagements with a real enemy, as Russian troops encroached ever further into the capital. Suddenly, everything that they had previously treated as just another 'sort of cross-country war-game' had become deadly serious; half a dozen of the boys were killed or wounded within the first couple of days.[108] The sight of dead bodies, at first shocking, became commonplace; some lay with photographs scattered from their already-plundered wallets. There were so many ways in which it was possible to die: enemy fire; Russian grenades hurled into the trenches in which the boys were hidden; once, even a German Tiger tank set its flame-thrower onto them.[109] Theo Jäckel remembered that, on 24 April, one of the *Erzieher*, Otto Möller, told him that he thought the whole thing was insane, using 'half children' to fight off an invincible enemy in a murderous final battle, and instructed him to gather together all the members of his class and set off for NPEA Plön. Yet Theo knew that they would have next to no chance; if they marched out west, armed and in uniform, they would simply be forced to join another fighting unit, or be treated as deserters. The situation seemed hopeless.[110]

However, on 26 April, an opportunity presented itself to break out from Spandau into the surrounding countryside, where the Potsdamer split up into small groups of three or four. Although some were taken prisoner by the Russians, others managed to find their way to safety. Gerd-Ekkehard Lorenz describes his own experience attempting to break through the Russian lines as follows:

> Everywhere bustle, agitation. Shouts of: 'The Russians are coming!'...There was still time to take off our military tunics. I threw the pistol and the belt with the dagger, which I had worn during the fighting, into the woods. As I, like the others, wanted to put my hands up, there came a couple of shots from a submachine gun. Barely a metre away...—I could have touched him with my

outstretched arm—Steinmann clutched his breast, groaned, and collapsed. We tried to help him; there were several bullet-holes in his chest; blood welled from the wounds. His face became wax-yellow..., his eyes glassy.

I was hit by a kick from behind. I fell on top of the dying man. '*Davai, Davai, pashol!*' I pulled myself up, saw in front of me a young Russian soldier, and attached to his gun a sharp, four-edged bayonet.

'But...' I stammered, and gestured to Steinmann, whom I had been trying to help. The Russian laughed. '*Kaputt! Voyna kaputt, Hitler kaputt! Dalli, Davai!*' I looked around. Günther and Otto had put up their hands. Then I took off my steel helmet and threw it into the woods. I gazed again at Steinmann and then looked the Russian full in the face. He was no older than 17 or 18. He stared at me.

'Oh,' he said, 'You no soldier, you children!' Then he reached into his haversack, took out a piece of damp, gluey bread, broke it, and gave me a piece. I took it, turned round, and followed the others across the meadow.

As I stepped out of the wood, I heard one more shot. The Captain. He did not wish to be captured either.[111]

Conclusion

Self-evidently, this chapter can only do justice to a fraction of the experiences which pupils at the Napolas had to undergo as the Second World War came to its cataclysmic close.[112] However, by looking at events which occurred in a number of different locations throughout the 'Greater German Reich', the variety of these experiences can be appreciated, as well as some of the similarities which they shared.

Of course, some elements of the pupils' narratives have much in common with the experiences of many refugees or evacuees in Germany during this time—the long treks westwards, the chaotic train journeys, the lack of sufficient transport with which to reach safety, and the constant fear for the welfare of absent family members.[113] Similarly, Napola pupils were not the only group of young people who were made to work on (often seemingly pointless) fortifications, trenches, and tank traps—members of the Hitler Youth, the BDM, and even local women and older men from the *Volkssturm* were often forced to do the same.[114]

However, other elements of these accounts do have a specific relevance to the pupils' status as members of the NPEA. One recurring theme which occurs in many of the recollections is the necessity of concealing one's real identity from the advancing Allies—whether by discarding obvious symbols of one's affiliation, such as a ceremonial dagger or uniform, or by going into hiding with local people who would keep one's connections with a Nazi elite school a secret. Another element which recurs repeatedly is the dubiety over whether the Napola pupils were really soldiers or children, which was not only remarked upon by many of the invaders who finally encountered them (such as the Russian who captured Gerd-Ekkehard Lorenz, or the Americans who found the Traiskirchner at Altaussee), but also made manifest in the actions and reactions of many of the boys themselves.

On one level, when tempered with youthful insouciance, the idea of going into battle could seem to be a mere extension of the pre-military and cross-country war-games which had formed such an important part of NPEA life; however, when the bitter realities of combat were finally encountered at first hand, and death came far too close for comfort, many boys (even two such valiant and well-indoctrinated individuals as Dietrich Schulz and Klaus Schikore) simply wished to escape and rejoin their loved ones. Once the ideological fetters of the Napola education had been shattered, confusion and chagrin might take their place, but the desire to immolate oneself in the ashes of the Nazi regime rarely retained its old intoxication. Clearly, the oldest pupils were those most fully invested in the idea of fighting and dying for folk, flag, and Führer; for younger boys such as Jürgen Schach von Wittenau, freedom from the Napola often seemed to be a blessed release.

Two other themes which feature in very many of the eyewitness accounts reflect the importance of the school authorities in the boys' eyes. When pupils felt that they had been betrayed by staff who refused to put their own ideological precepts into practice and fight to the last (the staff at Putbus providing the paradigm par excellence), their bitterness and bewilderment knew no bounds, and is still clearly discernible many decades after the fact. However, the corollary was a tendency, again present in many of the accounts, to stress the concern which NPEA staff had for their pupils' welfare (even in circumstances where it was highly questionable that positive intervention by the school authorities could actually have taken place). In tandem with such remarks, former pupils would often claim that it was only the tough training at the NPEA which had enabled them to endure the hardships of the last few months of the war (Paul Sch.'s recollections are a case in point).[115]

Whether this could ever be proved or not, it does seem at least probable that a certain amount of ingrained physical toughness could have been an important element in some of the boys' capacity for survival in difficult circumstances. Furthermore, it does seem that the school authorities were better able to regulate the circumstances of the Napolas' retreat than would have been the case for most civilian refugees. Even when Napolas were being evacuated from one school to another almost unceasingly for two or three months, there seem to have been very few casualties, even when the journeys themselves were protracted and chaotic. It was only after the schools disbanded that pupils were really left to fend for themselves, and even then, some of the staff would often attempt to find sanctuary for those who had no way of returning home. Those who were betrayed most grievously were the pupils who were sent into battle by their *Erzieher*—particularly the Potsdamer, who could so easily have been evacuated along with the Spandauer, but were instead left to the tender mercies of 'Ivan', quite probably in order simply to satisfy Inspector Heißmeyer's symbolic desire for a last stand. Heißmeyer himself fled to Bavaria, and, after less than two years in prison, became the director of a Coca-Cola bottling plant, living to the ripe old age of 82.[116]

Ultimately, however, the chaos of *Stunde Null*, Germany's so-called 'zero hour', claimed all the surviving former pupils of the Napolas, whether it found them at home, in hiding, or in prison. The future was devastatingly uncertain, but one thing was guaranteed—that their experiences at the NPEA would have a substantial impact on the rest of their lives.

Notes

1. This chapter necessarily draws predominantly on eyewitness testimonies, since these constitute the sole body of evidence which we possess for this aspect of the schools' history and their disintegration. In so doing, it is intended both to complement and augment the growing number of experiential histories of everyday life in Germany during World War II and the collapse of the Third Reich, which include Nicholas Stargardt, *Witnesses of War: Children's Lives under the Nazis* (London, 2006); Nicholas Stargardt, *The German War. A Nation under Arms, 1939–1945* (London, 2015); Ian Kershaw, *The End: Hitler's Germany, 1944–1945* (London, 2011); Dietmar Süß, *Death from the Skies: How the British and Germans Survived Bombing in World War II* (Oxford, 2014); Florian Huber, *Kind, versprich mir, dass du dich erschießt. Der Untergang der kleinen Leute 1945* (Berlin, 2015); and Thomas Brodie, *German Catholicism at War, 1939–1945* (Oxford, 2018), to name but a few. For an in-depth narratological analysis of the corpus of eyewitness testimonies in question, including full engagement with the relevant secondary literature, see my article 'Surviving "*Stunde Null*": Narrating the Fate of Nazi Elite-School Pupils during the Collapse of the Third Reich', *German History* 33, no. 4 (2015), 570–87. On ego-documents depicting this period, see also Stefan-Ludwig Hoffmann, 'Besiegte, Besatzer, Beobachter: Das Kriegsende im Tagebuch', in Daniel Fulda et al., eds, *Demokratie im Schatten der Gewalt: Geschichten des Privaten im deutschen Nachkrieg* (Göttingen, 2010), 25–55; and Michael Geyer, 'Die eingebildete Heimkehr: Im Schatten der Niederlage', in the same volume, 72–96.
2. Manfred Peter Hein, *Fluchtfährte: Erzählung* (Zürich, 1999), 92.
3. Horst Ueberhorst, *Elite für die Diktatur. Die Nationalpolitischen Erziehungsanstalten 1933–1945: Ein Dokumentarbericht* (Düsseldorf, 1969), 421–2, 425, 434–5; Stiftsarchiv Lambach, letter from Heißmeyer dated 23 September 1944. Although both Heißmeyer and his deputy, Otto Calliebe, claimed after the war that plans to 'avoid senseless bloodletting' and retreat from one NPEA to another (whilst dismissing all pupils who lived in the area) were carried out to the letter, declaring that (to quote Calliebe) 'not a single school was taken by surprise', other eyewitnesses were unconvinced. For

instance, Eugen Wittmann, the former head of NPEA Klotzsche, claimed that he had had no idea that NPEA Loben and Annaberg were going to descend upon his school for succour, and, more significantly, former pupils from NPEA Potsdam and Neuzelle were disgusted by both men's post-war denial that they had explicitly commanded the boys to defend NPEA Spandau, where Heißmeyer had decamped during the last days of the war—cf. Gerd-Ekkehard Lorenz, *Bis zum bitteren Ende. 'Kadetten' des Führers in der Schlacht um Berlin (April/Mai 1945). Ein Beitrag zum Ende der NAPOLA Potsdam* (1998), 7–8, 35. In any case, however orderly the series of evacuations had been to begin with, the schools were generally disbanded in chaotic circumstances as the war neared its close.

4. Here, I will only be considering the experiences of boys who were still nominally of school age (i.e., under 18) at this time, rather than those who had already left the schools and had become fully-fledged soldiers in Wehrmacht and SS units. For some older pupils' recollections of the Third Reich's collapse, see e.g. Rüdiger Bauer, *Wie und warum wir so waren? Erinnerungen an Damals—Schicksalsjahre 1925–1945* (Gelnhausen, 2009), 79–99; [Hermann K.], *Von der Napola zur Loge. Ein Weg in Umbruchzeiten* (n.d., *c.*1995), 89–100; Klaus Kleinau, *Im Gleichschritt, marsch! Der Versuch einer Antwort, warum ich von Auschwitz nichts wusste. Lebenserinnerungen eines NS-Eliteschülers der Napola Ballenstedt* (Hamburg, 2000), 77–86; Peter Meuer, *Linien des Lebens: Eine Kindheit und Jugend im Schwäbischen und anderswo* (Stuttgart, 1991), 164–8; Lothar Steinbach, *Ein Volk, ein Reich, ein Glaube? Ehemalige Nationalsozialisten und Zeitzeugen berichten über ihr Leben im Dritten Reich* (Bonn, 1995), 140–56 (quoting Klaus E.).
5. Karl-Heinz Lübke, private correspondence, 29 September 2011. For discussion of the types of discrimination which former Napola pupils on both sides of the incipient Iron Curtain experienced after the war's end, see Chapter 12.
6. E.g. Helmut Wigelbeyer, *Schicksal am Fluss. Autobiographischer Roman* (Berlin, 2012), 84–6, 96–7, 103.
7. Hein, *Fluchtfährte*, 93–4.
8. Hein, *Fluchtfährte*, 94.
9. Eckhard R., private correspondence, 25 February 2012.
10. Eckhard R., private correspondence, 25 February 2012. Eckhard R. also remembered that the constant hunger of those days led him and his companions to attempt to eat peelings of the trees' roots, though this upset his stomach for several days afterwards.
11. One former pupil, Manfred G., recalled travelling back to his mother in Berlin and being astounded at the destruction which had overtaken the city in the two months since the Christmas holidays (Manfred G., *Erinnerungen*, 7). For a contemporary diary account of another boy's time at Plön between 1 February and 3 March 1945, see Eberhard Vogel, *Wanderungen in Deutschland. Lebensstationen 1935–1948* (Berlin, 2007), 101–19. Vogel himself was dismissed from the school 'until further notice' on 16 April; on his way home, he was caught in an air raid on Schwerin station, where he saw a neighbouring soldier bleed to death before his eyes (p. 120).
12. Uwe Lamprecht, quoted in Johannes Leeb, *'Wir waren Hitlers Eliteschüler': Ehemalige Zöglinge der NS-Ausleseschulen brechen ihr Schweigen* (7th edn; Munich, 2005), 121; Matthias Paustian, *Die Nationalpolitische Erziehungsanstalt Plön 1933–1945* (Rostock, 1995), 77.

13. Uwe Lamprecht, quoted in Leeb, *Eliteschüler*, 121; Eckhard R., private correspondence, 25 February 2012.
14. Lamprecht, quoted in Leeb, *Eliteschüler*, 121.
15. Eckhard R., private correspondence, 25 February 2012.
16. Harald R., interview with the author, 22 August 2011.
17. Harald R., *Tagebuch der Zeit vom 7.9.1944—1.9.1945*, 23–4 (extract from letter to Hans Bernhard Kaufmann).
18. Harald R., *Tagebuch*, 26 (journal entry for 2 August 1946).
19. Martin Köhler, *Als Jungmann in der Napola Köslin 1942 bis zum bitteren Ende 1945* (n.d.), 10.
20. Bernhard von Gélieu, *1890—1990. Culm—Köslin. Kadettenhaus/Stabila/NPEA* (Butzbach-Maibach, 1990), 107.
21. Köhler, *Köslin*, 10–11.
22. Köhler, *Köslin*, 13. This is only Köhler's own speculation, however, and may have been added to his narrative in order to provide a gratuitous link with the *Gustloff* disaster—a recurring theme in many other refugee narratives, even when the narrators in question could not possibly have had any real connection with the *Gustloff* at all. For more on this, see Maren Röger, *Flucht, Vertreibung und Umsiedlung: Mediale Erinnerungen und Debatten in Deutschland und Polen seit 1989* (Marburg, 2011), 3, 5, 245–52.
23. Köhler, *Köslin*, 13.
24. Köhler, *Köslin*, 13. Jürgen Schach von Wittenau, a pupil of NPEA Rügen, corroborates this; cf. *Blown Away (or: Just Keep Walking...)* (n.d.), 65, 74–5. For more on the Kösliners' stay in Putbus, see Henner Menge, ed., *Chronik der ehemaligen Nationalpolitischen Erziehungsanstalt Rügen in Putbus für die Zeit von Oktober 1944 bis Mai 1945* (1999), Anhang A16.
25. von Gélieu, *Köslin*, 107.
26. von Gélieu, *Köslin*, 107.
27. von Gélieu, *Köslin*, 107–8.
28. von Gélieu, *Köslin*, 108.
29. von Gélieu, *Köslin*, 109. For more on the time in Heide, see Köhler, *Köslin*, 14–15.
30. Köhler, *Köslin*, 15–16.
31. Köhler, *Köslin*, 16.
32. Schach von Wittenau, *Blown Away*, 80; Hans F., private correspondence, 22 July 2011.
33. Schach von Wittenau, *Blown Away*, 80; cf. Klaus Schikore, private correspondence, May 2011; Menge, *Chronik*, Anhang A20, 1.
34. Menge, *Chronik*, Anhang A20, 1.
35. Menge, *Chronik*, Anhang A18. In his journal from this period, Dietrich Schulz commented: 'This *Bonbontransport* is probably important for the war-effort! One should not comment on the matter. In the Third Reich anything whatsoever may be commanded, and commands must be carried out.... We can only shake our heads over them....' cf. Dietrich Schulz, *Tagebuch—Kriegsjahr 1945—Napola—Putbus auf Rügen* (1945), 4.
36. Menge, *Chronik*, Anhang A17; Schach von Wittenau, *Blown Away*, 78; Schulz, *Tagebuch*, 4. The handful of pupils involved are adamant that the idea that they themselves should become 'were-wolves' had never been broached (though the symbol of

the movement had been scrawled on the door of one of the teachers' houses some while before, and many of them would have been more than happy to defend the area to the last). Most of the rest of the school did not have a clue that the bunkers even existed, and were able to proclaim with utter conviction to the Soviet authorities that they had never been involved with any potential 'were-wolf' activity. This was just as well, since when the Russians did come across teenagers with such a background, they often had them summarily executed.

37. Schulz, *Tagebuch*, 4.
38. For more on Klaus Schikore's experiences as a child-soldier in Stralsund, see his autobiography *Kennungen. Landmarken einer Wandlung* (Aachen, 1994), 87–101. N.B. Klaus Montanus also depicts the activities of Schulz and Schikore in his autobiographical novel *Die Putbusser* (Frankfurt am Main, 1998), using the barely veiled pseudonyms 'Schult' and 'Schikorra'; however, in the following pages, I have preferred to use the eyewitnesses' own accounts.
39. Schulz, *Tagebuch*, 8–9. For more on the preparations for the voyage west, see Menge, *Chronik*, Anhang A23.
40. Schulz, *Tagebuch*, 9–10. Interestingly, Wiers had just suggested that Schikore should flee with him and his new bride to Namibia. His plan, unbeknownst to Lüders, was to steal one of the school yachts and flee to a port in the west where he could find passage to his homeland, Holland, and thence to Africa (Klaus Schikore, private correspondence, 28 May 2011; cf. Schach von Wittenau, *Blown Away*, 91). Needless to say, Schikore was not amenable to the idea at the time, though he and his wife maintained a long-distance friendship with Fritz and Erna in later life. Wiers did manage to reach Holstein in the yacht *Walfisch*, but was then sent with Erna to a Displaced Persons camp, where he apparently had to undergo numerous interrogations by the Dutch-Jewish commandant before being allowed to proceed to Holland (Menge, *Chronik*, Anhang A29, 6). For a full account of Wiers' voyage, including accounts from the *Jungmannen* who helped him man the *Walfisch*, see Menge, *Chronik*, Anhang A29 *passim*.
41. Schulz, *Tagebuch*, 10.
42. Schulz, *Tagebuch*, 10. Klaus Schikore describes all these events in *Kennungen*, 103–4.
43. Schulz, *Tagebuch*, 10–11.
44. Schulz, *Tagebuch*, 11–12.
45. Schulz, *Tagebuch*, 13–14; cf. Schikore, *Kennungen*, 105–13.
46. For a full account of the voyage (including charts showing the course taken), put together from a number of different eyewitness accounts, see Menge, *Chronik*, Anhang A24.
47. Menge, *Chronik*, Anhang A24, 2 (quoting Peter Hubig); cf. Schach von Wittenau, *Blown Away*, 88–90. Schach von Wittenau describes the boats as follows (pp. 86–7): 'A cutter...isn't much, a small open clinker-built vessel of wooden planks, six by two metres. The boat has five thwarts and, accordingly, ten oars. There is no keel but a centreboard to minimize the side-drift; the boat can either be rowed or sailed. To this effect it is laid out to allow setting a mainsail and a foresail, thus single-mast, rigged like a sloop. It is slightly smaller than a lifeboat but quite adequate for learning the elementary lessons of seamanship if within the reaches of the coastline. Cutters of this type are not built for long-distance hauls.'

48. Menge, *Chronik*, Anhang A24, 2; Schach von Wittenau, *Blown Away*, 92.
49. Schach von Wittenau, *Blown Away*, 93.
50. Schach von Wittenau, *Blown Away*, 93–4.
51. Schach von Wittenau, *Blown Away*, 97–9.
52. Schach von Wittenau, *Blown Away*, 99–100.
53. Menge, *Chronik*, Anhang A25.
54. Menge, *Chronik*, Anhang A26, 1.
55. Menge, *Chronik*, Anhang A26, 2.
56. Jürgen Schach von Wittenau describes Lüders' post-war circumstances as follows (*Blown Away*, 66–7): 'After the war, Lüders applied to influential friends to issue letters of vindication describing him as an honest person uncontaminated by Nazi ideology. He re-entered the church and saw to it that he obtained once again the reputation of a respectable member of the parish....'
57. Quoted in Marieluise Conradt, *Vom Königlichen Württembergischen Lehrerseminar zum Staatlichen Aufbaugymnasium des Landes Baden-Württemberg. 1912 bis 1994 in Rottweil: Eine Schulchronik* (Rottweil, 1994), 47.
58. Conradt, *Rottweil*, 47.
59. Cf. the various accounts cited in Conradt, *Rottweil*, 46–8.
60. Conradt, *Rottweil*, 47 (quoting Hans Binder).
61. Fritz D., private correspondence, 21 July 2011.
62. Arnulf Moser, *Die Napola Reichenau. Von der Heil- und Pflegeanstalt zur nationalsozialistischen Eliteerziehung (1941–1945)* (Konstanz, 1997), 89.
63. Moser, *Reichenau*, 81.
64. For a diagram showing the exact evacuation movements of the schools involved, see Moser, *Reichenau*, 80.
65. Moser, *Reichenau*, 86–7.
66. Moser, *Reichenau*, 87.
67. Moser, *Reichenau*, 89.
68. Paul Sch., private correspondence, 29 April 2010. For further analysis of this passage, see Roche, 'Surviving "*Stunde Null*"', 580–1.
69. Water Knoglinger, *Stift Göttweig. Heimstätte einer 'Nationalpolitischen Erziehungsanstalt' in der Zeit von Jänner 1943 bis April 1945* (2000), 30. This pamphlet was put together by Knoglinger from the recollections of a large number of former pupils.
70. Knoglinger, *Göttweig*, 31. Nevertheless, the documents still received the NPEA Göttweig official stamp and the acting headmaster's signature—as if these symbols might yet have helped, rather than hindered, their bearers' progress.
71. Knoglinger, *Göttweig*, 31–2.
72. Knoglinger, *Göttweig*, 32–3.
73. Knoglinger, *Göttweig*, 33–4.
74. Knoglinger, *Göttweig*, 33–4.
75. Knoglinger, *Göttweig*, 35.
76. Knoglinger, *Göttweig*, 36.
77. Knoglinger, *Göttweig*, 36.
78. Alfred Strubegger, *Tagebuch-Aufzeichnungen*, 9.

79. Knoglinger, *Göttweig*, 37.
80. Wigelbeyer, *Schicksal*, 40–2.
81. Wigelbeyer, *Schicksal*, 50. For more on the preponderance of night-time exercises at Traiskirchen during this period, see Harald Ofner, quoted in Leeb, *Eliteschüler*, 225.
82. Harald Ofner, quoted in Leeb, *Eliteschüler*, 225.
83. Richard Picker, *Das Ende vom Lied. Positionen eines Lebens zwischen Hitlerjugend, Psychotherapie und Kirche* (Vienna, 2005), 58.
84. Picker, *Ende*, 59. In Catholic countries, it would be considered at best a *faux pas* (if not actually a sin) to eat meat on Good Friday.
85. For more detail on the trials and tribulations of the journey, see Wigelbeyer, *Schicksal*, 60–2.
86. Harald Ofner, quoted in Leeb, *Eliteschüler*, 225.
87. Wigelbeyer, *Schicksal*, 62–4.
88. Wigelbeyer, *Schicksal*, 84–6.
89. Wigelbeyer, *Schicksal*, 88–9.
90. Wigelbeyer, *Schicksal*, 89–90; 92–6.
91. Wigelbeyer, *Schicksal*, 92.
92. Wigelbeyer, *Schicksal*, 96–7.
93. Wigelbeyer, *Schicksal*, 97–103.
94. Wigelbeyer, *Schicksal*, 103–4.
95. Mike M., *NAPOLA—Ethos und Pathos* (2011), 17–18.
96. Mike M., *NAPOLA*, 18.
97. Mike M., *NAPOLA*, 18.
98. Mike M., *NAPOLA*, 18–19.
99. Lorenz, *Bis zum bitteren Ende*, 27–30. The account given in this pamphlet is put together from the recollections of a number of former pupils.
100. Lorenz, *Bis zum bitteren Ende*, 31–2.
101. Lorenz, *Bis zum bitteren Ende*, 34.
102. Lorenz, *Bis zum bitteren Ende*, 35. After the war, the Potsdamer could not understand why they had been transferred to Spandau in order to take part in the defence of Berlin, rather than being evacuated, as the Spandauer had been. Were they, as one of the very first Napolas to have been founded, supposed to have had the 'honour' of symbolically defending the final site of the Napola Inspectorate to the last? If their deployment was indeed part of a carefully arranged plan (see n. 3 in this chapter), then it seemed to have been a shockingly cynical one.
103. Lorenz, *Bis zum bitteren Ende*, 36.
104. Lorenz, *Bis zum bitteren Ende*, 37.
105. Lorenz, *Bis zum bitteren Ende*, 41–2.
106. Lorenz, *Bis zum bitteren Ende*, 42.
107. For a full depiction of Gellinek's experience of the march, see Christian Gellinek, *Northwest Germany in Northeast America: Immigration Waves from Central Europe and Their Reverberations until Today. Essays in Preparation of the 400 Year Celebration in A.D. 2007* (Münster, 1997), 135ff. For analysis of this account and other ex-pupils' eyewitness accounts of death marches, see Helen Roche, '"*Der Versuch einer Antwort, warum ich von Auschwitz nichts wußte*": The Evolution of Napola-pupils' Responses

to the Holocaust', in A. S. Sarhangi and Alina Bothe, eds, *Früher/später: Zeugnisse in der Zeit* (Berlin, forthcoming).

108. Lorenz, *Bis zum bitteren Ende*, 49. By the end of the war, over half Lorenz's classmates had been killed or were missing, presumed dead.
109. Lorenz, *Bis zum bitteren Ende*, 49–50.
110. Lorenz, *Bis zum bitteren Ende*, 54.
111. Lorenz, *Bis zum bitteren Ende*, 153–4. For another Potsdam pupil's experience of the war's end, see the final chapters of Hans Müncheberg, *Gelobt sei, was hart macht: Aus dem Leben eines Zöglings der Nationalpolitischen Erziehungsanstalt Potsdam* (Berlin, 2002). For the story of a pupil from Putbus who also got drawn into the fighting in Berlin, see Menge, *Chronik*, Anhang A22, 1–4.
112. For accounts of the end of the war as experienced by pupils of other Napolas, see e.g. Harald Schäfer, *NAPOLA. Die letzten vier Jahre der Nationalpolitischen Erziehungsanstalt Oranienstein bei Diez an der Lahn 1941–1945: Eine Erlebnis-Dokumentation* (Frankfurt am Main, 1997), 93–108, and 211–52 (extracts from the author's diary); Walter Becker, *Erinnerungen an die NAPOLA Naumburg: Ein über die 'Kadette Naumburg' hinausgehender Beitrag zur Geschichte der NPEA* (Neustrelitz, 2000), 83–121; Norbert Fiolka, 'Das Ende in Schulpforta—April 1945' in Lorenz, *Bis zum bitteren Ende*, 190–4. Jürgen Möller, *Der Kampf um Zeitz April 1945. Der Übergang der amerikanischen Truppen über die Weiße Elster im Raum Zeitz, der Einsatz der Napola-Schüler aus Naumburg und Schulpforta, der Kampf um die Flakstellungen und die Besetzung von Zeitz* (Bad Langensalza, 2010) also gives details of the fighting around Naumburg and Schulpforta in which Napola pupils were involved.
113. Interestingly, it is possible to compare former pupils' experiences of their westward evacuation treks favourably with those of families or individuals, which seem to have been characterized by total terror, chaos, and helplessness—cf. Michael Schwartz, 'Ethnische "Säuberung" als Kriegsfolge: Ursachen und Verlauf der Vertreibung der deutschen Zivilbevölkerung aus Ostdeutschland und Osteuropa 1941 bis 1950', in Rolf-Dieter Müller, ed., *Der Zusammenbruch des deutschen Reiches 1945. Zweiter Halbband: Die Folgen des zweiten Weltkrieges* (Munich, 2008), 509–656. Meanwhile, the Napolaner were always fleeing to a goal as well as from the enemy; they did not have to leave their home territory and all hope of return to their families behind, and hence their flight was far less marked by what Albrecht Lehmann has termed 'existential impact' (*Im Fremden ungewollt zuhaus: Flüchtlinge und Vertriebene in Westdeutschland 1945–1990*, Munich, 1991, 199). For more on the expulsions in general, see R. M. Douglas, *Orderly and Humane: The Expulsion of the Germans after the Second World War* (New Haven, 2012).
114. Cf. Kershaw, *The End*, 88.
115. Roche, 'Surviving "*Stunde Null*"', esp. 580–1. On such adumbrations as a key part of the formation of Napola collective memory, see Chapter 12.
116. On Heißmeyer's role as Coca-Cola's general representative (*Generalvertreter*) for South Germany, see Peter Hölzle, *Zwischen Krähwinkel und Kalifornien. Baden-Württemberg einmal ganz anders* (Stuttgart, 2008), 189. Hölzle notes pointedly that Coke is, nevertheless, a 'brown' drink ('*immerhin ein braunes Getränk*'), referring to the prevalent association of Nazism with the colour of the brown shirts worn by the SA.

12
Epilogue
Post-war

As we have seen, the human chaos wrought upon former staff and pupils of the NPEA by the travails of Germany's defeat was more than matched by the material chaos visited upon the schools' fabric as the Second World War ground towards its end. In many cases, the occupation authorities in each zone simply and summarily expropriated former Napola campuses for their own use; thus, the grounds of NPEA Klotzsche became a barracks for Red Army troops, and NPEA Neubeuern's estate was taken over by the United Nations Relief and Rehabilitation Administration (UNRRA), while NPEA Reichenau was requisitioned as a sanatorium for several hundred French children, many of whom apparently ended up wearing left-over pieces of NPEA uniform.[1] Meanwhile, NPEA Ilfeld was looted and sacked by unwelcome visitors who allegedly not only smeared the walls with excrement, but also stole or destroyed all of the buildings' surviving fixtures and fittings, including the school organ.[2]

From a bureaucratic perspective, local administrative and financial authorities were often left completely at a loss as to how to deal with the schools' surviving property and capital assets—an uncertainty which was frequently exacerbated when former school buildings had been consistently plundered by renegade members of the general public prior to their being requisitioned by the occupying forces.[3] Further confusion was also caused by the fact that many former staff were unwilling to reveal their NPEA affiliation even in order to regain control of school assets such as bank accounts. However, if they were once 'found out', they might then proceed to play the 'victim card', demanding hefty reparations for damage incurred to their property and former residences on campus. Thus, the ex-headmistress of the NPEA for girls at Achern, Margarete Wevers, who had previously attempted to pass herself off as a mere nursing-sister in the school infirmary, filed a series of vituperative complaints to the French occupation authorities to the effect that the convent which had re-taken the school's temporary premises at Hegne had illegally appropriated all of her furniture and her 2,000-volume library during her internment.[4]

As we shall see, this rather ambivalent attitude to the Napola past was by no means uncommon in the immediate post-war period. In their attempts to create non-incriminating and sufficiently 'usable' pasts, former administrators and teaching staff utilized the process of denazification to fabricate a veritable tissue

The Third Reich's Elite Schools: A History of the Napolas. Helen Roche, Oxford University Press. © Helen Roche 2021.
DOI: 10.1093/oso/9780198726128.003.0013

of half-truths, exonerating omissions, and outright lies, which arguably formed the basis for a specific form of Napola collective memory—for this explosion of exculpatory voices undoubtedly laid the foundation for the stories which alumni would later tell to make their own autobiographies seem socially and psychologically acceptable under the new post-war order. In giving way to this impulse, the self-styled 'Napolaner' were no different from the majority of their compatriots—nevertheless, the specific narratives and myths which they chose to foster still possessed a dynamic all their own; a phenomenon which Tim Müller has recently termed 'the Napolas' postwar legend'.[5] These myths were subsequently cultivated not only by individual alumni, but also at the level of the NPEA old boys' networks (*Traditionsgemeinschaften*), which deliberately sought to continue the 'comradeship' of the Napolas' wartime alumni associations, whilst at the same time explicitly dissociating themselves from any overtly 'political' affiliations or activities.[6] Finally, such notions were crucial in moulding many ex-pupils' receptions of cultural portrayals of the Napolas, both before and after the fall of the Berlin Wall. Thus, the Napolaner would often trenchantly criticize relevant books, films, and broadcasts, not least *Das Erbe der Napola* (*The Napolas' Legacy*—1996), a psycho-historical analysis of the trauma supposedly inflicted upon Napola-pupils and their families unto the third generation, and Dennis Gansel's 2005 film *Napola: Elite für den Führer* (screened in Anglophone countries as *Napola: Before the Fall*), which portrayed a fictional NPEA Allenstein (based on NPEA Stuhm), featuring a cast of more or less sadistic staff and downtrodden or potentially murderous pupils.[7]

Following a concise discussion of the fates which awaited ex-staff and -pupils immediately after '*Stunde Null*', post-war Germany's so-called 'zero hour', this chapter will then go on to consider both the formation of the NPEA old boys' networks, and the various stages in the development of Napola memory culture, taking into consideration how successful the 'Napolaner' may have been in creating a unique strand of collective memory all their own, defined by their own specific identification as a 'community of experience'.[8] The conclusion will then site these reflections within the context of relevant literature on Allied denazification policy, veterans' organizations in the Federal Republic, and post-war German memory.

'I Wonder What Happened to Them?': The Fate of Former Pupils after '*Stunde Null*'

As one might expect, the degree of leniency or scrutiny with which former Napola-staff and pupils were treated was largely dictated by which occupation zone they had ended up in, corresponding to the relative severity or otherwise of denazification measures employed by the occupying forces in each area.[9] Thus, in the Soviet Occupation Zone (SBZ), former elite-school pupils might well be forbidden to return to school at all; at the very least, the number of pupils allowed to attend any one institution was strictly limited, and their prospects for further study were doubtful, unless they were both willing and convincingly able to lie about their scholastic past.[10] Former elite-school pupils were also most likely to come under suspicion from the Soviet authorities as potential 'were-wolf' activists if political agitation happened to break out at their new schools. Thus, Klaus Schikore and two other former pupils from NPEA Rügen were arrested and interrogated by a Soviet Military Tribunal in 1948–9 on an erroneous charge of having distributed anti-Soviet leaflets at their high school in Stralsund; Schikore was initially sentenced to twenty-five years' imprisonment at the NKVD 'special camp' at Bautzen, although his sentence was later commuted, and he was allowed to return home thereafter.[11] Meanwhile, Arnulf Putzar, a former pupil of NPEA Spandau, was taken into Soviet captivity on suspicion of being a member of a National Socialist youth-group—he was only amnestied and permitted to return home in 1951.[12]

The official penalties for having attended a Nazi elite school in the other three occupation zones were rarely so severe, but could nevertheless still affect former pupils' prospects of entering higher education, at least in the short term. In the American zone, the so-called 'youth amnesty' ensured that no one under the age of 20 would have to undergo the full denazification process, and in any case, most of the remaining NPEA on German soil (apart from Neubeuern) had existed in the British or French sphere of influence, so it was only those pupils whose homes lay relatively far afield, or whose families had been displaced, who might inadvertently find themselves under American jurisdiction.[13] Until May 1953, the school-leaving certificates of former Napola-pupils in Bavaria appear to have been considered ineligible to qualify them for tertiary education, along with those of former pupils of the other Nazi elite schools; however, prospective students in these categories were still permitted to attend special courses for returning soldiers in order to gain a valid school-leaving certificate.[14]

In the British zone, it was more common for former elite-school pupils to be permitted to return to school, so long as the oldest among them joined the penultimate year-group rather than the final year (in order to give them time to 'unlearn' their previous political indoctrination), and with the proviso that only one former elite-school pupil could be accepted into any one class—any remaining applicants should be divided up amongst other schools in the area, to prevent potential conniving and sedition. For two months, such pupils were considered to be on probation, and they could only be firmly accepted for the duration of their course if the staff and administration at their new school had no qualms whatsoever about their political leanings.[15] Staff assessments held at the Staatsarchiv in Hamburg regarding readmitted pupils' deportment highlight the concerns which teachers were expected to raise; comments usually focused on pupils' behaviour, their achievements in class, and their relationship with classmates and staff, as well as any hints of politicization. For instance, a report on a former pupil of NPEA Plön by a teacher at the boys' high school in Hamburg-Rahlstedt stated that 'he takes part in class enthusiastically, demonstrates pleasing diligence in his homework, and is therefore able to work successfully with the class. His character is impeccable and he is thoroughly esteemed by his classmates. He has not attempted to exert any kind of National Socialist influence over his classmates.'[16] During the 1945–6 academic year, the Hamburg school authorities had to deal with a total of sixty-eight former elite-school pupils in this fashion, including sixteen pupils from NPEA Plön, three from NPEA Köslin, two from NPEA Naumburg and NPEA Raudnitz, and one each from NPEA Ballenstedt, Emsland, Potsdam, Putbus, Rufach, Schulpforta, Spandau, Stuhm, Türnitz, and Wartheland respectively.[17] Interestingly, in many cases, these reports do tend to bear out the contention that the majority of former Napola-pupils were able to match their peers academically, or even to surpass them—as well as revealing that they seemingly encountered few problems in readapting to the demands of a very different political regime.[18]

In the French zone, meanwhile, penalties were ostensibly rather graver—according to an order promulgated by the French Military Government on 13 December 1945, all former Hitler Youth and BDM leaders and all former elite-school pupils were automatically debarred from attending secondary and tertiary education institutions. However, anyone who came under one of these categories was given the right to apply for an exemption to be granted by the military government in their respective district.[19] This led to some unrest on both sides—while certain German officials who desired to present themselves as convinced antifascists claimed that all former Napola-pupils represented a heinous danger to the public and their potential future classmates, others argued that youngsters of this age could not be considered to be wholly responsible for their political behaviour, and that their potential extremist propensities might only be enhanced if they were unable to pursue their education any further.[20] In any event, the uncertainties caused by this ruling did leave their mark upon those former pupils who opted to take up a more technical trade, rather than pursuing a career which demanded degree-level qualifications.[21]

However, in more general terms, perusal of the numerous circumstantial (though scarcely statistically extensive) catalogues of post-war careers taken up by former pupils from various NPEA suggests that, overall, most Napolaner were able to go on to pursue an extremely wide and varied range of professions, from academia, law, medicine, journalism, and the military, to engineering, big business, and teaching, as well as trades ranging from book-selling to organ-building.[22] While some of these achievements may have entailed falsifying one's curriculum vitae, or simply concealing the fact that one had ever attended a Nazi elite school (especially in East Germany), it does appear that, on average, attending an NPEA appears to have had neither a wholly adverse nor a wholly affirmative effect on one's future career trajectory.[23] Thus, while Christian Schneider has claimed that the Napolaner were once seen as one of the Nazi regime's most dangerous legacies, since a startling number of former elite-school pupils ended up in leading positions in the media, the military, or the economy,[24] it seems that the unsung majority of former Napola-pupils enjoyed neither particularly stellar careers nor especially disadvantaged ones. Rather, they simply made their way as best they could—often with a little help from their old schoolfriends.

However, the situation which former staff at the Napolas faced appears in many cases to have been even less unfavourable, since the majority were permitted to return to their pedagogical careers after what was to all intents and purposes a fairly brief intermission for the purposes of denazification—it is to this process which we shall now turn.

'Schools Like Any Others'? Denazification, Exculpatory Narratives, and the Creation of Napola Collective Memory

As the occupation regime took hold,[25] staff at the NPEA, along with those who had taught at the Adolf-Hitler-Schools and the *Ordensburgen*, were officially classed as 'major offenders' and placed in the most culpable category (*Hauptbelastet*), signifying their status in the eyes of the occupation authorities as dyed-in-the-wool activists and militarists who had staunchly supported the Nazi regime by systematically poisoning the minds of Germany's youth.[26] However, by skilfully distancing themselves from these other self-avowedly Party-run educational institutions, former Napola-*Erzieher* were able to profit greatly from the inconsistencies and loopholes of the Allied denazification programme. In West Germany, at least, most former NPEA-*Erzieher*—or even *Anstaltsleiter*—experienced few problems in navigating the denazification process without its leaving any lasting stain on their characters, and were then usually able to regain some form of employment in the education sector.[27] The fact that the NPEA had often striven to keep their activities out of the public eye (as discussed in the Introduction) now proved a blessing in disguise, since accusatory antifascist voices at the denazification tribunals were often entirely unable to provide concrete evidence of how Nazified or otherwise life at the schools had really been.[28]

Indeed, as Tim Müller's detailed case study of the denazification of former Napola-*Erzieher* in the American zone of occupation has demonstrated, it was fairly simple for staff and administrators to 'play the system' when it came to pulling the wool over the eyes of the German-led tribunals or '*Spruchkammer*' which had the power to legally determine both one's degree of collaboration with the Nazi regime, and the penalties which one should accordingly have to pay.[29]

Former staff, administrators, personnel, and pupils began to produce an efficient carousel of mutually reinforcing exonerating affidavits, the so-called 'Persil certificates' (*Persilscheine*), in order to whitewash the highly politicized nature of the education which the NPEA had offered, and the extent of their complicity with the Nazi regime. These affidavits routinely stressed the notion that the NPEA had never had any connection with the NSDAP as such, and that the school authorities had been actively hostile to Party or Hitler Youth interference; they also suggested that the Napolas' affiliation with the SS was a mere formality, yet one which had in fact protected the schools from being taken over by 'the real Nazis'.[30] Particularly paradigmatic in this regard was a statement given by Bernhard Pein, the former *Anstaltsleiter* of NPEA Spandau, to his denazification tribunal in Bielefeld, which was subsequently quoted in *Der Spiegel*. Pein claimed that the Napolas had stood in complete opposition to the Party, that the SS uniform had been a mere cloak, and that his own promotion to the rank of SS-*Obersturmbannführer* was due to this entirely superficial and unwelcome affiliation. Astonishingly, *Der Spiegel* reported, 'the Bielefeld tribunal concurred with this opinion, and acquitted the defendant'.[31]

Other prime strategies of exculpation regarding the extent of 'National Socialism' and 'militarism' at the Napolas were evidently formulated in response to the specific wording of relevant charges and occupation laws, providing a paradigm which would later prove invaluable for the construction of subsequent narratives.[32] While the staff and former *Jungmannen* who provided 'Persil certificates' for their colleagues and superiors repeatedly stressed supposedly exonerating aspects of the schools' programme which possessed some foundation in fact, they still consistently omitted the whole truth.[33] The fact that pupils were given a free choice of career, or that the schools had been open to any pupil regardless of his parents' means or political background, were frequently presented as grounds for instant exoneration, as was the idea that the NPEA were neither 'militaristic', nor overtly 'political', since they had never explicitly been designated as 'National *Socialist* Education Institutes'. Even the American and British exchange programmes were frequently cited as proof that the education which the Napolas offered must have been without reproach, while the schools' increasingly anti-religious stance was repeatedly denied.[34] Despite the survival of explicit archival evidence to the contrary, it was insistently averred that the NPEA had never been hostile to Christianity, that all pupils had been permitted to attend confirmation classes unproblematically as a matter of course, and that the schools had been wholly characterized by their cultivation of 'freedom of opinion'.[35] Even the fact that the schools' 'national political' courses of instruction had often entailed the perusal of banned books was recast as proof of how 'liberal' and un-doctrinaire the Napola curriculum had been.

Meanwhile, former staff would frequently claim that they had been forced to take up employment or remain at a Napola against their will; that the atmosphere at their school had never been particularly political (and, in any case, their very presence had made it even less so), and that they had never taught any explicitly 'political' subjects or had any interest in politics anyway.[36] False logical propositions on a binary model also abounded in many of these statements—for instance, the contention that if a member of staff had been a 'wonderful pedagogue', or 'artistic', he therefore could not possibly have been a National Socialist, or that if he had ever come into conflict with the Party, the Hitler Youth, or the SS, then he necessarily could not have possessed any Nazi political sympathies whatsoever.[37]

Perhaps the most powerful trope of all, however, was that which relied explicitly upon the individual tradition and location of each NPEA to provide both a defence and an exoneration—stressing the school's religious or humanistic background, its regional loyalties, and, in those Napolas which had lain beyond Prussia, its absolute rejection of any hint of 'Prussian militarism'.[38] As we have seen in Chapter 5 and Chapter 6, such protestations would often come to form a mainstream part of these schools' memory culture later on. However, while claims that the previous traditions of the various NPEA had exerted a significant influence on their development certainly possessed some basis in fact, their deployment in this context was often tendentious and disingenuous, and frequently attempted to attribute any 'militaristic' elements whatsoever to NPEA in other regions—in these accounts, 'Prussia' was always elsewhere.[39] Thus, the honour of the Napolas in Württemberg could be defended by assertions that NPEA Backnang and Rottweil had had nothing whatsoever in common with schools such as NPEA Plön, which were devoted to an inhumane 'Prussian-militaristic drill-system' (again, considering the Plön *Anstaltsleiter* Brunk's obsessive devotion to war-games and paramilitary drills, there may have been more than a grain of truth in this claim—but not the whole truth).[40] Meanwhile, former adherents of NPEA Klotzsche accused the *Erzieher* who had been sent from Württemberg to take the school in hand, including acting *Anstaltsleiter* Eugen Wittmann, of being 'south-German SS-invaders' who had been sent to infect the Saxon school with their particularly nefarious brand of 'Prussian' militarism (see Chapter 5). From this perspective, Tim Müller's contention that the individual circumstances and location of each NPEA had a crucial role to play in forming their adherents' collective defence (and, later, their collective memory) is evidently well-founded.[41] Thus, in similar fashion to the exonerating myths cultivated by SS-veterans during and after the Nuremberg Trials, Allied intervention had inadvertently sown the fertile seed which would facilitate the subsequent flourishing of exculpatory narratives among the community of Napolaner.[42]

Even after the end of the denazification process, such convenient myths remained alive and well within the networks of former NPEA staff and pupils which were beginning to form, as those concerned began to take their first tentative steps into the brave new world of West German democracy. While maintaining contact between 'comrades' in the Soviet Zone and later GDR was considered dangerous to the point of impossibility, given that the formation of any kind of network might potentially lead to arrest by the NKVD, those on the Western side of the incipient Iron Curtain soon began to cultivate their old 'comradeship' in a new, ostensibly politically inoffensive guise—that of the NPEA *Traditionsgemeinschaften*.[43]

From *Jungmann* to 'Napolaner': The Foundation and Operation of the West German Old Boys' Networks

By the early 1950s, the seeds which had been sown by the wartime *Altkameradschaften* (alumni associations) had begun to flourish, though in a very different political soil. Adherents of many of the NPEA had coalesced into a number of more or less close-knit groups, most with analogous aims and preoccupations.[44] These groups uniformly emphasized their non-political nature, and the fact that they were wholly interested in cultivating nostalgia for their schooldays, commemorating their war-dead, and providing a helping hand for 'comrades' who had not yet found their feet practically or financially, rather than desiring to foster any kind of political extremism in the present.[45] Many of these groups adamantly refused to register themselves as any kind of formal 'organization' or 'association', contenting themselves with cultivating their 'comradeship' through regular reunions (*Treffen*), shared reminiscences, and the publication and distribution of round-robin newsletters and address lists.

However, for those alumni who were not wholly in tune with the organizations' objectives, or for those who simply had no desire whatsoever to rekindle their connection with their *alma mater*, the demands of this new 'comradeship' might not appear quite so appealing. Some of the *Traditionsgemeinschaften*, such as that pertaining to NPEA Oranienstein, displayed distinct displeasure when confronted with critical voices, even going so far as to castigate dissenting members of the younger year-groups (who had only experienced life at the Napola in wartime) as pharisees, mud-slingers, or mere parrots of left-wing '*Spiegel*-jargon', since they were clearly so susceptible to post-war influences.[46] Those who simply ignored the invitations to reunions which landed on their doorstep, or refused to send in updates for the associations' newsletters and address lists, were routinely treated to a guilt-tripping campaign every bit as resentful as that which had been visited upon those who had exercised their right to silence in the original school newsletters during World War II.[47]

In 1953, a number of Napolaner from various schools decided to attempt to found an official nationwide association of former NPEA pupils and staff as a sort of umbrella organization, something along the lines of the League of Former Prussian, Saxon, and Bavarian Cadets.[48] Originally conceived as an organization for former Napola-adherents who were based in the Ruhr area, by the time that the association was officially launched, the name had been changed simply to the 'Association of Members of Former National Political Education Institutes' (*Vereinigung der Angehörigen ehemaliger Nationalpolitischer Erziehungsanstalten*). The initial plans for the organization stated explicitly that it should not use any kind of alias, for fear of being considered some sort of politically questionable secret society. Its aims included 'nurturing comradeship'; assistance to comrades in the Eastern zone and the dependents of fallen comrades; regular meetings of individual subgroups and annual reunions; the organization of lecture series on economic and cultural topics; and discussions of current political problems, which might allow members to take on political responsibility and work to help their fatherland.[49] One of the Oranienstein board members went even further in his vision of the former pupils' future mission, stating that: 'we do not desire neo-Nazism nor any other form of restoration; rather, we want to help, through a pristine, strong, inwardly stable Germany, to create a Europe which will be worthy of its culture, and which will be a bulwark against Bolshevism.... We affirm every democratic government which thinks and acts in a fashion which is both German and European.'[50] The organization finally came into being on 13 February 1954, in the presence of twenty-two representatives from Oranienstein, sixteen from Naumburg, two from Stuhm, one from Bensberg, and one from Klotzsche.[51]

However, the organization does not appear to have enjoyed the success or longevity of many other veterans' associations—even the majority of the Oranienstеiner appear to have been sceptical and disengaged from the idea of a nationwide association which might seek to replace or destroy the intimacy of their specific Oranienstein '*Kameradschaft*'. There were also fears that the younger members would find the whole endeavour in poor taste, and the danger of being tarred with an adverse political brush was something which many were equally unwilling to risk.[52] Some were afraid that any attempt to found such an organization officially would inevitably lead to surveillance by the security services; even half a century later, the circulation of the initial regulations of the umbrella 'Association' as a historical curiosity 'sent a chill down the spine' of former pupils at other schools.[53] Thus, the nucleus of each *Traditionsgemeinschaft* remained resolutely localized around an individual school, or even an individual year-group—ex-pupils from different Napolas rarely evinced any desire to convene joint reunions, and the generational cleft between younger and older cohorts could also widen into a permanent rift.[54] By the 1960s, wives and children had also begun to attend the reunions regularly as a matter of course, lending them a more familial aspect.[55]

Over the years, the importance of place, and the Napolas' own place in history, also began to take on an ever greater significance, with plans afoot either to attempt to refound schools (as at Ilfeld), to commemorate their erstwhile presence with official plaques (as at Klotzsche), or, after German reunification in

1991, to rejoice in the possibility of finally revisiting those schools which had been out of bounds due to their location in the GDR (Potsdam being a key case in point). Alumni who were particularly interested in preserving the Napolas' history would frequently keep in touch with each other on an informal basis, and the urge to propagate a (suitably sanitized) version of the NPEA past was made manifest in projects such as the reprinting (with judicious excisions) of school newsletters, or the donation of (sufficiently censored) runs of relevant documents to local and regional archives. The Napolaner hoped in this way to be able to pass on their view of the schools' history to posterity—an endeavour which was also mirrored in the increasing number of (often self-published) Napola memoirs which began to appear from the 1990s onwards.

Even in the twenty-first century, some of the old boys' networks are still highly organized, with a constitution, Annual General Meetings, and an official spokesman or '*Sprecher*' who organizes reunions, facilitates contacts, and publishes newsletters and address lists; others are far less formal, and are based around loosely knit groups of friends or classmates. Still, despite the disparate nature of these groupings and associations, there still exists an overwhelming sense that, somehow, all of the former pupils share a bond which links them together, even if they have never met—as evidenced by the ease with which ex-pupils are able to instigate friendly correspondence with their comrades from different schools, almost immediately falling back on the familiar form of address ('*Du*' rather than '*Sie*'). Everyone knows *someone*, and there is a very strong feeling that all of the Napolaner automatically share similar assumptions—indeed, there is a strong sense of possessing a shared collective destiny, a *Schicksalsgemeinschaft*, that seems to have lasted long into the post-war era. The importance and symbolism of these reunions for some of their adherents may be demonstrated by the fact that one former pupil travelled for nine hours to attend his annual *Treffen* (including multiple train changes), before travelling a further nine hours back, even at an advanced age, while another twice made a round-trip all the way from Canada in order to attend.[56]

One of the consequences of this feeling of community is that those former pupils who are seen to be making an effort to preserve knowledge about the Napolas for the future, or those who are attempting to facilitate contacts between and within the various old boys' networks, are now quickly and easily welcomed into other groups, invited to reunions that are linked with schools other than their own, and so forth. At one point, such endeavours led not merely to former pupils themselves endeavouring to write their own histories of the schools—but even writing to esteemed public figures, including the (somewhat controversial) author Martin Walser, in order to beg them to take on the task.[57]

This situation has certainly been exacerbated by the very patchy and partial appearance of the Napolas in the post-war media landscape. Apart from a few much-hyped and often historically questionable publications or releases—such as

Das Erbe der Napola; Johannes Leeb's edited collection of reminiscences of Nazi elite-school pupils, *Wir waren Hitlers Eliteschüler* (1998); the documentaries *Hitler's Children* (*Hitlers Kinder*, directed by the notorious Guido Knopp [2000]) and *Herrenkinder* (2009), and Dennis Gansel's aforementioned Napola-film—the Napolas have rarely been brought into the limelight during the German post-Wall memory boom. Thus, one former pupil, Uwe L., tried to convince as many of his comrades as possible that it *must* be better to appear on a programme such as *Hitler's Children*, even just chopped for a few unrepresentative seconds out of the obligatory three-hour interview, in order to draw public attention to the schools, than not to have them represented at all. Meanwhile, in reaction to tendentious media coverage, sporting headlines such as 'Cadets of the Devil' or 'Brutality and Beethoven', or in relation to the Napola film, former pupils often become extremely defensive, writing whole screeds to the newspaper editors or the production companies in question concerning their manifold 'errors'. It is therefore to these sore points—and the tropes of Napola collective memory which underlie them—to which we shall now turn.

Napola-*Vergangenheitsbewältigung*? Napolaner and the Past in Reunified Germany

Often, the reappearance of the Napolas in the media landscape after the fall of the Wall, even (or especially) when portrayed in a negative or ahistorical light, seems to have given former pupils an impetus to reflect upon their schooldays, and to consider how much influence (or otherwise) their time at an NPEA might really have had upon their later life.[58] Thus, Manfred Gembalies was inspired to write his private memoirs and donate them to the German Diary Archive in Emmendingen after he had read the tie-in book which accompanied the broadcast of *Hitler's Children*, while Dieter Eschenhagen only began to reflect at length on the possible psychological effects of his schooling after having read *Das Erbe der Napola*.[59] Often, the newsletters of the *Traditionsgemeinschaften* would also feature pages of discussion and letters from alumni concerning such media events—the editors might make a habit of publishing a varied selection of members' views, or reprinting reproductions of relevant newspaper articles and reviews. At times, they would also deliberately attempt to stimulate more far-reaching reflections on the value and long-term effects of one's Napola education.[60]

In more belligerent vein, ex-pupils might also attempt to engage with authors, film-makers, and broadcasters, in order to find fault with their interpretation of the Napola past, taking great pains to point out all of their 'mistakes' or historical inaccuracies. Thus, Christian Schneider, the principal investigator of the *Erbe der Napola* project, frequently received vituperative critiques from former pupils who took issue with the scholarly basis of his study and accused him of politicizing his research, while one former pupil from NPEA Spandau was so enraged by Dennis Gansel's Napola-film that he even put together a self-published pamphlet entitled *Napola: Filmischer Schuss in den Ofen* ('Napola: A Cinematic Flop'). The pamphlet minutely detailed all of the ways in which the film had portrayed the Napolas 'falsely', ranging from erroneous deployment of uniforms and swastika-armbands, to the fact that the 'hero' of the film would never have been allowed to join an NPEA at the age of 17 anyway, no matter how great his boxing talent—not least because he had never studied Latin.[61] However, when the former pupil in question sent the pamphlet to the film's production company, they simply threatened to sue him for violation of copyright, since he had made the mistake of reproducing the official film poster on its cover. Meanwhile, ex-pupil Dieter P. went even further, collating all of the increasingly vitriolic (and inevitably unpublished) fulminations which he had sent to the editors of all of the newspapers which had reviewed the film, and forwarding copies of the entire collection to a number of other former pupils with whom he was acquainted. Dieter P.'s correspondence included a series of hymns of hate to the publicist Hellmuth Karasek, whose extremely unflattering autobiographical account of his brief time at NPEA Loben has long made him *persona non grata* in *Traditionsgemeinschaft* circles.[62] Karasek had deemed the film a passable reflection of his own experiences, since he, too, had been bullied for bed-wetting at a Napola; in response, Dieter P. denounced 'Quiz-show Karasek' as a mere 'four-month Napolaner', impugning his veracity as a witness, and denouncing any journalists who had been willing to publish his flawed commentary on the schools as unprofessional lackeys of the uniformly biased media machine.[63]

By contrast, Johannes Leeb's *Wir waren Hitlers Eliteschüler* (*We Were Hitler's Elite-School Pupils*), an edited volume which simply published retrospective accounts by former pupils from all of the Nazi elite schools, taking them more or less at face value, was hailed by many Napolaner as presenting a portrait which was pleasingly 'true to reality'.[64] Put simply, any film, book, or broadcast which portrayed the schools in a negative light was dismissed as an ideologically or politically motivated 'pathetic effort', while those which accorded with ex-pupils' own rosy-tinted view of the past were praised for possessing the requisite 'objectivity'—a symbolic term which recurs repeatedly in former pupils' critiques, and which reflects their very real anxieties about how the Napolas will be treated by posterity. In this context, an 'objective' portrayal means a 'positive' account which concurs with all the main tropes of the Napola memory narrative since denazification, in opposition to the so-called 'political correctness' of an often undifferentiated group of 'victimizers', who are generally dismissed as '68ers', 'leftists', and liberals of the 'Frankfurt brigade'.

From this perspective, whether one considers the increasing archive of memoir literature and autobiographical reflections penned by former Napola-pupils, or the ruminations preserved within the pages of the old boys' newsletters, certain themes repeatedly and insistently return to the fore—themes which, if combined, would arguably constitute the basis of an 'objective' account in the eyes of many Napolaner, as well as providing a framework for their own specific form of collective memory.[65] One of the most frequently recurring tropes is that of ex-pupils' victimhood; language denoting 'betrayal', 'manipulation', and 'seduction' by the Nazi regime is rife in their accounts—a discourse of passivity which also absolves them of any complicity. This discourse of force, compulsion, or even being 'bewitched' by political events beyond one's control commonly occurs in tandem with a systematic minimization of the political aspects of NPEA education—for example, the insistence that political teaching as such had never existed at the schools, or that it was something that pupils 'never noticed', and that those teachers who were most 'fanatical' were in any case those who were the most cordially disliked. In similar vein, the schools are repeatedly distanced from other, supposedly far more overtly 'National Socialist' organizations within the Nazi state, such as the NSDAP, the Hitler Youth, or the SS, and anecdotes are frequently rehearsed which demonstrate pupils' disdain for regime grandees and other so-called 'golden pheasants' (*Goldfasanen*; a disparaging term for Party dignitaries).[66] Ex-pupils often deny that any of their classmates ever desired to join the SS or the Party as a career, and claim that, in any event, attending a normal school or the Hitler Youth would have subjected them to an equal or even more formidable level of political indoctrination; favourable comparisons may also be made with the politicized state of education in the GDR. All in all, the Napola is presented as an 'ideal world' or an 'isle of the blessed' which was providentially able to preserve pupils from the worst of the regime's political and military excesses, even right up to the end of the war.[67]

The more militaristic or harsh aspects of Napola-education are also explained away, not merely through the old saws that it 'didn't do us any harm', or that the paramilitary training was 'just like the scouts', but through a form of positive mythologization which ascribes an extraordinary degree of personal competence both to the Napolaner as a group, and to former pupils as individuals.[68] The idea runs that such a tough training was wholly necessary in order to enable ex-pupils to survive the travails of the immediate post-war period (and often those of later life as well), and that all of the 'Prussian' or 'gentlemanly' virtues which they learnt at the Napola have stood them in excellent stead in later life.[69] This trope is often accompanied by negative comparisons with the present; for instance, the idea that the former pupil's own grandchildren would be far better able to cope with life if they had been instilled with similar virtues, or that contemporary liberal democracy is in dire need of an analogous form of elite education which could combat the selfish individualism of the present day. All in all, former pupils often contend that 'people nowadays can't possibly judge what it was like then', and any surviving evidence that National Socialist ideology had fundamentally infiltrated the schools (including politicized accounts of school activities in contemporary Napola newsletters) is explained away with reference to the ostensible gulf between 'conception and reality' at the NPEA in question. Indeed, it is highly likely that a significant proportion of those former pupils who eventually read this book will take issue with its overall findings on analogous grounds, asserting that, since its portrayal does not wholly match their current perceptions of previous lived realities, it cannot be deemed 'objective' on their own terms.

Nevertheless, such reactions merely lie at one end of a spectrum of ex-pupils' reactions to the Napola past which, in its entirety, is extremely broad and multifaceted. Indeed, there also exist a number of former pupils who have managed wholly to escape the comforting confines of these convenient narratives, and who are able to regard their experiences at the Napola more objectively, in the literal sense of the word. These eyewitnesses are fully aware of the fallibility of memory, the false seductions of exculpatory myths, and the inherent subjectivity of their own perceptions of the past. As one of them, Ernst-Christian G., put it: 'Perhaps it's enough, and a help to historical truth, if we can lay ready a few stones—authentic, as I hope—for the mosaic. Can we do more?'[70]

Conclusions

All in all, the Napolas' ambivalent position in post-war and post-Wall memory culture can be explained in a number of ways. Firstly, although former adherents of the NPEA were largely able to sidestep severe penalties under the denazification process by astutely distancing the schools from more self-evidently 'National Socialist' institutions, in the eyes of other members of the German public, former Napola-staff and pupils often made the perfect scapegoats. Thus, the denazification tribunal which tried the Mayor of the town of Diez an der Lahn was presented with the defence that the Mayor's opposition to the removal of the town museum from its home within the confines of Schloss Oranienstein, which had led to escalating conflict with the NPEA authorities, provided proof positive of his fundamental and wholehearted opposition to the Nazi regime—even though he had also been involved in facilitating forced sterilizations, the deportation of local Jewish families, and the desecration of Jewish graves in the area.[71] By accepting in such cases that adherents of the Napolas represented 'the real Nazis', the tribunals were ostensibly hoodwinked into believing that the NPEA were both politically harmless, and that they were simultaneously the most devilish incarnations of National Socialism, in opposition to which such allegedly 'upstanding citizens' could heroically hone their post-war credentials as 'resisters' who had 'always been against' Nazism. In similar vein, former *Erzieher* who had left a position at an NPEA prior to 1945 might castigate the schools' 'militarism' or hostility to Christianity as execrable manifestations of Nazification against which they, too, had staunchly resisted, leading inevitably to their dismissal—a convenient narrative which also presented the staff in question as undoubted victims of the regime.[72]

In similar vein, while the Napolaner consistently distanced themselves from 'the real Nazis', in the guise of members of the SS or Nazi grandees, the exculpatory narratives of other members of the 'Hitler Youth' generation might use the Napolaner themselves as expedient scapegoats—especially those who had attended other state-run National Socialist educational institutions such as the *Lehrerbildungsanstalten* (teacher-training colleges) or *Deutsche Heimschulen*.[73] This mixture of prurient curiosity and exculpatory disgust regarding the Napola past is still discernible in present-day journalistic depictions of the NPEA, which frequently tend to sensationalize and demonize, rather than treating the schools as rational objects of historical enquiry.[74]

How far, then, do the adherents of the NPEA conform to prevailing patterns in German post-war culture more generally? Many of the defining features of denazification pertaining to the Napolas certainly conformed to much broader trends among the German population at large—for instance, the selective crafting of occupational histories; the 'you testify for me and I'll testify for you' mentality, and even the existence of what was tantamount to a black market in exculpatory statements—that 'densely woven web of positive affidavits' which provided mutually exonerating certification of so many defendants' alleged anti-Nazi attitudes and activities.[75] As Steven P. Remy's detailed case study of the denazification of Heidelberg University has shown, analogous protestations regarding the institution's unblemished 'tradition' and its professors' secret 'opposition' to the regime (in contrast with the more or less mythical figure of the utterly fanatical and wholly irrational 'Nazi professor') allowed staff to construct a series of 'elaborate and remarkably similar narratives of defence and justification regarding their engagement with National Socialism', which subsequently contributed to the emerging political culture of selective memory, whilst also laying the foundations of future exculpatory accounts in memoirs throughout the 1950s and 1960s, and even beyond.[76] Moreover, similar conditions often pertained when it came to the denazification of West German primary- and secondary-school staff, where any conflict with higher authority during the Third Reich, however trivial, was disingenuously styled as 'resistance', and former pupils' testimonies were routinely used to dismiss or whitewash any accusations regarding teachers' previous ideological commitment.[77]

Meanwhile, Napola alumni culture, as represented by the West German old boys' networks, often bears a striking resemblance to the more mainstream veterans' culture fostered by the various military and regimental veterans' associations in the post-war period.[78] Former Napolaner in the Soviet Zone and later GDR, deprived of such means of cultivating their former comradeship, might be more likely to undergo what Frank Biess has termed 'antifascist conversions'—dedicating themselves wholeheartedly to a new form of ideology, as did Erich Honecker's righthand man in the East German youth organization, Hans Schoenecker.[79] However, in the Federal Republic, former pupils were usually able to rekindle a suitably sanitized version of their former '*Kameradschaft*' without any problems.

As Thomas Kühne's seminal account of post-war veterans' culture has shown, most of the military veterans' organizations followed a similar path to that of the NPEA *Traditionsgemeinschaften*, inasmuch as they had little interest in political lobbying, let alone a resurrection of far-right extremism; rather, they remained resolutely rooted in comradely nostalgia, which they generally preferred to cultivate at a local or regional rather than a national level. From this perspective, the failure of the overarching NPEA '*Vereinigung*' discussed above was mirrored in the military veterans' analogous failure to create a successful nationwide umbrella organization which could have emulated the influential *Kyffhäuserbund* association of the interwar period.[80] Just like the Napola old boys' networks, these ex-military organizations similarly thrived upon the notion of 'comradeship' as a form of reciprocity or obligation, expressed through regular attendance at annual reunions, subscriptions and contributions to membership journals, or donations to the associations' mutual aid funds. However, they were also similarly plagued by the problem of how to mobilize the silent majority of members who failed to show as much dedication to their association as the organizers would ideally have wished; moreover, the generational tensions prevalent in some of the NPEA *Traditionsgemeinschaften* also manifested themselves in the military veterans' organizations too.[81] Meanwhile, the plaints of the Napolaner regarding the shocking failure of veracity and objectivity in media portrayals of the NPEA followed an analogous playbook to military and Waffen-SS veterans' criticisms of cultural portrayals of the Wehrmacht, the SS, or the Third Reich in general—attempting to cast their merits into question by using partial (and often extremely nit-picking) criticism to discredit an entire production.[82]

At the same time, autobiographical accounts by the Napolaner also display many tropes of collective memory which were commonly found in German society at large—such as the desire to portray oneself above all as a 'victim' of the Nazi regime, or the desperation to distance oneself from National Socialism at all costs.[83] However, the simple truth was that, as potential future rulers and loyal servants of the regime, it was very difficult (if not impossible) for the Napolaner to convincingly cast themselves as victims of Nazism in the same way that the majority of German 'war children' had done.[84] Thus, while the turn-of-the-millennium discourse which declared that the 'Hitler Youth' or 'war child' generation had courageously been able to 'break a taboo' by finally publishing autobiographical accounts of the 'trauma' which they had suffered did apply to the Napolaner in some measure, their narratives could never be so sure of a positive reception.[85] Nevertheless, it is evident that the Napola-related projects instigated by Christian Schneider and Johannes Leeb respectively represented the psycho-historicizing, 'generational trauma'-exploring and 'taboo-breaking memoir' ends of the spectrum of 'war child literature', despite the fact that the psychologizing portrayal of former pupils' sufferings in *Das Erbe der Napola* was scarcely a sympathetic one.[86]

Finally, in terms of discursive strategies, the Napolaner of this generation are certainly not alone in their tendencies to depoliticize accounts of their education during this period, stressing the positive aspects of their Nazi schooldays or their time in the Hitler Youth, or highlighting the 'socialist' aspects of the National Socialist *Volksgemeinschaft*, which arguably granted them numerous opportunities for self-gratification and advancement which they might never otherwise have enjoyed.[87] Such distancing strategies are not necessarily actively or consciously motivated by a desire to dissemble or rehabilitate, but may well simply reflect the extreme cognitive dissonance which exists between former pupils' untroubled recollections of their childhood experiences, which often did not contain any explicitly political coding at the time, and the more conflicted view of their adult selves looking back with hindsight, now possessing full knowledge of the Nazi regime's crimes—and the ease with which they might subsequently have been implicated in them.[88]

At the same time, the Napolaner do seem to possess a more specific form of collective memory all their own, not only in terms of their frequent recourse to the suite of tropes described in the previous section, but also (and most especially) in terms of the extent to which they attribute their allegedly enhanced capacity to cope with all subsequent difficulties and challenges to their Napola education.[89] Therefore, even if the training offered at the NPEA never transformed the Napolaner into future leaders of Germany, as had once been promised, it nevertheless appears to have given many former pupils a lasting sense of leadership over their own lives.

Notes

1. Cf. Stadtarchiv Dresden, GV Klotzsche 8.20 147/05k, Bl. 1–2; Bayerisches Hauptstaatsarchiv München (BayHStA), MK53972, letter dated 10 September 1945; Arnulf Moser, *Die Napola Reichenau. Von der Heil- und Pflegeanstalt zur nationalsozialistischen Eliteerziehung (1941–1945)* (Konstanz, 1997), 89–90.
2. Klosterkammer Hannover, IIf. X. 4, Band I, Bl. 4.
3. For examples, see the relevant correspondence in Bundesarchiv Lichterfelde, R 87/142, and Staatsarchiv Freiburg (StAF), C 25/4 Nr. 106 and Nr. 117.
4. Cf. StAF, D 5/1 Nr. 2364. Needless to say, the French authorities were unimpressed by Wevers' asseverations.
5. Cf. Tim Müller, 'A Legal Odyssey: Denazification Law, Nazi Elite Schools, and the Construction of Postwar Memory', *History of Education* 46, no. 4 (2017), 498–513. For

some initial reflections on the creation of collective memory among former Napola-pupils, see also Helen Roche, 'Surviving "*Stunde Null*": Narrating the Fate of Nazi Elite-School Pupils during the Collapse of the Third Reich', *German History* 33, no. 4 (2015), 570–87; also Chapter 11.

6. From this perspective, we can make a clear distinction between the activities of the NPEA old boys' networks and the specifically military veterans' associations, such as the Waffen-SS' '*Hilfsgemeinschaft auf Gegenseitigkeit*' (HIAG). However, some former members of staff and some of the older Napolaner were also members of associations such as HIAG (including Eugen Wittmann, Heißmeyer's adjutant from Württemberg, and Claus Cordsen, a former pupil of NPEA Bensberg), and may therefore have been implicated in these bodies' more overt pursuit of right-wing identity politics in the post-war period.
7. Christian Schneider et al., *Das Erbe der Napola. Versuch einer Generationengeschichte des Nationalsozialismus* (Hamburg, 1996). On Gansel's film, see e.g. Daniel Kulle, '"Tut so was ein deutscher Junge?" Verantwortung und Mitleid in *Napola—Elite für den Führer*', in Margrit Frölich et al., eds, *Das Böse im Blick. Die Gegenwart des Nationalsozialismus im Film* (Nehren, 2007), 219–30; Markus Zöchmeister, 'Nazismus, Karneval und Perversion. Mediale Reproduktionen der NS-Welt', in the same volume, 30–42; Sebastian Winter, 'Arischer Antifaschismus. Geschlechterbilder als Medium der kulturindustriellen Bearbeitung der Erinnerung an den Nationalsozialismus am Beispiel der Filme "Der Untergang", "Sophie Scholl" und "Napola"', in kittkritik, ed., *Deutschlandwunder. Wunsch und Wahn in der postnazistischen Kultur* (Mainz, 2007), 52–68; Christian Mehr, 'NS-Volksgemeinschaft im Geschichtsunterricht: Der Spielfilm "Napola—Elite für den Führer"', in Uwe Danker and Astrid Schwabe, eds, *Die NS-Volksgemeinschaft. Zeitgenössische Verheißung, analytisches Konzept und ein Schlüssel zum historischen Lernen?* (Göttingen, 2017), 141–55.
8. Cf. Mary Fulbrook, 'History-Writing and "Collective Memory"', in Stefan Berger and Bill Niven, eds, *Writing the History of Memory* (London, 2014), 65–88; Mary Fulbrook, 'Guilt and Shame among Communities of Experience, Connection, and Identification', in Stephanie Bird et al., eds, *Reverberations of Nazi Violence in Germany and Beyond: Disturbing Pasts* (London, 2016), 15–31.
9. On this diversity of zonal experience when it came to denazifying youthful adherents of the regime more generally, see e.g. Michael Buddrus, 'A Generation Twice Betrayed: Youth Policy in the Transition from the Third Reich to the Soviet Zone of Occupation (1945–1946)', in Mark Roseman, ed., *Generations in Conflict: Youth Revolt and Generation Formation in Germany 1770–1968* (Cambridge, 1995), 247–68. On re-education policy in schools in the Soviet Occupation Zone, see Benita Blessing, *The Antifascist Classroom: Denazification in Soviet-occupied Germany, 1945–1949* (Basingstoke, 2006); on denazification policy more generally, see e.g. Perry Biddiscombe, *The Denazification of Germany: A History 1945–1950* (Stroud, 2007); Frederick Taylor, *Exorcising Hitler: The Occupation and Denazification of Germany* (London, 2011); Konrad Jarausch, *After Hitler: Recivilizing Germans, 1945–1995* (Oxford, 2006), ch. 2.
10. Cf. e.g. Heinz Kula, 'Was ich Arnfried verdanke', *Rundklotz* 53 (2003), 7–8; Klaus Schikore, private correspondence, May 2011.

11. Klaus Schikore, private correspondence, May 2011. For an account of Schikore's experiences in Soviet captivity, see Klaus Schikore, *Wir müssen ihre Last wohl tragen. Rückblicke eines Grenzgängers zwischen West und Ost* (Aachen, 2006), 9–14.
12. Cf. Arnulf H. K. Putzar, *Im Schatten einer Zeit* (Schwerin, 1998).
13. On the youth amnesty, see Michael R. Hayse, *Recasting West German Elites: Higher Civil Servants, Business Leaders, and Physicians in Hesse between Nazism and Democracy, 1945–1955* (Oxford, 2003), 149.
14. Cf. relevant correspondence in BayHStA, MK53972. Educational officials in Bavaria also attempted to claim that NPEA Neubeuern had not been a 'real' Napola in the same sense as the schools in Prussia (for more on this anti-Prussian exculpatory trope, which I have termed '*Preußen ist immer anderswo*', see below).
15. Cf. Staatsarchiv Hamburg (StAH), 361–2 VI Nr. 502, letter dated 15 August 1945.
16. StAH, 361–2 VI Nr. 502, letter dated 20 December 1945. For a full range of assessments, see further relevant correspondence in this file and in StAH, 362–2–30 Nr. 45 Bd. 5.
17. Cf. StAH, 361–2 VI Nr. 502.
18. On former pupils' boasting of the academic utility of their Napola education post-war, see Roche, 'Surviving "*Stunde Null*"'; on such youthful adaptability more generally, see e.g. Mary Fulbrook, *Dissonant Lives: Generations and Violence through the German Dictatorships* (Oxford, 2011).
19. Staatsarchiv Sigmaringen (StAS), Wü 80 T 1–2 Nr. 325, decree dated 13 December 1945. This decree replaced an order dated a month earlier, which had suggested that former Napola-pupils would normally be allowed to return to school unless it could be proven that they had been accepted at an NPEA solely due to party-political reasons, despite their academic achievements being insufficient (StAS, Wü 80 T 1–2 Nr. 325, decree dated 13 November 1945).
20. StAS, Wü 80 T 1–2 Nr. 325, esp. letters dated 18 September 1945, 8 January 1946, and 13 February 1946.
21. Moser, *Reichenau*, 91–2.
22. Cf. e.g. Landeshauptarchiv Koblenz (LHAKO), Bestand 662,008, Nr. 10, issues of *Wer ist Wo* (an address list published by former adherents of NPEA Ballenstedt); Walter Becker, *Erinnerungen an die NAPOLA Naumburg. Ein über die 'Kadette Naumburg' hinausgehender Beitrag zur Geschichte der NPEA* (Neustrelitz, 2000), 198–200; Heinz Winkler and Hans Worpitz, *Die Nationalpolitischen Erziehungsanstalten (NPEA) und ihre Jungmannen. Berichte, Entwicklungen und Erlebnisse von Jungmannen der NPEA Loben/Annaberg* (2003), 58. Many former pupils' memoirs also contain lists of the careers which former *Jungmannen* in their class or year-group pursued; however, these are often partial or contain self-confessed lacunae, and hence cannot offer a sufficient source base for a statistical analysis. Meanwhile, the lists contained in the newsletters of the old boys' networks (or in compilations of addresses such as the Ballenstedt *Traditionsgemeinschaft*'s directory *Wer ist Wo*) only mention those former pupils who were willing to supply the network with their occupational details.
23. For instance, Christian Gellinek, a former pupil of NPEA Potsdam and subsequently a successful academic, admitted that he had never revealed his time at the Napola prior to his retirement, any more than Günter Grass had spoken about his time in the SS

(private correspondence, 9 January 2013): 'In the Anglo-Saxon world...I would not have been supported with scholarships and fellowships if I had spoken of this in loyal German fashion.'

24. Christian Schneider, 'Karrierewege ehemaliger NS-Eliteschüler in der Bundesrepublik', in Albert Moritz, ed., *'Fackelträger der Nation'. Elitebildung in den NS-Ordensburgen* (Cologne, 2010), 228–31. In support of this thesis, Schneider cites the careers of NATO-Commander Leopold Chalupa, Austrian justice minister Harald Ofner, AEG-chairman Heinz Dürr, the diplomat Rüdiger Freiherr von Wechmar, and the journalists Mainhardt Graf von Nayhauß-Cormons, Jörg Andrees Elten, and Hellmuth Karasek, and suggests that their success in the context of the West German 'economic miracle' was partly due to their reformulation of the Nazified concept of '*Gemeinschaft*' to suit prevailing contemporary business models which hailed the merits of the corporatist, hierarchical 'team'. While the malleability of these thought-patterns may well have assisted those Napolaner who did go on to do well in business-related careers, the argument as a whole does not account for the thousands of former pupils who ended up pursuing far less high-flying professions and trades.
25. The title of the ensuing section alludes to the frequent claim by former members of the Waffen-SS that they were 'soldiers like any others'—cf. e.g. Jens Westermeier, '"Soldaten wie andere auch!" Der Einfluss von SS-Veteranen auf die öffentliche Wahrnehmung der Waffen-SS', in Jan Erik Schulte and Michael Wildt, eds, *Die SS nach 1945. Entschuldungsnarrative, populäre Mythen, europäische Erinnerungsdiskurse* (Göttingen, 2018), 269–88.
26. Cf. Landesarchiv Berlin, B Rep. 004 Nr. 1043, *Rang- und Organisationsliste der NSDAP mit Gliederungen, angeschlossenen Verbänden und betreuten Organisationen unter Beschreibung weiterer Verbände, Einrichtungen, Dienststellen und Personengruppen. Mit Angaben der Klassifizierung nach der Anlage zum Gesetz zur Befreiung von Nationalsozialismus und Militarismus vom 5. März 1946* (Stuttgart, 1946). This categorization was partly due to the schools' connection with the SS—cf. Müller, 'Legal Odyssey', 501–6.
27. This was also true of school and university teaching staff in general; cf. Benjamin Ortmeyer, *Schulzeit unterm Hitlerbild. Analysen, Berichte, Dokumente* (Frankfurt am Main, 1996), 146–7; Steven P. Remy, *The Heidelberg Myth: The Nazification and Denazification of a German University* (Cambridge, MA, 2002). It is unclear whether any former NPEA teaching staff would have been reemployed in the Soviet Occupation Zone, although this might not have been an impossibility for those who were able successfully to conceal their previous affiliation. On continuities in the education sector under Soviet rule in general, see Blessing, *Antifascist Classroom*; also Charles Lansing, *From Nazism to Communism: German Schoolteachers under Two Dictatorships* (Cambridge, MA, 2010).
28. Cf. Tim Müller, 'From Racial Selection to Postwar Deception: The Napolas and Denazification' (PhD thesis, McMaster University, 2016), 76; for an example of this, see former *Erzieher* Gerd Siegel's account of the denazification process in his memoir *Wechselvolle Vergangenheit* (Göttingen, 1980), 149, 168–70.
29. For an in-depth discussion of denazification law in the American zone and its relevance to former Napola-*Erzieher*, as well as an analysis of Heißmeyer's own denazification, see Müller, 'Legal Odyssey' and Müller, 'Deception'.

30. My analysis in this chapter is based on relevant denazification files and exculpatory testimonies held at the Staatsarchiv Sigmaringen, Landesarchiv Speyer, Hauptstaatsarchiv Stuttgart, Hessisches Staatsarchiv Darmstadt, Landeshauptarchiv Koblenz, Bundesarchiv Koblenz, Niedersächsisches Landesarchiv—Staatsarchiv Osnabrück, and the Institut für Zeitgeschichte in Munich, as well as my own private archive. However, my findings fully reinforce those which Tim Müller presented in his aforementioned article and in the second chapter of his doctoral dissertation, which relied on a more limited sourcebase.
31. StAS, Wü 13 T 2 Nr. 1771/028, DND 1948 cutting from *Der Spiegel*; for similar examples see also Bundesarchiv Koblenz, Z 42-IV/2809; Hessisches Staatsarchiv Darmstadt, H 52 Offenbach Nr. 21, Bl. 11.
32. On the US military government's 'Law for Liberation from National Socialism and Militarism' (OMGUS, 5 March 1946), see Müller, 'Legal Odyssey', 505–6. See also Beate Müller, '"Der Mann, den ich vergötterte, hat uns ins Unglück geführt": The Post-War Crisis of Consciousness as Mirrored in Essays and Questionnaires by Nuremberg's Schoolchildren in 1946', *German Life and Letters* 69, no. 4 (2016), 453–67, on schoolchildren in the immediate post-war period using tropes of exculpation which were already familiar from adult denazification narratives.
33. Cf. e.g. Hauptstaatsarchiv Stuttgart, EA 3/803 Bü 12, 'Bericht über die ehemalige Nationalpolitische Erziehungsanstalt in Backnang' (20 July 1946); StAS, Wü 13 T 2 Nr. 1015/008 and Wü 13 Bü 2644/023.
34. E.g. LHAKO, Bestand 856 Nr. 100392, affidavit from Udo S. dated 26 March 1946; Institut für Zeitgeschichte, München, Sp 26; Sowade, 'Erklärung'.
35. On the prevalence of 'religious Persil certificates' supplied by pastors, see Hayse, *Elites*, 163; Andrew H. Beattie, 'Verdiente Strafe des harten Kerns oder ungerechte Besatzungsmaßnahme? Die SS und die alliierte Internierung im besetzten Deutschland', in Schulte and Wildt, *Die SS nach 1945*, 57–74, 66.
36. StAS, Wü 13 T 2 Nr. 1015/008; Landesarchiv Speyer (LASP), H37 Nr. 1915.
37. The documents in StAS, Wü 13 T 2 Nr. 1015/008 provide a particularly rich sample of these tendencies.
38. E.g. the affidavits in LASP, H37 Nr. 1915, which took great pains to stress NPEA Weierhof's erstwhile Mennonite tradition, and the religious sympathies of those staff who were allegedly forced to stay on there as Napola-*Erzieher*. Indeed, such distancing from 'Prussianism' was hardly surprising, given its being treated as more or less synonymous with 'militarism' by denazification officers (cf. the *Fragebogen* evaluation key—my thanks to Mikkel Dack for this point). For adherents of the Prussian NPEA, meanwhile, the idea of 'Prussia' was soon reinterpreted as equating to resistance, freedom, and liberty, as espoused by Frederick the Great, and (later on) the resistance circle around Stauffenberg.
39. See also n. 14 in this chapter. We might also connect the emergence of this trope with Thomas Brodie's observation that regional identities increasingly began to take a prominent place within the exculpatory discourse of German victimhood in the immediate post-war era, thus prefiguring a central element of West German memory culture—cf. Thomas Brodie, *German Catholicism at War, 1939–1945* (Oxford, 2018), 209.
40. E.g. StAS, Wü 13 T 2 Nr. 1015/008, affidavit by the Dutch *Erzieher* Franz Happel dated 18 February 1947.

41. Müller, 'Deception', 236. However, in this connection, I would still suggest that although the narratives which former pupils tell are indeed situated 'within a specific localized context', shaped by the specificities of their individual NPEA, the *topoi* which recur within their narratives nevertheless adhere to wider overarching themes which can generally be found in the recollections of Napolaner from all of the schools (cf. Roche, 'Surviving "*Stunde Null*"').
42. Cf. Jan Erik Schulte, 'The SS as the "Alibi of a Nation"? Narrative Continuities from the Nuremberg Trials to the 1960s', in Kim Christian Priemel and Alexa Stiller, eds, *Reassessing the Nuremberg Military Tribunals: Transitional Justice, Trial Narratives, and Historiography* (New York, 2012), 134–60; Jan Erik Schulte, 'Wiege apologetischer Narrative. Die Organisationsverfahren gegen SS, Gestapo und SD vor dem Internationalen Militärgerichtshof in Nürnberg 1945/46', in Schulte and Wildt, *Die SS nach 1945*, 29–55.
43. On the risks inherent in making contact with other Napolaner in East Germany, see e.g. *Rundklotz* 4 (1959), 3; Johannes Leeb, '*Wir waren Hitlers Eliteschüler': Ehemalige Zöglinge der NS-Ausleseschulen brechen ihr Schweigen* (7th edn; Munich, 2005), 95–7.
44. The following account is largely based on the archives of the following old boys' networks: Ilfeld (Niedersächsisches Landesarchiv—Hauptstaatsarchiv Hannover); Klotzsche (Sächsisches Hauptstaatsarchiv Dresden); Oranienstein (LHAKO); newsletters from Spandau and Potsdam, and miscellaneous collections of documents from Ballenstedt, Köslin, and Putbus. N.B. I intend to investigate this topic in more depth, using a wider range of sources, at a later juncture.
45. That said, in 1952–3, one former teacher from Oranienstein was keen to involve some members of the network with a contribution to the far-right magazine *Nation Europa* (LHAKO, 662,008 Nr. 9, correspondence with and from Otto B.). The influence of former *Erzieher* in the networks' early years should not be underestimated—most seem to have had at least one former member of staff acting as a 'guiding influence'. Meanwhile, the concept of self-help has still persevered among the Napolaner to the present day, except that the recipients of the largesse of 'comradeship' may now be one's classmates' descendants who are in need of advice, placements, and internships, rather than the classmates themselves—cf. e.g. *Schulkameradschaft Hans Richert Schule—Staatl. Bildungsanstalt—N.P.E.A.-Berlin: Mitteilungsblatt* 19 (September 1986), 3.
46. Cf. correspondence in LHAKO, 662,008 Nr. 9.
47. Such attitudes and tensions were common in other types of post-war veterans' association too—cf. Thomas Kühne, *The Rise and Fall of Comradeship: Hitler's Soldiers, Male Bonding and Mass Violence in the Twentieth Century* (Cambridge, 2017), ch. 8. On the cadet-corps *Traditionsgemeinschaften*, see Helen Roche, *Sparta's German Children: The Ideal of Ancient Sparta in the Royal Prussian Cadet Corps, 1818–1920, and in National Socialist Elite Schools (the Napolas), 1933–1945* (Swansea, 2013), ch. 7.
48. Relevant correspondence is contained in LHAKO, 662,008 Nr. 9.
49. LHAKO, 662,008 Nr. 9, letter dated 18 September 1953.
50. LHAKO, 662,008 Nr. 9, letter dated 3 January 1954. On the prevalence of this kind of anti-communist rhetoric in other veterans' organizations, see Kühne, *Comradeship*, 243.
51. LHAKO, 662,008 Nr. 9, 'Kurzbericht über die Gründungsversammlung "Vereinigung der Angehörigen ehemaliger Nationalpolitischer Erziehungsanstalten"' (March 1954).
52. See further correspondence with Otto B. in LHAKO, 662,008 Nr. 9.

53. Letter from Henner M. to Karl I. dated 9 March 2004; Letter from Karl I. dated 28 January 2004 (Putbus collection). Even in more recent years, some ex-pupils are still paranoid that they would suffer severe adverse consequences if their Napola affiliation were ever to be mentioned on the internet or otherwise made public (cf. e.g. [Otto R.], private correspondence, 1 March 2011; [Hermann K.], private correspondence, 21 January 2011).
54. Cf. e.g. LHAKO, 662,008 Nr. 10, letter dated 23 May 1962.
55. This development was also common in the case of other veterans' organizations during this period; cf. Kühne, *Comradeship*, 228.
56. The reflections in this paragraph and the two following are based on my own personal experiences and conversations, since I was invited to attend a number of meetings and reunions with former pupils during the course of my research for this project. Individuals have been left anonymous for reasons of data protection.
57. On the Walser-Bubis debate, and the reasons why the Napolaner might have considered Walser to be sufficiently sympathetic to their cause to approach him, see e.g. Bill Niven, *Facing the Nazi Past: United Germany and the Legacy of the Third Reich* (London, 2002), ch. 7; Raphael Gross, *Anständig geblieben. Nationalsozialistische Moral* (Frankfurt am Main, 2010), ch. 9.
58. On the prevalence of this phenomenon in German memory culture more generally, where media reportage on a certain aspect of the Third Reich may subsequently stimulate a spate of private recollection and personal engagement with the past among surviving eyewitnesses, see Malte Thießen, 'Zeitzeuge und Erinnerungskultur. Zum Verhältnis von privaten und öffentlichen Erzählungen des Luftkriegs', in Lu Seegers and Jürgen Reulecke, eds, *Die 'Generation der Kriegskinder'. Historische Hintergründe und Deutungen* (Gießen, 2009), 157–82.
59. Manfred Gembalies, *Vom Hakenkreuz zu Schwarz Rot Gold. Episoden aus meinem Leben—der Versuch, Erlebtes zu überliefern* (2003, Deutsches Tagebucharchiv, Nr. 1007), 6; Dieter Eschenhagen, 'Auch ich war ein Eliteschüler Hitlers' (Oldenburg, 2000), 36–7.
60. E.g. *Potsdamer Kameradschaft* 62 (December 1997); *Rundklotz* 54 (2004), 11–13.
61. Mike M., *NAPOLA. Filmischer Schuss in den Ofen* (2005), Teil II.
62. Cf. Hellmuth Karasek, *Auf der Flucht: Erinnerungen* (Berlin, 2004); '"Ich war einer von Hitlers Elite-Schülern". Hellmuth Karasek besuchte eine "Napola". In diesen Kadetten-Anstalten sollten die zukünftigen Gauleiter von Chicago und Kapstadt gedrillt werden', *Berliner Zeitung am Sonntag*, 9 January 2005.
63. Collection of letters from Dieter P. (Putbus collection).
64. E.g. *Schulkameradschaft Hans Richert Schule—Staatl. Bildungsanstalt—N.P.E.A.-Berlin: Mitteilungsblatt*, 59. Nachkriegsausgabe (20 October 1998), 8.
65. This analysis is based on a close reading of all of the extant memoirs and autobiographical writings by former pupils to which I have had access during my research on this project, as well as the aforementioned material from the *Traditionsgemeinschaften*.
66. Thus, Harry Bolte claimed that pupils at NPEA Ilfeld referred to Himmler as the '*Reichsküchenchef*' (Reich Master Chef) because his portrait hung in the dining hall, and that they routinely treated Party assemblies with 'irreverent laughter' (*Ilfelder Erinnerungen 1936–1943*, 20).
67. The related trope of the 'caring school authorities' who allegedly saved pupils from being deployed as child soldiers during the last days of World War II, which is

discussed in more detail in Roche, 'Surviving "*Stunde Null*"', also appears to have its roots in the immediate post-war context of these denazification statements. Such assertions were intended to prove that, by protecting pupils from further state incursion at a crucial point, staff had in fact positioned themselves in opposition to the regime, and could therefore be credited with some form of 'resistance'.

68. For further discussion of this phenomenon, see Roche, 'Surviving "*Stunde Null*"'. We might also argue that the roots of this *topos* ultimately lie in a trope which can be frequently found in many of the original NPEA school newsletters—that of former pupils' extraordinary ease of adaptation to military life during World War II.
69. On the prevalence of praise of 'Prussian' virtues in the reminiscences of other members of this generation, see Heidi Rosenbaum, '*Und trotzdem war's 'ne schöne Zeit*': *Kinderalltag im Nationalsozialismus* (Frankfurt am Main, 2014), 267–9; Rüdiger Ahrens, *Bündische Jugend. Eine neue Geschichte 1918–1933* (Göttingen, 2015), 371–2.
70. Ernst-Christian G., private correspondence with Rüdiger B., May 2000.
71. LHAKO, Bestand 856 Nr. 100630/1 and Nr. 100630/2.
72. E.g. Archiv Gymnasium Schloss Plön, denazification documents for Erwin Schmidt; Niedersächsisches Landesarchiv—Staatsarchiv Osnabrück, Rep. 430 Dez 400 Akz 2003/018 Nr. 2.
73. For an example of this tendency, see Wolfram Hauer, 'Das Elsass als "Erziehungsproblem". Zur Umgestaltung des Schulwesens und der Lehrerbildung jenseits des Rheins nach badischem Vorbild (1940–1945)', in Konrad Krimm, ed., *NS-Kulturpolitik und Gesellschaft am Oberrhein 1940–1945* (Ostfildern, 2013), 161–260, esp. 239–40. On the trope of accusing other groups of bearing the 'true' culpability for Nazism, see Janosch Steuwer and Hanne Leßau, '"Wer ist ein Nazi? Woran erkennt man ihn?" Zur Unterscheidung von Nationalsozialisten und anderen Deutschen', *Mittelweg 36*, no. 1 (2014), 30–51.
74. Cf. Roche, *Sparta's German Children*, 2. On non-members of the SA and the SS portraying these organizations as the 'ugly faces' of National Socialism in order to deflect personal accusations of guilt in similar fashion, see Daniel Siemens, *Stormtroopers: A New History of Hitler's Brownshirts* (New Haven, 2017), xxxix, 308; Jan Erik Schulte and Michael Wildt, 'Die zweite Geschichte der SS—Einleitung', in Schulte and Wildt, *Die SS nach 1945*, 9–26. Meanwhile, older Germans might attempt to scapegoat the Hitler Youth generation *in toto* for their allegedly total indoctrination with fanatical National Socialist convictions, in what Jaimey Fisher has termed a 'dense discursive field of competing narratives [about youth and education..., which] paradoxically narrate[d] the past without incorporating overwhelming culpability into [German] postwar identity'—cf. Jaimey Fisher, *Disciplining Germany: Youth, Reeducation, and Reconstruction after the Second World War* (Detroit, 2007), 11; also Philipp Gassert and Alan E. Steinweis, eds, *Coping with the Nazi Past: West German Debates on Nazism and Generational Conflict, 1955–1975* (New York, 2006).
75. Cf. Hayse, *Elites*, 236; Jarausch, *After Hitler*, 52; Remy, *Heidelberg Myth*, 208; Taylor, *Exorcising Hitler*, 285.
76. Remy, *Heidelberg Myth*, 116–17, 177–8, 208–9. For more on defendants' use of denazification statements to underpin later exculpatory narratives, see the forthcoming monographs on this theme by Mikkel Dack and Hanne Leßau.
77. Ortmeyer, *Schulzeit*, 146–7. The relevant section of Ortmeyer's study is tellingly entitled 'After 1945: "As if Nothing at All Had Happened"'.

78. For more on veterans' culture in the Federal Republic, see Kühne, *Comradeship*, chs 7–9; also Karsten Wilke, *Die 'Hilfsgemeinschaft auf Gegenseitigkeit' (HIAG) 1950–1990. Veteranen der Waffen-SS in der Bundesrepublik* (Paderborn, 2011); Jörg Echternkamp, *Soldaten im Nachkrieg: Historische Deutungskonflikte und westdeutsche Demokratisierung 1945–1955* (Munich, 2014); Andreas Eichmüller, *Die SS in der Bundesrepublik. Debatten und Diskurse über ehemalige SS-Angehörige 1949–1985* (Berlin, 2018).
79. Frank Biess, *Homecomings: Returning POWs and the Legacies of Defeat in Postwar Germany* (Princeton, 2006), ch. 5; cf. Alexander von Plato, 'The Hitler Youth Generation and Its Role in the Two Post-War German States', in Roseman, *Generations in Conflict*, 210–26; Benjamin Möckel, *Erfahrungsbruch und Generationsbehauptung. Die 'Kriegsjugendgeneration' in den beiden deutschen Nachkriegsgesellschaften* (Göttingen, 2014). For Schoenecker's biography and an account of his time at NPEA Köslin, see Hans Schoenecker, *Lebenserinnerungen 1928–1960* (2007); also Hans S., 'Ein Blick von "unten", dann von "oben" und schließlich doch wieder von "ganz unten"', in Helga Gotschlich, ed., *'Und der eignen Kraft vertrauend...' Aufbruch in die DDR—50 Jahre danach* (Berlin, 1999), 259–72. Other former pupils might turn to less conventional forms of alternative ideology, including yoga, Buddhism, and freemasonry; cf. e.g. [Hermann K.], *Von der Napola zur Loge. Ein Weg in Umbruchzeiten* (n.d., *c.*1995); Jörg Andrees Elten, *Ganz entspannt im Hier und Jetzt: Tagebuch über mein Leben mit Bhagwan in Poona* (Reinbek bei Hamburg, 1979).
80. Kühne, *Comradeship*, 230.
81. Kühne, *Comradeship*, 232–3.
82. For instance, Waffen-SS veterans used such strategies to protest the TV series *Holocaust* and the film *Lebensborn*, writing enraged letters to the production companies in question, while Wehrmacht veterans were similarly defensive and hypercritical when it came to the infamous 'Wehrmacht exhibition'; cf. Wilke, *HIAG*, 308–11, 413; Niven, *Nazi Past*, 156.
83. Cf. Robert G. Moeller, *War Stories: The Search for a Usable Past in the Federal Republic of Germany* (Berkeley, 2001); Robert G. Moeller, 'Germans as Victims? Thoughts on a Post-Cold War History of World War II's Legacies', *History and Memory* 17, no. 1–2 (2005), 145–94; Bill Niven, ed., *Germans as Victims: Remembering the Past in Contemporary Germany* (Basingstoke, 2006); Marc J. Philipp, *'Hitler ist tot, aber ich lebe noch': Zeitzeugenerinnerungen an den Nationalsozialismus* (Berlin, 2010); Mikkel Dack, 'Retreating into Trauma: The Fragebogen, Denazification, and Victimhood in Postwar Germany', in Peter Leese and Jason Crouthamel, eds, *Traumatic Memories of the Second World War and After* (Basingstoke, 2016), 143–70.
84. Cf. Roche, 'Surviving "*Stunde Null*"'.
85. On the so-called '*Kriegskinder-boom*', see e.g. Lu Seegers, 'Einführung', in Seegers and Reulecke, *Generation der Kriegskinder*, 11–30; Michael Heinlein, *Die Erfindung der Erinnerung. Deutsche Kriegskindheiten im Gedächtnis der Gegenwart* (Bielefeld, 2010); Beate Müller et al., 'Cradle and Crucible of "Vergangenheitsbewältigung": Representations of the War Child in the Occupation Period (1945–9). An Introduction', *German Life and Letters* 69, no. 4 (2016), 417–36.
86. Cf. Lu Seegers, 'Die "Generation der Kriegskinder". Mediale Inszenierung einer "Leidensgemeinschaft"?', in Detlef Schmiechen-Ackermann, ed., *'Volksgemeinschaft': Mythos, wirkungsmächtige soziale Verheißung oder soziale Realität im 'Dritten Reich'?* (Paderborn, 2012), 335–54. Harald Welzer's *Opa war kein Nazi. Nationalsozialismus*

und Holocaust im Familiengedächtnis (Frankfurt am Main, 2002) may be considered the apotheosis of the former category, while the numerous best-selling works by Sabine Bode, such as *Die vergessene Generation. Die Kriegskinder brechen ihr Schweigen* (Stuttgart, 2004) are essentially representative of the latter.

87. Rosenbaum, *Kinderalltag*, 186, 486, 630–2. See also Gabriele Rosenthal, *Die Hitlerjugend-Generation. Biographische Thematisierung als Vergangenheitsbewältigung* (Essen, 1986); Welzer, *Opa war kein Nazi*; Philipp, *Hitler ist tot*; Malte Thießen, 'Schöne Zeiten? Erinnerungen an die "Volksgemeinschaft" nach 1945', in Frank Bajohr and Michael Wildt, eds, *Volksgemeinschaft. Neue Forschungen zur Gesellschaft des Nationalsozialismus* (Frankfurt am Main, 2009), 165–87.
88. Cf. Rosenbaum, *Kinderalltag*, 14, 31, 154. For an example of one former pupil's highly analytical and self-critical reflection on this theme, see Ernst-Christian G., private correspondence with Rüdiger B., May 2000.
89. Cf. Roche, 'Surviving "*Stunde Null*"'.

Conclusion

Delving into the total history of these total institutions can serve to illuminate the historical record in a number of ways. Firstly, and most significantly, the preceding chapters, taken as a whole, demonstrate the value of treating *Bildungsgeschichte* as both *Zeitgeschichte* and *Alltagsgeschichte*—that is, placing the history of education and the everyday life of children and young people at the centre of historical enquiry, rather than leaving such topics to languish on the margins, and treating them as the sole domain of their respective sub-disciplines.

In this instance, we have seen that the Napolas provide a window through which we can gain a fresh and fruitful perspective on many facets of the Third Reich's social and political history, ranging from gender politics to Germanization, from particularism to persecution, and even post-war memory. Analysing the history of the NPEA in depth can therefore grant us valuable new insights into ongoing debates concerning (for example) National Socialist racial policy, the nature of the *Volksgemeinschaft*, or the extent to which the Nazi dictatorship offered its citizens genuine opportunities for social advancement and self-realization. Indeed, within the Napola system, many of the mechanisms and characteristics of the National Socialist state are observable either in microcosm, or in hyper-concentrated form. Whether we consider the regime's attempts to realize the imperial dream of a New European Order, the polycratic wrangling between competing actors and bureaucracies within the state apparatus, the underlying tensions between centralization and federalism within the Reich, or the dictatorship's Janus-faced attitude towards the role of women, the history of the NPEA can shed light on all of these themes (and many more). From an analogous standpoint, equally pertinent insights can undoubtedly be gained by fusing the history of education and youth with political and social histories of everyday life when considering other regimes and political systems (totalitarian or otherwise). In this context, this study demonstrates paradigmatically that pedagogical histories, and enquiries into the training and socialization of elites, can usefully illuminate the history of the societies within which they exist from a plethora of new angles.

At the same time, in providing the first comprehensive account of the Napolas' history, this book also aims to revolutionize and revivify debate on the schools themselves, supplementing the existing scholarship (much of which is either outdated, or betrays a highly regional focus). Hence, it considers the schools not only within a more broadly transnational context, but (above all) investigates their antecedents, in order to paint a more nuanced picture of the Napola system's

The Third Reich's Elite Schools: A History of the Napolas. Helen Roche, Oxford University Press. © Helen Roche, 2021.
DOI: 10.1093/oso/9780198726128.003.0014

complexity, taking full account of that 'variety within unity' which individual schools displayed within the context of their distinctive traditions and trajectories. Even though many elements of these traditions would undoubtedly have become increasingly homogenized, had the Nazi dictatorship survived World War II, the different schools' past incarnations still shaped their ethos to a considerable degree throughout the duration of the Third Reich—as well as subsequently shaping their perception and reception in post-war memory culture. It was precisely this adaptability within the NPEA system, and the flexibility with which it could accommodate a multiplicity of varied educational traditions, which arguably made it so successful. In similar vein, the Napolas' effective fusion of the most enticing facets of the cadet-school, youth-movement, and reform-pedagogical traditions made use of elements which had long lain to hand, whilst simultaneously forging them into novel forms which contemporary observers perceived as uniquely seductive.

In this connection, my interpretation also seeks to provide an answer to the question of why staff and pupils genuinely found the education which the NPEA provided so attractive—taking the schools' aspirations seriously, and treating them to a certain extent on their own terms, rather than simply dismissing their programme as 'chaotic' or 'anti-pedagogical'. From this standpoint, however, one crucial question remains: how significant were the NPEA, and how 'effective' was the education which they provided, when compared with the Third Reich's other educational institutions?

From one standpoint, Rust and Haupt's assertions that the Napolas constituted the vanguard of a much more far-reaching National Socialist transformation of secondary education appear to have been at least partially justified. It was not only that the NPEA went further, and appeared to represent a greater innovation, than any of Rust's more generalized reforms to the secondary education system (including the dubious wartime introduction of the Austrian-style *Hauptschule*—a reform which was instigated at Hitler's behest).[1] Rather, when one looks in detail both at Rust's 'Selection Decree' (*Ausleseerlass*) from 27 March 1935, which implied that only those who were sufficiently physically fit should have access to secondary education at all, and at the Ministry's increasing emphasis on the provision of extra physical training at state secondary schools during the mid- to late 1930s, one finds clear echoes of the type of education and *Auslese* which the Napolas had already been putting into practice for several years.[2] From this perspective (as in so many others), the NPEA were clearly a bellwether for a series of Nazified educational innovations which would subsequently have been put into practice throughout the German secondary-school system as a whole.

This contention is also borne out by the creation in 1941—also at Hitler's instigation—of a system of non-elite state boarding schools along analogous lines to the NPEA (known first as *höhere Internatsschulen*, then *Deutsche Heimschulen*), run by an 'Inspectorate' which was also directly subordinate to Heißmeyer, and overseen by the Education Ministry.[3] That Hitler was pleased with the development of the NPEA up to this point is implied strongly by his nomination of Heißmeyer as Inspector of the *Deutsche Heimschulen* (DHS), commending him as a 'superbly capable' administrator in this regard.[4] By 1944, the new system comprised sixty-one DHS, and a further sixty-six 'subordinate boarding schools', including those schools for war orphans which had previously been run by the *Reichskriegerbund* (Reich War Veterans' Association).[5] Like the Napolas, the *Deutsche Heimschulen* were now recast as state schools with an explicitly National Socialist pedagogical mission, and staff working there had to possess a suitably Nazified political background.[6] Moreover, many of the ideas which had first been put into practice in an 'elite' context at the NPEA—using boarding schools as a medium for 'Germanizing' subject peoples in the occupied territories, or for subduing regions where 'political Catholicism' was allegedly rife, for instance—were now being extended to a far wider range of boarding schools, bringing as many children as possible under the sole control of the state.[7] Arguably, then, in the eyes of the Führer and his acolytes, the Napolas had proved the perfect experimental laboratory in which to try out a 'total education' of this kind, and the introduction of the *Deutsche Heimschulen* definitively proved the success of the NPEA experiment.

Meanwhile, although the Adolf-Hitler-Schools (AHS) swiftly evolved into the Napolas' most dangerous 'competition' in the elite-school stakes, it is less well-known that a significant proportion of the AHS' programme was simply cribbed from that of the NPEA.[8] A top-secret report from the schools' early planning stages clearly shows just how much Reich Organization Leader Robert Ley and Reich Youth Leader Baldur von Schirach planned to take over wholesale from the Napola system—even if surreptitious changes in terminology might be used to disguise some of the more glaring similarities.[9] Thus, the description of the *Anstaltsleiter*'s role admitted that this term was taken directly from the NPEA, and would have to be replaced with one which was 'less bland'; the description of the tasks allocated to the Director of Studies (*Unterrichtsleiter*) also admitted that this term was borrowed from Napola usage, but stated that, on this occasion, the designation could be retained.[10] Ley and von Schirach also treated the Napolas' methods of selection as a key model, and NPEA admission criteria, curricula, and budgets were closely scrutinized in order to see how they might best be adapted for the Party schools' purposes.[11] The only crucial differences in the AHS' conception were that pupils only joined at the age of 12, the schools did not charge fees at all, and they explicitly aimed to prepare graduates for Party leadership positions (though other careers could also be chosen, if so desired). Additionally, the AHS placed a particular emphasis on Hitler Youth membership and leadership, both during the selection process, and in everyday life, and the political probity of prospective candidates' families formed a key criterion of assessment.[12]

However, when it came to putting Ley and von Schirach's grand (and partially stolen) conception into practice, the reality at the AHS scarcely matched up to the propaganda. Although Ley had proudly claimed that (unlike the NPEA) every AHS would soon have its own monumental building complex, asserting that they must never be accommodated in the buildings of the past, in fact, none of the new buildings ever got further than the laying of foundation stones, despite the media frenzy surrounding their advent—the *Ordensburgen* had to be used as temporary residences instead.[13] Moreover, because the AHS had been set up so hastily, largely in order to outflank Rust, the schools' programme often felt hectic in its improvisatory quality—persistent rumour had it that Ley had only gone ahead with the idea because his own nephew had failed the NPEA entrance exam, and Ley and von Schirach had simply forged on and announced the AHS' opening to the press in January 1937 without even informing Rust in his capacity as Reich Education Minister.[14] The highly experimental nature of the academic curriculum, involving new lessons such as '*Volkskunde*' (Ethnology), which comprised a fusion of History, Geography, and German Studies, was stymied in particular by the lack of qualified teachers (especially as war conditions worsened).[15] Meanwhile, because the AHS boasted an entirely new form of school-leaving exam which entailed no written examination at all, the 'diploma' which graduates gained thereafter was only grudgingly accepted as an equivalent to the state 'school-leaving certificate' (*Reifezeugnis*) less than a year before the AHS' first graduation ceremony. In order to graduate, candidates had to undergo a week of practical contests, culminating in a *viva voce* exam where they were requested to pick an unseen topic from an urn and expatiate upon it in front of the examination commission.[16]

Overall, the inadequacies of the new curriculum appear to have led to pupils and graduates being seriously underqualified academically, and in any case, due to the outbreak of war, the number of years allotted for the AHS-course was soon reduced to five—only 1,240 pupils ever officially graduated.[17] In the end, those aspects of the AHS which functioned best were arguably those which had been cribbed wholesale from the NPEA, while the more anti-traditional and experimental aspects of the curriculum never really got off the ground. In any case, since their doors had only opened a year and a half before the outbreak of World War II, the AHS were disproportionately affected by the vagaries and exigencies of wartime, suffering from a combination of ineffective teaching and constantly having to squeeze into makeshift accommodation—to add insult to injury, the promised 'special sports programme' also never fully materialized.[18]

Meanwhile, although the *Ordensburgen* cannot strictly be considered analogous to the Napolas, given that they catered to an adult clientele, we might still argue that they were even less effective than the AHS in training a qualified National Socialist elite—the set-up appears to have favoured brawn and ideological fanaticism over brains, and the level of drop-outs on the relatively few courses which did take place was extremely high.[19] In any case, the full planned course of training across all four *Ordensburgen* never came to fruition, and, even when the course graduates or '*Ordensjunker*' were all called up to the Wehrmacht in 1939, most ended up serving in the ranks, rather than making it into the officer class (as was par for the course for Napola-graduates).[20] Thus, the Napolas' longevity, twinned with their comparative lack of aversion to existing educational traditions, meant that they ultimately fulfilled the requirements of a National Socialist 'total elite education' far more effectively than did either of these Party-run institutions.[21]

But how far did the NPEA compare with those other state mechanisms of education which encompassed almost the entirety of the youthful citizen population—'civilian' schools and the Hitler Youth?

While the level of academic education at schools throughout the Third Reich appears to have deteriorated progressively, especially during the war years, the 'National Socialist revolution' in schools was for the most part only partial.[22] Purges were rarely sufficient to remove all teachers who were opposed to or simply indifferent towards National Socialism, and the Nazification of staff often proceeded in a decentralized and piecemeal fashion.[23] As Charles Lansing has noted, many teachers were politically apathetic, and were generally unwilling to ideologize their subjects completely.[24] However, the NPEA were less constrained by the inherent instability or 'dysfunctionality' which prevented coherent new programmes being carried out in so many spheres of education during the Third Reich, and it was generally possible for a hard core of younger pedagogues to put their 'total' indoctrination into practice at the Napolas in a way that most civilian schools could never match (see Chapter 2).

Meanwhile, in comparison with the HJ, which was never successfully able to mobilize the entirety of German youth, the Napolas were not only able to provide a far more thorough and undiluted indoctrination in the National Socialist *Weltanschauung*, but their socialization was also self-evidently much more 'total', never suffering from the usual routine tensions with school or the parental home.[25] In addition, the HJ's provision of physical training, including 'special' sports and paramilitary activities, was never as systematic or frequent as at the NPEA. Moreover, it was impossible to ensure that every single Hitler Youth could be trained or indoctrinated into taking physical education seriously; by contrast, the Napola selection process swiftly weeded out any pupil who might not be sufficiently keen on (or capable of) cultivating physical excellence.[26]

Taking all of these considerations into account, then, it seems fair to conclude that pupils at the NPEA in many ways did represent the 'avant-garde of the *Volksgemeinschaft*', inasmuch as they had been far more thoroughly trained to conform to Nazi social, political, and physical ideals than the majority of their coevals.[27] Moreover, just as the Napola-pupils themselves constituted a physically and 'racially' elite group within the wider 'racial' or national community, having been subjected to an extremely rigorous selection process which placed physical fitness, sporting prowess, and sheer courage at a premium, the schools as institutions also held an extremely privileged position within the Third Reich's educational hierarchy, facing few of the problems which their non-elite counterparts in the secondary-school system had to suffer.[28]

Finally, we might also conclude that the Napolas were in fact rather more successful than institutions such as the Hitler Youth or the Reich Labour Service in promoting a sense of social equality between youths from different backgrounds, despite their inherent elitism.[29] For working-class families, the opportunities offered by the NPEA occupied a significant position within the constellation of Nazi social welfare programmes which offered middle-class opportunities and cultural practices to even the poorest 'racially valuable' citizen, rewarding individual achievement and encouraging a sense of upward mobility which could, in some cases, be completely genuine.[30] For the middle classes, too, the opportunities which the Napolas could provide for their sons' advancement, as potential future leaders of their nation, also seemed extremely attractive (even if this did mean that they were being schooled alongside a certain proportion of working-class boys)—thus helping to reinforce the idea that the new National Socialist society based on the *Volksgemeinschaft* could offer all of its citizens unprecedented opportunities for personal development. Therefore, although the Napolas' mission to 'widen participation' radically seems to have been only partially successful, inasmuch as middle-class pupils still predominated at the schools, it still seems highly likely that the Napolas would ultimately have become instrumental in helping to consolidate a new, National Socialist caste structure—a class system of stratification based not on pre-Nazi values, but on the uncompromising core ideals of the Nazi *Volksgemeinschaft*: 'racial purity' and the 'will to achieve' (*rassische Reinheit und Leistungsfähigkeit*).[31]

By interrogating the pedagogical and political assumptions which drove the Napola authorities on in this endeavour, then, we can undoubtedly gain new insights into the National Socialist mindset, in a way which the examination of 'normal' schooling during the Third Reich cannot achieve. And, while it is impossible now to tell whether the Napola system would ever have been wholly successful in its primary aim—creating an ideological and 'racial' elite in all spheres of German society—it was undoubtedly (and terribly) successful in its secondary aim—training ideologically schooled and highly skilled and self-sacrificial future officers in all branches of the military. In sum, then, taking the schools on their own terms, we can ultimately see the National Political Education Institutes as the Nazi dictatorship's most effective educational experiment.

Notes

1. Cf. Heidemarie Kemnitz and Frank Tosch, 'Zwischen Indoktrination und Qualifikation—Höhere Schule im Nationalsozialismus', in Klaus-Peter Horn and Jörg-W. Link, eds, *Erziehungsverhältnisse im Nationalsozialismus. Totaler Anspruch und Erziehungswirklichkeit* (Bad Heilbrunn, 2011), 109–34; Anne C. Nagel, *Hitlers Bildungsreformer. Das Reichsministerium für Wissenschaft, Erziehung und Volksbildung, 1934–1945* (Frankfurt am Main, 2012).
2. Helen Roche, 'Sport, Leibeserziehung und vormilitärische Ausbildung in den Nationalpolitischen Erziehungsanstalten: Eine "radikale" Revolution der körperlichen Bildung im Rahmen der NS-"Gesamterziehung"?', *Beiträge zur Geschichte des*

Nationalsozialismus 32 (2016), 173–96, 191–2; cf. Barbara Schneider, *Die höhere Schule im Nationalsozialismus: Zur Ideologisierung von Bildung und Erziehung* (Cologne, 2000), chs III.3.2 and III.3.3; Nagel, *Hitlers Bildungsreformer*, 156–7.

3. Cf. Anke Klare, 'Die Deutschen Heimschulen 1941–1945. Zur Gleichschaltung und Verstaatlichung kirchlicher, privater und stiftischer Internatsschulen im Nationalsozialismus', *Jahrbuch für historischen Bildungsforschung* 9 (2003), 37–58; for important primary sources on these schools, see also Bundesarchiv Lichterfelde (BArch), R 187/557, Bl. 331; BArch, R 43-II/956b; BArch, R 2/31684; BArch, R 2/12719.
4. BArch, R 43-II/956b, Bl. 93, letter from Bormann to Lammers dated 9 June 1941.
5. Klare, 'Heimschulen', 45–7. Over time, the DHS were often deemed a suitable dumping-ground for prospective NPEA candidates who had not quite made the grade; cf. e.g. BArch, NS 19/1556, Bl. 1; Staatsarchiv Freiburg, B 715/1 Nr. 765, correspondence concerning Frau Erasmia Burse and her son.
6. Klare, 'Heimschulen', 46; cf. Geheimes Staatsarchiv Preußischer Kulturbesitz (GStAPK), I. HA Rep. 151 IC, Nr. 7305, Bl. 53, 'Erläuterungen zum Kassenanschlag für eine Deutsche Heimschule' (20 April 1942).
7. For a similar argument, see also Harald Scholtz, *Nationalsozialistische Ausleseschulen. Internatsschulen als Herrschaftsmittel des Führerstaates* (Göttingen, 1973).
8. On the 'competition' (*Konkurrenz*) between the NPEA and the AHS, see e.g. BArch, R 2/12710, letter from Heißmeyer dated 12 December 1940; BArch, R 2/12711, letter from Heißmeyer to Reinhardt dated 17 February 1943; GStAPK, I. HA Rep. 151 Nr. 3929, Bl. 104–5; Generallandesarchiv Karlsruhe, Bestand 235, Nr. 35327, letter from Gärtner dated 25 October 1943; BArch, NS 2/64, Bl. 129; Staf., *10 Jahre NPEA Plön. Sonderheft der Kameradschaft* (Kiel, 1943), 122.
9. BArch, NS 22/1273, 'Die Aufbauschulen der Partei (vorläufige Richtlinien)' (8 December 1936), Bl. 3–12. At this stage, the schools were still known simply as '*Aufbauschulen*', since Hitler did not give the schools his eponymous blessing until 15 January 1937.
10. 'Aufbauschulen', Bl. 3–4. The descriptions of both roles also matched their analogous functions at the NPEA.
11. 'Aufbauschulen', Bl. 5–10.
12. '"Adolf-Hitler-Schulen" ab Ostern. Genehmigung durch den Führer—HJ. führt die neuen Aufbauschulen', *Berliner Tageblatt*, 19 January 1937 [BArch, R 2/12769]; for more on the schools' programme, see Robert Ley and Baldur von Schirach, *Die Adolf-Hitler-Schule* (Berlin, [1937]); Robert Ley, *Wir alle helfen dem Führer. Deutschland braucht jeden Deutschen* (4th edn; Munich, 1939).
13. Stefan Wunsch, 'Führer von übermorgen?—Die Adolf-Hitler-Schulen und das Erziehungsprojekt "Herrenmensch"', in Klaus Ring and Stefan Wunsch, eds, *Bestimmung: Herrenmensch. NS-Ordensburgen zwischen Faszination und Verbrechen* (Dresden, 2016), 210–27, 211–13; Anke Klare, 'Nationalsozialistische Ausleseschulen—"Stätten konzentrierter und auserlesener Menschenformung"', in Klaus-Peter Horn and Jörg-W. Link, eds, *Erziehungsverhältnisse im Nationalsozialismus. Totaler Anspruch und Erziehungswirklichkeit* (Bad Heilbrunn, 2011), 137–60, 148. Although it was intended that there should be an AHS in every Gau, in the end, only twelve of the schools were ever founded.

14. Rust only learned about the AHS' advent on the scene from a newspaper report. For more on the scandal surrounding the schools' foundation, see BArch, R 2/12769, especially the 'secret', outraged letter from Rust to Ley dated 21 January 1937, accusing both parties of the most shameful disloyalty in taking this unwarranted and potentially illegal step; also Wolfgang and Barbara Feller, *Die Adolf-Hitler-Schulen. Pädagogische Provinz versus ideologische Zuchtanstalt* (Weinheim, 2001); Rainer Hülsheger, *Die Adolf-Hitler-Schulen 1937–1945: Suggestion eines Elitebewusstseins* (Weinheim, 2015). On the AHS' 'hectic' quality, see Wunsch, 'Führer von übermorgen?'.
15. Klare, 'Ausleseschulen', 150–1.
16. Wunsch, 'Führer von übermorgen?', 212; Feller and Feller, *Adolf-Hitler-Schulen*, ch. 3.4.4.
17. Wunsch, 'Führer von übermorgen?', 212. On the insufficiency of the AHS' academic education, see Feller and Feller, *Adolf-Hitler-Schulen*, 175–6.
18. Cf. Harald Scholtz, 'Körpererziehung als Mittel der Mentalitätsprägung an den Adolf-Hitler-Schulen', *Sozial- und Zeitgeschichte des Sports* 3, no. 1 (1989), 33–49.
19. Cord Arendes, 'Burgansichten für alle?—Inszenierungen der Ordensburgen in Fotografien', in Ring and Wunsch, *Bestimmung: Herrenmensch*, 84–91; pp. 96–100 in the same volume; also Eckhard Bolenz, 'Improvisation und Rastlosigkeit—Die NS-Ordensburg Vogelsang als "unfertiger Ort" im System des NS-Führernachwuchses', 102–9; Kiran Klaus Patel, 'Alltag und Freizeit in den NS-Ordensburgen', 188–97; Edgar Wolfrum, 'Die Bedeutung der NS-Ordensburgen für das Verständnis des Nationalsozialismus', 20–7.
20. Bolenz, 'Improvisation', 107; Kiran Klaus Patel, '"Sinnbild der nationalsozialistischen Weltanschauung"? Die Gestaltung von Lagern und Ordensburgen im Nationalsozialismus', in Paul Ciupke and Franz-Josef Jelich, eds, *Weltanschauliche Erziehung in Ordensburgen des Nationalsozialismus. Zur Geschichte und Zukunft der Ordensburg Vogelsang* (Essen, 2006), 33–52, 50.
21. For a similar assessment, see H. W. Koch, *The Hitler Youth. Origins and Development 1922–1945* (New York, 1975), 203.
22. E.g. Konrad Jarausch, *The Unfree Professions: German Lawyers, Teachers, and Engineers, 1900–1950* (Oxford, 1990), 135–7, 181–2; Charles Lansing, *From Nazism to Communism: German Schoolteachers under Two Dictatorships* (Cambridge, MA, 2010), especially ch. 2, which catalogues the failure of the National Socialist Teachers' League's re-education camps (*Schulungslager*) and other similarly politicized initiatives.
23. Jarausch, *Unfree Professions*, 197–8; Lansing, *Nazism to Communism*, 26–7, 33.
24. Lansing, *Nazism to Communism*, 12.
25. For an analogous comparison with other National Socialist 'total education institutions', such as the Reich Labour Service (RAD) and the 'Year on the Land' (*Landjahr*) programme, see Chapter 3. On the Hitler Youth movement's inadequacies when it came to mobilizing German youth, see e.g. Michael Buddrus, *Totale Erziehung für den totalen Krieg: Hitlerjugend und nationalsozialistische Jugendpolitik, Teil 1* (Munich, 2003), lv; Michael H. Kater, *Hitler Youth* (Cambridge, MA, 2004), 28; Richard J. Evans, *The Third Reich in Power* (London, 2006), 275–81.
26. Cf. Roche, 'Sport, Leibeserziehung und vormilitärische Ausbildung', 192–4. Even the Hitler-Youth system of *Wehrertüchtigungslager* (military training camps), which could

in some measure be said to remedy the deficits in HJ pre-military training, was only established in 1942; in any case, the camps were intended for 16- to 18-year-olds only.

27. Cf. Patel, 'Sinnbild', 33; Patel is using this designation to describe the *Ordensjunker*, but it could arguably apply just as well, if not better, to the Napola-*Jungmannen*.
28. Roche, 'Sport, Leibeserziehung und vormilitärische Ausbildung', 194. On the Napolas' relatively privileged position even in wartime, see Chapter 10.
29. Cf. Norbert Frei, *1945 und wir. Das Dritte Reich im Bewußtsein der Deutschen* (Munich, 2009), 127–8; also Frank Bajohr and Michael Wildt, eds, *Volksgemeinschaft. Neue Forschungen zur Gesellschaft des Nationalsozialismus* (Frankfurt am Main, 2009), 9; Rüdiger Hachtmann, 'Social Spaces of the Nazi *Volksgemeinschaft* in the Making: Functional Elites and Club Networking', in Martina Steber and Bernhard Gotto, eds, *Visions of Community in Nazi Germany: Social Engineering and Private Lives* (Oxford, 2014), 200–14, 200.
30. Shelley Baranowski, *Strength through Joy: Consumerism and Mass Tourism in the Third* Reich (Cambridge, 2004), 2–12. On the real opportunities for youthful social advancement offered by the regime, particularly during the war years, see Ulrich Herbert, 'Echoes of the *Volksgemeinschaft*', in Steber and Gotto, *Visions of Community*, 60–9, 64–5; Peter Fritzsche, *Life and Death in the Third Reich* (Cambridge, MA, 2008), 105; Jürgen Reulecke, *Ich möchte einer werden so wie die…Männerbünde im 20. Jahrhundert* (Frankfurt am Main, 2001), 145.
31. Cf. Helen Roche, 'Schulische Erziehung und Entbürgerlichung', in Norbert Frei, ed., *Wie bürgerlich war der Nationalsozialismus?* (Göttingen, 2018), 154–72, 167–8.

Glossary

N.B. Terms in **bold** are only translated the first time that they appear, and will thereafter be used as terms of art. German plurals are only noted when they differ from the singular form, and appear within the text.

AHS (*Adolf-Hitler-Schule*, pl. *Adolf-Hitler-Schulen*): the Adolf-Hitler-Schools were a competing form of Nazi elite school, founded in 1937 by Reich Organization Leader Robert Ley and Reich Youth Leader Baldur von Schirach, and organized along Hitler Youth lines.

Alltagsgeschichte: the history of everyday life.

Altkamerad (pl. *Altkameraden*): lit. 'old comrade'; an old boy who had left the school.

Altkameradschaft: lit. 'old comradeship', referring to the Napola old boys' networks which were founded during the Third Reich, most often during World War II.

Altreich: the 'old Reich'; Germany's heartland, understood as existing within pre-1938 borders, as opposed to territories which had newly 'returned to the Reich' such as Austria or the Sudetenland, or those which were conquered during World War II.

Anstaltsleiter (f. *Anstaltsleiterin*): the official designation for the headmaster or principal of a Napola, often shortened to '*Alei*' in Napola slang (or '*Astl*' at the NPEA in Württemberg).

Aufbau: the process by which new Napolas were built up to full strength over a number of years, starting off with the younger year-groups, and (at least initially) led by staff and some pupils from the new foundation's 'mother school' (*Mutteranstalt*). As the initial year-groups moved upwards, new pupils would join at the beginning of each year to form the youngest year-group, until the usual number of classes for a secondary school had been reached. NPEA which had not yet completed this process were described as still '*im Aufbau*'.

Aufbauzug: a special class which was introduced at NPEA Naumburg, NPEA Klotzsche, and NPEA Ballenstedt (among others) for pupils aged around 13 or 14 who came from disadvantaged backgrounds, and who might not have been educated sufficiently to succeed in the admissions process at the age of 10.

Aufnahmeprüfung: entrance examination. The Napola examination was usually residential, lasting about a week.

Auslese: 'selection'; also used to denote the Napola selection process. For a more detailed discussion, see the Note on Terminology.

BDM (*Bund Deutscher Mädel*): the League of German Girls, the female counterpart of the Hitler Youth.

Bundeserziehungsanstalt (BEA, pl. *Bundeserziehungsanstalten*): Federal Education Institute; the name given to the former Habsburg imperial and royal (*k.u.k.*) cadet schools in Austria after they were turned into civilian boarding schools following World War I. At various points in their existence, the schools were also known as *Staatserziehungsanstalten* (see Chapter 7, n. 2). The *Bundeserziehungsanstalten* in the vicinity of Vienna were all transformed into Napolas in the wake of the Anschluss.

Deutsche Heimschulen (DHS): 'German Boarding Schools': a system of non-elite boarding schools which began to take shape during World War II, also run by August Heißmeyer in his capacity as 'Inspector of the German Boarding Schools'.

Deutsche Oberschule: a type of German secondary school.

Einsatz (pl. *Einsätze*): 'mission', used to denote the trips which the *Jungmannen* regularly took part in, especially those which involved their working for several weeks or months down mines (*Bergwerkseinsatz*), in factories (*Industrieeinsatz*), and on the land (*Landeinsatz*).

Erzieher (f. *Erzieherin*): trainer/educator. *Erzieher* were young men (usually in their mid-20s) whose task was to supervise and train pupils; they performed the function of teachers and housemasters.

Gau: region, an archaic term which was revived by the Nazis to denote a Party administrative district, each ruled by its *Gauleiter*.

Geländespiele (pl.; also known as *Geländesport/Geländedienst*): cross-country wargames.

Gleichschaltung: lit. 'coordination'; the term used for the Nazi takeover of institutions after the seizure of power.

Gymnasium (pl. *Gymnasien*): a traditional German secondary school which followed a humanistic curriculum, focusing on Latin and ancient Greek.

Hausdame (pl. *Hausdamen*): a house-matron who looked after the youngest year-groups at each school.

HJ (*Hitlerjugend*): the Hitler Youth, the Nazi Party youth organization.

Hundertschaft (pl. *Hundertschaften*): most Napolas were divided into two of these units, corresponding to the lower school and the upper school.

Hundertschaftsführer: lit. unit commander; a Napola teacher with responsibility for one of the *Hundertschaften*.

Jungmann (pl. *Jungmannen*; f. *Jungmädel*): the official designation for a pupil attending a Napola.

Jungmannzugführer/Jungmanngruppenführer/Jungmannhundertschaftsführer: ranks in the Napola hierarchy, roughly corresponding to the English school hierarchy of form prefect, senior prefect, and head boy.

Junkerschulen: elite military and ideological training academies for SS-officers.

Kameradschaft: comradeship.

KLV (*Kinderlandverschickung*): the German children's evacuation programme during World War II.

Kompetenzstreit (pl. *Kompetenzstreiten*): a power struggle or conflict of competence between competing organizations or institutions.

Kraft durch Freude (KdF): 'Strength through Joy'; the Nazi Party leisure organization.

Kreisleitung: the 'district' level of the National Socialist Party administration, led by the *Kreisleiter*.

Länder (pl. of *Land*): the German federal states, which possessed a good deal of regional autonomy. The NPEA in Saxony, Anhalt, and Württemberg could therefore be designated *Länder-NPEA*. Until April 1941, they were funded by their respective federal education ministries, rather than by the Reich.

Landjahr: 'Year on the Land'; a labour service programme for school-leavers established by Education Minister Bernhard Rust.

Landesverwaltung der Nationalpolitischen Erziehungsanstalten in Preußen (abbrev. *Landesverwaltung*): 'State Administration of the National Political Education Institutes in Prussia'; the initial name of the administrative bureau responsible for the Napolas. After the Anschluss with Austria, its remit extended beyond Prussia, and its designation therefore changed to the 'Inspectorate of the National Political Institutes' (*Inspektion der Nationalpolitischen Erziehungsanstalten*).

Landschulheim/Landerziehungsheim (pl. *Landerziehungsheime*): a form of country boarding school, usually run in accordance with the principles of reform pedagogy.

Luftwaffenhelfer (aka *Marinehelfer* or *Flakhelfer*): terms used for teenage pupils (and other young Germans) who were deployed as anti-aircraft auxiliaries in World War II.

Mädchen-Napola/NPEA für Mädchen: Napola for girls (as opposed to a *Jungen-Napola* or Napola for boys).

Napola (pl. *Napolas*): common abbreviation for *Nationalpolitische Erziehungsanstalt* (see Note on Terminology).

Napolaner: a colloquial term for Napola pupils or former pupils. A variant version, '*Napolitaner*', might be used at the schools in Württemberg.

Nationalpolitische Erziehungsanstalt (pl. *Nationalpolitische Erziehungsanstalten*): National Political Education Institute; the official name for the Napolas.

NPEA: the officially sanctioned abbreviation for *Nationalpolitische Erziehungsanstalt* (singular) or *Nationalpolitische Erziehungsanstalten* (plural).

NSDAP (*Nationalsozialistische Deutsche Arbeiterpartei*): the full name of the Nazi Party; the National Socialist German Workers' Party.

NSKK (*Nationalsozialistisches Kraftfahrkorps*): National Socialist Motoring Corps; a subsidiary of the Party organization.

NSV (*Nationalsozialistische Volkswohlfahrt*): National Socialist People's Welfare Organization, a Party caritative organization which organized state charity drives such as the annual 'Winter Help campaign' (WHW).

Obergruppenführer: a rank equivalent to that of Lieutenant General.

Ordensburgen (pl.): lit. 'Order-Castles'; Nazi Party elite academies for young men, which were intended to provide preparatory training for the planned 'Party University'.

RAD (*Reichsarbeitsdienst*): the Reich Labour Service.

Realschule (also *Realgymnasium*): a type of German secondary school which focused upon modern languages and science subjects (Latin was usually taught, but not Greek).

Reichsschule (pl. *Reichsschulen*): 'Reich School' or 'Imperial School': the name given to the Napolas in Flanders and the Netherlands.

Reichsdeutsche (pl.): 'Reich Germans'; i.e. Germans from the 'old Reich' as opposed to 'ethnic Germans' (*Volksdeutsche*).

Reichsführer-SS: Reich Leader of the SS, one of Himmler's many titles.

RJF (*Reichsjugendführung*): the Reich Youth Leadership of the HJ, headed by Baldur von Schirach.

Reichsreform: the process of centralization by which the Nazi regime aimed to bring the German federal states into line with Berlin, reducing their autonomous power and influence. See also *Verreichlichung*.

Reichsstatthalter: Reich Governor; an office which was often also held by the *Gauleiter*.

SA (*Sturmabteilung*): 'Stormtroopers'; the Nazi Party's paramilitary wing, which fell from favour after the so-called Röhm Putsch or 'Night of the Long Knives' in June–July 1934.

Schloss: palace/castle: a designation used for some of the buildings which housed the schools, including Schloss Bensberg and Schloss Oranienstein.

SS (*Schutzstaffel*): lit. 'Protection Squad'; Himmler's militarized network of repression and colonization organizations.

Staatliche Bildungsanstalt (pl. *Staatliche Bildungsanstalten*): State Education Institute; the name given to the former Prussian cadet schools after they were turned into civilian state boarding schools in the wake of the Treaty of Versailles. These institutions endured throughout the Weimar Republic, and were subsequently transformed into Napolas in 1933–4.

Stabila (pl. Stabilas): common abbreviation for *Staatliche Bildungsanstalt*.

Stube: 'room' comprising ten *Jungmannen*; the place where they would keep their belongings and do their homework.

Stubenältester: room captain; an older *Jungmann*, who was in charge of the boys in his *Stube* (room).

Traditionsgemeinschaft (pl. *Traditionsgemeinschaften*): post-war Napola old boys' network.

Treffen: reunion of a post-war old boys' network.

Unterrichtsleiter: Director of Studies; usually the *Anstaltsleiter*'s second-in-command—the member of staff responsible for all academic affairs, timetabling, and so forth.

VDA (*Verein für das Deutschtum im Ausland*): Association for Germandom Abroad; a revanchist and imperialist organization which founded branches in schools from the late nineteenth century onwards.

Verreichlichung: the process of centralization by which the Nazi regime aimed to bring the German federal states into line with Berlin, reducing their autonomous power and influence. See also *Reichsreform*.

Volksdeutsche (pl.): 'ethnic Germans'; a contemporary term used to denote those living beyond the borders of the German '*Altreich*' and Austria who could lay claim to German descent.

Volksgemeinschaft: lit. people's community or ethnic/national community; the propagandistic ideal of the national community of Nazi citizens, defined by race.

Volkstum: usually used during this period in the sense of racial heritage, culture, and customs. *Volkstumsarbeit* (work for the *Volkstum*) or *Volkstumspolitik* (politics for the *Volkstum*) generally involved colonialist or quasi-colonialist efforts to increase German cultural influence.

Waffen-SS: the military branch of the SS, which fought alongside the *Wehrmacht* in World War II.

Wehrmacht: the German armed forces.

Weltanschauung: worldview.

WHW (*Winterhilfswerk*): the annual winter charity scheme set up by the National Socialist People's Welfare Organization (NSV/*Nationalsozialistische Volkswohlfahrt*).

Zentraldirektion: the administrative body in charge of the Austrian *Bundeserziehungsanstalten*.

Zug: lit. platoon; the name for a year-group at the Napolas, replacing the civilian term *Klasse* (class).

Zugführer: lit. platoon commander; a Napola teacher responsible for a particular class or year-group. A senior teacher would be designated a ***Hauptzugführer***.

List of Eyewitnesses

Backnang

Gerhard F.

Kurt S.

Bensberg

Rolf Burmeister

Eike G.

Arne Heinich

Dietrich J.

Berlin-Spandau

Rudolf Arendt

Rüdiger B.

Manfred F.

Ernst-Christian G.

Heinrich H.

Erwin K.

Wilfried K.

Karl K.

Peter K.

Werner K.

Gerhard L.

Günter L.

Hans M.

Arnulf P.

Gerhard Richter

Anon.

[Hermann K.]

[Otto R.]

Göttweig

Engelbert L.

Alfred S.

Haselünne

Peter B.

Hans-Hermann H.

Hubertendorf-Türnitz

Christiane K.

Hannelore S. (Türnitz)

Ilfeld

Erika B. (support staff: maid)

Gerwalt B.

Walter K.
Hinrich Kattentidt
Hubertus M.
Martin Meissner

Klotzsche

Helmuth J.
Roman R.

Köslin

Erich Andrée (Stabila)
Manfred B.
Klaus B.
Rolf B.
Joachim D.
Bernhard G.
Walter K.
Kurt K.
Henning L.
Dietlef N.
Günter R.
Hans Schoenecker
Ulli Z.

Loben

Hans W.

Mokritz

Friedrich G. (Traiskirchen, Mokritz)

Naumburg

Friedrich-Wilhelm J.
Karl L.
Ekkehard P.
Günther P.
Hans-Dieter R.
Heiner S.

Neubeuern

Joachim Doedter
Günter B.O. (Schulpforta, Neubeuern)
Josef T.

Oranienstein

Klaus-Jürgen B.
Lothar J.
Karl L.
Kurt L.

Plön

Peter B.
Dietmar K.
Uwe L.

Harald R.
Wolfgang V.

Potsdam

Christian Gellinek
Hans L.

Raudnitz

Erwin W.

Reichenau

Gerhard B.
Fritz D. (Reichenau, Rottweil)
Klaus H. (Reichenau et al.)
Paul Sch.

Rottweil

H. B.
Manfred B.
Günther E.
Klaus E.
Paul F.
Theodor K.
Wolfgang T.

Rügen/Putbus

Hans F.
Al F.
Karl-Heinz Lübke
Klaus Montanus
Mike M. (Spandau, Rügen)
Hans-Hoyer von P.
Jürgen Schach von Wittenau
Klaus Schikore
Dietrich Schulz
Helmuth Z.

Schulpforta

Wolfgang Conrad
Günter F.
Hans Habermann
Hans-Joachim M.
Hans R.
Uwe S.
Hartmut V.

Stuhm

Eckhard R.
Herr S. (local HJ)

Sudetenland/Ploschkowitz

Rüdiger Bauer
Johannes K.

Traiskirchen

Harald O.

Friedrich P.

Helmut W.

Reinfried W.

Valkenburg

Armin Eise (Bensberg/Valkenburg)

Wahlstatt

Günter S. (Stabila/NPEA, also Bensberg)

Wartheland/Reisen

Wolfgang E.

Karl-Josef Franke

Eugen K.

Günter L.

Rolf R.

List of Archives Consulted

Mainland Europe

AEKR	Archiv der Evangelischen Kirche im Rheinland, Düsseldorf
AGSP	Archiv Gymnasium Schloss Plön
ALSP	Archiv der Landesschule Pforta
AMSW	Archiv Missionshaus St. Wendel
Apabiz	Antifaschistisches Pressearchiv und Bildungszentrum, Berlin
ASL	Archiv Stift Lambach, Austria
AUS	Archiv der Universität Saarbrücken
BAK	Bundesarchiv Koblenz
BAL	Bundesarchiv Außenstelle Ludwigsburg
BA-MA	Bundesarchiv-Militärarchiv Freiburg
BArch	Bundesarchiv Berlin-Lichterfelde
BayHStA	Bayerisches Hauptstaatsarchiv, München
BBF	Bibliothek für Bildungsgeschichtliche Forschung, Berlin
BLHA	Brandenburgisches Landeshauptarchiv, Potsdam
BWAF	Bergwerkarchiv Freiberg
DIPF	Deutsches Institut für Pädagogische Forschung, BBF, Berlin
DNB	Deutsche Nationalbibliothek, Leipzig
DTA	Deutsches Tagebucharchiv, Emmendingen
GLAK	Generallandesarchiv Karlsruhe
GStAPK	Geheimes Staatsarchiv Preußischer Kulturbesitz, Berlin
HAEK	Historisches Archiv des Erzbistums Köln
HHStAW	Hessisches Hauptstaatsarchiv Wiesbaden
HStAD	Hessisches Staatsarchiv Darmstadt
HStAM	Hessisches Staatsarchiv Marburg
HStAS	Hauptstaatsarchiv Stuttgart
IfZ	Institut für Zeitgeschichte, München
KAN	Kreisarchiv Nordhausen
KAP	Kreisarchiv Plön
KKH	Klosterkammer Hannover
LAB	Landesarchiv Berlin
LAK	Landesarchiv Kärnten, Austria
LAS	Landesarchiv Schleswig-Holstein
LASP	Landesarchiv Speyer
LHAKO	Landeshauptarchiv Koblenz
LHASA-DE	Landeshauptarchiv Sachsen-Anhalt, Abteilung Dessau
LHASA-M	Landeshauptarchiv Sachsen-Anhalt, Abteilung Merseburg

LHASA-MD	Landeshauptarchiv Sachsen-Anhalt, Abteilung Magdeburg
LKAS	Landeskirchliches Archiv Stuttgart
LNRW-D	Landesarchiv Nordrhein-Westfalen, Abteilung Rheinland, Duisburg
LNRW-M	Landesarchiv Nordrhein-Westfalen, Abteilung Westfalen, Münster
NADH	Nationaal Archief, Den Haag, Holland
NIOD	NIOD Institute for War, Holocaust, and Genocide Studies Archives, Amsterdam, Holland
NLA-HStAH	Niedersächsisches Landesarchiv—Hauptstaatsarchiv Hannover
NLA-StAOL	Niedersächsisches Landesarchiv—Staatsarchiv Oldenburg
NLA-StAOS	Niedersächsisches Landesarchiv—Staatsarchiv Osnabrück
NLA-StAW	Niedersächsisches Landesarchiv—Staatsarchiv Wolfenbüttel
NÖL	Niederösterreichisches Landesarchiv, St. Pölten, Austria
NSA	Neubeuern Schularchiv
ÖNB	Österreichische Nationalbibliothek, Vienna, Austria
ÖStA	Österreichisches Staatsarchiv, Vienna, Austria
PAAA	Politisches Archiv des Auswärtigen Amts, Berlin
PAAM	Privatarchiv Adolf Morlang, Diez
PASF	Privatarchiv Stefanie Flintrop, Solingen
PASW	Privatarchiv Steffen Wagner, Weierhof
SHStAD	Sächsisches Hauptstaatsarchiv Dresden
StaBi	Staatsbibliothek zu Berlin
StABG	Stadtarchiv Bergisch Gladbach
StAD	Stadtarchiv Dresden
StAF	Staatsarchiv Freiburg
StAH	Staatsarchiv Hamburg
StAL	Staatsarchiv Ludwigsburg
StAS	Staatsarchiv Sigmaringen
StASW	Stadtarchiv St. Wendel
UBV	Universitätsbibliothek, Vienna, Austria
WSA	Weierhof Schularchiv
ZABVP	Zentralarchiv des Bezirksverbands Pfalz

England, Ireland, and the United States

Archive of the Independent Association of Prep Schools (IAPS)
Bradfield College Archive
Dauntsey's School Archive
Harrow School Archive
Kingswood School Archive
Merton Heritage Centre
Shrewsbury School Archive
St. Paul's School Archive
The Leys School Archive

Tonbridge School Archive
St. Andrew's School Archive, Delaware, USA
St. Columba's College Archive, Dublin, Eire
Philips Academy, Andover, Archives and Special Collections, Massachusetts, USA
Tabor Academy Archive, Marion, Massachusetts, USA

List of Periodicals Consulted

General

Deutsches Bildungswesen
Die deutsche höhere Schule
Der Deutsche Volkserzieher
Deutsche Volksschule
Deutsche Wissenschaft, Erziehung und Volksbildung
Die Erziehung
Internationale Zeitschrift für Erziehung
Nationalsozialistisches Bildungswesen
Reichskadettenblatt
Volk im Werden
Weltanschauung und Schule
Zentrale NSLB-Zeitschrift

Backnang

Alte Kameradschaft: Feldpostbriefe der Nationalpolitischen Erziehungsanstalt Backnang (1939–44)

Ballenstedt

Ballenstedt. Schriftenfolge der Nationalpolitischen Bildungsanstalt Anhalt, Ballenstedt am Harz / Schriftenfolge der Nationalpolitischen Erziehungsanstalt Ballenstedt (1936–44)
Rundbrief (1940–2)
Wer ist Wo (1960–70)

Bensberg

Rundbrief der Nationalpolitischen Erziehungsanstalt Bensberg (1939–43)
Die Fackel (1944)

Berlin-Spandau

Staatliche Bildungsanstalt Berlin-Lichterfelde—Bericht über das Schuljahr (1924–9)
Blätter der Hans Richert-Schule—Staatliche Bildungsanstalt Berlin-Lichterfelde (1930–3)
Blätter der Hans Richert-Schule—Staatliche Bildungsanstalt Berlin-Spandau (1933)
Blätter der Nationalpolitischen Erziehungsanstalt Berlin-Spandau [abbreviated as *Spandauer Blätter*] (1934–45)
Mitteilungen für die ehemaligen Lehrer und Schüler der früheren Hans Richert-Schule Berlin-Lichterfelde und Berlin-Spandau (1952–83)
Schulkameradschaft Hans Richert Schule—Staatl. Bildungsanstalt—N.P.E.A.-Berlin: Mitteilungsblatt (1984–)

Haselünne

Nationalpolitische Erziehungsanstalt Emsland (1943–4)

Hubertendorf-Türnitz

Alles für Deutschland! Mitteilungen der Nationalpolitischen Erziehungsanstalt Hubertendorf-Türnitz (1941–3)

Ilfeld

Jahresbericht über das Königliche Pädagogium zu Ilfeld (1873)

Jahresbericht über die Königliche Klosterschule zu Ilfeld (1874–96)

Jahresbericht über die Klosterschule zu Ilfeld (1900–15)

Klosterschule Ilfeld—Bericht über das Schuljahr (1925–30)

Jahresbericht der Nationalpolitischen Erziehungsanstalt Ilfeld über das Schuljahr 1934/35 (1935)

Ilfelder Blätter (1926–34)

**Ilfeld. Nachrichtenblatt für ehemalige Angehörige der Klosterschule und der jetzigen Nationalpolitischen Erziehungsanstalt Ilfeld* (1934)

**Ilfelder Blätter* (1935–7) [N.B. This designation is also used as the abbreviated form for all of the subsequent editions.]

**Blätter der Nationalpolitischen Erziehungsanstalt Ilfeld* (1938–9, 1941)

**Ilfeld-Kriegsbrief* (1939–41)

**Ilfelder Altkameradschaft. Blätter der Nationalpolitischen Erziehungsanstalt Ilfeld* (1941–3)

**Ilfelder Kameradschaft. Blätter der Nationalpolitischen Erziehungsanstalt Ilfeld* (1943–4)

**NPEA Ilfeld. Blätter der Ilfelder Kameradschaft* (1944)

Ilfelder Blätter (1991–4)

* = contained in Rudolf Marggraf, ed., *Die Nationalpolitische Erziehungsanstalt Ilfeld. Sammlung der von 1934 bis 1944 herausgegebenen Ilfeld-Blätter—Ein Beitrag zur Zeitgeschichte* (2 vols). Page numbers in the notes refer to these volumes, not the original edition, and hence are placed in square brackets.

Klotzsche

Mitteilungen aus der Landesschule Dresden (1928–33)

Die junge Front. Kameradschaftsblätter der Staatlichen Nationalpolitischen Erziehungsanstalt Klotzsche (1938–40)

Mitteilungen der Nationalpolitischen Erziehungsanstalt Klotzsche (1939)

Nachrichtenblatt der Nationalpolitischen Erziehungsanstalt Klotzsche in Sachsen (1941)

Blätter der Nationalpolitischen Erziehungsanstalt Klotzsche in Sachsen (1942–4)

Mitteilungen ehemaliger LSDer (1960–2003)

Rundklotz. Mitteilungen ehemaliger Klotzscher Schröterknaben (1959–2010)

Köslin

Die Brücke. Nachrichten von der Stabila Köslin (1928–33)

Die Brücke. Nachrichten von der Nationalpolitischen Erziehungsanstalt Köslin (1933–44)

Die Brücke. Mitteilungsblatt des Gollenkreises (2001–)

Naumburg

Mitteilungen der Nationalpolitischen Erziehungsanstalt Naumburg/Saale (1939–44)

Neubeuern

Landschulheim Neubeuern—Schulzeitung ([1935]–1939)

Oranienstein

Der Jungmann. Blätter/Feldpostbericht der Nationalpolitischen Erziehungsanstalt Oranienstein/Lahn (1935–44)

Oranienstein Rundbrief (1951–*c*.1960)

Oranienstein Freundeskreis ehemaliger Jungmannen/Oranienstein Briefe (2000–3)

Plön

Schleswig-Holsteinische Bildungsanstalt Plön in Holstein (Kaiserin Auguste-Viktoria-Gymnasium und Staatliche Bildungsanstalt)—Bericht über das Schuljahr (1924–32)

Die Kameradschaft. Blätter der Nationalpolitischen Erziehungsanstalt Plön (1935–9)

Rundbrief [für alle Buten- und Binnenplöner] (1939–41)

Nationalpolitische Erziehungsanstalt Plön—Rundbrief (1942–4)

Potsdam/Potsdam-Neuzelle

Staatliche Bildungsanstalt Potsdam: Bericht über das Schuljahr (1924–30)

Stimmen aus der Stabila Potsdam (1930–3)

Mehr sein als scheinen. Nationalpolitische Erziehungsanstalt Potsdam-Neuzelle: Arbeitsbericht (1937–8)

Nationalpolitische Erziehungsanstalt Potsdam-Neuzelle—Kriegsbriefe (1940–4)

Potsdamer Kameradschaft. Blätter der Nationalpolitischen Erziehungsanstalt Potsdam (1940–5)

Potsdamer Kameradschaft (1953–)

Rottweil

Rundbrief der Nationalpolitischen Erziehungsanstalt Rottweil an die feldgrauen Erzieher und Altkameraden (1940)

Im Gleichschritt: Rundbrief der NPEA Rottweil (1940–5)

Rügen—Putbus

Putbusser Kameradschaft. Blätter der Nationalpolitischen Erziehungsanstalt Rügen (1943–4)

Rufach/Achern

Nationalpolitische Erziehungsanstalt—Reichsschule für Volksdeutsche Rufach/Achern (1941–3)

Schulpforta

Pförtner Blätter. Vierteljahrsblätter der Landesschule Pforta (1926–35)

Pförtner Blätter. Zeitschrift der Nationalpolitischen Erziehungsanstalt Schulpforta (1936–44)

Die Pforte. Neue Folge des 'Alten Pförtners'; Zeitschrift des Pförtner-Bundes ([1934]–1939)

Die Pforte. Schulpforta-Nachrichten. Zeitschrift des Pförtner Bundes e.V. ([1996]–)

Spanheim—St. Paul

Rundbrief der NPEA. Spanheim in Kärnten—Ehre ist Zwang genug! (1944)

Stuhm

Rundbrief der Stuhmer Altkameradschaft/Kriegsbrief der Stuhmer Kameradschaft (1938–43)

Sudetenland—Ploschkowitz

Blätter der Nationalpolitischen Erziehungsanstalt Sudetenland (1941–2)

Wahlstatt

Staatliche Bildungsanstalt Wahlstatt bei Liegnitz: Bericht über das Schuljahr (1924–30)

Wahlstatt: Blätter der Staatlichen Bildungsanstalt Wahlstatt (1931–3)

Wahlstatt-blätter: Blätter der Nationalpolitischen Erziehungsanstalt Wahlstatt (1935–6)

Wartheland—Reisen

Pflug und Schwert (1943–4)

Wien-Breitensee

Die Bundeserziehungsanstalt für Knaben Wien-Breitensee (1919–27)

Blätter der Bundeserziehungsanstalt Wien-Breitensee (1931–8)

Der Turm. Blätter der Bundes-Erziehungs-Anstalt für Knaben, Wien XVII. (1934–5)

Breitenseer Rundbriefe. Blätter der Nationalpolitischen Erziehungsanstalt Wien-Breitensee (1942–4)

Wien-Traiskirchen

Bundes-Erziehungsanstalt Traiskirchen: Heimjahr (1922–32)

Unser Heim. Heimzeitung der B.-E.-A. Traiskirchen (1925–37)

Traiskirchen. Berichte aus dem Heim und der Schule der Bundeserziehungsanstalt Traiskirchen samt 'Elternzeitung' und 'Alt-Beanerklub' (1937–8)

Der Traiskirchner Bericht (1944)

Bibliography

N.B. All newspaper articles, archival documents, unpublished correspondence, manuscripts, and theses are cited solely in the footnotes. If no archival provenance for an unpublished document is given, then it can be found in the author's personal archive.

Published Primary Sources

Anon., *Die wichtigsten Bestimmungen über die österreichischen Staats-Erziehungsanstalten* (Vienna, 1920).

Anon., *Die österreichischen Bundeserziehungsanstalten* (Vienna, 1931).

Anon., 'Aus den Nationalpolitischen Erziehungsanstalten. Ziel und Einrichtung der Nationalpolitischen Erziehungsanstalten Preußens', *Die deutsche höhere Schule* 1, no. 1 (1935), 18–19.

Anon., 'Herbstübung der Nationalpolitischen Erziehungsanstalten', *Weltanschauung und Schule* 1, no. 1 (1936), 27–34.

Anon., 'Erziehung und Zeit', *Der Deutsche Volkserzieher* 1 (1936), 371–5.

Anon., *Die österreichischen Bundeserziehungsanstalten* (Vienna, 1937).

Anon., 'Aufnahmeprüfung an den Nationalpolitischen Erziehungsanstalten', *Weltanschauung und Schule* 1, no. 5 (1937), 300–3.

Anon., 'Deutsche Jungen in England', *Weltanschauung und Schule* 1, no. 6 (1937), 372–3.

Anon., 'Anstaltsleitertagung der Nationalpolitischen Erziehungsanstalten in Ostpreußen vom 23. bis 27. Juni 1937', *Weltanschauung und Schule* 1, no. 7 (1937), 553–6.

Anon., 'Segelfahrt der Nationalpolitischen Erziehungsanstalt Köslin nach Schweden und Dänemark vom 15. bis 29. August 1937', *Weltanschauung und Schule* 1, no. 12 (1937), 710–17.

Anon., 'Deutsche Schule—mitten im Volk: Oktoberbericht der Nationalpolitischen Erziehungsanstalten Plön, Schulpforta und Stuhm', *Weltanschauung und Schule* 1, no. 14 (1937), 112–17.

Anon., 'Die Nationalpolitischen Erziehungsanstalten: Vier Jahre Arbeit für eine nationalsozialistische Erziehung!', *Volksaufklärung und Schule* 47/48 (1938), 2–4.

Arbeitsgruppe Stadtgeschichte am Internatsgymnasium Schloß Plön, *Alternativer Stadtführer zu den Stätten des Nationalsozialismus in Plön* (Plön, 1989).

Bauer, Rüdiger, *Wie und warum wir so waren? Erinnerungen an Damals—Schicksalsjahre 1925–1945* (Gelnhausen, 2009).

Bauer, Rüdiger, *Suche nach neuen Ufern 1945–1960. Studienjahre eines Sudetendeutschen im Nachkriegsdeutschland* (Norderstedt, 2012).

Becker, Peter, 'Erinnerungen an die NAPOLA Plön und das Kriegsende 1945. Von einer Reifezeit in Krieg und Nachkrieg', *Deutsche Geschichte*, Juli/August/September 2015/ Sonderausgabe 2 (2015), 57–62.

Becker, Walter, *Gestern* (1984).

Becker, Walter, *Unser Naumburg* (Essen, 1992).

Becker, Walter, *Erinnerungen an die NAPOLA Naumburg. Ein über die 'Kadette Naumburg' hinausgehender Beitrag zur Geschichte der NPEA* (Neustrelitz, 2000).

Belohoubek, Viktor, *Die österreichischen Bundeserziehungsanstalten. Ein Werk kulturellen Aufbaues der Republik Österreich* (Vienna, 1924).

Belohoubek, Viktor, *Die ersten zehn Jahren der österreichischen Bundes-Erziehungsanstalten. Ein Beitrag zur Geschichte der Mittelschule in Österreich* (Vienna, 1931).

Bergisch-Gladbach, Kreisleitung, 'Die Nationalpolitische Erziehungsanstalt in Bensberg', *Jahrbuch des Rheinisch-Bergischen Kreises* (1937), 63–5.

Bessel, Herbert, 'Hat Ilfeld mich geprägt?', in Rudolf Marggraf (ed.), *Die Nationalpolitische Erziehungsanstalt Ilfeld. Sammlung der von 1934 bis 1944 herausgegebenen Ilfeld-Blätter—Ein Beitrag zur Zeitgeschichte. Band II: Januar 1943 bis April 1944/45* (1998), 523–6.

Bewig, Gerwalt, 'Zum Gedenken an unseren Ilfelder Musiklehrer, Karl Bauche', in Rudolf Marggraf (ed.), *Die Nationalpolitische Erziehungsanstalt Ilfeld. Sammlung der von 1934 bis 1944 herausgegebenen Ilfeld-Blätter—Ein Beitrag zur Zeitgeschichte. Band II: Januar 1943 bis April 1944/45* (1998), 443.

Bleckmann, Alfred, 'Wie prägte Ilfeld durch den Unterricht seine Alumnen?', in Rudolf Marggraf (ed.), *Die Nationalpolitische Erziehungsanstalt Ilfeld. Sammlung der von 1934 bis 1944 herausgegebenen Ilfeld-Blätter—Ein Beitrag zur Zeitgeschichte. Band II: Januar 1943 bis April 1944/45* (1998), 483–5.

Bolte, Harry and Weihe, Justus (eds), *Ilfeld 1189–1989. Beiträge zur Festveranstaltung am 20. Mai 1989 im Kloster Walkenried anläßlich des Jubiläums der Gründung des Klosters Ilfeld vor 800 Jahren* (n.p., 1989).

Bremer, Dieter, 'Die letzten Monate in Ballenstedt—unser Erzieher, Hans Seidel, besorgt die rechtzeitige Heimkehr der in Ballenstedt verbliebenen Jüngsten', in Rudolf Marggraf (ed.), *Die Nationalpolitische Erziehungsanstalt Ilfeld. Sammlung der von 1934 bis 1944 herausgegebenen Ilfeld-Blätter—Ein Beitrag zur Zeitgeschichte. Band II: Januar 1943 bis April 1944/45* (1998), 441–2.

Calliebe, Otto, 'Die nationalpolitischen Erziehungsanstalten', *Deutsche Schulerziehung* (1940), 248–57.

Carstensen, Christian, *Emil Nolde in meinem Leben* (Flensburg, 1990).

Charlesworth, M. B., 'Football against the Nazis', *Old Salopian Newsletter*, May 1987 (1987).

Cnotka, Hans-Günter (ed.), *Vollständiges Personalverzeichnis der Schüler der Anstalt am Gollen in Köslin. Staatliche Bildungsanstalt (Stabila) 1920–1933; Nationalpolitische Erziehungsanstalt (N.P.E.A./Napola) 1933–1945* (Kiel, 1993).

Cnotka, Hans-Günter (ed.), *Chronik der Anstalt am Gollen. Teil 2: Staatliche Bildungsanstalt Stabila—Köslin 1920–1933* (Kiel, 2002).

Donnersberg, Realanstalt am, *Prof. Dr. Ernst Göbel—Lebensbild eines pfälzischen Schulmannes. Sonderdruck aus dem Jahresbericht der Realanstalt am Donnersberg 1934/35* (Kirchheimbolanden, 1935).

Drechsler, Karl, 'Napola-Jungmannen als Kumpel in der Grube', *Weltanschauung und Schule* 1, no. 11 (1937), 663–9.

Dürrschmidt, Karl, *Mit 15 in den Krieg. Ein Napola-Schüler berichtet* (Graz, 2004).

Eike, Siegfried J., 'Die Jungmannen der Nationalpolitischen Erziehungsanstalten (NPEA)', *Deutsches Soldatenjahrbuch* 38 (1990), 430–9.

Eike, [Siegfried] J., *Die Jungmannen-Kadetten—Eliten im Vergleich* (Hamburg, n.d.).

Elten, Jörg Andrees, *Ganz entspannt im Hier und Jetzt. Tagebuch über mein Leben mit Bhagwan in Poona* (Reinbek bei Hamburg, 1979).

Erfurt, Vereinigten Kirchen- und Klosterkammer, *Vereinigten Kirchen- und Klosterkammer Erfurt: 'Stiftung öffentlichen Rechts'* (Erfurt, 1972).

Fachgemeinschaft für Geschichte an der Nationalpolitischen Erziehungsanstalt Naumburg an der Saale, *Aufriß der deutschen Geschichte im 19. und 20. Jahrhundert. Von der französischen bis zur nationalsozialistischen Revolution und zur Gegenwart* (Leipzig, 1941).

Fadrus, Viktor (ed.), *Die österreichischen Bundeserziehungsanstalten* (Vienna, 1924).

Freyberg, Jutta von, et al. (eds), *'Wir hatten andere Träume.' Kinder und Jugendliche unter der NS-Diktatur* (Frankfurt am Main, 1995).

Fuhlroth, Oskar, 'Persönliche Erlebnisse in Ballenstedt bis März 1945 mit Kampfeinsatz am Führerbunker der Reichskanzlei in Berlin: Meine kurze Gastrolle in Ballenstedt und deren Folgen', in Rudolf Marggraf (ed.), *Die Nationalpolitische Erziehungsanstalt Ilfeld. Sammlung der von 1934 bis 1944 herausgegebenen Ilfeld-Blätter—Ein Beitrag zur Zeitgeschichte. Band II: Januar 1943 bis April 1944/45* (1998), 445–9.

Gélieu, Bernhard von, *1890—1990. Culm—Köslin. Kadettenhaus/Stabila/NPEA* (Butzbach-Maibach, 1990).

Gellinek, Christian, *Northwest Germany in Northeast America: Immigration Waves from Central Europe and Their Reverberations until Today. Essays in Preparation of the 400 Year Celebration in A.D. 2007* (Münster, 1997).

Gellinek, Christian, *Deutsches Elternland—Eine geographisch-historische Untersuchung. Essays* (Münster, 2013).

Geyer, Dietrich, *Reußenkrone, Hakenkreuz und roter Stern. Ein autobiographischer Bericht* (Göttingen, 1999).

Glöckel, Otto, *Drillschule—Lernschule—Arbeitsschule* (Vienna, 1928).

Glöckel, Otto, *Aus dem Leben eines großen Schulmannes—Otto Glöckel—Selbstbiographie. Sein Lebenswerk: Die Wiener Schulreform* (Zürich, 1939).

Glöckel, Otto, *Ausgewählte Schriften und Reden* (Vienna, 1985).

Goedewaagen, Tobie, 'Die Nationalpolitische Erziehungsanstalten in Deutschland', *Nieuw Nederland* (1938) [translation: BArch, NS 15/205, Bl. 73–85].

Goerke, Heinz, *Am Puls der Medizin: Arzt im 20. Jahrhundert. Eine Autobiographie* (Hildesheim, 1996).

Gräfer, Gustav, *Die Deutsche Schule. Sonderdruck aus Benze-Gräfer 'Erziehungsmächte und Erziehungshoheit im Großdeutschen Reich'* (Leipzig, [1940]).

Graffenberger, Günter, *Vom Memel bis Stockholm. Erinnerungen eines auslandsdeutschen Journalisten* (Osnabrück, 2002).

Gräter, Reinhold, et al., 'Die Nationalpolitischen Erziehungsanstalten in Württemberg', *Der Deutsche Erzieher* (1937), 234–50.

Gronau, Joachim, *Glocken, Ganter und Geschütze. Erinnerungen eines Ostpreußen* (Rendsburg, 1990).

Guericke, Konrad, 'Das Schlußkapitel der Napola Emsland', in Rudolf Marggraf (ed.), *Die Nationalpolitische Erziehungsanstalt Ilfeld. Sammlung der von 1934 bis 1944 herausgegebenen Ilfeld-Blätter—Ein Beitrag zur Zeitgeschichte. Band II: Januar 1943 bis April 1944/45* (1998), 341–2.

Haffner, Sebastian, *Defying Hitler: A Memoir* (London, 2002).

Haupt, Joachim, *Vom deutschen Nationalsozialismus* (Frankfurt am Main, 1921).

Haupt, Joachim, 'Das Bildungsziel im nationalsozialistischen Staat', *Nachrichtenblatt des N.S.L.B., Gau Südhannover-Braunschweig* 1, no. 1 (1933), 3–6.

Haupt, Joachim, 'The Educational Ideals of the German National Socialist Movement', *The Yearbook of Education* (1935), 923–30.

Haupt, Joachim, *Nationalerziehung* (Langensalza, 1936).

Haupt, Joachim, *Völkisch oder national? Eine grundlegende Auseinandersetzung mit der deutsch-'nationalen' Oberschicht* (Munich, n.d.).

Heck, Robert, *Schloß Oranienstein (Lahn) und sein Nassauisches Heimatmuseum* (Diez, 1937).

Hein, Manfred Peter, *Fluchtfährte. Erzählung* (Zürich, 1999).

Heinich, Arne, *'Niemand entgeht seiner Zeit': Erziehung, Lernen und Leben in der Nationalpolitischen Erziehungsanstalt (Napola) Bensberg bei Köln. September 1942 bis April 1945* (Norderstedt, 2007).

Heißmeyer, August, 'Auslese an den Nationalpolitischen Erziehungsanstalten', *Internationale Zeitschrift für Erziehung* 5 (1936), 222.

Heißmeyer, August, 'Über die Nationalpolitischen Erziehungsanstalten', *Der Altherrenbund* 1, no. 8 (1939), 201–3.

Heißmeyer, August, *Die Nationalpolitischen Erziehungsanstalten* (Berlin, 1939).

Heißmeyer, August, 'Wieviele Nationalpolitische Erziehungsanstalten gibt es?', *Weltanschauung und Schule* 3 (1939), 334–6.

Heißmeyer, August, 'Der Stand der NPEA', *Weltanschauung und Schule* 5, no. 6 (1941), 138–40.

Heißmeyer, August, 'Erziehung zur soldatischen Moral. Das Ziel der Nationalpolitischen Erziehungsanstalten', *Die Innere Front NSK. Pressedienst der NSDAP—Sonderdruck* (1942).

Hellmann, 'Jungmannen im Bergwerk', *Weltanschauung und Schule* 1, no. 3 (1937), 179–82.

Helms, Bodo, *Von Anfang an dabei. Mein abenteuerliches Fliegerleben 1939–1980* (Berg am Starnberger See, [2000]).

Herlyn, Carl, 'Was Ilfeld mir bedeutet hat?', in Rudolf Marggraf (ed.), *Die Nationalpolitische Erziehungsanstalt Ilfeld. Sammlung der von 1934 bis 1944 herausgegebenen Ilfeld-Blätter—Ein Beitrag zur Zeitgeschichte. Band II: Januar 1943 bis April 1944/45* (1998), 465–9.

Herlyn, Carl, et al., 'Nachbetrachtungen zur Klosterschule und zur Nationalpolitischen Erziehungsanstalt Ilfeld—Erinnerungen und Wertungen ehemaliger Schüler und Jungmannen', in Rudolf Marggraf (ed.), *Die Nationalpolitische Erziehungsanstalt Ilfeld. Sammlung der von 1934 bis 1944 herausgegebenen Ilfeld-Blätter—Ein Beitrag zur Zeitgeschichte. Band II: Januar 1943 bis April 1944/45* (1998), 463–557.

Heuer, Hermann, 'Englische und deutsche Jugenderziehung', *Zeitschrift für neusprachlichen Unterricht* 36 (1937), 215–26.

Hitler, Adolf, *Mein Kampf* (Munich, 1943 edn).

Hobohm, Kurt, 'Über Geist und Arbeit der Nationalpolitischen Erziehungsanstalt. Bericht von einer Besichtigung der Nationalpolitischen Erziehungsanstalt Potsdam', *Die Erziehung* 16 (1941), 223–5.

Hrazky, Josef, 'Rückschau auf die Jahre 1910–1938', *Realgymnasium der Theresianischen Akademie. Jahresbericht 1957/58* (1958), 24–30.

Itz., 'Erziehungswichtige Tatsachen: Die Lehrernachwuchsfrage wird geregelt', *Weltanschauung und Schule* 5, no. 5 (1939), 232–5.

Janssen, Horst, *Hinkepott. Autobiographische Hüpferei in Briefen und Aufsätzen* (Gifkendorf, 1987).

Janssen, Horst, *Johannes. Illustrierte Briefe 'Hinkepott II'* (Gifkendorf, 1989).

Jung, Willi, *Deutsche Arbeiterjugend. Auslese, Förderung, Aufstieg* (Berlin, 1940).

Junghans, Helmut, *Dawaj. Ein Echo der Vergangenheit: Tagebuchszenen aus russischer Gefangenschaft 1942–1945* (Rheine, 2010).

Kalckstein, Wilfried von, *Jahrgang 1920: Gestempelt und geprägt* (Rodowo, 2012).

Kamprath, Rainer, 'Unterricht und Erziehung im Krieg', *Die Pforte. Schulpforta-Nachrichten. Zeitschrift des Pförtner Bundes e.V.* 43 (1990), 20–4.

Karasek, Hellmuth, *Auf der Flucht. Erinnerungen* (Berlin, 2004).

Kemper, Wilhelm, 'Mehr sein als scheinen. Bensberg—die Nationalpolitische Erziehungsanstalt der Westmark', *Rheinische Blätter. Deutsche kulturpolitische Zeitschrift im Westen* 16, no. 9 (1939), 584–8.

Klaes, Michael, 'Die Napola Neubeuern 1942–1945', *Landschulheim Neubeuern—Jahrbuch* (1995), 42–3.

Kleinau, Klaus, *Im Gleichschritt, marsch! Der Versuch einer Antwort, warum ich von Auschwitz nichts wusste. Lebenserinnerungen eines NS-Eliteschülers der Napola Ballenstedt* (Hamburg, 2000).

Kleinschmidt, Hans, *Die 'Ilfelder Parteien'. Ein Beitrag zur deutschen Schul- und Erziehungsgeschichte. Quellenmäßiger Bericht über die Schülerverbindungen an der Klosterschule Ilfeld nach den Verbindungs- und Schulakten* (Nordhausen, 1924).

Kleint, Walter, 'Die Rudolf-Schröter-Schule: Nationalpolitische Erziehungsanstalt in Klotzsche bei Dresden', *Die höhere Schule* (1934), 213–20.

Kloppe, Fritz, *Nationalpolitische Erziehungsanstalten* (Leipzig, n.d.).

Klotz, Manfred, *Trotzdem groß geworden! Jugenderfahrungen eines kleinen Mannes* (Norderstedt, 2000).

Knoglinger, Walter, *Stift Göttweig. Heimstätte einer 'Nationalpolitischen Erziehungsanstalt' in der Zeit von Jänner 1943 bis April 1945* (2000).

Knüpffer, Philipp, 'Interview mit Hans Rettkowski (alumnus portensis 1936–42)', *Die Pforte. Schulpforta-Nachrichten. Zeitschrift des Pförtner Bundes e.V.* 55 (2002), 27–35.

Körber, Paul, *Erfahrungsaussagen—Wege und Umwege* (Celle, n.d.).

Koschatzky, Walter, *Faszination Kunst. Erinnerungen eines Kunsthistorikers* (Vienna, 2001).

Kraemer, Edgar, *Das Narrenschiff Germania* (n.p., 2000).

Kreitz, Erwin, 'Austausch der Nationalpolitischen Erziehungsanstalten mit Nordamerikanischen Academies', *Weltanschauung und Schule* 1, no. 4 (1937), 222–5.

Krieck, Ernst, *Nationalpolitische Erziehung* (Leipzig, 1932).

Lamprecht, Günther (ed.), *Wie es damals war. Napola Schloss Reisen, Wartheland. Erinnerungen und Berichte* (Hamburg, 2007).

Leeb, Johannes, *'Wir waren Hitlers Eliteschüler'. Ehemalige Zöglinge der NS-Ausleseschulen brechen ihr Schweigen* (7th edn; Munich, 2005).

Ley, Robert, *Wir alle helfen dem Führer. Deutschland braucht jeden Deutschen* (4th edn; Munich, 1939).

Ley, Robert and Schirach, Baldur von, *Die Adolf-Hitler-Schule* (Berlin, [1937]).

Loebe, Victor, *Putbus. Geschichte des Schlosses und der Entstehung und Entwickelung des Badeortes. Eine Festgabe zur Hundertjahrfeier der Gründung des Ortes Putbus* (Putbus, 1910).

Loge, Eckhard, 'Der Musikzug der Nationalpolitischen Erziehungsanstalt Wahlstatt', *Völkische Musikerziehung* 2 (1936), 228–32.

Loge, Eckhard, 'Das Fest der Waffenleite. Bericht über den Versuch einer Neugestaltung in einer Nationalpolitischen Erziehungsanstalt', *Völkische Musikerziehung* 6 (1940), 61–3.

Lübbert, Friedrich, 'Die körperliche Erziehung in den Nationalpolitischen Erziehungsanstalten', *Leibesübungen und körperliche Erziehung* 11 (1938), 273–9.

Männig, Hans-Joachim, 'Schulpforta: NPEA im Krieg', *Die Pforte. Schulpforta-Nachrichten. Zeitschrift des Pförtner Bundes e.V.* 51 (1998), 15–19.

Männig, Jochen, et al. (eds), *Das Tagebuch. Aufzeichnungen des 2. Zuges der N.P.E.A. Schulpforta 1943–1945* (n.p., 1997).

Marggraf, Rudolf, 'Zur Erinnerung an den OStDir. Dr. Erich von Drygalski', in Rudolf Marggraf (ed.), *Die Nationalpolitische Erziehungsanstalt Ilfeld. Sammlung der von 1934 bis 1944 herausgegebenen Ilfeld-Blätter—Ein Beitrag zur Zeitgeschichte. Band II: Januar 1943 bis April 1944/45* (1998), 519–22.

Mayer-Rosa, Eugen, 'Musikerziehung und Musik im Gemeinschaftsleben einer Nationalpolitischen Erziehungsanstalt', *Die deutsche höhere Schule* 5, no. 21 (1938), 702–10.

Meinken, Helmut, *Zwischen Bremen und Caracas* (Bremen, 2002).

Meister, Robert (ed.), *Diez-Oranienstein* (Diez, 1933).

Meuer, Peter, *Linien des Lebens. Eine Kindheit und Jugend im Schwäbischen und anderswo* (Stuttgart, 1991).

Montanus, Klaus, *Die Putbusser—Kadetten unter dem Hakenkreuz. Ein Napola-Schüler erzählt* (Frankfurt am Main, 1998).

Mücke, *Haus- und Schulordnung der Königlichen Klosterschule zu Ilfeld* (Göttingen, 1900).

Müller, Fritz Traugott, *Potsdamin Pojat (Potsdamer Jungens). Ein Finnland-Fahrt von Jungens der Nationalpolitischen Erziehungsanstalt in Potsdam* (Nürnberg, 1943).

Müncheberg, Hans, *Gelobt sei, was hart macht. Aus dem Leben eines Zöglings der Nationalpolitischen Erziehungsanstalt Potsdam* (Berlin, 1991).

Naumburg, Stabila, *Staatliche Bildungsanstalt Naumburg a.S.* (Berlin, *c.*1931).

Neufeldt, Sieghard and Halm, Regine, 'Interview des MB mit Herrn Rudolf von Ribbentrop am 22.6.09', *Das Ritterkreuz. Mitteilungsblatt der Ordensgemeinschaft der Ritterkreuzträger (OdR); Traditionsgemeinschaft des Eisernen Kreuzes* 55, no. 3 (2009), 2–4.

Oberle, Wilhelm, 'Die deutsche höhere Schule am Vorabend der großen Schulreform', *Die deutsche höhere Schule* 4, no. 4 (1937), 623–4.

Overesch, Manfred, et al. (ed.), *Das Dritte Reich im Gespräch* (Hildesheim, 1991).

Peters, Carl, *Lebenserinnerungen* (Hamburg, 1918).

Pfeiffer, Dieter, 'Jungmann in vier Nationalpolitischen Erziehungsanstalten—Wahlstatt, Bensberg, Traiskirchen, Spanheim—1936–1943', *Der Freiwillige* 39, no. 9 (1993) 22–4; no. 10, 13–16.

Pfeiffer, Dieter, 'Mit 16 in den letzten Kriegstagen', *Der Freiwillige* 45, no. 9 (1999), 8–10.

Pichl, Engelbert, *1945: Meine Lage war hoffnungslos. NAPOLA, Volkssturm, russische Gefangenschaft, Flucht mit 15 Jahren* (n.p., 2012).

Picker, Richard, *Das Ende vom Lied. Positionen eines Lebens zwischen Hitlerjugend, Psychotherapie und Kirche* (Vienna, 2005).

Prowaznik, Franz, 'Von unseren Schulkinos. Das Schulkino der Bundeserziehungsanstalt in Wien XIII', *Das Bild im Dienste der Schule u. Volksbildung. Drittes Tochterblatt der Zeitschrift Die Quelle* 6/7/8 (1929), 141–5.

Putzar, Arnulf H. K., *Im Schatten einer Zeit* (Schwerin, 1998).

Rau, Rolf, *Junge, das Einzige, was wir noch haben, ist dein Kopf. Erinnerung und Spurensuche* (Bremen, 2017).

Rautenberg, Wilhelm, 'Von der Klosterschule zur Nationalpolitischen Erziehungsanstalt. Ilfeld April 1932–April 1935', in Rudolf Marggraf (ed.), *Die Nationalpolitische Erziehungsanstalt Ilfeld. Sammlung der von 1934 bis 1944 herausgegebenen Ilfeld-Blätter—Ein Beitrag zur Zeitgeschichte. Band II: Januar 1943 bis April 1944/45* (1998), 487–517.

Rein, Erwin, '"Ilfeld"—wie es für mich 1945 endete', in Rudolf Marggraf (ed.), *Die Nationalpolitische Erziehungsanstalt Ilfeld. Sammlung der von 1934 bis 1944 herausgegebenen Ilfeld-Blätter—Ein Beitrag zur Zeitgeschichte. Band II: Januar 1943 bis April 1944/45* (1998), 455–6.

Reukauf, Irmfried, 'Das Ende des Krieges in Ballenstedt—Ein Rückblick im Dezember 1997', in Rudolf Marggraf (ed.), *Die Nationalpolitische Erziehungsanstalt Ilfeld. Sammlung der von 1934 bis 1944 herausgegebenen Ilfeld-Blätter—Ein Beitrag zur Zeitgeschichte. Band II: Januar 1943 bis April 1944/45* (1998), 451–2.

Ries, Hanns, *Erziehungsheim 'Schloß Oranienstein'* (Diez an der Lahn, 1928).

Rischmann, Kurt, 'Persönliche Erinnerungen und Eindrücke September 1944 bis zum Kriegsende', in Rudolf Marggraf (ed.), *Die Nationalpolitische Erziehungsanstalt Ilfeld. Sammlung der von 1934 bis 1944 herausgegebenen Ilfeld-Blätter—Ein Beitrag zur Zeitgeschichte. Band II: Januar 1943 bis April 1944/45* (1998), 437–40.

Rischmann, Kurt, et al., '"Wie Ilfelder Jungmannen das Ende des Krieges erlebten"—Ballenstedt November 1944 bis April 1945', in Rudolf Marggraf (ed.), *Die Nationalpolitische Erziehungsanstalt Ilfeld. Sammlung der von 1934 bis 1944 herausgegebenen Ilfeld-Blätter—Ein Beitrag zur Zeitgeschichte. Band II: Januar 1943 bis April 1944/45* (1998), 433–62.

Rommel, Otto, 'Die österreichischen Bundeserziehungsanstalten', *Erziehung und Unterricht* (1952), reprinted in Agnes Rudda (ed.), *Später Dank: Erinnerungen an die österreichischen Bundeserziehungsanstalten. Ein Beitrag zur Geschichte und Entwicklung des Bildungswesens von 1919 bis zur Gegenwart* (Heidenreichstein, 2007), 381–4.

Röttger, 'Warum Latein auch an Nationalpolitische Erziehungsanstalten?', *Der Deutsche Erzieher* 11 (1941), 326–7.

Rowan-Robinson, G. A., 'The German Nationalpolitische Erziehungsanstalt and the English Public School: I. A Comparison', *Internationale Zeitschrift für Erziehung* 6 (1937), 162–5.

Rowan-Robinson, G. A., 'The Training of the Nazi Leaders of the Future', *International Affairs* 17 (1938), 233–50.

Rudda, Agnes (ed.), *Später Dank: Erinnerungen an die österreichischen Bundeserziehungsanstalten. Ein Beitrag zur Geschichte und Entwicklung des Bildungswesens von 1919 bis zur Gegenwart* (Heidenreichstein, 2007).

Rust, Bernhard, 'Die Grundlagen der nationalsozialistischen Erziehung', *Hochschule und Ausland* 13, no. 1 (1935), 1–18.

Rust, Bernhard, 'Völkische Auslese und Aufbauschule', *Weltanschauung und Schule* 1, no. 1 (1936), 3–9.

Rust, Bernhard, 'Education in the Third Reich', in Joachim von Ribbentrop (ed.), *Germany Speaks. By 21 Leading Members of Party and State* (London, 1938), 97–117.

Rust, Bernhard, 'Erziehung zur Tat', *Deutsche Schulerziehung* 1941/2 (1943), 3–12.

Schäfer, Harald, *NAPOLA: Die letzten vier Jahre der Nationalpolitischen Erziehungsanstalt Oranienstein bei Diez an der Lahn 1941–1945. Eine Erlebnis-Dokumentation* (Frankfurt am Main, 1997).

Schäfer, Otto, 'Ziel und Gestalt der nationalpolitischen Erziehungsanstalten', *Nationalsozialistisches Bildungswesen* 7, no. 1 (1942), 19–31.

Schikore, Klaus, *Kennungen. Landmarken einer Wandlung* (2nd edn; Aachen, 1994).

Schikore, Klaus, *Trennungen. Zwischen Verbannung und Heimkehr* (Schwerin, 2000).

Schikore, Klaus, *Wir müssen ihre Last wohl tragen. Rückblicke eines Grenzgängers zwischen West und Ost* (Aachen, 2006).

Schikore, Klaus, *Aus bewegter Zeit. Gesammelte Gedichte 1949–1999* (Wetzlar, 2009).

Schirmeister, F. M., 'Ziel und Sinn der Nationalpolitischen Erziehungsanstalt Potsdamsches Großes Waisenhaus', *Der Deutsche Volkserzieher* 1 (1936), 3–4.

Schlegel, Fritz Peter, 'Ein Tagesablauf', *Die Pforte. Schulpforta-Nachrichten. Zeitschrift des Pförtner Bundes e.V.* 43 (1990), 15–19.

Schlottke, Hartmut, *Kreuze, Katzen, Kinderkram. Kleine Tag- und Nachtgeschichten* (Munich, 2006).

Schlunke, *First English Textbook* (Potsdam, n.d.).

[Schoenecker], Hans, 'Ein Blick von "unten", dann von "oben" und schließlich doch wieder von "ganz unten"', in Helga Gotschlich (ed.), *'Und der eignen Kraft vertrauend…' Aufbruch in die DDR—50 Jahre danach* (Berlin, 1999), 259–72.

Sidgwick, Christopher, 'The German Nationalpolitische Erziehungsanstalt and the English Public School: III. German Journey: To Backnang!', *Internationale Zeitschrift für Erziehung* 6 (1937), 170–3.

Siegel, Gerd, *Wechselvolle Vergangenheit* (Göttingen, 1980).

Skroblin, Gustav, 'Erzieher und Jungmannen der Nationalpolitischen Erziehungsanstalten mit ihren Feldküchen beim Einmarsch in das Sudetenland', *Weltanschauung und Schule* 2 (1938), 526–7.

Skroblin, Gustav, 'Vom Sinn der Gemeinschaftserziehung in den Nationalpolitischen Erziehungsanstalten', *Frauen-Warte* 6 (1941).

Skroblin, Gustav, 'Tradition und Zukunft. Aufgabe der Nationalpolitischen Erziehungsanstalten', *Die Pforte. Neue Folge des 'Alten Pförtners'; Zeitschrift des Pförtner-Bundes* 19, no. 1 (1942), 3–6.

Skroblin, Gustav, 'Die Nationalpolitischen Erziehungsanstalten', *Deutsche Schulerziehung* 1941/2 (1943), 211–18.

Sommer, Geb, 'Is Freedom Failing?', *KLV-Rundbrief* 103 (2006), 15–20.

Spreckelsen, Otto, *Plöner Liederbuch für die marschierende Jugend. Im Auftrage der Nationalpolitischen Erziehungsanstalt Plön von deutschen Jungen gesammelt und für den Schulgebrauch zusammengestellt* (Itzehoe, 1933).

Stehle, Gerd, *Fliegen—nichts als fliegen. Pilot in Krieg und Frieden* (Berg am Starnberger See, 2001).

Steinbach, Lothar, *Ein Volk, ein Reich, ein Glaube? Ehemalige Nationalsozialisten und Zeitzeugen berichten über ihr Leben im Dritten Reich* (Bonn, 1995).

Stifter, Herbert, 'Wir Jungen steh'n bereit. Unsere Bundes-Erziehungsanstalten', *ÖWB: Österreich in Wort und Bild. Monatshefte des Heimatdienstes* 1, no. 1 (1937), 1–5.

Stigulinszky, Roland, *Von Hundertsten ins Tausendste. Lebensgeschichte(n) zwischen Hitler und Heute* (Saarbrücken, 1997).

Strauss, Felix F., *Bilder von der Wiener Neustädter Burg zwischen zwei Weltkriegen. Ansichten von fünfzehnjährigen Augenzeugen in den Jahren 1932/1933, ergänzt durch Darstellungen aus dem Jahre 1923. Ein Beispiel der Schulreform von Otto Glöckel an der Bundeserziehungsanstalt 'Schule am Turm'* (Vienna, 1985).

Strauss, Felix F., 'Schule und Heim in der Bundeserziehungsanstalt Wiener Neustadt im Rahmen der österreichischen Reformpädagogik', in Agnes Rudda (ed.), *Später Dank: Erinnerungen an die österreichischen Bundeserziehungsanstalten. Ein Beitrag zur Geschichte und Entwicklung des Bildungswesens von 1919 bis zur Gegenwart* (Heidenreichstein, 2007), 439–51.

Strauss, Felix F., 'Die Bundeserziehungsanstalt "Schule am Turm": Ein Interludium in der Geschichte der Neustädter Burg zwischen den beiden Weltkriegen', in Agnes Rudda (ed.), *Später Dank: Erinnerungen an die österreichischen Bundeserziehungsanstalten. Ein Beitrag zur Geschichte und Entwicklung des Bildungswesens von 1919 bis zur Gegenwart* (Heidenreichstein, 2007), 387–425.

Strubegger, Alfred, 'Wie ich in die Napola kam', in Gregor M. Lechner (ed.), *Stift Göttweig und seine Kunstschätze* (St. Pölten, 1983).

Tate, J. W., 'The German Nationalpolitische Erziehungsanstalt and the English Public School: II. The Public Schools of Germany', *Internationale Zeitschrift für Erziehung* 6 (1937), 165–70.

Taubeneder, Josef, '"Napola"-Schüler in Neubeuern', *Landschulheim Neubeuern—Jahrbuch* (1995), 43.

Teichert, Friedrich, 'Die Staatlichen Bildungsanstalten in Preußen', *Der neue Weg. Österreichische Monatshefte für pädagogische Forschung und Bildung* (1931), 172–9.

Tesar, Ludwig Erik, 'Probleme der österreichischen Bundeserziehungsanstalten', *Die Erziehung. Monatsschrift für den Zusammenhang von Kultur und Erziehung in Wissenschaft und Leben* 4 (1929), 500–13.

Tesar, Ludwig Erik, 'Vom Zeichenunterricht. Erfahrungen aus einer österreichischen Bundeserziehungsanstalt', *Die Erziehung. Monatsschrift für den Zusammenhang von Kultur und Erziehung in Wissenschaft und Leben* 6 (1931), 644–54.

Tesar, Ludwig Erik, 'Die österreichischen Bundes-Erziehungs-Anstalten. Gleichzeitig ein Beitrag zum Problem der Erziehung durch den Staat', *Internationale Zeitschrift für Erziehungswissenschaft* 2, no. 4 (1933), 610–21.

Thaller, Franz (ed.), *50 Jahre österreichische Bundeserziehungsanstalt* (Saalfelden, 1969).

Thimme, Adolf, *Ilfelder Klosterleben um 1870* (Göttingen, 1928).

Tischendorf, Gerhard, *Zwischen Überzeugung und Aufbegehren. Biographischer Bericht eines Freiberger Mineralogen* (Schkeuditz, 1999).

Trepte, Helmut, 'Die Nationalpolitische Erziehungsanstalt', *Internationale Zeitschrift für Erziehung* 3, no. 4 (1934), 489–92.

Trepte, Helmut, 'Erziehungswichtige Tatsachen: Die Nationalpolitischen Erziehungsanstalten', *Weltanschauung und Schule* 1, no. 2 (1936), 105–9.

Trepte, Helmut, 'Engländer über Nationalpolitische Erziehungsanstalten', *Weltanschauung und Schule* 1, no. 7 (1937), 423–7.

Trepte, Helmut, 'USA-Austausch der Nationalpolitischen Erziehungsanstalten', *Weltanschauung und Schule* 1, no. 13 (1937), 54–61.

Tzöbl, Josef A., *Vaterländische Erziehung. Mit einem Geleitwort von Bundesminister Dr. Kurt v. Schuschnigg* (2nd edn; Vienna, 1933).

Vahl, Hartmut, *Napola Schulpforta 1943–1945. Erinnerungen eines Schülers* (Hamburg, 2000).

Vahlbruch, Heinz, 'Was verdanke ich Ilfeld?', in Rudolf Marggraf (ed.), *Die Nationalpolitische Erziehungsanstalt Ilfeld. Sammlung der von 1934 bis 1944 herausgegebenen Ilfeld-Blätter—Ein Beitrag zur Zeitgeschichte. Band II: Januar 1943 bis April 1944/45* (1998), 479–82.

Vogel, Eberhard, *Wanderungen in Deutschland. Lebensstationen 1935–1948* (Berlin, 2007).

Vormbrock, Wolfgang, *Miniaturen. Wahllos niedergeschriebene Erinnerungen, Geschichten und Anekdoten aus meinem Leben*, 2 vols (Norderstedt, 2011–12).

Walle, Dirk G. van de, *Memories of My Youth in National Socialist Germany* (n.p., 2018).

Wassermann, Ernst, 'Schulpforta 1935–1945: Nationalsozialistische Erziehung unter humanistischem Deckmäntelchen oder Kontinuität humanistischer Bildungstradition hinter NS-Fassade?', *Die Pforte. Schulpforta-Nachrichten. Zeitschrift des Pförtner Bundes e.V.* 51 (1998), 12–15.

Watzke, Adolf, 'Unsere Bundeserziehungsanstalten', *Monatshefte für Deutsche Erziehung* 1, no. 1 (1923), 12–16.

Weber, Herbert, 'Gedanken um den Biologieunterricht an einer Nationalpolitischen Erziehungsanstalt', *Weltanschauung und Schule* 5, no. 12 (1941), 274–81.

Wechmar, Rüdiger von, *Akteur in der Loge. Weltläufige Erinnerungen* (Berlin, 2000).

Wehrhan, Kurt, 'Nationalpolitische Erziehung, insbesondere die nationalpolitischen Erziehungsanstalten', *Die neue deutsche Schule* 9 (1935), 99–105.

Weihe, Justus, 'Die Umstellung der Landesschule in die Nationalpolitische Erziehungsanstalt 1935', *Die Pforte. Schulpforta-Nachrichten. Zeitschrift des Pförtner Bundes e.V.* 41 (1988), 15–20.

Weihe, Justus, 'Die Erziehung in der Nationalpolitischen Erziehungsanstalt Schulpforte', *Die Pforte. Schulpforta-Nachrichten. Zeitschrift des Pförtner Bundes e.V.* 43 (1990), 24–8.

Weihe, Justus, 'Die Nationalpolitische Erziehungsanstalt Schulpforta 1935 bis 1945', in Hans Heumann (ed.), *Schulpforta. Tradition und Wandel einer Eliteschule* (Erfurt, 1994), 231–58.
Wenke, Hans, 'Die pädagogische Lage in Deutschland', *Die Erziehung* 16, no. 11–12 (1941), 257–67.
Wiebach (ed.), *Festschrift: 700 Jahre Stadt Plön am See 1236–1936* (Plön, 1936).
Wigelbeyer, Helmut, *Schicksal am Fluss. Autobiographischer Roman* (Berlin, 2012).
Windschild, Günther and Schmid, Helmut (eds), *Mit dem Finger vor dem Mund. Ballenstedter Tagebuch des Pfarrers Karl Fr. E. Windschild 1931–1944* (Dessau, 1999).
Worpitz, Hans, *Roter und schwarzer Moloch. Erkenntnisse des Napola-Schülers Benjamin—Russische Kriegsgefangenschaft 1945–1950* (Norderstedt, 2005).
Zempelin, Hans Günther, *Des Teufels Kadett: Napola-Schüler von 1936 bis 1943. Gespräch mit einem Freund* (Frankfurt am Main, 2000).

Published Secondary Literature[1]

Abels, Kurt, *Kadetten: Preußenfilm, Jugendbuch und Kriegslied im 'Dritten Reich'* (Bielefeld, 2002).
Abrams, Lynn, *Oral History Theory* (London, 2010).
Abrams, Lynn, 'Memory as both Source and Subject of Study: The Transformations of Oral History', in Stefan Berger and Bill Niven (eds), *Writing the History of Memory* (London, 2014), 89–109.
Abrams, Lynn and Harvey, Elizabeth (eds), *Gender Relations in German History: Power, Agency and Experience from the Sixteenth to the Twentieth Century* (London, 1996).
Achs, Oskar and Krassnigg, Albert, *Drillschule—Lernschule—Arbeitsschule. Otto Glöckel und die österreichische Schulreform in der Ersten Republik* (Vienna, 1974).
Adam, Erik, 'Austromarxismus und Schulreform', in Erik Adam and Primus-Heinz Kucher (eds), *Die Schul- und Bildungspolitik der österreichischen Sozialdemokratie in der Ersten Republik. Entwicklung und Vorgeschichte* (Vienna, 1983), 271–416.
Adam, Erik and Kucher, Primus-Heinz (eds), *Die Schul- und Bildungspolitik der österreichischen Sozialdemokratie in der Ersten Republik. Entwicklung und Vorgeschichte* (Vienna, 1983).
Ahrens, Rüdiger, *Bündische Jugend. Eine neue Geschichte 1918–1933* (Göttingen, 2015).
Alexander, Kristine, 'Agency and Emotion Work', *Jeunesse: Young People, Texts, Cultures* 7, no. 2 (2015), 120–8.
Alexander, Kristine and Sleight, Simon, 'Introduction', in Kristine Alexander and Simon Sleight (eds), *A Cultural History of Youth in the Modern Age* (London, forthcoming).
Amlung, Ulrich, 'Landesschule Dresden—Entstehung, Konzeption und Praxis (1920–1933)', in DGUV (ed.), *Lernräume. Von der Landesschule Dresden zur Akademie* (Dresden, 2009), 24–49.
Andresen, Sabine, *Mädchen und Frauen in der bürgerlichen Jugendbewegung. Soziale Konstruktion von Mädchenjugend* (Neuwied, 1997).
Arendes, Cord, 'Burgansichten für alle?—Inszenierungen der Ordensburgen in Fotografien', in Klaus Ring and Stefan Wunsch (eds), *Bestimmung: Herrenmensch. NS-Ordensburgen zwischen Faszination und Verbrechen* (Dresden, 2016), 84–91.

[1] N.B. Works of an unscholarly and/or journalistic character have generally been excluded from this bibliography.

Arnhardt, Gerhard, 'Schulpforte im faschistischen Deutschland—der Bruch mit einer 400jährigen humanistischen Bildungstradition', *Jahrbuch für Erziehungs- und Schulgeschichte* 22 (1982), 121–38.

Arnhardt, Gerhard, *Schulpforte—Eine Schule im Zeichen der humanistischen Bildungstradition* (Berlin, 1988).

Arnhardt, Gerhard, 'Reformerisches im Denken und Handeln an den Fürsten- und Landesschulen Meißen, Schulpforte und Grimma zwischen 1900 und 1930—Motive, Quellen, Erscheinungsbilder', in Hermann Röhrs and Andreas Pehnke (eds), *Die Reform des Bildungswesens im Ost-West Dialog. Geschichte, Aufgaben, Probleme* (Frankfurt am Main, 1994), 87–100.

Arnhardt, Gerhard and Reinert, Gerd-Bodo, *Die Fürsten- und Landesschulen Meißen, Schulpforte und Grimma: Lebensweise und Unterricht über Jahrhunderte* (Weinheim, 2002).

Arnold, Egon, *Joachim Daerr (1909–1986). Autobiographische Texte eines Rügener Künstlers* (Putbus, 2011).

Assmann, Aleida, *Der lange Schatten der Vergangenheit. Erinnerungskultur und Geschichtspolitik* (Munich, 2006).

Aumüller-Roske, Ursula, 'Weibliche Elite für die Diktatur? Zur Rolle der Nationalpolitischen Erziehungsanstalten für Mädchen im Dritten Reich', in Ursula Aumüller-Roske (ed.), *Frauenleben—Frauenbilder—Frauengeschichte* (Pfaffenweiler, 1988), 17–44.

Aumüller-Roske, Ursula, 'Die Nationalpolitischen Erziehungsanstalten für Mädchen im "Großdeutschen Reich": Kleine Karrieren für Frauen?', in Lerke Gravenhorst and Carmen Tatschmurat (eds), *Töchter-Fragen. NS-Frauengeschichte* (2nd edn; Freiburg im Breisgau, 1995), 211–36.

Bahro, Berno, *Der SS-Sport. Organisation—Funktion—Bedeutung* (Paderborn, 2013).

Bair, Jeanette, 'Nationalsozialismus als Gegenstand bildungshistorischer Forschung—Ein Überblick über Neuanfänge, Kontinuitäten, Brüche und ihre disziplinäre Rezeption', in Klaus-Peter Horn and Jörg-W. Link (eds), *Erziehungsverhältnisse im Nationalsozialismus. Totaler Anspruch und Erziehungswirklichkeit* (Bad Heilbrunn, 2011), 13–26.

Bajohr, Frank, *'Unser Hotel ist judenfrei'. Bäder-Antisemitismus im 19. und 20. Jahrhundert* (Frankfurt am Main, 2003).

Bajohr, Frank, 'Dynamik und Disparität. Die nationalsozialistische Rüstungsmobilisierung und die "Volksgemeinschaft"', in Frank Bajohr and Michael Wildt (eds), *Volksgemeinschaft. Neue Forschungen zur Gesellschaft des Nationalsozialismus* (Frankfurt am Main, 2009), 78–93.

Bajohr, Frank and Pohl, Dieter, *Der Holocaust als offenes Geheimnis. Die Deutschen, die NS-Führung und die Alliierten* (Munich, 2006).

Bajohr, Frank and Wildt, Michael (eds), *Volksgemeinschaft. Neue Forschungen zur Gesellschaft des Nationalsozialismus* (Frankfurt am Main, 2009).

Bannack, Siegfried, '"Stadt der Flieger"—Klotzsches Erhebung zur Stadt 1935', in Konstantin Herrmann (ed.), *Führerschule, Thingplatz, 'Judenhaus'. Topografien der NS-Herrschaft in Sachsen* (Dresden, 2014), 194–7.

Baranowski, Shelley, *Strength through Joy: Consumerism and Mass Tourism in the Third Reich* (Cambridge, 2004).

Baranowski, Shelley, *Nazi Empire: German Colonialism and Imperialism from Bismarck to Hitler* (Cambridge, 2011).

Barnouw, David, *Van NIVO tot Reichsschule. Nationaal-socialistische onderwijsinstellingen in Nederland* ('s-Gravenhage, 1981).

Barteszko, Dieter, 'Bollwerke im Höhenrausch—Die Ordensburgen des "Dritten Reiches"', in Klaus Ring and Stefan Wunsch (eds), *Bestimmung: Herrenmensch. NS-Ordensburgen zwischen Faszination und Verbrechen* (Dresden, 2016), 66–79.

Bartov, Omer, *Hitler's Army: Soldiers, Nazis, and War in the Third Reich* (Oxford, 1991).

Bastian, Alexander and Stagge, Christiane, 'Forschungsbericht zur Geschichte des heutigen Bundeslandes Sachsen-Anhalt im Nationalsozialismus', in Detlef Schmiechen-Ackermann and Steffi Kaltenborn (eds), *Stadtgeschichte in der NS-Zeit. Fallstudien aus Sachsen-Anhalt und vergleichende Perspektiven* (Münster, 2005), 150–79.

Baumeister, Stefan, *NS-Führungskader. Rekrutierung und Ausbildung bis zum Beginn des Zweiten Weltkriegs 1933–1939* (Konstanz, 1997).

Beattie, Andrew H., 'Verdiente Strafe des harten Kerns oder ungerechte Besatzungsmaßnahme? Die SS und die alliierte Internierung im besetzten Deutschland', in Jan Erik Schulte and Michael Wildt (eds), *Die SS nach 1945. Entschuldungsnarrative, populäre Mythen, europäische Erinnerungsdiskurse* (Göttingen, 2018), 57–74.

Beller, Steven, *A Concise History of Austria* (Cambridge, 2006).

Bendel, Rainer (ed.), *Die katholische Schuld? Katholizismus im Dritten Reich—Zwischen Arrangement und Widerstand* (Münster, 2002).

Beniston, Judith and Vilain, Robert (eds), *Culture and Politics in Red Vienna* (Leeds, 2006).

Benz, Wolfgang (ed.), *Wie wurde man Parteigenosse? Die NSDAP und ihre Mitglieder* (Frankfurt am Main, 2009).

Benz, Wolfgang, 'Einleitung: Die NSDAP und ihre Mitglieder', in Wolfgang Benz (ed.), *Wie wurde man Parteigenosse? Die NSDAP und ihre Mitglieder* (Frankfurt am Main, 2009), 7–17.

Berg, Christa, '"Wer aber vor der Vergangenheit die Augen verschließt, wird blind für die Zukunft." Zur Einführung in diesen Band', in Christa Berg and Sieglinde Ellger-Rüttgart (eds), *'Du bist nichts, Dein Volk ist alles.' Forschungen zum Verhältnis von Pädagogik und Nationalsozialismus* (Weinheim, 1991), 9–21.

Berg, Christa and Ellger-Rüttgart, Sieglinde (eds), *'Du bist nichts, Dein Volk ist alles.' Forschungen zum Verhältnis von Pädagogik und Nationalsozialismus* (Weinheim, 1991).

Berg, Matthew Paul (ed.), *The Struggle for a Democratic Austria: Bruno Kreisky on Peace and Social Justice* (New York, 2000).

Bergen, Doris, 'The "Volksdeutschen" of Eastern Europe, World War II and the Holocaust: Constructed Ethnicity, Real Genocide', *Yearbook of European Studies* 13 (1999), 70–93.

Berger, Karin, *Zwischen Eintopf und Fließband. Frauenarbeit und Frauenbild im Faschismus: Österreich 1938–1945* (Vienna, 1984).

Berger, Stefan, 'Prussia in History and Historiography from the Nineteenth to the Twentieth Centuries', in Philip G. Dwyer (ed.), *Modern Prussian History 1830–1947* (Harlow, 2001), 21–40.

Berger, Stefan, 'On Taboos, Traumas and Other Myths: Why the Debate about German Victims of the Second World War Is Not a Historians' Controversy', in Bill Niven (ed.), *Germans as Victims: Remembering the Past in Contemporary Germany* (Basingstoke, 2006), 210–24.

Berger, Stefan and Niven, Bill (eds), *Writing the History of Memory* (London, 2014).

Berndt, Michael (ed.), *Kreisgymnasium St. Ursula Haselünne 1854–2004. Festschrift zum 150-jährigem Bestehen* (Haselünne, 2004).

Bernett, Hajo, *Sportunterricht an der nationalsozialistischen Schule. Der Schulsport an den höheren Schulen Preußens 1933–1940* (Sankt Augustin, 1985).

Besier, Gerhard, *Die Kirchen und das Dritte Reich. Spaltungen und Abwehrkämpfe 1934–1937* (Berlin, 2001).

Biddiscombe, Perry, *The Denazification of Germany: A History 1945–1950* (Stroud, 2007).

Biess, Frank, *Homecomings: Returning POWs and the Legacies of Defeat in Postwar Germany* (Princeton, 2006).

Bird, Stephanie, et al. (eds), *Reverberations of Nazi Violence in Germany and Beyond: Disturbing Pasts* (London, 2016).

Bird, Stephanie, et al., 'Introduction: Disturbing Pasts', in Stephanie Bird et al. (eds), *Reverberations of Nazi Violence in Germany and Beyond: Disturbing Pasts* (London, 2016), 1–12.

Birn, Ruth Bettina, 'Die SS—Ideologie und Herrschaftsausübung. Zur Frage der Inkorporierung von "Fremdvölkischen"', in Jan Erik Schulte (ed.), *Die SS, Himmler und die Wewelsburg* (Paderborn, 2009), 60–75.

Black, Peter, 'Indigenous Collaboration in the Government General: The Case of the Sonderdienst', in Pieter M. Judson and Marsha L. Rozenblit (eds), *Constructing Nationalities in East Central Europe* (New York, 2005), 243–66.

Blackburn, Gilmer W., *Education in the Third Reich. A Study of Race and History in Nazi Textbooks* (Albany, 1985).

Blesse, Hanka, 'Die Rudolf-Schröter-Schule—Nationalpolitische Erziehungsanstalt Dresden-Klotzsche', in Kuratorium Gedenkstätte Sonnenstein (ed.), *'Es war ein Welt von Befehl und Gehorsam.' Nationalsozialistische Elitebildung und die Adolf-Hitler-Schule Sachsen in Pirna-Sonnenstein (1941 bis 1945)* (Pirna, 2008), 107–29.

Blesse, Hanka, 'Die Anfänge der Rudolf-Schröter-Schule, Staatliche Nationalpolitische Erziehungsanstalt Klotzsche', *Dresdner Hefte: Beiträge zur Kulturgeschichte* 97, no. 1 (2009), 54–63.

Blesse, Hanka, 'Rudolf-Schröter-Schule—Die Staatliche Nationalpolitische Erziehungsanstalt (1934–1945)', in DGUV (ed.), *Lernräume. Von der Landesschule Dresden zur Akademie* (Dresden, 2009), 94–113.

Blesse, Hanka, 'Die Anstaltsleiter der sächsischen Napola Dresden-Klotzsche', in Christine Pieper, Mike Schmeitzner, and Gerhard Naser (eds), *Braune Karrieren. Dresdner Täter und Akteure im Nationalsozialismus* (Dresden, 2012), 238–45.

Blesse, Hanka, 'Die Nationalpolitische Erziehungsanstalt in Dresden-Klotzsche', in Konstantin Herrmann (ed.), *Führerschule, Thingplatz, 'Judenhaus'. Topografien der NS-Herrschaft in Sachsen* (Dresden, 2014), 118–21.

Blessing, Benita, *The Antifascist Classroom: Denazification in Soviet-Occupied Germany, 1945–1949* (Basingstoke, 2006).

Bock, Gisela, 'Nazi Gender Politics and Women's History', in Françoise Thébaud (ed.), *A History of Women in the West. V. Toward a Cultural Identity in the Twentieth Century* (Cambridge, MA, 1994), 149–76.

Bock, Gisela, 'Ordinary Women in Nazi Germany: Perpetrators, Victims, Followers, and Bystanders', in Dalia Ofer and Lenore J. Weitzman (eds), *Women in the Holocaust* (New Haven, 1998), 85–100.

Bode, Sabine, *Die vergessene Generation. Die Kriegskinder brechen ihr Schweigen* (Stuttgart, 2004).

Böhler, Jochen and Gerwarth, Robert, 'Non-Germans in the Waffen-SS: An Introduction', in Jochen Böhler and Robert Gerwarth (eds), *The Waffen-SS: A European History* (Oxford, 2017), 1–15.

Böhler, Jochen and Gerwarth, Robert, *The Waffen-SS: A European History* (Oxford, 2017).

Bohn, Robert (ed.), *Die deutsche Herrschaft in den 'germanischen' Ländern 1940–1945* (Stuttgart, 1997).

Bolenz, Eckhard, 'Improvisation und Rastlosigkeit—Die NS-Ordensburg Vogelsang als "unfertiger Ort" im System des NS-Führernachwuchses', in Klaus Ring and Stefan

Wunsch (eds), *Bestimmung: Herrenmensch. NS-Ordensburgen zwischen Faszination und Verbrechen* (Dresden, 2016), 102–9.

Böltken, Andrea, *Führerinnen im 'Führerstaat'. Gertrud Scholtz-Klink, Trude Mohr, Jutta Rüdiger und Inge Viermetz* (Pfaffenweiler, 1995).

Bornemann, Manfred, *Ilfeld 1940–1950* (Hamburg, 1984).

Botz, Gerhard, *Die Eingliederung Österreichs in das Deutsche Reich. Planung und Verwirklichung des politisch-administrativen Anschlusses (1938–1940)* (Vienna, 1972).

Bouvier, Herma and Geraud, Claude, *NAPOLA: Les écoles d'élites du troisième Reich* (Paris, 2000).

Boyd, Julia, *Travellers in the Third Reich: The Rise of Fascism through the Eyes of Everyday People* (London, 2017).

Brandes, Detlef, *Die Tschechen unter deutschem Protektorat*, 2 vols (Munich, 1969–75).

Brandes, Detlef, *'Umvolkung, Umsiedlung, rassische Bestandsaufnahme'. NS-'Volkstumspolitik' in den böhmischen Ländern* (Munich, 2012).

Bräutigam, Helmut (ed.), *Spandau 1945. Das Kriegsende in einem Berliner Bezirk: Ein Lesebuch* (Berlin-Spandau, 1997).

Breitschuh, Gernot, 'Das Schulwesen im NS-Staat. Spezialuntersuchungen: Schulzeugnis', in Max Liedtke (ed.), *Handbuch der Geschichte des Bayerischen Bildungswesens Bd. 3—Geschichte der Schule in Bayern von 1918 bis 1990* (Bad Heilbrunn, 1997), 453–73.

Bremen, Schulgeschichtliche Sammlung, *Am Roland hing ein Hakenkreuz: Bremer Kinder und Jugendliche in der Nazizeit. Katalog zur Ausstellung* (Bremen, 2002).

Bridenthal, Renate, Grossmann, Atina, and Kaplan, Marion (eds), *When Biology Became Destiny: Women in Weimar and Nazi Germany* (New York, 1984).

Brockhaus, Gudrun, 'Einführung: Attraktion der NS-Bewegung—Eine interdisziplinäre Perspektive', in Gudrun Brockhaus (ed.), *Attraktion der NS-Bewegung* (Essen, 2014), 7–28.

Brockhaus, Gudrun, 'Der deutsche Herrenmensch—ein attraktives Angebot', in Klaus Ring and Stefan Wunsch (eds), *Bestimmung: Herrenmensch. NS-Ordensburgen zwischen Faszination und Verbrechen* (Dresden, 2016), 164–73.

Brodie, Thomas, *German Catholicism at War, 1939–1945* (Oxford, 2018).

Broszat, Martin, *Nationalsozialistische Polenpolitik 1939–1945* (Stuttgart, 1961).

Bryant, Chad, *Prague in Black: Nazi Rule and Czech Nationalism* (Cambridge, MA, 2007).

Buddrus, Michael, 'A Generation Twice Betrayed: Youth Policy in the Transition from the Third Reich to the Soviet Zone of Occupation (1945–1946)', in Mark Roseman (ed.), *Generations in Conflict: Youth Revolt and Generation Formation in Germany 1770–1968* (Cambridge, 1995), 247–68.

Buddrus, Michael, *Totale Erziehung für den totalen Krieg. Hitlerjugend und nationalsozialistische Jugendpolitik Teil 1* (Munich, 2003).

Buddrus, Michael, 'Das letzte Jahr, der letzte Jahrgang. Zu einigen Aspekten des Kriegseinsatzes der Hitlerjugend in der Endphase des Zweiten Weltkrieges', in Ulrich Herrmann and Rolf-Dieter Müller (eds), *Junge Soldaten im Zweiten Weltkrieg. Kriegserfahrungen als Lebenserfahrungen* (Weinheim, 2010), 240–72.

Bude, Heinz, *Deutsche Karrieren. Lebenskonstruktionen sozialer Aufsteiger aus der Flakhelfer-Generation* (Frankfurt am Main, 1987).

Buggeln, Marc and Wildt, Michael (eds), *Arbeit im Nationalsozialismus* (Munich, 2014).

Bugiel, Gerhard, et al. (eds), *150 Jahre Weierhof—(mindestens) 150 Facetten. Festschrift des Gymnasiums Weierhof am Donnersberg zum 150. Jubiläum 1867–2017* (Göllheim, 2017).

Bukey, Evan Burr, *Hitler's Austria: Popular Sentiment in the Nazi Era, 1938–1945* (Chapel Hill, 2000).

Bunnenberg, Christian, '"Daher sieht es die Partei als ihre vornehmste Aufgabe an...". "Schulungen" als Instrumente der Differenzierung und Kontrolle', in Nicole Kramer and Armin Nolzen (eds), *Ungleichheiten im 'Dritten Reich'. Semantiken, Praktiken, Erfahrungen* (Göttingen, 2012), 139–54.

Burleigh, Michael, *Germany Turns Eastwards: A Study of* Ostforschung *in the Third Reich* (Cambridge, 1988).

Burleigh, Michael and Wippermann, Wolfgang, *The Racial State: Germany 1933–1945* (Cambridge, 1991).

Buruma, Ian, *The Wages of Guilt: Memories of War in Germany and Japan* (London, 1994).

Canning, Kathleen, et al. (eds), *Weimar Publics/Weimar Subjects: Rethinking the Political Culture of Germany in the 1920s* (New York, 2010).

Caplan, Jane, *Government without Administration: State and Civil Service in Weimar and Nazi Germany* (Oxford, 1988).

Caplan, Jane (ed.), *Nazi Germany* (Oxford, 2008).

Carsten, Francis L., *Fascist Movements in Austria: From Schönerer to Hitler* (London, 1977).

Casagrande, Thomas, et al., 'The Volksdeutsche: A Case Study from South-Eastern Europe', in Jochen Böhler and Robert Gerwarth (eds), *The Waffen SS: A European History* (Oxford, 2017), 209–51.

Century, Rachel, *Female Administrators of the Third Reich* (Basingstoke, 2017).

Christensen, Claus Bundgård, et al., 'Germanic Volunteers from Northern Europe', in Jochen Böhler and Robert Gerwarth (eds), *The Waffen SS: A European History* (Oxford, 2017), 42–75.

Chroust, Peter, 'Universität und Studium', in Klaus-Peter Horn and Jörg-W. Link (eds), *Erziehungsverhältnisse im Nationalsozialismus. Totaler Anspruch und Erziehungswirklichkeit* (Bad Heilbrunn, 2011), 205–28.

Chu, Winson, 'National Socialism and Hierarchical Regionalism: The German Minorities in Interwar Poland', in Claus-Christian W. Szejnmann and Maiken Umbach (eds), *Heimat, Region and Empire. Spatial Identities under National Socialism* (Basingstoke, 2012), 72–90.

Chu, Winson, *The German Minority in Interwar Poland* (Cambridge, 2012).

Ciupke, Paul and Jelich, Franz-Josef, '"Steinerner Zeuge des Ewigkeitswillens"? Zur Diskussion um Geschichte und künftige Gestaltung der NS-Ordensburg Vogelsang—eine Einleitung', in Paul Ciupke and Franz-Josef Jelich (eds), *Weltanschauliche Erziehung in Ordensburgen des Nationalsozialismus. Zur Geschichte und Zukunft der Ordensburg Vogelsang* (Essen, 2006), 7–13.

Ciupke, Paul and Jelich, Franz-Josef (eds), *Weltanschauliche Erziehung in Ordensburgen des Nationalsozialismus. Zur Geschichte und Zukunft der Ordensburg Vogelsang* (Essen, 2006).

Clark, Christopher, *Iron Kingdom: The Rise and Downfall of Prussia, 1600–1947* (London, 2006).

Conrad, Claus W., 'Nationalsozialistische Erziehung. Die Reichsschulen für Volksdeutsche in Achern und Rufach', *Geschichte und Region* 4 (1995), 245–69.

Conradt, Marieluise, *Vom Königlichen Württembergischen Lehrerseminar zum Staatlichen Aufbaugymnasium des Landes Baden-Württemberg. 1912 bis 1994 in Rottweil: eine Schulchronik* (Rottweil, 1994).

Conway, J. S., *The Nazi Persecution of the Churches 1933–45* (London, 1968).

Conze, Vanessa, '"Unverheilte Brandwunden in der Außenhaut des Volkskörpers". Der deutsche Grenz-Diskurs der Zwischenkriegszeit (1919–1939)', in Wolfgang Hardtwig (ed.), *Ordnungen in der Krise. Zur politischen Kulturgeschichte Deutschlands 1900–1933* (Munich, 2007), 21–48.

Coser, Lewis A., *Greedy Institutions: Patterns of Undivided Commitment* (New York, 1974).

Czech, Michaela, *Frauen und Sport im nationalsozialistischen Deutschland. Eine Untersuchung zur weiblichen Sportrealität in einem patriarchalen Herrschaftssystem* (Berlin, 1994).

Dachs, Herbert, *Schule und Politik. Die politische Erziehung an den österreichischen Schulen 1918 bis 1938* (Vienna, 1982).

Dachs, Herbert, 'Schule in der "Ostmark"', in Emmerich Tálos et al. (eds), *NS-Herrschaft in Österreich. Ein Handbuch* (Vienna, 2002), 446–66.

Dack, Mikkel, 'Retreating into Trauma: The Fragebogen, Denazification, and Victimhood in Postwar Germany', in Peter Leese and Jason Crouthamel (eds), *Traumatic Memories of the Second World War and After* (Basingstoke, 2016), 143–70.

Dagnino, Jorge, Feldman, Matthew, and Stocker, Paul (eds), *The 'New Man' in Radical Right Ideology and Practice, 1919–45* (London, 2018).

Dahm, Volker, 'Nationale Einheit und partikulare Vielfalt. Zur Frage der kulturpolitischen Gleichschaltung im Dritten Reich', *Vierteljahrshefte für Zeitgeschichte* 43, no. 2 (1995), 221–65.

Deutsche Gesetzliche Unfallversicherung e.V. (ed.), *Lernräume. Von der Landesschule Dresden zur Akademie* (Dresden, 2009).

Deutsches Historisches Museum, '"Bildberichterstatterin" im "Dritten Reich". Fotografien aus den Jahren 1937 bis 1944 von Liselotte Purper', *DHM Magazin* 7, no. 20 (1997).

Didczuneit, Veit, et al. (eds), *Schreiben im Krieg, Schreiben vom Krieg. Feldpost im Zeitalter der Weltkriege* (Essen, 2011).

Dierker, Wolfgang, *Himmlers Glaubenskrieger. Der Sicherheitsdienst der SS und seine Religionspolitik 1933–1941* (Paderborn, 2002).

Dietz, Burkhard, et al. (eds), *Griff nach dem Westen. Die 'Westforschung' der völkisch-nationalen Wissenschaften zum nordwesteuropäischen Raum (1919–1960) (Vol. 1)* (Münster, 2003).

Dillon, Christopher, *Dachau and the SS: A Schooling in Violence* (Oxford, 2015).

Ditt, Karl, 'Regionalismus in Demokratie und Diktatur. Die Politisierung der kulturellen Identitätsstiftung im Deutschen Reich 1919–1945', *Westfälische Forschungen* 49 (1999), 421–36.

Dluhosch, Ursula and Rotte, Ralph, 'Das Kultusministerium als Machtfaktor in der NS-Schulpolitik: Bürokratische Friktionen am Beispiel Bayerns', *Paedagogica Historica: International Journal of the History of Education* 37, no. 2 (2001), 317–40.

Dodd, Lyndsey, 'Mon petit papa chéri: Children, Fathers and Family Separation in Vichy France', *Essays in French Literature and Culture* 54 (2017), 97–116.

Dodd, Lyndsey, 'Children's Citizenly Participation in the National Revolution: The Instrumentalization of Children in Vichy France', *European Review of History/revue européenne d'histoire* 24, no. 5 (2017), 759–80.

Doerfel, Marianne, 'Der Griff des NS-Regimes nach Elite-Schulen. Stätten klassischer Bildungstradition zwischen Anpassung und Widerstand', *Vierteljahrshefte für Zeitgeschichte* 37, no. 3 (1989), 401–55.

Domansky, Elisabeth, 'A Lost War: World War II in Postwar German Memory', in Alvin H. Rosenfeld (ed.), *Thinking about the Holocaust—After Half a Century* (Bloomington, 1997), 233–72.

Dorfmüller, Petra and Konetzny, Rudolf, *'Damit es an gelahrten Leuten in unsern Landen nicht Mangel gewinne.' Schulpforta 1543–1993: Ein Lesebuch* (Leipzig, 1993).

Douglas, R. M., *Orderly and Humane: The Expulsion of the Germans after the Second World War* (New Haven, 2012).

Dreetz, Dieter (ed.), *Kriegsende. Erlebnisse von Schülern der Körner- und späteren Hegelschule vom Januar bis Mai 1945* (Berlin, 2006).

Dreyfus, Jean-Marc, 'Germanisierungspolitik im Elsass 1940–1945', in Jerzy Kochanowski and Maike Sach (eds), *Die 'Volksdeutschen' in Polen, Frankreich, Ungarn und der Tschechoslowakei. Mythos und Realität* (Osnabrück, 2006), 205–23.

Duff, Shiela Grant, *A German Protectorate: The Czechs under Nazi Rule* (London, 1942).

Dülffer, Jost, 'Die Erschließung von Vogelsang. Wissenschaftlicher Stand, sprachlicher Umgang und historischer Rahmen', in Albert Moritz (ed.), *'Fackelträger der Nation'. Elitebildung in den NS-Ordensburgen* (Cologne, 2010), 9–19.

Dwyer, Philip G. (ed.), *Modern Prussian History 1830–1947* (Harlow, 2001).

Dwyer, Philip G., 'Introduction: Modern Prussia—Continuity and Change', in Philip G. Dwyer (ed.), *Modern Prussian History 1830–1947* (Harlow, 2001), 1–20.

Ebner, Christopher (ed.), *Festschrift 75 Jahre Abteigymnasium der Benediktiner in Seckau mit Öffentlichkeitsrecht (1931–2006)* (Seckau, 2006).

Echternkamp, Jörg (ed.), *Germany and the Second World War, Volume IX/I. German Wartime Society 1939–1945: Politicization, Disintegration, and the Struggle for Survival* (Oxford, 2008).

Echternkamp, Jörg, *Soldaten im Nachkrieg: Historische Deutungskonflikte und westdeutsche Demokratisierung 1945–1955* (Munich, 2014).

Egger, Franz, 'Schüler der "NAPOLA Wien-Theresianum" 1941–45', in Gerhard Moser (ed.), *Das Stadtbuch St. Johann im Pongau* (St. Johann im Pongau, 2005), 298–302.

Eichmüller, Andreas, *Die SS in der Bundesrepublik. Debatten und Diskurse über ehemalige SS-Angehörige 1949–1985* (Berlin, 2018).

Eickhoff, Thomas, *Politische Dimensionen einer Komponisten-Biographie im 20. Jahrhundert—Gottfried von Einem* (Stuttgart, 1998).

Elvert, Jürgen, *Mitteleuropa! Deutsche Pläne zur europäischen Neuordnung (1918–1945)* (Stuttgart, 1999).

Engehausen, Frank, 'Ehemalige Ordensburgangehörige vor Gericht—Ermittlungen und Prozesse der bundesdeutschen Strafjustiz', in Klaus Ring and Stefan Wunsch (eds), *Bestimmung: Herrenmensch. NS-Ordensburgen zwischen Faszination und Verbrechen* (Dresden, 2016), 340–7.

Engelbrecht, Helmut, 'Tendenzen der österreichischen Schulpolitik in der Zwischenkriegszeit', in Manfred Heinemann (ed.), *Sozialisation und Bildungswesen in der Weimarer Republik* (Stuttgart, 1976), 203–29.

Engelbrecht, Helmut, 'Die Eingriffe des Dritten Reiches in das österreichische Schulwesen', in Manfred Heinemann (ed.), *Erziehung und Schulung im Dritten Reich. Teil 1: Kindergarten, Schule, Jugend, Berufserziehung* (Stuttgart, 1980), 113–59.

Engelbrecht, Helmut, *Geschichte des österreichischen Bildungswesens. Erziehung und Unterricht auf dem Boden Österreichs Band 5: Von 1918 bis zur Gegenwart* (Vienna, 1988).

Epstein, Catherine, *Model Nazi: Arthur Greiser and the Occupation of Western Poland* (Oxford, 2010).

Erfurt, Vereinigten Kirchen- und Klosterkammer, *800 Jahre Stift Ilfeld—1189–1989* (Heiligenstadt, 1989).

Esden-Tempska, Carla, 'Civic Education in Authoritarian Austria', *History of Education Quarterly* 30, no. 2 (1990), 187–211.

Evans, Richard J., *The Coming of the Third Reich* (London, 2003).

Evans, Richard J., *The Third Reich in Power* (London, 2006).

Evans, Richard J., *The Third Reich at War* (London, 2008).

Evans, Richard J., 'The Emergence of Nazi Ideology', in Jane Caplan (ed.), *Nazi Germany* (Oxford, 2008), 26–47.

Fass, Paula S., 'Introduction: Is There a Story in the History of Childhood?', in Paula S. Fass (ed.), *The Routledge History of Childhood in the Western World* (New York, 2013), 1–14.

Förderverein Fürstliches Pädagogium zu Putbus, *175 Jahre Bildungstradition am Putbusser Circus. Die Geschichte des Königlichen Pädagogiums und seiner nachfolgenden Einrichtungen bis zum IT-College Putbus* (3rd edn; Putbus, 2011).

Frauengruppe Faschismusforschung (ed.), *Mutterkreuz und Arbeitsbuch. Zur Geschichte der Frauen in der Weimarer Republik und im Nationalsozialismus* (Frankfurt am Main, 1981).

Feiten, Willi, *Der Nationalsozialistische Lehrerbund: Entwicklung und Organisation. Ein Beitrag zum Aufbau und zur Organisationsstruktur des nationalsozialistischen Herrschaftssystems* (Weinheim, 1981).

Feller, Barbara and Feller, Wolfgang, *Die Adolf-Hitler-Schulen. Pädagogische Provinz versus ideologische Zuchtanstalt* (Weinheim, 2001).

Feltz, Nina and Meyer-Lenz, Johanna, 'Franz P. (Jahrgang 1934) "Sei stark, werde nicht schwach—Du kannst noch einsamer sein, als Du denkst!" Zu den Einflüssen des nationalsozialistischen Männlichkeitsbildes in der Nachkriegszeit', in Johanna Meyer-Lenz (ed.), *Die Ordnung des Paares ist unbehaglich. Irritationen um und im Geschlechterdiskurs nach 1945* (Hamburg, 2000).

Fichtner, Klaus-Dieter, *Schulpforte. Geschichte und Geschichten* (Schulpforte, 2011).

Finger, Jürgen, 'Gaue und Länder als Akteure der nationalsozialistischen Schulpolitik. Württemberg als Sonderfall und Musterbeispiel im Altreich', in Jürgen John, Horst Möller, and Thomas Schaarschmidt (eds), *Die NS-Gaue. Regionale Mittelinstanzen im zentralistischen 'Führerstaat'* (Munich, 2007), 159–76.

Finger, Jürgen, *Eigensinn im Einheitsstaat. NS-Schulpolitik in Württemberg, Baden und im Elsass 1933–1945* (Baden-Baden, 2016).

Fischl, Hans, *Schulreform, Demokratie und Österreich 1918–1950* (Vienna, n.d.).

Fisher, Jaimey, *Disciplining Germany: Youth, Reeducation, and Reconstruction after the Second World War* (Detroit, 2007).

Flessau, Kurt-Ingo, *Schule der Diktatur. Lehrpläne und Schulbücher des Nationalsozialismus* (Munich, 1977).

Flessau, Kurt-Ingo, 'Schulen der Partei(lichkeit)? Notizen zum allgemeinbildenden Schulwesen des Dritten Reichs', in Kurt-Ingo Flessau, Elke Nyssen, and Günter Patzold (eds), *Erziehung im Nationalsozialismus. '... und sie werden nicht mehr frei ihr ganzes Leben!'* (Cologne, 1987), 65–82.

Flessau, Kurt-Ingo, Nyssen, Elke, and Patzold, Günter (eds), *Erziehung im Nationalsozialismus. '... und sie werden nicht mehr frei ihr ganzes Leben!'* (Cologne, 1987).

Flöter, Jonas, 'Prestige und Kalkül. Das Stiftungswesen an den sächsischen Fürsten- und Landesschulen im 19. Jahrhundert', in Jonas Flöter (ed.), *Bildungsmäzenatentum. Privates Handeln, Bürgersinn, kulturelle Kompetenz seit der Frühen Neuzeit* (Cologne, 2007), 251–310.

Flöter, Jonas, 'Religiöse Bildung und Erziehung. Die Landesschule Pforta und das Joachimsthalsche Gymnasium im Kaiserreich und in der Weimarer Republik', in Michael Berger, Jonas Flöter, and Markus Hein (eds), *Christlicher Glaube und weltliche Herrschaft* (Leipzig, 2008), 355–67.

Flöter, Jonas, 'Der Wert der humanistischen Bildung. Zur Diskussion um Kultur und Curriculum an den Fürsten- und Landesschulen Grimma, Meißen, Schulpforte und Joachimsthal in der Zwischenkriegszeit', *Das Altertum* 53 (2008), 3–20.

Flöter, Jonas, *Eliten-Bildung in Sachsen und Preußen. Die Fürsten- und Landesschulen Grimma, Meißen, Joachimsthal und Pforta (1868–1933)* (Cologne, 2009).

Flöter, Jonas, 'Reformpädagogik in der religiösen Bildung und Erziehung. Religionsunterricht und Alumnatserziehung an der Landesschule Pforta und am Joachimsthalschen Gymnasium im ersten Drittel des 20. Jahrhunderts', in Michael

Wermke (ed.), *Religionspädagogik und Reformpädagogik. Brüche, Kontinuitäten, Neuanfänge* (Jena, 2010), 155–75.
Flöter, Jonas, 'Von der Landesschule zur Nationalpolitischen Erziehungsanstalt—Transformationsprozesse in Schulpforte und deren Rückwirkungen auf den Religionsunterricht', in Michael Wermke (ed.), *Transformation und religiöse Erziehung. Kontinuitäten und Brüche der Religionspädagogik 1933 und 1945* (Jena, 2011), 35–52.
Flöter, Jonas and Pesenecker, Marita (eds), *Erziehung zur Elite. Die Fürsten- und Landesschulen zu Grimma, Meißen und Schulpforte um 1900. Publikation zur Ausstellung* (Leipzig, 2003).
Föllmer, Moritz, 'Which Crisis? Which Modernity? New Perspectives on Weimar Germany', in Jochen Hung, Godela Weiss-Sussex, and Geoff Wilkes (eds), *Beyond Glitter and Doom: The Contingency of the Weimar Republic* (Munich, 2012), 19–30.
Föllmer, Moritz, 'The Subjective Dimension of Nazism', *The Historical Journal* 56, no. 4 (2013), 1107–32.
Föllmer, Moritz, *Individuality and Modernity in Berlin: Self and Society from Weimar to the Wall* (Cambridge, 2013).
Föllmer, Moritz, *'Ein Leben wie im Traum': Kultur im Dritten Reich* (Munich, 2016).
Förschler, Andreas, 'Die Nationalpolitische Erziehungsanstalt (NPEA) in Backnang', *Backnanger Jahrbuch* 15 (2007), 202–42 (Teil I); *Backnanger Jahrbuch* 16 (2008), 147–80 (Teil II).
Frei, Norbert, *Adenauer's Germany and the Nazi Past: The Politics of Amnesty and Integration* (New York, 2002).
Frei, Norbert, *1945 und wir: Das Dritte Reich im Bewußtsein der Deutschen* (Munich, 2009).
Frevert, Ute, *Women in German History: From Bourgeois Emancipation to Sexual Liberation* (New York, 1990).
Fritzsche, Peter, *Rehearsals for Fascism: Populism and Political Mobilization in Weimar Germany* (New York, 1990).
Fritzsche, Peter, 'Did Weimar Fail?', *Journal of Modern History* 68, no. 3 (1996), 629–56.
Fritzsche, Peter, 'The NSDAP 1919–1934: From Fringe Politics to the Seizure of Power', in Jane Caplan (ed.), *Nazi Germany* (Oxford, 2008), 48–72.
Fritzsche, Peter, *Life and Death in the Third Reich* (Cambridge, MA, 2008).
Fröhlich, Elke, 'Die drei Typen der nationalsozialistischen Ausleseschulen', in Johannes Leeb (ed.), *'Wir waren Hitlers Eliteschüler'. Ehemalige Zöglinge der NS-Ausleseschulen brechen ihr Schweigen* (Munich, 2005), 241–63.
Fuhrmann, Horst, *Einladung ins Mittelalter* (Munich, 1997).
Fulbrook, Mary, *German National Identity after the Holocaust* (Cambridge, 1999).
Fulbrook, Mary, *Dissonant Lives: Generations and Violence through the German Dictatorships* (Oxford, 2011).
Fulbrook, Mary, 'History-Writing and "Collective Memory"', in Stefan Berger and Bill Niven (eds), *Writing the History of Memory* (London, 2014), 65–88.
Fulbrook, Mary, 'Guilt and Shame among Communities of Experience, Connection and Identification', in Stephanie Bird et al. (eds), *Reverberations of Nazi Violence in Germany and Beyond: Disturbing Pasts* (London, 2016), 15–31.
Fulbrook, Mary and Rublack, Ulinka, 'In Relation: The "Social Self" and Ego-Documents', *German History* 28, no. 3 (2010), 263–72.
Fulda, Daniel, et al. (eds), *Demokratie im Schatten der Gewalt. Geschichten des Privaten im deutschen Nachkrieg* (Göttingen, 2010).
Gailus, Manfred, *Protestantismus und Nationalsozialismus. Studien zur nationalsozialistischen Durchdringung des protestantischen Sozialmilieus in Berlin* (Cologne, 2001).

Gailus, Manfred and Nolzen, Armin (eds), *Zerstrittene 'Volksgemeinschaft'. Glaube, Konfession und Religion im Nationalsozialismus* (Göttingen, 2011).

Gallin, Isabel, 'Machtstrukturen im Reichskommissariat Niederlande', in Robert Bohn (ed.), *Die deutsche Herrschaft in den 'germanischen' Ländern 1940–1945* (Stuttgart, 1997), 145–57.

Gassert, Philipp and Steinweis, Alan E. (eds), *Coping with the Nazi Past: West German Debates on Nazism and Generational Conflict, 1955–1975* (New York, 2006).

Gebel, Ralf, *'Heim ins Reich!' Konrad Henlein und der Reichsgau Sudetenland (1938–1945)* (2nd edn; Munich, 2000).

Gehmacher, Johanna, *Jugend ohne Zukunft. Hitler-Jugend und Bund Deutscher Mädel in Österreich vor 1938* (Vienna, 1994).

Gehmacher, Johanna, 'Illegale nationalsozialistische Jugendorganisierung in Österreich 1933–1938: Mobilisierungsmuster im Regionalvergleich', in Thomas Albrich and Werner Matt (eds), *Geschichte und Region. Die NSDAP in den 30er Jahren im Regionalvergleich: Forschungsberichte—Fachgespräche* (Dornbirn, 1995), 101–13.

Gehmacher, Johanna, 'Jugendbewegung und Jugendorganisation in der Ersten Republik', in Emmerich Tálos et al. (eds), *Handbuch des politischen Systems Österreichs: Erste Republik 1918–1933* (Vienna, 1995), 292–303.

Gehmacher, Johanna, 'Fluchten, Aufbrüche: Junge Österreicher und Österreicherinnen im nationalsozialistischen Deutschland 1933–1938', in Traude Horvath and Gerda Neyer (eds), *Auswanderungen aus Österreich: Von der Mitte des 19. Jahrhunderts bis zur Gegenwart* (Vienna, 1996), 211–32.

Gehmacher, Johanna, 'Zukunft, die nicht vergehen will: Jugenderfahrungen in NS-Organisationen und Lebensentwürfe österreichischer Frauen', in Christina Benninghaus and Kerstin Kohtz (eds), *'Sag mir, wo die Mädchen sind...' Beiträge zur Geschlechtergeschichte der Jugend* (Vienna, 1999), 261–74.

Gehmacher, Johanna, 'Biografie, Geschlecht und Organisation: Der "Bund Deutscher Mädel" in Österreich', in Dagmar Reese (ed.), *Die BDM-Generation: Weibliche Jugendliche in Deutschland und Österreich im Nationalsozialismus* (Berlin, 2007), 159–213.

Gellott, Laura, 'Recent Writings on the Ständestaat, 1934–1938', *Austrian History Yearbook* 26 (1995), 207–38.

Gentsch, Dirk, 'Potsdam—ein Standort nationalsozialistischer Eliteschulen. "Die Politik macht die Schule—nicht die Pädagogik!" Rousseau "Emile" (1762)', *Pädagogik und Erziehungswissenschaft* 49, no. 4 (1994), 478–82.

Geyer, Michael, 'The Stigma of Violence, Nationalism, and War in Twentieth-Century Germany', *German Studies Review* 15 (1992), 75–110.

Geyer, Michael, 'The Place of the Second World War in German Memory and History', *New German Critique* 71 (1997), 5–40.

Geyer, Michael, 'Die eingebildete Heimkehr: Im Schatten der Niederlage', in Daniel Fulda et al. (eds), *Demokratie im Schatten der Gewalt. Geschichten des Privaten im deutschen Nachkrieg* (Göttingen, 2010), 72–96.

Giesecke, Hermann, *Hitlers Pädagogen. Theorie und Praxis nationalsozialistischer Erziehung* (Weinheim, 1993).

Goffman, Erving, *Asylums: Essays on the Social Situation of Mental Patients and Other Inmates* (London, 2007).

Goltermann, Svenja, *The War in Their Minds: German Soldiers and Their Violent Pasts in West Germany* (Ann Arbor, 2017).

Goossen, Benjamin W., *Chosen Nation: Mennonites and Germany in a Global Era* (Princeton, 2017).

Göpfert, Rebekka, 'Oral History: Über die Zusammensetzung individueller Erinnerung im Interview', in Clemens Wischermann (ed.), *Die Legitimität der Erinnerung und die Geschichtswissenschaft* (Stuttgart, 1996), 101–11.

Gotto, Klaus and Repgen, Konrad (eds), *Die Katholiken und das Dritte Reich* (Mainz, 1990).

Gretzel, Peter, *'Klostersturm' im Gau 'Niederdonau'. Die Geschicke des nicht enteigneten Zisterzienserstiftes Zwettl* (St. Pölten, 2017).

Griffiths, Richard, *Fellow Travellers of the Right: British Enthusiasts for Nazi Germany, 1933–1939* (London, 1980).

Grill, Johnpeter Horst, 'Local and Regional Studies on National Socialism: A Review', *Journal of Contemporary History* 21 (1986), 253–94.

Groppe, Carola, 'Reformpädagogik und soziale Ungleichheit', in Wolfgang Keim, Ulrich Schwerdt, and Sabine Reh (eds), *Reformpädagogik und Reformpädagogik-Rezeption in neuer Sicht. Perspektiven und Impulse* (Bad Heilbrunn, 2016), 73–95.

Gross, Jan Tomasz, *Polish Society under German Occupation: The Generalgouvernement, 1939–1944* (Princeton, 1979).

Gross, Raphael, *Anständig geblieben. Nationalsozialistische Moral* (Frankfurt am Main, 2010).

Großruck, Johann, *Benediktinerstift Lambach im Dritten Reich 1938–1945. Ein Kloster im Fokus von Hitlermythos und Hakenkreuzlegende* (Linz, 2011).

Gruber, Helmut, *Red Vienna: Experiment in Working-Class Culture, 1919–1934* (Oxford, 1991).

Grüttner, Michael, 'Hochschulpolitik zwischen Gau und Reich', in Jürgen John, Horst Möller, and Thomas Schaarschmidt (eds), *Die NS-Gaue. Regionale Mittelinstanzen im zentralistischen 'Führerstaat'* (Munich, 2007), 177–93.

Guglia, Eugen, *Das Theresianum in Wien. Vergangenheit und Gegenwart* (Vienna, 1996).

Gulick, Charles A., *Austria from Habsburg to Hitler. Volume I: Labor's Workshop of Democracy* (Berkeley, 1948).

Gutmann, Martin R., *Building a Nazi Europe: The SS's Germanic Volunteers* (Cambridge, 2017).

Hachmeister, Lutz, *Der Gegnerforscher. Die Karriere des SS-Führers Franz Alfred Six* (Munich, 1998).

Hachtmann, Rüdiger, '"Volksgemeinschaftliche Dienstleister"? Anmerkungen zu Selbstverständnis und Funktion der Deutschen Arbeitsfront und der NS-Gemeinschaft "Kraft durch Freude"', in Detlef Schmiechen-Ackermann (ed.), *'Volksgemeinschaft': Mythos, wirkungsmächtige soziale Verheißung oder soziale Realität im 'Dritten Reich'?* (Paderborn, 2012), 111–31.

Hachtmann, Rüdiger, 'Social Spaces of the Nazi *Volksgemeinschaft* in the Making: Functional Elites and Club Networking', in Martina Steber and Bernhard Gotto (eds), *Visions of Community in Nazi Germany: Social Engineering and Private Lives* (Oxford, 2014), 200–14.

Hachtmann, Rüdiger and Süß, Winfried (eds), *Hitlers Kommissare. Sondergewalten in der nationalsozialistischen Diktatur* (Göttingen, 2006).

Hagemann, Karen and Schüler-Springorum, Stefanie (eds), *Heimat-Front. Militär und Geschlechterverhältnisse im Zeitalter der Weltkriege* (Frankfurt am Main, 2002).

Hansen, Georg (ed.), *Schulpolitik als Volkstumspolitik. Quellen zur Schulpolitik der Besatzer in Polen 1939–1945* (Münster, 1994).

Hansen, Georg, *Ethnische Schulpolitik im besetzten Polen: der Mustergau Wartheland* (Münster, 1995).

Hansen, Georg, 'Schulpolitik im besetzten Polen 1939–1945', *bildungsforschung* 3, no. 1 (2006).

Harrison, E. D. R., 'The Nazi Dissolution of the Monasteries: A Case Study', *English Historical Review* CIX (1994), 323–55.

Hart, Bradley W., *Hitler's American Friends: The Third Reich's Supporters in the United States* (New York, 2018).

Harten, Hans-Christian, *De-Kulturation und Germanisierung. Die nationalsozialistische Rassen- und Erziehungspolitik in Polen 1939–1945* (Frankfurt am Main, 1996).

Harten, Hans-Christian, *Himmlers Lehrer. Die Weltanschauliche Schulung in der SS 1933–1945* (Paderborn, 2014).

Harvey, Elizabeth, *Youth and the Welfare State in Weimar Germany* (Oxford, 1993).

Harvey, Elizabeth, *Women and the Nazi East: Agents and Witnesses of Germanization* (New Haven, 2003).

Harvey, Elizabeth, '"Ich war überall". Die NS-Propagandaphotographin Liselotte Purper', in Sybille Steinbacher (ed.), *Volksgenossinnen. Frauen in der NS-Volksgemeinschaft* (Göttingen, 2007), 138–53.

Hauer, Wolfram, 'Das Elsass als "Erziehungsproblem". Zur Umgestaltung des Schulwesens und der Lehrerbildung jenseits des Rheins nach badischem Vorbild (1940–1945)', in Konrad Krimm (ed.), *NS-Kulturpolitik und Gesellschaft am Oberrhein 1940–1945* (Ostfildern, 2013), 161–260.

Hauptverband der gewerblichen Berufsgenossenschaften, *Zur Geschichte des Standortes der Berufsgenossenschaftlichen Akademie für Arbeitssicherheit und Gesundheitsschutz: Landesschule Dresden in Klotzsche (1927–1933)* (Dresden, 2001).

Hayse, Michael R., *Recasting West German Elites: Higher Civil Servants, Business Leaders, and Physicians in Hesse between Nazism and Democracy, 1945–1955* (Oxford, 2003).

Heggen, Alfred, 'Die offizielle Einweihung der Nationalpolitischen Erziehungsanstalt "Ernst Röhm" in Plön am 28. Oktober 1933', *Jahrbuch für Heimatkunde im Kreis Plön* 37 (2007), 46–62.

Heggen, Alfred, 'Joachim Haupt (1900–1989): Ein früher NSDAP-Aktivist in Schleswig-Holstein', *Zeitschrift der Gesellschaft für Schleswig-Holsteinische Geschichte* 134 (2009), 193–203.

Hehl, Ulrich von, 'Nationalsozialismus und Region. Bedeutung und Probleme einer regionalen und lokalen Erforschung des Dritten Reiches', *Zeitschrift für bayerische Landesgeschichte* 56, no. 1 (1993), 111–29.

Hein, Bastian, *Elite für Volk und Führer? Die Allgemeine SS und ihre Mitglieder 1925–1945* (Munich, 2012).

Hein, Bastian, 'Eine "Tat-Elite" in der "Volksgemeinschaft". Vergemeinschaftung im Rahmen der Auslese und Praxis der Allgemeinen SS', in David Reinicke et al. (eds), *Gemeinschaft als Erfahrung. Kulturelle Inszenierungen und soziale Praxis 1930–1960* (Paderborn, 2014), 113–28.

Heineman, Elizabeth D., *What Difference Does a Husband Make? Women and Marital Status in Nazi and Postwar Germany* (Berkeley, 1999).

Heinemann, Isabel, *'Rasse, Siedlung, deutsches Blut'. Das Rasse- und Siedlungshauptamt der SS und die rassenpolitische Neuordnung Europas* (Göttingen, 2003).

Heinemann, Isabel, '"Until the Last Drop of Good Blood": The Kidnapping of "Racially Valuable" Children and Nazi Racial Policy in Occupied Eastern Europe', in A. Dirk Moses (ed.), *Genocide and Settler Society: Frontier Violence and Stolen Indigenous Children in Australian History* (New York, 2004), 244–66.

Heinen, Franz Albert, '"Des Führers treueste Soldaten und seiner Idee glühendste Prediger". Das System der NS-Ordensburgen', in Albert Moritz (ed.), *'Fackelträger der Nation'. Elitebildung in den NS-Ordensburgen* (Cologne, 2010), 20–46.

Heinlein, Michael, *Die Erfindung der Erinnerung. Deutsche Kriegskindheiten im Gedächtnis der Gegenwart* (Bielefeld, 2010).

Heinsohn, Kirsten, 'Germany', in Kevin Passmore (ed.), *Women, Gender and Fascism in Europe, 1919–45* (Manchester, 2003), 33–56.

Heinsohn, Kirsten, Vogel, Barbara, and Weckel, Ulrike (eds), *Zwischen Karriere und Verfolgung. Handlungsräume von Frauen im nationalsozialistischen Deutschland* (Frankfurt am Main, 1997).

Helmreich, E. C., *The German Churches under Hitler: Background, Struggle, and Epilogue* (Detroit, 1979).

Herbert, Ulrich, 'Echoes of the *Volksgemeinschaft*', in Martina Steber and Bernhard Gotto (eds), *Visions of Community in Nazi Germany: Social Engineering and Private Lives* (Oxford, 2014), 60–9.

Hering, Sabine and Schilde, Kurt, *Das BDM-Werk 'Glaube und Schönheit'. Die Organisation junger Frauen im Nationalsozialismus* (Berlin, 2000).

Hermann, Konstantin (ed.), *Führerschule, Thingplatz, 'Judenhaus'. Topografien der NS-Herrschaft in Sachsen* (Dresden, 2014).

Hermann, Konstantin, 'Erzgebirge—Brauch und Missbrauch einer Region', in Konstantin Hermann (ed.), *Führerschule, Thingplatz, 'Judenhaus'. Topografien der NS-Herrschaft in Sachsen* (Dresden, 2014), 26–33.

Herrmann, Ulrich (ed.), *'Neue Erziehung': 'Neue Menschen'. Ansätze zur Erziehungs- und Bildungsreform in Deutschland zwischen Kaiserreich und Diktatur* (Weinheim, 1987).

Herrmann, Ulrich and Müller, Rolf-Dieter (eds), *Junge Soldaten im Zweiten Weltkrieg. Kriegserfahrungen als Lebenserfahrungen* (Weinheim, 2010).

Herrmann, Ulrich and Nassen, Ulrich, 'Die ästhetische Inszenierung von Herrschaft und Beherrschung im nationalsozialistischen Deutschland. Über die ästhetischen und ästhetik-politischen Strategien nationalsozialistischer Herrschaftspraxis, deren mentalitäre Voraussetzungen und Konsequenzen', in Ulrich Herrmann and Ulrich Nassen (eds), *Formative Ästhetik im Nationalsozialismus: Intentionen, Medien und Praxisformen totalitärer ästhetischer Herrschaft und Beherrschung* (Weinheim, 1994), 9–12.

Herrmann, Ulrich and Oelkers, Jürgen, 'Zur Einführung in die Thematik "Pädagogik und Nationalsozialismus"', in Ulrich Herrmann and Jürgen Oelkers (eds), *Pädagogik und Nationalsozialismus* (Weinheim, 1989), 9–17.

Herrmann, Ulrich and Oelkers, Jürgen (eds), *Pädagogik und Nationalsozialismus* (Weinheim, 1989).

Heumann, Hans, *Schulpforta. Tradition und Wandel einer Eliteschule* (Erfurt, 1994).

Heydemann, Günther, et al., 'Sachsen und der Nationalsozialismus. Zur Vielfalt gesellschaftlicher Teilhabe—Einführung', in Günther Heydemann, Jan Erik Schulte, and Francesca Weil (eds), *Sachsen und der Nationalsozialismus* (Göttingen, 2014), 9–19.

Heydemann, Günther, Schulte, Jan Erik, and Weil, Francesca (eds), *Sachsen und der Nationalsozialismus* (Göttingen, 2014).

Hirschfeld, Gerhard, *Nazi Rule and Dutch Collaboration: The Netherlands under German Occupation 1940–1945* (Oxford, 1988).

Hirschfeld, Gerhard, 'Formen nationalsozialistischer Besatzungspolitik im Zweiten Weltkrieg', in Joachim Tauber (ed.), *'Kollaboration' in Nordosteuropa. Erscheinungsformen und Deutungen im 20. Jahrhundert* (Wiesbaden, 2006), 40–55.

Hirschfeld, Gerhard and Kettenacker, Lothar, *The 'Führer State'. Myth and Reality. Studies on the Structure and Politics of the Third Reich* (Stuttgart, 1981).

Hochstetter, Dorothee, *Motorisierung und 'Volksgemeinschaft'. Das Nationalsozialistische Kraftfahrkorps (NSKK) 1931–1945* (Munich, 2005).

Hockerts, Hans Günter, 'Zugänge zur Zeitgeschichte: Primärerfahrung, Erinnerungskultur, Geschichtswissenschaft', in Konrad Jarausch and Martin Sabrow (eds), *Verletztes Gedächtnis: Erinnerungskultur und Zeitgeschichte im Konflikt* (Frankfurt am Main, 2002), 39–73.

Hoffmann, Gabriele, *NS-Propaganda in den Niederlanden. Organisation und Lenkung der Publizistik unter deutscher Besatzung 1940–1945* (Munich-Pullach, 1972).

Hoffmann, Stefan-Ludwig, 'Besiegte, Besatzer, Beobachter: Das Kriegsende im Tagebuch', in Daniel Fulda et al. (eds), *Demokratie im Schatten der Gewalt. Geschichten des Privaten im deutschen Nachkrieg* (Göttingen, 2010), 25–55.

Höhne, Julia, 'Napola—Elite für den Führer', in Charlotte Jacke and Rainer Winkel (eds), *Die gefilmte Schule* (Hohengehren, 2008), 58–68.

Hölzle, Peter, *Zwischen Krähwinkel und Kalifornien. Baden-Württemberg einmal ganz anders* (Stuttgart, 2008).

Hopfer, Ines, *Geraubte Identität. Die gewaltsame 'Eindeutschung' von polnischen Kindern in der NS-Zeit* (Vienna, 2010).

Horn, Daniel, 'The National Socialist *Schülerbund* and the Hitler Youth, 1929–1933', *Central European History* 11, no. 4 (1978), 355–75.

Horn, Klaus-Peter, '"Unsere Jungen". Zur Darstellung der Praxis der Nationalpolitischen Erziehungsanstalten im Film', in Klaus-Peter Horn et al. (eds), *Pädagogik im Militarismus und Nationalsozialismus. Japan und Deutschland im Vergleich* (Bad Heilbrunn, 2006), 141–9.

Horn, Klaus-Peter, '"Immer bleibt deshalb eine Kindheit im Faschismus eine Kindheit"—Erziehung in der frühen Kindheit', in Klaus-Peter Horn and Jörg-W. Link (eds), *Erziehungsverhältnisse im Nationalsozialismus. Totaler Anspruch und Erziehungswirklichkeit* (Bad Heilbrunn, 2011), 29–56.

Horn, Klaus-Peter and Link, Jörg-W. (eds), *Erziehungsverhältnisse im Nationalsozialismus. Totaler Anspruch und Erziehungswirklichkeit* (Bad Heilbrunn, 2011).

Hövelmanns, Friederike, 'Zwischen Weimarer Republik und Zweitem Weltkrieg. Die Bürgerliche Jugend in Sachsen am Beispiel der Sächsischen Jungenschaft', in Günther Heydemann, Jan Erik Schulte, and Francesca Weil (eds), *Sachsen und der Nationalsozialismus* (Göttingen, 2014), 335–48.

Huber, Florian, *Kind, versprich mir, dass du dich erschießt. Der Untergang der kleinen Leute 1945* (Berlin, 2015).

Hübner-Funk, Sybille, *Loyalität und Verblendung. Hitlers Garanten der Zukunft als Träger der zweiten deutschen Demokratie* (Potsdam, 1998).

Hübner-Grützsch, Ulrike and Hübner, Ulrich, 'Kramer und Tessenow—Bau und Architektur der Landesschule (1925–1927)', in DGUV (ed.), *Lernräume. Von der Landesschule Dresden zur Akademie* (Dresden, 2009), 60–83.

Huerkamp, Claudia, *Bildungsbürgerinnen. Frauen im Studium und in akademischen Berufen 1900–1945* (Göttingen, 1996).

Huisken, Freerk, 'Scham—Abwehr—Verdrängung: Täterorte als Störfälle der deutschen Erinnerungskultur', in Albert Moritz (ed.), *'Fackelträger der Nation'. Elitebildung in den NS-Ordensburgen* (Cologne, 2010), 232–44.

Hülsheger, Rainer, *Die Adolf-Hitler-Schulen 1937–1945: Suggestion eines Elitebewusstseins* (Weinheim, 2015).

Hummel, Karl-Joseph and Kißener, Michael (eds), *Die Katholiken und das Dritte Reich. Kontroversen und Debatten* (Paderborn, 2009).

Hung, Jochen, 'Beyond Glitter and Doom. The New Paradigm of Contingency in Weimar Research', in Jochen Hung, Godela Weiss-Sussex, and Geoff Wilkes (eds), *Beyond Glitter and Doom: The Contingency of the Weimar Republic* (Munich, 2012), 9–15.

Hung, Jochen, Weiss-Sussex, Godela, and Wilkes, Geoff (eds), *Beyond Glitter and Doom: The Contingency of the Weimar Republic* (Munich, 2012).
Hunzinger, Silke, *Schloß Plön. Residenz—Adliges Armenhaus—Erziehungsanstalt* (Plön, 1997).
Hürter, Johannes, 'The Military Elite and *Volksgemeinschaft*', in Martina Steber and Bernhard Gotto (eds), *Visions of Community in Nazi Germany: Social Engineering and Private Lives* (Oxford, 2014), 257–69.
Hutz, Ferdinand, 'Die Vorauer Stiftskirche als Hallenbad. Ein geplanter Umbau aus dem Jahre 1941', *Blätter für Heimatkunde* 71 (1997), 81–4.
Jacob, Ulf, 'Die Oberlausitz—Beobachtungen zur Motivik eines medialen Regionalbildes im "Dritten Reich"', in Konstantin Herrmann (ed.), *Führerschule, Thingplatz, 'Judenhaus'. Topografien der NS-Herrschaft in Sachsen* (Dresden, 2014), 34–41.
Jansen, Christian and Weckbecker, Arno, *Der 'Volksdeutsche Selbstschutz' in Polen 1939/40* (Munich, 1992).
Jarausch, Konrad, *The Unfree Professions: German Lawyers, Teachers, and Engineers, 1900–1950* (Oxford, 1990).
Jarausch, Konrad, '1945 and the Continuities of German History: Reflections on Memory, Historiography, and Politics', in Geoffrey J. Giles (ed.), *Stunde Null: The End and the Beginning Fifty Years Ago* (Washington, DC, 1997), 11–24.
Jarausch, Konrad, 'Zeitgeschichte und Erinnerung. Deutungskonkurrenz oder Interdependenz?', in Konrad Jarausch and Martin Sabrow (eds), *Verletztes Gedächtnis: Erinnerungskultur und Zeitgeschichte im Konflikt* (Frankfurt am Main, 2002), 9–37.
Jarausch, Konrad, *After Hitler: Recivilizing Germans, 1945–1995* (Oxford, 2006).
Jarausch, Konrad and Geyer, Michael, *Shattered Past: Reconstructing German Histories* (Princeton, 2003).
Jarausch, Konrad and Sabrow, Martin (eds), *Verletztes Gedächtnis: Erinnerungskultur und Zeitgeschichte im Konflikt* (Frankfurt am Main, 2002).
Jodda-Flintrop, Stefanie, *'Wir sollten intelligente Mütter werden'. Nationalpolitische Erziehungsanstalten für Mädchen* (Norderstedt, 2010).
John, Jürgen, 'Die Gaue im NS-System', in Jürgen John, Horst Möller, and Thomas Schaarschmidt (eds), *Die NS-Gaue. Regionale Mittelinstanzen im zentralistischen 'Führerstaat'* (Munich, 2007), 22–55.
John, Jürgen, Möller, Horst, and Schaarschmidt, Thomas (eds), *Die NS-Gaue. Regionale Mittelinstanzen im zentralistischen 'Führerstaat'* (Munich, 2007).
Jureit, Ulrike, 'Generationen-Gedächtnis. Überlegungen zu einem Konzept kommunikativer Vergemeinschaftungen', in Lu Seegers and Jürgen Reulecke (eds), *Die 'Generation der Kriegskinder'. Historische Hintergründe und Deutungen* (Gießen, 2009), 125–37.
Jürgens, Birgit, *Zur Geschichte des BDM (Bund Deutscher Mädel) von 1923 bis 1939* (Frankfurt am Main, 1994).
Kansteiner, Wulf, 'Generation and Memory: A Critique of the Ethical and Ideological Implications of Generational Narration', in Stefan Berger and Bill Niven (eds), *Writing the History of Memory* (London, 2014), 111–34.
Kasberger, Erich, *Heldinnen waren wir keine: Alltag in der NS-Zeit* (Hamburg, 1995).
Kasdorff, Hans and Schmidt, Erwin (eds), *100 Jahre Erziehung der Jugend auf Schloss Plön: 1868–1968* (Plön, 1968).
Kater, Michael H., *Hitler Youth* (Cambridge, MA, 2004).
Keil, Theo (ed.), *Die deutsche Schule in den Sudetenländern. Form und Inhalt des Bildungswesens* (Munich, 1967).
Keim, Wolfgang, *Erziehung unter der Nazi-Diktatur Band I: Antidemokratische Potentiale, Machtantritt und Machtdurchsetzung* (Darmstadt, 1995).

Keim, Wolfgang, *Erziehung unter der Nazi-Diktatur Band II: Kriegsvorbereitung, Krieg und Holocaust* (Darmstadt, 1997).

Keim, Wolfgang, 'Bildung versus Ertüchtigung. Gab es einen Paradigmenwechsel im Erziehungsdenken unter der Nazi-Diktatur?', in Hartmut Lehmann and Otto Gerhard Oexle (eds), *Nationalsozialismus in den Kulturwissenschaften: Band 2—Leitbegriffe—Deutungsmuster—Paradigmenkämpfe—Erfahrungen und Transformationen im Exil* (Göttingen, 2004), 223–58.

Keim, Wolfgang, 'Kontinuitäten und Traditionsbrüche. Die Inkorporation des Weimarer Erziehungswesens in den NS-Staat', in Albert Moritz (ed.), *'Fackelträger der Nation'. Elitebildung in den NS-Ordensburgen* (Cologne, 2010), 47–80.

Keim, Wolfgang, '100 Jahre Reformpädagogik-Rezeption in Deutschland im Spannungsfeld von Konstruktion, De-Konstruktion und Re-Konstruktion—Versuch einer Bilanzierung', in Wolfgang Keim, Ulrich Schwerdt, and Sabine Reh (eds), *Reformpädagogik und Reformpädagogik-Rezeption in neuer Sicht. Perspektiven und Impulse* (Bad Heilbrunn, 2016), 19–69.

Keim, Wolfgang, Schwerdt, Ulrich, and Reh, Sabine (eds), *Reformpädagogik und Reformpädagogik-Rezeption in neuer Sicht. Perspektiven und Impulse* (Bad Heilbrunn, 2016).

Keller, Anne, 'Das Deutsche Volksspiel. Jugendliche Propagandisten im Visier und Dienst der "Volksgemeinschaft"', in Detlef Schmiechen-Ackermann et al. (eds), *Der Ort der 'Volksgemeinschaft' in der deutschen Gesellschaftsgeschichte* (Paderborn, 2018), 375–83.

Kellerhoff, Sven Felix, 'Die Erfindung des Karteimitglieds. Rhetorik des Herauswindens: Wie heute die NSDAP-Mitgliedschaft kleingeredet wird', in Wolfgang Benz (ed.), *Wie wurde man Parteigenosse? Die NSDAP und ihre Mitglieder* (Frankfurt am Main, 2009), 167–80.

Kemnitz, Heidemarie and Tosch, Frank, 'Zwischen Indoktrination und Qualifikation—Höhere Schule im Nationalsozialismus', in Klaus-Peter Horn and Jörg-W. Link (eds), *Erziehungsverhältnisse im Nationalsozialismus. Totaler Anspruch und Erziehungswirklichkeit* (Bad Heilbrunn, 2011), 109–34.

Kershaw, Ian (ed.), *The Nazi Dictatorship: Problems and Perspectives of Interpretation* (4th edn; London, 2000).

Kershaw, Ian, *The End: Hitler's Germany 1944–45* (London, 2011).

Kershaw, Ian, '*Volksgemeinschaft*: Potential and Limitations of the Concept', in Martina Steber and Bernhard Gotto (eds), *Visions of Community in Nazi Germany: Social Engineering and Private Lives* (Oxford, 2014), 29–42.

Kettenacker, Lothar, *Nationalsozialistische Volkstumspolitik im Elsaß* (Stuttgart, 1973).

Kettenacker, Lothar, 'Hitler und die Kirchen. Eine Obsession mit Folgen', in Günther Heydemann and Lothar Kettenacker (eds), *Kirchen in der Diktatur. Drittes Reich und SED-Staat* (Göttingen, 1993), 67–87.

Kinz, Gabriele, *Der Bund Deutscher Mädel. Ein Beitrag über die außerschulische Mädchenerziehung im Nationalsozialismus* (Frankfurt am Main, 1991).

Kipp, Martin, 'Militarisierung der Lehrlingsausbildung in der "Ordensburg der Arbeit"', in Ulrich Herrmann and Ulrich Nassen (eds), *Formative Ästhetik im Nationalsozialismus. Intentionen, Medien und Praxisformen totalitärer ästhetischer Herrschaft und Beherrschung* (Weinheim, 1994), 209–19.

Kipp, Martin and Miller-Kipp, Gisela, *Erkundungen im Halbdunkel. Fünfzehn Studien zur Berufserziehung und Pädagogik im Nationalsozialismus* (Kassel, 1990).

Kipp, Michaela, *'Großreinemachen im Osten'. Feindbilder in deutschen Feldpostbriefen im Zweiten Weltkrieg* (Frankfurt am Main, 2014).

Kißener, Michael, 'Katholiken im Dritten Reich: eine historische Einführung', in Karl-Joseph Hummel and Michael Kißener (eds), *Die Katholiken und das Dritte Reich. Kontroversen und Debatten* (Paderborn, 2009), 13–35.

Kißener, Michael and Scholtyseck, Joachim, 'Nationalsozialismus in der Provinz: Zur Einführung', in Michael Kißener and Joachim Scholtyseck (eds), *Die Führer der Provinz. NS-Biographien aus Baden und Württemberg* (Konstanz, 1997), 11–29.

Kißener, Michael and Scholtyseck, Joachim (eds), *Die Führer der Provinz. NS-Biographien aus Baden und Württemberg* (Konstanz, 1997).

Kitchen, Martin, *The Coming of Austrian Fascism* (London, 1980).

Klafki, Wolfgang, 'Typische Faktorenkonstellationen für Identitätsbildungsprozesse von Kindern und Jugendlichen im Nationalsozialismus im Spiegel autobiographischer Berichte', in Christa Berg and Sieglinde Ellger-Rüttgart (eds), *'Du bist nichts, Dein Volk ist alles.' Forschungen zum Verhältnis von Pädagogik und Nationalsozialismus* (Weinheim, 1991), 159–72.

Klare, Anke, 'Die Deutschen Heimschulen 1941–1945. Zur Gleichschaltung und Verstaatlichung kirchlicher, privater und stiftischer Internatsschulen im Nationalsozialismus', *Jahrbuch für historischen Bildungsforschung* 9 (2003), 37–58.

Klare, Anke, 'Nationalsozialistische Ausleseschulen—"Stätten konzentrierter und auserlesener Menschenformung"', in Klaus-Peter Horn and Jörg-W. Link (eds), *Erziehungsverhältnisse im Nationalsozialismus. Totaler Anspruch und Erziehungswirklichkeit* (Bad Heilbrunn, 2011), 137–60.

Klaus, Martin, *Mädchen im 3. Reich. Der Bund Deutscher Mädel* (Cologne, 1998).

Kleiber, Lore, '"Wo ihr seid, da soll die Sonne scheinen!"—Der Frauenarbeitsdienst am Ende der Weimarer Republik und im Nationalsozialismus', in Frauengruppe Faschismusforschung (ed.), *Mutterkreuz und Arbeitsbuch. Zur Geschichte der Frauen in der Weimarer Republik und im Nationalsozialismus* (Frankfurt am Main, 1981), 188–214.

Klein, Gerhard, 'Die NS-Ordensburg Sonthofen 1934 bis 1945', in Paul Ciupke and Franz-Josef Jelich (eds), *Weltanschauliche Erziehung in Ordensburgen des Nationalsozialismus. Zur Geschichte und Zukunft der Ordensburg Vogelsang* (Essen, 2006), 65–84.

Kleinöder, Eva-Maria, 'Der Kampf um die katholische Schule in Bayern in der NS-Zeit', in Georg Schwaiger (ed.), *Das Erzbistum München und Freising in der Zeit der nationalsozialistischen Herrschaft* (Vol. 1; Munich, 1984), 596–638.

Kletzin, Birgit, *Europa aus Rasse und Raum. Die nationalsozialistische Idee der neuen Ordnung* (Münster, 2002).

Klönne, Arno, *Jugend im Dritten Reich. Die Hitler-Jugend und ihre Gegner* (Munich, 1990).

Klönne, Irmgard, *'Ich spring' in diesem Ringe'. Mädchen und Frauen in der deutschen Jugendbewegung* (Pfaffenweiler, 1990).

Klönne, Irmgard, 'Kontinuitäten und Brüche: Weibliche Jugendbewegung und Bund Deutscher Mädel', in Dagmar Reese (ed.), *Die BDM-Generation. Weibliche Jugendliche in Deutschland und Österreich im Nationalsozialismus* (Berlin, 2007), 41–85.

Kluge, Ulrich, *Der österreichische Ständestaat 1934–1938. Entstehung und Scheitern* (Munich, 1984).

Kluke, Paul, 'Nationalsozialistische Europaideologie', *Vierteljahrshefte für Zeitgeschichte* 3, no. 3 (1955), 240–75.

Kneller, George Frederick, *The Educational Philosophy of National Socialism* (New Haven, 1941).

Knoch, Habbo, 'Gemeinschaften im Nationalsozialismus vor Ort', in Dietmar von Reeken and Malte Thießen (eds), *'Volksgemeinschaft' als soziale Praxis. Neue Forschungen zur NS-Gesellschaft vor Ort* (Paderborn, 2013), 37–50.

Knüpfer, Volker, 'Die "Sächsische Logenmuseum" in Chemnitz—Inszenierung im Dienst der "Gegnerbekämpfung"', in Konstantin Herrmann (ed.), *Führerschule, Thingplatz, 'Judenhaus'. Topografien der NS-Herrschaft in Sachsen* (Dresden, 2014), 218–23.

Koch, H. W., *The Hitler Youth. Origins and Development 1922–1945* (New York, 1975).

Kochanowski, Jerzy and Sach, Maike (eds), *Die Volksdeutschen in Polen, Frankreich, Ungarn und der Tschechoslowakei. Mythos und Realität* (Osnabrück, 2006).

Kock, Gerhard, *'Der Führer sorgt für unsere Kinder…' Die Kinderlandverschickung im Zweiten Weltkrieg* (Paderborn, 1997).

Kock, Lisa, *'Man war bestätigt und man konnte was!' Der Bund Deutscher Mädel im Spiegel der Erinnerungen ehemaliger Mädelführerinnen* (Münster, 1994).

Kösters, Christoph, 'Katholiken im Dritten Reich: eine wissenschafts- und forschungsgeschichtliche Einführung', in Karl-Joseph Hummel and Michael Kißener (eds), *Die Katholiken und das Dritte Reich. Kontroversen und Debatten* (Paderborn, 2009), 37–59.

Koll, Johannes, *Arthur Seyß-Inquart und die deutsche Besatzungspolitik in den Niederlanden (1940–1945)* (Vienna, 2015).

Kollmeier, Katrin, *Ordnung und Ausgrenzung. Die Disziplinarpolitik der Hitler-Jugend* (Göttingen, 2007).

Kollmeier, Katrin, 'Erziehungsziel "Volksgemeinschaft"—Kinder und Jugendliche in der Hitler-Jugend', in Klaus-Peter Horn and Jörg-W. Link (eds), *Erziehungsverhältnisse im Nationalsozialismus. Totaler Anspruch und Erziehungswirklichkeit* (Bad Heilbrunn, 2011), 59–76.

Kompisch, Kathrin, *Täterinnen. Frauen im Nationalsozialismus* (Cologne, 2008).

Koonz, Claudia, *Mothers in the Fatherland: Women, the Family and Nazi Politics* (New York, 1987).

Koop, Volker, *Dem Führer ein Kind schenken. Die SS-Organisation Lebensborn* (Cologne, 2007).

Kraas, Andreas, *Lehrerlager 1932–1945. Politische Funktion und pädagogische Gestaltung* (Bad Heilbrunn, 2004).

Kraas, Andreas, '"Den deutschen Menschen in seinen inneren Lebensbezirken ergreifen"—Das Lager als Erziehungsform', in Klaus-Peter Horn and Jörg-W. Link (eds), *Erziehungsverhältnisse im Nationalsozialismus. Totaler Anspruch und Erziehungswirklichkeit* (Bad Heilbrunn, 2011), 295–317.

Kramer, Nicole, *Volksgenossinnen an der Heimatfront. Mobilisierung, Verhalten, Erinnerung* (Göttingen, 2011).

Kramer, Nicole and Nolzen, Armin, 'Einleitung', in Nicole Kramer and Armin Nolzen (eds), *Ungleichheiten im 'Dritten Reich'. Semantiken, Praktiken, Erfahrungen* (Göttingen, 2012), 9–26.

Kramer, Nicole and Nolzen, Armin (eds), *Ungleichheiten im 'Dritten Reich'. Semantiken, Praktiken, Erfahrungen* (Göttingen, 2012).

Krantz, Robert, *'…Auf ausdrücklichen Befehl des Führers als kriegsentscheidende Erziehungseinrichtung…' Materialien zur 'Nationalpolitischen Erziehungsanstalt Kolmar-Berg' vom Einzug in das ehemalige großherzogliche Schloss (1941) bis zur Auflösung in Reichenau (1945)* (Luxembourg, 2007).

Kraul, Margret and Schmidtke, Adrian, 'Mädchen und Jungen in der Eliteerziehung des Nationalsozialismus. Eine Annäherung über Fotografien', in Barbara Friebertshäuser, Heide von Felden, and Burkhard Schäffer (eds), *Bild und Text. Methoden und Methodologien visueller Sozialforschung in der Erziehungswissenschaft* (Opladen, 2007), 239–59.

Krier, Emile, 'Die deutsche Volkstumspolitik in Luxemburg und ihre sozialen Folgen', in Wacław Długoborski (ed.), *Zweiter Weltkrieg und sozialer Wandel* (Göttingen, 1981), 224–41.

Kroener, Bernhard R., Müller, Rolf-Dieter, and Umbreit, Hans, *Germany and the Second World War, Volume V/I—Organization and Mobilization of the German Sphere of Power: Wartime Administration, Economy, and Manpower Resources 1939–1941* (Oxford, 2000).

Krzoska, Markus, 'Bromberger Blutsonntag. Unklare Fakten, klare Interpretationen', in Hans Henning Hahn and Robert Traba (eds), *Deutsch-Polnische Erinnerungsorte. Bd. 2. Geteilt/Gemeinsam* (Paderborn, 2014), 351–63.

Kühl, Stefan, *Ganz normale Organisationen. Zur Soziologie des Holocaust* (Berlin, 2014).

Kühne, Thomas, *Belonging and Genocide: Hitler's Community, 1918–1945* (New Haven, 2010).

Kühne, Thomas, *The Rise and Fall of Comradeship: Hitler's Soldiers, Male Bonding and Mass Violence in the Twentieth Century* (Cambridge, 2017).

Kuhn, Annette (ed.), *Frauenleben im NS-Alltag. Bonner Studien zur Frauengeschichte* (Pfaffenweiler, 1994).

Kuhnke, Wolf, *Blaue Blume und Spinnrocken. Die Geschichte des Bundes Deutscher Pfadfinderinnen 1912–1933* (Gießen, 1984).

Kulle, Daniel, '"Tut so was ein deutscher Junge?" Verantwortung und Mitleid in Napola—Elite für den Führer', in Margrit Frölich, Christian Schneider, and Karsten Visarius (eds), *Das Böse im Blick. Die Gegenwart des Nationalsozialismus im Film* (Nehren, 2007), 219–30.

Kuller, Christiane, '"Kämpfende Verwaltung". Bürokratie im NS-Staat', in Dietmar Süß and Winfried Süß (eds), *Das 'Dritte Reich'* (Munich, 2008), 227–45.

Kundrus, Birthe, 'Regime der Differenz. Volkstumspolitische Inklusionen und Exklusionen im Warthegau und im Generalgouvernement 1939–1944', in Frank Bajohr and Michael Wildt (eds), *Volksgemeinschaft. Neue Forschungen zur Gesellschaft des Nationalsozialismus* (Frankfurt am Main, 2009), 105–23.

Kupfer, Torsten, 'Umfeldbedingungen des Aufstieges der anhaltischen NSDAP zur Regierungspartei (1918–1932)', in Werner Freitag, Klaus Erich Pollmann, and Matthias Puhle (eds), *Politische, soziale und kulturelle Konflikte in der Geschichte von Sachsen-Anhalt. Beiträge des landesgeschichtlichen Kolloquiums am 4./5. September 1998 in Vockerode* (Halle am Saale, 1999), 175–94.

Kwiet, Konrad, *Reichskommissariat Niederlande. Versuch und Scheitern nationalsozialistischer Neuordnung* (Stuttgart, 1968).

Lamberti, Marjorie, 'German Schoolteachers, National Socialism, and the Politics of Culture at the End of the Weimar Republic', *Central European History* 34, no. 1 (2001), 53–82.

Lamberti, Marjorie, *The Politics of Education: Teachers and School Reform in Weimar Germany* (New York, 2002).

Langewiesche, Dieter and Tenorth, Heinz-Elmar (eds), *Handbuch der deutschen Bildungsgeschichte—Band V: 1918–1945. Die Weimarer Republik und die nationalsozialistische Diktatur* (Munich, 1989).

Lansing, Charles, *From Nazism to Communism: German Schoolteachers under Two Dictatorships* (Cambridge, MA, 2010).

Lapp, Benjamin, *Revolution from the Right: Politics, Class, and the Rise of Nazism in Saxony, 1919–1933* (Boston, 1997).

Larass, Claus, *Der Zug der Kinder. KLV—Die Evakuierung 5 Millionen deutscher Kinder im 2. Weltkrieg* (Munich, 1983).

Latzel, Klaus, 'Tourismus und Gewalt. Kriegswahrnehmungen in Feldpostbriefen', in Hannes Heer and Klaus Neumann (eds), *Vernichtungskrieg. Verbrechen der Wehrmacht 1941 bis 1944* (Hamburg, 1995), 447–59.

Latzel, Klaus, *Deutsche Soldaten—nationalsozialistischer Krieg? Kriegserlebnis—Kriegserfahrung 1939–1945* (Paderborn, 1998).

Lauridsen, John T., *Nazism and the Radical Right in Austria, 1918–1934* (Copenhagen, 2007).

Lehmann, Albrecht, 'Militär und Militanz zwischen den Weltkriegen', in Dieter Langewiesche and Heinz-Elmar Tenorth (eds), *Handbuch der deutschen Bildungsgeschichte—Band V: 1918–1945. Die Weimarer Republik und die nationalsozialistische Diktatur* (Munich, 1989), 407–29.

Lehmann, Albrecht, *Im Fremden ungewollt zuhaus. Flüchtlinge und Vertriebene in Westdeutschland 1945–1990* (Munich, 1991).

Lehnstaedt, Stephan, *Okkupation im Osten. Besatzeralltag in Warschau und Minsk 1939–1944* (Munich, 2010).

Lejeune, Carlo, '"Des Deutschtums fernster Westen". Eupen-Malmedy, die deutschen Dialekt redenden Gemeinden um Arlon und Montzen und die "Westforschung"', in Burkhard Dietz, Helmut Gabel, and Ulrich Tiedau (eds), *Griff nach dem Westen. Die 'Westforschung' der völkisch-nationalen Wissenschaften zum nordwesteuropäischen Raum (1919–1960)* (Vol. 1; Münster, 2003), 493–538.

Leniger, Markus, *Nationalsozialistische 'Volkstumsarbeit' und Umsiedlungspolitik 1933–1945. Von der Minderheitenbetreuung zur Siedlerauslese* (Berlin, 2006).

Leser, Gérard, et al., *Rouffach—De l'asile au centre hospitalier: 90 ans de psychiatrie* (Strasbourg, 1999).

Lichtenberger-Fenz, Brigitte, '"Es läuft alles in geordneten Bahnen". Österreichs Hochschulen und Universitäten und das NS-Regime', in Emmerich Tálos (ed.), *NS-Herrschaft in Österreich. Ein Handbuch* (Vienna, 2002), 549–69.

Lilienthal, Georg, *Der 'Lebensborn e.V.': Ein Instrument nationalsozialistischer Rassenpolitik* (Frankfurt am Main, 2003).

Link, Jörg-W., '"Erziehungsstätte des deutschen Volkes"—Die Volksschule im Nationalsozialismus', in Klaus-Peter Horn and Jörg-W. Link (eds), *Erziehungsverhältnisse im Nationalsozialismus. Totaler Anspruch und Erziehungswirklichkeit* (Bad Heilbrunn, 2011), 79–106.

Linton, Derek S., *'Who Has the Youth, Has the Future': The Campaign to Save Young Workers in Imperial Germany* (Cambridge, 1991).

Liulevicius, Vejas Gabriel, *War Land on the Eastern Front: Culture, National Identity, and German Occupation in World War I* (Cambridge, 2000).

Liulevicius, Vejas Gabriel, *The German Myth of the East: 1800 to the Present* (Oxford, 2009).

Livi, Massimiliano, *Gertrud Scholtz-Klink: Die Reichsfrauenführerin. Politische Handlungsräume und Identitätsprobleme der Frauen im Nationalsozialismus am Beispiel der 'Führerin aller deutschen Frauen'* (Münster, 2005).

Livi, Massimiliano, *Führerinnen del Terzo Reich. Nascita, sviluppo, funzione e struttura dell'élite politica femminile nazionalsocialista (1918–1939)* (Münster, 2012).

Lloyd, Alexandra, '"Wir wollten doch wissen, wie groß die Gefahr war": The German War Child as Icon and Agent in Berlin School Essays, 1946', *German Life and Letters* 69, no. 4 (2016), 437–52.

Löffler, Klara, *Aufgehoben: Soldatenbriefe aus dem Zweiten Weltkrieg. Eine Studie zur subjektiven Wirklichkeit des Krieges* (Bamberg, 1992).

Longerich, Peter, *Die braunen Bataillone. Geschichte der SA* (Munich, 1989).

Longerich, Peter, *Heinrich Himmler* (Oxford, 2012).

Loock, Hans-Dietrich, 'Zur "Großgermanischen Politik" des Dritten Reiches', *Vierteljahrshefte für Zeitgeschichte* 8, no. 1 (1960), 37–63.

Loock, Hans-Dietrich, 'Nationalpolitische Erziehungsanstalten', *Gutachten des Instituts für Zeitgeschichte* (1966), 138–42.

Lower, Wendy, *Hitler's Furies: German Women in the Nazi Killing Fields* (London, 2013).

Lüder, Ludwig, *Ilfeld. Ein Blick in die Geschichte des Fleckens* (Nordhausen, 2002).

Lüdtke, Alf, '"Coming to Terms with the Past": Illusions of Remembering, Ways of Forgetting Nazism in West Germany', *Journal of Modern History* 65, no. 3 (1993), 542–72.
Lüdtke, Alf (ed.), *The History of Everyday Life: Reconstructing Historical Experiences and Ways of Life* (Princeton, 1995).
Lukas, Richard C., *The Forgotten Holocaust: The Poles under German Occupation* (New York, 1997).
Lumans, Valdis O., *Himmler's Auxiliaries: The* Volksdeutsche Mittelstelle *and the German National Minorities of Europe, 1933–1945* (Chapel Hill, 1993).
Malinowski, Stephan, *Vom König zum Führer. Deutscher Adel und Nationalsozialismus* (Frankfurt am Main, 2004).
Margies, Dieter, *Das höhere Schulwesen zwischen Reform und Restauration. Die Biographie Hans Richerts als Beitrag zur Bildungspolitik in der Weimarer Republik* (Rheinstetten, 1972).
Marquardt, Axel and Rathsack, Heinz (eds), *Preußen im Film. Eine Retrospektive der Stiftung Deutsche Kinemathek* (Rheinbek bei Hamburg, 1981).
Martin, Benjamin, *The Nazi-Fascist New Order for European Culture* (Cambridge, MA, 2016).
Matthäus, Jürgen (ed.), *Approaching an Auschwitz Survivor. Holocaust Testimony and Its Transformations* (Oxford, 2009).
Matthes, Eva, 'Die aufgegebene Aufklärung. Höhere Schulen im NS-Staat', in Johanna Hopfner and Michael Winkler (eds), *Die aufgegebene Aufklärung. Experimente pädagogischer Vernunft* (Weinheim, 2004), 124–42.
Maubach, Franka, 'Führerinnen-Generationen? Überlegungen zur Vergesellschaftung von Frauen im Nationalsozialismus', *H-Soz-Kult* (2003): www.hsozkult.de/debate/id/diskussionen-331 (accessed November 2018).
Maubach, Franka, 'Expansionen weiblicher Hilfe: Zur Erfahrungsgeschichte von Frauen im Kriegsdienst', in Sybille Steinbacher (ed.), *Volksgenossinnen. Frauen in der NS-Volksgemeinschaft* (Göttingen, 2007), 93–111.
Maubach, Franka, *Die Stellung halten. Kriegserfahrungen und Lebensgeschichten von Wehrmachthelferinnen* (Göttingen, 2009).
Mazower, Mark, *Hitler's Empire: Nazi Rule in Occupied Europe* (London, 2008).
McElligott, Anthony (ed.), *Weimar Germany* (Oxford, 2009).
McElligott, Anthony, *Rethinking the Weimar Republic: Authority and Authoritarianism, 1916–1936* (London, 2014).
Mehr, Christian, 'NS-Volksgemeinschaft im Geschichtsunterricht: Der Spielfilm "Napola—Elite für den Führer"', in Uwe Danker and Astrid Schwabe (eds), *Die NS-Volksgemeinschaft. Zeitgenössische Verheißung, analytisches Konzept und ein Schlüssel zum historischen Lernen?* (Göttingen, 2017), 141–55.
Mejstrik, Alexander, 'Die Erfindung der deutschen Jugend. Erziehung in Wien 1938–1945', in Emmerich Tálos et al. (eds), *NS-Herrschaft in Österreich: Ein Handbuch* (Vienna, 2002), 494–522.
Mertens, Annette, *Himmlers Klostersturm. Der Angriff auf katholische Einrichtungen im Zweiten Weltkrieg und die Wiedergutmachung nach 1945* (Paderborn, 2006).
Meyer, Beate, 'Erfühlte und erdachte "Volksgemeinschaft". Erfahrungen "jüdischer Mischlinge" zwischen Integration und Ausgrenzung', in Frank Bajohr and Michael Wildt (eds), *Volksgemeinschaft. Neue Forschungen zur Gesellschaft des Nationalsozialismus* (Frankfurt am Main, 2009), 144–64.
Meyer, Karl-Heinz, 'Eine Schule—zwei Geschichten. Von der Nationalpolitischen Bildungsanstalt Ballenstedt zur Bezirksparteischule der SED "Wilhelm Liebknecht"', in

Justus H. Ulbricht (ed.), *Schwierige Orte. Regionale Erinnerung, Gedenkstätten, Museen* (Halle am Saale, 2013), 153–70.

Mezger, Caroline, '"Denn du bist die Zukunft deines Volkes": Youth, Nation, and the Nazi Mobilization of Southeastern Europe's *Donauschwaben*, 1930s–1944', in Burkhard Olschowsky and Ingo Loose (eds), *Nationalsozialismus und Regionalbewusstsein im östlichen Europa: Ideologie, Machtausbau, Beharrung* (Berlin, 2016), 105–26.

Mezger, Caroline, 'Entangled Utopias: The Nazi Mobilization of Ethnic German Youths in the Batschka, 1930s–1944', *The Journal of the History of Childhood and Youth* 9 (2016), 87–117.

Michel, Anette, '"Führerinnen" im Dritten Reich. Die Gaufrauenschaftsleiterinnen der NSDAP', in Sybille Steinbacher (ed.), *Volksgenossinnen. Frauen in der NS-Volksgemeinschaft* (Göttingen, 2007), 115–37.

Miller, Susan A., 'Assent as Agency in the Early Years of the Children of the American Revolution', *The Journal of the History of Childhood and Youth* 9, no. 1 (2016), 48–65.

Miller-Kipp, Gisela, 'Die ausgebeutete Tradition, die ideologische Revolution und der pädagogische Mythos', in Ulrich Herrmann and Jürgen Oelkers (eds), *Pädagogik und Nationalsozialismus* (Weinheim, 1989), 21–37.

Miller-Kipp, Gisela, *'Auch Du gehörst dem Führer'. Die Geschichte des Bundes Deutscher Mädel (BDM) in Quellen und Dokumenten* (2nd edn; Weinheim, 2001).

Miller-Kipp, Gisela, '"Klasse Schule—immer genug zu essen, wenig Mathematik". Elitebildung im "Dritten Reich" oder über die Herstellung von Elite-Bewusstsein', in Jutta Ecarius and Lothar Wigger (eds), *Elitebildung—Bildungselite. Erziehungswissenschaftliche Diskussionen und Befunde über Bildung und soziale Ungleichheit* (Opladen, 2006), 44–66.

Miller-Kipp, Gisela, '"Deutsche Jungs, die dem Führer helfen, das Reich zu tragen". Elite-Bildung und Elite-Bewusstsein in der Adolf-Hitler-Schule nebst Erinnerungsspuren zur "Ordensburg" Vogelsang', in Paul Ciupke and Franz-Josef Jelich (eds), *Weltanschauliche Erziehung in Ordensburgen des Nationalsozialismus. Zur Geschichte und Zukunft der Ordensburg Vogelsang* (Essen, 2006), 53–64.

Miller-Kipp, Gisela, *'Der Führer braucht mich'. Der Bund Deutscher Mädel (BDM): Lebenserinnerungen und Erinnerungsdiskurs* (Weinheim, 2007).

Miller-Kipp, Gisela, 'Elitebildung in den Elite-Schulen des "Dritten Reiches". Praxis und Systemfunktion', in Kuratorium Gedenkstätte Sonnenstein (ed.), *'Es war ein Welt von Befehl und Gehorsam.' Nationalsozialistische Elitebildung und die Adolf-Hitler-Schule Sachsen in Pirna-Sonnenstein (1941 bis 1945)* (Pirna, 2008), 17–36.

Möckel, Benjamin, *Erfahrungsbruch und Generationsbehauptung. Die 'Kriegsjugendgeneration' in den beiden deutschen Nachkriegsgesellschaften* (Göttingen, 2014).

Möding, Nori, '"Ich muß irgendwo engagiert sein—fragen Sie mich bloß nicht, warum." Überlegungen zu Sozialisationserfahrungen von Mädchen in NS-Organisationen', in Lutz Niethammer and Alexander von Plato (eds), *'Wir kriegen jetzt andere Zeiten'. Auf der Suche nach der Erfahrung des Volkes in nachfaschistischen Ländern* (Bonn, 1985), 256–304.

Moeller, Robert G., *War Stories: The Search for a Usable Past in the Federal Republic of Germany* (Berkeley, 2001).

Moeller, Robert G., 'Germans as Victims? Thoughts on a Post-Cold War History of World War II's Legacies', *History and Memory* 17, no. 1–2 (2005), 145–94.

Moll, Martin, 'Der Reichsgau Steiermark 1938–1945', in Jürgen John, Horst Möller, and Thomas Schaarschmidt (eds), *Die NS-Gaue. Regionale Mittelinstanzen im zentralistischen 'Führerstaat'* (Munich, 2007), 364–77.

Möller, Horst, 'Regionalismus und Zentralismus in der neueren Geschichte. Bemerkungen zur historischen Dimension einer aktuellen Diskussion', in Horst Möller, Andreas

Wirsching, and Walter Ziegler (eds), *Nationalsozialismus in der Region. Beiträge zur regionalen und lokalen Forschung und zum internationalen Vergleich* (Munich, 1996), 9–22.

Möller, Horst, Wirsching, Andreas, and Ziegler, Walter (eds), *Nationalsozialismus in der Region. Beiträge zur regionalen und lokalen Forschung und zum internationalen Vergleich* (Munich, 1996).

Möller, Jürgen, *Der Kampf um Zeitz April 1945. Der Übergang der amerikanischen Truppen über die Weiße Elster im Raum Zeitz, der Einsatz der Napola-Schüler aus Naumburg und Schulpforta, der Kampf um die Flakstellungen und die Besetzung von Zeitz* (Bad Langensalza, 2010).

Moncure, John, *Forging the King's Sword: Military Education between Tradition and Modernization—The Case of the Royal Prussian Cadet Corps, 1871–1918* (New York, 1993).

Moritz, Albert (ed.), *'Fackelträger der Nation'. Elitebildung in den NS-Ordensburgen* (Cologne, 2010).

Morlang, Adolf, *'Neuer Stil im alten Schloss'. Die Napola/NPEA Oranienstein 1934–1945* (Diez, 2002).

Morlang, Adolf, 'Als Frau in einer Männerwelt: Das Tagebuch der sog. "Hausdame" der NPEA Oranienstein', *Heimatjahrbuch Rhein-Lahn-Kreis* (2016), 64–7.

Morsches, Max, 'Nutzungsgeschichte des Neuen Schlosses Bensberg. Vom Tod des Erbauers 1716 bis zum Kauf durch die Aachener und Münchener Lebensversicherung 1997', in Albert Eßer and Wolfgang Vomm (eds), *Bürgerburg und Musenvilla. Zugänge zu historischen Herrschaftsbauten in Bergisch Gladbach* (Bergisch Gladbach, 2006), 91–115.

Moser, Arnulf, 'Von der Euthanasie zur Eliteerziehung. Die Napola Reichenau 1941–1945', *Badische Heimat* 76, no. 2 (1996), 271–85.

Moser, Arnulf, *Die Napola Reichenau. Von der Heil- und Pflegeanstalt zur nationalsozialistischen Eliteerziehung (1941–1945)* (Konstanz, 1997).

Moser, Arnulf, 'Die Napola in Rottweil—ein Zwischenbericht', *Rottweiler Heimatblätter* 60, no. 4 (1999).

Moser, Arnulf, 'Von der Mennoniten-Schule zur Nationalpolitischen Erziehungsanstalt. Weierhof am Donnersberg im Dritten Reich', *Pfälzer Heimat* 53, no. 2 (2002), 55–61.

Moser, Arnulf, 'Die Illenau im 2. Weltkrieg. Quellen zur nationalsozialistischen Schul- und Volkstumspolitik', *Acherner Rückblicke* 2 (2002), 70–7.

Moser, Arnulf, 'Die Reichsschule für Volksdeutsche in Achern/Illenau 1940–44', *Die Ortenau. Veröffentlichungen des Historischen Vereins für Mittelbaden* (2003), 107–16.

Moser, Arnulf, 'Die Nationalpolitische Erziehungsanstalt (Napola) Neubeuern im Zweiten Weltkrieg', *Das bayerische Inn-Oberland. Zeitschrift des Historischen Vereins Rosenheim* 57 (2004), 130–9.

Moser, Arnulf, 'Nationalsozialistische Mädchenschulen in der ehemaligen Heil- und Pflegeanstalt Reichenau (1944/45)', *Hegau: Zeitschrift für Geschichte, Volkskunde und Naturgeschichte des Gebietes zwischen Rhein, Donau und Bodensee* 63 (2006), 197–212.

Moses, Dirk, 'Der nichtdeutsche Deutsche und der deutsche Deutsche: Stigma und Opfer-Erlösung in der Berliner Republik', in Daniel Fulda et al. (eds), *Demokratie im Schatten der Gewalt. Geschichten des Privaten im deutschen Nachkrieg* (Göttingen, 2010), 354–79.

Mouton, Michelle, *From Nurturing the Nation to Purifying the Volk: Weimar and Nazi Family Policy, 1918–1945* (Cambridge, 2007).

Mühlenberg, Jutta, *Das SS-Helferinnenkorps. Ausbildung, Einsatz und Entnazifizierung der weiblichen Angehörigen der Waffen-SS 1942–1949* (Hamburg, 2010).

Mühlenfeld, Daniel, 'The Pleasures of Being a "Political Soldier": Nazi Functionaries and Their Service to the "Movement"', in Pamela E. Swett, Corey Ross, and Fabrice d'Almeida (eds), *Pleasure and Power in Nazi Germany* (Basingstoke, 2011), 204–33.

Müller, Alwin, *Geschichte und Geschichten der Jahre 1925–1950. 50 Jahre Landschulheim Neubeuern 1925–1975* (Fischbach, 1975).

Müller, Beate, '"Der Mann, den ich vergötterte, hat uns ins Unglück geführt": The Post-War Crisis of Consciousness as Mirrored in Essays and Questionnaires by Nuremberg's Schoolchildren in 1946', *German Life and Letters* 69, no. 4 (2016), 453–67.

Müller, Beate, Pinfold, Debbie, and Wölfel, Ute, 'Cradle and Crucible of "Vergangenheitsbewältigung": Representations of the War Child in the Occupation Period (1945–9). An Introduction', *German Life and Letters* 69, no. 4 (2016), 417–36.

Müller, Rolf-Dieter, Ueberschar, Gerd R., and Wette, Wolfram (eds), *Wer zurückweicht wird erschossen! Kriegsalltag und Kriegsende in Südwestdeutschland 1944/45* (Freiburg im Breisgau, 1985).

Müller, Sven Oliver, *Deutsche Soldaten und ihre Feinde. Nationalismus an Front und Heimatfront im Zweiten Weltkrieg* (Frankfurt am Main, 2007).

Müller, Thomas, 'Der Gau Köln-Aachen und Grenzlandpolitik im Nordwesten des Deutschen Reiches', in Jürgen John, Horst Möller, and Thomas Schaarschmidt (eds), *Die NS-Gaue. Regionale Mittelinstanzen im zentralistischen 'Führerstaat'* (Munich, 2007), 318–33.

Müller, Tim, 'A Legal Odyssey: Denazification Law, Nazi Elite Schools, and the Construction of Postwar Memory', *History of Education* 46, no. 4 (2017), 498–513.

Müller-Römer, Dieter (ed.), *Die Stiftung Schulpforta 1990–2006. Eine Chronik (Beilage zu 'Die Pforte' Nr. 60/2007)* (Naumburg, 2007).

Naake, Erhard, 'Die Heranbildung des Führernachwuchses im faschistischen Deutschland', *Zeitschrift für Geschichtswissenschaft* 21, no. 2 (1973), 181–95.

Nagel, Anne C., *Hitlers Bildungsreformer. Das Reichsministerium für Wissenschaft, Erziehung und Volksbildung, 1934–1945* (Frankfurt am Main, 2012).

Nagel, Anne C., *Johannes Popitz (1884–1945): Görings Finanzminister und Verschwörer gegen Hitler. Eine Biographie* (Cologne, 2015).

Nath, Axel, *Die Studienratskarriere im Dritten Reich* (Frankfurt am Main, 1988).

Niehuis, Edith, *Das Landjahr. Eine Jugenderziehungseinrichtung in der Zeit des Nationalsozialismus* (Nörten-Hardenberg, 1984).

Niven, Bill, *Facing the Nazi Past: United Germany and the Legacy of the Third Reich* (London, 2002).

Niven, Bill (ed.), *Germans as Victims: Remembering the Past in Contemporary Germany* (Basingstoke, 2006).

Noakes, Jeremy, '"Viceroys of the Reich"? Gauleiters 1925–45', in Anthony McElligott and Tim Kirk (eds), *Working towards the Führer: Essays in Honour of Sir Ian Kershaw* (Manchester, 2003), 118–52.

Nolzen, Armin, 'Inklusion und Exklusion im "Dritten Reich". Das Beispiel der NSDAP', in Frank Bajohr and Michael Wildt (eds), *Volksgemeinschaft. Neue Forschungen zur Gesellschaft des Nationalsozialismus* (Frankfurt am Main, 2009), 60–77.

Nolzen, Armin and Schlüter, Marnie, 'Das Reichsministerium für Wissenschaft, Erziehung und Volksbildung im nationalsozialistischen Herrschaftssystem', in Klaus-Peter Horn and Jörg-W. Link (eds), *Erziehungsverhältnisse im Nationalsozialismus. Totaler Anspruch und Erziehungswirklichkeit* (Bad Heilbrunn, 2011), 341–55.

Norwood, Stephen H., *The Third Reich in the Ivory Tower: Complicity and Conflict on American Campuses* (Cambridge, 2009).

Oelkers, Jürgen, 'Erziehung und Gemeinschaft. Eine historische Analyse reformpädagogischer Optionen', in Christa Berg and Sieglinde Ellger-Rüttgart (eds), *'Du bist nichts, Dein Volk ist alles.' Forschungen zum Verhältnis von Pädagogik und Nationalsozialismus* (Weinheim, 1991), 22–45.

Orlow, Dietrich, *The Lure of Fascism in Western Europe: German Nazis, Dutch and French Fascists, 1933–1939* (Basingstoke, 2009).

Ortmeyer, Benjamin, *Schulzeit unterm Hitlerbild. Analysen, Berichte, Dokumente* (Frankfurt am Main, 1996).

Overmans, Rüdiger, 'Jugendliche in Kriegsgefangenschaft', in Ulrich Herrmann and Rolf-Dieter Müller (eds), *Junge Soldaten im Zweiten Weltkrieg. Kriegserfahrungen als Lebenserfahrungen* (Weinheim, 2010), 273–86.

Pahlke, Georg and Pohlmann, Wilhelm (eds), *Jugendhaus Hardehausen: 40 Jahre* (Paderborn, 1985).

Pammer, Thomas, 'Austrofaschismus und Jugend: gescheiterte Beziehung und lohnendes Forschungsfeld?', in Florian Wenninger and Lucile Dreidemy (eds), *Das Dollfuß/Schuschnigg-Regime 1933–1938. Vermessung eines Forschungsfeldes* (Vienna, 2013), 395–410.

Papanek, Ernst, *The Austrian School Reform: Its Bases, Principles and Development—The Twenty Years between the Two World Wars* (New York, 1962).

Patel, Kiran Klaus, *Soldiers of Labor: Labor Service in Nazi Germany and New Deal America, 1933–1945* (Cambridge, 2005).

Patel, Kiran Klaus, '"Sinnbild der nationalsozialistischen Weltanschauung"? Die Gestaltung von Lagern und Ordensburgen im Nationalsozialismus', in Paul Ciupke and Franz-Josef Jelich (eds), *Weltanschauliche Erziehung in Ordensburgen des Nationalsozialismus. Zur Geschichte und Zukunft der Ordensburg Vogelsang* (Essen, 2006), 33–52.

Patel, Kiran Klaus, '"Auslese" und "Ausmerze". Das Janusgesicht der nationalsozialistischen Lager', *Zeitschrift für Geschichtswissenschaft* 54 (2006), 339–65.

Patel, Kiran Klaus, 'Die "Volkserziehungsschule"—Der Arbeitsdienst für Männer und Frauen', in Klaus-Peter Horn and Jörg-W. Link (eds), *Erziehungsverhältnisse im Nationalsozialismus. Totaler Anspruch und Erziehungswirklichkeit* (Bad Heilbrunn, 2011), 187–203.

Patel, Kiran Klaus, 'Alltag und Freizeit in den NS-Ordensburgen', in Klaus Ring and Stefan Wunsch (eds), *Bestimmung: Herrenmensch. NS-Ordensburgen zwischen Faszination und Verbrechen* (Dresden, 2016), 188–97.

Pauley, Bruce F., *Hitler and the Forgotten Nazis: A History of Austrian National Socialism* (London, 1981).

Paustian, Matthias, *Die Nationalpolitische Erziehungsanstalt Plön 1933–1945* (Rostock, 1995).

Pedersen, Ulf, *Bernhard Rust: Ein nationalsozialistischer Bildungspolitiker vor dem Hintergrund seiner Zeit* (Braunschweig, 1994).

Perchinig, Elisabeth, *Zur Einübung von Weiblichkeit im Terrorzusammenhang. Mädchenadoleszenz in der NS-Gesellschaft* (Munich, 1996).

Perry, Joe, 'Christmas as Nazi Holiday: Colonising the Christmas Mood', in Lisa Pine (ed.), *Life and Times in Nazi Germany* (London, 2016), 263–89.

Pfefferle, Roman, *Schule—Macht—Politik. Politische Erziehung in österreichischen Schulbüchern der Zwischenkriegszeit* (Marburg, 2010).

Philipp, Marc J., *'Hitler ist tot, aber ich lebe noch': Zeitzeugenerinnerungen an den Nationalsozialismus* (Berlin, 2010).

Pine, Lisa, *Education in Nazi Germany* (Oxford, 2010).

Plato, Alexander von, 'The Hitler Youth Generation and Its Role in the Two Post-War German States', in Mark Roseman (ed.), *Generations in Conflict: Youth Revolt and Generation Formation in Germany 1770–1968* (Cambridge, 1995), 210–26.

Plön, Staatl. Internatsoberschule, *Festschrift der Staatl. Internatsoberschule Schloß Plön zur Erinnerung an die Gründung der Plöner Lateinschule vor 250 Jahren 1704–1954* (Plön, 1954).

Poensgen, Ruprecht, 'Die Schule Schloß Salem im Dritten Reich', *Vierteljahrshefte für Zeitgeschichte* 44, no. 1 (1996), 25–54.

Ponzio, Alessio, *Shaping the New Man: Youth Training Regimes in Fascist Italy and Nazi Germany* (Madison, 2015).

Poßekel, Kurt, 'Verein für das Deutschtum im Ausland (VDA) 1881–1945', in Dieter Fricke (ed.), *Die bürgerlichen und kleinbürgerlichen Parteien und Verbände in Deutschland (Bd. 4)* (Leipzig, 1986), 282–97.

Puchinger, Günther, *Von der Kadettenschule zum Flüchtlingslager. Die k. u. k. Artillerie-Kadettenschule in Traiskirchen und ihre Verwendung nach dem Zusammenbruch der Monarchie* (Traiskirchen, 1991).

Rahden, Till van, 'Clumsy Democrats: Moral Passions in the Federal Republic', *German History* 29, no. 3 (2011), 485–504.

Raphael, Lutz, 'Die nationalsozialistische Ideologie', in Paul Ciupke and Franz-Josef Jelich (eds), *Weltanschauliche Erziehung in Ordensburgen des Nationalsozialismus. Zur Geschichte und Zukunft der Ordensburg Vogelsang* (Essen, 2006), 15–32.

Raphael, Lutz, 'Pluralities of National Socialist Ideology: New Perspectives on the Production and Diffusion of National Socialist *Weltanschauung*', in Martina Steber and Bernhard Gotto (eds), *Visions of Community in Nazi Germany: Social Engineering and Private Lives* (Oxford, 2014), 73–86.

Ras, Marion E. P. de, *Body, Femininity and Nationalism: Girls in the German Youth Movement 1900–1934* (London, 2008).

Rath, R. John, 'Training for Citizenship, "Authoritarian" Austrian Style', *Journal of Central European Affairs* 3, no. 2 (1943), 121–46.

Rath, R. John, 'History and Citizenship Training: An Austrian Example', *The Journal of Modern History* 21, no. 3 (1949), 227–38.

Rau, Petra, *English Modernism, National Identity and the Germans, 1890–1950* (Farnham, 2009).

Rau-Kühne, Cornelia and Ruck, Michael (eds), *Regionale Eliten zwischen Diktatur und Demokratie. Baden und Württemberg 1930–1952* (Munich, 1993).

Reagin, Nancy R., *Sweeping the German Nation: Domesticity and National Identity in Germany, 1870–1945* (Cambridge, 2007).

Reeken, Dietmar von and Thießen, Malte (eds), *'Volksgemeinschaft' als soziale Praxis. Neue Forschungen zur NS-Gesellschaft vor Ort* (Paderborn, 2013).

Reese, Dagmar, 'Emancipation or Social Incorporation: Girls in the *Bund Deutscher Mädel*', in Heinz Sünker and Hans-Uwe Otto (eds), *Education and Fascism: Political Identity and Social Education in Nazi Germany* (London, 1997), 102–20.

Reese, Dagmar, 'Verstrickung und Verantwortung. Weibliche Jugendliche in der Führung des Bundes Deutscher Mädel', in Kirsten Heinsohn, Barbara Vogel, and Ulrike Weckel (eds), *Zwischen Karriere und Verfolgung. Handlungsräume von Frauen im nationalsozialistischen Deutschland* (Frankfurt am Main, 1997), 206–22.

Reese, Dagmar, *Growing up Female in Nazi Germany* (Ann Arbor, 2006).

Reese, Dagmar (ed.), *Die BDM-Generation. Weibliche Jugendliche in Deutschland und Österreich im Nationalsozialismus* (Berlin, 2007).

Reese, Dagmar and Sachse, Carola, 'Frauenforschung zum Nationalsozialismus: Eine Bilanz', in Lerke Gravenhorst and Carmen Tatschmurat (eds), *Töchter-Fragen. NS-Frauen-Geschichte* (Freiburg im Breisgau, 1990), 73–106.

Rehberger, Karl, 'Die Stifte Oberösterreichs unter dem Hakenkreuz', in Rudolf Zinnhobler (ed.), *Das Bistum Linz im Dritten Reich* (Linz, 1979), 244–94.

Reichardt, Sven and Seibel, Wolfgang (eds), *Der prekäre Staat. Herrschen und Verwalten im Nationalsozialismus* (Frankfurt am Main, 2011).

Reichel, Peter, *Der schöne Schein des Dritten Reiches. Gewalt und Faszination des deutschen Faschismus* (Hamburg, 2006).

Reinicke, David, et al. (eds), *Gemeinschaft als Erfahrung. Kulturelle Inszenierungen und soziale Praxis 1930–1960* (Paderborn, 2014).

Rellecke, Werner and Zehrer, Eva-Maria (eds), *Unauslöschlich. Erinnerungen an das Kriegsende 1945: Ein Lesebuch* (Dresden, 1995).

Rempel, Gerhard, *Hitler's Children: The Hitler Youth and the SS* (Chapel Hill, 1989).

Remy, Steven P., *The Heidelberg Myth: The Nazification and Denazification of a German University* (Cambridge, MA, 2002).

Reulecke, Jürgen, *'Ich möchte einer werden so wie die...' Männerbünde im 20. Jahrhundert* (Frankfurt am Main, 2001).

Reulecke, Jürgen, 'Die Ordensjunker im Kontext ihrer Generation', in Klaus Ring and Stefan Wunsch (eds), *Bestimmung: Herrenmensch. NS-Ordensburgen zwischen Faszination und Verbrechen* (Dresden, 2016), 148–57.

Rhode, Gotthold, 'The Protectorate of Bohemia and Moravia 1934–1945', in Victor S. Mamatey and Radomír Luža (eds), *A History of the Czechoslovak Republic, 1918–1948* (Princeton, 1973), 296–321.

Ring, Klaus, 'Fanatischer Idealist und pragmatischer Organisator der NSDAP—Robert Ley', in Klaus Ring and Stefan Wunsch (eds), *Bestimmung: Herrenmensch. NS-Ordensburgen zwischen Faszination und Verbrechen* (Dresden, 2016), 44–9.

Ring, Klaus and Wunsch, Stefan (eds), *Bestimmung: Herrenmensch. NS-Ordensburgen zwischen Faszination und Verbrechen* (Dresden, 2016).

Rinnerthaler, Alfred, 'Die Orden als Feindbilder des NS-Staates', in Maximilian Liebermann et al. (eds), *Staat und Kirche in der 'Ostmark'* (Frankfurt am Main, 1998), 351–94.

Ritter, Ernst, *Das Deutsche Ausland-Institut in Stuttgart 1917–1945. Ein Beispiel deutscher Volkstumsarbeit zwischen den Weltkriegen* (Wiesbaden, 1976).

Roche, Helen, '*Spartanische Pimpfe*: The Importance of Sparta in the Educational Ideology of the Adolf Hitler Schools', in Stephen Hodkinson and Ian Macgregor Morris (eds), *Sparta in Modern Thought: Politics, History and Culture* (Swansea, 2012), 315–42.

Roche, Helen, *Sparta's German Children: The Ideal of Ancient Sparta in the Royal Prussian Cadet Corps, 1818–1920, and in National Socialist Elite Schools (the Napolas), 1933–1945* (Swansea, 2013).

Roche, Helen, '"*Wanderer, kommst du nach Pforta...*": The Tension between Classical Tradition and the Demands of a Nazi Elite-School Education at Schulpforta and Ilfeld, 1934–45', *European Review of History/revue européenne d'histoire* 20, no. 4 (2013), 581–609.

Roche, Helen, '"Anti-Enlightenment": National Socialist Educators' Troubled Relationship with Humanism and the Philhellenist Tradition', *Publications of the English Goethe Society* 82, no. 3 (2013), 193–207.

Roche, Helen, '*Zwischen Freundschaft und Feindschaft*: Exploring Relationships between Pupils at the Napolas (*Nationalpolitische Erziehungsanstalten*) and British Public Schoolboys', *Angermion: Yearbook for Anglo-German Literary Criticism, Intellectual History and Cultural Transfers/Jahrbuch für britisch-deutsche Kulturbeziehungen* 6 (2013), 101–26.

Roche, Helen, 'Surviving "*Stunde Null*": Narrating the Fate of Nazi Elite-School Pupils During the Collapse of the Third Reich', *German History* 33, no. 4 (2015), 570–87.

Roche, Helen, 'Sport, Leibeserziehung und vormilitärische Ausbildung in den Nationalpolitischen Erziehungsanstalten: Eine "radikale" Revolution der körperlichen Bildung im Rahmen der NS-"Gesamterziehung"?', in Frank Becker and Ralf Schäfer (eds), *Beiträge zur Geschichte des Nationalsozialismus*, 32—*Sport und Nationalsozialismus*, (2016), 173–96.

Roche, Helen, '*Herrschaft durch Schulung*: The *Nationalpolitische Erziehungsanstalten im Osten* and the Third Reich's Germanising Mission', in Burkhard Olschowsky and Ingo Loose (eds), *Nationalsozialismus und Regionalbewusstsein im östlichen Europa: Ideologie, Machtausbau, Beharrung* (Berlin, 2016), 127–51.

Roche, Helen, '*Blüte und Zerfall*: "Schematic Narrative Templates" of Decline and Fall in *völkisch* and National Socialist Racial Ideology', in Lara Day and Oliver Haag (eds), *The Persistence of Race: Change and Continuity in Germany from the Wilhelmine Empire to National Socialism* (Oxford, 2017), 65–86.

Roche, Helen, 'Classics and Education in the Third Reich: *Die Alten Sprachen* and the Nazification of Latin- and Greek-Teaching in Secondary Schools', in Helen Roche and Kyriakos Demetriou (eds), *Brill's Companion to the Classics, Fascist Italy and Nazi Germany* (Leiden, 2018), 238–63.

Roche, Helen, 'Die Klosterschule Ilfeld als Nationalpolitische Erziehungsanstalt', in Detlef Schmiechen-Ackermann et al. (eds), *Die Klosterkammer Hannover 1931–1955. Eine Mittelbehörde zwischen wirtschaftlicher Rationalität und Politisierung* (Göttingen, 2018), 605–26.

Roche, Helen, 'Antisemitismus und Eliteerziehung in den Nationalpolitischen Erziehungsanstalten', *Stiftung Niedersächsische Gedenkstätten. Jahresbericht 2017. Schwerpunktthema: Kindheit im Nationalsozialismus* (2018), 12–17.

Roche, Helen, 'Schulische Erziehung und Entbürgerlichung', in Norbert Frei (ed.), *Wie bürgerlich war der Nationalsozialismus?* (Göttingen, 2018), 154–72.

Roche, Helen, '"*Der Versuch einer Antwort, warum ich von Auschwitz nichts wußte*": The Evolution of Napola-Pupils' Responses to the Holocaust', in A.S. Sarhangi and Alina Bothe (eds), *Früher/später: Zeugnisse in der Zeit* (Berlin, forthcoming).

Röger, Maren, *Flucht, Vertreibung und Umsiedlung. Mediale Erinnerungen und Debatten in Deutschland und Polen seit 1989* (Marburg, 2011).

Rohkrämer, Thomas, *Die fatale Attraktion des Nationalsozialismus. Zur Popularität eines Unrechtsregimes* (Paderborn, 2013).

Rohn, Hendryk, 'Nationalpolitische Erziehungsanstalten', in Wolfgang Benz (ed.), *Handbuch des Antisemitismus. Judenfeindschaft in Geschichte und Gegenwart* (Berlin, 2012), 423–5.

Römer, Felix, *Kameraden. Die Wehrmacht von innen* (Munich, 2012).

Roseman, Mark, 'Introduction: Generation Conflict and German History 1770–1968', in Mark Roseman (ed.), *Generations in Conflict: Youth Revolt and Generation Formation in Germany 1770–1968* (Cambridge, 1995), 1–46.

Roseman, Mark (ed.), *Generations in Conflict: Youth Revolt and Generation Formation in Germany 1770–1968* (Cambridge, 1995).

Roseman, Mark, 'Surviving Memory: Truth and Inaccuracy in Holocaust Testimony', in Robert Perks and Alistair Thomson (eds), *The Oral History Reader* (2nd edn; London, 2006), 230–43.

Rosenbaum, Heidi, *Formen der Familie. Untersuchungen zum Zusammenhang von Familienverhältnissen, Sozialstruktur und sozialem Wandel in der deutschen Gesellschaft des 19. Jahrhunderts* (Frankfurt am Main, 1982).

Rosenbaum, Heidi, *'Und trotzdem war's 'ne schöne Zeit'. Kinderalltag im Nationalsozialismus* (Frankfurt am Main, 2014).

Rosenthal, Gabriele (ed.), *Die Hitlerjugend-Generation. Biographische Thematisierung als Vergangenheitsbewältigung* (Essen, 1986).

Rosenthal, Gabriele (ed.), *'Als der Krieg kam, hatte ich mit Hitler nichts mehr zu tun': Zur Gegenwärtigkeit des 'Dritten Reiches' in Biographien* (Opladen, 1990).

Rosenthal, Gabriele, 'German War Memories: Narrability and the Biographical and Social Functions of Remembering', *Oral History* 19, no. 2 (1991), 34–41.

Roth, Thomas and Wunsch, Stefan, 'Vogelsang in der Region. Die NS-Ordensburg im Fokus der regionalgeschichtlichen Forschung', in Albert Moritz (ed.), *'Fackelträger der Nation'. Elitebildung in den NS-Ordensburgen* (Cologne, 2010), 136–98.

Rother, Wolfgang, 'Die ehemalige Landesschule Dresden in Klotzsche—Ein architekturgeschichtlicher Rückblick und Betrachtungen zu den restaurierten bauplastischen Arbeiten am ehemaligen Lehrgebäude', in Hauptverband der gewerblichen Berufsgenossenschaften (ed.), *Zur Geschichte des Standortes der Berufsgenossenschaftlichen Akademie für Arbeitssicherheit und Gesundheitsschutz. Landesschule Dresden in Klotzsche (1927–1933)* (Dresden, 2001), 3–24.

Rovere, Luca la, 'Totalitarian Pedagogy and the Italian Youth', in Jorge Dagnino, Matthew Feldman, and Paul Stocker (eds), *The 'New Man' in Radical Right Ideology and Practice, 1919–45* (London, 2018), 19–38.

Ruck, Michael, 'Zentralismus und Regionalgewalten im Herrschaftsgefüge des NS-Staates', in Horst Möller, Andreas Wirsching, and Walter Ziegler (eds), *Nationalsozialismus in der Region. Beiträge zur regionalen und lokalen Forschung und zum internationalen Vergleich* (Munich, 1996), 99–122.

Rudloff, Wilfried, 'Einleitung: Dimensionen der Regionalität in der Bildungs- und Wissenschaftsgeschichte', *Westfälische Forschungen* 60 (2010), 1–17.

Sabrow, Martin, 'Der Zeitzeuge als Wanderer zwischen zwei Welten', in Martin Sabrow and Norbert Frei (eds), *Die Geburt des Zeitzeugen nach 1945* (Göttingen, 2012), 13–32.

Saldern, Adelheid von, 'Victims or Perpetrators? Controversies about the Role of Women in the Nazi State', in David F. Crew (ed.), *Nazism and German Society, 1933–1945* (London, 1994), 141–65.

Sauer, Walter, 'Loyalität, Konkurrenz oder Widerstand? Nationalsozialistische Kultuspolitik und kirchliche Reaktionen in Österreich 1938–1945', in Emmerich Tálos et al. (eds), *NS-Herrschaft in Österreich. Ein Handbuch* (Vienna, 2002), 159–86.

Saxton, Martha, 'Introduction to the First Volume of *The Journal of the History of Childhood and Youth*', in Heidi Morrison (ed.), *The Global History of Childhood Reader* (New York, 2012), 103–4.

Scapinelli, Paul, 'Die Zeit von 1938 bis 1957: Ein nüchterner Tatsachenbericht', *Realgymnasium der Theresianischen Akademie. Jahresbericht 1957/58* (Vienna, 1958), 31–7.

Schaarschmidt, Thomas, 'Regionalität im Nationalsozialismus—Kategorien, Begriffe, Forschungsstand', in Jürgen John, Horst Möller, and Thomas Schaarschmidt (eds), *Die NS-Gaue. Regionale Mittelinstanzen im zentralistischen 'Führerstaat'* (Munich, 2007), 13–21.

Schaarschmidt, Thomas, 'Die Zentrale des "Heimatwerks Sachsen" im ehemaligen Ständehaus, Schloßstraße 1—"Sachsen marschiert wieder einmal an der Spitze..."', in Konstantin Herrmann (ed.), *Führerschule, Thingplatz, 'Judenhaus'. Topografien der NS-Herrschaft in Sachsen* (Dresden, 2014), 166–9.

Schaat, Julia and Krause, Markus, 'Zur Konzeption der Dauerausstellung "Bestimmung: Herrenmensch. NS-Ordensburgen zwischen Faszination und Verbrechen"', in Klaus Ring and Stefan Wunsch (eds), *Bestimmung: Herrenmensch. NS-Ordensburgen zwischen Faszination und Verbrechen* (Dresden, 2016), 28–35.

Schanetzky, Tim, *'Kanonen statt Butter'. Wirtschaft und Konsum im Dritten Reich* (Munich, 2015).

Scheck, Raffael, *Mothers of the Nation: Right-Wing Women in Weimar Germany* (Oxford, 2004).

Schiedeck, Jürgen and Stahlmann, Martin, 'Totalizing of Experience: Educational Camps', in Heinz Sünker and Hans-Uwe Otto (eds), *Education and Fascism: Political Identity and Social Education in Nazi Germany* (London, 1997), 54–80.

Schildt, Axel, 'The Long Shadows of the Second World War: The Impact of Experiences and Memories of War on West German Society', *Bulletin of the German Historical Institute London* 29, no. 1 (2007), 28–49.

Schilling, René, *'Kriegshelden'. Deutungsmuster heroischer Männlichkeit in Deutschland 1813–1945* (Paderborn, 2002).

Schlüter, Marnie, 'Das Preußische Kultusministerium zwischen Reichsexekution und Reichsministerium (Juli 1932–Mai 1934). Vom Nutzen der Verwaltungsgeschichte für die Bildungsgeschichte', in Gisela Miller-Kipp and Bernd Zymek (eds), *Politik in der Bildungsgeschichte—Befunde, Prozesse, Diskurse* (Bad Heilbrunn, 2006), 149–63.

Schmeitzner, Mike, 'Dresden: Landtag und Staatskanzlei', in Konstantin Herrmann (ed.), *Führerschule, Thingplatz, 'Judenhaus'. Topografien der NS-Herrschaft in Sachsen* (Dresden, 2014), 58–61.

Schmidt, Daniel, '"Der Osten ist ein Bewährungsfeld für Pioniere in jeder Hinsicht."—Angehörige der NS-Ordensburgen im Weltanschauungs- und Vernichtungskrieg 1939–1945', in Klaus Ring and Stefan Wunsch (eds), *Bestimmung: Herrenmensch. NS-Ordensburgen zwischen Faszination und Verbrechen* (Dresden, 2016), 316–23.

Schmiechen-Ackermann, Detlef, 'Das Potenzial der Komparatistik für die NS-Regionalforschung—Vorüberlegungen zu einer Typologie von NS-Gauen und ihren Gauleitern anhand der Fallbeispiele Süd-Hannover-Braunschweig, Osthannover und Weser-Ems', in Jürgen John, Horst Möller, and Thomas Schaarschmidt (eds), *Die NS-Gaue. Regionale Mittelinstanzen im zentralistischen 'Führerstaat'* (Munich, 2007), 234–53.

Schmiechen-Ackermann, Detlef (ed.), *'Volksgemeinschaft': Mythos, wirkungsmächtige soziale Verheißung oder soziale Realität im 'Dritten Reich'?* (Paderborn, 2012).

Schmiechen-Ackermann, Detlef, 'Social Control and the Making of the *Volksgemeinschaft*', in Martina Steber and Bernhard Gotto (eds), *Visions of Community in Nazi Germany: Social Engineering and Private Lives* (Oxford, 2014), 240–53.

Schmiechen-Ackermann, Detlef and Kaltenborn, Steffi, 'Stadtgeschichte und NS-Zeit in Sachsen-Anhalt und im regionalen Vergleich. Forschungsstand, Fragen und Perspektiven', in Detlef Schmiechen-Ackermann and Steffi Kaltenborn (eds), *Stadtgeschichte in der NS-Zeit. Fallstudien aus Sachsen-Anhalt und vergleichende Perspektiven* (Münster, 2005), 7–38.

Schmiechen-Ackermann, Detlef and Schaarschmidt, Thomas, 'Regionen als Bezugsgröße in Diktaturen und Demokratien', *Comparativ* 13, no. 1 (2003), 7–16.

Schmiechen-Ackermann, Detlef, et al. (eds), *Der Ort der 'Volksgemeinschaft' in der deutschen Gesellschaftsgeschichte* (Paderborn, 2018).

Schmiechen-Ackermann, Detlef, et al. (eds), *Die Klosterkammer Hannover 1931–1955. Eine Mittelbehörde zwischen wirtschaftlicher Rationalität und Politisierung* (Göttingen, 2018).

Schmitz, Klaus, 'Gründung und Aufbau der "Nationalpolitischen Erziehungsanstalt" in Bensberg im Rahmen der NS-Schulpolitik in Preußen (1933–1940)', *Zeitschrift des Bergischen Geschichtsvereins* 93 (1987/8), 133–69.

Schmitz, Klaus, 'Auf Spurensuche in der jüngeren Vergangenheit: Das Außenlager Bensberg des KZ-Buchenwald', *Rheinisch-Bergischer Kalender* 59 (1989), 209–15.

Schmitz, Klaus, *Militärische Jugenderziehung. Preußische Kadettenhäuser und Nationalpolitische Erziehungsanstalten zwischen 1807 und 1936* (Frankfurt am Main, 1997).

Schneider, Barbara, *Die höhere Schule im Nationalsozialismus. Zur Ideologisierung von Bildung und Erziehung* (Cologne, 2000).

Schneider, Barbara, 'Die sächsischen Fürstenschulen unter dem Einfluß nationalsozialistischer Bildungspolitik. Ein Beitrag zum Verhältnis von Schulkultur und Politik', in Jonas Flöter and Günther Wartenberg (eds), *Die sächsischen Fürsten- und Landesschulen. Interaktion von lutherisch-humanistischem Erziehungsideal und Eliten-Bildung* (Leipzig, 2004), 141–63.

Schneider, Christian, 'Sehen, Hören, Glauben. Zur Konstruktion von Authentizität', in Margrit Frölich, Christian Schneider, and Karsten Visarius (eds), *Das Böse im Blick. Die Gegenwart des Nationalsozialismus im Film* (Nehren, 2007), 15–29.

Schneider, Christian, 'Karrierewege ehemaliger NS-Eliteschüler in der Bundesrepublik', in Albert Moritz (ed.), *'Fackelträger der Nation'. Elitebildung in den NS-Ordensburgen* (Cologne, 2010), 228–31.

Schneider, Christian, Stillke, Cordelia, and Leineweber, Bernd, *Das Erbe der Napola. Versuch einer Generationengeschichte des Nationalsozialismus* (Hamburg, 1996).

Schneider, Michael, 'Nationalsozialismus und Region', *Archiv für Sozialgeschichte* 40 (2000), 423–39.

Schnurr, Stefan, 'Vom Wohlfahrtsstaat zum Erziehungsstaat. Sozialpolitik und soziale Arbeit in der Weimarer Republik und im Nationalsozialismus', *Widersprüche* 8 (1988), 47–64.

Schnurr, Stefan and Steinacker, Sven, 'Soziale Arbeit im Nationalsozialismus—*Auslese* und *Ausmerze* im Dienste der *Volkspflege*', in Klaus-Peter Horn and Jörg-W. Link (eds), *Erziehungsverhältnisse im Nationalsozialismus. Totaler Anspruch und Erziehungswirklichkeit* (Bad Heilbrunn, 2011), 253–73.

Schoenbaum, David, *Hitler's Social Revolution: Class and Status in Nazi Germany* (New York, 1966).

Scholtyseck, Joachim, 'Der "Schwabenherzog". Gottlob Berger, SS-Obergruppenführer', in Michael Kißener and Joachim Scholtyseck (eds), *Die Führer der Provinz. NS-Biographien aus Baden und Württemberg* (Konstanz, 1997), 77–110.

Scholtyseck, Joachim, 'Nationalsozialismus im Raum Bergisch Gladbach, 1933–1945', in Albert Eßer (ed.), *Bergisch Gladbacher Stadtgeschichte* (Bergisch Gladbach, 2006), 353–400.

Scholtz, Harald, '*Unsere Jungen*. Ein Film der Nationalpolitischen Erziehungsanstalten', *Filmdokumente zur Zeitgeschichte* (1969), 285–302.

Scholtz, Harald, *Nationalsozialistische Ausleseschulen. Internatsschulen als Herrschaftsmittel des Führerstaates* (Göttingen, 1973).

Scholtz, Harald, *Erziehung und Unterricht unterm Hakenkreuz* (Göttingen, 1985).

Scholtz, Harald, 'Schule unterm Hakenkreuz. Zum Aufarbeiten von Erinnerungen', *Universitas. Zeitschrift für Wissenschaft, Kunst und Literatur* 43, no. 4 (1988), 466–73.

Scholtz, Harald, 'Pädagogische Reformpraxis im Sog einer totalitären Bewegung. Versuche zur Anpassung und Instrumentalisierung', in Ulrich Herrmann and Jürgen Oelkers (eds), *Pädagogik und Nationalsozialismus* (Weinheim, 1989), 221–41.

Scholtz, Harald, 'Das nationalsozialistische Reich—kein Erziehungsstaat', in Dietrich Benner, Jürgen Schriewer, and Heinz-Elmar Tenorth (eds), *Erziehungsstaaten. Historisch-vergleichende Analysen ihrer Denktraditionen und nationaler Gestalten* (Weinheim, 1998), 131–44.

Scholtz, Harald, 'Körpererziehung als Mittel zur Mentalitätsprägung an den Adolf-Hitler-Schulen', in Paul Ciupke and Franz-Josef Jelich (eds), *Weltanschauliche Erziehung in Ordensburgen des Nationalsozialismus. Zur Geschichte und Zukunft der Ordensburg Vogelsang* (Essen, 2006 [orig. 1989]), 85–100.

Schörken, Rolf, '"Schülersoldaten"—Prägung einer Generation', in Rolf-Dieter Müller and Hans-Erich Volkmann (eds), *Die Wehrmacht: Mythos und Realität* (Munich, 1999), 456–73.

Schörken, Rolf, *Die Niederlage als Generationserfahrung. Jugendliche nach dem Zusammenbruch der NS-Herrschaft* (Weinheim, 2004).

Schörken, Rolf, *Jugend 1945. Politisches Denken und Lebensgeschichte* (Frankfurt am Main, 2005).

Schreckenberg, Heinz, *Erziehung, Lebenswelt und Kriegseinsatz der deutschen Jugend unter Hitler. Anmerkungen zur Literatur* (Münster, 2001).

Schröter, Roland, 'Die Staatliche Bildungsanstalt zu Berlin-Lichterfelde von 1920 bis 1933', *Steglitzer Heimat* 31 (1986), 13–22.

Schulte, Jan Erik, 'The SS as the "Alibi of a Nation"? Narrative Continuities from the Nuremberg Trials to the 1960s', in Kim Christian Priemel and Alexa Stiller (eds), *Reassessing the Nuremberg Military Tribunals: Transitional Justice, Trial Narratives, and Historiography* (New York, 2012), 134–60.

Schulte, Jan Erik, Lieb, Peter, and Wegner, Bernd (eds), *Die Waffen-SS. Neue Forschungen* (Paderborn, 2014).

Schulte, Jan Erik, 'Wiege apologetischer Narrative. Die Organisationsverfahren gegen SS, Gestapo und SD vor dem Internationalen Militärgerichtshof in Nürnberg 1945/46', in Jan Erik Schulte and Michael Wildt (eds), *Die SS nach 1945. Entschuldungsnarrative, populäre Mythen, europäische Erinnerungsdiskurse* (Göttingen, 2018), 29–55.

Schulte, Jan Erik and Wildt, Michael, *Die SS nach 1945. Entschuldungsnarrative, populäre Mythen, europäische Erinnerungsdiskurse* (Göttingen, 2018).

Schulte, Jan Erik and Wildt, Michael, 'Die zweite Geschichte der SS—Einleitung', in Jan Erik Schulte and Michael Wildt (eds), *Die SS nach 1945. Entschuldungsnarrative, populäre Mythen, europäische Erinnerungsdiskurse* (Göttingen, 2018), 9–26.

Schulze, Hagen, 'Democratic Prussia in Weimar Germany, 1919–33', in Philip Dwyer (ed.), *Modern Prussian History 1830–1947* (Harlow, 2001), 211–29.

Schwartz, Michael, 'Ethnische "Säuberung" als Kriegsfolge: Ursachen und Verlauf der Vertreibung der deutschen Zivilbevölkerung aus Ostdeutschland und Osteuropa 1941 bis 1950', in Rolf-Dieter Müller (ed.), *Der Zusammenbruch des deutschen Reiches 1945. Zweiter Halbband: Die Folgen des zweiten Weltkrieges* (Munich, 2008), 509–656.

Schwarz, Angela, *Die Reise ins Dritte Reich. Britische Augenzeugen im nationalsozialistischen Deutschland 1933–1939* (Göttingen, 1993).

Schwarz, Gudrun, *Eine Frau an seiner Seite. Ehefrauen in der 'SS-Sippengemeinschaft'* (Hamburg, 1997).

Seegers, Lu, 'Einführung', in Lu Seegers and Jürgen Reulecke (eds), *Die 'Generation der Kriegskinder'. Historische Hintergründe und Deutungen* (Gießen, 2009), 11–30.

Seegers, Lu, 'Die "Generation der Kriegskinder". Mediale Inszenierung einer "Leidensgemeinschaft"?', in Detlef Schmiechen-Ackermann (ed.), *'Volksgemeinschaft': Mythos, wirkungsmächtige soziale Verheißung oder soziale Realität im 'Dritten Reich'?* (Paderborn, 2012), 335–54.

Seegers, Lu and Reulecke, Jürgen (eds), *Die 'Generation der Kriegskinder'. Historische Hintergründe und Deutungen* (Gießen, 2009).

Segar, Kenneth and Warren, John (eds), *Austria in the Thirties: Culture and Politics* (Riverside, 1991).

Seitter, Wolfgang, 'Verdrängung, Eingliederung, Aufwertung—Erwachsenenbildung im Nationalsozialismus', in Klaus-Peter Horn and Jörg-W. Link (eds), *Erziehungsverhältnisse im Nationalsozialismus. Totaler Anspruch und Erziehungswirklichkeit* (Bad Heilbrunn, 2011), 275–93.

Semmens, Kristin, *Seeing Hitler's Germany: Tourism in the Third Reich* (Basingstoke, 2005).

Showalter, Dennis, 'Prussia's Military Legacy in Empire, Republic and Reich, 1871–1945', in Philip G. Dwyer (ed.), *Modern Prussian History 1830–1947* (Harlow, 2001), 230–52.

Siemens, Daniel, *Stormtroopers: A New History of Hitler's Brownshirts* (New Haven, 2017).

Simms, Brendan, 'Prussia, Prussianism and National Socialism, 1933–1947', in Philip G. Dwyer (ed.), *Modern Prussian History 1830–1947* (Harlow, 2001), 253–73.

Šimůnek, Michal, 'Poslední "vůdcovska škola" nacistické diktatury: tzv. Nacionálně politický výchovný ústav Čechy (Nationalpolitische Erziehungsanstalt Böhmen) v Kutné Hoře, 1943–1945 [Die "NPEA Böhmen" in Kuttenberg 1943–1945: Letzte "Führerschule" der national-sozialistischen Diktatur]', *Acta Universitatis Carolinae* 51, no. 1 (2011), 59–81.

Šimůnek, Michal, '"Tschechische Studentenaktion"—Das medizinische Universitätsstudium der Protektoratsangehörigen in Deutschland, 1941–1945', in Ursula Ferdinand, Hans-Peter Kröner, and Ioanna Mamali (eds), *Medizinische Fakultäten in der deutschen Hochschullandschaft 1925–1950* (Heidelberg, 2013), 283–93.

Smelser, Roland and Syring, Enrico, *Die SS. Elite unter dem Totenkopf: 30 Lebensläufe* (Paderborn, 2000).

Spannenberger, Norbert, 'The Ethnic Policy of the Third Reich toward the Volksdeutsche in Central and Eastern Europe', in Marina Cattaruzza, Stefan Dyroff, and Dieter Langewiesche (eds), *Territorial Revisionism and the Allies of Germany in the Second World War: Goals, Expectations, Practices* (Oxford, 2013), 56–71.

Sperling, Christoph, *Joachim Haupt (1900–1989). Vom Aufstieg eines NS-Studentenfunktionärs und Sturz des Inspekteurs der Nationalpolitischen Erziehungsanstalten* (Berlin, 2018).

Spicer, Kevin P., *Hitler's Priests: Catholic Clergy and National Socialism* (DeKalb, 2008).

Stachura, Peter, *Nazi Youth in the Weimar Republic* (Santa Barbara, 1975).

Städtisches Gymnasium Laurentianum, *Die höheren Schulen Arnsbergs im Dritten Reich. Schulalltag am Staatlichen Gymnasium Laurentianum, am Evangelischen Lyzeum und an der Städtischen Oberschule für Mädchen (1933 bis 1945)* (Arnsberg, 2001).

Stadtmuseum Schwedt/Oder, *Wir wollten eigentlich nicht fliehen... Schwedt im Frühjahr 1945* (Schwedt/Oder, 2007).

Stargardt, Nicholas, 'German Childhoods: The Making of a Historiography', *German History* 16, no. 1 (1998), 1–15.

Stargardt, Nicholas, *Witnesses of War: Children's Lives under the Nazis* (London, 2006).

Stargardt, Nicholas, *The German War: A Nation under Arms, 1939–45* (London, 2015).

Starke, Holger, 'Die Vereidigung des Dresdner Volkssturms auf der Ilgen-Kampfbahn', in Konstantin Herrmann (ed.), *Führerschule, Thingplatz, 'Judenhaus'. Topografien der NS-Herrschaft in Sachsen* (Dresden, 2014), 291–3.

Stearns, Peter N., 'Challenges in the History of Childhood', *The Journal of the History of Childhood and Youth* 1, no. 1 (2008), 35–42.

Steber, Martina, 'Fragiles Gleichgewicht. Die Kulturarbeit der Gaue zwischen Regionalismus und Zentralismus', in Jürgen John, Horst Möller, and Thomas Schaarschmidt (eds), *Die NS-Gaue. Regionale Mittelinstanzen im zentralistischen 'Führerstaat'* (Munich, 2007), 141–58.

Steber, Martina and Gotto, Bernhard, '*Volksgemeinschaft*: Writing the Social History of the Nazi Regime', in Martina Steber and Bernhard Gotto (eds), *Visions of Community in Nazi Germany: Social Engineering and Private Lives* (Oxford, 2014), 1–25.

Steber, Martina and Gotto, Bernhard (eds), *Visions of Community in Nazi Germany: Social Engineering and Private Lives* (Oxford, 2014).
Steigmann-Gall, Richard, *The Holy Reich: Nazi Conceptions of Christianity, 1919–1945* (Cambridge, 2003).
Steinbach, Stefanie, *Erkennen, erfassen, bekämpfen—Gegnerforschung im Sicherheitsdienst der SS* (Berlin, 2018).
Steinbacher, Sybille (ed.), *Volksgenossinnen. Frauen in der NS-Volksgemeinschaft* (Göttingen, 2007).
Steinbacher, Sybille, 'Differenz der Geschlechter? Chancen und Schranken für die "Volksgenossinnen"', in Frank Bajohr and Michael Wildt (eds), *Volksgemeinschaft. Neue Forschungen zur Gesellschaft des Nationalsozialismus* (Frankfurt am Main, 2009), 94–104.
Steinbacher, Sybille, 'Zeitzeugenschaft und die Etablierung der Zeitgeschichte in der Bundesrepublik Deutschland', in Martin Sabrow and Norbert Frei (eds), *Die Geburt des Zeitzeugen nach 1945* (Göttingen, 2012), 145–56.
Steinert, Marlis G., *Hitler's War and the Germans: Public Mood and Attitude during the Second World War* (Athens, OH, 1977).
Stelzner-Large, Barbara, *Der Jugend zur Freude? Untersuchungen zum propagandistischen Jugendspielfilm im Dritten Reich* (Weimar, 1996).
Stephenson, Jill, *The Nazi Organisation of Women* (London, 1981).
Stephenson, Jill, *Women in Nazi Germany* (London, 2001).
Stephenson, Jill, *Hitler's Home Front: Württemberg under the Nazis* (London, 2006).
Stephenson, Jill, 'Der Arbeitsdienst für die weibliche Jugend', in Dagmar Reese (ed.), *Die BDM-Generation. Weibliche Jugendliche in Deutschland und Österreich im Nationalsozialismus* (Berlin, 2007), 255–87.
Stephenson, Jill, 'Inclusion: Building the National Community in Propaganda and Practice', in Jane Caplan (ed.), *Nazi Germany* (Oxford, 2008), 99–121.
Stern, Kathrin, 'Vom Volksschullehrer zum Volkserzieher—Ostfriesische Lehrkräfte im Einsatz für die nationalsozialistische "Volksgemeinschaft"?', in Dietmar von Reeken and Malte Thießen (eds), *'Volksgemeinschaft' als soziale Praxis. Neue Forschungen zur NS-Gesellschaft vor Ort* (Paderborn, 2013), 225–39.
Steuwer, Janosch, *'Ein Drittes Reich, wie ich es auffasse'. Politik, Gesellschaft und privates Leben in Tagebüchern 1933–1939* (Göttingen, 2017).
Steuwer, Janosch and Leßau, Hanne, '"Wer ist ein Nazi? Woran erkennt man ihn?" Zur Unterscheidung von Nationalsozialisten und anderen Deutschen', *Mittelweg 36*, no. 1 (2014), 30–51.
Stibbe, Matthew, *Women in the Third Reich* (London, 2003).
Stier, P. Elmar, 'Das Missionshaus St. Wendel zur NS-Zeit', *Heimatbuch des Landkreises St. Wendel* 19 (1981/2), 181–6.
Stiller, Alexa, 'On the Margins of the *Volksgemeinschaft*: Criteria for Belonging to the Volk within the Nazi Germanization Policy in the Annexed Territories, 1939–1945', in Claus-Christian W. Szejnmann and Maiken Umbach (eds), *Heimat, Region and Empire. Spatial Identities under National Socialism* (Basingstoke, 2012), 235–51.
Stiller, Alexa, 'Gewalt und Alltag der Volkstumspolitik. Der Apparat des Reichskommissars für die Festigung deutschen Volkstums und andere gesellschaftliche Akteure der veralltäglichten Gewalt', in Jochen Böhler and Stephan Lehnstaedt (eds), *Gewalt und Alltag im besetzten Polen 1939–1945* (Osnabrück, 2012), 45–66.
Stolle, Michael, 'Der schwäbische Schulmeister. Christian Mergenthaler, Württembergischer Ministerpräsident, Justiz- und Kultminister', in Michael Kißener and Joachim Scholtyseck (eds), *Die Führer der Provinz. NS-Biographien aus Baden und Württemberg* (Konstanz, 1997), 445–75.

Stone, Dan, *Responses to Nazism in Britain, 1933–1939: Before War and Holocaust* (Basingstoke, 2012).

Strien, Renate, *Mädchenerziehung und -sozialisation in der Zeit des Nationalsozialismus und ihre lebensgeschichtliche Bedeutung. Lehrerinnen erinnern sich an ihre Jugend während des Dritten Reiches* (Opladen, 2000).

Strippel, Andreas, *NS-Volkstumspolitik und die Neuordnung Europas. Rassenpolitische Selektion der Einwandererzentralstelle des Chefs der Sicherheitspolizei und des SD 1939–1945* (Paderborn, 2011).

Strippel, Andreas, 'Race, Regional Identity and *Volksgemeinschaft*: Naturalization of Ethnic German Resettlers in the Second World War by the Einwandererzentralstelle/Central Immigration Office of the SS', in Claus-Christian W. Szejnmann and Maiken Umbach (eds), *Heimat, Region and Empire: Spatial Identities under National Socialism* (Basingstoke, 2012), 184–98.

Sünker, Heinz and Otto, Hans-Uwe (eds), *Education and Fascism: Political Identity and Social Education in Nazi Germany* (London, 1997).

Süß, Dietmar, *Death from the Skies: How the British and Germans Survived Bombing in World War II* (Oxford, 2014).

Süß, Dietmar, *'Ein Volk, ein Reich, ein Führer'. Die deutsche Gesellschaft im Dritten Reich* (Munich, 2017).

Svašek, Maruška, 'Gewähltes Trauma: Die Dynamik der erinnerten und (wieder-) erfahrenen Emotion', in Elisabeth Fendl (ed.), *Zur Ikonographie des Heimwehs. Erinnerungskultur von Heimatvertriebenen* (Freiburg im Breisgau, 2002), 55–78.

Swett, Pamela E., Ross, Corey, and d'Almeida, Fabrice (eds), *Pleasure and Power in Nazi Germany* (Basingstoke, 2011).

Szejnmann, Claus-Christian W., *Nazism in Central Germany: The Brownshirts in 'Red' Saxony* (New York, 1999).

Szejnmann, Claus-Christian W., 'Verwässerung oder Systemstabilisierung? Der Nationalsozialismus in Regionen des Deutschen Reichs', *Neue politische Literatur* 48 (2003), 208–51.

Szejnmann, Claus-Christian W., 'Regionalgeschichte und die Erforschung des Nationalsozialismus. Forschungsstand und Forschungsperspektiven', in Günther Heydemann, Jan Erik Schulte, and Francesca Weil (eds), *Sachsen und der Nationalsozialismus* (Göttingen, 2014), 21–40.

Szepansky, Gerda, *'Blitzmädel', 'Heldenmutter', 'Kriegerwitwe'. Frauenleben im Zweiten Weltkrieg* (Frankfurt am Main, 1986).

Szodrzynski, Joachim, 'Die "Heimatfront" zwischen Stalingrad und Kriegsende', in Forschungsstelle für Zeitgeschichte in Hamburg (ed.), *Hamburg im 'Dritten Reich'* (Göttingen, 2005), 633–85.

Tálos, Emmerich, *Das austrofaschistische Herrschaftssystem. Österreich 1933–1938* (Vienna, 2013).

Tálos, Emmerich, et al. (eds), *NS-Herrschaft in Österreich. Ein Handbuch* (Vienna, 2002).

Taylor, Frederick, *Exorcising Hitler: The Occupation and Denazification of Germany* (London, 2011).

Tenorth, Heinz-Elmar, 'Grenzen der Indoktrination', in Peter Drewek et al. (eds), *Ambivalenzen der Pädagogik. Zur Bildungsgeschichte der Aufklärung und des 20. Jahrhunderts—Harald Scholtz zum 65. Geburtstag* (Weinheim, 1995), 335–50.

Tenorth, Heinz-Elmar, '"Erziehungsstaaten". Pädagogik des Staates und Etatismus der Erziehung', in Dietrich Benner, Jürgen Schriewer, and Heinz-Elmar Tenorth (eds), *Erziehungsstaaten. Historisch-vergleichende Analysen ihrer Denktraditionen und nationaler Gestalten* (Weinheim, 1998), 13–54.

Tenorth, Heinz-Elmar, 'Pädagogik der Gewalt. Zur Logik der Erziehung im Nationalsozialismus', *Jahrbuch für historischen Bildungsforschung* 9 (2003), 7–36.

Thamer, Hans-Ulrich, 'Der "Neue Mensch" als nationalsozialistisches Erziehungsprojekt. Anspruch und Wirklichkeit in den Eliteeinrichtungen des NS-Bildungssystems', in Albert Moritz (ed.), *'Fackelträger der Nation'. Elitebildung in den NS-Ordensburgen* (Cologne, 2010), 81–94.

Thamer, Hans-Ulrich, 'Die Dauerausstellung "Bestimmung: Herrenmensch. NS-Ordensburgen zwischen Faszination und Verbrechen"—Geschichtsort und zeitgeschichtliche Forschung', in Klaus Ring and Stefan Wunsch (eds), *Bestimmung: Herrenmensch. NS-Ordensburgen zwischen Faszination und Verbrechen* (Dresden, 2016), 14–19.

Thamer, Hans-Ulrich, 'Heilversprechen und Sendungsbewußtsein—Der "Neue Mensch" in der Ikonografie und im politischen Kult der NS-Ordensburgen', in Klaus Ring and Stefan Wunsch (eds), *Bestimmung: Herrenmensch. NS-Ordensburgen zwischen Faszination und Verbrechen* (Dresden, 2016), 274–81.

Thamer, Hans-Ulrich, '"Volksgemeinschaft" in der Debatte. Interpretationen, Operationalisierungen, Potenziale und Kritik', in Detlef Schmiechen-Ackermann et al. (eds), *Der Ort der 'Volksgemeinschaft' in der deutschen Gesellschaftsgeschichte* (Paderborn, 2018), 27–36.

Thieler, Kerstin, 'Gesinnungskontrolle in Göttingen. Die NSDAP-Kreisleitung und die Beurteilung der "politischen Zuverlässigkeit"', in Nicole Kramer and Armin Nolzen (eds), *Ungleichheiten im 'Dritten Reich'. Semantiken, Praktiken, Erfahrungen* (Göttingen, 2012), 117–38.

Thieler, Kerstin, 'Gemeinschaft, Erfahrung und NS-Gesellschaft—eine Einführung', in David Reinicke et al. (eds), *Gemeinschaft als Erfahrung. Kulturelle Inszenierungen und soziale Praxis 1930–1960* (Paderborn, 2014), 7–20.

Thieme, Sarah, *Nationalsozialistischer Märtyrerkult. Sakralisierte Politik und Christentum im westfälischen Ruhrgebiet (1929–1939)* (Frankfurt am Main, 2017).

Thießen, Malte, 'Schöne Zeiten? Erinnerungen an die "Volksgemeinschaft" nach 1945', in Frank Bajohr and Michael Wildt (eds), *Volksgemeinschaft. Neue Forschungen zur Gesellschaft des Nationalsozialismus* (Frankfurt am Main, 2009), 165–87.

Thießen, Malte, 'Zeitzeuge und Erinnerungskultur. Zum Verhältnis von privaten und öffentlichen Erzählungen des Luftkriegs', in Lu Seegers and Jürgen Reulecke (eds), *Die 'Generation der Kriegskinder'. Historische Hintergründe und Deutungen* (Gießen, 2009), 157–82.

Thompson, Paul, *The Voice of the Past. Oral History* (3rd edn; Oxford, 2000).

Thorpe, Julie, 'Austrofascism: Revisiting the "Authoritarian State" 40 Years On', *Journal of Contemporary History* 45, no. 2 (2010), 315–43.

Thorpe, Julie, 'Pan-Germanism after Empire: Austrian "Germandom" at Home and Abroad', in Günter Bischof, Fritz Plasser, and Peter Berger (eds), *From Empire to Republic: Post-World War I Austria* (New Orleans, 2010), 254–72.

Thorpe, Julie, *Pan-Germanism and the Austrofascist State, 1933–38* (Manchester, 2011).

Thorpe, Julie, 'Education and the Austrofascist State', in Florian Wenninger and Lucile Dreidemy (eds), *Das Dollfuß/Schuschnigg-Regime 1933–1938. Vermessung eines Forschungsfeldes* (Vienna, 2013), 381–93.

Threuter, Christina, 'Nackte Helden. Die "Ordensburg Vogelsang" und das Gedächtnis der Bilder', in Albert Moritz (ed.), *'Fackelträger der Nation'. Elitebildung in den NS-Ordensburgen* (Cologne, 2010), 95–119.

Tiefenbrunner, Friedrich, *Colloquium Theresianum. Festschrift zum 250jährigen Jubiläum der Theresianischen Akademie* (Vienna, 1996).

Tiffert, Juliane, '"Wer mit hinübergeht, muß ein Jungmann mit guter innerer Haltung sein". Über die Fahrten Nationalpolitischer Erziehungsanstalten zu den "Auslandsdeutschen" in Südosteuropa', in Daniel Drascek (ed.), *Kulturvergleichende Perspektiven auf das östliche Europa. Fragestellungen, Forschungsansätze und Methoden. Konferenz der Fachkommission Volkskunde des Johann Gottfried Herder-Forschungsrates in Regensburg, 22. bis 23. November 2013* (Münster, 2017), 113–28.

Tiffert, Juliane, 'Der "volksdeutsche Bildgedanke". Über den Einsatz von Fotografien bei den Fahrtenberichten der Nationalpolitischen Erziehungsanstalten', in Markus Tauschek (ed.), *Handlungsmacht, Widerständigkeit und kulturelle Ordnungen: Potenziale kulturwissenschaftlichen Denkens. Festschrift für Silke Göttsch-Elten* (Münster, 2017), 249–60.

Timpe, Julia, *Nazi-Organized Recreation and Entertainment in the Third Reich* (London, 2017).

Tooze, Adam, *The Wages of Destruction: The Making and Breaking of the Nazi Economy* (London, 2007).

Torrie, Julia S., *'For Their Own Good': Civilian Evacuations in Germany and France, 1939–1945* (New York, 2010).

Tröger, Annemarie, 'Die Frau im wesensgemäßen Einsatz', in Frauengruppe Faschismusforschung (ed.), *Mutterkreuz und Arbeitsbuch. Zur Geschichte der Frauen in der Weimarer Republik und im Nationalsozialismus* (Frankfurt am Main, 1981), 246–72.

Tröger, Annemarie, 'The Creation of a Female Assembly-Line Proletariat', in Renate Bridenthal, Atina Grossmann, and Marion Kaplan (eds), *When Biology Became Destiny: Women in Weimar and Nazi Germany* (New York, 1984), 237–70.

Ueberhorst, Horst, *Elite für die Diktatur. Die Nationalpolitischen Erziehungsanstalten 1933–1945: Ein Dokumentarbericht* (Düsseldorf, 1969).

Uhl, Heidemarie, 'Vom Pathos des Widerstands zur Aura des Authentischen. Die Entdeckung des Zeitzeugen als Epochenschwelle der Erinnerung', in Martin Sabrow and Norbert Frei (eds), *Die Geburt des Zeitzeugen nach 1945* (Göttingen, 2012), 224–46.

Ulbricht, Gunda, 'Kommunalverfassung und Kommunalpolitik', in Clemens Vollnhals (ed.), *Sachsen in der NS-Zeit* (Leipzig, 2002), 85–103.

Ulbricht, Justus H., 'Inseln im Meer des "deutschen Verfalls"—Knotenpunkte im Netzwerk der völkischen "Szene" Sachsens', in Konstantin Herrmann (ed.), *Führerschule, Thingplatz, 'Judenhaus'. Topografien der NS-Herrschaft in Sachsen* (Dresden, 2014), 18–23.

Usborne, Cornelie, 'Social Body, Racial Body, Woman's Body. Discourses, Policies, Practices from Wilhelmine to Nazi Germany, 1912–1945', *Historical Social Research* 36, no. 2 (2011), 140–61.

Vahlbruch, Heinz, 'Klosterschule Ilfeld—alte Kulturstätte', *Nordhäuser Nachrichten* 16, no. 43 (1966).

Veld, N.K.C.A. In't (ed.), *De SS en Nederland. Documenten uit SS-archieven 1935–1942*, 2 vols ('s-Gravenhage, 1976).

Venken, Machteld and Röger, Maren, 'Growing up in the Shadow of the Second World War: European Perspectives', *European Review of History/revue européenne d'histoire* 22, no. 2 (2015), 199–220.

Vermandel, Georges, '"Lausbuben" vernichteten europäisches Kulturgut. Der Brand im Nordflügel des Bensberger Schlosses im März 1942—Damaliger Ablauf nach 50 Jahren erstmals genau rekonstruiert—Ein "Jungenstreich"', *Rheinisch-Bergischer Kalender* 65 (1995), 30–5.

Vogel, Barbara, 'Eliten—Ein Thema der Frauenforschung?', in Günther Schulz (ed.), *Frauen auf dem Wege zur Elite* (Munich, 2000), 15–40.

Volk, Ludwig, *Katholische Kirche und Nationalsozialismus* (Mainz, 1987).

Völker, Bernhard, 'Christian Mergenthaler. Kultminister und Überzeugungstäter', in Hermann G. Abmayr (ed.), *Stuttgarter NS-Täter. Vom Mitläufer bis zum Massenmörder* (Stuttgart, 2009), 296–301.

Völker, Bernhard, 'Wilhelm Gschwend. "Politischer Vertrauensmann" im Kultministerium', in Hermann G. Abmayr (ed.), *Stuttgarter NS-Täter. Vom Mitläufer bis zum Massenmörder* (Stuttgart, 2009), 302–9.

Vollnhals, Clemens, 'Der gespaltene Freistaat. Der Aufstieg der NSDAP in Sachsen', in Clemens Vollnhals (ed.), *Sachsen in der NS-Zeit* (Leipzig, 2002), 9–40.

Vollnhals, Clemens (ed.), *Sachsen in der NS-Zeit* (Leipzig, 2002).

von Zedlitz und Neukirch, Conrad-Dieter and Weske, Hans Heinrich, *Wahlstatt. Einstige Propstei der Benediktiner—Das Kadettenhaus (1838–1920)—Die Staatliche Bildungsanstalt (1920–1934)* (Lorch, 1989).

Vondung, Klaus, *Deutsche Wege zur Erlösung. Formen des Religiösen im Nationalsozialismus* (Munich, 2013).

Vonwald, Franz and Kainig-Huber, Margarethe (eds), *Wie es bei uns in Niederösterreich war 1938–1945: Spurensuche im Nationalsozialismus. Materialien zur Zeitgeschichte* (Berndorf, 2015).

Wagner, Andreas, *Mutschmann gegen von Killinger. Konfliktlinien zwischen Gauleiter und SA-Führer während des Aufstiegs der NSDAP und der 'Machtergreifung' im Freistaat Sachsen* (Beucha, 2001).

Wagner, Andreas, 'Partei und Staat. Das Verhältnis von NSDAP und innerer Verwaltung im Freistaat Sachsen 1933–1945', in Clemens Vollnhals (ed.), *Sachsen in der NS-Zeit* (Leipzig, 2002), 41–56.

Wagner, Andreas, *'Machtergreifung' in Sachsen. NSDAP und staatliche Verwaltung 1930–1935* (Cologne, 2004).

Wagner, Leonie, *Nationalsozialistische Frauenansichten. Vorstellungen von Weiblichkeit und Politik führender Frauen im Nationalsozialismus* (Frankfurt am Main, 1996).

Wagner, Leonie, 'Perspektiven von Frauen 1933–1945', in Günther Schulz (ed.), *Frauen auf dem Wege zur Elite* (Munich, 2000), 117–38.

Wagner, Monika, 'Erinnern und Beteiligen als Strategie der Gemeinschaftsstiftung. Die Ausmalung der Karlsruher Helmholtz-Schule', in Ulrich Hermann and Ulrich Nassen (eds), *Formative Ästhetik im Nationalsozialismus. Intentionen, Medien und Praxisformen totalitärer ästhetischer Herrschaft und Beherrschung* (Weinheim, 1994), 123–37.

Wagner, Steffen, '"Aus weltanschaulichen Gründen besonders bekämpft und gehaßt"? Die Weierhöfer Schule und ihre Umwandlung in eine NS-Eliteanstalt im Jahr 1936', *Mennonitische Geschichtsblätter* 68 (2011), 89–160.

Wahle, Manfred, 'Berufsausbildung—Zum Widerspruch zwischen nationalsozialistischer Gesinnungsschulung und moderner Ausbildungspraxis', in Klaus-Peter Horn and Jörg-W. Link (eds), *Erziehungsverhältnisse im Nationalsozialismus. Totaler Anspruch und Erziehungswirklichkeit* (Bad Heilbrunn, 2011), 231–51.

Warkus-Thomsen, Dirk, '"Jüdische Kinder gehören in jüdische Heime." Von einem jüdischen Kinderheim und einer "Judenaustreibung" in Wyk auf Föhr', in Gerhard Paul and Miriam Gillis-Carlebach (eds), *Menora und Hakenkreuz. Zur Geschichte der Juden in und aus Schleswig-Holstein, Lübeck und Altona 1918–1998* (Neumünster, 1998), 387–96.

Warmbrunn, Werner, *The German Occupation of Belgium, 1940–1944* (New York, 1993).

Wassermann, Janek, *Black Vienna: The Radical Right in the Red City, 1918–1938* (Ithaca, 2014).

Weaver, William N., '"A School-Boy's Story": Writing the Victorian Public Schoolboy Subject', *Victorian Studies* 46, no. 3 (2004), 455–87.

Weckel, Ulrike, 'Shamed by Nazi Crimes: The First Step towards Germans' Re-education or a Catalyst for Their Wish to Forget?', in Stephanie Bird et al. (eds), *Reverberations of Nazi Violence in Germany and Beyond: Disturbing Pasts* (London, 2016), 33–46.

Wegehaupt, Phillip, 'Funktionäre und Funktionseliten der NSDAP. Vom Blockleiter zum Gauleiter', in Wolfgang Benz (ed.), *Wie wurde man Parteigenosse? Die NSDAP und ihre Mitglieder* (Frankfurt am Main, 2009), 39–59.

Wegner, Bernd, *The Waffen-SS: Organisation, Ideology and Function* (Oxford, 1990).

Wegner, Gregory Paul, 'Mothers of the Race: The Elite Schools for German Girls under the Nazi Dictatorship', *Journal of Curriculum and Supervision* 19, no. 2 (2004), 169–88.

Weidenfeller, Gerhard, *VDA—Verein für das Deutschtum im Ausland. Allgemeiner deutscher Schulverein (1881–1918): Ein Beitrag zur Geschichte des deutschen Nationalismus und Imperialismus im Kaiserreich* (Frankfurt am Main, 1976).

Weigel, Björn, '"Märzgefallene" und Aufnahmestopp im Frühjahr 1933. Eine Studie über den Opportunismus', in Wolfgang Benz (ed.), *Wie wurde man Parteigenosse? Die NSDAP und ihre Mitglieder* (Frankfurt am Main, 2009), 91–109.

Welzer, Harald, 'Vom Zeit- zum Zukunftszeugen. Vorschläge zur Modernisierung der Erinnerungskultur', in Martin Sabrow and Norbert Frei (eds), *Die Geburt des Zeitzeugen nach 1945* (Göttingen, 2012), 33–48.

Welzer, Harald, Moller, Sabine, and Tschuggnall, Karoline, *'Opa war kein Nazi': Nationalsozialismus und Holocaust im Familiengedächtnis* (Frankfurt am Main, 2002).

Wenninger, Florian and Dreidemy, Lucile (eds), *Das Dollfuß/Schuschnigg-Regime 1933–1938. Vermessung eines Forschungsfeldes* (Vienna, 2013).

Werther, Steffen, '"Volksgemeinschaft" vs. "Rassengemeinschaft". Nationalsozialisten in der dänischen Grenzregion Nordschleswig/Sønderjylland 1933–39', in David Reinicke et al. (eds), *Gemeinschaft als Erfahrung. Kulturelle Inszenierungen und soziale Praxis 1930–1960* (Paderborn, 2014), 35–61.

Westermeier, Jens, '"Soldaten wie andere auch!" Der Einfluss von SS-Veteranen auf die öffentliche Wahrnehmung der Waffen-SS', in Jan Erik Schulte and Michael Wildt (eds), *Die SS nach 1945. Entschuldungsnarrative, populäre Mythen, europäische Erinnerungsdiskurse* (Göttingen, 2018), 269–88.

Wetzel, Juliane, 'Die NSDAP zwischen Öffnung und Mitgliedersperre', in Wolfgang Benz (ed.), *Wie wurde man Parteigenosse? Die NSDAP und ihre Mitglieder* (Frankfurt am Main, 2009), 74–90.

Weyrather, Irmgard, *Muttertag und Mutterkreuz. Der Kult um die 'deutsche Mutter' im Nationalsozialismus* (Frankfurt am Main, 1993).

Wierling, Dorothee, '"Kriegskinder": westdeutsch, bürgerlich, männlich?', in Lu Seegers and Jürgen Reulecke (eds), *Die 'Generation der Kriegskinder'. Historische Hintergründe und Deutungen* (Gießen, 2009), 141–55.

Wieviorka, Annette, *The Era of the Witness* (Ithaca, 2006).

Wildt, Michael, 'Die Ungleichheit des Volkes. "Volksgemeinschaft" in der politischen Kommunikation der Weimarer Republik', in Frank Bajohr and Michael Wildt (eds), *Volksgemeinschaft. Neue Forschungen zur Gesellschaft des Nationalsozialismus* (Frankfurt am Main, 2009), 24–40.

Wildt, Michael, *An Uncompromising Generation: The Nazi Leadership of the Reich Security Main Office* (Madison, 2009).

Wildt, Michael, *Hitler's* Volksgemeinschaft *and the Dynamics of Racial Exclusion: Violence against Jews in Provincial Germany, 1919–1939* (New York, 2012).

Wildt, Michael, '*Volksgemeinschaft*: A Modern Perspective on National Socialist Society', in Martina Steber and Bernhard Gotto (eds), *Visions of Community in Nazi Germany: Social Engineering and Private Lives* (Oxford, 2014), 43–59.

Wildt, Michael, '"Volksgemeinschaft" und Führer—Der Beitrag der NS-Ordensburgen zur Elitebildung im Nationalsozialismus', in Klaus Ring and Stefan Wunsch (eds), *Bestimmung: Herrenmensch. NS-Ordensburgen zwischen Faszination und Verbrechen* (Dresden, 2016), 128–35.

Wilke, Karsten, *Die 'Hilfsgemeinschaft auf Gegenseitigkeit' (HIAG) 1950–1990. Veteranen der Waffen-SS in der Bundesrepublik* (Paderborn, 2011).

Wilke, Karsten, 'Veteranen der Waffen-SS in der frühen Bundesrepublik. Aufbau, gesellschaftliche Einbindung und Netzwerke der "Hilfsgemeinschaft auf Gegenseitigkeit"', in Jan Erik Schulte and Michael Wildt (eds), *Die SS nach 1945. Entschuldungsnarrative, populäre Mythen, europäische Erinnerungsdiskurse* (Göttingen, 2018), 75–97.

Williams, Maurice, *Gau, Volk and Reich: Friedrich Rainer and the Paradox of Austrian National Socialism* (Klagenfurt, 2005).

Willmot, Louise, 'Zur Geschichte des Bundes Deutscher Mädel', in Dagmar Reese (ed.), *Die BDM-Generation. Weibliche Jugendliche in Deutschland und Österreich im Nationalsozialismus* (Berlin, 2007), 89–154.

Winter, Martin Clemens, 'Die SS als Negativfolie in Narrativen der Todesmärsche', in Jan Erik Schulte and Michael Wildt (eds), *Die SS nach 1945. Entschuldungsnarrative, populäre Mythen, europäische Erinnerungsdiskurse* (Göttingen, 2018), 99–115.

Winter, Sebastian, 'Arischer Antifaschismus. Geschlechterbilder als Medium der kulturindustriellen Bearbeitung der Erinnerung an den Nationalsozialismus am Beispiel der Filme "Der Untergang", "Sophie Scholl" und "Napola"', in kittkritik (ed.), *Deutschlandwunder. Wunsch und Wahn in der postnazistischen Kultur* (Mainz, 2007), 52–68.

Wirsching, Andreas, 'Nationalsozialismus in der Region. Tendenzen der Forschung und methodische Probleme', in Horst Möller, Andreas Wirsching, and Walter Ziegler (eds), *Nationalsozialismus in der Region. Beiträge zur regionalen und lokalen Forschung und zum internationalen Vergleich* (Munich, 1996), 25–46.

Wirsching, Andreas, '*Volksgemeinschaft* and the Illusion of "Normality" from the 1920s to the 1940s', in Martina Steber and Bernhard Gotto (eds), *Visions of Community in Nazi Germany: Social Engineering and Private Lives* (Oxford, 2014), 149–56.

Wissmann, Sylvelin (ed.), *Geh zur Schul und lerne was: 150 Jahre Schulpflicht in Bremen 1844–1944. Buch zum Ausstellungszyklus* (Bremen, 1994).

Withuis, Jolande, 'Zeitzeugen des Zweiten Weltkriegs in den Niederlanden', in Martin Sabrow and Norbert Frei (eds), *Die Geburt des Zeitzeugen nach 1945* (Göttingen, 2012), 157–75.

Wolf, Gerhard, *Ideologie und Herrschaftsrationalität. Nationalsozialistische Germanisierungspolitik in Polen* (Hamburg, 2012).

Wolf, Gerhard, 'Suitable Germans—Enforced Assimilation Policies in Danzig-West Prussia, 1939–1945', in Claus-Christian W. Szejnmann and Maiken Umbach (eds), *Heimat, Region and Empire. Spatial Identities under National Socialism* (Basingstoke, 2012), 213–34.

Wolfrum, Edgar, 'Die Bedeutung der NS-Ordensburgen für das Verständnis des Nationalsozialismus', in Klaus Ring and Stefan Wunsch (eds), *Bestimmung: Herrenmensch. NS-Ordensburgen zwischen Faszination und Verbrechen* (Dresden, 2016), 20–7.

Worschech, Rudolf, 'Frühling für Hitler: "Der Untergang" und andere. Wie der deutsche Film das "Dritte Reich" und seine Täter darstellt', *Augen-Blick: Marburger Hefte zur Medienwissenschaft* 36 (2004), 102–10.

Wunsch, Stefan, 'Führer von übermorgen?—Die Adolf-Hitler-Schulen und das Erziehungsprojekt "Herrenmensch"', in Klaus Ring and Stefan Wunsch (eds), *Bestimmung: Herrenmensch. NS-Ordensburgen zwischen Faszination und Verbrechen* (Dresden, 2016), 210–27.

Zahra, Tara, 'Reclaiming Children for the Nation: Germanization, National Ascription, and Democracy in the Bohemian Lands, 1900–1945', *Central European History* 37, no. 4 (2004), 501–43.

Zahra, Tara, *Kidnapped Souls: National Indifference and the Battle for Children in the Bohemian Lands, 1900–1948* (Ithaca, 2008).

Zakić, Mirna, *Ethnic Germans and National Socialism in Yugoslavia in World War II* (Cambridge, 2017).

Zeidler, Manfred, 'Luftkriegsschule Dresden-Klotzsche', in Konstantin Herrmann (ed.), *Führerschule, Thingplatz, 'Judenhaus'. Topografien der NS-Herrschaft in Sachsen* (Dresden, 2014), 284–7.

Zeps, Michael J., *Education and the Crisis of the First Republic* (New York, 1987).

Ziegler, Walter, 'Gaue und Gauleiter im Dritten Reich', in Horst Möller, Andreas Wirsching, and Walter Ziegler (eds), *Nationalsozialismus in der Region. Beiträge zur regionalen und lokalen Forschung und zum internationalen Vergleich* (Munich, 1996), 139–59.

Zimmermann, Volker, *Die Sudetendeutschen im NS-Staat. Politik und Stimmung der Bevölkerung im Reichsgau Sudetenland (1938–1945)* (Essen, 1999).

Zimmermann, Volker, '"Volksgenossen" erster und zweiter Klasse? Reichs- und Sudetendeutsche in Böhmen und Mähren 1938–1945', in Jerzy Kochanowski and Maike Sach (eds), *Die 'Volksdeutschen' in Polen, Frankreich, Ungarn und der Tschechoslowakei. Mythos und Realität* (Osnabrück, 2006), 257–71.

Zöchmeister, Markus, 'Nazismus, Karneval und Perversion. Mediale Reproduktionen der NS-Welt', in Margrit Frölich, Christian Schneider, and Karsten Visarius (eds), *Das Böse im Blick. Die Gegenwart des Nationalsozialismus im Film* (Nehren, 2007), 30–42.

Zymek, Bernd, 'War die nationalsozialistische Schulpolitik sozialrevolutionär? Praxis und Theorie der Auslese im Schulwesen während der nationalsozialistischen Herrschaft in Deutschland', in Manfred Heinemann (ed.), *Erziehung und Schulung im Dritten Reich. Teil 1: Kindergarten, Schule, Jugend, Berufserziehung* (Stuttgart, 1980), 264–74.

Index

Note: Figures are indicated by an italic '*f*', respectively, following the page number.

For the benefit of digital users, indexed terms that span two pages (e.g., 52–53) may, on occasion, appear on only one of those pages.